Revised and Expanded Edition

Textbook
Of
FISH HEALTH

Dr. George Post

t.f.h.

T.F.H. Publications, Inc.

Title page photo: An African Cichlid of the genus *Haplochromis* with severe fin rot. The entire caudal fin is already destroyed. Photo by Ruda Zukal.

Photos not individually credited in the color section:
Dr. G Post: Plates 1-5 (except 5F); 6B, C, E, F; 8B, C, E, F; 9A, C-F; 10 A-E; 11A, C; 12A, C; 14A, B, F; 15 C-F; 16B; 17 A, C; 18C; 19A, C; 22 A, C, D; 24A, B, D, F; 26 A-F 27 A, B, D; 28 A-F; 29A, C-F; 30A, B, E, F; 31 A-F; 32 A-C, E, F. Dr. J. D. Hendricks: Plate 29 B, Plate 30 D. Yasutake: Plate 16 A. Nose: Plate 27 C. Courtesy of the U.S. Fish & Wildlife Service: Plate 30 C. Dr. A. Woolf: Plate 32 D. All others from books published by T.F.H. Publications.

Distributed in the UNITED STATES by T.F.H. Publications, Inc., 211 West Sylvania Avenue, Neptune City, NJ 07753; in CANADA to the Pet Trade by H & L Pet Supplies Inc., 27 Kingston Crescent, Kitchener, Ontario N2B 2T6; Rolf C. Hagen Ltd., 3225 Sartelon Street, Montreal 382 Quebec; in CANADA to the Book Trade by Macmillan of Canada (A Division of Canada Publishing Corporation), 164 Commander Boulevard, Agincourt, Ontario M1S 3C7; in ENGLAND by T.F.H. Publications Limited, 4 Kier Park, Ascot, Berkshire SL5 7DS; in AUSTRALIA AND THE SOUTH PACIFIC by T.F.H. (Australia) Pty. Ltd., Box 149, Brookvale 2100 N.S.W., Australia; in NEW ZEALAND by Ross Haines & Son, Ltd., 18 Monmouth Street, Grey Lynn, Auckland 2 New Zealand; in SINGAPORE AND MALAYSIA by MPH Distributors (S) Pte., Ltd., 601 Sims Drive, #03/07/21, Singapore 1438; in the PHILIPPINES by Bio-Research, 5 Lippay Street, San Lorenzo Village, Makati Rizal; in SOUTH AFRICA by Multipet Pty. Ltd., 30 Turners Avenue, Durban 4001. Published by T.F.H. Publications Inc. Manufactured in the United States of America by T.F.H. Publications, Inc.

CONTENTS

Color Plates Begin on Page 113

PREFACE

The subject of fish health was first introduced to me in 1951 when the Wyoming Game and Fish Department started participation in the then-new Federal Aid to Fish Restoration Act. My supervisor, Mr. Floyd M. Blunt, coerced me into examining the relationship among diseases, parasites, nutrition and fish health. I had previously studied various diseases of wild mammals and birds and assisted with research on several zoonotic diseases for the U.S. Army Chemical Corp. I had also worked as a hospital medical technologist and was well aware of the then most modern laboratory methods used for human disease diagnosis. I was not sure I wanted to work with fish health at the time Mr. Blunt suggested I do so, but he gently persuaded me to at least work for a year with the Wyoming state fish cultural system. I could then either continue to work with fish health or return to research with higher vertebrates. I found the study of fish health a fascinating and rewarding vocation, a nearly untouched field to which only a few people in the world were devoting full-time efforts at that time.

I attended study sessions at the Cortland, New York, laboratory of fish nutrition and the Leetown, West Virginia, fish disease research laboratory during that first year. There I met Drs. Arthur M. Phillips, Jr. and Stanislas F. Snieszko, two people who made a profound impression upon me and have been responsible for my continued interest in both pathogenic organisms and basic nutrition of fishes.

I do not know when I first realized the great need for educators in fish health. Possibly the inability to find laboratory technicians trained in the field of fish health gradually demonstrated this need. I began teaching what I knew of fish health to fish culture personnel in Wyoming while working for the Wyoming Game and Fish Department and in Utah while directing the Utah Department of Fish and Game's experimental fish cultural laboratory. I began to teach a formal course on fish health in 1965 at Colorado State University and a course in fish nutrition in 1967. Both courses continued to be offered each year until my retirement in 1984. Neither course has been offered since 1984.

I have been most impressed with the need for undergraduate education for those students interested in fish health. Initial studies on fish health should begin during early academic training, much as a pre-veterinary curriculum prepares students for veterinary studies. Consequently, a fish disease technology curriculum was developed for the interested undergraduate student and was offered as a four-year academic plan at Colorado State University until 1983.

Another part of undergraduate education was the need for a suitable textbook. There was no textbook for the fish health student until Dr. Erwin Amlacher's *Textbook of Fish Diseases* was translated from German in 1970. This textbook has served well but is in need of updating and revision or replacement. I took the time under persuasion of the late Dr. S. F. Snieszko and of Dr. Herbert Axelrod, president of T.F.H. Publications to write this textbook. Dr. Axelrod urged that I use as many color illustrations as possible. Some have been replaced and others have been improved for this revision. This basic text book has attempted to bring my knowledge together with information scattered in journals, leaflets and monographs, special reports and books into a single-volume summary. I have selected references for a list at the end of each chapter so the student may find additional reading on each subject. These reference lists are not intended to be all-conclusive. I take full responsibility for making specific disease or parasite selections used as illustrations on how fishes become diseased, how the selected diseases may be diagnosed and controlled and some of the practical aspects of each disease.

I wish to offer thanks to all those people in the fish health field who, over the years, contributed information for this book. I especially wish to express my appreciation to everyone who answered my request for their published articles necessary tor this revision, because I am now 65 miles away from a complete scientific library. Thanks are also given to all my past students, friends and my wife who continually urged that I write the book. I am also grateful to the Departments of Fishery and Wildlife Biology and of Microbiology at Colorado State University who made time available for preparation of the original manuscript, and to Miss. Phyllis Turner, the secretary who assisted with the original manuscript. I had no secretarial assistance for the revision. My hope is that this revision will make the book more useful.

George Post, Ph. D.
Board Certified Fish Pathologist

INTRODUCTION

Diseases have no doubt occurred among fishes over the millenia these animals have occupied a place on the earth. Scientific efforts have been made to understand causes of diseases in fishes, and to attempt control, only during the last two-thirds of a century.

Fishes, as with other animals, are subject to a wide spectrum of diseases. Diagnosis of fish diseases and understanding of their epizootiology have involved the efforts of relatively few people compared to the large number of people working with human and domestic animal diseases.

Diseases of fishes require a somewhat different approach to problem solving than diseases involving terrestrial animals. Aquatic animals are in an entirely different environment than air-breathing animals. Fishes are poikilothermic, and their internal biological systems are tremendously altered by water temperature. Their internal and external biology is also altered by other physical factors of the environment: pH, osmotic pressure, dissolved gases, ions or elements, and others. These factors also determine if an etiological agent (disease-causing agent) can or will cause disease among fishes. The fish disease diagnostician must have a broad knowledge of the aquatic environment in order to relate clinical findings to disease entities.

There was an awareness of fish diseases prior to 1900, however, most cases of disease among these animals were probably viewed as interesting but of little practical significance. The advent of more successful fish culture, in which fishes were produced in large numbers for sport fishing, culinary use, ornamental value, laboratory research and other uses, has enhanced the study of fish health and disease problems.

There are documented epizootics of diseases among wild fish populations. However, most modern-day wild fish losses can be attributed to environmental alteration by man. This is contrasted to the extreme conditions of population density in most fish culture facilities. These overcrowded conditions are conducive to the movement of pathogens from host to host and to the development of extremes of water contamination detrimental to the health of each individual fish in the population. So, the art of fish disease diagnostics and the science of the disease process in fishes have been closely associated with fish culture in the United States, Europe, Japan and other countries. Studies of diseases among fishes in many countries have enriched the knowledge of fish health and disease.

Fish health and disease have become subjects offered by many schools of higher learning and continuing education courses in the United States and the world. An attempt is made here to supply a reference and textbook for assistance of the student of fish health and disease.

Chapter I

FISH HEALTH AND DISEASE

Study of any subject should start with an overview of the history of that subject. This is true of the subject of fish health and disease. No attempt will be made here to examine all of the contributions made to the knowledge of fish disease; rather only some of the incidents of the past will be mentioned which have implications on present understanding of fish health and disease.

There are several bibliographies of literature derived from studies on fish health and disease available to the serious historian. Locating the literature listed in some of these bibliographies is difficult, especially those written prior to the turn of this century. There are two early bibliographies of note which can be used to assist the reader in establishing the early history of fish health. One bibliography was prepared by Freund[11] in 1923 and another by McGregor[22] in 1963. The latter has a title which catches the eye by stating that it lists those publications on fish parasites and disease from the year 330 B.C., when Aristotle[1a] wrote of a crustacean parasite of tuna and swordfish, to a reference in 1923 A.D.

The study and identification of animal parasites received the most attention from early researchers and authors. Probably this was because animal parasites were easily seen by the observer. Fungal organisms were also mentioned in early literature[4,17] for the same reason. Reference to bacterial pathogens did not occur until the last 25 years of the 19th century. The first reference to viral diseases of fishes, except for postulation of viral presence, was not until 1955.[32]

Many of the early epizootics which occurred among

fish populations and were noted by individuals interested in animal disease were related in some way to a disease in humans or their domesticated animals. Such was the case of a disease which occurred in 1867 and again in 1868 among the perch population of Lake Geneva in Switzerland. The disease was referred to as typhus (possibly typhoid) because of a yellow discharge from the anus of dead and dying fish.[25] Disease signs in the fish were those usually associated with septicemia. However, a yellow discharge from the anus is not surprising, since this usually happens in fishes that have not eaten for a long period of time and fluids passed are stained with bile. No doubt these epizootics caused some apprehension among people living around the lake, especially if proof could be obtained that fishes can harbor the etiological agent of human typhus (or typhoid). The actual cause of the epizootics has never been determined.

A disease called *"Pestis salmonum"* in salmon or *"Pestis rubra anguillarum"* in eels was first described in 1868.[2,14,16,22,24,28] The disease is presently called vibriosis. Early-day research people found the disease in salmon of Scotland and other parts of the British Isles[5,16] and in eels in Italy.[22,29] The bacterium was proved to be psychrophilic and to have no connection with a human infection. Study of vibriosis has continued, being one of the important diseases among many fish species of the world today.

Another example of finding bacteria which might be transmissable to humans occurred in 1896.[3] Acid-fast bacteria were found in fishes from a lake in France, and a tuberculosis sanitarium was located on the shores of the lake. Imagine the headlines in newspapers of the day when tuberculosis (mycobacteriosis) in fishes was thought to be associated with human tuberculosis. The probable reaction of bacteriologists of the time may have brought about the thorough study of this bacterium. The studies indicated that *Mycobacterium marinum* (the bacterium responsible for piscine mycobacteriosis) is not transmissible to homeothermic animals.

Furunculosis is the name of a disease originally described in 1894 from cultured trout in Germany.[8] The cause of the disease was named *Bacterium salmonicida* or *Bacterium truttae*[19] by authors of the day. The organism has been known by other names over the intervening years, but the presently accepted name is *Aeromonas salmonicida*.[7] The disease may have occurred in German cultured trout prior to 1894, because after publication of a description of the disease it was recognized by fish culturists of the day as being a common disease among trout culture installations.[20] Extensive studies among wild fish populations in central and western Europe from 1909 to 1911 revealed the presence of this bacterium in many countries.[12,26] The disease was found in the British Isles in 1911.[9] Surprisingly, the first reference to the disease in the United States was in 1902.[19]

The known distribution and recognition of the seriousness of furunculosis by the mid-1920's brought about the formation of a "Furunculosis Committee" in Great Britain in 1928.[20] Formation of this committee was certainly a milestone in the recognition of fish diseases, because it was the first time a concerted effort was made among interested people to study and combat a fish disease. The committee remained active until 1933.

Meanwhile, the study of animal parasites of fishes continued. Publications appeared describing parasites in or on fishes in many locations of the world.[22] Many of the host-parasite descriptions, life cycle studies and other data obtained during the early part of this century continue to be valid and have formed the basis of today's parasitological studies with fishes.

The Furunculosis Committee brought about an interest in other diseases of fishes. It made many people aware that fishes do have diseases, just as do all other animals. The period of time between the 1930's and 1950's became one of awakening to an interest in fish health and disease. Research people began to observe the pathological changes in fishes when certain etiological agents were involved. Infectious organisms were studied more carefully, and each catalogued into a logical system of nomenclature. A number of different diseases known today were identified, named and their etiology determined during that time.

There is an indication that people working with fish health and disease prior to 1925 did so as an avocation, their true interest being parasitology, bacteriology, zoology or a vocation which led them to observe fishes. There were only a few people, by 1930, who had taken up fish health and disease as a major occupation. These people brought the interest to others, and even though the fish health specialist profession is small, it is growing.

Fish culturists became aware of the relationship between disease epizootics among fishes and fish stocking levels in troughs, tanks, raceways and ponds. Non-infectious disease occurring as a result of fish culture mismanagement were prevalent. The relationship was noted between the overcrowding of fishes and infections of opportunist bacteria, fungi and animal parasites. Disinfectants such as salt, acetic acid, copper sulfate and potassium permanganate were used in an attempt to control these infections. Lime, calcium hypochlorite and similar disinfectants were used to disinfect utensils and fish holding facilities. However, the only means of control of some of the primary pathogenic organisms in fish culture facilities was found to be the cessation of fish production and allowing the fish hatchery to dry under the sun for a year or two. Another practice prevalent during this period was to *solve* infectious disease problems among fishes, especially those being reared for sport fishing, by stocking them into streams and lakes. This practice served to spread infectious organisms into wild fish populations and created disastrous results in some geographical areas.[15]

The occurrence of fish diseases caused by toxic substances in water had been known as early as the 1860's. However, only with the advent of synthetic insecticidal and herbicidal substances in the late 1930's did fish health specialists begin to examine the effects of these substances on fishes. These studies continue as new pesticidal substances are synthesized and used in the environment of fishes.[23]

The years between 1947 and 1960 were years of rapid progress in the study of fish health and disease. Studies were initiated on proper nutrition and nutritional requirements of several of the most important cultured fish species. The therapeutic compounds used during earlier times were examined and new ones made available. Sulfonamides were used to control furunculosis by 1947.[13] Other antibiotics and chemotherapeutic compounds were found useful for control of infectious diseases. More suitable disinfectants began to be used, and dose levels established.

Viral agents of disease in fishes had been postulated prior to 1955. One example of such a probable viral disease was known as acute catarrhal enteritis. A publication in 1941 mentioned its possible viral cause,[21] but proof was not demonstrated. A report on the viral nature of infectious pancreatic necrosis in brook trout[32] and further studies on the disease indicated that it was the same as acute catarrhal enteritis. A fishery leaflet prepared in 1958[30] gave the disease both names but suggested the use of infectious pancreatic necrosis, a name which continues to be used.

Results of important research on the study of viral diseases of fishes were published in 1960.[31] The virus which causes infectious pancreatic necrosis was successfully transmitted to a culture of trout gonad cells. The use of various cell cultures from fishes continues to be a primary method of studying fish viruses and maintaining many viral pathogens of fishes today.

Fishes and fish products were being moved indiscriminately about the world. Fishes raised in Europe, Japan and other countries were imported into the United States. Fishes from the United States were shipped to other parts of the world. No attention was given to pathogens being transported along with the fishes. Millions of pounds of French, Danish, Belgian and Japanese trout were imported into the United States each year. These same countries were the best source of trout eggs for trout culture in the United States, because the trout egg volume necessary to support United States trout culture had not been developed domestically. Hundreds of millions of trout eggs were brought into the United States each year without concern for pathogen transmission.[15] A philosophy developed during the 1960's by many fish health specialists, and which has been of great importance to fish health and disease to-day, advocated control of the movements of fishes or fish eggs. This philosophy reached into many states of the United States, provinces of Canada and other countries of the world.

The American Fisheries Society, a professional society, formed an *ad hoc* committee on fish disease in 1964. The charge to the Fish Disease Committee (FDC) was to examine disease problems among fishes and to make recommendations on methods of control. The FDC remained an active group until 1972.

The FDC invited fish health specialists of the world to meet at annual meetings. Up-to-date reports were given by these experts on fish disease problems. The best methods of approach to be made in the study and control of fish health and disease problems were examined. Each year a report was made to the parent society on fish disease status. These reports were published in the transactions of society meetings.

One major accomplishment of the FDC was the annual preparation of a list of the most troublesome and special interest diseases of fishes. Restriction of movement of fishes exposed to these diseases was urged; this included intercontinental, interstate and interprovincial movement. The results of these efforts brought into existence the U.S. Fish and Wildlife Service Title 50 restriction for movement of certain food or sport fishes or their products from countries of the world which have pathogens unknown in fishes of the United States. The restriction became effective in 1969. Similar legislation by the Canadian government became effective in 1971, thus eliminating the possibility of fishes shipped from various countries of the world into Canada subsequently crossing the United States/Canadian border.[6]

Title 50 does allow certain fish species to be brought into the United States from other parts of the world. The restrictions apply only to food and sport fishes, including live fishes, dead fishes, fish parts and fish eggs. They do not include ornamental fishes. The ornamental fish industry of the United States has remained comparatively free from quarantine and importation restrictions.

Several states have also approved restriction-of-movement legislation for fishes from other states known to harbor specific pathogens. Such legislation should lessen the chances of moving transmittable diseases indiscriminately about the United States. Experience had demonstrated the possibility of such movement by the fact that a disease known as bacterial kidney disease was present in the states along the east and west coasts of the country in 1950. The disease is now known throughout much of the United States where salmonids are raised. Furunculosis had been moved throughout the salmonid raising areas of the country from its probable east coast origin. State legislation may be enacting embargoes too late to stop the spread of some diseases, but it will certainly control movement of those not already widespread.

The FDC was replaced by a Fish Health Section (FHS) of the American Fisheries Society in 1972. Most of the same philosophies were carried through into the newly formed section. Some of the goals of the FDC which had not been accomplished were continued by the FHS. One example was efforts to obtain federal legislation regulating the interstate movement of fishes. No less than eight bills have been introduced into the two houses of Congress, and each has been denied passage by legislative action.

The FHS has its own roster of members, which includes many of the fish health specialists from throughout North America, as well as members in all other continents of the world. The Section has advocated professionalization of fish pathologists (fish health specialists) by board certification. A Board of Certification was first appointed in 1976, but the certification procedure for fish pathologists was not active until 1984. A Board Certified Fish Pathologist has proved competence through academic background and experience, and will continue to be examined for competence each five years of practice. The Board has certified fish health inspectors since 1972. A Certified Fish Health Inspector examines fish which will subsequently be transported across state lines with importation regulations. The Section has prepared publications on standardized diseases diagnostic procedures, [10] a glossary of fish health terms to assist in maintaining a commmon language of fish diseases, [27] and a newsletter—*Fish Health News*—publication designed to inform the membership of the most recent developments in fish health, often before publication in more formal literature.

Fish health specialists throughout the world continue to publish scientific findings in their field(s) of interest.

This has led to great progress since the early awareness of diseases of fishes. Examination of past accomplishments indicates that much of the truly scientific progress has been made during the past 50 to 75 years. Much remains to be done in the future in order to bring knowledge of fish diseases to the competency of knowledge of diseases in other domesticated animals. There is a need to initiate more research on location, proving efficacy and assuring availability of therapeutic drugs for controlling diseases in fish populations. No matter how successful quarantine, restriction of fish movement, immunization or use of resistant fish strains may be, there will be times when drug therapy will be the only method of controlling epizootics. [23]

Research on epizootiology of fish diseases is badly needed. Epizootiological research must be accompanied by further investigations of pathogens and host-pathogen relationships. More knowledge is needed on the pathological processes in fishes, and histopathology needs to become part of disease diagnosis in fishes, especially since publications on normal fish histology and micronanatomy are now available. [1,12a,13a,33] Immunological knowledge of fishes has been slow in developing, and more needs to be done in developing methods for controlling certain diseases. Fish nutrition has advanced tremendously over the past, but more needs to be done on the relationship between nutrition and infectious diseases. Fish culture management and toxicology are responsible for many epizootics and should receive the attention of future fish health research programs. [18] There is also a need for the development of simplified diagnostic procedures. Last, but by no means less important, is the need for a disease reporting service to keep fish specialists informed of epizootics and disease among fishes of the world. [23]

Selected References

1. Anderson, B.G. and D.L. Mitchum. 1974. *Atlas of Trout Histology*. Wyoming Game & Fish Dept., Cheyenne, WY. 110p.

1a. Aristotle. 330 B.C. *De historia animalium*. Published in 50 volumes (only references to these volumes seem to be available today).

2. Arthur, W. 1882/83. "Notes on the salmon diseases in the Tweed and other rivers and its remedy," *Nat. Zool. J. Sci.*, Volume 1.

3. Battaillon, E.D. and L. Terry. 1897. "Un nouveau type de tuberculose," *Compt. Rend. Soc. Biol.*, (Paris), 4:446.

4. Bennett, J.H. 1844. "On vegetable structures found growing in living animals. Parasitic fungi in living animals, "*Trans. Roy. Soc. Edinburgh*, 15:284-287.

5. Brook, G. 1879. "Notes on the salmon disease in the Esk and Eden," *Trans. Bot. Soc. Edinburgh*, Volume 13.

6. *Canadian Fisheries Act of 1932, the Salmonidae Import Regulations* (P.C. 1969-1417) annexed under *Section 34 of the Fisheries Act and Amendment*, P.C. 1971-479.

7. Cowan, S.T., J.G. Holt, J. Liston, R.G.E. Murray, C.F. Niven, A.W. Ravin and R.W. Stanier. 1974. *Bergey's manual of determination bacteriology, 8th Ed.* Williams & Wilkins Co., Baltimore, MD. 1,246p.

8. Emmerich, R. and C. Weibel. 1894. "Uber eine durch Bakterien erzeugte Seuche unter den Forellen," *Arch. f. Hygiene*, 21:1-21.

9. Fish, F.F. 1937. "Furunculosis in wild trout" *Copeia*, 37-40.

10. Fish Health Section, McDaniel, D. (ed.). 1979. *Procedures for the detection and identification of certain fish pathogens: revised*, Am. Fish. Soc., Bethesda, MD 118p.

11. Freund, L. 1923. *Bibliographia pathologiae piscium.* Druck: A. Hopfer, Burg Bz. Mgdgb. p. 188-263.

12. Fuhrman, O. 1909. "La Furunkulose," *Bull. Suisse de Peche et Pisciculture*, 12:193-195.

12a. Groman, D.B. 1982. *Histology of the striped bass.* Amer. Fish. Soc. Monog. No.3, Bethesda, MD. 116p

13. Gutsell, J.S. 1947. "The value of certain drugs, especially sulfa drugs in the treatment of furunculosis in brook trout (*Salvelinus fontinalis*)," *Trans. Am. Fish. Soc.*, 75:186-199.

13a. Hibiya, T. 1982 *An atlas of fish histology. Normal and pathological features.* Kodansha Ltd., Tokyo, Japan and Gustav Fisher Verlag, Stuttgart, East Germany and New York City, NY. 147p

14. Hofer, B. and F. Doflein. 1898. "Die Rotseuche de Aales," *Allg. Fischztg.*, Number 1.

15. Hoffman, G.L. 1970. "Intercontinental and transcontinental dissemination and transfaunation of fish parasites with emphasis on whirling disease (*Myxosoma cerebralis*)," In *A symposium or diseases on fishes and shellfishes*, S.F. Snieszko, ed. Am. Fish. Soc., Bethesda, MD. p. 69-81.

16. Huxley, T.H. 1882. "A contribution to the pathology of the epidemic known as 'salmon disease'," *Proc. Roy. Soc. London*, Volume 33.

17. Huxley, T. 1882. "*Saprolegnia* in its relation to an epidemic in salmon," *Quart. J. Microbiol. Soc.*, 22 (New Series):311.

18. MacPhee, C. and R. Ruelle. 1969. *Lethal effects of 1888 chemicals upon four species of fish from western North America.* Univ. of Idaho, For., Wildl. and Rnge. Expt. Stn., Moscow, ID. Bull. No. 3. 112p.

19. Marsh, M.C. 1902. "*Bacterium truttae*, a new species of bacterium pathogenic to trout," *Science*, (N.S.) 16:706-707.

20. McCraw, B.M. 1952. *Furunculosis in fish. U.S. Dept. Int. Fish & Wildl. Serv. Spec. Sci. Rpt.:Fisheries, No. 84.* 87p.

21. McGonigle, R.H. 1940. "Acute catarrhal enteritis of salmonid fingerlings," *Trans. Am. Fish. Soc.*, 70: 297-303.

22. McGregor, E.A. 1963. *Publications on fish parasites and diseases, 330 B.C.-A.D. 1923. U.S. Dept. Int., Fish & Wildl. Spec. Sci. Rpt.:Fisheries, No. 474.* 84p.

23. National Academy of Sciences. 1973. *Aquatic Animal Health. Nat. Acad. Sci.*, Washington, DC. 46p.

24. Ninni, A. 1868. "Sulla mortalita delle anguille." *Atti e mem. R. Soc. Agr. Gorcia*, 4. 4 p.

25. Petavel, J. 1868. "Etudes sur le typhus de perches, epizooties de 1867-1868," *Gaz. hop. Paris*, 41:487.

26. Plehn, M. 1910. "Die Furunkulosepidemie der Salmoniden in Suddeutschland," *Ztrbl. Bakt. Paraskde. I.*, 52:468.

27. Post, G. 1977. *Glossary of fish health terms.* Am. Fish. Soc., Bethesda, MD. 48p.

28. Rutherford, J. 1881. "Observations on the salmon disease," *Trans. Dumfr. Gallow, Soc.*, Volume 2.

29. Sennebogen, E. "Sulla malattia delle anguille," *Neptunia*, Venezia, 18:39-41.

30. Snieszko, S.F. and K. Wolf. 1958. *Infectious pancreatic necrosis of salmonid fishes (acute catarrhal enteritis). U.S. Fish & Wildl. Serv., Fish. Leaf. No. 453.* 3p.

31. Wolf, K., C.E. Dunbar and S.F. Snieszko. 1960. "Infectious pancreatic necrosis of trout. I. A tissue culture study," *Prog. Fish-Cult.*, 22:64-68.

32. Wood. E.M., S.F. Snieszko and W.T. Yasutake. 1955. "Infectious pancreatic necrosis in brook trout," *Arch. Path.*, 60:26-28.

33. Yasutake, W.T. and J.H. Wales. 1983. *Microscopic anatomy of salmonids: An atlas.* U.S. Fish & Wild. Serv. Resource Publ. No. 150. U.S. Department of the Interior, Washington, DC. 188p.

Chapter II
DIAGNOSIS
OF DISEASES

Diagnosis of diseases in fishes should be a step by step procedure. Observation of the behavior of ailing fishes may be of diagnostic assistance and should become a part of the diagnostic procedure whenever possible. Fish with certain illnesses may be listless or lethargic, seek the sides of the holding facility or the surface of the water, refuse to take food, breath rapidly, rub against the sides or bottom of the holding facility and be blind or appear blind. The gills may protrude from under the opercula or the opercula may not close. These observations should be noted by the diagnostician and kept in mind throughout the diagnostic process.

Collection and Preservation of
Diagnostic Specimens

Careful attention should be given to the selection of suitable diagnostic specimens from the fish population. Fishes near death or freshly dead should be used in most cases. Fishes with common signs of disease should be used in the case of epizootics. Specimens should be examined as soon as possible following removal from the water. However, several methods of preservation can be used to save specimens for future investigation when immediate examination is impossible.

The individual who selects diagnostic specimens, in those cases when immediate examination is impractical, must first make an assumption of the general cause of the disease or epizootic in order to use the most suitable method of preservation. Specimens should be preserved differently for diseases caused by bacterial, viral or fungal organisms than for tumors, abnormal tissue growths or abnormal structures. Bacteria, viruses and fungi should be preserved by chilling or freezing because chemical preservatives destroy them and isolation and identification will not be possible. Freezing of tissue samples destroys cells on thawing and makes diagnosis by histopathology difficult or impossible. The method used for preservation of diagnostic specimens may be responsible for accurate diagnosis or failure to find the correct etiology. Therefore, great care must be taken to preserve specimens which cannot be examined immediately. The methods of preservation used for diagnostic specimens are listed below along with probable uses for each method.

Chilling of specimens can be used when freezing will destroy the usefulness of the specimen. An example is the preservation of whole blood. Whole blood can be preserved for a short time (up to two or three days) by chilling without destroying the blood cells. Whole fishes or fish parts may be preserved by chilling if laboratory examination will be done within a few hours of collecting the specimens. The best procedure for chilling specimens is to place them into a waterproof container and place the container directly onto wet ice for shipment or in a refrigerator for storage.

Freezing as a method of preserving diagnostic specimens is used in those cases when living organisms are thought to be present in the specimen and destruction of tissue cells is not important. Most bacteria, viruses and fungi are not killed by freezing, and specimens of fishes thought to be harboring these organisms can be preserved by freezing. There are several ways of freezing fishes or fish parts. The best method is to place the specimen in a waterproof container which fits snuggly and place the container on dry ice or into a mechanical freezer. Fishes or fish tissues should be frozen as quickly as possible to avoid the overgrowth of contaminating organisms. Large fishes or large pieces of fish tissue should be frozen on dry ice or liquid nitrogen to assure rapid freezing. The practice of placing a whole fish into water in a plastic or paper container and freezing the fish, water and container together should be avoided. Signs of disease on the fish will be completely eliminated upon thawing. Frozen tissues should remain frozen until ready for examination in the laboratory.

Chemical preservatives can be used when viability of organisms is not necessary. There are many suitable chemical preservatives; a selected list of those most useful are given in Table 1.[7] Diagnostic specimens selected for chemical preservation should be small enough to allow penetration of the preservative within a short time. Postmortem change continues in specimens until the preservative destroys the autolyzing enzymes. The process of preservation is called "fixing," and the more rapidly fixation can occur in tissues the better will be the observation of tissue changes caused by the etiological agent. Usually fishes up to 5 cm in length can be placed directly into the preservative. Fishes larger than 5 cm should be opened along the abdomen or the length of the swim bladder (see "Necropsy Procedures") before being placed into the preservative. This allows the fixative to enter the body cavity and fix all tissues more rapidly. Pieces of tissue no thicker than 1 to 2 cm on the smallest axis should

TABLE 1

Selected chemical preservatives used for fixation of histological and parasitic specimens[a]

Name	Method of Preparation	Suggested Use	Remarks
10% Formalin	Mix 1 part saturated (37-40%) formaldehyde solution with 9 parts water	All tissue specimens; large animal parasites	Best results from tissues held in the preservative under 30 days
10% Neutral Formalin	Same as 10% formalin except sodium hydroxide solution is added to a phenolphthalein endpoint	All tissue specimens; large animal parasites	Specimens can be held indefinitely without adverse effects
Bouin's Fluid	Mix 15 parts saturated aqeous solution of picric acid with 5 parts 37-40% formaldehyde solution and 1 part glacial acetic acid	All tissue specimens; large animal parasites	Animal parasites can be held in this preservative indefinately. Keeps organisms soft and flexible for easy manipulation
Schaudinn's Fluid	Just before use, mix 2 parts saturated solution of mercuric chloride in 0.85% aqueous sodium chloride and enough glacial acetic acid to equal 1% solution; discard after 24hrs.	Smears of protozoa	Place wet smears of protozoans in Schaudinn's fluid for 24 hrs., transfer to 70% ethyl alcohol and store indefinitely

[a]Other fixatives and preservatives are given in:
  Preece, A. 1972. *A manual for histological technicians, Third Ed..*
  Little, Brown & co., Boston. 428 p.

be removed from large fishes and placed directly into the preservative. The characteristics of the preservative determine the length of time whole fishes or fish tissues can remain in fixatives (Table 1).

Drying can be used to preserve certain specimens. Blood smears can be dried and sent directly to the laboratory. Blood smears to be held for over one to two days should be air-dried, placed in absolute methanol for about four minutes, redried and held almost indefinitely without further preservation.

Normal Anatomy and Histology

The fish diseases diagnostician needs to know the normal anatomy and normal histology of fishes. The large number of fishes and the varying anatomy of the different fish species makes knowledge of the anatomy of all species difficult. The fish disease diagnostician usually becomes adept at the anatomy of commonly examined fish species. However, knowledge of the anatomy of one fish species is easily related to the anatomy of other fishes (Pl. 33).

Disease diagnosis among fishes is assisted by the use of histology or histopathology. The competent fish disease diagnostician should become familiar with the normal microanatomy of the various organs of fishes in order to detect pathological changes caused by a disease.[1,3,3a,3b,10] Normal histology of several organs of a salmonid species can serve to demonstrate normal fish histology (Pl. 1A through Pl. 3A).

Necropsy Procedure

The purpose of a necropsy is to obtain information by observing external structures and gaining access to internal organs in a systematic way. There is no standard necropsy procedure. However, the necropsy technique which follows has been found to be satisfactory, with maximum opportunity to observe the organs and structures of the fish.

Performance of a necropsy on a fish, as with all animals, requires suitable instruments. Cultured fishes range in size from almost microscopic (alevins of small ornamental fishes) to fishes of several kilograms. Necropsy tools satisfactory for dissection of all life stages of the most common fishes should be included in the necropsy kit. Knives, scalpels and scissors should be sharp in order to reduce the tearing of tissues or the contamination of organs because tissues cannot be cut without great difficulty. Several sizes of scissors will be needed if necropsies are to be performed on fishes of various sizes. Forceps with sharp points which are directly opposed are essential to proper necropsy. Dissecting needles, eyedroppers, inoculating loops and other instruments will be useful. Plate 3B demonstrates a necropsy kit suitable for most of the fish species commonly found in fish culture facilities or aquariums.

Live fishes must be killed prior to proceeding with a necropsy. Euthanasia can be performed by thrusting the blade of a scalpel or knife through the top of the skull to the point where the skull attaches to the first vertebrae. A lateral movement of the blade will sever the spinal cord at the base of the brain and cause almost immediate paralysis. Another method of euthanasia must be employed if the brain is to be used for bacterial culture of histological examination. Anesthetics can be used but must be at greater concentration than is usually acceptable for anesthesia. Tricaine methanesulfonate (MS-222) at 100-200 mg/L has been found to be satisfactory for euthansia of fishes. Carbonic acid is an excellent euthanizing material. Add 100 ml of 6.75% w/v aqueous sodium bicarbonate solution to 4 liters of water followed by 100 ml of 3.95% w/v aqueous sulfuric acid solution. This mixture yields approximately 1,000 mg/L of carbonic acid and will kill fish within a few minutes.[2,4,5,6,8,9]

A necropsy should begin by examination of the exterior of the fish (Pl. 3C). The color of the skin, gills and fins may be of assistance in diagnosis. Note the presence of redness (erythema) on any part of the body. Look for light colored areas of skin or small white spots. Observe white to gray mucus or filaments on the skin. Look into the mouth for abnormal signs. Note whether the fish is emaciated or whether the eyes are protruding or sunken. Look for skeletal deformations and general skin, fin and scale abnormalities. Note the presence of external lesions, abnormal growths, swellings or the presence of inflammation. All external observations must be made before proceeding to the next step of the necropsy.

Careful gill observation should be made by clipping an operculum away and exposing the gills underneath (Pl. 3D). Note any swelling of gill tissue, presence of small or large white to gray areas and extreme redness or paleness. A section of the gill arch can be removed, placed on a microscope slide with a drop or two of water, covered with a cover glass and examined under the microscope (Pl. 3E). Look for abnormalities of the filaments and lamellae or for the presence of bacteria or parasites. Additional sections of gill arch may be removed and placed into a chemical fixative to be used for preparation of histological sections.

The next step in the necropsy is to open the body cavity. This should be done in a way which reduces contamination, especially in those cases where bacterial or fungal etiology of disease is suspected. The best procedure is to open the body cavity through the skin and into the swim bladder. All instruments used to make this cut should be disinfected if cultures are to be taken, and the entire side of the fish should be disinfected prior to making the first cut (Pl. 3F). The most distinguishing feature to use as a guide for opening the body cavity of most fishes is the lateral line. Locate the lateral line and then place the point of the scissors approximately one-fourth of the distance ventrally between the lateral line and the ventral abdominal surface (Pl. 4A). Thrust the point of the scissors through the skin and

into the swim bladder. Extend the cut posteriorly, using the lateral line as a guide, until the cut has extended the full length of the swim bladder, and then turn the cut ventrally to a point just anterior to the anus. Returning to the starting point, extend the cut anteriorly, using the lateral line as a guide, until the anterior end of the swim bladder is reached, and then turn the cut diagonally toward the pectoral fin. Keep the point of the scissors high to avoid cutting structures under the body wall.

Use disinfected forceps to turn the flap of the body wall ventrally to expose visceral organs. If bacterial cultures are to be taken, to avoid contamination, they should be taken as soon as the body cavity is opened. The kidneys are usually the best source of those bacterial pathogens which cause septicemia or kidney abscesses. A loop full of kidney tissue is removed using a sterile inoculating loop (Pl. 4B). This can be done by twirling the inoculating loop in a small area of the kidney. Prepare a smear of the kidney tissue using two microscope slides pressed together with the kidney tissue between them (Pl. 4C). Stain the kidney smear and examine it under the microscope for the presence of bacteria. If bacteria are found, use a sterile inoculating loop to remove additional kidney tissue from the same part of the kidney which is known to harbor bacteria and streak the tissue onto an appropriate culture medium (Pl. 4D). If bacteria are not seen in the stained kidney smear, use a sterile inoculating loop to remove small bits of kidney tissue from other parts of the kidney, preparing stained kidney smears as before. Cultures can then be prepared from the area of kidney known to harbor bacteria. This practice will save much culture medium.

Bacterial cultures should be made from organs other than kidneys prior to proceeding with a complete examination of the visceral organs. Note any indications of disease anywhere in the body cavity. Gently lift the alimentary tract, gonads, liver or other organs so that all parts of the abdominal cavity can be seen (Pl. 4E). Open the pericardium with scissors to expose the heart for examination. Blood smears may be made by gently opening the atrium, thus releasing blood from the atrial cavity. Parts of organs may be removed for gross and microscopic examination. Whole organs or parts of organs may be taken for virological isolation. Parasites may be separated from tissues and observed for identification or preserved for future examination.

Whole organs or parts of organs may be removed and placed into fixative for future histological preparation (Pl. 4F & 5A). Notes should be made of the color and consistency of each organ, the presence of abnormal fluids in the body cavity or organs, abscesses or abnormal growths, hemorrhages and other abnormal appearances. Muscles should be examined by making cuts through the skin and muscle along the entire length of the body (Pl. 5B).

The eyes should be removed and observed for pres-

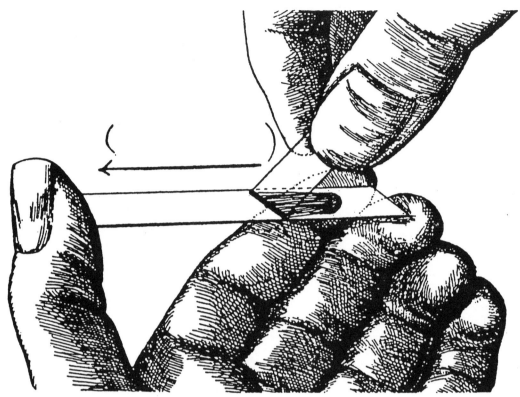

Fig. 1: A blood smear can be prepared from a small drop of blood. From *Textbook of Fish Diseases* by E. Amlacher, T.F.H. Publications, Neptune City, New Jersey.

ence of parasites or preserved for histological examination. The brain can be exposed by clipping away one side of the skull (Pl. 5C). Disinfected instruments must be used if cultures of brain are to be taken. Note abnormalities of the brain and cerebral fluid. Place the entire brain or parts of the organ in a fixative if histological examination is intended.

Blood needed for blood chemistry or hematology should be taken from living fishes. Blood from very small fishes can be taken by severing the caudal peduncle of the fish and collecting blood as it flows from the caudal vein (Pl. 5D & Fig. 1). Blood can be collected from larger fishes by entering the caudal vein or by heart puncture using a syringe and needle (Pl. 5E & 5F). Fish blood clots much more rapidly than blood of other animals. An anticoagulant-treated syringe and needle (heparin, EDTA, citric acid or potassium oxalate) may be used to stop or reduce coagulation.

All diagnostic samples taken during the necropsy should be preserved in some way if immediate examination is not possible. Tissue samples should be either chilled, frozen or preserved in a chemical preservative (fixative). The time between death of the fish and pres-

ervation of tissues should be reduced as much as possible to lessen postmortem autolysis. Animal parasites can be preserved in any good chemical fixative, but glycerin-alcohol is preferred by some parasitologists because it keeps the preserved organisms soft and pliant (Table 1). Parasitic flatworms (cestodes and trematodes) should be relaxed in hot water (about 60° C) for approximately five minutes before being placed into a fixative. Smears of protozoan parasites may be preserved in Schaudinn's fluid (Table 1). Blood smears should be fixed in absolute methanol if staining is not done within 24 to 48 hours after collection.

Necropsy, sample collection and sample preservation are important parts of disease diagnosis. The procedures are complicated by the fact that there are many sizes and shapes of fishes. Each fish species has anatomical conformations and organ locations or organ structures which are different from other fishes. The fish disease diagnostician usually must become familiar with these variations in many fish species. Knowledge of fish anatomy is essential in order to perform an acceptable necropsy. Selection of correct methods of sample preservation also becomes an essential part of the step by step procedure so necessary for accurate disease diagnosis.

Selected References

1. Anderson, B.G. and D.L. Mitchum. 1974. *Atlas of trout histology*. Wyo. Game and Fish Dept., Cheyenne, WY. 110p.

2. Bell, G.R. 1964. "A guide to the properties, characteristics, and uses of some general anesthetics for fish, "*J. Fish. Res. Bd. Can., Bull.* 148. 2nd Ed. revised. 11p.

3. Grizzle, J.M. and W.A. Rogers. 1976. *Anatomy and histology of the channel catfish*. Agric. Exp. Sta., Auburn University, Auburn, AL. 94p.

3a. Groman, D.B. 1982 *Histology of the striped bass*. Amer. Fish. Soc. Monog. No. 3., Bethesda, MD. 116p.

3b. Hibiya, T 1982 *An Atlas of fish histology. Normal and pathological features*. Kodansha Ltd., Tokoyo, Japan and Gustav Fisher Verlag, Stuttgart, East Germany and New York City, NY. 147p.

4. Klontz, G.W. 1964. "Anesthesia of fishes," *Proc. Symp. Expt. Animals Anesth.*, 13p.

5. Nelson, P.R. 1953. "Use of three anesthetics on juvenile salmon and trout," *Prog. Fish-Cult.*, 15:74.

6. Post, G. 1979. "Carbonic acid anesthesia for aquatic organisms," *Prog. Fish.-Cult.*, 41:142-144.

7. Preece, A. 1972. *A manual for histologic technicians, 3rd Ed.* Little, Brown & Co., Boston, MA. 428p.

8. Schoettger, R.A. 1967. "Annotated bibliography on MS-222," *U.S. Fish Wildl. Serv. Resource Publ.*, 22:1-15.

9. Schoettger, R.A., C.R. Walker, L.L. Marking and A.M. Julin. 1967. "MS-222 as an anesthetic for channel catfish: Its toxicity, efficiency and muscle residues," *U.S. Fish Wildl. Serv. Resource Publ.*, 33:1-14.

10. Yasutake, W.T. and J.H. Wales. 1983. *Microscopic anatomy of salmonids: An atlas*. U.S. Fish & Wildl. Serv. Resource Publ. 150, U.S. Dep. of the Interior, Washington, DC. 188 p.

Chapter III
CONTROL OF
FISH DISEASES

Methods of Disease Control in Fishes

Disease control procedures for fishes employ many of the same principles of therapy used for other animals. Certain modifications of therapeutic procedures have been adapted to the treatment of fishes in water. The mucus layer on the skin of fishes offers a major line of protection, but the fragility of this structure when fishes are removed from water has limited some of the techniques used for administration of therapeutic compounds to terrestrial animals. The mass rearing of fishes in fish culture excludes the use of parenteral injection of therapeutic compounds for the control of infectious diseases. Systemic drugs are usually added to the food of fishes when systemic therapy is required. Immunization of fishes for disease control has restrictions because injecting immunizing agents is impossible in large fish culture facilities where millions of fish are involved. There are a few cases in which parenteral injection can be used, such as in the case of a few valuable ornamental fishes or a few brood fishes in a fish hatchery. Other methods of immunization or mass systemic therapy have been developed.

There are at least six general methods of disease control in fishes. Some are used extensively in the culture of aquarium fishes and for limited disease control in wild fish populations. Some methods are used effectively, while others are less effective but offer alternative procedures when others fail or cannot be used. Six of the most used methods are:

1. Test and slaughter;
2. Quarantine and restriction of movement;
3. Drug therapy and sanitation;
4. Immunization and disease resistance;
5. Destruction or reduction of a link in the transmission cycle; and
6. Limitation or control of the release of toxic substances

Test and slaughter has been and will continue to be one of the most effective methods of disease control in fishes. Test and slaughter means that fish are examined and, if an infectious organism which has no known control is found or fish have excessively high levels of certain toxic compounds, the entire population will be killed and the carcasses disposed of in such a way that the etiological agent of the disease will be removed from other fish populations or other animals. Test and slaughter is the most distasteful method of disease control but has been found to be the most effective when

there is a necessity for absolute control. This method of disease control has been used successfully for animals other than fishes. It is not a newly developed procedure but probably has been used since animals have been domesticated by man.

There are several examples of the effectiveness of test and slaughter as a method of disease control in fishes. A disease known as whirling disease, caused by a sporozoan (*Myxosoma cerebralis*), has a limited distribution in the United States. Each time it has occurred in a new geographical location from which it could easily spread, the entire fish population has been slaughtered and the carcasses burned and deep-buried. Test and slaughter procedures combined with other methods of disease control have limited whirling disease distribution in the United States. Furunculosis has been controlled in many fish hatcheries by use of test and slaughter combined with other methods. Successful elimination of infectious pancreatic necrosis from many fish hatcheries has been possible by the use of test and slaughter and other disease control methods. Populations of fish with excessively high body burdens of chlorinated hydrocarbon insecticides or mercury have been slaughtered to prevent the fish from passing these toxic materials to animals which may use the fish for food. Test and slaughter is the only feasible method of disease control in limited wild fish populations.

Test and slaughter is not usually the complete answer to control of a disease, but when combined with other methods it has been one of the most useful and most successful methods for absolute disease control among fish populations.

Quarantine and restriction of movement has been used extensively for control of fish diseases.[11a] Quarantine and restriction of movement means that either: (1) fish which are to be moved from a suspected or infected geographical area to a noninfected geographical area must be held in detention for a period of time, at least as long as the incubation period of the suspected disease and then moved into the new geographical area, if the suspected disease does not develop; or (2) all movement of fishes is restricted between two geographical areas.

Unfortunately this method of disease control was not initiated until several diseases which originated on the European continent were brought to the United States and certain diseases originating in the United States were transported to other countries of the world. Quarantine and restriction of movement cannot be used successfully as a method of disease control without cooperation between fish culturists, sport fishery managers, fish health specialists, state and federal agencies and everyone interested in controlling fish diseases.

The most effective use of quarantine and movement restriction for disease control has been through legislative regulation of the intercontinental, interstate or interprovincial movement of fishes. Regulating intrastate fish movements for purposes of disease control has not been successful in most of the states of the United States. Several state agencies have placed state fishery operations under quarantine and movement restrictions when fishes were known to have quarantinable infectious diseases, but these restrictions have not applied to commercial fish culture or privately owned fishes.

Quarantine and restriction of movement is especially effective for the control of fish diseases when used with other methods of control. Transmissible diseases with no known cure may be controlled by restricting the movement of fishes, fish parts or fish products from the effected population until other disease control methods can be employed. Quarantine and restriction of movement has been found to be especially effective when combined with test and slaughter and sanitation and disinfection.

Quarantine and restriction of movement has limited the geographical distribution of several very important fish diseases. Examples are viral hemorrhagic septicemia, whirling disease (a protozoan disease), European gill rot (a fungal disease) and enteric redmouth (a bacterial disease). These diseases have limited distribution outside the continent of origin but continue to be spread within the continent of origin. Wise use of quarantine and restriction of movement can be an effective method of disease control in fishes.

Drug therapy and sanitation is a method of disease control which comes to mind whenever treatment of a disease is mentioned. Therapeutic drugs have been found to be effective in the control of certain diseases of humans and domestic animals. However, drugs used for systemic or topical therapy, disease prophylaxis and disinfectant procedures have been of limited use for diseases of fishes.[14] Certainly fish health specialists working with curable fish diseases have had a desire to use therapeutic compounds, but there are a limited number of therapeutic drugs proven useful for the control of these diseases. The search for acceptable drugs has been extremely limited. Funds have been available from government agencies and commercial drug manufacturers for therapeutic drug research on humans and domestic animals, but not on fishes. The reason for the scarcity of funding for therapeutic drug research in fishes is the limited volume of sales of the drugs used for control of fish diseases in comparison to the large volume of drugs used to control diseases in humans or domestic animals.

There are an extermely large number of known therapeutic compounds available from pharmaceutical manufacturers which have not been applied to the control of fish diseases. There are a great number of synthetic compounds prepared by chemists and pharmacologists each year which may be potentially effective in the control of pathogenic organisms. Only a very limited number of all of these compounds have been examined for possible usefulness as therapeutic compounds for fish disease control.

There is another reason why many of the potentially usable therapeutic compounds have not been used for fish disease control in the United States. The Federal Food, Drug and Cosmetic Act of 1915 and the revised act of 1956 limit the use of most substances until safety to animals (including fishes) can be proved.[6] All compounds, natural and synthetic, must be registered as safe to use in or on animals by the Food and Drug Administration (FDA), an administrative part of the U.S. Department of Health and Human Services. Each potentially effective therapeutic compound must be examined for its effectiveness in the control of a specific disease, toxicity of the compound and the time of clearance of the compound or its metabolites from the tissues of the same animal species. Data must be obtained on these three variables to satisfy the FDA that the compound is effective for the disease intended, is safe to use in the animal species at a prescribed dosage for a prescribed time and that the compound will be eliminated from the animal's tissues in a specified length of time. Tissue clearance regulation is of special interest in those animals which will be used as the food of other animals, including humans.

The revised act of 1956 included a "food additives" section necessary to control the addition of various substances to the foods of animals. The myriad of substances used in the modern technology of food preparation, preservation and storage is covered under the revised act. The addition of therapeutic substances to foods which are subsequently fed to any animal is regulated. Systemic therapeutic compounds for use in fishes are also included. Most of the systemic disease control in fishes is through the use of therapeutic compounds in food.

Food additives registration with the FDA is necessary for each drug to be added to the food of fishes. Therapeutic drugs administered in the diet require the additional registration as a food additive, which includes information on dosage and withdrawal time between the last dose given to the fish and the time fish can be used as food. This information must appear on a "tag" which must be attached to each container of fish food. Fishes used as experimental animals may be given unregistered drugs, but the fish must be destroyed and the entire body of the fish eliminated from possible use as food.

FDA control of all therapeutic substances, including external disinfectants, used in or around fish is possible by taking samples of marketed food fish or cultured sport fish which have been treated with therapeutic compounds at the prescribed dosage for the dosage time and withdrawn from the drug as directed. Analysis of these samples should indicate correct use of the therapeutic compound. Analysis may also indicate illegal use of therapeutic compounds or compounds not registered for use in or around fish.

Regulation of the Federal Food, Drug and Cosmetic Act, as revised, has definitely curtailed the use of antibiotics, chemotherapeutic compounds and, to some extent, external disinfectants for control of fish diseases. The regulations appear as a nuisance to fish culturists and fish disease disgnosticians but are an essential part of the modern way of life, which is to protect all animals from indiscriminate use of toxic substances in food.

Immunization and disease resistance has been of limited use when compared to the successful use of immunizing agents for disease control in humans and domestic animals other than fish. Many devastating infectious diseases of certain domestic animals and humans have been controlled or eliminated by immunization techniques. The reasons why fish immunization has been of limited success are because: (1) fishes are not as immunologically competent as higher animals, especially at lower temperatures; and (2) there are limited methods for mass immunization of cultured fishes.

Injection of all fishes in a fish culture facility is usually an insurmountable task. Parenteral injections used for successful immunization against most infectious agents require anamnestic dosages of the immunizing agent to stimulate and restimulate the immune system of the animal being immunized. Research has demonstrated that certain fishes require two or more injections of an immunizing agent at extended time intervals to maintain protective immunity against certain pathogens.[12,20,21] This means that the usually impossible task of mass injecting fishes in a fish culture facility must be followed at regular time intervals with additional immunizing agent injections for each fish. Parenteral injections of immunizing agents have been used as a successful method when small numbers of fishes require vaccination, however.

The oral method of immunizing large numbers of fishes against bacterial pathogens has been of limited use.[5,15,21,14a] The procedure used for oral immunization has been to add the immunizing agent to fish food and feed at prescribed time intervals.

A method of vacuum infiltration of the immunizing agent has been suggested for the mass immunization of fish. Fishes are placed in a bacterin which is contained in a pressure vessel. A partial vacuum is established inside the vessel and then released. The rapid change in pressure causes some of the bacterin to enter tissues of the fishes. This method has been used experimentally but holds little promise for mass immunization of fishes.[2]

Mass immunizing techniques in which fish are submersed in an hypertonic solution containing the immunizing agent, or by spraying the hypertonic immunizing preparation against the fish as they pass along a downward sloping pan, are more adaptable to delivery of the immunizing agent to large numbers of fish over a short period of time. These two method of mass immunizing fish are being developed rapidly and will become more useful as more acceptable vaccines and bacterins prepared from a wider variety of infectious pathogens are developed.[9,11,11b,19a]

Resistant strains of fish species have been used to control disease. Some fish species have a natural resistance to certain pathogens. An example is the natural resistance of rainbow trout to *Aeromonas salmonicida* if the water temperature is below 11 °C. The fish will become infected but will usually remain asymptomatic.[8] Brown trout are known to be resistant to whirling disease (caused by *Myxosoma cerebralis*). Therefore, brown trout can be reared without excessive losses in culture facilities known to harbor this organism. Other trout species may develop the disease and suffer excessive mortality if held in the same facility.

Attempts have been made to develop strains of fish species which are resistant or immune to certain pathogens. This method of disease control holds promise but requires much more research to be effective.

Destruction or reduction of a link in the transmission cycle has been used to control infectious diseases of fishes to a limited extent when involving animal parasites. Metazoan parasites of fishes have a definite transmission cycle involving the fish at some stage of development. Many of these parasites require one or more other animal host species to complete the life cycle. Each stage of development in each host offers a possible means of disrupting the transmission of the parasite. However, eliminating a link in the transmission cycle may not be feasible, because it may mean the elimination of a protected mammal or bird, or of a crustacean or mollusc which cannot be eliminated. Destruction or reduction of the life cycle of a fish pathogen should always be considered when methods of disease control are being judged.

Limit or control of the release of toxic substances has been one of the most effective methods of disease control in the more technologically oriented countries of the world. Study of the toxic effects of various substances in the water surrounding fishes has been the subject of research for the past half century. There have been tremendous losses of fishes in streams, lakes and reservoirs from the release of toxic substances from industries, agriculture and domestic wastes. The myriad of toxic substances such as heavy metals, organic solvents, pesticides, oxygen-depleting chemicals, toxic gases and other toxic substances which have found their way into the environment of fishes act in many detrimental ways to fish-life. These toxic substances may reduce survivability or kill fishes, alter or eliminate reproduction, reduce or destroy the food supply or adversely affect fishes in other ways. Release of many of these substances can be controlled to reduce fish loss.[10,16]

Toxic substances occur in the water of fish culture facilities. Some of these substances are derived from outside sources, but many are the metabolic waste products from the fishes themselves. Limiting or controlling these toxic materials will assist in the disease control of cultured fishes.

External Treatment of Fish Diseases

External disinfectants are used to control infections of organisms on the outside surface of fishes and to eliminate or reduce potential pathogens from fish-holding facilities as well as utensils used for the maintenance of the fishes. External disinfectants used to control disease organisms on fishes must be miscible with water or capable of being suspended in water at a therapeutic concentration. These compounds must control the growth of or destroy the target organism at a concentration below the lethal level for the fish being treated. The compounds should resist absorption by the fish and should be capable of being used for multiple treatments without observable harm to the fish. The compounds should also be economically acceptable for use in fish culture facilities.

The success of any disinfectant is a time-concentration ratio. Fish must be capable of being held in water within this time-concentration ratio in order to allow removal of infectious organisms from them without undue harm. There are several disinfectants known to be suitable for use in water surrounding fishes. However, there are many other disinfecting compounds in general use today which have not been examined for potential use as external disinfectants for fishes.

Time and dose level (concentration in the water) data have been established for several disinfectants known to reduce or eliminate external pathogen populations on fishes without undue toxicity. The time of treatment is usually given in seconds, minutes or hours. Concentrations of each disinfectant can usually be increased for short treatment periods or reduced for increased treatment times. Usually fishes can withstand a higher concentration of a disinfectant for a short period of time or a lower concentration for an extended disinfection time (Table 2).

Natural products such as table salt (NaCl) and acetic acid have been used for external therapy of fish diseases for many years. Other disinfectant compounds have come into use which are much better bactericides, fungicides or parasiticides. However, registration for their use is required in the United States and certain other countries of the world. The fish health specialist, aquarist or fish culturist must limit use of these compounds to those accepted for safe use by governing agencies responsible for their control (the FDA and the Environmental Protection Agency in the United States).

Some of the most useful disinfectants for external control of fish disease organisms have stable molecules which resist breakdown in water. Some are absorbed into fish tissue and remain there for long periods of time. In both cases, the two United States federal agencies attempt to reduce the possibility of water pollution from water released from fish culture facilities or elimination of contaminated food fish. The small quantity of water used by the aquarist is not usually a problem where water pollution standards are concerned nor are the fishes used as food of other animals, yet each aquarist should comply with registration regulations for each disinfectant compound. A selection of compounds found useful as external therapeutic agents for fishes is given in Table 2.

There are some disinfectants which cannot be used in water surrounding fishes. Chlorine, as an example, has approximately the same toxicity to fishes as it has to microorganisms. Chlorine is acceptable for disinfection of facilities used for holding fishes or for utensils used for maintenance of fishes. Chlorine has been found to be one of the most useful disinfectants for elimination of pathogens from fish-holding facilities. Care must be taken to completely detoxify chlorine before returning fish to the holding facility after disinfection.

Fish eggs can be disinfected to reduce or eliminate pathogenic bacteria which may be on the external surface of the eggs. Three disinfectants have been used: acriflavin, polyvinylpyrolidone-iodine (iodophor) and merthiolate (Table 2).[2,3,7] The practice has been responsible for reducing the spread of certain infectious diseases.[26,28]

Methods for external disinfection and disease therapy include dip, flush, bath (static) and dynamic (flow-through) procedures. The treatment of fishes using the dip procedure is accomplished by mixing the required quantity of disinfectant in a measured volume of water. Fish are taken from the holding tank in a net, held in the dip for the specified time and returned to the holding tank. The dip procedure is generally used for small numbers of fish and for those disinfectants which can be used for a short treatment time. Malachite green, salt and acetic acid dips are acceptable because high concentrations of the disinfectants can be used effectively for short treatment times. Most fish species can withstand

TABLE 2

Disinfectants used for control of external pathogens of fishes

Disinfectant	Type of Disinfectant	Use	Concentration/Time for Safe Use
Acetic acid[a]	Organic compound	Bactericide, parasiticide	1:20 (5%) for 1 minute
Acriflavin[27]	Organic dyestuff	Bactericide (for fish egg disinfection)	1:2,000 (500 mg/L) for 20 minutes
Anti-Stain X	Organic mercurial (1.2% mercury)	Bactericide	1:1,000,000 (1 mg/L) for 1 hour, use no oftener than once a week
Chloramine-T[10a]	Organic compound	General disinfectant	1:154,000 to 1:225,000 (4.5 to 6.5 mg/L) for 1 to 8 hours
Chlorine	Inorganic gas	Complete disinfectant	$\geq$1:100,000 (10 mg/L) for 30 minutes
Copper sulfate[a]	Inorganic compound	Bactericide, parasiticide	1:250,000 to 1:1,000,000 (1 to 4 mg/L) for 1 hour, depends upon dissolved elements in the water
Crystal violet	Organic dyestuff	Fungicide	1:200,000 (5 mg/L) for 1 hour
Diquat[27a]	Organic compound	Algicide (for use on bacterial gill disease)	1:120,000 to 1:240,000 (8.4 to 16.8 mg/L) for 1 hour
Erythromycin phosphate[14b]	Antibiotic	Bacteristat (for control of bacterial kidney disease in salmonid eggs)	1:500,000 (2 mg/L) to water harden salmonid eggs
Formalin[a] (37-40% formaldehyde gas in water)	Organic gas in water	Protozoacide, parasiticide and fungicide	1:4,000 (250 mg/L) for 1 hour
Furanace[b] (P-7138)	Nitrofuran compound	Myxobactericide	1:500,000 (2 mg/L) for 1 hour
Hyamin 3500 (10% liquid)	Quaternary ammonium	General bactericide	1:50,000 (20 mg/L) for 1 hour
Hyamin 2389 (50% liquid)	Quaternary ammonium	General bactericide	1:250,000 (4 mg/L) for 1 hour
Hyamin 1622 (100% powder)	Quaternary ammonium	General bactericide	1:500,000 (2 mg/L) for 1 hour
Malachite green (zinc-free)	Organic dyestuff	Fungicide, parasiticide	1:15,000 (66.7 mg/L) for 10 to 30 seconds; 1:200,000 (5 mg/L) for 1 hour
Masoten[b]	Organophophate	Copepod parasites	1:4,000,000 (0.25 mg/L) for 1 hour, up to four times a week

TABLE 2

(continued)

Disinfectant	Type of Disinfectant	Use	Concentration/Time for Safe Use
Merthiolate [29] (Thimerosal)	Organic mercurial (49.55% mercury)	Bactericide (for fish egg disinfection)	1:5,000 (200 mg/L) for 10 minutes
Methylene blue	Organic dyestuff	Ichthyophthiriasis parasiticide	1:200,000 to 1:500,000 (2 to 5 mg/L) permanent bath
Metronidazole	Organic compound	Protozoacide (flagellates)	1:250,000 4 mg/L) for 1 hour, 3 to 5 consecutive days
Nitrofurazone (Furacin®)	Organic compound	Myxobactericide	1:50,000 to 1:200,000 (5 to 20 mg/L) for 1 hour
Polyvinylpyrolidone iodine[c]	Organic iodine complex	Bactericide (for fish egg disinfection)	1:100 (1%) for 10 minutes
Potassium permanganate [a]	Inorganic compound	Bactericide	Up to 1:250,000 (up to 4 mg/L) for 1 hour; depends upon BOD[d] and COD[e] of the water
Purina disinfectant 1X	Quaternary ammonium	General bactericide	1:56,000 (17.86 mg/L) for 1 hour
Purina disinfectant 2X improved	Quaternary ammonium	General bactericide	1:112,000 (8.9 mg/L) for 1 hour
Purina disinfectant 4X improved	Quaternary ammonium	General bactericide	1:225,000 (4.45 mg/L) for 1 hour
Purina disinfectant 8X improved	Quaternary ammonium	General bactericide	1:450,000 (2.22 mg/L) for 1 hour
Quinine hydrochloride	Natural alkaloid	Ichthyophthiriasis	1:50,000 (20 mg/L) permanent bath
Roccal (10% liquid)	Quaternary ammonium	General bactericide	1:50,000 (20 mg/L) for 1 hour
Roccal (50% liquid)	Quaternary ammonium	General bactericide	1:250,000 (4 mg/L) for 1 hour
Sodium chloride[a]	Natural compound	Selective bactericide, fungicide and parasiticide	1:33 to 1:20 (3 to 5%) for 1 to 2 minutes; 1:100 to 1:66.7 (1 to 1.5%) for 20 to 30 minutes

[a]Registered by the FDA for use on food fish
[b]Registered by the FDA for non-food fish use only
[c]Examples are Betadine® and Wescodyne®
[d]Biochemical Oxygen Demand
[e]Chemical Oxygen Demand

a high concentration of these disinfectants for a short time.

Flush treatments are similar to dip treatments in that disinfectant concentration is high and the fish remain in the disinfectant for only a short period of time. The fish are not handled in the flush treatment procedure. Flush treatments are used in troughs, tanks, raceways and ponds with direct water flow; for example, water enters at one end of the container, flows directly through and leaves at the lower end of the container. A high concentration of the disinfectant is prepared at the upper end of the container and allowed to "flush" through as a high disinfectant concentration area. The fish move into and out of the high disinfectant concentration. Colored compounds, such as potassium permanganate or copper sulfate, are especially useful for flush treatment because the high disinfectant concentration area can be observed and the length of time most fish are treated can be determined. A demonstration of the flush treatment procedure is given in Example 1.

Treatment of fish using the bath or static procedure is accomplished by measuring the volume of water and fish in the container, calculating the quantity of disinfectant required, adding and mixing the disinfectant and allowing the disinfectant/water mixture to remain with the fish for the designated length of time. The disinfectant/water mixture is then removed and replaced with fresh water. An advantage of the bath procedure is that a more precise treatment can be given to the fish. An exact quantity of disinfectant can be added to a more exact quantity of water, and fish are held in the more precise disinfecting bath for a more carefully regulated length of time. There are several disadvantages to the bath treatment procedure. Baths used in troughs, tanks, raceways or ponds require that inflow water be shut off during the treatment time. Fishes suffering with respiratory diseases may become more anoxic during the treatment period, especially in overcrowded fish-holding facilities. The bath treatment procedure requires that the disinfectant/water mixture be removed from the fish-holding facility very rapidly at the end of the treatment time. Large ponds usually drain slowly, which leaves fish in contact with the disinfecting solution for an excessively long period of time. The bath treatment procedure is most useful for the treatment of fishes in relatively small holding facilities or in those which can be drained rapidly. Example 2 is a demonstration of the bath treatment procedure.

The dynamic or flow-through treatment procedure can only be used in fish-holding facilities which have inflow and outflow water. Disinfectant is added at a *constant rate* to the inflow water for the desired treatment time. The disinfectant/water mixture forms at the inflow end of the container and moves through and out of the container to be replaced by fresh water. A requirement for the dynamic treatment procedure is that the inflow water can be measured and the volume of inflow remains constant during the treatment period. The major advantage of the dynamic treatment procedure is that water does not need to be shut off during treatment, thus being advantageous for the therapy of respiratory diseases or for overcrowded fish-holding facilities. A disadvantage of the procedure is that the fish-holding container must have direct flow throughout its length. Usually irregularly shaped raceways or large ponds cannot be treated satisfactorily using the dynamic procedure. A demonstration of the dynamic treatment procedure is given in Example 3.

Disinfecting Fish Culture Facilities

Sanitizing entire fish culture facilities as well as nets, brooms, brushes, grading equipment or other paraphernalia used to manage fishes is a common practice when the facilities and utensils are contaminated with an economically important or exceptionally obnoxious pathogen. The sanitizing procedure is usually done when there are no fishes in the facility. The troughs, tanks, raceways and ponds are filled completely with water, the overflow is blocked and the inflow shut off. Each container is sanitized by adding sodium hypochlorite so that a residual chlorine strength of at least 10 mg/L remains after 30 minutes. The tops of the tanks and raceways are kept wet with the disinfecting solution during the 30-minute period. All utensils and equipment used around fishes not harmed by chlorine are soaked in the sanitizing solution.

The inside of hatchery buildings or other buildings used for fishes are sanitized by spraying a strong solution of sodium hypochlorite into cracks in floors, walls, incubator frames or any place where the pathogen could occur.

Residual chlorine is allowed to dissipate to less than 0.01 mg/L, and then water held in troughs, tanks, raceways and ponds is released. Usually the facilities can be returned to fish production immediately after the sanitizing procedure is completed.

Systemic Treatment of Fish Diseases

Systemic therapy of fish diseases is primarily through the oral route. Most systemic therapeutic compounds are administered in the food. Occasionally these drugs are administered parenterally, but only when small numbers of fish are involved.

Therapeutic drugs used for control of fish diseases must be capable of controlling reproduction of the pathogen under conditions found in the fishes. The therapeutic dose level must be safely below the toxic level of the drugs. The compounds should also be economically acceptable for use in cultured fishes. The most commonly used systemic drugs for fish disease control are given in Table 3.

There are constraints which apply to the use of systemic therapeutic drugs for control of fish diseases.

Example 1: Demonstration of the flush treatment procedure for therapy of fish in holding facilities having constant inflow water.

Inflow of water to container: 10 liters (2.64 gallon) per minute

Disinfectant to be used: malachite green

Disinfectant concentration (approx.): 1:15,000

Stock malachite green solution: 2 g per 3,785 ml (1 gallon)

Desired Treatment time: 1 minute

Calculation:

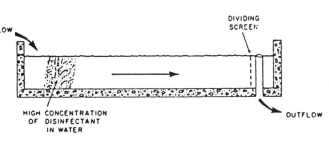

10 liter per minute = 10,000 ml per minute

10,000 ml ÷ 15,000 = 0.67 g malachite green required for treatment and

2 g : 3,785 :: 0.67 g : X ml

X = 1,268 ml

1,268 ml of stock malachite green are added to the inflow water over a period of one minute. The high concentration of malachite green flushes downstream, allowing fish to remain in the disinfectant for a short period of time.

Example 2: Demonstration of the static (bath) procedure for treatment of external diseases of fishes

Tank dimensions: 25 X 1.5 meters (82 X 5 feet)

Average water depth: 61 cm (24 inches)

Disinfectant to be used: Purina disinfectant 4X improved

Disinfectant concentration: 1:225,000

Treatment time: 1 hour

Calculations:

25 m X 1.5 m X 0.61 m = 22.875 cu m

22.875 cu m X 1,000,000 cc/cu m = 22,875,000 cc (ml)

22,875,000 ml ÷ 225,000 = 102 ml of disinfectant required

The inflow water to the tank is shut off. 102 ml of Purina disinfectant are added to the tank so that an even distribution of disinfectant is possible. The disinfectant is thoroughly mixed with the water in the tank. The water-disinfectant mixture is allowed to remain in contact with the fishes for one hour. Inflow water is turned on at the end of one hour and the drain opened completely to release disinfectant as rapidly as possible. The drain is closed after most of the disinfectant has been removed and the tank is allowed to fill with fresh water.

Example 3: Demonstration of the dynamic (flow through) procedure for treatment of external diseases of fishes

Volume of inflow: 190 liters (50 gallons) per minute

Disinfectant to be used: formalin

Disinfectant concentration: 1:4,000

Treatment time: 1 hour

Calculations:

190 L/min X 60 min = 11,400 L/hr

11,400 L X 1,000 = 11,400,000 ml/hr

11,400,000 ÷ 4,000 = 2,850 ml of formalin (37-40% formaldehyde) required

2,850 ml of formalin are placed into a carefully regulated constant flow device and allowed to flow at the rate of 47.5 ml per minute into the stream of inflow water. The disinfectant mixture, in a one-hour-long train, flows downstream through the tank and out the drain. Additional tanks below the initially treated tank may receive the outflow of disinfectant and be treated as the train of disinfecting solution moves along.

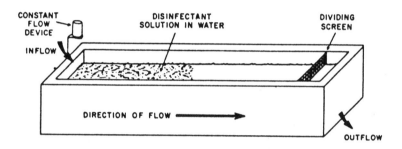

These constraints must be adhered to for best results when attempting to treat systemic diseases. The therapeutic compound must be mixed evenly and thoroughly into the food. There must be a consistent feeding level of the therapeutic drug-food mixture. The therapeutic drug-food must be fed so each fish receives the required amount of mixture at prescribed intervals. The mixture must be fed over a long enough period of time to be effective in controlling the pathogen.

The nutrients in the ration must meet all nutritional requirements of the fish during the treatment period. The reason for a balanced ration during the treatment period is that many systemic drugs are given for 10 to 21 days to yield best therapeutic results (Table 3). Nutritional deficiencies could occur in the fish during these relatively long treatment times. This means that not only must the required quantity of therapeutic drug be added per unit of ration, but the unit quantity of ration must meet nutritional requirements of the fish. Examples of these calculations are given in Examples 4 and 5.

Orally administered systemic drugs must be absorbed from the alimentary tract of the fish and produce a therapeutic concentration of the drug in all tissues without reaching a toxic concentration. Most antibiotic and chemotherapeutic compounds do not destroy the pathogens directly but reduce or stop their replication. Therefore, the therapeutic level of drug in tissues must be maintained for a long enough period of time to allow defense mechanisms of the fish (primarily phagocytes) to remove the static pathogens.

There are a limited number of drugs which can be administered orally for control of systemic diseases of fishes (Table 3). The reason for the small number of effective drugs is partially because research on new drugs has not kept up with drug production and partially because of apathy or lack of interest, since the few drugs being used have been effective and economical. The nature of systemic pathogens and the poikilothermic system of fishes combine to make many of the antibiotic and chemotherapeutic drugs used for disease control in other animals unsuitable for use with fishes. However, there are certainly many potential systemic drugs which could be used for this purpose. There is a need for research to locate suitable drugs, establish effective dosage and determine toxic quantities and clearance times from fish tissue.

**Example 4: Sulfamerazine (SM) therapy for 1,000 kg (2,200 lb) of fish
at a feeding level of 1.3 for balanced nutrition**

SM dose level: 0.26 g/kg (12 g/100 lb) of fish per day for 3 days
Then: 0.15 g/kg (7 g/100 lb) of fish per day for 11
additional days

Total SM requirement: 260 g per day for the first 3 days
150 g per day for the next 11 days

Feeding level: 1.3 (1.3% of total fish body weight per day)
1,000 kg (2,200 lb) of fish receive 13 kg (28.6 lb)
of ration per day

Requirement for drug and ration:
260 g SM in 13 kg (28.6 lb) ration for 3 days
150 g SM in 13 kg (28.6 lb) ration each day for
11 additional days

**Example 5: Terramycin (TM) therapy for 1,000 kg (2,200 lb) of fish at a
feeding level of 1.3 for balanced nutrition using TM-50 Premix
@ 50 g TM per 454 g (lb)**

TM dose level: 55 mg/kg (2.5 g/100 lb) of fish per day for 10 days

Total TM requirement: 55 g per day for 10 days

Total TM-50 Premix: 50 : 454:: 55 : X
X = 500 g

Feeding level: 1.3 (1.3% of total body weight per day)
1,000 kg (2,200 lb) of fish receive 13 kg (28.6 lb)
of ration per day

Requirements for drug and ration:
500 g TM-50 in 13 kg (28.6 lb) ration each day for
10 days

A second major factor which limits the number of suitable systemic drugs which can be used for control of disease in fishes in the United States is federal regulations. Each drug found usable for disease control must pass the U.S. Food and Drug Administration (FDA) registration procedures, which is both time consuming and costly.[30]

Alimentary pathogens (those organisms which remain in the alimentary tract) require a somewhat different approach to therapy of the diseases caused by these organisms. Alimentary organisms are controlled in fishes by adding the therapeutic drug to the food. The drugs should remain in the alimentary tract, and absorption into the blood or other tissues should be in minor quantities or not at all. The drugs should kill the pathogens *in situ* or render them incapable of remaining in place. Some drugs used for control of alimentary pathogens may do so by causing violent peristalsis of the intestinal tract and mechanical removal from the fish.

There are a limited number of effective therapeutic drugs for control of alimentary pathogens of fishes (Table 3). The reason for the small number is mainly lack of research and lack of interest among fish health specialists, fish culturists and other fishery workers. As with other drugs used for disease control in fishes, therapeutic compounds used for the control of alimentary pathogens must receive FDA registration for safety and effectiveness.

TABLE 3

Therapeutic drugs used for control of systemic and alimentary diseases of fishes

Drug	Therapeutic Dose	Suggested Use
Aureomycin[28]	55 mg/kg (2.5 g/100 lb) of fish per day for 10 days	Diseases caused by certain *Aeromonas* and *Pseudomonas* bacteria
Carbarsone[8]	0.2% of the diet for 3 days	Infections of intestinal flagellated protozoa
Chloramphenicol[28]	55 mg/kg (2.5 g/100 lb) of fish per day for 10 days	Motile aeromonad disease and furunculosis
Chlortetracycline	See aureomycin	
Cyzine[17]	20 mg/kg (9.1 mg/lb) of diet for 3 days	Infections of intestinal flagellated protozoa
Di-N-Butyl Tin Oxide[1,19]	250 mg/kg (114 mg/lb) of the diet for 3 days	Cestode (tapeworm) and trematode (fluke) infections
Enheptin[24]	0.1% of the diet for 3 days	Infections of intestinal flagellated protozoa
Epsom salts	3.0% of the diet for 2 to 3 days	Infections of intestinal flagellated protozoa
Erythromycin[31]	0.1 g/kg (4.5 g/100 lb) of fish per day for 20 days	Renibacterial kidney disease, and streptococcal infections
Furazolidone [22,23]	35 mg/kg (1.6 g/100 lb) of fish per day for 21 days	Furunculosis
	75 mg/kg (3.4 g/100 lb) of fish per day for 10 to 14 days	Hexamitiasis and coccidiosis
Furanace[26]	0.5 to 1.0 g/kg of the diet for 10 to 14 days	Vibriosis and *Aeromonas* sp.
Kamala[18a]	1 g/kg (45 g/100 lb) of fish per day for 7 to 14 days	Cestode infestations
Kanamycin[4]	20 mg/kg (0.91 g/100 lb) of fish per day for up to 20 days	Mycobacteriosis and diseases caused by certain *Aeromonas* and *Pseudomonas* bacteria
Mebendazole[6a,18a]	100 mg/kg (4.5 g/100 lb) of fish per day for 14 days	Cestode infestations
Metronidazole	1% of the diet fed every 12 hours for 3 days	Infections of intestinal flagellated protozoa
Nitrofurazone (Furacin®)	75 mg/kg (3.4 g/100 lb) of fish per day for 14 days	Furunculosis and internal *Flexibacter* infections

TABLE 3

(continued)

Drug	Therapeutic Dose	Suggested Use
Oxolinic Acid[8a]	5 mg/kg (227 mg/100 lb) of fish per day for 10 days	Furunculosis
★Oxytetracycline[28]	55 mg/kg (2.5 g/100 lb) of fish per day for 10 days	Furunculosis, ulcer disease and certain other diseases caused by gram-negative bacteria
★Ormetoprim + Sulfadimethoxine (Romet-30®)	50 mg/kg (2.27 g/100 lb) of fish per day for 10 days	Furunculosis and enteric redmouth disease
Sulfisoxazole[4]	0.22 g/kg (10 g/100 lb) of fish per day for 10 days	Systemic myxobacterial infections
Sulfadiazine[13,25]	0.26 g/kg (12 g/100 lb) of fish per day for 7 days followed by 0.13 g/kg (6 g/100 lb) of fish per day for 21 additional days	Renibacterial kidney disease and other selected bacterial diseases
Sulfaguanadine[10]	Add sulfaguanadine to sulfamerazine at the rate of 0.13 g/kg (6 g/100 lb) of fish per day for 3 days, then 0.09 g/kg (4 g/100 lb) of fish per day for 11 additional days	Furunculosis and other bacterial diseases in which there are septicemia and alimentary bacteremia
★Sulfamerazine	0.26 g/kg (12 g/100 lb) of fish per day for 3 days followed by 0.15 g/kg (7 g/100 lb) of fish per day for an additional 11 days	Many diseases caused by gram-negative bacterial pathogens of fishes
Sulfamethazine	Same as sulfamerazine	Same as sulfamerazine
Terramycin	See oxytetracycline	
Tiamulin[20a]	5 mg/kg (227 mg/100 lb) of fish per day for 14 days	Enteric redmouth disease
Tribressen®[6b,20a]	1 mg/kg (45 mg/100 lb) of fish per day for 14 days	Enteric redmouth disease
Yomesan[18a]	50 mg/kg (2.27 g/100 lb) of fish per day for 3 days	Intestinal nematodes and cestodes

★Registered by the FDA for food fish use[18-30]

Selected References

1. Allison, R. 1957. "A preliminary note on the use of di-n-butyl tin oxide to remove tapeworms from fish,"*Prog. Fish-Cult.*, 19:128-130.

2. Amend, D.F. 1976. "Prevention and control of viral diseases of salmonids," *J. Fish. Res. Bd. Can.*, 33:1059-1066.

3. Amend, D.F. and J.P. Pietsch. 1972. "Virucidal activities of two iodophors to salmonid viruses," *J. Fish. Res. Bd. Can.*, 29:61-65.

4. Amlacher, E. 1970. *Textbook of fish diseases*. T.F.H. Publ., Neptune, NJ, p. 75.

5. Anderson, D.P. and J.R. Nelson. 1974. "Comparison of protection in rainbow trout (*Salmo gairdneri*) inoculated with and fed Hagerman redmouth bacterin," *J. Fish. Res. Bd. Can.*, 31:214-216.

6. Anonymous. 1972. *Federal Food, Drug and Cosmetic Act* as amended. U.S. Health, Education and Welfare. Available from: U.S. Government Printing Office, Washington, DC. (Contains the *Act* and all amendments through the year 1972). 94p.

6a. Boonyaratpalin, S. and W.A. Rogers. 1984 "Control of the bass tapeworm, *Proteocephalus ambloplitis*, with mebendazole." *J. Fish Dis.*, 7:449-456.

6b. Bosse, M.P. and G. Post. 1983. Tribressen® and tiamulin for control of enteric redmouth disease. *J. Fish Dis.*, 6:27-32.

7. Bullock, G.L., R.R. Rucker, D. Amend, K. Wolf and H.M. Stuckey. 1976. "Infectious pancreatic necrosis: Transmission with iodine-treated and nontreated eggs of brook trout (*Salvelinus fontinalis*)," *J. Fish. Res. Bd. Can.*, 33:1197-1198.

8. Davis, H.S. 1953. *Culture and diseases of game fishes*. Univ. of Calif. Press, Berkeley and Los Angeles. p. 247.

8a. Endo, T., K. Ogishima, H. Hayasaki, S. Kaneko and S. Oshima. 1973. "Application of oxolinic acid as a chemotherapeutic agent for treating infectious diseases in fish. I. Antibacterial activity, chemotherapeutic effect and pharmacokinetic effect of oxolinic acid in fish." *Bull. Jpn. Soc. Sci. Fish.*, 2:165-171.

9. Fender, D.C. and D.F. Amend. 1978. "Hyperosmotic infiltration: Factors influencing uptake of bovine serum albumin by rainbow trout (*Salmo gairdneri*)," *J. Fish. Res. Bd. Can.*, 35:871-874.

10. Flakas, K.G. 1950. "Sulphonamide therapy of furunculosis in brown trout," *Trans. Am. Fish. Soc.*, 78 (1948):117-127.

10a. From, J. 1980. "Chloramine-T for control of bacterial gill disease." *Prog. Fish-Cult.*, 42:85-86.

11. Fryer, J.L., D.F. Amend, L.W. Harrell, A.J. Novotony, J.A. Plumb, J.S. Rohovec and G.L. Tebbit. 1977. *Development of bacterins and vaccines for control of infectious diseases in fish*. Publ. No. ORESU-T-77-012. Ore. St. Univ., Sea Grant Coll. Prog. 10 p.

11a. Fryer, J.L., J.S. Rohovec, E.F. Pulford, R.E. Olson, D.P. Ransom, J.R. Winton, C.N. Lannan, R.P. Hedrick and W.J. Groberg. 1979. "Proceedings from a conference on disease inspection and certification of fish and fish eggs." *Ore. St. Univ. Sea Grant Prog. Publ. No. ORESU-W-79-001*, Corvallis, OR. 40p.

11b. Gould, R.W., P.J. O'Leary, R.L Garrison, J.S. Rohovec and J. L. Fryer 1978. "Spray vaccination for the immunization of fish." *Fish Pathol*, 13:63-68.

12. Heartwell, C.M., III. 1975. *Immune response and antibody characterization of the channel catfish (Ictalurus punctatus) to a naturally pathogenic bacterium and virus. U.S. Dept. Int., Fish & Wildl. Serv. Tech. Paper No. 85.* 34p.

13. Herman, R.L. 1970. "Chemotherapy of fish diseases: a review," *J. Wildl. Dis.*, 6:31-34.

14. Herwig, N. 1979. *Handbook of drugs and chemicals used in the treatment of fish diseases.* Charles C. Thomas, Springfield, IL. 272p.

14a. Kawano, K., T. Aoki and T. Kitao. 1984. "Duration of protection against vibriosis in ayu (*Plecoglossus altivelis*) vaccinated by immersion and oral administration with *Vibrio anguillarum*." *Bull. Jpn. Soc. Sci. Fish.*, 50:771-774.

14b Klontz, G.W. 1980. "*Control of bacterial kidney disease in adult and juvenile spring chinook salmon at the Rapid River Salomon Hatchery.* Univ. Idaho Press, Moscow, ID.

15. Kusuda, R., K. Kawai, Y.J. Yasuhiko, T. Akizuki, M. Fukunaga and N. Kotake. 1978. "Efficacy of oral vaccination for vibriosis in cultured ayu," *Bull. Jap. Soc. Sci. Fish.*, 44:21-25.

16. McPhee, C. and R. Ruelle. *Lethal effects of 1,888 chemicals upon four species of fish from western North America. For. Wildl. Rang. Expt. Stn. Bull. No. 3.* Univ. Idaho, Moscow, ID, 112p.

17. McElwain, I. and G. Post. 1968. "Efficacy of cyzine for trout hexamitiasis," *Prog. Fish-Cult.*, 30:84-91.

18. Meyer, F.P. and R.A. Schnick. 1978. "The approaching crisis in the registration of fishery chemicals," *Proc. Ann. Conf. S.E. Assoc. Fish & Wildl. Agencies*, 30:5-14.

18a. Mitchell, A.J. and G.L. Hoffman. 1980. "Important tapeworms of North American freshwater fishes." *U.S. Dept. Int., Fish & Wild. Serv. Fish Dis. Leafl.* 59, 18p.

19. Mitchum, D.L. and T.D. Moore. 1966. "Efficacy of di-n-butyl tin oxide on an intestinal fluke, *Crepidostomum farionus*, in golden trout," *Prog. Fish-Cult.*, 31:143-148.

19a. Nelson, J.S., J.S. Rohovec and J.L. Fryer. 1985. "Tissue location of vibrio bacterin delivered by intraperitoneal injection, immersion and oral routes." *Fish Pathol.,* 19:263-269

20. Paterson, W.D. and J.L. Fryer. 1974. "Immune response of juvenile coho salmon (*Oncorhynchus kisutch*) to *Aeromonas salmonicida* cells administered intraperitoneally in Freund's complete adjuvant," *J. Fish. Res. Bd. Can.,* 31:1751-1755.

20a. Post, G. 1981. "Two potentially useful drugs for control of ERM." *Salmonid,* 4:4-5,7.

21. Post, G. 1966. "Response of rainbow trout (*Salmo gairdneri*) to antigens of *Aeromonas hydrophila,*" *J. Fish. Res. Bd. Can.,* 23:1487-1494.

22. Post G. 1962. "Furazolidone (nf-180) for control of furunculosis in trout," *Prog. Fish-Cult.,* 24:182-183.

23. Post, G. 1959. "A preliminary report on the use of nitrofuran compounds for furunculosis of trout, with special emphasis on furoxone," *Prog. Fish-Cult.,* 21:30-33.

24. Post, G. and M.M. Beck. 1966. "Toxicity, tissue residue and efficacy of enheptin given orally to rainbow trout for hexamitiasis," *Prog. Fish-Cult.,* 28:83-88.

25. Rucker, R.R., A.F. Bernier, W.J. Whipple and R.E. Burrows. 1951. "Sulfadiazine for kidney disease," *Prog. Fish-Cult.,* 13:135-137.

26. Shiraki, K., F. Miyamoto, T. Sato, I. Sonezaki and Y. Kuniichro. 1970. "Studies on a new chemotherapeutic agent nifurprazine (HB-115) against infectious diseases. Part I," *Fish Pathol,* 4:130-137.

27. Smith, W.W. 1942. "Action of alkaline acriflavine solution on *Bacterium salmonicida* and trout eggs," *Proc. Soc. Exp. Biol. Med.,* 51:324-326.

27a. Snieszko, S.F. 1981. "Bacterial gill disease of freshwater fishes." *U.S. Dept. Int., Fish & Wild. Serv. Fish Dis. Leafl.,* 62, 11p.

28. Snieszko, S.F. 1959. "Antibiotics in fish disease and fish nutrition," *Antibio. Ther.,* 9:541-545.

29. Snieszko, S.F. and S.B. Friddle. 1948. "Disinfection of trout eggs with sulfo-merthiolate," *Prog. Fish-Cult.,* 10:143-149.

30. Schnick, R.A., F.P. Meyer and H.D. Van Meter. 1978. "Quarterly highlights of FWS registration activities involving fishery use chemicals," *Fish. Health Sec., Am. Fish. Soc.,* 6(4):1-10. (July-Sept. 1978)

31. Wolf, K. and C.E. Dunbar. 1959. "Test on 34 therapeutic agents for control of kidney disease in trout," *Trans. Am. Fish. Soc.,* 88:117-124.

Chapter IV
BACTERIAL DISEASES
OF FISHES

Characteristics of Bacteria Pathogenic to Fishes

Bacteria are single cell organisms which reproduce by binary fission. Bacteria occur in three shapes: rod (bacillus), spherical (cocci) and helical (spirillum).[17] Most bacteria pathogenic to fishes are rod-shaped, only a few species of spherical pathogens are known and there are no known helical forms. Bacteria have a cell wall which maintains cellular shape and an inner membrane which allows diffusion of nutrients and metabolites into and out of the cell. Organisma of the genus *Mycoplasma* (bacteria without call walls) have been isolated form fish but only rarely.[17] Rickettsia and Chlamydia (intracellular bacterial parasites) are rarely found in fish, those known to infect fish are considered the epitheliocystis agent in some cases.[127] Some bacterial pathogens of fish develop a capsule outside of the cell wall which is usually associated with the virulence of the organism. None form spores, although some may form microcysts. Many of the bacterial pathogens of fishes are flagellated, but a few have no flagella for locomotion. Some move by body flexing or gliding.

Many bacteria pathogenic to fishes are psychrophilic. Only a few species will grow above 35°C. Most have a maximum growth temperature of 35°C or less. Many of the psychrophilic species have an optimum growth temperature of 10°C and continue to replicate at 4°C.

Many can exist at a broad range of osmotic pressure. Some are especially halophilic, with an optimum sodium chloride tolerance of 3.5%, but can replicate at salt concentrations above 7.0%. All reproduce better if at least 0.5% salt is present.

Many of the pathogenic bacteria of fishes grow at a wide range of pH. Opportunistic or secondary pathogens of fishes can replicate at a pH range of 5.5 to 10.0. The primary pathogens of fishes usually have a more narrow pH tolerance, generally 6.0 to 9.0.

Nearly all of the bacteria infecting fishes are aerobic or facultative anaerobic. Rarely are strictly anaerobic bacteria found to be associated with a fish disease.

Some of the organisms are chromogenic. There are a wide variety of pigments produced, such as brown, yellow, orange or red, and some are fluorescent. Occasionally the pigment produced by a bacterium is useful for identification.

Many of the bacteria capable of causing disease in fishes are saprophytic. They become pathogens when fishes are physiologically unbalanced, nutritionally deficient or there are other abnormalities which allow opportunistic organisms to invade.

Some bacterial pathogens of fishes are fastidious and require special growth media for laboratory culture. However, the greatest number of bacterial species found as fish pathogens grow well on common laboratory media.

Classification of Bacteria Pathogenic to Fishes

There are members of the true bacteria (Eubacteriales), the ray bacteria (Actinomycetales) and the gliding bacteria (Cytophagales) associated with disease in fishes (Table 4).[32] The taxonomic classification and the disease caused by each organism will be discussed as the major subjects of this chapter.

The identification of bacterial pathogens of fishes is essential to diagnosis of the disease. Definitive identification can be accomplished by using several laboratory procedures. Morphology, staining and biochemical activity continue to be the usual procedures for identification. A number of schematic keys of bacterial pathogens of fishes are of assistance in identification of the bacteria.[65,101] Other laboratory procedures can be used for limited assistance in the diagnosis of certain bacterial diseases: slide agglutination tests, immunodiffusion tests and fluorescent antibody tests. Some of the bacterial pathogens of fishes require species identification for definitive diagnosis and proper treatment. Others require identification to genus for effective diagnosis and therapy.

PATHOGENIC AEROMONADS:

Furunculosis

The fish disease known as furunculosis was first reported in 1890 and the etiology identified in 1894.[37] The disease was named furunculosis at the time because of the formation of furuncles, boil-like lesions, in various tissues of the body. Other diseases caused by variant strains of the etiological agent of furunculosis have been reported; goldfish ulcerative disease, carp erythrodermatitis, and ulcerative diseases have dissimilar disease signs from furunculosis but limited information about their etiology suggests their relationship to the furunculosis complex.[19a] Typical furunculosis is an acute, subacute, chronic or latent disease.[51] It has been considered a scourge of salmonid culture. Furunculosis was of such

TABLE 4

Classification of bacterial pathogens of fishes[32]

Order	Family	Genus
Eubacteriales (Gram-negative, rod-shaped)	Enterobacteriaceae	*Edwardsiella* *Yersinia*
	Pseudomonadaceae	*Pseudomonas*
	Vibrionaceae	*Aeromonas* *Plesiomonas* *Vibrio*
	Uncertain	*Flavobacterium* *Haemophilus*
Actinomycetes (Gram-positive, rod- and spherical-shaped)	Coryneform Group	*Renibacterium*
	Nocardiaceae	*Nocardia*
	Mycobacteriaceae	*Mycobacterium*
	Streptococcaceae	*Streptococcus*
Cytophagales (Gram-negative, long rod-shaped)	Cytophagaceae	*Cytophaga* *Flexibacter*

importance among trout in European trout culture and among wild fish populations during the mid-1920's that a Furunculosis Committee was formed in 1928 to study the disease and to attempt control of its etiological agent.[68] Thus, furunculosis became the first fish disease in history to receive the combined efforts of scientists, fish culturists, government agencies and sportsmen of the time. The work of the Furunculosis Committee was responsible for much of the early knowledge of the disease and demonstrated the definite need for professional fish health people. Furunculosis continues to be studied, and new evidence of epizootiology, mode of action on the host, etiological characteristics and other information are established each year.

Etiological Agent:

The etiological agent of furunculosis is *Aeromonas salmonicida*. Several synonymous names have been give to the organism since it was first identified: *Bacterium salmonicida*, 1894[37,103] *Bacterium truttae*, 1902[66]; and finally *Aeromonas salmonicida*, 1957.[18] *Aeromonas salmonicida* is said to differ in several respects from the motile aeromonads, and there are efforts to place it into a genus of its own and call it *Necromonas*. This generic name will be seen occasionally in literature.

The species name has remained unchanged. However, the isolation of achromogenic strains of the bacterium has led to subspecies designation.[32] The names given to the non-pigment producing strains are *A. s.*

achromogens,[40,56,67] and *A. s. masoucida*,[59] the latter an isolate from *Oncorhynchus masou* ("sakuramasu," a Japanese salmon). The pigmented strains of the organism are correctly designated *A. s. salmonicida*. Research has also demonstrated the bacterium *Hemophilus piscium* (etiology of brook trout ulcer disease) is serologically indistinguishable from *A. salmonicida*, its guanine to cytosine ratio is similar, and it is sensitive to *A. salmonicida* bacteriophages. *H. piscium* has similar biochemical activities to nonpigmented strains of *A. salmonicida*.[80a]

A. salmonicida is a gram-negative short to oval (1 micrometer wide and 1.7 to 2 micrometers long) rod-shaped bacterium. Some strains approach coccus form (approximately 1 micrometer in diameter).[47] All have rounded ends. The organism is non-spore forming, non-acid-fast and usually does not have a capsule. It is non-motile.

A. salmonicida is aerobic but is capable of growth as a facultative anaerobe. It has an optimum growth temperature of 20 to 22°C, with a range from 6 to 34.5°C. It grows best between pH 6.4 and 8.0 but is capable of growth between pH 5.3 and 9.0.

Chromogenic strains of *A. salmonicida*, which include nearly all known strains, produce a brown to red-brown pigment when cultured on media containing tyrosine or phenylalanine. The pigment is melanin-like and soluble in water and absolute alcohol. The pigment is not observable in infected fish tissue. Chromogenic strains of

A. salmonicida have been known to lose the ability to produce pigment after prolonged subculture on agar medium but regain pigment production on changing the medium to one containing blood serum.[35] The ability to produce pigment is also inhibited by extremes of pH and incubation temperature. Some strains of *A. salmonicida* produce little or no pigment when grown on nutrient agar but are highly chromogenic when grown on media with a rich supply of tyrosine and phenylalanine (brain heart infusion agar or trypticase yeast extract agar, for example). The pigment production of most strains of *A. salmonicida* is used as a part of the presumptive diagnosis of furunculosis.

The biochemical reactions of *A. salmonicida* have been well documented.[18,19,68] The organism attacks glucose fermentatively, producing gas, but does not produce 2,3 butanediol.[47,51] It is cytochrome oxidase positive. Most strains of the organism do not produce indol, acetylmethylcarbinol or hydrogen sulfide, although *A. s. masoucida* produces all three and *A. s. achromogenes* produces indol but not acetylmethylcarbinol or hydrogen sulfide.[32] There are other biochemical characteristics which indicate the two achromogenic subspecies are actually not subspecies of *A. salmonicida* but should be classified specifically under the suggested genus *Necromonas*.[102]

The pathogenic effect of *A. salmonicida* is associated with several of the biochemical characteristics of the organism. The rapid utilization of glucose led some researchers to believe that much of the pathogenic effect of the organism was through hypoglycemic shock to the host. The organism also produces several proteolytic enzymes, which accounts for much of the tissue breakdown in furuncular lesions.[46] Early observers noted a repression of the inflammatory response, especially the response associated with leucocytic infiltration into and around the lesions. Additional research demonstrated that *A. salmonicida* produces a leucocytolytic response in susceptible fishes[60] and that the response occurs early in infections (within 56 hours). A saline extract of *A. salmonicida* will produce the same leucocytolytic response. The effect of the endotoxin extends beyond the area where the extract is inoculated. A complete loss of hematopoiesis occurs in the kidney and spleen, with a repression of lymphocytopoiesis.[60] Thus the organism has the capability of repressing the defenses of the susceptible fish and assists in increasing its own invasiveness. Another primary virulence property is an array of proteins in the so called A-layer in the cell wall which protects the bacterial cell from defenses of the fish host. The A-layer is also involved in ferric iron metabolism. *A. salmonicida* has an absolute requirement for ferric iron and virulent strains of *A. salmonicida* sequester required iron from various host sources (transferrin, lactoferrin, and possibly others) through holes in the A-layer proteins of the cell wall.[116a]

Geographical Distribution:

A. salmonicida is, or has been, present in much of the United States where salmonid fishes are raised. It occurs among wild fishes of many areas of the United States, in most cases having been transported through the stocking of cultured fishes or from release of infected effluents from culture facilities. Some authors hold that furunculosis was brought to the North American continent with brown trout from Germany, but others feel the disease was present in the western United States as a disease of rainbow trout.[35,68]

The disease has been reported in Canadian fish culture facilities and in wild fishes of British Columbia as early as 1933.[35] The disease occurs over much of Europe. It was present but has been eliminated from Switzerland. The organism occurs in Japan, which is the only known geographic area known to support *A. s. masoucida*.[59] It has never been reported in Australia or New Zealand, an area of the world which remains free of the disease by restricting movement of salmonids or salmonid eggs into the countries.

Susceptible Species:

All species of the family Salmonidae are considered to be susceptible to furunculosis. This means that all salmon, trouts, chars, grayling and whitefishes are susceptible to the disease. There are variations in susceptibility within each group of fishes. The cutthroat trout appears to be the most susceptible of the trouts, with brown trout being less susceptible than cutthroat trout and the rainbow trout being the least susceptible. Some authors suggest that the rainbow trout is immune to furunculosis.[66,68] This is far from the truth, because epizootics of furunculosis occur in rainbow trout in which large numbers succumb to the disease. Usually the water temperature must be higher than 13 to 14°C before furunculosis can become a devastating disease among rainbow trout.

The eastern brook trout, one of the chars, is considered to be the most susceptible of all fishes. However, there is a wide range of susceptibility between strains of brook trout. The lake trout, another char, is susceptible, but not as highly so as the brook trout.

All of the Pacific and Atlantic salmon are susceptible. Epizootics have occurred in these fishes both among wild fish populations and under culture. Furunculosis has been diagnosed in whitefishes and grayling. All species of these two groups are considered to be more or less susceptible. *Aeromonas salmonicida* has been isolated from cultivated American eels, and in one case was thought to be the primary pathogen.[34a]

A. salmonicida has been isolated from a wide variety of fishes other than the salmonids.[33,40,56] Nonclinical cases of the disease have been found in chubs, dace, tench, carp, catfish, pike, sculpins, perch and other fish species. Usually no disease signs occur in these fishes, but the bacterium can be isolated from either the intestinal tract or from internal structures. At least two isolations have been made from marine fish, Pacific sable fish and Atlantic cod which were being held in seawater.[31a,40]

Young fish are more susceptible to furunculosis than are older fish. The disease is definitely temperature-related, and it rarely occurs if water temperatures are below 8 to 9°C. The organism may be present in the intestinal tract and other body organs. Usually the bacterium can be isolated from water and fecal material in the water of fish culture facilities in which the water temperature is below these temperatures and the disease is in a latent form.

Epizootiology:

A. *salmonicida* can be isolated from the environment of fish where furunculosis is enzootic. Large numbers of the organism are shed in feces of infected fish which no doubt serves to maintain a high pathogen population in the environment. Dead and disintegrating fish are also a source of the pathogen.

There is much evidence to indicate A. *salmonicida* is transmitted from host to host by the oral route, although brook trout in one experiment failed to develop the disease following feeding of the organism. Transmission can occur through injuries of the skin. Normal gills are apparently not a usual route of transmission [28a]

The incubation period for furunculosis is dependent on water temperature. Susceptible fishes at water temperatures of 20°C will develop furunculosis cases within four to 12 days following release of viable A. *salmonicida* into the water supply. Outward signs of the disease may never develop among susceptible fishes at water temperatures below 8°C.

Fishes with acute furunculosis may or may not develop furuncles. Usually the more chronic or subacute cases do so, and furuncles appear under the skin over various parts of the body (Pl. 6A). Furuncles may or may not rupture to the outside spontaneously. The organisms released from furuncles or shed in the feces serve as a source of infection for other fish in the population and for fishes in water downstream from the infected fish. Water was found to be a vehicle for spread of furunculosis very early in the study of the disease (1911).[82]

Furunculosis lends itself well to development of carriers of the disease. Any fish with a latent or chronic infection must be considered as a carrier of the disease. An example of probable carrier state in brook trout, usually thought of as being the fish most susceptible to furunculosis, occurred when a number of brook trout were stocked from a fish hatchery into ponds formed by beavers at the headwaters of a stream and at an altitude of approximately 3,000 m. Brook trout in the source hatchery from the same lot of fish were subsequently found to be infected with the organism. No indication of the disease was present until a summer period when water temperatures increased to above 12.5°C. An epizootic of furunculosis occurred in the brown trout and brook trout populations in the stream several miles downstream and at least 800 m lower in altitude from the original stocking point. The time span between stocking of the diseased fish and the epizootic was six years. There had been no indication that A. *salmonicida* had survived in the stream fish. A carrier state must have developed in brook trout and in brown trout, two highly susceptible fish species, only to develop into an epizootic when the environmental temperature increased to give the bacterium an advantage over the host.[84]

The temperature requirements for replication of A. *salmonicida* are responsible for the seasonal occurrence of furunculosis, especially among wild fish populations. Many fish culture facilities are located on a water supply which remains at or above the incubation temperature for the bacterium. These facilities may have a continuous epizootic throughout the year.

One of the epizootiological problems with furunculosis has been the stocking of infected fishes into previously noninfected water courses. Fish culture offers a more fertile ground for development of diseases such as furunculosis. Fishes are crowded together more closely than in the wild, so the pathogen can be transmitted from fish to fish easily. Fish leaving such an environment are potentially infected, and every fish in the group may have the disease, thus making its transmission more possible on being stocked into streams, lakes and ponds.

The migratory nature of some fishes susceptible to furunculosis must be considered in examining the epizootiology of this disease. Most trout species tend to move upstream from lakes as well as in streams. Those infected with A. *salmonicida* will carry the organism into previously noninfected parts of the stream. There is no evidence that high-seas salmon can transmit the organism under marine conditions. Evidence by the Furunculosis Committee indicated that salmon did not become infected at sea, but obtained the infection after entering fresh water or in fish culture facilities.[68]

Other poikilothermic animals (amphibians, reptiles and invertebrates) have been considered as sources of infection for A. *salmonicida*. These organisms may harbor the bacterium in the intestine or body organs but do not succumb to the infection. Most evidence of the carrier nature of these animals indicates involvement, but possibly of only minor importance.

A. *salmonicida* can be found in the ovaries of infected trout. The organism is passed at the time of spawning to become a source of infection to other eggs and to other fishes. The bacterium apparently remains on the surface of the egg and is destroyed by external disinfectants. Salmonid eggs have been responsible for transportation of furunculosis over great distances by modern transportation systems.

Disease Signs:

Fishes with furunculosis become more lethargic as the infection progresses. They usually seek the sides of the holding facility, remain near the surface of the water and are swept downstream to dividing screens. They are usually dark in color and will not take food, especially near termination of the disease.[67a]

External signs of furunculosis are erythema (redness) at the base of fins, in the mouth, in the grooves under the lower jaw, sometimes in the opercula and around the anus. Internally, there will be erythema in tissues of the body wall, visceral organs and adipose (fat) tissue. There may be petechial hemorrhages in the adipose tissue, gonads, stomach wall, pericardium, swim bladder, peritoneum and muscles. There may be discrete furuncles in the liver, kidney, spleen and muscles. Some furuncles may be visible through the skin (Pl. 6A). Chronic or subacute cases may have grayish areas in the kidney and liver where the organisms have necrotized (killed and liquified) the tissues, but this is not usually a sign in acute cases, however. The intestine may be filled with bloody partially digested food or fecal material.

Diagnosis:

Disease signs, bacterial identification and histopathology are used for diagnosis of furunculosis. Isolation and identification of *A. salmonicida* are essential for definitive diagnosis. Epizootics of the disease in fish culture facilities usually mean a financial loss to the owner. Rapid diagnosis is necessary to determine correct therapeutic measures which can be taken and to reduce mortality as soon as possible. *A. salmonicida* can be presumptively identified, usually within 14 to 24 hours, after cases of the epizootic have been examined and bacterial cultures prepared. Squash smear preparations should be made from infected tissue, usually the kidney. Gram staining of the smears will demonstrate short to oval gram-negative rod-shaped bacteria in positive cases of furunculosis (Pl. 6B). Bacterial cultures of positive cases of infection should be made on solid media containing tyrosine and/or phenylalanine. The cultures should be incubated between 20 and 22°C for the most rapid growth of *A. salmonicida*.

The presumptive test for *A. salmonicida* includes four parameters: morphology, staining, motility and pigment production. *A. salmonicida* is gram-negative, a short to oval rod-shaped organism, non-motile and produces a brown pigment in media containing tyrosine or phenylalanine.

Pigment production by *A. salmonicida* usually develops slowly and may delay the presumptive test. There are tests which can be performed to aid in rapid presumptive identification of the bacterium. A colony of bacteria on the medium can be treated with a drop of freshly prepared 0.1% aqueous paraphenylenediamine-HC1. *A. salmonicida* colonies will become purple-brown

in color usually within 30 seconds to one minute after application. Colonies of other bacterial species may react in the same way, but usually more slowly than *A. salmonicida*.

Diagnosis of atypical furunculosis in which nonpigment producing *A. salmonicida* is the pathogen, is more difficult. Those nonpigmented strains of *A. salmonicida* associated with goldfish ulcer disease and carp erythrodermatitis are usually more fastidious and slow growing. The culture media of choice for first isolation is blood agar or modified blood agar into which ampicillan (5 ug/ml) and polymyxin-B sulfate (5 IU/ml) has been added to supress contaminants.[16a,36a]

Gram staining characteristics and cell morphology can be done as soon as enough growth appears on culture media. Cells should also be examined for motility to complete the presumptive test. Another rapid presumptive test is a macroscopic slide agglutination test. A colony or two are picked from the media and mixed with two drops of saline (0.95% sodium chloride) on a microscope slide. One drop of *A. salmonicida* antiserum (Available from: U.S. Fish and Wildlife Service, National Fisheries Center, Route 3, Box 50, Kearneysville, West Virgina 25430) is mixed with the cell suspension. Agglutination of the cells within a few minutes is a positive presumptive test for *A. salmonicida*.[22,86]

Definitive diagnosis of furunculosis should continue following presumptive identification of the bacterium. There are several biochemical tests which can be used for definitive identification (Table 5). Diagnostic schemes used to differentiate gram-negative pathogens of fishes usually do not consider achromogenic *A. salmonicida*[22,101] or the possibility of bacteria which may occur as opportunistic pathogens or contaminants from the environment and have presumptive characteristics similar to *A. salmonicida*. Usually the diagnostic schemes for gram-negative bacterial pathogens of fishes are acceptable. Additional biochemical characteristics may be desired for bacteria isolated from suspected furunculosis in those cases where there is doubtful identification.

A. salmonicida produces distinctive pathology, and histological preparations of tissues selected during the necropsy of suspected cases of furunculosis can be of assistance in diagnosis. Acute cases usually have rather small lesions. Chronic cases reveal large areas of necrosis and tissue liquefactions. There is a paucity of leucocytic infiltration and large numbers of bacteria can be seen (Pl. 6C).

Therapy and Control:

Test and slaughter, quarantine and restriction of movement, and drug therapy and sanitation have been and will continue to be the methods of controlling furunculosis among cultured fishes. Each fish culture facility must be studied to determine the best method of control. Facilities with a spring or well water system

TABLE 5

Characteristics of *Aeromonas salmonicida* used for identification

Characteristic or Test Media	Results
Solid media with tyrosine/phenylalanine	Colonies round, complete, convex and semitranslucent; brown pigment develops after 24 to 48 hours or not at all in achromogenic strains
Morphology	Short to oval rod-shaped; nonsporeforming
Staining	Gram-negative; non-acid-fast
Glucose broth	Acid and gas produced
Lactose broth	No change
Maltose broth	Acid and gas produced
Mannitol broth	Acid and gas produced
Sucrose broth	No change (Acid by some atypical strains)
Xylose broth	No change
Sorbitol broth	No change
Nitrate broth	Nitrite produced
SIM medium	Hydrogen sulfide not produced; indol not produced; motility is negative
Clark and Lubs medium	Methyl red test negative; Voges-Poskauer test negative
Nutrient gelatin	Crateriform to saccate liquefaction in 1 to 5 days; complete liquefaction within 21 days
O/F medium with glucose	Oxidative positive; fermentative positive
Cytochrome oxidase	Positive

(i.e., water taken from a spring which can be covered or from a relatively deep well) are acceptable to complete removal of the bacterium through test and slaughter and sanitation of the entire facility, including the water supply. The facility can remain free of the disease by quarantine and movement restriction of fish into the facility and by proper use of disinfectants.

Facilities using stream water or with recirculation of water cannot be disinfected because reinfection will occur. Fish culture facilities of this nature must rely on drug therapy for control of the disease, but not for elimination of the pathogen.

Fish culture facilities which are free of *A. salmonicida* can remain free of the pathogen by restricting movement of potentially infected fishes into the facility. Fish eggs brought into the facility should be obtained from a source known to be free of the disease, and all eggs should be disinfected regardless of where they originate.

Fish-hauling equipment brought onto the grounds of noninfected fish culture facilities should be carefully disinfected prior to arrival.

Drug therapy for furunculosis has been useful in controlling the disease. Usually the disease cannot be eliminated from the treated fishes without very special attention to the water supply, type of construction in the fish-holding facilities and the therapeutic drug to be used. Fishes infected with *A. salmonicida* and experiencing mortality can be treated with sulfamerazine (Table 3). Many strains of the bacterium are resistant to this drug, and the treatment may be of little value. Fish with sulfonamide-susceptible strains of *A. salmonicida* when treated with sulfamerazine may demonstrate reduced or cessation of mortality but not elimination of the pathogen from the fish. Mortality from the disease will usually recur.

Combinations of the sulfonamide drugs may be of assistance for control of some cases of furunculosis. Sulfaguanidine is relatively insoluble, and most will remain in the intestinal tract. Sulfamerazine used with sulfaguanidine offers a soluble drug to assist in control of the pathogen in the body tissue.

Oxytetracycline (terramycin) and chloramphenicol have been used to treat furunculosis (Table 3). Mortality from the disease may or may not be controlled with these antibiotics. Combinations of these antibiotics and sulfonamides may be effective.

Sulfamerazine and oxytetracyckline are the only drugs cleared by the United States Food and Drug Administration (FDA) for control of furunculosis. Other compounds have been found to be effective for control of the disease but not cleared by the FDA. Furazolidone (NF-180 or Furoxone) has been used to treat cases of furunculosis. A. salmonicida has been eliminated from fish culture facilities and fishes within the facilities by use of furazolidone and sanitation combined. The water supply must be closed or capable of being closed to reinfection from extraneous fishes, birds or other aquatic organisms. Each of the fish-holding structures within the entire facility must have a lining material which can be disinfected (fine grained cement, fiberglass, glass or butyl rubber, for example). Furazolidone is fed to the fish at the rate of 35 mg of the drug per kg of fish body weight per day for 20 days (Table 3). Care must be taken to be sure the drug is carefully mixed into the ration and the ration is given at the prescribed feeding level. The last three days of drug therapy must be accompanied by one-hour treatments of a good external disinfectant (the quarternary disinfectants are especially useful). All utensils used around the fishes, equipment, supplies and other objects which could be contaminated, including the tops of tanks and raceways, should be kept wet with the disinfectant during each of the hour-long disinfecting treatments. Each of the fish-holding units should be treated statically for best results.[85] Care must be taken to prevent reinfection once the pathogen has been eliminated.

Potentiated sulfonamides such as Romet-30 and Tribressen show promise as therapeutans for furunculosis.[19b,67b] Neither have been cleared for legal use in the United States. Oxolinic acid has been used in Europe and Japan for experimental control of furunculosis (Table 3).[10b]

Immunization as a method of controling furunculosis has received much study over the past 20 to 30 years. Bacterins have been prepared which stimulate production of protective antibodies when injected into fish. Four extracellular compounds released by A. salmonicida into culture media have been found to enhance immune response when added to whole-cell bacterins and injected into fish. The success of an injectable vaccine is important but of little practical value to fish culture.[19a]

Several attempts have been made to immunize fish

susceptable to furunculosis using immersion bacterins but with limited success. The most successful immersion bacterin was prepared from chloroform inactivated bacteria added to extracellular compounds produced by the bacteria. Brown trout treated by 60 second immersion in this bacterin and challenged 30 days later, demonstrated 2.1% mortality as compared to 28.9% mortality in the experimental control group of fish. These results demonstrate a potential for mass immunization against furunculosis but much more research is needes.[28b]

Several attempts have been made to produce a satisfactory oral bacterin which can be added to food. Results indicate that even though low levels of A. salmonicidea antibodies are produced by orally immunized fish, there is little or no actual protection against the disease.[19a]

Prognosis:

Mortality as high as 85% may occur among young, more susceptible fishes. Little or no mortality may occur among the least susceptible fish species. Sanitation and drug treatment can usually reduce mortality among even the most susceptible.

The morbidity among fish in fish culture facilities usually reaches 100% but is very low among wild-ranging fish populations. This is because of the ease of transmission among hosts at a fish hatchery as compared to the relatively large space occupied by individual fish in wild populations and the difficulty of pathogen transmission from host to host.

Practical Aspects of Furunculosis:

Extreme care should be taken when transporting or moving fishes from furunculosis-infected geographic areas to noninfected areas. Individuals interested in fishery problems, and especially those problems involving salmonid fishes, should be aware of the ease of moving A. salmonicida with fishes and the difficulty of eliminating it from contaminated fish culture facilities or open waters.

The spread of A. salmonicida can be inadvertent and unknowing. That is one reason why there is a need for a reporting service for fish diseases. There should be a system in which a disease like furunculosis could be listed as a "reportable" disease. Fishery workers would then know the dangers of moving fishes from one geographic area to another. An example of how such a reporting service could have been used to reduce transportation of A. salmonicida from an infected geographic area to another comes to mind and involves a lake used as a source of salmonid eggs for fish culture. Trout eggs from the lake were given to a neighboring state and placed into a fish hatchery without disinfection, partly because neither state was aware that furunculosis occurred in the lake. The eggs were incubated and hatched in a fish hatchery building also containing young brook trout. No attention was given to disinfecting brushes used to clean troughs and tanks, egg-picking devices and other utensils in the hatchery building. The pathogen was transmitted to the brook trout. The water temperature at the fish culture facility was about 9.5°C, a temperature at which *A. salmonicida* does not replicate rapidly. The disease was unnoticed for some time, partly because of the low water temperature and partly because of inexperience of the fish culturists. Fishes were moved from the one hatchery to four others belonging to the state agency. Some of the other fish hatcheries had water temperatures more conducive to replication of the bacterium, and furunculosis became more obvious. The disease was diagnosed and a decontamination and disinfection program was developed. Furunculosis was eliminated from two of the hatcheries within a year. Two of the facilities were using a spring water and stream water mixture. Infected fishes and water going into the stream created an opportunity for the bacterium to reenter the facilities, even after disinfection. Both of the facilities were rebuilt at great expense to eliminate the source of infection from the stream by developing the springs and disinfecting or reconstructing the fish-holding facilities. The remaining fish hatchery was disinfected twice over a period of a few years, and the disease was finally eliminated. This example serves to demonstrate the insidious nature of *A. salmonicida* and the effort and expense involved in eliminating it from fish hatcheries once it occurs.

Furunculosis is probably partly responsible for elimination of brook trout from many of the streams of the eastern United States. Rainbow trout, being much more resistant to furunculosis, are now stocked into these streams for the sport fisherman.

Efforts should be made to eliminate furunculosis wherever it occurs. Efforts should be made by fish health specialists, fish culturists, fishery managers and fishery administrators to control this disease and reduce its geographical distribution.

Motile Aeromonad Disease

Bacteria of the genus *Aeromonas* are found in water and soils in nature. Most are saprophytes. All grow at the wide range of temperature normally occupied by fishes. Fishes may become hosts to aeromonads when their defenses allow invasion.

The name motile aeromonad disease was accepted in 1974[69] for a disease previously reported under several synonymous names: hemorrhagic septicemia,[113] red sore of pike,[87] redmouth disease,[120] red-leg disease of frogs[120] and bacterial septicemia.[7] It occurs as an acute, subacute, chronic or latent disease of fishes, amphibians and reptiles.

Etiological Agents:

The taxonomy of motile aeromonads has not been fully settled. However, there are two recognized species. *Aeromonas hydrophila* and *Aeromonas punctata*. The two species are quite similar; some countries list *A. hy-*

drophila and others *A. punctata* as fish pathogens. These organisms, although not obligate pathogens, are primary pathogens of many cultured freshwater fishes. Other unspeciated bacteria are present in soil and water with characteristics of the genus *Aeromonas*. Some may become involved as secondary pathogens of fishes. There is evidence to indicate that unsatisfactory environmental conditions or debilitations of the fish are conducive to epizootics caused by any of the motile aeromonads.

Motile aeromonads, such as *A. hydrophila*, *A. punctata* and the unspeciated aeromonads, have been described as primary or secondary pathogens of fishes throughout the world. Thus, the etiological agent of motile aeromonad disease may be found under various synonyms. Synonymous names for *A. hydrophila* have been given as: *Bacillus hydrophilus* (1891), *Aerobacter liquefaciens* (1900), *Proteus hydrophilus* (1923), *Pseudomonas hydrophila* (1952) and *Aeromonas hydrophila* (1957).[18] *A. punctata* has also had numerous synonymous names: *Bacillus punctatus* (1890), *Bacterium punctatum* (1896), *Pseudomonas punctatum* (1901) and *Aeromonas punctata* (1957).[18] The name *A. liquefaciens* occurs in much of the literature concerning motile aeromonad disease, but it now has the accepted names *A. hydrophila* or *A. punctata*.[32]

Two subspecies have been designated for *A. punctata*: *A. p. punctata* and *A. p. caviae*. The suggestion has been made that the fish pathogens formerly named *A. liquefaciens* (those isolates producing acid from lactose and sorbitol and having an optimum temperature of 25 to 30°C) or *A. hydrophila* (isolates not producing acid from lactose or sorbitol and having an optimum temperature of 25 to 30°C) both be designated as *A. punctata*. A further suggestion was made that if a subspecies is needed for *A. punctata* isolates which are partly anaerogenic, glyconate or acetylmethylcarbinol negative, the subspecies of *A. punctata caviae* could be used for them.[32]

The etiological agents of motile aeromonad disease are rod-shaped bacteria, motile by polar flagella and generally monotrichous. None are spore-forming. All are gram-negative and non-acid-fast. The cells are usually not capsulated. All are aerobic and facultatively anaerobic. Some produce brown to red-brown water soluble pigment. (Pl. 6D)

Geographic Distribution:

The etiological agents of motile aeromonad disease are world-wide in distribution. Most occur in fresh water, but there are some halophilic organisms in brackish or sea water. *A. hydrophila* (*liquefaciens*) and *A. punctata* are not ubiquitous, there being many water courses and fish culture facilities in which neither has been found. Aeromonads may be spread on the plumage of birds, by terrestrial animals and by amphibians or reptiles from one part of the world to another.

Susceptible Species:

All freshwater fishes (warmwater, coolwater and coldwater) are susceptible to motile aeromonad disease. Saltwater fishes may be susceptible to halophilic aeromonads. Snakes, turtles and frogs are susceptible to the disease, especially when caused by *A. hydrophila*. This aeromonad species has also been associated with infections of the skin and as septicemic infections in humans.

Epizootiology

Most epizootics of motile aeromonad disease are stress-related. Overcrowding fish in a fish culture facility or in aquariums causes reduction of oxygen, presence of large quantities of excretory products from the fishes and general conditions conducive to invasion of opportunistic bacteria. Nutritionally deficient fishes are especially susceptible to secondary infections, as are fishes with injuries or damaged skin or gills.

Motile aeromonad disease is somewhat seasonal in occurrence. This is especially true in the temperate zones. Rising water temperature in spring and summer combined with stress, causes increases in epizootics of the disease.

There is usually no seasonal occurrence in fish culture facilities located on a relatively constant-temperature water supply. Facilities of this type, with *A. hydrophila* or *A. punctata* present, may develop epizootics of motile aeromonad disease whenever fishes become susceptible. Losses of fish under these circumstances can usually be associated to the single bacterial species. The organisms become septicemic, and pure cultures of the bacterium can be isolated from each case of the disease.

The organisms are usually transmitted orally except in those instances when fish have skin or gill abrasions and the organism may enter through these routes. External parasites of fishes which abrade skin and gills have also been implicated in the transmission of *A. hydrophila* or *A. punctata*. The organisms multiply in the intestine or at the site of invasion and are spread throughout the body by the blood stream. The incubation period between initial infection and appearance of disease signs is dependent upon the temperature of the environment. Acute cases may appear within four to ten days after infection. Subacute or chronic cases may take much longer to develop. Chronic and latent cases do occur and serve as a source of the infective bacterium. No research has been done to determine the importance of carrier fishes with motile aeromonad disease. However, experience indicates that latent cases and carrier fishes become an important factor when *A. hydrophila* and *A. punctata* are involved. Young fishes are more susceptible and can be infected by fishes with a chronic or latent infection or from carrier fishes remaining in the pond or aquarium.

Fishes with infections of *A. hydrophila* or *A. punctata* may never develop the disease when held at water temperatures below 7 to 8°C. Epizootics can occur in these fishes when the water temperature is increased above 12 to 14°C. In this way, latent infections of the bacteria may be responsible for increases in mortality as the wa-

ter temperature rises and decreases in mortality as water temperature decreases.

The disease can develop rapidly in infected and susceptible fishes, especially when the fishes are stressed. Large numbers of the organism are shed into the water from acute or subacute cases, thus becoming a significant source of bacteria.

Transportation of fishes and fish eggs is a part of the epizootiology of motile aeromonad disease, especially when *A. hydrophila* or *A. punctata* are involved. The organism apparently is carried on the outside of the egg and can be removed by egg disinfection. Fishes with *A. hydrophila* should not be transported into geographical areas which do not have the bacterium.

The nonspecific aeromonads which occur in water and become associated with fishes in fish culture or aquariums usually are not as important in the epizootiology of motile aeromonad disease as *A. hydrophila* or *A. punctata*. Little or no importance may be given to movement of fish or fish eggs known to be infected with those aeromonads usually considered opportunists.

Disease Signs:

External signs of motile aeromonad disease (Pl. 7A) include erythema (redness) at the base of fins, in the mouth, in the grooves under the lower jaw, within the opercula and around the anus. Internal signs include erythema and petechial hemorrhages in the peritoneum and most of the visceral organs. Slicing through the muscle may reveal petechia. The intestine is usually erythemic and there may be bloody mucus and fluid in the lumen.

Diagnosis:

Motile aeromonad disease can be diagnosed from the appearance of the infected fish and through isolation and identification of the bacterium. Histopathology is similar to that caused by other gram-negative bacteria (especially *Vibrio* sp. and *Pseudomonas* sp.) and may only indicate that septicemic infection has occurred.

All motile aeromonads are gram-negative and can usually be located in squash preparations made from various body organs. Squash preparations of kidney are especially useful when searching for the etiological agent of this disease (Pl. 6D). The organisms appear as rod-shaped bacteria which usually vary from 1 X 2.0 to 4.5 micrometers. There are a few coccoid forms or short rods. The organisms usually occur as singles or pairs in tissue squash preparations, rarely in short chains or filaments. They grow well on most common laboratory media. Growth is usually profuse and appears within 24 to 36 hours after inoculation when incubated between 20 and 22°C. Most motile aeromonads do not produce pigment, neither in the colony nor soluble in the culture media. There are no specific antisera which can be used for rapid identification. The organisms are motile and can be presumptively separated from *A. salmonicida* in this way. Definitive diagnosis of motile aeromand dis-

— *Can occur at any temp.*

38

ease must be accomplished by biochemical activity of the organism (Table 6).

A. hydrophila, A. punctata and soil and water opportunistic aeromonads can be definitively separated from *Vibrio* sp. and *Pseudomonas* sp. by observing growth and metabolic products on special media. Diagnostic keys may be of assistance.[65,101] *A. hydrophila* and *A. punctata* produce cytochrome oxidase, attack glucose oxidatively and fermentatively and produce indole and hydrogen sulfide. *A. hydrophila* produces 2,3-butanediol, *A. punctata* does not.

Many of the extraneous species of *Aeromonas* which occur as opportunistic pathogens of fishes are biochemically similar to *A. hydrophila* and *A. punctata*, so additional special media must be used for separation. Presence of arginine and lysine decarboxylase activity by the unspeciated aeromonads and not by the two speciated *Aeromonas* has been suggested.[65] Use of various carbohydrate broths, nutrient gelatin, SIM and other common media may also serve to separate these organisms (Table 6).

Therapy and Control:

Epizootics of motile aeromonad disease caused by either *A. hydrophila* or *A. punctata* among cultured fishes may respond to oxytetracycline treatment used in the food at the rate of 55 mg per kg of fish (2.5 g per 100 lb) per day for 10 days. Sulfamerazine at 264 mg per kg of fish (12 g per 100 lb) given in the food for three days, followed by 154 mg per kg of fish (7 g per 100 lb) per day for 11 additional days, may also be an effective treatment.

Many of the nonspecific aeromonads which cause epizootics of motile aeromonad disease as opportunistic pathogens may not respond to either of the therapeutic compounds given above. Plate inhibition tests may be of assistance for identification of a suitable therapeutic drug. A culture plate is heavily streaked with a pure culture of the bacterium and small sterile circles of filter paper impregnated with the test drug are placed on the medium. Glass or stainless steel cups may be placed on the medium if a solution of the drug is to be tested. The plate is incubated long enough to demonstrate growth of the organism on the surface of the medium. A zone of inhibition around the test drug indicates the ability of the drug to control growth of the bacterium (Pl. 6E). *In vitro* (in laboratory culture containers) results only indicate the possible *in vivo* (in the living animal) effect of the drug. Active *in vitro* drugs may have little or no therapeutic effect *in vivo*, especially if the drug is given by the oral route in food.

Secondary infections of motile aeromonads resulting from nutritional deficiency, physiological imbalance, injuries or physical stress may be treated with therapeutic drugs during the time between diagnosis of the absolute cause of the secondary infection and the time when fishes are capable of withstanding further infections.

The use of prophylactic treatments at regular intervals may reduce the chances of stressed fishes being infected by aeromonad opportunists. External disinfectants used as weekly or twice weekly treatments may reduce the population of these bacteria in environmental water, thus reducing the possibility of secondary infection. Also, the disinfectant may soothe damaged gills or external injuries and help reduce secondary infections by these routes.

Control of motile aeromonad disease by immunization has not been successful. This is because of the large number of serotypes of *A. hydrophila* and *A. punctata* as well as the large number of nonspecific motile aeromonads which complicates production of multivalent bacterin broad enough to immunize against all of them.[121a]

Overcrowding of fishes in holding facilities, transportation containers or other similar stress situations may be conducive to epizootics of motile aeromonad disease. Methylene blue added at the rate of 1:250,000 (4 mg/L) may reduce bacterial populations in the water and also reduce secondary infections.

Prognosis:

Mortality as high as 80% may occur among physically stressed, nutritionally deficient, anoxious or injured young fish. Older fishes tend to be capable of withstanding infections of *A. hydrophila, A. punctata* or other aeromonads, although mortalities of 20 to 35% are not uncommon in older fishes without external or systemic therapy.

Morbidity among fish populations demonstrating infections of either *A. hydrophila* or *A. punctata* may approach 100%, and the pathogen may be isolated from tissues or the intestinal tract of all fishes. Morbidity among susceptible fish populations from some of the nonspecific aeromonads may be quite low, depending to some extent on the extenuating problems in the fish.

Practical Aspects:

Fishes or fish eggs with either *A. hydrophila* or *A. punctata* should not be moved from infected geographical areas to noninfected areas. There are many fish culture facilities or aquariums which do not have either of these bacteria. Moving the organisms to such a facility or aquarium adds another possible pathogen for fishes.

Stressful activities on fishes in facilities known to have these bacteria endogenous to the facility should be limited to times when fishes are least vulnerable to secondary infection. As an example, fishes should be handled during low water temperature times of the year and not handled at all during warm water periods.

Both *A. hydrophila* and *A. punctata* can be removed by egg disinfection. Fish eggs being moved into any facility should receive disinfection. The polyvinyl-pyrolidone-iodine disinfectants are considered by some to be most satisfactory for the two bacteria (Table 3).[70]

Fishes can be protected from the nonspecific aeromo-

TABLE 6

Characteristics of *Aeromonas hydrophila*, *Aeromonas punctata* and an example of an unspeciated aeromonad which may be of use for identification[9,18]

Characteristic or Test Media	Results		
Solid media	All aeromonads have round, complete, convex or flat and semitranslucent colonies		
Pigment	Most aeromonads do not produce pigment in either the colony or soluble in the media; a few produce brown or red-brown soluble pigment		
Morphology	Rods, usually 2.0 to 4.5 times longer than wide; coccoid forms may occur; non-spore-forming		
Staining	All are gram-negative; some are bipolar staining; non-acid-fast		
	Aeromonas hydrophila	*Aeromonas punctata*	Unspeciated [a] aeromonad
Optimum temperature (°C)	37	25-30	28
Glucose broth	AG[b]	AG	AG
Lactose broth	–	A	A[c]
Maltose broth	AG	AG	AG
Mannitol broth	AG	AG	AG
Sucrose broth	AG	AG	A
Sorbitol broth	A or –	A	AG
Nitrate broth	NO$_2$ produced	NO$_2$ produced	NO$_2$ produced
SIM medium			
Hydrogen sulfide	+ or –	+	+
Indol	+	+	+
Motility	+	+	+
Clark and Lubs medium			
Methyl red test	–	–	+
Voges-Poskauer test	+	–	+
O/F medium with glucose	+/+[d]	+/+	+/+
2,3-Butanediol production	+	–	+
Nutrient gelatin	Napiform	Crateriform	Saccate
Cytochrome oxidase test	+	+	+
0/129 Vibriostat	Growth	Growth	Growth
Novobiocin	Growth	Growth	Growth

[a]From an epizootic among nutritionally deficient aquarium cichlids
[b]Acid and gas produced
[c]Acid produced
[d]Attacks glucose oxidatively/attacks glucose fermentatively

nads which occur as saprophytes and potential secondary fish pathogens by reducing physical stress, nutritional deficiencies, injuries or other conditions leading to epizootics. No restrictions may be necessary in the transportation of fishes known to carry nonspecific aeromonads.

PATHOGENIC VIBRIO

Vibriosis of Fishes

Vibriosis is a disease of many marine and freshwater fishes of the world. It has been called red pest of eels, red sore, red boil and pike pest. Vibriosis was given as the accepted name for the disease in 1974.[69]

There are many vibrios associated with the marine environment, much like the aeromonads and pseudomonads in the freshwater environment. *Vibrio anguillarum*, although not an obligate parasite, is a primary pathogen of fishes, and if present in or around fishes will sooner or later cause vibriosis. Other vibrios may be capable of causing disease in fishes as opportunistic pathogens.[9,102]

V. anguillarum (or closely related strains) is a common bacterial pathogen of marine and brackish water fishes. The organism has caused severe losses in marine and estuarine aquaculture. It has also been a problem to the saltwater aquarist. The organism causes acute, subacute and chronic vibriosis among various fishes in these environments. The bacterium has also been found in the gut flora of certain apparently normal marine fishes,[1] thus indicating the possibility of latent disease or a carrier state among certain fishes.

Etiological Agent:

The etiological agent of vibriosis is considered to be *V. anguillarum*. There are a number of biotypes of *V. anguillarum*. Some biotypes differ enough from *V. anguillarum* to receive specific classification. *Vibrio ordalii* is the name proposed for Biotype-2 *V. anguillarum*. Some authors classify the etiological agent of vibriosis in fish as being *V. anguillarum* and *V. ordalii*.[121a,100a] There has been confusion over the nomenclature of *V. anguillarum* since its first isolation in 1893.[19] It has been called *Bacterium anguillarum* (1893), *Vibrio anguillarum* (1909), *Vibrio piscium* (1927), *Achromobacter ichthyodermis* (1934) and *Pseudomonas ichthyodermis* (1944).[19] The name *Vibrio piscium*, with various subspecies and varieties, was suggested between 1948 and 1974.[18,19,32] The name *Vibrio anguillarum* was made official in 1974,[32] and all variants and strains of *V. piscium* are to be known as *V. anguillarum*.

V. anguillarum is a non-spore-forming rod-shaped bacterium, either curved or straight. It is motile by a single polar flagellum, is gram-negative and non-acid-fast. The organism does not produce pigment. Its optimum growth temperature is 18 to 20°C, but it will grow at 5°C and rarely at 37°C.[18-32] It grows well on most common laboratory media, usually more profusely in the presence of 1.5 to 3.5% salt. Most strains of the bacterium will grow in the presence of 7% salt, but not at 10%. Some strains will grow with 0.5% salt added to the media, but with difficulty.[32] It is a facultative anaerobe. Biochemical characteristics may be used to separate this organism from other fish pathogens.

There are three commonly recognized biochemical variants of *V. anguillarum*. Studies have demonstrated that one variant produces acid but no gas from sucrose and mannitol, and produces indol (Type A). A second biochemical variant will not attack sucrose or mannitol and does not produce indol (Type B). A third biochemical variant ferments sucrose and mannitol but does not produce indol (Type C).[44]

Further research to justify variants of *V. anguillarum* has demonstrated three serological types: Serotype 1—from Pacific Northwest salmonids; Serotype 2—from diseased fishes in European waters; and Serotype 3—from Pacific Northwest herring.[77] There is some evidence that the biochemical types are similar to the suggested serotypes.[44]

Geographic Distribution:

Vibriosis occurs worldwide in susceptible fishes.[91] It has been reported in North America, South America, in many countries of Europe and from at least three countries in Asia. It usually occurs in marine or estuarine environments, although it has been reported in freshwater fish culture facilities and aquariums.[44,91] It has also been reported from high seas fishes.[102]

Susceptible Species:

At least 48 species of fishes are known to be susceptible to *V. anguillarum* infection.[9] Most are marine and estuarine fishes (cod, herring, four species of salmon, pompano, puffer, croaker, mackerel, flounder, turbot, three species of sole and others). Freshwater fishes known to be susceptible to vibriosis include rainbow trout, carp, pike, eel, tilapia, guppy, tiger barb, tetra and loach.[9,48.]

Epizootiology:

V. anguillarum may be ubiquitous to marine and estuarine environments, and fishes in these localities may be continually exposed to the pathogen. There is evidence that herring and other fishes may be carriers of the bacterium.[91]

There is no information on the route of transmission from fish to fish, but the oral route is highly suspect. The organism is known to occur in the intestinal tract of apparently normal fishes,[1] suggesting oral transmission. Those pathogens in the gut may be capable of invasion of the host under any condition of stress (physical, physiological or nutritional). There is evidence to indicate the organism can enter susceptible fishes through external injuries. External parasites may also play a role in infection through the dermal route.

The incubation period following exposure to the bacteria may be as short as three days, depending on virulence of the pathogen and susceptibility of the fish. Bacteria becomes septicemic after invasion and can be demonstrated in blood, kidney, liver and other organs. Bacteria may be transmitted to water in feces at this time. Dead fishes become a source of infection to other fishes. Close crowding of fish in fish culture makes exposure to a high population of the pathogen likely, and transmission under these conditions will be more direct. The disease has been a special problem in the rearing of salmon for release.

Another route of transmission in fish culture has been through the feeding of infected fishes or fish viscera to hatchery fishes. This practice constitutes a direct transmission cycle and should be avoided.

There is no evidence that vibriosis is transmitted with fish eggs. However, *V. anguillarum*—contaminated fish eggs are surely possible, especially when eggs are taken from sea-run salmon or other fishes which have been exposed to the bacterium.

Disease Signs:

External signs of vibriosis are similar to those caused by other gram-negative bacteria, i.e., erythema at the base of fins, in the mouth, along the grooves of the lower jaw, the opercles and around the anus. There may be boil-like lesions under the skin and in muscles, not much different from furuncles. Many times these boils break to the exterior and the necrotic skin is lifted away, leaving large open sores (Pl. 6F).

Internal signs of the disease include petechia and erythema in the peritoneum and visceral organs. The intestine is usually erythemic and filled with fluid. Cut surfaces of muscle may demonstrate petechial hemorrhages to large red boil-like lesions.

Diagnosis:

Diagnosis of vibriosis is by disease signs, isolation and identification of the bacterium and histopathology. Disease signs are not too different from those of other diseases caused by septicemic bacteria. Squash preparations of kidney, liver, spleen, necrotic muscle tissue and other organs reveal the bacterium. Usually the organism is of the curved vibrio shape (Pl. 8A), although certain strains of *V. anguillarum* may be straight.

The pathogen can usually be isolated from infected organs in pure culture if care is taken in the selection of diagnostic sample fish and disinfection practiced on entering the fish. Growth on laboratory media will be apparent within 24 to 36 hours at 22°C.

Separation of *V. anguillarum* from anaerogenic aeromonads is difficult. Both are cytochrome oxidase positive, both attach glucose oxidatively and fermentatively and both are motile with one polar flagellum. The characteristic curved rod morphology usually associated with the *Vibrio* bacteria is of little or no value in separating the two genera. The use of 2,4-diamino-6,7-diisopropyl pteridine (0/129) vibriostat and novobiocin is useful, as addition of either of these two compounds to the media will suppress growth of most strains of *V. anguillarum* but not the aeromonads or pseudomonads (Table 6, 7 and 8).[18,19,32,48,74a]

Histopathological findings may be of assistance for diagnosis of vibriosis. Contrasted to furunculosis, the boil-like lesions in muscle tissue are well populated with leucocytes. Liver degeneration throughout the organ is usually apparent in subacute or chronic cases. All visceral organs are hyperemic, especially the spleen. Hemorrhages occur throughout most tissues, including muscle, kidney, liver, intestine and heart. This is especially true in the acute or subacute cases.

Therapy and Control:

Vibriosis epizootics can be prevented in cultured fishes, even though the pathogen is enzootic. Overcrowding, reduced dissolved oxygen, increased quantities of excretory products in the water and all conditions usually found in present-day culture places stress on the fishes and make them more susceptible to infection. Rearing of fishes in relatively high water temperatures (greater than 18°C) may also be conducive to development of vibriosis epizootics. Careful culture techniques will reduce the requirements for drug therapy.

Sulfonamide and antibiotic therapy have been useful in controlling the mortality during epizootics of vibriosis in cultured fishes. Sulfamerazine and oxytetracycline are the drugs of choice. Various dosages of sulfamerazine have been used, but the 14-day treatment regimen used for other gram-negative fish pathogens (264 mg per kg, 12 g per 100 lb, of fish per day for three days; followed by 154 mg per kg, 7 g per 100 lb, of fish for 11 days) appears to be the best procedure. Oxytetracycline at 77 mg per kg (3.5 g per 100 lb) of fish per day for ten days will reduce or eliminate mortality from vibriosis.

Some of the nitrofuran compounds are useful for controlling vibriosis. Nitrofurazone (furacin) used at 56 mg per kg (2.5 g per 100 lb) of fish per day for ten days controlled the disease in cultured yellow tail.[62] Furazolidone added to the diet at the rate of 0.02% and fed over a two-week period prevented development of vibriosis in cultured rainbow trout.[49] Furanace added to the diet at the rate of 0.05 to 1 g per kg and fed for ten days may give satisfactory control if the fishes will eat the ration.

Control of vibriosis by immunization is possible and effective bacterins have been developed to do so. The immersion route appears to be the more practical route of bacterin delivery, although the intraperitoneal route is more effective.[64] Research continues on the use of oral bacterins.

Immersion bacterins are usually prepared by growing the organisms in broth and ajusting the number of cells per milliliter prior to use. Research has demonstrated that the antigen is found on gill surfaces, in the alimentary tract and in the kidneys following immersion of fish in the bacterin.[1a,74b,96a]

TABLE 7

Characteristics of *Vibrio anguillarum* and *Vibrio ordalii* used for identification[18,19,32,48,65,100a,101]

Characteristic or Test Media	V. anguillarum	V. ordalii
Solid media	Colonies round, complete, convex and semi translucent	Same as *V. anguillarum*
Pigment	Usually none	Usually none
Morphology	Curved to straight rod, asporogenous 0.5 x 1.5-3.0 micrometers; usually 1 polar flagellum	Same as *V. anguillarum*
Optimum temperature (°C)	18 to 20	18 to 20
Glucose broth	A[a]	A
Glycerol	A	−
Lactose	−	−
Maltose	A	A
Mannitol	A	A
Sucrose	A	A
Sorbitol	A	−
Trehalose	A	−
Starch hydrolysis	+	−
Nitrate broth	No_2 produced	−
Citrate test (Christensen)	+	−
SIM medium		
Hydrogen sulfide	−	−
Indol	+	−
Motility	+	+
Clark and Lubs medium		
Methyl red test	−	−
Voges-Poskauer test	+	−
O/F medium with glucose	+/+[b]	+/+
2.3 Butanediol production	−	unknown
Nutrient gelatin hydrolysis	+	+
Cytochrome oxidase test	+	+
O/129 Vibriostat	No growth	No growth
Novobiocin	No growth	unknown

[a]Acid produced
[b]Attacks glucose oxidatively/attacks glucose fermentatively

Oral bacterins are prepared by adding killed bacteria to the ration and fed to fish. Usually these bacterins will not give complete elimination of mortality from the disease but do reduce losses.[44,45] There are reports of successful use of oral bacterins, for example, an oral *V. anguillarum* bacterin added to food and fed at 0.4g wet-weight bacteria per kg of ayu fish per day for 15 days gave protection for 50 days after withdrawal of the bacterin.[63a]

The use of oral bacterins has many advantages over other methods of developing acquired immunity in cultured fish. Many serious problems must be overcome before they are generally acceptable for vibriosis control.

Fish egg disinfection may control the spread of vibriosis. This is especially true when fish eggs taken from sea-run fishes are transported to noninfected freshwater fish culture facilities.

Fish culture facilities receiving water from springs or wells and having hard-lined tanks, raceways and ponds (fine-grained cement, fiberglass or butyl rubber) may be disinfected and *V. anguillarum* eliminated. Chlorine is the disinfectant of choice, used in the manner prescribed earlier.

Prognosis:

Mortality among susceptible fishes may reach 80%.[45] The average loss in Danish eel culture was given as 30%, varying somewhat from year to year, before the use of antibiotic or chemotherapeutic treatment (1932).[95]

Morbidity may reach 100% of a population where *V. anguillarum* is enzootic in overcrowded fish culture facilities. Morbidity is probably lower among free-ranging fishes. As an example, plaice removed from a natural vibrio-infected environment and held in an aquarium had 49% infected, 29% possibly infected and 22% not infected with vibrio organisms. Seventy percent of the fish eventually died from vibriosis.[95]

Practical Aspects:

Vibriosis is a greater problem in marine and estuarine environments. The development of fish culture in these surroundings increases the necessity for management of vibriosis. Proper management in facilities known to harbor *V. anguillarum* or other pathogenic vibrios is necessary to avoid epizootics. Great care should be taken in handling or overcrowding the fish in order to reduce stress.

Fishes from vibriosis-infected fish culture facilities should not be moved to noninfected geographical areas. Eggs taken from brood fishes suspected of being infected with *V. anguillarum* should be disinfected prior to being moved to other areas.

Feeding raw ocean fish or fish viscera to cultured fishes should be avoided. These products can be used but should be pasteurized prior to feeding to vibriosis-susceptible fishes.

PATHOGENIC PSEUDOMONADS

Pseudomonad Septicemia

Bacteria of the genus *Pseudomonas* are ubiquitous in water. Most are freshwater bacteria, but there are saltwater and brackish water species. Most of these organisms are saprophytic. Some are capable of becoming opportunistic pathogens of fishes.[25] Pseudomonad septicemia occurs primarily among cultured and aquarium fishes, but occassionally appears among wild-ranging fishes. The disease among cultured fishes is usually the result of improper management or stress. Reduced dissolved oxygen, increased water temperature, poor nutrition and other factors predispose the fishes to pseudomonad septicemia.

Pseudomonad septicemia offers a different diagnostic and management challenge from septicemias caused by other gram-negative bacterial pathogens of fishes. There is usually no need for harsh control methods such as test and slaughter, restriction movement or quarantine of fishes suffering from pseudomonad septicemia. This is because there usually is a different species or strain of pseudomonad associated with each epizootic. Quite often there is no drug choice for treatment of the disease because of the difference in species or strain of pseudomonad, and each may be controlled by a different therapeutic compound.

Etiological Agent:

The etiological agents of pseudomonad septicemia are secondary pathogens belonging to the genus *Pseudomonas*. *Pseudomonas fluorescens* is one of those organisms. Other pseudomonads have been isolated from fish septicemia, but most resemble *P. fluorescens*.[25] Therefore, much of the discussion given here will be about *P. fluorescens* and closely related forms.

There are four recognized biotypes and several miscellaneous strains of *P. fluorescens*. *P. fluorescens* was first identified as *Bacillus fluorescens liquifaciens* in 1886. The name was changed to *Bacillus fluorescens* in 1889. It became *Pseudomonas fluorescens* in 1895.[18,19,32]

P. fluorescens and related species are non-spore-forming, gram-negative, rod-shaped bacteria, generally 0.5 to 1 micrometer by 1.5 to 4.0 micrometers in size. All are motile, usually by one polar flagellum, but some forms may have three polar flagella. They attack glucose oxidatively, never fermentatively. Most are cytochrome oxidase positive. Many produce diffusable pigments which fluoresce under ultraviolet light. The optimum temperature for growth of the biotypes associated with fish diseases is 20 to 25°C. Most of the strains or species will grow to 4°C, but not at 41°C. These organisms grow well on most common laboratory media. Many grow on very simple mineral media with a single organic compound as the source of carbon and energy. Some require addition of amino acids or vitamins. Most are strict aerobes. Biochemical characteristics serve to separate the biotypes and miscellaneous forms of *P. fluorescens* from other species of *Pseudomonas* and from other similar genera (*Vibrio* and *Aeromonas*) among the fish pathogens.

Geographic Distribution:

The biotypes and miscellaneous strains of *P. fluorescens* and the other species of *Pseudomonas* capable of opportunistic infections of fishes are worldwide in distribution. There are freshwater and saltwater strains or species involved with fishes in these aquatic environments. The reported cases of pseudomonad septicemia are primarily found in cultured or aquarium fishes.

Susceptible Species:

Probably all species of fishes are susceptible to pseudomonad infections under certain conditions. Cultured fishes, fishes held in aquariums, those being subjected to stress of transport and captive fishes in general are the most susceptible. Wild-ranging fishes do become susceptible during extremes of temperature, pH, pollution and other factors in environmental water.

Epizootiology:

Secondary infections of pseudomonads occur when defenses of the fish are disturbed in some way. Physical stresses such as excesses of pH or toxic substances in the water, injuries or damage to skin or scales, reduced dissolved oxygen, overcrowding of fishes in fish-holding containers and other factors predisposing the fishes to infections are of primary importance. Malnutrition and physiological alteration are also factors leading to pseudomonad septicemia.

Pseudomonad septicemia can occur as single-fish cases or as epizootics. Epizootics occur when all fishes in a population become more or less vulnerable to infection at the same time, such as the epizootics resulting from malnutrition.

The pathogen enters the host either through the oral route or through broken or abraded skin. Damaged gills are also routes of infection. The organisms are carried throughout the fish's body by the blood stream. The bacteria and their toxins serve to destroy body tissues, organs and functions. Infected fishes probably release large numbers of the bacteria into the water in the feces, thus increasing the bacterial population among groups of fishes and increasing chances of other fishes receiving overwhelming infections.

The incubation period for pseudomonad septicemia varies with the biotype or species of pseudomonad. An epizootic may be slow in developing or in some instances may "happen over night." Only a few fishes in a population may develop the disease or the epizootic may effect all fishes. Morbidity is difficult to predict in pseudomonad septicemia epizootics.

Fishes surviving an epizootic will probably be free of the bacterium within a short time. There is doubt that carrier fishes are involved to any great extent in outbreaks of pseudomonad septicemia. Usually pseudomonad septicemia is a "one-time-thing" if care is taken to keep fishes healthy and under normal conditions.

Disease Signs:

External disease signs of pseudomonad septicemia are similar to those caused by other gram-negative bacterial pathogens of fishes (Pl. 7A). There usually will be erythema at the base of the fins, in the mouth, along the grooves under the lower jaw and around the anus. Internally there will be general erythema and possibly hemorrhages in the peritoneum and visceral organs. The intestine will be erythemic and there may be bloody fluid in the lumen. Muscles may be hemorrhagic, but there are usually no large lesions or hemorrhages.

Diagnosis:

Diagnosis of pseudomonad septicemia is difficult. Separation of this disease from motile aeromonad disease or vibriosis relies on isolation and identification of the bacterium. Disease signs indicate that a general septicemia has occurred, but no judgement can be made on the identification of the causative bacterium. Histopathology is only useful to indicate a general infection.

Specimens of fishes used for diagnosis should be recently dead or still living but moribund. Care should be taken to disinfect the fish and use sterile instruments to open the specimen. Squash preparations of kidney or other affected organs will usually serve to demonstrate gram-negative rod-shaped bacteria. Cultures of organs can be made. Growth of the organism usually will appear within 24 to 36 hours after inoculation at 20 to 22°C incubation temperature. Fluorescent pigments may be obvious within 48 hours for many pseudomonads, although some require up to ten days to develop. The pigment from some species develops quickly, within one day, and breaks down rapidly so that within two days it is no longer obvious.

These organisms are motile and can be presumptively separated from *A. salmonicida* as soon as growth appears, but not motile aeromonads or vibrios. Definitive diagnosis of pseudomonad septicemia must be made from biochemical characteristics of the bacterium.

P. fluorescens biotypes and miscellaneous strains, as well as other species of *Pseudomonas* infecting fishes, do not attack glucose fermentatively; some will not even attack glucose oxidatively. The oxidation-fermentation test thus becomes a prime method for separation of the pseudomonads from the aeromonads and vibrios. Other biochemical characteristics serve to identify species of *Pseudomonas* (Table 8).[72] Bacterial keys may be used to differentiate biotypes of *P. fluorescens*.[32,65]

Part of the diagnosis of pseudomonad septicemia is to determine the primary cause for the infection. Observation of management practices or estimation of malnutrition may be necessary.

TABLE 8

Characteristics of pseudomonads isolated from diseased fishes

Characteristic or Test Media	Results	
Solid media	Most pseudomonads produce round, complete, convex or flat translucent colonies	
Pigment	Yellow, yellow-green or blue fluorescent pigment produced, usually soluble	
Morphology	Rods, 0.5 to 1.0 micrometers by 1.5 to 4.0 micrometers; non-spore-forming	
Staining	Gram-negative, non-acid-fast	
	Pseudomonas fluorescens	*Nonspecific pseudomonad* [a]
Glucose broth	A[b]	A
Lactose broth	No change	A
Maltose broth	No change	A
Mannitol broth	A	A
Sucrose broth	A	A
Sorbitol broth	No change	No change
Nitrate broth	No change	NO_2 produced
SIM Medium		
Hydrogen sulfide	–	–
Indol	–	+
Motility	+	+
Clark and Lubs Medium		
Methyl red test	+	+
Voges-Poskauer test	+	+
O/F medium with glucose	–/–[c]	–/–
Nutrient gelatin	Saccate	No liquefaction
Cytochrome oxidase test	+	+
0/129 Vibriostat	Growth	Growth
Novobiocin	Growth	Growth

[a]From an epizootic among wild yellow perch in a lake
[b]Acid production in the medium
[c]No change oxidatively/no change fermentatively

Therapy and Control:

Prevention is the best control method of pseudomonad septicemia. Maintaining the health of cultured or aquarium fishes is of utmost importance. Management of fish populations to reduce overcrowding, using an adequate water supply and reducing injuries will also decrease the possibility of pseudomonad septicemia epizootics.

Drug therapy and disinfection have been used for control of pseudomonad septicemia when it does occur among cultured or aquarium fishes.[72] Usually a prediction of the drug of choice for therapy of pseudomonad septicemia is not possible. A drug sensitivity test using a bacterial isolate from the epizootic may be of assistance in determining which drug may be of value for treatment of that epizootic. (Pl. 6E)

External bactericides may be useful for therapy of pseudomonad septicemia in those epizootics which develop slowly. External disinfection reduces the bacterial population in the water surrounding the fishes and soothes injuries if they occur. This will limit chances of secondary infection of fishes in the population. External bactericides can also be used during epizootics for which no systemic therapy is used or when morbidity and mortality cannot be reduced with systemic drugs.

Prognosis:

Setting exact figures for morbidity and mortality from pseudomonad septicemia is impossible. Each epizootic or case is different. Observant fish culturists and aquarists may notice changes in fish activity when only a few fishes are infected. Quick action to isolate and identify the pathogen and to determine the primary cause of the disease, may reduce morbidity and mortality from the disease. Contrast the rapid diagnosis and control of pseudomonad septicemia with a major epizootic in which no attempt is made to diagnose the disease or correct the primary cause until 100% morbidity and 60 to 70% mortality occur.

Practical Aspects:

There are no restrictions on transporting fishes harboring potentially pathogenic pseudomonads from one geographic area to another. These organisms are present in water throughout the world.

Stocking of sport fishes while an epizootic of pseudomonad septicemia is present is certainly unwise. The old practice of doing this very thing usually did not create a bacterial hazard to the environment where the fishes were stocked, but most of the fishes may die and be of no value to the sportsman.

Dealers in ornamental fishes sometimes sell fishes suffering from pseudomonad septicemia. This also is an unwise practice. Fishes with pseudomonad septicemia may not survive and may create a hazard to other fishes when placed into the home aquarium.

Careful diagnostic procedures may locate a therapeutic drug for systemic control of a pseudomonad pathogen involved with an epizootic. The disease may respond well to treatment during that epizootic. If the primary cause of the epizootic is not determined and corrected, a second epizootic may occur in the same fishes. The second epizootic may be caused by a different strain or species of pseudomonad. The therapeutic drug yielding good results for the first epizootic may be of no value for control of the second epizootic. Fish culturists and aquarists should keep this in mind whenever pseudomonad septicemia becomes a disease problem.

PATHOGENIC YERSINIA

Enteric Redmouth Disease (Yersiniosis)

Enteric redmouth disease (or yersiniosis) is an acute to subacute or chronic bacterial disease of rainbow trout. It has been known by the names Hagerman redmouth, pinkmouth or redthroat disease.

Enteric redmouth (ERM) disease is somewhat stress-related, although the etiological agent has produced spontaneous ERM disease without obvious stress factors. The disease was first reported in 1958[51] but was probably present prior to that time. The disease has primarily been associated with cultured trout.

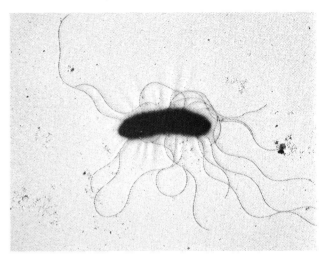

Fig. 1a: Electron micrograph of *Yersinia ruckeri* demonstrating peritrichous flagellation. (X 7140) (From Ross et al, 1964)[94]

Etiological Agent:

The etiological agent of ERM disease is *Yersinia ruckeri*.[41] The name was given in 1978.[41] It had previously been called by its family name (Enterobacteriaceae). The first description of the organism was published in 1966.[94]

Two major *Y. ruckeri* serotypes (Serotype I and Serotype II) have been demonstrated. The two serotypes differ antigenically in cross agglutination tests and by immunizations tests on fish.[74d]

Y. ruckeri is a gram-negative, non-spore-forming, straight rod-shaped bacterium. The organism is motile and peritrichously flagellated (Fig. 1a). It grows well on most common laboratory media.

Y. ruckeri does not produce cytochrome oxidase, but attacks glucose both oxidatively and fermentatively. It produces acid but no gas from glucose and mannitol but does not act on most other carbohydrates. It does not produce hydrogen sulfide, indol or acetymethylcarbinol. It does not produce pigment. The organism has an optimum temperature of 22°C. It will grow slowly at 8°C and at 35°C.

Geographical distribution:

ERM disease was first identified in south-central Idaho in the late 1950's. The etiological agent has been transported with fishes or fish products to most of the western part of the United States including Alaska, at least two midwestern states and three east-central states.[36] It has been reported in Saskatchewan and Nova Scotia, Canada. The disease has been found in Great Britain, Germany and France. It may be in other parts of Europe and in Australia.[45b,64a,122] The range of ERM disease continues to be extended as carrier fish are transported into noninfected areas.

Susceptible Species:

ERM disease is primarily a disease of rainbow trout, including the sea-going steelhead rainbow trout. Spontaneous disease has been reported in cutthroat trout, coho salmon and chinook salmon. It has been transmitted experimentally to Atlantic salmon.[26] Crayfishes have been implicated as a reservoir of infection but do not develop clinical signs of the disease.[36]

Epizootiology

Y. ruckeri is an obligate parasite. It does not survive well outside its host. A study in the laboratory indicated that it can survive only two to three weeks in water without plants or animals and up to two months in pond mud.[36]

Carrier fishes and other aquatic organisms (crayfishes for example) have been proven to be capable of supporting nonclinical infections of *Y. ruckeri*. These carriers are primarily responsible for maintenance of the organism within infected fish culture facilities. Carriers of *Y. ruckeri* are known to shed large numbers of the organisms into the water. Research has demonstrated that infected crayfish contained up to 500 or more viable *Y. ruckeri* per gram of visceral hemogenate.[36] The outfall water from fish culture facilities with active epizootics of ERM disease may have 100 to 1,000 viable *Y. ruckeri* per milliliter. Epizootics of disease within the facility increase these numbers 25 to 30 fold.[36]

The route of transmission of *Y. ruckeri* from fish to fish is probably by the oral route, although injuries or damaged skin, scales or gills may also be entry routes into noninfected fishes. The bacterium can lie dormant in the alimentary tract (more commonly in the lower intestine). Stress of handling, overcrowding with reduced dissolved oxygen and other stresses allow the organism to invade. Epizootics of ERM disease may follow within three or more days the handling of the fishes for sorting, transfer to other ponds or other necessary cultural procedures, indicating latent infections in the fishes.

The incubation period for experimentally induced ERM disease was found to be five to ten days at 13 to 15°C. *Y. ruckeri* introduced into the environment of noninfected fishes being held at 14.5°C resulted in an epizootic on the sixteenth day,[36] and on the ninth day at 18.3°C. Water temperature and fish susceptibility alter the incubation period in all cases.

The disease can develop into acute, subacute or chronic cases depending on environmental and physical factors. Epizootics of acute ERM disease may follow handling stresses. Subacute or chronic cases occur in overcrowded fish culture facilities or in facilities with reduced dissolved oxygen.

Latent cases of ERM disease and nonclinical carriers have no doubt been responsible for transmission of the disease to noninfected geographical areas. These fishes appear and act normal; no indication of *Y. ruckeri* is apparent.

Another source of *Y. ruckeri* transmission from infected geographical areas to noninfected areas has been the clinical cases of ERM disease which have been arrested by use of systemic drugs. Reduction or elimination of mortality has been the signal for transporting the fishes to the predetermined location. The bacterium has been moved long distances in this way.

No work has been done to indicate if *Y. ruckeri* can be transmitted in or on fish eggs. This is a possible source of infection which should be examined. Disinfection of eggs coming into a fish hatchery is recommended as a control procedure for ERM disease.

Most epizootics of ERM disease occur at water temperatures between 11 and 18°C. Epizootics of subacute or chronic ERM disease may be noted between 8 and 11°C.

Disease Signs:

Two forms of ERM disease are common, depending on whether the case is acute, subacute or chronic. Acute cases usually develop rapidly with little or no external signs. Occasionally fishes may demonstrate erythema in the mouth, at the base of the fins, in the opercula and around the anus. Hemorrhages may occur in the skin of various parts of the body.

Internally, acute cases demonstrate much erythema and petechial hemorrhages in the peritoneum, body fat, gonads, mesenteries, swim bladder and other organs. The intestinal tract is usually erythemic and filled with bloody mucus. The kidney and spleen may be somewhat swollen. The liver may be pale in color, and muscle tissue may or may not have petechiae.

Subacute cases are similar to the acute cases in many respects. The disease signs may be more advanced, with definite petechiae in skin and fins. The subacute cases may also demonstrate either unilateral or bilateral exophthalmos. Internally, disease signs of subacute cases are similar to the acute forms, except more advanced: the kidney and spleen are much more swollen and general erythema is more apparent (Pl. 8B, Pl. 34A).

Chronic cases of ERM diseases have a much different appearance from the acute or subacute cases. These fishes quite often demonstrate partial or total blindness, exophthalmos in one or both eyes and the dark skin color which usually accompanies blindness. These fish are lethargic and float aimlessly about the pond. Some may show a distended abdomen, others may be emaciated. There may or may not be erythema at the base of fins, in the mouth or in the opercula. The gills are usually pale in color. There may be an accumulation of serous fluid around the viscera and a general erythema, but usually no hemorrhages. The kidney is quite swollen and the spleen enlarged. The liver is usually pale in color. The alimentary tract is quite often completely free of food or feces, but there may be yellowish bile-stained mucus in the lumen of the intestine. There is usually no visceral fat in the chronic cases of ERM disease.

Diagnosis:

Disease signs, bacterial isolation and identification, and histopathology are useful in the diagnosis of ERM disease. History of past occurrences of the disease or of importation of fishes from enzootic ERM disease areas is also of diagnostic assistance.

Kidney, spleen or liver squash preparations of ERM disease will reveal gram-negative, straight rod-shaped bacteria (Pl. 8C). The organisms can be isolated onto most laboratory media. Visible growth appears within 16 to 24 hours after inoculation of cultures. The bacterium is motile, especially when taken from young, rapidly growing cultures. Motility will presumptively separate the bacterium from *A. salmonicida*. The early visible growth can also be tested for cytochrome oxidase production. *Y. ruckeri* is cytochrome oxidase negative, which presumptively separates it from the aeromonads, pseudomonads and vibrios. Definitive identification of *Y. ruckeri* can be made from other biochemical characteristics (Table 9).

Histopathology of ERM disease is not distinctive from that caused by other gram-negative bacterial septicemic fish pathogens. The kidney, spleen, liver and other organs may reveal more edematous change than some of the other similar diseases, but this is not reliable for diagnosis, only an indication.

Other nonspecific findings which may be of assistance in the diagnosis of ERM disease are the decreased hematocrit and reduced serum protein which usually accompany *Y. ruckeri* infections.[36] The diagnostician must be aware that similar clinical results will also be found in other septicemic bacterial diseases, excessive parasitism and malnutrition.

A hemagglutination test has been suggested for definitive diagnosis of ERM disease. This test, an inert particle agglutination test and a fluorescent antibody test all show promise for diagnosis of ERM disease, but more research is necessary before they are widely accepted.

Therapy and Control:

Sulfamerazine and oxytetracycline have been the drugs of choice for therapy of ERM disease. The usual 14-day course of sulfamerazine therapy (265 mg per kg, 12 g per 100 lb, of fish per day for three days; followed by 154 mg per kg, 7 g per 100 lb, of fish per day for an additional 11 days) is an effective treatment. Oxytetracycline used at 55 mg per kg (2.5 g per 100 lb) of fish per day for ten days is also effective. Romet-30 (ormetoprim plus sulfadimethoxine) is effective when used at 50 mg per kg (2.27 g per 100 lb) of fish per day for 14 days. The three drugs given above have been cleared by the U.S. Food and Drug Administration for use in control of ERM disease.

Two other drugs have been found effective for control of ERM disease but have not been cleared for use in the United States: Tiamulin used at 5 mg per kg (227 mg per 100 lb) of fish per day for 14 days, and Tribressen® used at 1 mg per kg (45 mg per 100 lb) of fish per day for 14 days.[16b]

Prophylactic use of external bactericides is also useful to remove or reduce the pathogen population in water, thus reducing transmission from host to host. Some of the quaternary ammonium compounds are excellent for this purpose.

Many fish culturists have not used either sulfamerazine or oxytetracycline as recommended. Therapy is terminated as soon as mortality from ERM disease is controlled. Sometimes systemic therapy has been stopped after only three days of treatment. Repeated short-term treatment is usually not entirely effective and may also be responsible for stimulation of drug resistance in the bacterium. Certain enzootic ERM disease areas of the United States now have *Y. ruckeri* strains completely resistant to both sulfamerazine and oxytetracycline. A concerted effort is being made to find other drugs which will control the disease in affected fishes.

The apparent low number of *Y. ruckeri* biotypes makes immunization of susceptible fish an acceptable practice for control of ERM disease. The progress in preparation of better immunizing agents for control of ERM disease has been phenomenal during the late 1970's and early 1980's.[74c] The first bacterins were expensive and only small fish could be immunized economically. Effective immersion type bacterins have been improved to the point where larger fish can be treated and booster doses given. These products are commercially available in the United States. The most useful method of immunizing large numbers of any size fish against ERM disease has been the use of spray bacterins. Fish are allowed to slide down an inclined plane while the bacterin is sprayed over their bodies. The twisting, turning fish are sprayed over every side as they move down the chute.

Research continues on methods of preparing effective oral bacterins for control of ERM disease. Laboratory experiments using these bacterins often give acceptable results, but the same bacterins used in field trials are ineffective.

Prognosis:

Young fishes are somewhat more susceptible to ERM disease than older fishes. Morbidity may reach 100% in any age class of fishes. Mortality is usually higher in younger fishes but is dependent upon fish culture management. Those fish hatcheries which tend to overcrowd

TABLE 9

Characteristics of *Yersinia ruckeri* used for identification

Characteristic or Test Media	Results
Solid media	Colonies round, complete, convex and translucent
Pigment	No pigment is produced
Morphology	Rods 0.8 micrometer by 1.5 to 2.3 micrometers; non-spore-forming; peritrichous flagella
Staining	Gram-negative; non-acid-fast
Optimum temperature (°C)	22
Glucose broth	A[a]
Lactose broth	No change
Maltose broth	No change
Mannitol broth	A
Sucrose broth	No change
Sorbitol broth	No change (A produced by Serotype II)[74c]
Nitrate broth	NO₂ produced
SIM medium	
Hydrogen sulfide	—
Indol	—
Motility	+
Clark and Lubs medium	
Methyl red test	+
Voges-Poskauer test	—
O/F Medium with glucose	+/+[b]
Nutrient gelatin	Stratiform
Cytochrome oxidase test	—

[a]Acid produced
[b]Attacks glucose oxidatively/attacks glucose fermentatively

the fishes become more prone to epizootics of ERM disease than those which do not. Fish culture facilities on a limited water supply, and especially a water supply which fluctuates from season to season, tend to have higher mortality from ERM disease during periods of extreme overcrowding or low flow.

ERM disease is not a highly fatal disease. Mortality in any single epizootic may not exceed 50% of a population, even under the most overcrowded and unsatisfactory conditions. Ideal management of fish culture in *Y. ruckeri*-infected culture facilities may continue with little or no mortality from ERM disease.

Practical Aspects:

ERM disease control should begin with quarantine and restriction of movement of carrier fishes. Fish culturists with enzootic *Y. ruckeri* in the culture facility should be extremely careful of moving live fishes, some fish products and fish eggs to non-infected geographical areas. Much more research is needed on the epizootiology of ERM disease to determine how *Y. ruckeri*-infected fishes can be used without continually widening the geographical range of the disease. Canadian, European and Japanese trout cultures are vulnerable to this disease, and acceptable restrictions of infected fish movement are definitely needed to eliminate the possibility of moving the disease to all parts of the world.

Fish culture facilities with enzootic ERM disease should be examined for possible removal of the pathogen. Those facilities using springs or wells for a water supply may be disinfected so that the disease is no longer a problem to them and to other noninfected geographical areas.

No research has been done on the effect of stocking *Y. ruckeri*-infected fishes into wild fish populations. The nature of ERM disease and the fact that epizootics and mortality occur under improper management conditions indicates that mortality from the disease in wild-ranging susceptible fishes would be unlikely. However, *Y. ruckeri*-infected wild fishes could continue to be a source of infection for those fish culture facilities using water from the same stream or lake containing the infected fishes.

PATHOGENIC CYTOPHAGALES

Bacteria belonging to the order Cytophagales and family Cytophagaceae have previously been called "myxobacteria," a name appearing in much of the literature on fish diseases prior to 1978.[16] The cytophagales commonly occur in soil and water; they are saprophytes but may also become opportunistic pathogens of fishes and other aquatic organisms.

The cytophagales are long, slender or filamentous rod-shaped bacteria. All are motile by gliding. The exact mechanism of motility is not known, but some members of the order can move 10 or more micrometers per minute.[32] Only species of a single genus of Cytophagaceae are known to be involved as secondary pathogens of fishes. Members of other genera may also be opportunistic fish pathogens, but little is known about them.

All bacteria of the family Cytophagaceae involved as fish pathogens are fastidious. Most will grow on only specially prepared media or not at all. Little is known of the biochemical activity of these organisms because of this characteristic.

Columnaris Disease

Columnaris disease was first described in 1922 and named after the etiological agent, a bacterium called *Bacillus columnaris* at that time. Columnaris disease has also been called cotton-wool disease and mouth-fungus, the latter being a misnomer because the disease is in no way caused by a fungus.

Columnaris disease is a chronic to subacute disease in natural infections of most freshwater fishes. The disease affects the external structures of the fish body, although case histories of systemic columnaris disease have been reported.[125]

Etiological Agent:

The etiological agent of columnaris disease is *Flexibacter columnaris*. The name *Bacillus columnaris* was proposed in 1922[34] but was never accepted. The bacterium was named *Chondrococcus columnaris* in 1944[76] and *Flexibacter columnaris* in 1974.[32]

F. columnaris is an unbranched rod- or filament-shaped bacterium usually 0.5 to 0.7 micrometer by 5 to 100 or more micrometers (Pl. 8D, Pl. 34B). Early literature on the organism suggested the presence of resting stages (called fruiting bodies or microcysts).[8,76] However, these spheroplasts have been

shown to be slime with rod-shaped cells within the circular structures, and this has been the reason for the nomenclatural change from genus *Chondrococcus* to genus *Flexibacter*.[32] The bacterium is motile by gliding on solid, moist surfaces.

F. columnaris is somewhat fastidious. It will not grow on most common laboratory media. It is inhibited by as little as 0.1% salt and will not grow at all in media which contains 0.5 to 1.0% salt. Cytophaga medium which contains tryptone, yeast extract, beef extract and sodium acetate has been found best for primary isolation of *F. columnaris*.[8] The organism will grow between 4° and 35°C.[78] It seldom causes disease in susceptible fish below 10°C, but causes explosive infections in susceptible fish above 18°C.[53a] It is actively proteolytic, ferments glucose, fructose, maltose, sucrose and a few other less common carbohydrates. It produces cytochrome oxidase and catalase. It is a strict aerobe. *F. columnaris* produces hydrogen sulfide, does not reduce nitrate to nitrite and does not produce indole.

There are four recognized groups, each with varying serological characteristics. Differences in pathogenicity between groups have been reported.[121a] Antisera are available for separating the groups.[13]

The bacterium grows on the surfaces of fishes, producing column-like structures. It also produces a characteristic "stacked" appearance of organisms when grown on bits of fish tissue in sterile water.[78] The organisms tend to lie parallel to each other when grown on cytophaga agar.

The organism produces a yellow-green pigment. Colonies are flat, spreading and with uneven edges. General biochemical characteristics are not used for identification of *F. columnaris*.

Geographic Distribution:

Columnaris disease was first described in warmwater fishes of the Mississippi River.[34] The disease has subsequently been reported in freshwater fishes throughout the world.

Susceptible Species:

All freshwater fishes are susceptible to *F. columnaris* infection. The disease has been reported as a mortality factor in several species of cultured salmonids, cultured catfishes, bait minnows, goldfish, carp, eel, basses, sunfishes and most other cultured fishes. It is a problem among nearly all freshwater aquarium and ornamental fishes, probably because of the high temperature of aquaria (28 to 35°C, an optimum growth temperature for many *F. columnaris* strains). The disease has occurred among wild-ranging fishes, but to a lesser degree than cultured fishes, probably because mass injuries or malnutrition is not as prevalent among most wild fishes.[13]

Epizootiology:

The disease does not usually occur as a spontaneous

infection but results from injuries to the fish, or physical and nutritional deficiencies. Severity of infection among susceptible fishes depends on severity of injury or deficienty and virulence of the strain of *F. columnaris*. Most normal and healthy fishes are quite resistant to *F. columnaris*.[119]

F. columnaris is ubiquitous to most freshwaters of the world. The organism first invades the skin of the head region of the body, including the mouth, lips, cheeks, opercles, fins and gills as the primary site of infection of susceptible fishes. Injuries anywhere on the body also serve as the primary infection site.

Bacterial growth on the skin, fins and gills releases many organisms into the water. Thus, the overcrowded conditions of fish in culture facilities and aquaria and congregations of migrating fishes at the base of dams along rivers are conducive to a self-perpetuating infection among the fish. Infected fishes release large numbers of bacteria which infect other hosts. These hosts then begin to release more pathogens which increase the severity of infections on the present hosts or attack new hosts until every member of the population has the disease. The results are a fulminating infection and increase of case numbers in the population until overcrowding is reduced or therapeutic measures taken to decrease the bacterial population in the water.

F. columnaris carrier fishes may develop and serve as a source of infection for younger, more susceptible fishes. Older hatchery-reared fishes usually demonstrate circulating antibodies against this bacterium, as indication that they have been in contact with the organism.

The incubation period of columnaris disease is variable. Overcrowding of facilities or nutritional deficiencies develop gradually. *F. columnaris* can invade at any time during the development of these conditions. Several isolates of *F. columnaris* have proven to be highly virulent. One strain of the organism was reported to be capable of causing mortality in young fishes in less than 24 hours following parenteral injection.[96] The incubation period for most strains of *F. columnaris* is much longer than this, even following parenteral injection.

Development of columnaris disease in susceptible fishes is temperature-related. There usually will be little or no indication of the disease at water temperatures below 10°C and certainly none below 7°C. The optimum temperature is near 28° to 30°C, but epizootics do occur in cultured or aquarium fishes at 15° to 17°C. Blueback salmon, as an example, which had been intentionally injured suffered 100% mortality at 21°C, 60% mortality at 15.5°C and no mortality at 10°C.[43]

Stocking and transporting fish infected with *F. columnaris* have probably not been important to the spread of columnaris disease. This bacterium is so widely distributed in nature that movement of infected fishes will only serve to distribute certain virulent strains of the organism.

Disease Signs:

The earliest disease sign of columnaris disease in fish is a thickening of the mucus at various spots on the head, opercula, fins and in and around injuries. The mucus continues to become thicker until definite areas of skin involvement appear as circular areas of fluffy, grayish opalescent growth. The gills may be involved and demonstrate light-colored areas at the tips of the gill filaments initially, followed by an overgrowth of the outer parts of filaments as the infection progresses. Fins affected by columnaris disease usually have necrotic lesions on the outer edges initially which progress down the rays of the fin.

Well-developed columnaris disease on the skin usually has tiny erythemic spots or petechiae within the lesions. The lesions are circular, as if spreading from a single focus in all directions at the same rate.

Fringes of gill filaments are lost to advancing necrosis and sloughing of gill tissue (Pl. 7B). There is actual loss of respiratory tissue in these cases. The bacterium may invade the blood stream through gill or skin lesions in cases of columnaris disease in which gill damage is minimal and enough vital respiratory tissue remains to support life. The disease is usually terminal within a relatively short time following bacteremia.

Diagnosis:

Columnaris disease can be presumptively diagnosed from disease signs on the skin and gills of the host and from squash preparations made from scrapings of the affected areas or gills. Presence of long, slender, possibly filamentous, rod-shaped, gram-negative bacteria assists in presumptive diagnosis. Examination of gill arches may reveal piles of *F. columnaris* at various locations on the gill filament (Pl. 8E).

Definitive diagnosis requires isolation of the bacterium on cytophaga medium[32] or a slide agglutination test using *F. columnaris* antiserum. The growth of *F. columnaris* on solid media is usually yellow-green, with flat, rough, spreading colonies which adhere to the media. Sometimes the growth is unsatisfactory for use in the slide agglutination test. The suggestion has been made that these unsatisfactory isolates may become usable by transferring to cytophaga broth medium incubating until moderate growth appears, centrifuging the broth, resuspending the cells in saline and heating the suspension for five minutes at 55°C prior to use in the agglutination test. There are no growth media useful for biochemical identification of *F. columnaris*.

Therapy and Control:

Columnaris disease had been one of those annoying diseases of cultured and aquarium fishes which seemed to defy therapeutic approaches until furanace (P7138) was used for the disease. Furanace is a nitrofuran derivative which is absorbed from the water, yielding therapeutic tissue levels as well as acting as a topical therapeutic. *F. columnaris* is sensitive to this chemotherapeutic. Furanace has another characteristic which makes it acceptable to use for fish disease control—it may be absorbed rapidly from the water, but it also leaves the fish tissue rapidly, usually within a few hours.[6] Furanace has received U.S. Food and Drug Administration registration as an acceptable drug for disease control in nonfood fishes. Registration for use against columnaris disease of food fishes has not been accepted.

The dosage of furanace for control of columnaris disease is 1:750,000 (1.5 mg/L) for one hour. The treatment can be given for one day or up to three consecutive days, depending on the progress of the disease.

Columnaris disease can also be treated with a wide variety of other therapeutic compounds. None of the drugs, other than furanace, treat the fish systemically as well as topically. Those given systemically reduce or eliminate systemic *F. columnaris*; those given topically as a bath reduce or eliminate the external pathogens.

Oxytetracycline given at 50 mg per kg (2.5 g per 100 lb) of fish per day for ten days has been found effective in the control of some epizootics of columnaris disease. Sulfamerazine will also prove somewhat effective when used at a rate of 264 mg per kg (12 g per 100 lb) of fish per day for three days, followed by 154 mg per kg (7 g per 100 lb) of fish per day for 11 days. Neither of these drugs treat the surface infection.

Dip or bath treatments have been used to treat columnaris disease topically. The quaternary ammonium compounds used according to directions will reduce infections of *F. columnaris* on skin and gills. Copper sulfate has been used both as a 20-minute dip at 1:25,000 (40 mg/L) or a one-minute dip at 1:2,000 (500 mg/L). Potassium permanganate used at 1:500,000 (2 mg/L) has been added to ponds and aquariums and left indefinitely for columnaris disease therapy. Oxolinic acid has been used at 1:1,000,000. (1 mg/L) for 24 hours.[107]

Control of *F. columnaris* in fishes may be possible by immunization. Research has demonstrated that fishes produce a high antibody titer against the bacterium when injected either subcutaneously or intramuscularly. No acceptable immunizing agents are available, although research continues in attempts to develop mass immunizing procedures for delivery of a columnaris bacterin for fish.[100]

Other control procedures involve proper management practices. Overcrowded fishes become more susceptible to columnaris disease, especially when the fishes are nutritionally deficient or are handled. Prophylactic treatments with external disinfectants may be given to fishes prior to physical handling to reduce possibilities of later infections with *F. columnaris*. There is some indication that removing older fishes, which sometimes find their way into the water supply of fish culture facilities, assists in reducing the infection of small, young fish in the water below them.

The ubiquitous nature of *F. columnaris* precludes the elimination of the organism from fish culture facilities or aquariums. Therefore, the disease threat will always be present in culture facilities and aquariums. Management around the bacterial population is necessary for control of the disease.

Prognosis:

Morbidity for columnaris disease in overcrowded or unsanitary conditions may reach 100% of the fishes. Mortalities under these same unsatisfactory conditions may reach 70% or higher among the young and most susceptible fishes.

F. columnaris infection of wild-ranging fishes can best be demonstrated by the studies performed on Columbia River salmon between 1955 and 1962. The Columbia River salmon are not typical of wild fishes, but give an indication of the wide distribution of *F. columnaris* in nature. Columnaris disease morbidity in the salmon at Bonneville Dam was less than 1%. These same fish examined higher up the river system demonstrated morbidity between 28 and 75%.[78] The water temperature in the upper streams reached 21°C and higher. Mortalities were high in the upper warmer waters. *F. columnaris* also occurred in other fishes of the streams.

Practical Aspects:

The fish culturist and the aquarist should be aware of columnaris disease. Overcrowding of fishes, handling them in nets and moving from pond to pond or tank to tank makes them vulnerable to *F. columnaris* infection and should be avoided. Nutritionally deficient fishes are also susceptible to *F. columnaris* infection. Maintenance of nutritional health of the fishes will reduce the possibility of columnaris disease.

Rapid diagnosis and treatment of columnaris disease are necessary for practical control of the disease. Infections of this pathogen become involved in the lower layers of skin and the gills as they progress. The organisms are more easily removed during the early infection stage than at the more advanced stage. Prophylactic use of external disinfectants will be found most useful if applied at the early onset of columnaris disease. Fish showing thickened, grayish opalescent mucus on the head region of the body, outer margins of fins and in and around injured areas or sloughed scales should be examined for presence of long slender or filamentous rod-shaped gram-negative bacteria. Treatment should be initiated when a positive presumptive test for *F. columnaris* is obtained.

Columnaris disease can be a tremendous problem among wild-ranging fishes, too, and the fish manager should be aware of this disease. The Columbia River salmon population is thought to have been adversely affected by the placement of dams along the main river and its tributaries, but columnaris disease has no doubt been another vital factor in the decline. Columnaris disease in native fishes in streams and lakes can be a mortality or morbidity factor when water temperatures increase to above 15°C and the fish are overcrowded in any way. Spawning runs of fishes are especially vulnerable to this disease because they usually are congested in streams or at the edges of lakes. The incidence of infection rises under these conditions. Many of the infections are mistaken for fungal infections by spawning crews working with the fishes. Microscopic examination of skin scrapings from these fishes may be of assistance in planning spawning operations.

Peduncle Disease, Fin Rot or Coldwater Disease

Peduncle disease is a chronic disease of fishes. The etiological agents are several species or subspcies of *Cytophaga* (formerly called myxobacteria).[16] The bacteria invade the fins, causing necrosis of tissue. Confinement of the necrosis to the fins alone is sometimes called fin rot disease, but when the necrosis enters tissue at the base of the caudal fin (the caudal peduncle) it is referred to as peduncle disease.[118]

Peduncle disease occurs more often in coldwater fishes and, therefore, it is sometimes referred to as coldwater disease. The disease may also be found among coolwater and warmwater fishes, but is much more prevalent in coldwater fishes. The disease appears more often in coldwater fishes kept at environmental temperatures between 4 and 10°C.

Peduncle disease is usually of a secondary nature. Predisposing conditions of the fishes such as malnutrition, presence of toxic substances or any physiological imbalance make them susceptible to secondary epithelial infections of flexibacteria.

Etiological Agent:

The etiological agents of peduncle disease are long, slender or filamentous, gram-negative rod-shaped bacteria belonging to the genus *Cytophaga*. The most commonly found bacteria in coldwater cases of peduncle disease is *Cytophaga psychrophilia*.[32,121a] The etiological agent is often referred to as the "myxobacteria of peduncle disease" or the "myxobacteria of fin rot".[32,121a] There are cytophaga-like organisms which cause a similar disease among warmwater fish and aquarium fish.

The etiological bacteria of this disease complex range in size from 0.7 to 1.5 micrometers by 5 to 100 micrometers. They occur as singles, pairs and long filaments. The exact classification of the bacteria differs from case to case. Some cases of peduncle disease demonstrate prolific numbers of bacteria in the infected tissues of the caudal peduncle and caudal fin (Pl. 8F), while other cases may have limited numbers of organisms which do not stain well and are difficult to locate. Some of the cases yield flexibacteria which grow well on cytophaga agar[32] or on highly enriched media such as blood agar or brain heart infusion agar. Flexibacteria from other cases

of the disease may be fastidious and incapable of being cultured.

The flexibacteria causing coldwater disease usually have an optimum growth temperature of 4 to 10°C. These bacteria do not grow at 12 to 15°C. Warmwater strains of flexibacteria causing peduncle disease among aquarium fishes have a much higher optimum growth temperature of 25 to 32°C.

All of the bacteria found in cases of peduncle disease are opportunistic pathogens. Mismanagement of cultured and aquarium fishes, as well as injuries and malnutrition, must be considered as an important component of the etiology of peduncle disease.

Geographical Distribution:

Peduncle disease has been reported often in the cultured salmonids, especially under coldwater conditions. The disease should be considered as one of temperate zone distribution, except for the warmwater strains of flexibacteria involved with aquarium and ornamental fishes. The disease is present among wild fish populations whenever conditions are conducive for invasion by pathogens.

Susceptible Species:

Probably all coldwater and coolwater fishes are susceptible to peduncle disease when their resistance to infection has been reduced. The disease has been reported in cultured salmon,[4] brook trout[23] (Pl. 9A), rainbow trout,[33] brown trout, lake trout, several sucker species, whitefish, dace, carp and many others.

Most aquarium fishes are also susceptible to peduncle disease (Pl. 9B). The disease is secondary among these fishes, too, the primary cause being nutritional deficiencies or rough handling.

Epizootiology:

The disease starts as fin rot but may proceed to peduncle disease if not arrested. Fins of fishes may be subjected to abrasion and injury from other fishes in the population, sloughing of epithelial tissue and mucus from malnutrition, high water pH, irritation from toxic materials in the water and a whole range of conditions which alter external surfaces of the host. The bacteria invade the first few layers of cells on the edges of the fins or under scale pockets (Pl. 1A).[4]

The flexibacteria destroy more epithelial cells on the margin of fins or where scales have been loosened, gradually destroying tissue and moving into uninfected tissue. The disease progresses until arrested by therapeutic measures or the condition which caused the original infection is reduced or eliminated, or else the fish dies.

The flexibacteria responsible for peduncle disease may be present in the water supply of most fish culture facilities. Increases in the number of cases also increase the number of bacteria available for infection of other hosts or increase the infection in already infected hosts.

Water temperature is very important in most cases of

peduncle disease among the coldwater fishes. The disease will not usually develop even in the most susceptible fishes unless the water temperature is below 10 or 11°C. Cases of the disease in aquarium fishes are not as temperature-related, but some epizootics have been known to occur in these species as the result of aquarium heater malfunction, which allows temperature to drop below that usually maintained in the aquarium.

Transporting fishes or fish eggs has probably been of no importance on the epizootiology of peduncle disease. The etiological bacteria are common in most waters, and movement of fishes may only serve to broaden the distribution of various strains or subspecies of flexibacteria.

Disease Signs:

Early signs of peduncle disease are a general rough appearance of the skin and a loss of integrity of the tips of fins. This is because the condition responsible for the susceptibility to the opportunistic pathogen usually affects all of the external epithelium, including skin, scale pockets and fins. Bacterial invasion first appears as a white to gray line along the margin of the fins. Fin rays may also begin to separate.

The invasion of epithelial tissue continues if the primary cause of the infection is not removed. The line of involvement appears as a line of necrotic tissue, usually with a line of erythemic or inflammatory tissue inside the line of necrosis. The line of erythema is the area of most active bacterial infection. The area is eventually destroyed, thus moving the line of invasion inward with sloughing of necrotic tissue. The disease progresses inwardly on the fins until the base of attachment of the fins is reached. The invasion process is usually halted at the base of all fins except the caudal fin, where the invasion may continue to progress into the caudal peduncle. Extremely advanced cases of peduncle disease may demonstrate necrosis and sloughing of necrotic tissue until the caudal vertebrae are exposed (Pl. 9A). Meanwhile, other surfaces of the body, even though not invaded by flexibacteria, appear rough and ragged (Pl. 9B).

Diagnosis:

Presumptive diagnosis of peduncle disease can be made from disease signs and appearance of bacteria in squash preparations made from the inflammatory and necrotic tissue of fins or caudal peduncle.[23] Definitive diagnosis is the same as the presumptive diagnosis with possible identification of the bacteria. These organisms are long, slender or filamentous gram-negative rod-shaped bacteria. Growth on solid media will demonstrate gliding movement or a lining up of bacteria within colonies. The organisms may or may not produce a yellow to greenish yellow pigment. Most of the flexibacteria responsible for peduncle disease have a tendency to adhere to the surface of the culture medium. Most of them are aerobic, but a few may be microaerophilic. Most will not grow on differential media.

Therapy and Control:

The usual sequence of therapy for peduncle disease is to use a course of drug treatment while the primary cause of infection is determined. Peduncle disease, like columnaris disease, was difficult to control before the use of furanace. Most of the flexibacteria which cause peduncle disease can be successfully treated with furanace used at 1:750,000 (1.5 mg/L) in the water for one hour. The treatment can be given for one to three days, depending on the course of the disease.

Furanace has not been registered for use in the control of food fish diseases, so other methods of treatment must be used in these cases. The usual sequence of therapy is to give a systemic drug and to treat externally at the same time. The bacteria are present in necrotic tissue of the fins or caudal peduncle as well as in the tissue of these organs which has a blood supply. The systemic drug acts within the tissue with a blood supply, and the external disinfectant affects the necrotic tissue on the surface.

Sulfamerazine combined with a quaternary ammonium disinfectant is useful for reducing or eliminating lesions of peduncle disease while the primary cause of the disease is determined. The usual 14-day course of sulfamerazine should be used: i.e., 264 mg per kg (12 g per 100 lb) of fish per day in the ration for three days, followed by 154 mg per kg (7 g per 100 lb) of fish per day for an additional 11 days. The external disinfectant should be used every third day during the systemic drug treatment.

Oxytetracycline in the food at a dose rate of 50 mg per kg (2.5 g per 100 lb) of fish per day for ten days has been found to be effective. The external disinfectant is used with oxytetracycline every third day of systemic treatment.

Sulfisoxazole added to the ration and given at a drug dose level of 220 mg per kg (10 g per 100 lb) of fish per day has also been found satisfactory.[5] External disinfection used every third day of the systemic treatment will assist in the control of the disease.

Determination and elimination of the primary cause for the disease are necessary to the cure of peduncle disease. Malnutrition and other physiological changes can be detected by hematology, blood chemistry, histopathology and disease signs. Presence of irritants in the water, unacceptable pH or other toxic conditions which lead to the disease can be detected by water chemistry analysis.

Raising the water temperature in those cases of peduncle disease which occur among coldwater or coolwater fishes may aid in controlling the disease. Increasing the temperature in aquaria may also be beneficial.

Prognosis:

Morbidity from peduncle disease may be very low (less than 1% of the population) or may involve the entire population in a tank, raceway or pond. The mortality may be extremely low but continuous, several fish dying each day to be replaced by new cases of the disease in the population, thus maintaining number of cases in the facilities at all times.

Peduncle disease progresses slowly, which gives the fish culturist or aquarist time to determine the primary cause and alleviate the problem. There are epizootics of peduncle disease in which 50% or more of the fishes are affected. This is especially true in cold water facilities with water temperatures below 10°C and low physiological resistance in the fishes. The coldwater factor of the disease is especially a problem in salmon hatcheries with a streamwater supply and cold seasonal temperatures. There have been instances of very high morbidity from flexibacteria infections in sac-fry. The primary cause of the infection is unknown in many of these epizootics, and mortality may reach 75%.

Fish with fin rot will usually survive if treated correctly. Fish with advanced fin rot, to the stage of peduncle disease, may not survive even with proper treatment.

Practical Aspects:

Peduncle disease occurring in fish culture facilities and aquaria should be an indication that something is amiss with the fish or the environment. The disease should alert the culturist or aquarist that the primary cause of physiological imbalance should be found and corrected.

There are cases of peduncle disease which occur in a single fish among a large population, especially in aquaria. The entire population may not need to be examined because the single case may be in a fish with a physical ailment (malformed body structures, internal injuries not obvious on the outside of the fish or another condition not found in the other fishes in the aquarium). Sick fishes should be removed to avoid increasing the opportunistic pathogen population to the point it may become invasive to other fishes.

Fishes with peduncle disease may be safely stocked into wild fish populations. However, survival of fishes with this disease may be low in open water. The usual suggestion is to determine the cause of the disease or of the rough and ragged appearance of the fishes and attempt to correct it prior to release.

Placing a new fish which has this disease into an aquarium with normal healthy fishes should be avoided. The bacteria present in the necrotic fin tissue of the new fish may be transmissible to the fishes present in the aquarium.

Bacterial (Environmental) Gill Disease

Bacterial (environmental) gill disease, usually referred to simply as "gill disease," is a chronic to acute disease primarily among cultured and aquarium fishes. The disease is often called "bacterial gill disease" but in actual-

ity it should be called "environmental gill disease." The latter name is more appropriate because most epizootics of the disease are caused by an environmental irritant resulting in derangement and damage to gill epithelium. Often bacteria invade the damaged gill tissue late in the course of the disease, thus the name "bacterial gill disease."

Etiological Agents:

Bacterial (environmental) gill disease is of mixed etiology. The major cause of the disease is damage to gill membranes by irritants in the water, followed by invasion of opportunistic bacteria. There is much evidence that products of fish metabolism, particularly ammonia, are the primary environmental factors predisposing fish to bacterial gill disease.

Most species of fish excrete a high percentage of their nitrogenous body wastes as ammonium ions from the gills. Small amounts are excreted as urea, uric acid, creatin, creatinine and a few other nitrogenous compounds from the kidney. Ammonium ions released into the water directly from the gills, and alteration of some of the other nitrogenous compounds to ammoniacal nitrogen by saprophytic bacteria, may reach concentrations which are highly irritating to gills, especially when fish are overcrowded in fish culture facilities or aquaria.

Flexibacteria and other opportunistic soil and water bacteria such as pseudomonads and flavobacteria are present in most waters which harbor fishes.[21,104a] These organisms may invade irritated gill membranes, resulting in bacterial gill disease. The bacteria involved are all gram-negative and rod-shaped. Some are fastidious but others will grow on most common laboratory media. However, the usual experience with bacterial gill disease is the presence of different species or strains of either flexibacteria, pseudomonads, flavobacteria or aeromonads in different epizootics of this disease. Often a single species or strain of bacteria is involved during any one epizootic.[21]

Geographical Distribution:

Environmental or bacterial gill disease is worldwide in its distribution. The disease is found more often in those parts of the world where fishes are held under crowded conditions or where other factors conducive to gill irritation and damage are present.

Susceptible Species:

All species of fishes are susceptible to environmental or bacterial gill disease. However, various species of fishes differ in resistance to this disease. Fishes which have evolved in water supplies rich in detritus and organic matter seem to be more resistant. The common carp, channel catfish, fathead minnow and other similar fishes will develop the disease but to a lesser degree than some of the salmonids, graylings, whitefishes or other fishes which have evolved in relatively clean water. Cultured salmonids are especially susceptible to environmental or bacterial gill disease, and the disease becomes of great economic importance in salmonid culture.

Epizootiology:

Understanding the anatomy of the fish gill is essential to understanding the epizootiology of environmental or bacterial gill disease. Fish gills include gill arches, those curved structures laying under the operculum. The gill arch has a cartilaginous or bony support structure. An afferent blood vessel enters on the ventral side of the arch and an efferent blood vessel leaves the arch at the dorsal side. Many gill filaments are attached to the gill arch, each by a cartilaginous structure. The cartilaginous structure of a filament is surrounded by tissue which also has afferent and efferent blood vessels (Pl. 9C). A gill filament has many capillaries attached on structures known as gill lamellae. The lamellae have unoxygenated blood entering at the afferent end and oxygenated blood leaving at the efferent end. The capillary wall of the gill lamella is a structure comprised of flat (squamous) epithelial cells. There are normally one or two of these flat epithelial cells between the blood supply in the lamella and the water (Pl. 1D, Pl. 9D). Oxygen in the water is transferred across the gill membranes to the blood. Breathing activity of the fish pushes water from the mouth posteriorly across the gills and out through the opercula. Water is circulated between the gill lamellae for oxygenation:

Ammoniacal gill excretions are the most important in the development of gill disease, especially during overcrowding in fish culture facilities or in aquaria. Ammonia in the un-ionized forms is a strong irritant to gill tissue. The ammonia-ammonium complex has a reaction constant when dissolved in water:[69]

$$NH_3 + H^+ \rightleftharpoons NH_4^+$$

The quantity of each is affected primarily by pH, there being a shift from ammonium ion to ammonia, and ammonia to ammonium ion, with alterations of pH and to a lesser degree water temperature (Fig. 2). The quantities of each are dependent on excretory quantities of ammonium ion from the fish, which is related to the biomass of fish in the water. Thus, the unit biomass of fish per unit volume of water is important in estimating the quantity of ammonia-ammonium ion complex present at any one time. The pH of a water supply to a fish culture facility or in an aquarium determines the quantity of nitrogenous excretory wastes which can be tolerated by the fishes.

Notice in Fig. 2 that a water supply to a fish hatchery or in an aquarium which approaches pH 9.2 will have 50% of all ammoniacal compounds and ions in the water as un-ionized ammonia. The holding capacity (biomass of fish per volume of water) in water supplies nearing pH 9.2 will be far less than at pH 7.6, where nearly all ammoniacal compounds and ions are the less toxic ammonium ion.

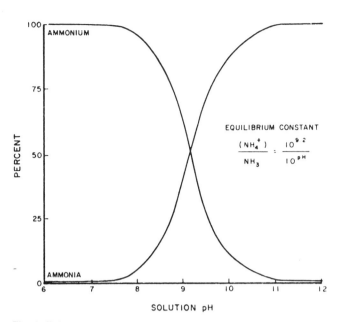

Fig. 2: Relationship between unionized ammonia (NH_3) and ammonium ion (NH_4^+) at various pH and at 15°C.

The acute toxicity (96-hour LC_{50}, the concentration where 50% of the fish die in 96 hours) for rainbow trout ranged between 0.5 and 0.8 mg of un-ionized ammonia per liter at a pH of 7.8.[116] The total ammoniacal compounds and ions under this test was 43.6 mg per liter. These data demonstrate that estimation of total ammoniacal nitrogen in a water supply for fishes is of value only if the pH is known and an estimation made for un-ionized ammonia. These data also indicate that the ammonium ion (approximately 43.5 mg per liter in the above example) is much less toxic to fishes than the un-ionized ammonia.

Environmental gill disease develops when gill irritants are present in the water supply at concentrations high enough to alter gill epithelium. Overcrowding of fishes, especially when accompanied by reduced water exchange in the holding facility, is one of the major causes of gill irritation. Placing more food into the water than can be eaten by the fishes with subsequent decomposition of the excess food, adds gill irritants to the water. Rough handling of the fishes may damage gill tissue. Irritated gills usually result in a condition known as hyperplasia.[54] Hyperplasia is a condition where epithelial cells on the lamellar surface increase in numbers in response to the irritant. The excess cells are not sloughed as rapidly as they are formed, so a thickening of gill lamellar surfaces results. The gill tissue thus becomes a classic example of hyperplasia: i.e., an increase in organ size (or volume) with a corresponding increase in cell numbers (Pl. 9E). The hyperplastic lamellae obstruct flow of water between them so that blood cannot be oxygenated. The severity of the hyperplasia determines the ability of the fishes to survive.

Hyperplastic cells have no direct blood supply and are a target for invasion of microorganisms. Classic bacterial gill disease develops from environmentally induced gill hyperplasia. Most opportunistic bacteria in the water may invade, but flexibacteria, pseudomonads and flavobacteria are most commonly found.[104a]

Development of either environmental gill disease or the secondary bacterial gill invasion may result in loss of fishes, thus reducing the biomass per unit volume of water. The excretory product (especially ammonia—ammonium) is reduced because of reduction in biomass. Fishes surviving are subjected to lower concentrations of these irritants and gill lamellar tissue heals. Survivors usually return to normal within a short time. Therefore, the disease is self-limiting; i.e., overcrowding and excessive excretory products are alleviated by death of fishes and reduction of excretory products to the concentration acceptable for gill normalcy.

A second episode of mortality may occur when fishes continue to grow in the water supply and reach the limiting biomass to volume ratio, with corresponding excretory product concentration. Mortality is followed by reduction of biomass and excretory products concentration and a period of gill normalcy. The severity of gill hyperplasia and the extent of the mortality is dependent on the interrelationship of all factors (biomass to volume ratio, water flow into the holding facility, pH of the water, water temperature, excess food, collections of fecal material in the facility, population of nitrifying bacteria in the facility, rough handling or injury to the fish gills and others).

Disease Signs:

The first signs of environmental gill disease are fishes remaining near the surface of the water, moving to the edge of the pond or piping for air. They usually swim aimlessly but slowly. They may break the surface to obtain a mouthful of air.

The gills appear swollen. The opercula may not close normally: red gill tissue may protrude from under the opercula or remain in sight when opercula are supposed to be closed. The posterior part of the head may appear thickened because of the swollen gills and protruding opercula. These signs can usually be seen by observing the fishes from a distance, especially as the fishes swim and turn through the water.

Signs of bacterial gill disease are white to gray spots on the gills. These spots are apparent as the fish swims and turns in the water.

Examination of fishes with environmental gill disease will indicate swelling of the gills to a greater than normal mass. Bacterial gill disease will have patches of bacterial growth firmly adhering to the gill filaments and lamellae (Pl. 9F). Bacterial invasion may be unilateral or bilateral, depending on the severity of the gill damage.

Diagnosis:

Disease signs, gross appearance of the gills, microscopic appearance of whole mounts of gill tissue and histopathology can be used to definitively diagnose environmental gill disease (Pl. 9F, 10A).[83] Water chemistry to determine the source of gill irritant may also be helpful in the diagnosis.

The severity of gill hyperplasia is important in the diagnosis of environmental gill disease. Fishes with minor hyperplasia are not as susceptible to secondary bacterial gill invasion as are fishes with advanced hyperplasia. The diagnostician should judge the severity to determine if the use of external therapy is needed or if relieving overcrowding, increasing water flow or other physical manipulation is all that will be required to cure the disease. A system found most useful for estimating severity of gill hyperplasia and recommending treatment is given in Table 10 (Pl. 1C, 1D, 10B, 10C, 10D). A representative sample of fishes should be taken from the affected fish population for making an estimate of severity.

Disease signs and bacterial isolation and identification can be used to diagnose bacterial gill disease. Direct squash preparations from the bacterial mass on the gills can be used to determine the morphology and staining of the bacteria. The growth which occurs may be towering and slender if flexibacteria are the etiology (Pl. 8E) or flat and leathery if pseudomonads or flexibacteria are the etiology (Pl. 10E). Pseudomonads and flexibacteria may be accompanied by flexibacteria in the bacterial mass or the infection may be of a single species. Occasionally pure cultures of pseudomonads can be isolated directly from affected gills, almost as if these organisms are capable of excluding growth of all others.

Therapy and Control:

Therapy of gill disease should be initiated as soon as possible after diagnosis. The disease is usually best controlled by use of an external disinfectant. The quaternary ammonium compounds soothe damaged gill tissue and reduce the bacterial population in water, which reduces the chance of bacterial invasion if the condition has not progressed to bacterial gill disease. The external disinfectant will also reduce bacterial plaque on gills as well as limit additional bacterial invasion. Salt or acetic acid dips are useful for soothing gills and reducing bacterial plaque on gills. Potassium permanganate is acceptable if the concentration can be held above 5 mg per liter for one hour. Relatively large quantities of organic matter usually present in fish tanks, raceways and ponds may decompose potassium permangenate much too rapidly for acceptable bactericidal action.

Most epizootics of gill disease must be treated two or three consecutive days for best control. Dynamic or flow-through treatment is much superior to a static or bath treatment when the therapeutic time is one hour. Fishes with gill hyperplasia have difficulty in the oxy-

TABLE 10

**Estimation of the severity of gill hyperplasia and treatment
recommendation for environmental gill disease[83]**

Designation of Hyperplastic Severity	Distinctive Characteristics	Recommended Treatment
Grade I	Lamellae swollen but not fused	Reduce gill irritants by increasing water exchange or reduce fish biomass in water
Grade II	Some but not all lamellae fused, primarily at distal ends of filaments (Pl. 10B)	External disinfectant used; reduce gill irritants by increasing water exchange or reducing fish biomass
Grade III	Most lamellae fused but no filaments fused (Pl. 10C)	One or more daily treatments of external disinfectant; reduce gill irritants by increasing water exchange; delay reducing biomass until fishes can be moved safely
Grade IV	Most lamellae fused, some filaments fused (Pl. 10D)	Usually two to three consecutive daily treatments of external disinfectant; reduce gill irritants by increasing water exchange; delay reducing biomass until fishes can be moved safely

Note: External disinfection is suggested in all cases when bacterial invasion is observed on the gills

genation of blood, and holding them in water of poor quality and with overcrowded conditions usually will result in high mortality.

Therapy of either environmental or bacterial gill disease prior to mortality may be completely successful if administered soon enough. Alleviating the cause of gill irritation after the fishes have partially or completely recovered will eliminate recurrence of the disease.

Prognosis:

Prognosis of environmental gill disease depends on many factors. Usually morbidity is high and may reach 100% of a population in a crowded raceway or pond. Mortality in an overcrowded fish population may be 25 to 30%.

Morbidity and mortality from bacterial gill disease are usually more severe than for environmental gill disease. There may not be a high incidence of bacterial gill invasion, but mortality among the fishes may reach 35 to 40% of the population.

Practical Aspects:

Environmental or bacterial gill disease is usually the result of mismanagement of the fish population in the holding facility. Correct management of the biomass of fish to volume of water eliminates or precludes the possibility of this disease developing in the fishes. There are several methods used to estimate the fish-holding capacity of a facility or tank. Some fish culturists use a fish biomass to water volume ratio based on kilograms of fish per cubic meter of water (or pounds of fish per cubic foot of water). Practical experience with the facility is essential to be assured that the water being supplied to the facility does not change from time to time or this method will not be successful.

Another method of estimating the fish biomass which can be held in a facility is based on inflow or circulation of water into the structure. Kilogram of fish per liter per minute flow (pounds of fish per gallon per minute flow) can be used to estimate maximum holding capacity of a facility. Practical experience with the facility is also needed for this method to be assured the water supply does not change in chemistry and quantity.

Chemistry of water being used for the fishes is important in estimating maximum holding capacity and permitting development of environmental or bacterial gill disease. Some waters have a great buffering capacity, others do not. Buffering capacity is especially needed in pond culture or with aquarium fishes. Aquatic plants release or absorb carbonaceous materials during respiration. These carbonaceous materials become a part of the dissolved elements in the water and alter pH during the daylight hours and in the dark. The pH of ponds or aquaria may rise to very high levels during daylight respiration of aquatic plants; a pH of 9.5 or 10.0 is not uncommon during long, sunny days of summer. Much of the excreted ammonium ions from fishes in the water will be converted to un-ionized ammonia. Thus, an ammonia—ammonium ion complex which is acceptable to fishes at night becomes a source of gill irritation during the daylight hours (Fig. 2). The water pH is reduced during the dark of night but may never fall below 7.8. Ponds with aquatic plants may have a much lower fish biomass to volume ratio than ponds without aquatic plants, primarily because of the ease at which environmental or bacterial disease can occur. The same pond may have a higher fish-holding capacity during the winter months, partly because of the reduction in aquatic plant respiration and partly because of the change in light and dark periods of the day.

Aquarists can use a ratio to determine the holding capacity of an aquarium to reduce the possibility of environmental or bacterial gill disease in the fish. The most often used method is based on centimeters (inches) of fish length per liter (gallon) of water. The usual rule is no more than 5 cm (2 inches) of fish per 3.8 liters (one gallon) of water. This, too, depends on the quality of the water in the aquarium, plants in the aquarium, type of bottom gravel in the aquarium and possibly other factors. Aquatic plants in aquaria will shift pH, accompanied by the ammonia—ammonium ion shift. Carbonate-containing bottom gravel in the aquarium continues to give bicarbonate to the water, which can be shifted to carbonate if the water pH increases to above 7.8. Aquarium water with a high buffering capacity can resist the pH shift and thus maintain the ammonia—ammonium ion ratio toward the less irritating ammonium ion.

Fishes with environmental or bacterial gill disease can be stocked into open water or transported without the chance of moving unwanted pathogens from one geographical area to another because the bacteria associated with bacterial gill disease are more or less ubiquitous. Transporting fishes may serve only to extend the range of certain species or strains of common soil and water bacteria.

Transporting fishes which have advanced environmental or bacterial gill disease should be avoided because of losses which may be incurred in the move. The recommendation is made to reduce the gill disease problem before transportation.

PATHOGENIC ACTINOMYCETES

The Actinomycetes are gram-positive and some are acid-fast to varying degrees. They range from short to long, sometimes curved, rod-shaped organisms to branched mycelial growths. Some reproduce by fission, others from mycelial fragments and others by production of spores. Members of at least three genera have been found to be associated with disease in fishes: *Renibacterium*, *Mycobacterium* and *Nocardia*.

Bacterial Kidney Disease

Bacterial kidney disease is usually a chronic to latent disease but can be acute to subacute when the most susceptible fishes are involved or water quality permits. Synonymous names for bacterial kidney disease are corynebacterial kidney disease and Dee disease. Bacterial kidney disease is the preferred name in North America and Europe, but Dee disease is preferred in the British Isles.[24] The disease was first reported by the Furunculosis Committee in 1933. Lesions of the disease were observed in salmon from the Dee and Spey Rivers of Scotland.[24] A first report of the disease in North America was in 1935.[14,75]

The disease was thought to be limited to cultured fishes in North America.[14,75] However, it was diagnosed in a wild-ranging population of brook trout in 1970. Transmission to wild fish may be more prevalent than previously thought, considering the wide distribution of infected cultured fishes over the past decades.[74,88]

Etiological Agent:

The etiological agent of bacterial kidney disease had been classified as a *Corynebacterium*, but no species was designated for many years until the name *Corynebacterium salmoninus* was recommended in 1978.[99] A new genus and species, *Renibacterium salmoninarum*, was accepted in 1980.[98] It is an obligate parasite and is not thought to survive well outside of a host. The bacterium is small (0.4 micrometer by 0.8 micrometer), gram-positive, non-acid-fast, non-motile and rod-shaped. It usually occurs in pairs, thus the usual morphological description as being a diplobacillus.[24] The optimum growth temperature is 15°C. It will grow at 5°C but not above 20°C. Only one serotype has been identified.[45a]

The bacterium is fastidious but can be grown in the laboratory on selected highly fortified media containing cystine or cysteine. It was grown first by addition of defibrinated blood to nutrient agar,[14] but a more satisfactory medium was devised in 1956 using tryptose (1.0%), beef extract (0.3%), sodium chloride (0.5%), yeast extract (0.5%), cysteine-HCl (0.1%), human blood (20%) and agar (1.5%).[75] Blood serum has subsequently been found to be an acceptable replacement for whole blood.[39] The use of blood serum also allows elimination of beef extract and sodium chloride from the medium. Meuller-Hinton medium with 0.1% cysteine-HCl will also support the growth of the bacterium. Some strains of the bacterium will grow on cystine-heart agar. It grows best at pH 6.5.

R. salmoninarum grows slowly, even on special media. Usually the initial culture of the bacterium is incubated at 15°C. Subcultures of the isolate can then be grown at 18°C, but even at the advanced temperature, it grows slowly. Growth will usually appear on each of the above-mentioned media within five to 18 days. Colonies are round, very convex, smooth to glistening, usually white in color and with complete margins. Old cultures of the bacterium may become somewhat granular and dry.

Geographical Distribution:

Bacterial kidney disease is known to occur in Europe, having been reported in Scotland in 1933 and in France in 1974.[24,88,103] The disease occurs in Spain, Italy, Yugoslavia and Iceland.[45a] It was found in Japan in 1973.[58] The bacterium was reported in the United States along both the east and west coasts prior to 1955.[111] The only locations outside of the two seaboard areas of the country reported by 1956 were Michigan, Minnesota, Wisconsin, Iowa, South Dakota, Nebraska and Wyoming.[123] The organism was found only in limited parts of the above-mentioned states. Subsequently, the disease has been found in almost all the states of the United States in which salmonids are cultured. The disease has been reported from many fish culture facilities in Canada.

Susceptible Species:

Probably all species of the family Salmonidae are susceptible to bacterial kidney disease. The bacterium has been isolated from cases of the disease in at least four species of Pacific salmon and from Atlantic salmon. Brook trout are the most susceptible of the trout. The disease has been diagnosed in four other trout species. The rainbow trout appears to be the most resistant to bacterial kidney disease. It has not been reported in the whitefishes or graylings. There have been no reports of bacterial kidney disease from fishes other than the salmonids.

Epizootiology:

The route of transmission of *R. salmoninarum* is not positively known. British researchers transmitted the disease by feeding infected trout tissue to trout.[75] Positive transmission was demonstrated in experiments in Oregon when infected salmon viscera were fed to fingerling chinook salmon.[126] Several attempts to experimentally transmit the disease orally to brook trout by feeding infected fish tissue met with failure.[24] Transmission of the disease to brook trout could be done by either abrading the skin with sandpaper covered with the bacteria or by allowing the fishes to abrade themselves against bricks and adding bacteria to the water.

Experiments designed to demonstrate routes of transmission of bacterial kidney disease suggest two possible routes, either orally or cutaneously. Orally could certainly occur under conditions of practical fish culture. Cutaneously could also occur as the result of injuries to the fish with infection of the wound or skin damage from external parasites and infection of the injury.

Water chemistry has been found to have an effect on occurrence of bacterial kidney disease.[121] The disease is more prevalent among susceptible fishes in soft water conditions than in hard water conditions.[121] This may account for the presence of bacterial kidney disease in some fish hatcheries situated very near other hatcheries in which the disease is unknown and in which a known transfer of fishes has occurred. The mode of action of water hardness on the presence of bacterial kidney disease is unknown. More research is needed to determine if the hardness elements (primarily calcium and magnesium) are the only dissolved elements with an effect on transmission of the disease.

Fishes with chronic or latent bacterial kidney disease are likely carriers of the disease. The disease continues from generation to generation among those fishes present in an infected fish culture facility. Bacteria are passed in the feces of infected fishes, supplying a continuous source of bacteria in the water which infect fishes with skin injuries or by the oral route. Bacterial kidney disease lesions in the skin and underlying muscle sometimes rupture to the outside, yielding another source of bacteria to the water supply.

Feeding infected salmon viscera from high-seas or spawning run salmon to cultured salmon fry was a common practice during the first half of this century. This custom yielded a perfect closed system for supplying infective bacteria to salmon; the bacterium fed to the fry resulted in infected smolts released to return later as infected adults. Pasteurization of salmon viscera prior to being fed to salmon fry was initiated in the early 1960's and has reduced transmission of this disease, as well as other diseases, from the source of infection.

Infected feral fishes in the spring water supply of fish culture facilities are also a source of the bacteria. The use of stream water sustains the infection by continually supplying renibacteria to susceptible fishes in the fish culture facility.

R. salmoninarum infected Pacific and Atlantic salmon continue to harbor the organism as they migrate into salt water. Mortality from the disease continues in salt water, possibly even at an accelerated rate when compared to fish remaining in fresh water.[45a]

Spontaneous bacterial kidney disease is not often found among wild-ranging fish. Possibly low pathogen concentration in large bodies of water is not conducive to transmission from fish to fish.[3] There have been a few cases in which definite transmission has occurred.

Bacterial kidney disease among a wild brook trout population in a mountain stream in Wyoming, just a few miles from an infected U.S. Fish and Wildlife Service fish hatchery, has received much study. The original source of *R. salmoninarum* was no doubt from the infected fish hatchery. The disease has continued in the fish population for many years, being transmitted from host to host in the relatively sparse population of the habitat. Specific evidence on exact routes of transmission has not been possible. However, a few assumptions can be made. The water in the stream is exceptionally soft, which could account for increased bacterial survival outside of a host. Also, much of the generation to generation transmission from parent to offspring is no doubt through the egg.[74] Bacterial kidney disease-free brook trout, brown trout and rainbow trout were stocked into the stream and became infected from the wild population. Mortality in the stocked fish began within nine months after stocking. *R. salmoninarum* was found in dead stocked fish and also in a sample of living fish.[73a]

There is evidence to indicate *R. salmoninarum* is transmitted inside the egg. Eggs known to be surface-contaminated, as evidenced by large numbers of *R. salmoninarum* in ovarian fluid taken with the eggs, were disinfected with povidone-iodine. The bacterium was found in approximately 10 to 20% of the surface-sterile eggs.[40a]

Bacterial kidney disease, usually being a chronic to subacute disease, develops slowly in susceptible fishes. The organism, like certain other non-motile bacteria, tends to produce abscesses. Some of the abscesses may break to the outer surfaces of the fish or into the lumen of the gut. Such a fish is a dangerous carrier of the disease.

Bacterial kidney disease may be seasonal, being more prevalent in late winter, spring and early summer in those trout and salmon culture facilities with fluctuating water temperature. Disease signs and mortality may be reduced or disappear completely during summer warm water periods. The infected fishes continue to carry a bacterial load until the water temperature becomes more conducive to resumption of bacterial growth. Disease signs reappear and mortality increases in the same fishes which had survived the previous outbreak of bacterial kidney disease.

Latent cases of bacterial kidney disease during high water temperature periods, and other periods when the disease is repressed, are the greatest problem in the absolute control and epizootiology of this disease. The search for latent cases and bacterial kidney disease carriers continues in many parts of the United States and Canada, because this disease is classified as a reportable disease among the state and federal agencies of both countries.

Disease Signs:

External signs of bacterial kidney disease may be limited to a few fishes in the infected population or 25 to 50% of the fishes may outwardly demonstrate the disease. External signs may be limited to the fishes being listless and lethargic. They may be dark in color, partially blind, seek the sides of the pond or raceway and generally appear sick. Other infected fishes may appear normal externally.

The obviously ill fish may have abscesses under the skin which may open into the water (Pl. 10F). Many of the fish may have unilateral or bilateral exophthalmos. Removal of the protruding eyeballs will usually reveal either granulation tissue or edematous fluid or both. The blind or partially blind fish will usually have signs of malnutrition because they have not been feeding properly.

Internal signs of bacterial kidney disease may include presence of white to gray-white abscesses in one or more visceral organs or tissues. These lesions may be filled with a thick, nearly white or sometimes blood-stained purulent mixture of bacteria, tissue cells and cellular debris (Pl. 11A). Fish with the most advanced disease will have little or no visceral fat.

Diagnosis:

Diagnosis of obviously ill fishes with bacterial kidney disease is dependent on disease signs, identification of the bacterium taken from the purulent lesions and histopathological findings. Presence of gram-positive small rods or diplobacilli in squash preparations of discrete lesions of the disease is a presumptive diagnosis for bacterial kidney disease (Pl. 11B).

Histopathology of a typical bacterial kidney disease lesion also assists in the presumptive diagnosis. The lesion usually contains a central area of liquefaction or coagulation necrosis which is later replaced by fibrous tissue. All stages of necrosis are present outside the area of liquefaction or coagulation necrosis. Karyolysis and karyorrhexis are evident. Cells in the outer fringes of the lesion are pyknotic, and cloudy swelling is evident (Pl. 11C).

Isolation of the bacterium and appearance of colonies on specially enriched media may also be of assistance in the presumptive diagnosis of bacterial kidney disease. Histopathology of tissues other than those containing obvious bacterial kidney disease lesions may also aid diagnosis. The presence of granulomatous inflammatory tissue behind the eyeballs of exophthalmic fishes may prove of assistance since this condition is not known in other diseases of fishes.[50]

Presumptive diagnosis is usually all that is required for bacterial kidney disease. This is because there are no other bacteria similar to *R. salmoninarum* known in salmonid fishes. However, diagnosis of the disease in latent infections and carrier fishes requires location of the bacterium in squash preparations from suspected infected tissues, either by direct microscopic examination of stained material or by use of a fluorescent antibody technique.[27] A drop plate test has also been suggested using tissue homogenates and direct culture.[38] An immunodiffusion procedure has also been used to detect latent disease cases and carriers.[28] Each of the procedures is acceptable, and preference of the method of use remains with the investigator. The direct microscopic examination of stained squash preparations is tedious, requires many hours at the microscope for location of a few bacterial cells present in latent cases of carrier fishes.

The fluorescent antibody technique is more rapid and one of the most sensitive procedures but it does require specialized equipment to perform the microscopic observation phase. Squash preparations are subjected to R. salmoninarum antibodies conjugated with fluorescent dyes. The preparations are washed to remove the free conjugate, and the slide is examined under a fluorescent microscope. The antibacterial kidney disease-bodies with the fluorescent dye adhere to homologous bacteria, which fluoresce under light excitement.

The drop plate method is performed with a minimum of special equipment. Suspected tissue is homogenized and washed with peptone-saline. The supernatant suspension is dropped onto surface-dried plates of culture medium and incubated. Growth appears between seven and 20 days. This method has one advantage in that cultures of the pathogen are available for further testing. The main disadvantage is the time required for appearance of bacterial growth on the medium.

The immunodiffusion procedure is accomplished with a minimum of special equipment also. Tissues from suspected bacterial kidney disease cases or carriers are frozen and thawed. This breaks tissue cells and releases bacterial antigens. The fluid from the tissue is placed in wells in diffusion agar. One well of the plate is filled with antiserum homologous to R. salmoninarum. The diffusion plate is allowed to incubate and precipitin lines appear in the agar between the antiserum well and the test tissue wells, indicating positive bacterial kidney disease carriers.

A counterimmunoelectrophoresis test has also been used in which R. salmoninarum antibody (rabbit antiserum) is placed in a well cut into a gel plate and material taken from suspect fish (antigen) is placed in an opposing well in the same gel plate. A visible precipitin line between the antigen and antibody wells following electrophoresis and incubation is positive evidence of the bacterium in the fish.[28a]

Studies have been made to compare sensitivity of these diagnostic procedures in locating carriers of bacterial kidney disease. The smear-gram stain procedure is usually the least sensitive and the counterimmunoelectrophoresis test the most sensitive.[28c]

Therapy and Control:

Bacterial kidney disease is one of the most difficult bacterial diseases of fishes to treat with drugs or chemotherapeutic compounds. The disease is chronic in nature and the bacterium may be intracellular. Also, the organism is not highly sensitive to the usual antibiotics or chemotherapeutic drugs.

Two researchers in 1959 tested 34 therapeutic agents for systemic control of bacterial kidney disease.[124] Only erythromycin gave control of the mortality. The drug was given at 190 to 220 mg per kg (9 to 10 g per 100 lb) of fish per day for 21 days. Some toxic effects were noticed from the drug. However, the drug is not equally effective against the various strains of R. salmoninarum.

Another study examined the effectiveness of over 70 drugs used both *in vitro* (in glass) and *in vivo* (in fish). Clindamycin, erythromycin, kitasamycin, penicillin-G and spiramycin were found to control growth of R. salmoninarum and may be effective in early clinical cases.[10a] Much more research is needed on these potentially effective compounds.

Some of the sulfonamide drugs have been found of value for controlling bacterial kidney disease. Sulfamerazine given at the rate of 45 mg per kg (2 g per 100 lb) of fish per day continuously may control mortality but will not eliminate the disease. This treatment regimen has been used to control mortality until water warms in late summer and the normal seasonal occurrence of bacterial kidney disease subsides. The longest time the low dose of sulfamerazine has been given to reduce mortality was about two months. The low dose level of sulfamerazine is conducive to developing drug resistance by the bacterium and should be used only as a last resort.

Fishes have been treated with various dosages of sulfadiazine or combinations of sulfadiazine, sulfaguanadine, sulfamethazine and sulfisoxazole. Results have been inconsistent.

Dietary modification has been investigated as a method of reducing incidence of bacterial kidney disease in fish populations. Experimental evidence demonstrated liver vitamin A, and serum zinc, iron and copper were lower than normal in fish infected with the disease. Fish being used to determine iodine requirements had significantly less bacterial kidney disease when given high iodine levels in the diet, as compared to those getting low dietary iodine levels. Likewise, dietary fluoride was thought to have significant effect on bacterial kidney disease incidence. Further experiments demonstrated fish being fed high iodine (4.5 mg/kg of ration) and fluorine (4.5 mg/kg of ration) had much reduced incidence of bacterial kidney disease, when compared to fish being fed a commercial ration with no additional supplementation of these two trace nutrients. There was no significant incidence change in fish fed increased vitamin A, zinc, iron, copper, manganese and cobalt.[14a,63b]

No acceptable bacterin for immunizing susceptible fish has been found. Research continues to develop and evaluate a suitable immunogen.[80b]

Prevention is the best method of control for bacterial kidney disease. Quarantine and restriction of movement has been an acceptable method for controlling relocation of the disease into noninfected geographical areas.

Test and slaughter used with complete disinfection has been used to eliminate bacterial kidney disease from infected fish culture facilities. There have been some instances when fishes known to carry bacterial kidney disease were stocked into open water to remove them from the culture facility while disinfection proceeded. This method opens up the opportunity for spreading the bacterium into previously noninfected areas.

Eggs from brood stock fish known to have or suspected of having bacterial kidney disease should not be transported into areas known to be free of the disease. Also, the usual procedures used for egg disinfection are ineffective in removing this bacterium from eggs. Erytromycin phosphate (1.0 mg/L) in water for water-hardening eggs has been used in attempts to destroy *R. salmoninarum* within the egg. Early results in Idaho suggested this may be an acceptable procedure, but subsequent work demonstrated the treatment to be ineffective.[40a]

Prognosis:

Estimating prognosis of a disease with the characteristics of bacterial kidney disease is difficult. The fish culturist or the fish disease diagnostician observing fishes with active bacterial kidney disease is never really aware of the morbidity or latent cases of the disease present in a population. The seasonal nature of the disease also adds another variable to prognostication of the year to year expectations. There does not seem to be reference to morbidity or mortality in literature on bacterial kidney disease except to state "often been the cause of severe mortality," "often results in high mortality," "often causes significant mortality" or "catastrophic mortalities result." Attempting to put a more exact figure to severe, high, significant or catastrophic is impossible.

The nature of bacterial kidney disease, as compared to some of the more acute diseases in which mortalities seem to "happen over night," excludes the appearance of great mortality at one time and in one place. Experience has demonstrated a continuous day to day and week to week low level mortality which may account for up to 50% or more of the population. The morbidity among a fish population suffering from this slow but continuous mortality may or may not reach 100%. Fish populations known to have carrier fish may demonstrate as little as 1% or as high as 50 to 60% carriers of the pathogen.

The work with wild fishes exhibiting seasonal bacterial kidney disease indicated nearly every fish was infected with *R. salmoninarum*. Mortality among the wild population, directly related to the disease, is impossible to assess. Certainly the disease will reduce vitality in the fishes, making them more open to predation, starvation or other rigors associated with survival under natural (wild) conditions.

Practical Aspects:

Experience has demonstrated that bacterial kidney disease can be transported with fishes and fish eggs over wide distances. The pathogen has also been demonstrated to be capable of transmission to susceptible fishes in wild-ranging fish populations. Bacterial kidney disease-infected salmon smolts released to the sea still carried the bacterium when the anadromous fishes returned from the ocean to spawn in fresh water. The presence of a significant number of infected fishes in a wild-ranging brook trout population indicated that the disease can be a significant survival factor when natural elements work toward the advantage of the pathogen. All criteria demonstrate that fishes infected with *R. salmoninarum*-caused bacterial kidney disease should not be moved into other geographic areas, streams, lakes, reservoirs or ponds in which the disease has not been diagnosed among the fishes. Also, fish culture facilities known to harbor *R. salmoninarum* should be examined critically for possibilities of eliminating the pathogen by disinfection and sanitation procedures.

There is a continuing disease surveillance program at all of the United States government owned and operated fish culture facilities. The fish health inspector is alert for presence of bacterial kidney disease during each inspection of the facilities. A few state fishery agencies of the United States also have a similar fish disease surveillance program, bacterial kidney disease being one of the diseases on the surveillance list. Those commercially owned and operated trout and salmon culture facilities which transport live fishes and fish eggs across state lines into states with fish importation restrictions are also inspected each year for the presence of certain diseases. Bacterial kidney disease is one of those diseases. The entire surveillance program should be expanded to include all trout and salmon culture facilities. Facilities which harbor *R. salmoninarum* could be placed on a list for assistance in the elimination of the disease if at all possible. Transportation of fishes or fish eggs from any bacterial kidney disease-infected facility should be controlled. *R. salmoninarum* is an obligate parasite and apparently cannot survive for extended periods of time without a host. This characteristic of the pathogen should assist in its elimination.

The existence of bacterial kidney disease in wild fish populations may be controlled by test and slaughter procedures. An effort made to use this method of disease control for bacterial kidney disease-infected brook trout in a small stream in Wyoming. The entire fish population was destroyed using a piscicide and restocked in a year. However, bacterial kidney disease was demonstrated in the restocked population.[73a]

Mycobacteriosis of Fishes

Fish mycobacteriosis is a chronic to subacute disease of many fishes. The disease is found among fishes in fresh water, brackish water and salt water.

The name fish mycobacteriosis was suggested in 1960 after a comprehensive study of the etiological bacterium.[80] Previously the disease had been known as fish or piscine tuberculosis.[7] Justification for the name change was on the basis that the bacterial characteristics made the name fish leprosy as scientifically acceptable as fish tuberculosis. The argument was that if the disease in fish could be called either name, then mycobacteriosis was a more justified single name.

The disease was first described from mycobacteriosis lesions in carp from a small lake in France.[11] The lake received pollution from human tubercular patients in a sanitarium on its shores. The doctors in the hospital were probably very much aware of acid-fast bacteria and routinely performed acid-fast staining on material from various sources. Preparations from the fish were probably also examined. The bacteria taken from the lesions in the fish were acid-fast and could be transmitted to frogs and lizards but not to guinea pigs or pigeons. A better description of the mycobacterial organism was given in 1902.[12]

Etiological Agent:

The etiological agents of mycobacteriosis are considered to be *Mycobacterium marinum* in marine fishes and *Mycobacterium fortuitum* in freshwater and brackish water fishes.[105] The former name first appeared in the literature in 1926 for isolates taken from several marine fish species.[19,32] Older literature mentioned *M. piscium* and *M. platypoecilus*, both of which are now considered as *M. marinum* or *M. fortuitum*. Several references are made to *M. anabanti*, but this name is considered to be a synonym for *M. marinum*.[15,32] *M. salmoniphilum* was suggested for the name of an isolate from kidneys of salmon, but the name was never accepted.[24,93] *M. balnei* has also been found to be immunoelectrophoretically similar to *M. marinum*.

M. chelonei has been isolated from cutthroat trout, mountain whitefish, and two species of Pacific salmon from Oregon and Montana. The organism was transmitted to, and caused relatively high mortality in rainbow trout.[9a] The significance of this organism as a fish pathogen has not been evaluated but does demonstrate the potential for other primarily soil saprophitic mycobacteria which may be associated with disease in fish.

M. marinum and *M. fortuitum* are long rod-shaped bacteria 0.3 to 0.7 micrometer wide by 1 to 4 micrometers long.[12,105] They are gram-positive, non-spore-forming, non-motile and acid-fast. They are relatively fastidious, growing on only a few special media, and they grow slowly even on those media which support growth. The bacteria are non-pigmented unless grown on inspissiated (thickened) egg medium and in the light, when they may produce yellow colonies. Colonies of both bacteria are round and very convex at the center but flattened at the edges. The edges are complete. The optimum growth temperature is given as 25 to 35°C,[2] but they will grow well at 18 to 20°C. They usually will not grow at 37°C.[79]

M. marinum and *M. fortuitum* will grow on glycerol agar, Dorset's medium, Petroff's medium, glycerated egg medium, Lowenstein's medium and Loeffler's medium of glycerated potato. Many of these media are difficult to prepare and store. Experience has demonstrated that a very good growth medium for the two mycobacterium species is CGY medium (casitone 0.2%, glucose 2%, yeast extract 0.2%, agar 1.5%, dissolve in water to make 100 ml, autoclave and pour). Growth appears in five to ten days, becoming heavy and thick within three weeks at 22°C.

Geographical Distribution:

M. marinum and *M. fortuitum* are worldwide in distribution.[4,105] The bacteria are found more often among crowded fish populations but do occur in wild-ranging fishes. *M. fortuitum* may be found on freshwater aquarium walls, in swimming pools and in various other aquatic habitats. *M. marinum* may be found in saltwater aquaria and in many marine environments.

Susceptible Species:

Probably all fish species and most amphibians and reptiles are susceptible to *M. marinum* or *M. fortuitum* infection.[4,105] The organisms have been reported in a large number of fishes.[79] One author listed susceptible fishes from ten orders, 34 families, 84 genera and 120 species from all over the world.[119] They have been reported from a wide variety of frogs, toads and salamanders, as well as snakes, lizards, alligators and turtles. *M. marinum* occurs among ocean-caught fishes taken for human consumption. One of the greatest economic problems with mycobacteriosis was among Pacific salmon, but the disease is much reduced since feeding unpasteurized fish to cultured salmon has been suspended. This disease is a problem to aquarists among fishes in both freshwater and saltwater systems.

Strains of these organisms may invade the skin of humans, especially the skin on elbows and knees, to produce a disease known as swimming pool granuloma. Pigeons and mice have been found to be susceptible to *M. marinum*.[79] The bacterium produces granulomatous lesions in skin at the site of injection in the peritoneum when inoculated intraperitoneally.

Epizootiology:

The most probable route of transmission for these bacteria is orally. The feeding of fish viscera or fish products contaminated with the organisms has served to transmit the disease to hatchery salmon. The disease was prevalent among returning salmon which had been marked and released from hatcheries using raw, contaminated fish products for the diet. The disease was not found in those salmon hatcheries which did not feed raw fish products. Guppies fed infected chinook salmon viscera developed caseous lesions within two and a half months.[92]

The feeding of pasteurized salmon viscera and other fish products has dramatically reduced the incidence of mycobacteriosis among cultured Pacific salmon. This evidence has proved beyond doubt that the oral route of transmission is very important in the epizootiology of mycobacteriosis.

Another route of transmission for *M. marinum* and *M. fortuitum* is through injuries or abrasions of the skin. External parasites may be involved with the cutaneous route.

Presence of mycobacteriosis lesions in the ovaries and testes of spawning chinook salmon led to experiments on the possibility of transovarian transmission. No indication of mycobacteriosis could be found in either chinook salmon or steelhead rainbow trout 18 months after eggs were spawned from infected and non-infected male and female chinook salmon and including all possible crosses. The eggs were hatched and the offspring reared in separate non-contaminated water supplies.[92]

The transovarian route may be of greater importance among the viviparous fishes. Acid-fast bacteria have been reported in embryos taken from gravid females or in the very young offspring of viviparous fishes.[30]

The incubation period for mycobacteriosis is not known but must be quite long (six weeks or more). Incubation is probably somewhat dependent on resistance of the fishes to infection and on the optimum temperature requirements of the strain of bacteria involved in the infection. Data obtained in salmon culture stations in the western United States substantiate a long incubation. Salmon fry, fingerlings and smolts fed infected salmon products seldom demonstrated mycobacteriosis prior to release. The same fish returning with the spawning run had a mycobacteriosis infection rate of 12 to 55% at one fish culture facility.[92] Fishes had not demonstrated infection prior to release because of the long incubation period, but the years at sea had given time for the disease to develop.

Cases of mycobacteriosis demonstrate granulomatous, caseous or necrotic lesions in many organs of the body, the kidney, spleen and liver being the most often infected organs. Mycobacteriosis lesions occurring along the gut or in the skin and gills may be responsible for release of pathogens into the water. There probably is little or no release of infective bacteria from other organs until the fish dies and disintegrates.

Mycobacteriosis in other aquatic vertebrates is a source of infection to fishes. Frogs, snakes and turtles may become involved in the transmission cycle. Snails are also thought to be a reservoir for the bacteria,[73] especially among aquarium fishes.

There has been much investigation into the possibility of acid-fast bacteria of poikilothermic vertebrates being transmissible to homeothermic animals (including humans) and from homeotherms to fishes. Research in 1902 led to the conclusion that the human tubercle bacterium can adapt to growth in fishes, but only the suggestion was made that the piscine bacteria could adapt to humans.[115] However, there is little likelihood that cases of mycobacteriosis of homeothermic animals are involved in the epizootiology of the disease among fishes.

Movement of warmwater ornamental fishes about the world in the ornamental fish industry is a common practice. Thus, ornamental fishes with mycobacteriosis become a definite part of the epizootiology of the disease and transmit the organism over long distances, even from continent to continent.

The chronic nature of mycobacteriosis makes every fish, other aquatic vertebrates and possibly some aquatic invertebrates carriers of the disease. Each of the animals is thus involved with the maintenance and transmission of the disease.

The temperature requirements of *M. marinum* and *M. fortuitum* are important in the epizootiology of mycobacteriosis. Most strains of the bacteria are more adaptable to the higher temperature ranges of fishes. Maintenance of 25 to 32°C is common in aquaria. Temperature alone is no doubt responsible for mycobacteriosis being more common among ornamental fishes than other confined fishes. Those strains of the bacteria adaptable to temperatures as low as 15°C have been the ones most commonly found among cultured salmonids. *M. marinum* has been isolated from ocean-caught halibut and cod. One such isolate grew well at 20°C.[92] Isolates from sea bass, croakers and sergeant majors grew at 28 to 20°C.[10]

Disease Signs:

There may or may not be external signs of mycobacteriosis. Fishes with mycobacteriosis exhibit a wide range of diagnostic characteristics. They may be listless and lethargic or may separate from other fishes to become solitary individuals in the corner of the holding facility. Some may attempt to hide or suspend themselves head-down and maintain this position in the water much of the time. They may refuse to eat and become emaciated. Some fishes may have skin ulcerations where lesions lying in the muscle directly below the skin rupture to the outside. Others may have pigment alterations, being brighter in color or duller (Pl. 11D). They may develop spinal curvature (Pl. 11E) or be stunted and small. Some may not develop sexually and lack secondary sexual characteristics. They may develop unilateral or bilateral exophthalmos.

Gross internal pathology of mycobacteriosis is generally similar in all fishes. Gray-white lesions of various sizes may be present in most organs or tissues of the body. The kidney and liver are more often involved, with spleen, mesentery, stomach, ceca, intestine, peritoneum, heart, gills and other organs occasionally involved. Lesions may occasionally occur in the muscle tissue. The kidneys may have so many lesions that they appear speckled throughout their length. Usually the posterior kidney is swollen.

Many of the mycobacterial lesions are purulent, others are necrotic. Some lesions may contain dark yellow or brown material in the centers.

Diagnosis:

Diagnosis of mycobacteriosis depends on disease signs, identification of the bacterial pathogen and histopathology. Presence of discrete gray-white lesions in various organs and tissues of the body suggests mycobacteriosis. Squash preparations of these lesions will demonstrate long rod-shaped bacteria which are gram-positive and acid-fast (Pl. 7C, Pl. 34C). These organisms must be distinguished from other acid-fast rod-shaped bacteria. *M. marinum* and *M. fortuitum* are relatively fastidious, growing slowly on special media. The other acid-fast rod-shaped bacteria which may be found in fishes with somewhat similar lesions (*Nocardia* sp.) are not usually as fastidious. Great care is needed to distinguish between the two genera.

Diagnosis of subclinical mycobacteriosis and location of carriers of the diseasee is difficult. The bacterial concentration method has to be used for this purpose.[31] Kidney or liver tissue is the best for this test. The tissue is digested with 4% sodium hydroxide for 30 to 40 minutes at 25°C. It is centrifuged, the supernatant removed and the solid material resuspended in a small amount of sterile distilled water and neutralized with 6% hydrochloric acid. The material is washed several times with sterile distilled water by centrifugation. The solid material from the final washing is placed onto microscope slides for staining and examination or onto suitable culture media.

Histopathology of mycobacteriosis lesions is similar to that found in other chronic, suppurative diseases (bacterial kidney disease, for example). The lesions may have necrotic centers with various stages of necrosis appearing in the outer portions. There may be caseation necrosis in the center and sometimes a fibrous membrane around the exterior of the lesion. The lesions tend to combine into large masses in some cases of advanced mycobacteriosis. This is especially true of kidney and liver tissue in salmonids. There is a paucity of inflammatory response around the lesion. Acid-fast staining of cut sections of lesions reveal masses of acid-fast bacilli (Pl. 12A, 12B).

Therapy and Control:

Sanitation, disinfection and destruction of carrier fishes are the primary methods of controlling mycobacteriosis. Restricting the movement of infected fishes into the habitat of noninfected fishes is also an important control procedure.

The histological nature of mycobacteriosis (necrotic lesions with no blood supply and pathogens within them) renders drug therapy of limited value for this disease. One laboratory tested 39 chemotherapeutic agents against ten strains of mycobacteria. None of the agents was effective.[92] However, other experiments using Kanamycin *in vitro* against mycobacteria isolated from fishes indicated the drug should be effective. Experience has demonstrated that Kanamycin will give limited control when used at 100 mg per kg (4.5 g per 100 lb) of fish per day for five to ten days. Usually the disease recurs after a short subsidence.[105] Kanamycin was thought to be successful in the treatment of platies with 0.01% of the drug in food for four days because no acid-fast bacteria was found in the fish after therapy.[31]

Location and destruction of fishes carrying the pathogen is difficult. Removing feces from individual fishes and concentration the material by digestion, centrifugation and washing, as discussed above, may demonstrate carriers. These fishes can then be eliminated from the population.[7]

Mycobacteriosis has been almost completely eliminated from cultured Pacific salmon by feeding pasteurized salmon or other fish products in the diets. Rarely are acid-fast bacteria seen in these cultured fishes today, where large numbers of infected fishes were present a few years ago.[92]

Prognosis:

Mycobacteriosis is such a slow-developing and chronic disease that mortality directly attributable to the disease is difficult to establish. Morbidity among aquarium fishes may reach 10 to 100% when pathogens are known to be present in the habitat. Infection levels depend on the care given to sanitize and disinfect the habitat, nets, brushes and other utensils.

Mycobacteriosis lesions developing in some tissues of the body do not create difficulties for the host, but lesions in vital areas (heart, brain, aorta or other essential parts of the body) may be responsible for an early death.

Fishes infected with mycobacteria may refuse food and actually die from malnutrition. The disease may cause structural deformities which make the fishes incapable of obtaining food, with malnutrition as the cause of death. The disease may create disabilities and make the host susceptible to predation.

Surveys among cultured Pacific salmon during the time raw, unpasteurized salmon products were being fed revealed morbidity levels up to 55%.[92] Surveys of wild-ranging salmon from streams in the western United States demonstrated a morbidity of less than 1% infected fish in some surveys.

Practical Aspects:

There are three practices which should be followed by

fish culturists and aquarists to reduce or eliminate the possibility of mycobacteriosis occurrence among fishes. 1) No fishes should be brought into the holding facilities containing noninfected fishes without suitable quarantine. Quarantine should be for at least two months, during which time stringent care should be taken to reduce chances of cross-infection. 2) Prevent overcrowding of fishes, especially in aquaria. Use at least four liters of water for each 5cm of fish length. 3) Do not feed diets which may be contaminated with *M. marinum* or *M. fortuitum*. Some fishes require a live fish diet. Select such food carefully to be most assured of freedom from mycobacteria.

Cultured fishes known to harbor these bacteria should not be moved to other geographical areas outside of the drainage in which they are confined. The best approach to mycobacteriosis control in a *Mycobacterium*-infected fish culture facility or aquarium is to eliminate all fishes and attempt complete disinfection. Feral fishes in the water supply of fish culture facilities should also be eliminated, if at all possible.

Nocardiosis

Nocardiosis came to the attention of fish disease diagnostician during the early and middle part of the 1960's. The disease was not suspected previously. Probably some of the reported cases of mycobacteriosis may have actually been nocardiosis, as the two diseases cause similar disease signs and both etiological agents are acid-fast. Consequently, the importance of nocardiosis as a disease among fishes will not be known until more evidence is obtained on its incidence, susceptible species, morbidity and mortality among fishes.

Etiological Agent:

The etiological agent of nocardiosis is *Nocardia asteroides*. The organism was first described in 1891.[18,19] Many synonymous names have been given over the years, including *Streptothrix asteroides* (1892), *Oospora asteroides* (1892), *Actinomyces asteroides* (1894), *Cladothrix asteroides* (1895), *Discomyces asteroides* (1902) and others. The organism closely resembles the mycotic (fungal) group of microorganisms, although one reference to it mentions the "bacterium-like growth."[18] *N. asteroides* grows into mycelium-like branched filaments 0.2 to 0.7 micrometer in diameter. The filaments break into coccoid- and bacillus-shaped reproductive units. Aerial cells may appear on older colonies.

N. asteroides is gram-positive and acid-fast. It is nonmotile and does not produce spores. The organism grows well on most common laboratory media. Colonies are rough, folded and leathery appearing on solid media. Colonies are yellow to yellow-orange, especially in older cultures. No soluble pigment is produced. The optimum temperature for growth is given as 37°C.[18,19] Those strains of *N. asteroides* involved as fish pathogens will grow on laboratory media at 22°C and in fishes at temperatures lower than 22°C. The organism is aerobic.

Geographic Distribution:

N. asteroides distribution is probably worldwide. The distribution of this organism as a fish pathogen is unknown. It has been reported in fishes in the United States,[109] Argentina[117] and Germany.[52] The disease is probably more widely distributed but has remained undetected.

Susceptible Species:

The known susceptible species for nocardiosis are rainbow trout, brook trout and neon tetras. Many homeothermic animals, including humans, are susceptible to *N. asteroides* infection.

Epizootiology:

The mode of transmission of *N. asteroides* is unknown. Attempts to transmit the disease from infected to non-infected rainbow trout by feeding commercial pelleted trout food onto which rainbow trout *N. asteroides* isolates were placed met with failure after seven months of observation.[109] Some fishes injected with organisms from the same source developed necrotic, inflamed lesions. These experiments suggest that the route of transmission may not be orally, but through injuries and skin abrasions.

The incubation period of nocardiosis is apparently quite long. The disease did not develop in injected rainbow trout for one to three months. Fish injected intramuscularly with *N. asteroides* isolates developed swellings at the site of injection which regressed within one to two weeks.[108]

Infections of *N. asteroides* which occur in fishes may be self-limiting. Rainbow trout with demonstrated nocardiosis were proved free of the nocardia after seven months in the laboratory. The environmental temperature of the laboratory and fish culture facility was 12 to 15°C.[109]

Nothing is known of the carrier state among fishes with nocardiosis. Higher environmental temperatures found in aquaria may increase the probability of organisms being transmitted from fish to fish. Thus, carrier fishes may be of more importance in the epizootiology of the disease among ornamental fishes.

Disease Signs:

Signs of known cases of nocardiosis resemble mycobacteriosis. There may or may not be external signs of the disease. Those fishes which do develop nocardiosis may become emaciated, lethargic and dark in color. They may have body swelling where nocardial lesions occur under the skin. Neon tetras may develop external ulcers.[117]

Internal disease signs include the development of discrete gray-white or hemorrhagic lesions in the kidney or other organs or tissues.[24] The posterior kidney is the most affected organ, sometimes being swollen, hard or rubbery.[52]

Diagnosis:

Diagnosis of nocardiosis depends on disease signs, isolation and identification of the causative organism and histopathology. Disease signs may be confused with other diseases causing miliary or nodular necrotic lesions (mycobacteriosis and bacterial kidney disease). *N. asteroides* can be grown on most laboratory media, which will presumptively differentiate it from mycobacteriosis. It is variably acid-fast, which may be useful in presumptively differentiating it from *Renibacterium salmoninarum*. *N. asteroides* will appear as branched filaments in young cultures, but its tendency to break into coccobacillus or bacillus forms as cultures age must be kept in mind. *N. asteroides* reduces nitrate to nitrite and does not usually yield proteolytic action on milk or other protein media. It is readily transmissible to rabbits and guinea pigs, but not to mice. Cut sections of tissues containing nocardial lesions will have masses of acid-fast organisms within the tissues.

Therapy and Control:

There is no known therapy for nocardiosis in fishes. Fishes known to harbor *N. asteroides* should be removed from the fish population to reduce possibilities of cross-transmission. Fishes with signs of nocardiosis should not be transported and placed into fish populations known to be free of the pathogen.

Prognosis:

The morbidity of nocardiosis is usually quite low, even among fish populations known to harbor the pathogen. Usually only a few fishes will have the infection at any one time.[52,109,117] Mortality among infected fishes is also quite low. The disease may regress in many of the obvious cases of nocardiosis.

Practical Aspects:

Nocardia are present in many of the soils and waters of the world. *N. asteroides*, among these organisms, has caused disease in many animals. The organism has been isolated from brain abscesses and lung lesions of humans. Thus, cases of nocardiosis in fishes should receive more care in handling the infected fishes by the fish disease diagnostician than is usually given to the other diseases of fishes.

N. asteroides infections develop slowly in fishes, as in other animals. Evidence indicates that spontaneous cure of these infections is possible. Therefore, any fish with nocardiosis should first be removed from among other fishes and, if it is a valuable fish, held at a lower temperature to assist in the elimination of the infection. Careful sanitation must be a part of any quarantine procedure at all times.

Miscellaneous Bacterial Diseases of Fishes
Ulcer Disease

Ulcer disease is an acute to subacute or chronic disease of trout. A description of a disease suggesting ulcer disease was first given in 1899, but the exact nature was not known until 1950.[112] Several descriptions of the disease were given in the 1930's and 1940's, but each time protozoa, *Aeromonas* (*Bacterium*) *salmonicida* or *Aeromonas* (*Pseudomonas*) *hydrophila* was given as the etiology. A *Haemophilus*-like bacterium was regularly isolated from cases of the disease in 1950 from brook trout in many of the eastern states.[110] Disease signs of ulcer disease resemble those of furunculosis, which may explain why ulcer disease has often been mistaken for furunculosis.

Ulcer disease has become of less economic importance during the past two decades because of reduction in brook trout culture within the geographical range of the disease.

Etiological Agent:

The etiological bacterium of ulcer disease is *Haemophilus piscium*. It was first isolated from trout with ulcer disease in 1948.[110] The bacterium is rod-shaped with rounded ends, 0.5 to 0.7 micrometer wide by 2.0 micrometers long. The organism is gram-negative and uniformly bipolar stained with Giesma stain. The bacterium is non-motile, non-spore-forming and a facultative anaerobe. It does not have an absolute requirement for hemin as do other *Haemophillus*, but presence of hemin stimulates growth response when media are enriched with cocarboxylase or adenosine triphosphate. Media containing fish peptone (prepared as a peptic digest of trout tissue), cocarboxylase or adenosine triphosphate will support the growth of this bacterium. The taxonomic position of *H. piscium* is somewhat in doubt because of these differences in growth requirements from other *Haemophilus* bacteria. Also, research indicates that *H. piscium* is immunologically similar to *Aeromonas salmonicida*. Consequently these findings may give further reason for placing *A. salmonicida* into the proposed genus *Necromonas*. *H. piscium* could also be placed into such a genus because it is more taxonomically similar to achromogenic strains of *A. salmonicida* than to other species of *Haemophilus*.[18,32,89]

H. piscium does not produce nitrate, indole or sulfide. The organism is methyl red positive and Voges-Poskauer negative. It produces acid from maltose and mannose but not from several other carbohydrates. The organism has an optimum growth temperature between 20 and 25°C. It will not grow below 7°C or at 35°C.[110]

Susceptible Species:

Brook trout are the most susceptible to *H. piscium*. Brown trout are less susceptible than brook trout, and rainbow trout are the most resistant of the trouts. The bacterium may cause ulcer disease in lake trout.[106]

Disease Signs:

H. piscium produces ulcers or open sores on the surface of the body of susceptible fishes (Pl. 11F). The lesions begin as a small papilla and then the top of the papilla erodes away leaving the open ulcer. The open ulcers have whitened skin around the periphery and a dark center. There are no internal signs of ulcer disease.

Diagnosis:

Disease signs will assist in the diagnosis of ulcer disease, However, isolation and identification of *H. piscium* are necessary for definitive diagnosis of this disease. Squash preparations made from unopened papillae and from ulcers should reveal gram-negative small rod-shaped bacteria. Careful disinfection of the skin around an unopened papilla and subsequent culture of underlying tissue onto trypticase soy agar or nutrient agar which has been fortified with fish peptone will usually result in a pure culture of *H. piscium*.

Histopathology of the papillae and the ulcers may be of assistance in diagnosis of this disease. However, the ulcer of ulcer disease is not specifically different from that of injuries or other ulcers. There will be much necrotic debris within the ulcer, the myomeres will be in various stages of degeneration and necrosis and there will be a marked inflammatory response within the ulcer of ulcer disease (Pl. 12C).

Therapy and Control:

Chloramphenicol or oxytetracycline given orally in the food at the rate of 35 to 75 mg per kg (2.5 to 3.5 g per 100 lb) of fish per day for ten to 15 days has been found to be effective for therapy of ulcer disease.[81]

Ulcer disease can be controlled by use of drug therapy combined with sanitation and disinfection. Carrier fishes in the water supply of the fish culture facility should be removed. Egg disinfection is effective in removing the causative bacterium and should be practiced whenever eggs are moved from enzootic ulcer disease geographic areas to noninfected areas. All brushes, nets and other utensils used around fish infected with *H. piscium* should be disinfected after each use. Adult fish may act as carriers of ulcer disease and should be examined for presence of the bacterium and treated or destroyed as necessary.

Edwardsiella Septicemia

Epizootics of edwardsiella septicemia have been investigated since 1969. The nature of the disease led to the suggested name of "emphysematous putrefactive disease of catfish."[71] This name, even though it describes the disease well, has not received acceptance. The name edwardsiella septicemia was adopted in 1974.[69]

Edwardsiella septicemia occurs during the midsummer and early autumn, when water temperature exceeds 30°C. It develops slowly in the larger fish (28 to 50 cm in length). Morbidity levels in channel catfish populations in ponds may reach 5%. A major problem arises when fish from the pond are collected and held for processing. The disease spreads rapidly and morbidity rates increase to near 50% of the population. Fish with the disease entering processing plants, if not detected and removed prior to processing, contaminate processing equipment. The equipment must then be stopped, sterilized and deodorized, creating a financial problem for the processor, even though few fish are involved.[71]

Etiological Agent:

A group of the family Enterobacteriaceae which did not conform to any others in the family was described in 1962.[97] These organisms were dissimilar from the *Escherichia*, *Citrobacter*, *Proteus* and *Salmonella*. The name *Edwardsiella* was given to this genus. The type species was named *Edwardsiella tarda* in 1965.[42] *E. tarda* was the bacterium found to be associated with edwardsiella septicemia of channel catfish in 1969.[71]

E. tarda is a gram-negative, peritrichously flagellated, motile, non-spore-forming, rod-shaped bacterium. It produces acid and gas from glucose and acid from mannitol but does not attack other carbohydrates. It produces hydrogen sulfide and indole, does not liquefy gelatin and does not produce cytochrome oxidase.[32] The bacterium grows well on most common laboratory media. It is facultatively anaerobic. The optimum growth temperature is probably about 35°C.

E. tarda can be distinguished from the *Aeromonas* and *Vibrio* by the fact that members of the latter two genera have polar flagella and produce cytochrome oxidase. It can be separated from *Flavobacterium* by the fact that the latter is a strict aerobe. Activity on various carbohydrates may also be of assistance. Host susceptibility and growth temperature may be necessary to distinguish *E. tarda* and *Y. ruckeri* without antigenic typing.

Geographical Distribution:

E. tarda has been identified as a fish pathogen in the southeastern United States and Japan. It is a normal inhabitant of the intestine of snakes and is occasionally found in human feces. Therefore, it probably has a very wide distribution, but more information will be needed to determine the world distribution of *E. tarda* as a fish pathogen.

Susceptible Species:

E. tarda produces septicemia in channel catfish in the United States and eels in Japan, as well as certain other warmwater fishes. It has not been found in other species of catfish (blue catfish and white catfish) being reared at the same installation with infected channel catfish but not in the same ponds.[71] Snake feces may contaminate catfish ponds.

Disease Signs:

External signs of edwardsiella septicemia are lesions under the skin. Abscesses develop in the muscles, especially along the sides and caudal peduncle. The abscesses may increase in size into large cavities filled with foul-smelling gas. The fish eventually loses control of the posterior part of the body (Pl. 12D, 12E).[71]

Experimentally infected channel catfish exhibited hemorrhages in the visceral organs. None of the usual external signs found among fish with natural infections were noted in experimentally inoculated fish. *E. tarda* suspensions injected into rainbow trout failed to produce the disease at 13°C.

Diagnosis:

Disease signs and bacterial isolation and identification are necessary for diagnosis of edwardsiella septicemia. The presence of subcutaneous abscesses along the posterior parts of the body of channel catfish being held at water temperatures of 30°C or higher and information on the abscesses (i.e., partially filled with foul-smelling gas and cellular débris) are presumptively positive for this disease. The bacterium must be isolated and identified for definitive diagnosis.

Therapy and Control:

Edwardsiella septicemia has been controlled by administering oxytetracycline orally in the diet at the rate of 55 mg per kg (2.5 g per 100 lb) of fish per day for 10 days. Mortality from the disease will usually be reduced within 48 to 72 hours in those fish receiving the drug. The lesions will gradually heal.[71]

The only control procedure known for edwardsiella septicemia in ponds of fish not severely affected is to locate and eliminate fish demonstrating signs of the disease. This is especially true among fish being held for market. Elimination of sources of feces of other animals (i.e., snakes and humans) may assist in control of this disease.

Flavobacteriosis

Members of the genus *Flavobacterium* are widely distributed in soil and water (both fresh water and salt water). They are commonly found as inhabitants of the skin of fishes.

The flavobacteria are not usually pathogenic. They become opportunistic pathogens when fish are injured, in poor physiological condition, in a state of malnutrition or in other conditions which reduce defenses of the body.

Etiological Agent:

The flavobacteria are a widely divergent pigment-producing group of bacteria. Some resemble *Flexibacter* or *Cytophaga* and some have characteristics far removed from these two genera. Thus the separation of flavobacteria from the above-mentioned genera takes considerable data and information.

The flavobacteria are gram-negative non-spore-forming bacteria. They range from coccobacilli to long, slender rod-shaped organisms. They may be motile with peritrichous flagellation or non-motile. The flagellated species do not show swarming or gliding movement. They may or may not grow well on laboratory media. Those that do may be difficult to subculture unless special media are used (additional nitrogen sources, additional vitamins or reduction of agar in solid media). Some do not grow well on liquid media unless shaken occasionally to increase oxygen tension in the depths of the media. Most are aerobic; only a few are facultatively anaerobic.

The flavobacteria produce yellow, orange, red or brown pigmented colonies on solid media. The pigment is not soluble in the medium. Pigment production usually occurs at lower incubation temperatures (10 to 20°C). Most isolates will not grow at temperatures above 30°C. A few species will grow at 37°C.

Susceptible Species:

Probably all fishes are susceptible to secondary infections of *Flavobacterium* sp.

Disease Signs:

The disease signs of flavobacteriosis are similar to many of the other septicemias. Externally there will be erythema at the base of fins, in the mouth, along the folds of the lower jaws and within the opercula. There are usually erythema and petechiae internally in the peritoneum, mesenteries, visceral organs and in muscle tissue. The intestine may or may not be hemorrhagic.

Diagnosis:

Diagnosis of flavobacteriosis is dependent upon disease signs and isolation and identification of the bacterium. Presence of general septicemic signs in or on the fishes, growth of pigmented colonies of bacteria on solid media and data on motility and morphology of the bacterium are used for presumptive diagnosis of flavobacteria.

The ubiquitous nature of the flavobacteria complicates identifying the species of pathogen involved. Usually a different strain or species of *Flavobacterium* is isolated from fishes during different epizootics of the disease. The divergent nature of these organisms also causes great difficulty in relating the pathogen associated with each epizootic of flavobacteriosis with known *Flavobacterium*. The problem is also complicated by the inconsistencies of biochemical characteristics in known species of the bacteria. Therefore, identification of flavobacteria to genus only is usually considered as definitive diagnosis of the disease. Attempts may be made to relate the pathogen found in an epizootic to known *Flavobacterium* sp.[18,19,32]

Therapy and Control:

The primary control of flavobacteriosis is prevention. Reducing fish susceptibility to opportunistic pathogens will usually eliminate the possibility of flavobacteriosis epizootics. This may be achieved by reduction of crowding, supplying acceptable water, careful handling of the fishes and complete nutrition.

Therapy during epizootics of flavobacteriosis includes the use of external disinfectants and sanitation. Oral administration of the most probable chemotherapeutic or antibiotic agent as obtained from plate inhibition tests (Pl. 6E) may also be of assistance in controlling epizootics of this disease.

Streptococcus Septicemia

Streptococcus sp. are uncommon pathogens of fishes. There have been occasional reports of bacteria of this genus causing fish disease, and there is therefore a need for some discussion.

Members of the genus *Streptococcus* are widely distributed in the world. Many are saprophytes and others are present in the various tracts of animals (the alimentary tract, genital tract or respiratory tract for example). They may be released in excreta from animals and into water with fishes. Probably those infections of streptococcus septicemia which have occurred in fishes were of a secondary nature. No information is available on the physiological or physical status of fishes infected with these organisms.

Most species of *Streptococcus* have an optimum growth temperature of about 37°C, but some will grow at temperatures as low as 10°C. This characteristic alone precludes their general appearance as pathogens of fishes. Streptococcal septicemia has been reported in warmwater fish in the United States when water temperature was near 30°C, and in saltwater fish in Japan. A report of the disease in rainbow trout in Japan was caused by a species which tolerated and grew at a lower temperature.

Etiological Agent:

Reported epizootics of streptococcus septicemia of fishes involve either group B[90] or group D[53] *Streptococcus* (Table 11). All streptococci are gram-positive, oval or spherical-shaped (approximately 0.5 to 1.0 micrometer in diameter), usually non-motile and non-spore-forming bacteria. They usually grow in pairs or chains. Most will grow on common laboratory media, but addition of blood or tissue extracts enhances growth. Many are hemolytic. They attack glucose oxidatively and fermentatively. They are facultatively anaerobic. *Streptococcus* reported in the United States more nearly resemble *S. agalactiae* and those in Japan more nearly resemble *S. faecalis* or *S. faecium.*[53,62a]

Susceptible Species:

Spontaneous epizootics of streptococcus septicemia have occurred in bait minnow culture (golden shiners in the United States) and rainbow trout (in Japan). The isolate from golden shiners was also found to be lethal for bluegills, green sunfish and the American toad but had no effect on channel catfish, largemouth bass, goldfish and bigmouth buffalo fish. It did not affect chicks, white mice or hamsters.[90]

Disease Signs:

Fishes with streptococcus septicemia may become lethargic. There may be erythema around the anus and inflamed areas along the dorsal surfaces, especially in the vicinity of the caudal peduncle. The intestine is usually hemorrhagic and filled with pink mucus. The kidney may be swollen and the liver dark and congested.

TABLE 11

Characteristics of groups B and D *Streptococcus*[17]

Characteristic	Group B	Group D
Growth in 6.5% sodium chloride	−	+
Growth in bile esculin medium	−	+
Growth at 10°C	−	+
Growth at 45°C	−	+
Hydrolysis of sodium hippurate	+	−
Growth in presence of bacitracin	+	+
Growth at pH 9.6	−	+
Growth in 0.1% methylene blue	−	+

There may also be inflammation in the muscle tissue.[90]

Diagnosis:

Diseases signs may be of assistance in suggesting presence of a septicemic disease. Isolation and identification of the bacterium are necessary for definitive diagnosis. The diagnostician should remember that *Renibacterium salmoninarum* is a gram-positive, very short rod-shaped bacterium which could be confused with streptococcus infections. There should be little or no chance for confusion with other bacterial pathogens of fishes.

Squash preparations from the kidney, liver or other organs may reveal gram-positive cocci. Careful transfer of specimens from infected fishes will yield pure cultures of the bacterium. The colonies will usually be small, translucent and without pigment.

Isolates of *Streptococcus* sp. from golden shiners produced acid from maltose and sucrose but not from 12 other carbohydrates. They did not reduce methylene blue and would not grow in the presence of 10% bile salts or with 6.5% sodium chloride in trypticase soy agar.

Therapy and Control:

Therapy of streptococcus septicemia has not been determined. Acriflavine used in aquaria at 1:333,000 (3 mg/L) prevented spread of infection when the golden shiner isolate was present. Oxytetracycline and chloramphenicol were used in aquaria at 13.2 mg/L (50 mg/gallon) and effectively controlled the disease.[90] Plate inhibition tests indicated the golden shiner isolate was sensitive to penicillin, erythromycin, tetracycline and novobiocin in addition to the two antibiotics mentioned previously.

Control measures for streptococcus septicemia in fishes should include removal of sources of fecal contamination from other animals. Although the epizootic of the disease in rainbow trout in Japan was definitely not from contaminated water, it could possibly have been obtained from feeding *S. faecalis*-contaminated food.[53]

Pasteurellosis

Bacteria of the genus *Pasteurella* had been suspected of causing disease in fishes, but not until 1963 did an epizootic of pasteurellosis occur. The epizootic involved the entire Chesapeake Bay area of the United States. The epizootic began in the lower Potomac River, a tributary of Chesapeake Bay, in June and gradually spread to the entire bay area and all its tributaries by July and August. Millions of white perch and a lesser number of striped bass were killed during the epizootic.[24] Large numbers of gram-negative, bipolar staining, rod-shaped bacteria were observed in kidney squash preparations taken from white perch. The bacterium was identified as a *Pasteurella* species.

The white perch population was high at the time. The bay and tributaries were heavily polluted with organic matter and algae.[24] Studies following the epizootic demonstrated the *Pasteurella* bacterium to be a part of the normal flora of white perch, indicating the source of infection.[2] A combination of conditions during the summer (high water temperature, high pollution levels, low dissolved oxygen, overpopulation of white perch and presence of an opportunistic pathogen) served to cause the epizootic.

The incident involving the Chesapeake Bay white perch is a classic example of host susceptibility, environmental circumstances and secondary infection. The incident demonstrates that disease epizootics can occur within populations of wild-ranging fishes very similarly to secondary disease epizootics within a crowded population of cultured fishes.

Pasteurellosis has also become an important bacterial disease in Japan, especially among cultured marine fishes. The disease has often been called tuberculosis or pseudotuberculosis in that country.[63] Pasteurellosis may become a more important bacterial disease as more marine fishes are subject to culture.[55]

Etiological Agent:

The cause of pasteurellosis is *Pasteurella piscicida*.[57] Twenty-seven isolates taken from moribund and dead white perch from Chesapeake Bay and its tributaries were identical in all respects. Most isolates from Japan and Europe have conformed to the characteristics of those found in the United States.[55,61] However, a bacterium isolated from a pasteurellosis epizootic in cultured ayu in Japan was named *Pasteurella plecoglosacida* n. sp. because it was dissimilar to *P. piscicida*.[20]

P. piscicida is a gram-negative, non-motile, encapsulated, rod-shaped bacterium with rounded ends and bipolar staining. The usual size is 0.5 micrometer by 1.5 micrometers. Colonies on agar medium are round, convex, glistening, with entire edges, translucent and gray-white to gray-yellow. There is no soluble pigment. It grows best on media with 1.5% sodium chloride, but is limited by greater than 3.0% salt. The organism produces acid only from glucose, maltose, mannose and sucrose. Lactose, sorbitol, xylose, manitol and 15 other carbohydrates are not attacked. The bacterium grows at pH 6.3 to pH 7.6, the optimum pH being 6.8. The growth temperature range is 17 to 31°C. It does not grow at 37°C. The organism does not reduce nitrate to nitrite and does not produce hydrogen sulfide or indole.

Susceptible Species:

White perch of the Chesapeake Bay area are susceptible to *P. piscicida*. An estimated 50% of the population of this species died from pasteurellosis during the summer of 1963. A lesser number of striped bass died during the epizootic.[24] Cultured yellowtail and ayu are known to be susceptible. Pasteurellosis has also been diagnosed in brown trout and Atlantic salmon.[55]

Disease Signs:

Pasteurellosis develops into a rapidly fatal septicemia. Typical external signs which accompany most septicemias have been noted, such as erythema at the base of fins, in the mouth and along the folds of the lower jaw and opercula. The internal signs include erythema with petechiae in organs and tissues.

Diagnosis:

Determination of the cause of epizootics such as the Chesapeake Bay area pasteurellosis epizootic is always a challenge for the diagnostician. Disease signs in moribund fish found at the time indicated an etiological agent other than a bacterium because of the tremendous morality. Toxic algae blooms, pollution and toxic agents were first suspected.[24] Observation of large numbers of bipolar staining, gram-negative, rod-shaped bacteria in kidney squash preparations and pure cultures of the organism taken directly from the fish demonstrated the bacterial etiology. Definitive diagnosis was dependent on bacterial identification. *P. piscicida* resembles nonpigment producing *Aeromonas salmonicida* in morphology and staining. The two organisms can be separated by use of a slide agglutination or fluorescent antibody test.[20]

Therapy and Control:

An interaction of factors usually combine to control mortalities within fish populations when infectious agents are the etiology. Reduction in population numbers quite often is responsible for reducing mortality levels in epizootics. Transmission of the pathogen is unlikely because hosts are farther apart. Some fishes develop nonfatal cases and become resistant to a second infection of the pathogen. Other factors may also be involved with controlling the epizootic.

Pasteurellosis can be controlled in cultured fishes by drug therapy, sanitation and proper management to avoid overcrowding. Sulfamerazine used at 200 to 400 mg per kg (9 to 18 g per 100 lb) of body weight per day for six days has been used to control epizootics. Chloramphenicol used at 20 to 40 mg per kg (0.9 to 1.8 g per 100 lb) of body weight per day for six days has also been found useful.[20]

Selected References

1. Aiso, K., U. Simidu and K. Hasuo. 1968. "Microflora in the digestive tract of inshore fish in Japan," *J. Gen. Microbiol.*, 52:361-364.

1a. Alexander, J. R., A. Bowers, G. A. Ingram and S. M. Shamshoon. 1982. "The portal of entry of bacteria into fish during hyperosmotic infiltration and the fate of antigens." *Dev. Comp. Immunol.*, 2:41-46.

2. Allen, N. and M. Pelczar, Jr. 1967. "Bacteriological studies on the white perch *Roccus americanus*," *Chesapeake Sci.*, 8:135-154.

3. Allison, L. N. 1961. "The fate of kidney disease among hatchery brook trout stocked in natural water," *Prog. Fish-Cult.*, 23:76-78.

4. Amend, D. F. 1970. "Myxobacterial infection of salmonids: prevention and treatment," *In* S. F. Snieszko, ed. *A symposium on diseases of fishes and shellfishes. Am. Fish. Soc. Spec. Publ., No.* 5:258-265.

5. Amend, D. F., J. L. Fryer and K. S. Pilcher. 1965. "Production trials utilizing sulfonamid drugs for control of 'cold-water' disease in juvenile salmon," *Research Briefs, Fish. Comm. of Oregon*, 11:14-17.

6. Amend, D. F. and A. J. Ross. 1970. "Experimental control of columnaris disease with a new nitrofuran drug, P 7138," *Prog. Fish-Cult.*, 32:19-25.

7. Amlacher, E. 1970. *Textbook of fish diseases*. T.F.H. Publ., Neptune, NJ. 302p.

8. Anacker, R. L. and E. J. Ordal. 1959. "Studies on the myxobacterium *Chondrococcus columnaris*. I. Serological typing," *J. Bacteriol.*, 78:25-32.

9. Anderson, J. I. W. and D. A. Conroy. 1969. "Vibrio diseases in marine fishes," *In* S. F. Snieszko, ed. *A symposium on disease of fishes and shellfishes. Am. Fish. Soc. Spec. Publ, No.* 5:266-272.

9a. Arakawa, C. K. and J. L. Fryer. 1984. "Isolation and characterization of a new subspecies of *Mycobacterium cheloni* infectious for salmonid fish. *Helgolander Meeresunter.*, 37:329-342.

10. Aronson, J. D. 1926. "Spontaneous tuberculosis in saltwater fish," *J. Inf. Dis.*, 39:315-320.

10a. Austin, B. 1985. "Evaluation of antimicrobial compounds for control of bacterial kidney disease in rainbow trout, *Salmo gairdneri* Richardson." *J. Fish Dis.*, 8:209-220.

10b. Austin, J. R. and D. J. Alderman. 1983. "Control of furunculosis by oxolinic acid." *Aquacult.*, 31:101-108.

11. Bataillon, E., Dubard and L. Terre. 1897. "Un nouveau type de tuberculose," *Compt. Rend. Soc. Biol.*, 4:446-449.

12. Bataillon, E., A. Moeller and L. Terre. 1902. "Uber die Identitat des Bacillus des Karpfens (Bataillon, Dubard and Terre) und des Bacillus der Blind- schleiche (Moeller)," *Z. Tuberk.*, 3:467-469.

13. Becker, C. D. and M. P. Fujihara. 1978. "The bacterial pathogen *Flexibacter columnaris* and its epizootiology among Columbia River fish," *Am. Fish. Soc., Mon. No. 2.* 92p.

14. Belding, D. L. and B. Merrill. 1935. "A preliminary report upon a hatchery disease of Salmonidae," *Trans. Am. Fish. Soc.*, 65:76-84.

14a. Bell, G. R., D. A. Higgs and G. S. Traxler, 1984. "The effect of dietary ascorbate, zinc and manganese on the development of experimentally induced bacterial kidney disease in sockeye salmon (*Oncorhynchus nerka*)." *Aquacult.*, 36:293-311.

15. Besse, P. 1949. "Epizootie a bacilles acido-resistants chez de poisson exotique," *Bull. Acad. Vet. France*, 23:151-154.

16. Borg, A. 1960. "Studies on myxobacteria associated with diseases in salmonid fishes," *Wildl. Dis. No. 8.* 85p. (Microcards).

16a. Bootsma, R., N. Fijan and J. Blommaert. 1977. "Isolation and preliminary identification of the causative agent of carp erythrodermatitis." *Vet. Arh.*, 47:291-302.

·16b. Bosse, M. P. and G. Post. 1983. "Tribressen® and tiamulin for control of enteric redmouth disease." *J. Fish Dis.*, 6:27-32.

17. Boyd, R. F. and B. G. Hoerl. 1977. *Basic medical microbiology.* Little, Brown & Co., Boston, MA. 518p.

18. Breed, R. S., E. G. D. Murray and N. R. Smith. 1957. *Bergey's manual of determinative bacteriology, 7th Ed.* Williams & Wilkins Co., Baltimore, MD. 1,094p.

19. Breed, R. S., E. G. D. Murray and A. P. Hitchens. 1948. *Bergey's manual of determinative bacteriology, 6th Ed.* Williams & Wilkins Co., Baltimore, MD. 1,529p.

19a. Bullock, G. L., R. C. Cipriano and S. F. Snieszko. 1983. "Furunculosis and other diseases caused by *Aeromonas salmonicida*." *U.S. Fish Wildl. Serv. Fish Dis. Leafl.*, 66. 29p.

19b. Bullock, G. L., G. Maestrone, C. Starliper and B. Schill. 1983. "Furunculosis: Results of field trials for therapy with RO5-0037, a potentiated sulfonamide." *Prog. Fish-Cult.*, 45:51-53.

20. Bullock, G. L. 1978. *Pasteurellosis of fishes. U.S. Fish Wildl. Ser. Fish Leaflet, FDL-54.* 7p.

21. Bullock, G. L. 1972. *Studies on selected myxobacteria pathogenic for fishes and on bacterial gill disease in hatchery-reared salmonids. U.S. Fish & Wildl. Serv. Tech. Paper 60.* 30p.

22. Bullock, G. L. 1971. *Diseases of fish, Book 2B: Identification of pathogenic bacteria.* S. F. Snieszko and H. R. Axelrod, eds. T.F.H. Publ., Neptune, NJ. 41p.

23. Bullock, G. L. 1968. "The bacteriology of brook trout with tail rot," *Prog. Fish-Cult.*, 30:19-22.

24. Bullock, G. L., D. A. Conroy and S. F. Snieszko. 1971. *Diseases of fishes, Book 2A: Bacterial diseases of fishes.* T.F.H. Publ., Neptune, NJ. 151p.

25. Bullock, G. L. and J. J. A. McLaughlin. 1970. Advances in knowledge concerning bacteria pathogenic to fishes (1954-1968)," *In* S. F. Snieszko, ed. *A symposium on diseases of fishes and shellfishes. Am. Fish. Soc. Spec. Publ.*, No. 5:231-242.

26. Bullock, G. L. and S. F. Snieszko. 1975. *Hagerman redmouth, a disease of salmonids caused by a member of the Enterobacteriaceae. U.S. Fish & Wildl. Serv. Fishery Leaflet FDL-42.* 5p.

27. Bullock, G. L., B. R. Griffen and H. M. Stuckey. 1980. "Detection of *Corynebacterium salmoninus* by direct fluorescent antibody test," *J. Fish. Res. Bd. Can.*, 37:719-721.

28. Chen, P. K., G. L. Bullock, H. M. Stuckey and A. C. Bullock. 1974. "Serological diagnosis of corynebacterial kidney disease of salmonids," *J. Fish. Res. Bd. Can.*, 31:1939-1940.

28a. Cipriano, R. C. 1982. "Furunculosis in brook trout: Infections by contact." *Prog. Fish-Cult.*, 44:12-14.

28b. Cipriano, R. C., J. K. Morrison and C. E. Starliper. 1983. "Immunization of salmonids against the fish pathogen, *Aeromonas salmonicida*." *J. World Maricul. Soc.*, 14:201-211.

28c. Cipriano, R. C., C. E. Starliper and J. H. Schachte. 1985. "Comparative sensitivies of diagnostic procedures used to detect bacterial kidney disease in salmonid fishes." *J. Wildl. Dis.*, 21:144-148.

29. Conestrini, G. 1893. "La malattia dominante delle anguille," *Atti. Ist. Veneto Sci.*, 7:809-814.

30. Conroy, D. 1966. "A report on the problems of bacterial fish diseases in the Argentine Republic," *Bull. Off. Int. Epiz.*, 65:755-768.

31. Conroy, D. A. 1966. "Observaciones sobre casos espontaneos de tuberculosis ictica," *Microbiol.*

Espan., 19:93-113.

31a. Cornick, J. W., C. M. Morrison, B. Zuicker and G. Shum. 1984. "Atypical *Aeromonas salomonicida* infection in Atlantic cod, *Gadus morhua* L. *J. Fish Dis.*, 7:495-499.

32. Cowan, S. T., J. G. Holt, J. Liston, R. G. E. Murray, C. F. Niven, A. W. Ravin and R. W. Stanier. 1975. *In* Buchanen, R. E. and N. E. Gibbons, eds. *Bergey's manual of determinative bacteriology. 8th Ed.* Williams & Wilkins Co., Baltimore, MD. 1,268p.

33. Davis, H. S. 1953. *Culture and diseases of game fishes.* Univ. of Calif. Press, Berkeley and Los Angeles, CA. 332p.

34. Davis, H. S. 1922. "A new bacterial disease of freshwater fishes," *Bull. U.S. Bur. Fish., 1921-22*, 38:261-280.

34a. Davis, J. F. and S. S. Hayasaka. 1983. "Pathogenic bacteria associated with cultured American eels, *Anguilla rostrata* le Sueur." *J. Fish Biol.*, 23:557-564.

35. Duff, D. C. B. and B. J. Stewart. 1933. "Studies on furunculosis of fish in British Columbia," *Contrib. Can. Biol. and Fish.*, 8:103-122.

36. Dulin, M. P., T. Huddleston, R. E. Larson and G. W. Klontz. 1976. *Enteric redmouth disease. Forest, Wildlife and Range Expt. Sta. Bull. No. 8* and 1976 update. Univ. of ID, Moscow, ID. 15p.

36a. Elliott, D. and E. B. Shotts, Jr. 1980. "Aetiology of an ulcerative disease in goldfish *Carassius auratus* (L): Microbiological examination of diseased fish from seven locations." *J. Fish Dis.*, 3:133-143.

37. Emmerich, R. and C. Weibel. 1894. "Uber eine durch Bakterien erzeugte Seuche unter den Forellen," *Arch. f. Hygiene*, 21:1-24.

38. Evelyn, T. P. T. 1978. "Sensitivities of bacterial kidney disease detection methods with special remarks on the culture method," *Trans. 3rd Biannual Fish Health Sec., Am. Fish. Soc.*, 1978 (contact the author at Dept. of Fish. Envir., Fish. Mar. Serv., Pac. Biol. Sta., Nanaimo, British Columbia, Canada).

39. Evelyn, T. P. T. 1977. "An improved growth medium for the kidney disease bacterium and some notes on using the medium," *Bull. Off. Int. Epiz.*, 87:511-513.

40. Evelyn, T. P. T. 1971. "An aberrant strain of the bacterial fish pathogen *Aeromonas salmonicida* isolated from a marine host, the sablefish, *Anoplopoma fimbria*, and from two species of cultured Pacific salmon," *J. Fish. Res. Bd. Can.*, 28:1629-1634.

40a. Evelyn, T. P. T., J. E. Ketcheson and L. Prosperi-Porta. 1984. "Further evidence for the presence of *Renibacterium salmoninarun* in salmonid eggs and for the failure of povidone-iodine to reduce the intra-ovum infection rate in water-hardened eggs." *J. Fish Dis.*, 7:173-182.

41. Ewing, W. H., A. J. Ross, D. J. Brenner and G. R. Fanning. 1978. "*Yersinia ruckeri*: sp. nov., the redmouth (RM) bacterium," *Int. J. Syst. Bact.*, 28: 37-44.

42. Ewing, W. H. and A. C. McWorter. 1965. "Genus *Edwardsiella* and *E. tarda*," *In* Ewing, W. H., A. C. McWorter, Escobar and Lubin, "*Edwardsiella*, a new genus of *Enterobacteriaceae* based on a new species, *E. tarda*," *Int. Bull. Bacteriol. Nomencl. Taxon.*, 15:33-38.

43. Fish, F. F. and R. R. Rucker. 1944. "Columnaris as a disease of cold-water fishes," *Trans. Am. Fish. Soc.*, 73:32-36.

44. Fryer, J. L., J. S. Nelson and R. L. Garrison. 1972. "Vibriosis in fish," *Prog. Fish. Food Sci.* (Univ. WA, Seattle, WA), 5:129-133.

45. Fryer, J. L., J. S. Rohovec, G. L. Tebbit, J. S. McMichael and K. S. Pilcher. 1976. "Vaccination for control of infectious diseases in Pacific salmon," *Fish. Pathol.*, 10:155-164.

45a. Fryer, J. L. and J. E. Sanders. 1981. "Bacterial kidney disease of salmonid fish." *Ann. Rev. Microbiol.*, 35:273-298.

45b. Fuhrmann, H., K. H. Böhm and H. J. Schlotfeldt. 1983. "An outbread of enteric redmouth disease in West Germany." *J. Fish Dis.*, 6:309-311.

46. Griffin, P.J. 1954. "The nature of bacteria pathogenic to fish," *Trans. Am. Fish. Soc.*, 83(1953):241-253.

47. Griffin, P. J., S. F. Snieszko and S. B. Friddle. 1953. "A more comprehensive description of *Bacterium salmonicida*," *Trans. Am. Fish. Soc.*, 82(1952):129-138.

48. Hacking, M. A. and J. Budd. 1971. "Vibrio infection in tropical fish in a freshwater aquarium," *J. Wildl. Dis.*, 7:273-280.

49. Hayashi, K., S. Kobayashi, T. Kamata and H. Ozaki. 1964. "Studies on the vibrio-disease of rainbow trout (*Salmo gairdneri irideus*). I. Therapeutic effect of the nitrofuran deviates," *J. Fac. Fish. Perfect. Univ. Mie, Japan*, 6:171-180.

50. Hendricks, J. D. and S. L. Leek. 1975. "Kidney disease postorbital lesions in spring chinook salmon (*Oncorhynchus tshawytcha*)," *Trans. Am. Fish. Soc.*, 104:805-807.

51. Herman, R. L. 1968. "Fish furunculosis 1952-1966," *Trans. Am. Fish. Soc.*, 97:221-230.

52. Heuschmann-Brunner, G. 1965. "Nocardiose bei Fischen des Susswasser und des Meeres," *Tierarztl. Wochensch.* 78 Jahrgang, Heft 5:94-95.

53. Hochino, T., T. Sano and Y. Morimoto. 1958. "A streptococcus pathogenic to fish," *J. Tokyo Univ. Fish.*, 44:57-68.

53a. Holt, R. A., J. E. Sanders, J. L. Zinn, J. L. Fryer and K. S. Pilcher. 1975. "Relation of water temperature to *Flexibacter columnaris* infection in steelhead trout (*Salmo gairdneri*), coho (*Oncorhynchus kisutch*) and chinook (*O. tshawytsche*)." *J. Fish. Res. Bd. Can.*, 32:1553-1559.

54. Hopps, H. C. 1964. *Principles of pathology, second ed.* Appleton-Century-Crofts, New York City, NY. 403p.

55. Hastein, T. and G. L. Bullock. 1976. "An acute septicemic disease of brown trout (*Salmo trutta*) and Atlantic salmon (*Salmo salar*) caused by a *Pasteurella*-like organism," *J. Fish. Biol.*, 8:23-26.

56. Hastein, T., S. J. Saltveit and R. J. Roberts. 1978. "Mass mortality among minnows *Phoxinus phoxinus* (L.) in Lake Tveitevatn, Norway, due to an aberrant strain of *Aeromonas salmonicida*," *J. Fish. Dis.*, 1:241-249.

57. Janssen, W. A. and M. J. Surgalla. 1968. "Morphology, physiology and serology of a *Pasteurella* species pathogenic to white perch (*Roccus americanus*)," *J. Bacteriol.*, 96:1606-1610.

58. Kimura, T. 1978. "Bacterial kidney disease of salmonids," *Fish. Pathol.*, 13:43-52.

59. Kimura, T. 1970. "Studies on a bacterial disease occurred in the adult Sakuramasu (*Oncorhynchus masou*) and pink salmon (*O. gorbuscha*) rearing for maturity," *Sci. Rep. Hakkaido Sal. Hatchery*, 24:9-100. (Hokkaido Univ., Hokodate, Hokkaido, Japan).

60. Klontz, G. W., W. T. Yasutake and A. J. Ross. 1966. "Bacterial diseases of the Salmonidae in the Western United States. Pathogenesis of furunculosis in rainbow trout," *Am. J. Vet. Res.*, 27:1455-1460.

61. Koike, Y., A. Kuwahara and H. Fujiwara. 1975. "Characterization of *Pasteurella piscicida* isolated from white perch and cultivated yellowtail," *Jpn. J. Microbiol.*, 19:241-247.

62. Kubota, S. S. and K. Hagita. 1963. "Studies on the diseases of marine-culture fishes. II. Pharmacodynamic effects of nitrofurazone for fish disease," *J. Fac. Fish. Prefect. Univ. Mie, Japan*, 6:125-144.

62a. Kusuda, R. and I. Kamatsu. 1978. "A comparative study of fish pathogenic *Streptococcus* isolated from saltwater and freshwater fishes." *Bull. Jpn. Soc. Sci. Fish.*, 44:1073-1078.

63. Kusuda, R. and M. Yamaoka. 1972. "Characteristics of a *Pasteurella* sp. pathogenic for pond cultured ayu," *Fish Pathol.*, 7:51-57.

63a. Kwano, K., T. Aoki and T. Kitao. 1984. "Duration of protection against vibrio in ayu, *Plicoglossus altivelis*, vaccinated by immersion and oral administration of *Vibrio anguillarum*." *Bull. Jpn. So. Sci. Fish.*, 50:771-774.

63b. Lall, S. P., W. D. Paterson, J. A. Hines and N. J. Adams. 1985. "Control of bacterial kidney disease in Atlantic salmon, *Salmo salar* L. by dietary modification. *J. Fish Dis.*, 8:113-124.

64. Lannan, J. E. 1978. "Vibriosis vaccination of chum salmon by hyperosmotic infiltration," *Prog. Fish-Cult.*, 40:43-45.

64a. Lesel, R., M. Lesel, F. Gavine and A. Vuillaume. 1983. "Outbreak of enteric redmouth disease in rainbow trout, *Salmo gairdneri* Richardson, in France. *J. Fish Dis.*, 6:385-387.

65. Lewis, D. H. 1973. *Predominant aerobic bacteria of fish and shellfish. Bull. TAMU-SG-73-401.* 102p. (Texas A&M Uni. Sea Grant College, Dept. of Vet. Microbiol., College Station, TX)

66. Marsh, M. C. 1902. "*Bacterium truttae*, a new species of bacterium pathogenic to trout," *Science, News Letter*, 16:706-707.

67. McCarthy, D. H. 1975. "Fish furunculosis caused by *Aeromonas salmonicida* var. *achromogenes*," *J. Wildl. Dis.*, 11:489-493.

67a. McCarthy, D. H. and R. J. Roberts. 1980. "Furunculsis of fish—the present state of our knowledge." *Adv. Aquat. Microbiol.*, 2:293-342.

67b. McCarthy, D. H., J. P. Stevenson and A. W. Salisbury. 1974. "Combined in vitro activity of trimethoprim and sulphonamides for fish pathogenic bacteria." *Aquacult.*, 3:87-91.

68. McCraw, B. M. 1952. *Furunculosis of fish. U.S. Fish and Wildl. Serv., Spec. Sci. Rep. Fisheries No. 84*, 87p.

69. McDaniel, D. 1979. *Procedures for detection and identification of certain fish pathogens. (Revised).* Am. Fish. Soc., Bethesda, MD. 118p.

70. McFadden, T. W. 1969. "Effective disinfection of trout eggs to prevent egg transmission of *Aeromonas liquefaciens*," *J. Fish. Res. Bd. Can.*, 26:2311-2318.

71. Meyer, F. P. and G. L. Bullock. 1973. "*Edwardsiella tarda*, a new pathogen of channel catfish (*Ictalurus punctatus*)," *Appl. Microbiol.*, 25:155-156.

72. Meyer, F. P. and J. D. Collar. 1964. "Description and treatment of a *Pseudomonas* infection in white catfish," *Appl. Microbiol.*, 12:201-203.

73. Michelson, E. 1961. "An acid-fast pathogen of freshwater snails," *Am. J. Tropic. Med. Hyg.*, 10:423- 433.

73a. Mitchum, D. L. and L. E. Sherman. 1981. "Transmission of bacterial kidney disease from wild to stocked hatchery trout." *Can. J. Aquacult. Sci.*, 38:547-551.

74. Mitchum, D. L., L. E. Sherman and G. T. Baxter. 1979. "Bacterial kidney disease in feral populations of brook trout (*Salvelinus fontinalis*), brown trout (*Salmo trutta*) and rainbow trout (*Salmo gairdneri*)," *J. Fish. Res. Bd. Can.*, 36:1370-1376.

74a. Muroga, K., N. Yoneyama and Y. Jo. 1979. "Vibriostatic agent-nonsensitive *Vibrio anguillarum* isolated from ayu." *Fish Pathol.*, 13:159-162.

74b. Nelson, J. S., J. S. Rohovec and J. L. Freyer. 1985. "Tissue location of vibrio bacterin delivered by intraperitoneal injection, immersion and oral routes to *Salmo gairdneri*." *Fish Pathol.*, 19:263-269.

74c. Newman, S. G. and J. J. Majnarich. 1982. "Direct immersion vaccination of juvenile rainbow trout, *Salmo gairdneri* Ricardson, and juvenile coho salmon, *Oncorhynchus kitsutch* (Walbaum), with *Yersinia ruckeri* bacterin." *J. Fish Dis.*, 5:339-341.

74d. O'Leary, P. J., J. S. Rohovec, J. E. Sanders and J. L. Fryer. 1982. "Serotypes of *Yersinia ruckeri* and their immunogenic properties." *ORESU-T-82-001*. Oregon State University, Corvallis, OR. 14p.

75. Ordal, E. J. and B. J. Earp. 1956. "Cultivation and transmission of the etiological agent of kidney disease in salmonid fishes," *Proc. Soc. Expt. Biol. Med.*, 92:85-88.

76. Ordal, E. J. and R. R. Rucker. 1944. "Pathogenic myxobacteria," *Proc. Soc. Expt. Biol. Med.*, 56:15-18.

77. Pacha, R. E. and E. D. Kiehn. 1969. "Characteristics and relatedness of marine vibrios pathogenic to fish: physiology, serology and epidemiology," *J. Bact.*, 100:1242-1247.

78. Pacha, R. E. and E. J. Ordal. 1970. "Myxobacterial diseases of salmonids," *In* S. F. Snieszko, ed. *A symposium on diseases of fishes and shellfishes. Am. Fish. Soc. Spec. Publ.*, No. 5:243-257.

79. Parisot, T. J. 1958. "Tuberculosis of fish," *Bact. Revs.*, 22:240-245.

80. Parisot, T. J. and E. M. Wood. 1960, "A comparative study of the causative agent of mycobacterial disease of salmonid fishes. II. A description of the histopathology of the disease in chinook salmon (*Oncorhynchus tshawytcha*) and a comparison of the staining characteristics of the fish disease with leprosy and human tuberculosis," *Am. Rev. Resp. Dis.*, 82:212-222.

80a. Paterson, W. D., D. Dovey and D. Desautels. 1980. "Relationship between selected strains of typical and atypical *Aeromonas salmonicida*, *Aeromonas hydrophila* and *Hemophilus piscium*." Can. *J. Microbiol.*, 26:588-598.

80b. Paterson, W. D., S. P. Lall and D. Desautels. 1981. "Studies on bacterial kidney disease in Atlantic salmon (*Salmon salar*) in Canada." *Fish Pathol.*, 15:283-292.

81. Piper, R. G. 1970. *Ulcer disease in trout. U.S. Fish & Wildl. Serv. Fishery Leaflet, FDL-24.* 3p.

82. Plehn, M. 1911. "Die furunculose der salmoniden," *Centrabl. f. Bakterial. Abt. I. Orig.*, 60:609-624. (After McCraw, 1952).

83. Post, G. 1971. "Systematic grading of gill hyperplasia," *Prog. Fish-Cult.*, 33:61

84. Post, G. 1959. *Trout from Douglas Creek, Albany County. FA-Wyo. Proj. No. FW-3-R-6:4-5.*

85. Post, G. 1962. "Furazolidone (nf-180) for control of furunculosis in trout," *Prog. Fish-Cult.*, 24:182- 184.

86. Rabb, L., J. W. Cornick and L. A. McDermott. 1964. "A macroscopic-slide agglutination test for presumptive diagnosis of furunculosis in fish," *Prog. Fish-Cult.*, 26:118-120.

87. Reed, G. B. and G. C. Toner. 1941. "Red sore disease of pike," *Can. J. Res., Sec. D., Zool. Sci.*, 19:139-143.

88. Reichenbach-Klinke, H. H. 1973. *Fish pathology*. T.F.H. Publ., Neptune, NJ. 512p.

89. Roberts, R. J., ed. 1978. *Fish pathology*. Bailliere Tindall, London, England. 318p.

90. Robinson, J. A. and F. P. Meyer. 1966. "Streptococcal fish pathogen," *J. Bacteriol.*, 92:512.

91. Ross, A. J. 1970. *Vibriosis in fish. U.S. Fish & Wildl. Serv., Fish Leaflet, FDL-29.* 3p.

92. Ross, A. J. 1970. "Mycobacteriosis among Pacific salmonid fishes," *In* S. F. Snieszko, ed. *A symposium on diseases of fishes and shellfishes. Am. Fish. Soc. Spec. Publ., No. 5:279-283.*

93. Ross, A. J. 1960. "*Mycobacterium salmoniphilum* sp. nov. from salmonoid fishes," *Am. Rev. Resp. Dis.*, 81:241-250.

94. Ross, A. J., R. R. Rucker and W. H. Ewing. 1966 "Description of a bacterium associated with redmouth disease of rainbow trout (*Salmo gairdneri*)," *Can. J. Microbiol.*, 12:763-769.

95. Rucker, R. R. 1959. "Vibrio infections among marine and freshwater fish," *Prog. Fish-Cult.*, 21:22-25.

96. Rucker, R. R., B. J. Earp and E. J. Ordal. 1954. "Infectious diseases of Pacific salmon," *Trans. Am. Fish. Soc.*, 83:297-312.

96a. Sakai, M., T. Aoki and T. Kitao. 1984. "Comparison of the cellular immune response of fish vaccinated by immersion and injection of *Vibrio anguillarum*." *Bull. Jpn. Soc. Sci. Fish.*, 50:1187-1192.

97. Sakazaki, R. 1962. "The new group of Enterobact-

eriaceae, the Asakusa group," *Jpn. J. Bacteriol.*, 17: 616-617.

98. Sanders, J. E. and J. L. Fryer. 1980. "*Renibacterium salmoninarum* gen. nov., sp. nov., the causative agent of bacterial kidney disease in salmonid fishes," *Internat. J. Syst. Bacteriol.*, 30:496-502.

99. Sanders, J. E. and J. L. Fryer. 1978. "*Corynebacterium salmoninus* sp. nov. The causative agent of bacterial kidney disease; selected biochemical properties and pathogenesis in salmonid fishes," *Proc. 3rd Biennial Fish. Health Sec., Am. Fish. Soc.*, 28-33.

100. Schachte, J. H., Jr. and E. C. Mora. 1973. "Production of agglutinating antibodies in the channel catfish (*Ictalurus punctatus*) against *Chondroccocus columnaris*," *J. Fish. Res. Bd. Can.*, 30:116-118.

100a. Shiew, M. H., T. J. Trust and J. H. Crosa. 1981. "*Vibrio ordali* sp. nov.: Causative agent of vibriosis in fish." *Curr. Microbiol.*, 6:343-348.

101. Schotts, E. B., Jr. and G. L. Bullock. 1975. "Bacterial disease of fishes: diagnostic procedures for gram-negative pathogens," *J. Fish. Res. Bd. Can.*, 32:1243-1247.

102. Simidu, I. and K. Hasuo. 1968. "Salt dependency of the bacterial flora of marine fish," *J. Gen. Microbiol.*, 52:347-354.

103. Smith, I. W. 1964. "The occurrence and pathology of Dee disease," *Freshwater and Salmon Fisheries Res.*, 34:1-12.

104. Smith, I. 1943. "The classification of *Bacterium salmonicida*," *J. Gen. Microbiol.*, 33:263-274.

104a. Snieszko, S. F. 1981. "Bacterial gill disease of freshwater fishes." *U.S. Dep. Int.; Fish & Wildl. Serv. Fish Dis. Leafl. 62.* 11p.

105. Snieszko, S. F. 1978. *Mycobacteriosis (tuberculosis) of fishes. U.S. Fish Wildl. Ser. Fish Leaflet, FDL- 55.* 9p.

106. Snieszko, S. F. 1952. "Ulcer disease in brook trout (*Salvelinus fontinalis*): its economic importance, diagnosis, treatment and prevention," *Prog. Fish-Cult.*, 14:43-49.

107. Snieszko, S. F. and G. L. Bullock. 1976. *Columnaris disease of fishes. Fish Dis. Leaf. 45.* U.S. Fish and Wildlife Serv., Div. of Fish-Cult. Res., Washington, DC. 10p.

108. Snieszko, S. F. and G. L. Bullock. 1976. *Diseases of freshwater fishes caused by bacteria of the genera Aeromonas, Pseudomonas and Vibrio. U.S. Fish & Wildl. Serv., Fish. Leaflet. FDL-40.* 10p.

109. Snieszko, S. F., G. L. Bullock, C. E. Dunbar and L. L. Pettijohn. 1964. "Nocardial infection in hatchery-reared fingerling rainbow trout (*Salmo gairdneri*)," *J. Bacteriol.*, 88:1809-1810.

110. Snieszko, S. F. and S. B. Friddle. 1950. "A contribution to the etiology of ulcer disease of trout," *Trans. Am. Fish. Soc.*, 78:56-63.

111. Snieszko, S. F. and P. J. Griffin. 1955. "Kidney disease in brook trout and its treatment," *Prog. Fish-Cult.* 17:3-13.

112. Snieszko, S. F., P. J. Griffin and S. B. Friddle. 1950. "A new bacterium (*Hemophilus piscium* n. sp.) from ulcer disease of trout," *J. Bacteriol.*, 59:699-710.

113. Snieszko, S., W. Piotrowska, B. Kocylowski and K. Marek. 1938. *Bacteriological and serological studies on bacteria of the carp hemorrhagic septicemia.* Lab. Microbial, Ichthyol. Fish. Jagellonian Univ., Krakow, Poland, 16:15pp. (Trans. by S. F. Snieszko, Fish Res. Cent., Route 3, Box 41, Kearneysville, WV)

114. Stumm, W. and J. J. Morgan. 1970. *Aquatic chemistry.* Wiley-Interscience Publ., New York City, NY. 585p.

115. Terre, L. 1902. "Essai sur la tuberculose der vertebres a sang froid. Etude de pathologie experimentale et comparee," *Zbl. Bakt. Abt. l, Orig.*, 33:210.

116. Thurston, R. V., R. C. Russo and C. E. Smith. 1978. "Acute toxicity of ammonia and nitrite to cutthroat trout fry," *Trans. Am. Fish. Soc.*, 107:361-368.

116a. Trust, T. J., E. E. Ishiguro, H. Chart and W. H. Kay. 1983. "Virulence properties of *Aeromonas salmonicida*." *Proc. Wold Maricult, Soc.*, 14:193-200.

117. Valdez, I. and D. A. Conroy. 1963. "The study of a tuberculosis-like condition in neon tetras (*Hyphessobrycon innesi*). II. Characteristics of the bacterium isolated," *Microbiol. Espan.*, 16:249-253.

118. van Duijn, C., Jr. 1973. *Diseases of fishes.* Charles C. Thomas, Publ. Springfield, IL. 372p.

119. Vogel, H. 1958. "Mycobacteria from cold blooded animals," *Am. Rev. Tuberc. Pulm. Dis.*, 77:823-838.

120. Wagner, E. D. and C. L. Perkins. 1952. "*Pseudomonas hydrophila*, the cause of 'red-mouth' disease in rainbow trout and 'red-leg' disease in frogs," *Prog. Fish-Cult.*, 14:127-128.

121. Warren, J. 1963. "Kidney disease of salmonid fishes and the analysis of hatchery waters," *Prog. Fish-Cult.*, 25:121-131.

121a. Winton, J. R., J. S. Rohovec and J. L. Fryer. 1983. "Bacterial and viral diseases of cultured salmonids in the Pacific Northwest." *Ore. St. Univ. Sea Grant Prog. ORESU-R-83-018:1-20.*

122. Wobeser, G. 1973. "An outbreak of redmouth disease in rainbow trout (*Salmo gairdneri*) in Saskat-

chewan," *J. Fish. Res. Bd. Can.*, 30:571-575.

123. Wolf, K. 1956. *Survey on the occurrence of kidney disease in trout in some inland states.* Unpubl. Memo. Eastern Fish Disease Lab, U.S. Fish & Wildl. Serv., Leetown, WV. 11p.

124. Wolf, K. E. and C. E. Dunbar. 1959. "Test of 34 therapeutic agents for control of kidney disease in trout," *Trans. Am. Fish. Soc.*, 88:117-124.

125. Wood, J. W. 1968. *Diseases of Pacific salmon: their prevention and treatment.* State of Washington, Dept. of Fisheries, Division of Hatcheries, Olympia, WA. 78p.

126. Wood, J. W. and J. Wallis. 1955. "Kidney disease in adult chinook salmon and its transmission by feeding to young chinook salmon," *Research Briefs, Fish Comm. of Oregon*, 6:32-40.

127. Zachary, A. and I. Paperna. 1977. "Epitheliocystis from the striped bass (*Morone saxatilis*) from the Chesapeake Bay." *Can. J. Microbiol.*, 23:1404-1414.

Chapter V

MYCOTIC DISEASES
OF FISHES

The word mycosis (or mycotic) is derived from the Greek word "mykeş," meaning "mushroom" in English. The word "fungi" is used interchangeably, because this is the word for mushroom in Latin. There are two major types of fungi: *saprobes* (those utilizing dead organic matter for sustenance) and *parasites* (those obtaining nutrients by infecting living organisms). The story of mycotic diseases is further complicated by the fact that many saprobes are facultative parasites, and many fungal parasites are facultative saprobes. All fungi have one thing in common: they are heterotrophic (organisms requiring preformed organic matter for growth and reproduction). This characteristic is different from green plants in that fungi are incapable of synthesizing their own nutrients.

The fungi are more complete organisms than the bacteria. Each fungal cell has one or more nuclei, minute in size but nevertheless nuclei. The cell wall of fungi may contain cellulose, chitin and/or callose through which nutrients are absorbed. Fungal cells liberate digestive enzymes into the surroundings to reduce organic matter into absorbable nutrients.[23]

The structure of fungi is extremely variable from species to species, genus to genus and especially from family to family. Some entire fungal organisms are made up of a single cell (the yeasts). Others are made up of many cells joined together into long filaments or *hyphae*. The filamentous or hyphal fungi usually branch in all directions, and the tangled mass of filaments is called a mycelium or thallus. Each cell of a hypha is separate; those more distinctly separate are called septate hyphae, while those without visible septa are called non-septate or aseptate. The septa in non-septate hyphae are actually there but are delicate and perforated so that they do not appear to be present.[36]

Fungi reproduce sexually or asexually. Either way, most fungi produce spores, usually zoospores because of flagellation, at some stage of the life cycle. Spores are the primary unit of transmission. Asexual reproduction (sometimes called somatic or vegetative reproduction) does not involve the union of other cells in any way. Sexual reproduction involves the union of the nuclei of two cells. A reproductive hypha is called a fertile hypha. A fertile hypha contains the reproductive unit (usually containing spores). Spores are released from the reproductive structure as the infecting units in the case of parasitic or facultatively parasitic fungi. The fungal spore is resistant to heat, drying, disinfectants and the defense mechanisms of the host.

Many of the fungi are capable of vegetative reproduction from a fragment of mycelium separated from the main fungal mass. The mycelial fragment continues to grow under favorable conditions, such as on the surface or inside of hosts.

Classification of fungi, in cases of mycotic diseases of fishes, is an important part of the diagnosis. Fungal classification is based on the life cycle, morphology of the hyphae, morphology of the reproductive units and the type of spores produced. The nomenclature and taxonomic classification of the fungi have been, and will continue to be, in a state of indecision. This taxonomic hesitancy is caused by individual interpretations of morphological, physiological and genetic information on the particular fungus in question or because of fragmentary knowledge of the fungal organism.

Relatively few genera and species of fungi are known to cause disease in fishes. Epizootics or rare cases of fungal infections have been reported.[11,15,26,30,31] Often these rare occurrences of fungal diseases are caused by facultative saprobes. Most epizootics of mycotic origin are facilitated by poor environmental conditions, malnutrition or other primary disease.

A selection of the most common mycotic diseases will be discussed here. These examples demonstrate the complexity of fungal pathogens, how parasitic fungi cause disease in the host and what may be done to reduce the effects on the host.

Saprolegniasis

Saprolegniasis is a fungal disease of fishes and fish eggs caused by a member of the family Saprolegniaceae.[25] This name has been broadly accepted when the etiology is a species of the genus *Saprolegnia*, *Achlya* or *Dictyuchus*.[37] Sometimes the name "achlyaiasis" is used when the diagnostician knows a species of *Achlya* is involved. However, the *Achlya* and the *Saprolegnia* which cause disease on fishes or fish eggs are so similar morphologically that even expert mycologists may disagree on classification. The reproductive units of *Dictyuchus* sp. are usually distinct from those of *Saprolegnia* sp. or *Achlya* sp. The gross appearance of dictyuchiasis on fishes or fish eggs is similar to infections of members of the other two genera. Only microscopic examination will distinguish the actual etiology of the disease. Therapy for the disease, no matter from which etiology, is similar. Therefore, the name "saprolegniasis" will be used here for convenience, even if not always taxonomically correct.

Saprolegniasis has been called by other names. The

term "fish fungus disease" or just "fungus disease" is broadly used because of its common occurrence.

Etiological Agent:

The family Saprolegniaceae is ubiquitous to the world, all of its species being classified as "water molds." Members of the family are primarily in fresh water, but some species can grow in brackish water to a salinity of about 2.8 0/00 (2.8 parts per thousand).[36] There are no marine species (sea water has a salinity of more than about 3.5 0/00). Many of the Saprolegniaceae are present in moist soils.

Most species of the family are saprophytic on dead organic matter. Even those species involved as fish pathogens are saprobes and facultative parasites.

Saprolegnia parasitica, Achlya hoferi and *Dictyuchus* sp. are the major etiological agents of saprolegniasis. There are several other species of each genus which cause diseases in various parts of the world. These fungi have long, branched, non-septate hyphae. They reproduce primarily asexually, forming zoosporangia on fertile hyphae. The zoosporangia are long, slender and usually slightly larger in diameter than the hyphae to which they are attached. The zoosporangia are double-walled and contain spherical zoospores (sometimes called sporangiospores). The zoosporangia of *S. parasitica* and *A. hoferi* opens to discharge zoospores into the water or soil while remaining attached to the hyphae. The zoosporangia of *Dictyuchus* sp. usually fall from the hyphae at maturity. Primary zoospores of *S. parasitica* or *A. hoferi* may form cysts which release many secondary zoospores. The secondary zoospores germinate to produce new hyphae. The zoosporangia of *Dictyuchus* sp. remain intact, the zoospores encysting and producing secondary zoospores prior to release. Thus, the species of Saprolegniaceae mentioned here have the capability of producing enormous numbers of infectious units either as saprophytes in the water supply containing the fishes or while on fishes or fish eggs.

Sexual reproduction of *S. parasitica, A. hoferi* and *Dictyuchus* sp., does occur, although asexual reproduction is far more common. Sexual reproduction among these fungi is by contact between the male gamete and the female gametangium, with fertilization taking place through a fertilization tube or antheridium. The end reproductive unit is called an oogonium and is of value for specific identification.[36]

Geographical Distribution:

Zoospores and mycelia of *S. parasitica, A hoferi* or *Dictyuchus* sp. are ubiquitous to the world. The zoospores can be carried on the feathers of birds, pellage of animals, by the wind and in flowing water. Therefore, the potential for saprolegniasis among susceptible fishes or fish eggs is continuous.

Susceptible Species:

All freshwater and brackish water fishes and fish eggs are potentially susceptible to saprolegniasis. Living fish eggs are not usually susceptible to invasion by any of the saprolegnia. Dead fish eggs are growth medium for the fungi, and fungal growth on dead eggs may be responsible for killing normal eggs by suffocation and invasion.

Epizootiology:

There apparently are no primary cases of saprolegniasis among fishes. Malnutrition among cultured fishes has been and continues to be a primary cause of saprolegniasis. Presence of toxic substances in the food or water or damage to skin, fins or gills from external parasites may lead to secondary invasion by the saprolegnia. Physical injuries are targets for the invasion of the saprolegnia. Physical stresses such as reduced water temperature, high or low pH or high salinity may be responsible for secondary invasion by the saprolegnia.

Saprolegniasis may be secondary to other infections. It accompanies fin rot or peduncle disease, ulcer disease, open furuncles of furunculosis and other bacterial diseases. Saprolegnia may appear in cases of environmental or bacterial gill disease.

Zoospores of the saprolegnia finding a fertile area on susceptible fish germinate and begin to produce vegetative hyphae. The mycelium grows to cover the injured tissue or place of invasion, spreading to the more normal tissue surrounding the initial invasion site. Digestive enzymes produced by the fungi destroy the surrounding tissue, allowing invasion of the dead and dying cells. The mycelium continues to spread, sending up hyphae into the surrounding water until the fish appears as if tufts of cotton were attached to its body (Pl. 13A). Only the skin may be involved and infection may be localized where an injury had occurred previously (Pl. 13B). The gills may become covered with the mycelium. The fungal growth may overwhelm the host by suffocation if on the gills or by destruction of skin and scales to the point of mortal injury.

Dead fishes are a fertile medium for more fungal growth and production of zoospores. The presence of dead fishes in water increases the numbers of infective zoospores enormously, thus making possible invasion of other living fishes with only minor injuries or deficiencies.

Saprolegniasis among fishes of a fish culture facility or in an aquarium may be confined to one fish, a few fish or the entire population, depending on the reason for the fungal invasion. Each case of the disease becomes a source of zoospores for the surrounding water and an increased possibility of invasion onto other fishes. There are no true carriers of the saprolegnia, only sources of increased zoospore population.

Dead fish eggs are a fertile medium for growth of saprolegnia (Pl. 12F). A single saprolegnia zoospore can initiate growth on a dead fish egg. The mycelial mass extends from the egg into the water surrounding the egg. A single dead egg with fungal growth can be the medium which produces a suffocating mycelial growth over living eggs. The partially suffocated eggs around the dead egg then die, to be directly invaded by the fungi. The suffocating effect is spread until eggs in the entire redd, nest or incubator tray are killed. The tremendous increase in zoospore production from fungal growth on dead eggs yields plenty of infective units for each additional dead and dying egg. The invasion of eggs appears to increase in tempo until all eggs in the group are killed and invaded by the fungi.

Rapidity of fungal growth on susceptible fishes or fish eggs is related to environmental temperature. Most of the saprolegnia have a minimum growth temperature between 0 and 5°C. The optimum growth temperature is between 15 and 30°C. Growth progresses more slowly at temperatures between 5 and 15°C, is much more rapid in the mid-range of optimum growth (18 to 26°C) and is reduced at higher temperatures (28 to 35°C).

Disease Signs:

Presence of fluffy, cotton-like, white to gray or gray to gray-brown growth on the skin, fins, gills or eyes of fishes or on fish eggs is the sign of saprolegniasis. Occasionally the fungi may invade the muscle tissue under the skin of fungus-infected fishes. There have been reports of saprolegnia invading fishes from the inside and extending hyphae through the skin to the outside.[11] External signs of this route of transmission are similar to disease signs derived from surface invasion.

Diagnosis:

Appearance of cotton-like white to gray-white or gray-brown growth on exterior surface structures of fishes or on dead fish eggs is a presumptively positive diagnosis for saprolegniasis. The usual practice is to accept the presumptive diagnosis and initiate therapy.

Identification of the fungi is necessary for definitive diagnosis of this disease. A small mycelial sample taken from the fish or fish eggs and mounted on a microscope slide with a few drops of water is examined microscopically. The fungal organisms causing saprolengiasis have branched, nonseptate hyphae. Asexual reproduction is completed by these organisms from a zoosporangium at the tip of fertile hyphae (Pl. 14A). Mature primary zoospores have two flagella; encystment occurs, and secondary zoospores also with two flagella are produced by all *Saprolegnia* sp. *Achlya* sp. do not produce secondary zoospores,[30] and *Dictyuchus* sp. do not release primary zoospores but release secondary zoospores.[36]

Therapy and Control:

The wide distribution and general occurrence of saprolegniasis have been responsible for the development of many therapeutic procedures for control of the disease. However, the efficiency of the therapeutic procedure depends on removal of the primary cause or the environmental condition.

One of the most effective fungicides for use in the therapy of saprolegniasis on fishes and fish eggs is zinc-free malachite green. Malachite green is an aniline dye product and has been found to be a teratogen (anomaly producing) and a mutagen (cell altering) compound. It has not, nor will it probably ever, receive acceptance by the United States Food and Drug Administration (FDA) for us as a therapeutic compound on or in food fish reared in the United States. Malachite green alone and in combination with formalin has been the primary fungicide used in fish culture.

Malachite green can be used for control of saprolegniasis on nonfood fish. The recommended treatment is to use a bath at 1:200,000 (5 mg/L) for one hour or 10 to 30 second dips at 1:15,000 (66.7 mg/L).

Saprolegniasis can be treated by dipping infected fishes into 5% salt (sodium chloride) solution for one to two minutes. Some species of fish cannot tolerate high salt concentrations and longer treatment times (20 to 30 minutes) in a bath containing 1 to 1.5% salt may be more suitable.[1a]

Dipping fish in 5% acetic acid solution for 30 seconds to one minute may reduce fungal growth. Formalin has been used to treat saprolegniasis at 1:4,000 (250 mg/L) for one hour, but with limited success. Combining formalin at 1:10,000 (100 mg/L) with 1:400,000 (2.5 mg/L) malachite green solution and treating for one hour has been found to be effective in some cases.

Saprolegnia control on incubating fish eggs can be achieved by either removing dead eggs at regular intervals during incubation or by flowing fungicidal solution over the eggs. The usual procedure for prophylactic malachite green treatment of incubating fish eggs is to dissolve two grams of the dye in 3.785 liters (one gallon) of soft or distilled water. The stock solution is used to "flush treat" eggs incubating in troughs or incubators. An aliquot of the stock solution is added to inflowing water of the incubator and allowed to flush past the eggs. Usually the prophylactic treatment is given once each day during the entire incubation period.

The ruling by the FDA to limit use of malachite green on food fish prompted the U.S. Fish and Wildlife Service and other agencies to examine potential replacement fungicides. Malachite green was used in a study as a standard against 25 candidate fungicides. None had an antifungal spectrum index (ASI) greater than 50% the ASI of malachite green. Two of the compounds (Duter® and copper oxychloride sulfate) were recommended for further study.[4a] A study in Great Britain involved 30 candidate compounds against *S. parasitica* and *Aphanomyces astaci*, an often fatal fungal pathogen of freshwater crayfish. Malachite green was the most effective, even at concentrations as low as 1.0 mg per liter. One other compound controlled both fungi at 1.0 mg per liter, dichlorphen sodium. However, this compound has an extremely high toxicity to fish which prohibits its use.[1a]

Tests run to determine the most acceptable fungicidal

compounds for prophylactic control of saprolegnia on incubating salmonid eggs indicated malachite green to be superior to seven other compounds used.[8] One-hour treatments with malachite green at concentrations ranging from 2 to 16 mg per liter given on five consecutive days completely controlled saprolegnia growth on dead eggs. Dead eggs without treatment were 100% infected on the sixth day of the study. Formalin used at 150 and 300 mg per liter controlled fungal growth, but 75 mg per liter did not. No other compounds used in the study were effective (Karmex, benzaldehyde, glutaraldehyde, Dowicide A, Cutrine and Doxine).

Prognosis:

Morbidity of saprolegniasis among susceptible fishes in a fish culture facility or aquarium may vary from less than 1% to all fishes in the population. The morbidity level is dependent on the severity of the primary cause of fungal infection. Handling fishes with rough nets may break scale pockets and loosen scales, producing large numbers of portals for saprolegnia spores to enter. The result may be a high incidence of saprolegniasis. A few nutritionally deficient fishes in a population may be the only susceptible fishes, with a low incidence of saprolegniasis.

Saprolegniasis is not usually a direct mortality factor unless the fungal mycelium covers vital areas of the body or causes extensive tissue damage. Excessive fungal growth on the gills may be responsible for suffocating the fish. Fungal growth on the cornea of the eye causes blindness and an inability to seek food or elude predators. Fishes with extensive saprolegnial mycelium on skin, fins, gills or other parts of the body are not usually able to compete with the more normal fishes in the holding facility and may be lost because of that disability.

Practical Aspects:

Signs of extensive saprolegniasis among cultured or aquarium fishes is an indication that something else is wrong. The fish culturist or aquarist should attempt to determine why fishes are susceptible to saprolegnia infection. Evidence of malnutrition, physical injury, bacterial or parasitic infection and any other possible factor should be investigated. Detecting the actual cause of saprolegniasis may be found quickly or absolute diagnosis may be extremely difficult. An example of a difficult diagnosis occurred in Japan. Eel culture had recurrent saprolegniasis for many years. A report was written in 1956 that this disease was no doubt primary in nature. Observations and experiments had not demonstrated any satisfactory prophylaxis or treatment for the control of the disease. *S. parasitica* was identified as the primary pathogen.[20] Ten years of studying the recurring disease developed a conclusion that eel saprolegniasis was secondary to a chronic infection of *Aeromonas* (*liquifaciens*) *hydrophila*. The bacterium was the primary pathogen.[13] Ten years is a long time to arrive at the etiology of a disease.

Transporting fishes with slight to moderate infections of saprolegnia from one geographical area to another is acceptable. These fungi are widely distributed in the world, and no danger exists in moving unwanted pathogens. Fishes with extreme saprolegniasis should not be moved until the primary cause of the disease is found and controlled. Stocking of sport fishes with saprolegniasis poses no threat to a wild population already in the stream, lake or pond, unless the primary cause of saprolegniasis is a serious primary pathogen.

Single fish with saprolegniasis in an aquarium should be removed and placed in quarantine and treated. Such a fish is a constant source of zoospores, and other slightly susceptible fishes may become infected. Also, an aquarium fish with saprolegniasis usually has reduced vitality and becomes a target for attack by the other fishes.

Ichthyophonus Disease

The name "ichthyophonus disease" was accepted by the Fish Health Section of the American Fisheries Society in 1974 as the official name for a fungal disease which had previously been known as ichthyosporidiosis as well as ichthyophonus disease. The difficulty in nomenclature of the disease is related to the nomenclature of the etiological agent. The disease was first described in 1893, but the etiology was not fully understood.[19] A similar disease was described in 1905 and the organism given the name *Ichthyosporidium gastrophilum*, as if it were a microsporidian protozoan.[7] The fungal nature of the disease was recognized in 1911, and an attempt was made to settle the nomenclature controversy by suggesting the name of the fungus be *Ichthyophonus hoferi*.[28] Studies were made in 1914 on a haplosporidian protozoa which causes similar disease signs and is rightfully named *Ichthyosporidium gastrophilum*.[1] These findings should have laid the nomenclature problem to rest, but did not. The two names continued to be used interchangeably. One author stated that the fungus was apparently called by the name *Ichthyosporidium* prior to the protozoa being called by that name, therefore prior rights for the fungus to be called by this name had been set.[27] The name ichthyosporidium disease and ichthyosporidiosis continued to be used interchangeably with ichthyophonus disease through 1965.[9,12,14,32] Possibly all authors were correct, except that each researcher was unsure of whether a fungus was involved or a protozoan. Better descriptions of an *Ichthyosporidium* species of protozoa have been given during the 1960's,[34] and very convincing arguments given for calling the fungus *Ichthyophonus hoferi*. Thus the name ichthyophonus disease is valid and will be used in the following discussion.

Etiological Agent:

The cause of ichthyophonus disease is *Ichthyophonus*

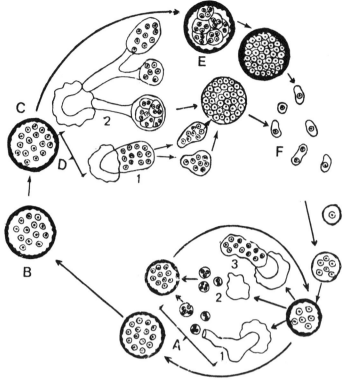

Fig. 3: Life cycle of *Ichthyophonus hoferi*
Germination in fish tissue:
    A. Parenchymal reproductive cycle
        1. Filamentium
        2. Direct endospores
        3. Plasmodium
    B. Quiescent cysts
Dead fish tissue or fish feces:
    C. Ripened cyst
    D. Germination
        1. Plasmodial germination
        2. Filamentous germination
Alimentary tract of a new host:
    E. Amoeboblast
    F. Amoeboid embryos
(Adapted from Dorier and Degrange)[12]

hoferi. This fungus is an obligate parasite with a complicated life cycle. It has an optimum growing temperature of 10°C and will grow between 3 and 20°C, but not at 30°C. The organism will grow on selected laboratory media (Sabouraud's dextrose agar with 1% bovine serum added or glycerine-peptone agar with 1% bovine serum).[2]

The stage in the life cycle of *I. hoferi* usually observed in fish tissue is the spherical quiescent or resting stage cyst. These cysts range in size from 10 to over 300 micrometers in diameter (Pl. 14B). The interior of the resting stage cyst contains an amorphous mass appearing somewhat disorganized. The cyst has a thick double wall usually surrounded by a connective tissue capsule formed by the host.

More advanced cysts demonstrate distinct nuclei, ranging from a few to several hundred. Endospores germinate within the cyst. Pseudopodia-like hyphae emerge from the wall of the cyst and extend into new host tissue. This method of reproduction is usually referred to as filamentous germination. A second form of reproduction called endogenous or plasmodial germination may also be observed in maturing cysts in which plasmodia penetrate the cyst wall and extend into the host tisuue, usually no more than two or three times the diameter of the mother cyst (Pl. 14C). Each young organism continues to develop into a resting stage cyst until the host tissue rejects further development.

Transmission from one host to another occurs when quiescent cysts are released in the feces or the host dies.

The cysts on the pond bottom or within dead fish tissue mature through filamentous or plasmodial germination to become amoeboblasts within the mother cyst (Fig. 3). The amoeboblasts remain at this stage of development until taken orally by a new host fish. Amoeboid bodies are released from the amoeboid cyst and actively pass through the intestinal wall. They are circulated by the blood to develop into a quiescent cyst wherever they are deposited.

Geographical Distribution:

I. hoferi probably occurs throughout the world, in fresh water and salt water.[33] The organism has been reported most often from parts of Europe, the North Atlantic Ocean and from various parts of the United States.

Susceptible Species:

Probably all fishes are susceptible to infections of *I hoferi*. The known susceptible species include over 73 different fishes, 21 of which are marine fishes.[30] Infections of *I. hoferi* have been found in many species of aquarium fishes, in fresh water or salt water, and among coldwater and warmwater species. The pathogen has also been reported in certain amphibians and copepods.[30,33]

Significant losses have occurred among wild fishes and in cultured fishes. The most notable losses among wild fish populations have been among Atlantic herring. Studies on these fish during two epizootic years (1931 and 1947) indicated that up to 70% of the population was infected during the epizootics. Mortality levels are not given, but heavy losses occurred.[2]

Epizootics of ichthyophonus disease among cultured rainbow trout in the United States during 1962 and 1963 led to increased mortality among the fish, reduced marketability and significant financial losses.[18]

Epizootiology:

The primary route of transmission for *I. hoferi* is oral. Raw fish, fish products or other food containing mature amoeboblasts taken by the fish enter the intestine, where digestive juices rupture the amoeboblast wall. Amoeboid bodies are released in large numbers (Fig. 3). Some of the amoeboid bodies enter the intestinal epithelium and others are released in the feces. Those from the feces are capable of entering other fishes through wounds, skin abrasions or damaged gills. The amoeboid bodies in the blood stream are swept to various organs of the body. Organs of the body with the greatest blood supply are most heavily infected, indicating direct blood transport. The heart, liver, kidney and spleen are the major target organs, but the brain, gills, muscle and other tissues are also commonly infected.

The amoeboid bodies are thought to be phagocytized within two days after entering the blood stream or host tissue.[12] The intraleucocytic stage may continue up to nine days, at which time the connective tissue capsule replaces the leucocyte wall. The developing quiescent bodies continue to enlarge within the connective tissue capsule (Pl. 14B). Asexual reproduction through filamentous or plasmodial germination (Fig. 3) continues with formation of additional quiescent cysts until host tissue prevents further reproduction.

Quiescent cysts remain in the host tissue for the life of the host. Some cysts may be present in the epithelial lining of the stomach, ceca or intestine. These may leave the body of the host in feces and become a part of the flora of the pond or aquarium bottom. They mature to amoeboblasts and are capable of infecting new hosts if taken orally.

The time required for maturation of amoeboblasts in dead fish tissue or on the pond bottom is not known, but experimental evidence indicates between one week and one and a half months. Environmental temperature may be involved in maturation of the cysts. Fishes held in ponds known to contain maturing cysts will develop infections within the time period already noted. Epizootics among cultured trout in the United States during 1962 and 1963 were caused by feeding ground raw carp and other rough fishes seined from Utah Lake, Utah, to trout being reared in Idaho trout farms. No records were kept on time between capture of infected fish from the lake and feeding flesh to cultured fish, but quite often the transfer was direct, *i.e.*, within a few days to a few weeks, depending on whether the rough fishes were ground and fed directly after transport to the fish farm or frozen to be ground and fed within a few weeks.

The length of time an amoeboblast can remain viable in pond bottom detritus or in frozen fish tissue is unknown. Experience indicates the time to be quite extensive, one or more years.

All fishes infected with *I. hoferi* should be considered as carriers of the disease. Each carrier is a potential source of amoeboblasts, either to be shed from the alimentary epithelium and discharged in feces or to mature in the fish tissues on death of the fish. Carriers with slight to moderate infections of the organism may remain unnoticed in a group of fishes and be a source of infection to others. Definite cases of the disease among fishes in a population are certainly potential sources of the etiological agent.

Overcrowding of fishes infected with *I. hoferi* in a fish culture facility or aquarium is conducive to transmission of the organism. Epizootics of ichthyophonus disease among wild-ranging Atlantic herring indicated the highest incidence of infection (average 70%) occurred among fry and fingerlings in shallow water prior to joining offshore sea herring. Reduced water depth and close confinement of young fish was thought to be responsible for increased transmission. The disease incidence among offshore sea herring was much less because of greater water volume and continuous movement of fish into areas with a reduced population of infective stages of the parasite.[16]

The etiological agent of ichthyophonus disease has been transported in infected fishes and infected fish products by humans over long distances. The role of aquatic birds and mammals in the epizootiology of ichthyophonus disease is not known. Amoeboblasts attached to the pellage or feathers of these animals and later be released at another site may be possible. The role of fish-eating birds and mammals as a source of the infective stage of *I. hoferi* has not been investigated. There is the possibility that quiescent cysts with the heavy protective cyst wall could pass through the alimentary tract of these animals to be released as infective units in the feces.

Copepods and other planktonic organisms are involved with the epizootiology of ichthyophonus disease. Experiments proved that intermediate stages of *I. hoferi* eaten by copepods will go through hyphal development, but whether or not they are infective to fishes is not known.[16] There may also be other aquatic organisms besides crustaceans capable of transporting *I. hoferi*.

There is no evidence of transmission of *I. hoferi* infective units in or on fish eggs.

Disease Signs:

Fishes with a slight to moderate infection of *I. hoferi* demonstrate no external signs of the disease. Fishes with marked or extreme infections of the fungus usually have rough or granulomatous skin. The term "sandpaper effect" is used to describe the granulomatous appearance. It is caused by numerous infective units under the skin and underlying muscle, each a swelling necrotic lesion. Some may rupture through the skin, leaving minute openings.

Some fishes, and especially the salmonids, demonstrate marked scoliosis and lordosis (lateral or dorsoventral bending of the body). Deformation of the vertebral column can be severe and interfere with swimming ability (Pl. 14D & Add 3).

Internal signs of ichthyophonus disease depend to some extent on the severity of infection. The kidney, liver, spleen and ventricle of the heart may be swollen and demonstrate white to gray-white lesions. These organs may appear granulomatous if large numbers of lesions are present. The gills, brain, spinal cord and other organs may also have white to gray-white lesions. Muscle tissue may have large purulent necrotic lesions filled with cellular debris, muscle fibers and the fungus. Lordotic and scoliotic fishes will not have excessive numbers of quiescent cysts in and around bendings of the body, as would be expected. Scoliosis and lordosis are usually caused by brain or spinal cord damage or possibly damage to myomeric structures which pull the vertebral column out of line.

Diagnosis:

Ichthyophonus disease is diagnosed by external and internal signs and identification of the fungus. Pieces of infected organs can be excised and placed on a microscope slide with a few drops of water. The tissue sample is squashed with a cover glass or another microscope slide and examined under the microscope. Presence of spherical bodies with double refractive walls, and external signs of the disease are presumptively positive (Pl. 14E). Specific identification and definitive diagnosis of the disease can be accomplished by histopathological examination of infected tissues. Various life stages of the fungus will be noted (Fig. 3). Further identification may be required by culture of the organism. Growth of the organism on solid culture medium may be apparent within five days to two weeks at 10°C. Identification of the same structures usually found in fishes is definitive diagnosis for the disease.

Therapy and Control:

There are no therapeutic procedures for cure of ichthyophonus disease. Fishes with *I. hoferi* infections will carry the infection for life.

Prevention of infection is the only control procedure known. Feeding raw fish or raw fish products to cultured fishes or fishes in aquaria is strongly discouraged. This is especially true if marine fishes or fishes from a body of water in which the fungus is known to exist are used in the feeding regimen. All raw fish or fish products should be cooked until the life stages of the fungus are destroyed before being fed. Any fishes exhibiting signs of ichthyophonus disease in a population should be removed and destroyed. Dead fishes from tanks, raceways, ponds or aquaria known to have *I. hoferi* should be removed daily or more often and destroyed.

The disease can be eliminated from fish culture facilities with cement-lined tanks or raceways or from aquaria, by complete disinfection with chlorine or other strong disinfectants. All nets, brushes and utensils used around infected fishes must also be disinfected at the same time that the facilities are being disinfected.

Ponds with dirt or gravel bottoms pose a difficult task for elimination of *I. hoferi*.[14] Removal of fishes and water, with several months or years of drying under sunshine, may be necessary to eliminate the pathogen from soil or gravel ponds.

Prognosis:

Morbidity levels from ichthyophonus disease may reach 100% of a population among cultured or aquarium fishes. Trout in some trout farms were 100% infected during epizootics of the disease in Idaho during 1962 and 1963. There were no infected trout at trout farms where no raw fish or fish products were used in the trout diet.

Examination of offshore herring indicated a 20% morbidity with greater than 70% morbidity among shoreline herring.[16] The morbidity of ichthyophonus disease in other wild fish populations is unknown. Probably the infection level is quite low, except in those instances when fishes are unnaturally crowded.

Mortality from ichthyophonus disease may be quite low even though all fishes in a population are known to be infected. A description of "excessive mortalities" has been given for trout in infected trout farms.

Mortality levels reached tremendous numbers during epizootics of this disease among Atlantic herring. The shore of bays and coves were white with the bodies of dead fish.[32] The actual percentage mortality was not given because the population size was unknown.

Mortality among aquarium fishes is usually low, with a few fishes dying over a long period of time.

Practical Aspects:

The most important practical aspect of ichthyophonus disease is prevention. Fishes or fish products with a dubious history or demonstrated presence of spherical cysts should be thoroughly cooked before being fed to other fishes. An example to demonstrate an unwise practice in a fish culture facility happened in the large trout-growing area of south-central Idaho. Trout in at least one facility were fed ground, raw rough fishes (suckers, chubs, carp and others) taken from the Snake River. The water from the fish culture facility returned directly to the Snake River. The practice made a perfect transmission circle for the pathogen—from river fishes to cultured fish and back to river fishes. The practice was eliminated when the consequences became evident by appearance of ichthyophonus disease among the cultured fish.

Fishes known to harbor *I. hoferi* should not be transported from one geographic area to another. Fishes cultured for sport should not be stocked into open waters if an *I. hoferi* infection is known or suspected. The organism is not transmissible to humans or other homeothermic animals but can be transmitted to other fishes at water temperatures up to 30°C.

Branchiomycosis

Branchiomycosis is a fungal disease involving gill tissue. It was first described in 1912 in carp in Europe.[29] The disease is acute, subacute or chronic in severity. The fungus reduces the blood supply to the gills, causing loss of oxygenation of the blood and death (necrosis) of gill tissues. Necrotic gill tissue sloughs away, leading to the more common names of "gill rot" or "European gill rot." The disease has been of great importance among cultured fishes of Europe. The pathogen is an opportunistic parasite, and the disease it causes is primarily environmentally induced. Presence of organic contaminants, algal blooms and water temperatures above 20°C are conducive to epizootics in those geographical areas where the fungus is enzootic.[2] Low dissolved oxygen and low pH have a definite role in epizootics of the disease.

Etiological Agent:

There are two organisms associated with branchiomycosis, *Branchiomyces sanguinis* and *Branchiomyces demigrans*.[29,38] *B. sanguinis* is found primarily in the gill filaments and gill lamellar capillaries, and *B. demigrans* is found in the parenchymal tissues of the gills. Both produce branched, non-septate hyphae. The reproductive unit for both species is a syncytium, an enlargement of a portion of the hyphae within which asexual spores are produced. *B. sanguinis* hyphae have a thin hyphal wall (0.2 micrometer; the *B. demigrans* hyphal wall is much thicker (0.5-0.7 micrometer). Spores of *B. sanguinis* are 5 to 9 micrometers in diameter, those of *B. demigrans* 12 to 17 micrometers). These two characteristics and the location within gill tissues are used for identification of the two species.

Both species release spores from the syncytium through an extramatrical discharge tube. *B. sanguinis* spores are usually released into the capillary of the lamella or filament, those of *B. demigrans* through the tube to the environmental water.

Both species of fungi grow at temperatures between 14 and 35°C. The optimum growth temperature appears to be between 25 and 32°C; at least these two temperatures are more conducive to rapid development of epizootics among fishes.

The nutrient requirements of the two species are not complex. A simple medium prepared from peptone water and glucose, with the pH adjusted to 5.8, will support growth and reproduction. A medium prepared from 10% broth of duck dung, 10% gelatin and 0.1% citric acid (final pH 5.8) supported growth and reproduction of *B. sanguinis*.[4] Both species will grow on Sabouraud's dextrose agar.[10]

Geographical Distribution:

Branchiomycosis has been reported from many parts of Europe (Germany, Czechoslovakia, Poland, Italy and Russia[4,5,17,21,38]), Japan,[3] India[35] and the United States.[3,22,24] Its first appearance in the United States was apparently in 1972, but the disease was not specifically identified until 1973 when it occurred in Arkansas.[22] So far the disease has been limited to the central and south-central United States.

Susceptible Species:

Probably all freshwater fishes are susceptible to branchiomycosis. The number of species in which the disease has been reported increases as fish disease diagnosticians become more aware of the disease signs and diagnostic procedures used for identification of the etiological agent.

Branchiomycosis has been diagnosed in European carp, crucian carp, European catfish, northern pike, tench, sheath fish, Japanese eels, guppies, great muraena, channa fish, largemouth bass, striped bass, golden shiner and rainbow trout.[3,6] Investigations in several lakes of northern Italy demonstrated the fungus to be present in the gill tissues of 11 fish species. There had been heavy mortality among bleak fish, and curiosity led to the investigations of the pathogen among other fishes in the lakes.[18] Perch, burbot and shad in the lakes were the only species not infected.

Epizootiology:

Branchiomycosis is transmitted from water to gill tissue. Fungal spores attach to the gills, germinate and produce hyphae. The hyphae penetrate gill epithelium and, depending on species, locate in the gill epithelium or within capillaries. *B. demigrans* seeks tissue with lower oxygen tension (gill epithelium), and *B. sanguinis* apparently requires a higher oxygen supply. Fungal mycelium extends into gill tissue, reducing the blood supply and causing necrosis of gill tissue. The necrotic tissues, containing fungal hyphae and syncytia with maturing spores, are sloughed and spores released into the water. The spores are probably capable of transmitting directly back to fishes without further maturation because material from necrotic gills will produce the fungus on laboratory media very shortly after preparation of cultures.[18]

Some fungal hyphae and spores may be released into the blood stream of the fish. The spores and individual hyphae have been reported in sections of liver and spleen taken from fishes with infected gills.[4] The organisms confined to internal organs have no route of spore transmission and probably have no relationship to the epizootiology of the disease but contribute to mortality.

Spores released from necrotic gill tissue, and which do not return directly to gills of fishes, remain suspended in the water or fall to the bottom of the pond. They remain there as a part of the pond flora, capable of continuing the infection among fishes of the pond. Ponds with bottom sediments rich in organic matter support the continued growth of the fungi, increasing the spore population within the pond.

Environmental characteristics of a body of water control the success or failure of the pathogen to maintain the disease in fishes. Branchiomycosis occurs in carp ponds in early spring, when water temperature reaches 14°C or higher. Presence of organic matter, algal blooms and dissolved fertilizer in the body of water all contribute to the early seasonal epizootics. Water temperatures exceeding 20°C, and especially temperatures between 25 and 32°C, are responsible for increased growth of the fungi within the fish gills and in organic matter of the pond. Water temperature in late summer (July and August) which is favorable to rapid fungal growth is responsible for most epizootics of branchiomycosis reported among fishes of the northern hemisphere.

Growth of the two *Branchiomyces* species is stimulated by slightly acid pH of the water. The most devastating epizootics among fish populations occur when the pH is between 5.8 and 6.5[10] Low dissolved oxygen, reduced water flow or volume and crowded conditions among fishes will also enhance morbidity and mortality from branchiomycosis.

Fishes with chronic branchiomycosis act as carriers of the disease. Clinical cases are responsible for maintenance of a high spore population within the environment and in direct transmission of water-borne spores to gills.

The incubation period for branchiomycosis is temperature-related. The disease has been known to develop rapidly (two to four days) under favorable conditions.[2] Laboratory cultures of *B. sanguinis* held at room temperature (probably in the middle 20's°C) produced spores on the fourteenth day of culture.[4] A similar incubation period could be assumed in living fish tissue.

Transportation of fishes with branchiomycosis infections from infected geographical areas to noninfected areas may spread the disease. Chronic cases of the disease may demonstrate few signs yet be capable of releasing viable fungal spores before, during and after being moved. Raw fish products, especially those containing gill tissue infected with *Branchiomyces* sp., can also be a potential source of fungal spores to be moved from one geographical area to another. There is no indication that fish eggs are infected with the pathogen, except fungal spores may be carried with water in which eggs are maintained.

Movement of spores from one geographical area to another on the feathers of aquatic birds is possible but has not been investigated. The main source of infection or reinfection among fishes is fungal spores in water and detritus on the pond bottom.

Disease Signs:

Fishes with acute to subacute branchiomycosis may be weak and lethargic. They may be in respiratory distress and cannot tolerate handling.[22] The acute course of the disease is usually observed during the warm months of the year. The fungus developing on or in gill tissue penetrates blood vessels, causing obstruction, congestion and necrosis. Gills may appear bright red from impaired circulation. Some areas of the gill may be white to brown depending on the stage of necrosis (Pl. 14F). Subacute cases of the disease develop more slowly, and definite marbling appears on different sections of the gills as necrotic disintegration advances. The gills become ragged and corroded in appearance.

There are usually no disease signs during chronic cases of branchiomycosis.[4] Pale areas of the gills may or may not be present. Some lamellae may appear swollen with fungal thrombi and slight to moderate necrosis.[2]

Diagnosis:

Three findings are essential for the diagnosis of branchiomycosis: history of presence of the disease in a geographical area, disease signs noted in the infected fish and detection and identification of fungus in gill tissue. Signs of respiratory distress in fishes located in a branchiomycosis enzootic area, especially during the warm period of the year, are suspect for the disease or other similar respiratory disease.

Pieces of gill arch mounted in water on microscope slides and examined microscopically may reveal gill necrosis in cases of branchiomycosis. Necrotic tissues may slough, leaving gill arches without soft tissue.[22] Squash preparations of gill tissue examined under subdued light through the microscope or by phase microscopy may reveal fungal hyphae and spores within the tissue. Sections cut and stained from gills suspected of being infected with *B. sanguinis* or *B. demigrans* should demonstrate the hyphae, syncytia and spores in cases of branchiomycosis (Pl. 15A, 15B). Disease signs and presence of fungus in parenchymal gill tissue or gill capillaries are presumptively positive for branchiomycosis.

The two species of *Branchiomyces* can be identified from cut and stained sections of infected gills and measurements made of hyphae and spores.[32] Position of fungal elements in gill tissue also may aid in identification. Pieces of infected gill tissue can be cultured on Sabouraud's dextrose agar, peptone-dextrose agar or other media. The pH of the media should be about 5.8 and the cultures should be incubated at 25 to 30°C. Separation of the fungal growth from contaminating bacteria is usually difficult.

Measurements of hyphae and spores taken from cultures can be used to identify the organisms to species.[22],[38] The hyphal wall of *B. demigrans* is 0.5 to 0.7 micrometer thick; the spores are 12 to 17 micrometers in diameter. The hyphal wall of *B. sanguinis* is near 0.2 micrometer thick and spores 5 to 9 micrometers in diameter. Diameter of filaments cannot be used for species identification because the measurements overlap (*B. demigrans*, 13 to 38 micrometers; *B. sanguinis* 8 to 30 micrometers.

Therapy and Control:

Strict sanitation and disinfection are essential for disease control in those fish-holding facilities with enzootic branchiomycosis. Dead fishes should be collected daily or more often if possible during acute to subacute epizootics and burned or deeply buried. Ponds with enzootic branchiomycosis should be dried and treated with calcium oxide (quicklime) or 2 to 3 kg of copper sulfate per hectare (1.78 to 2.42 lb per acre).[2,37]

Epizootics of the disease among nonfood fishes can be treated with malachite green at 1:10,000,000 (0.1 mg/L) for extended periods of time or 1:3,300,000 (0.3 mg/L) for 12-hour treatments.[10,22] Formalin has been used at 1:67,000 (15 mg/L) in a continuous bath when gill tissues are extremely damaged and at 1:40,000 (25 mg/L) when gills are more nearly normal.

Fishes known to harbor branchiomycosis should not be transported into geographical areas known to be free of the pathogens. *B. sanguinis* has been identified in a limited area of the central and south-central United States, and great care should be taken to prevent movement of the fungus into noninfected areas.

Prognosis:

Morbidity levels among fish populations with epizootics of branchiomycosis usually reach 100%, depending on fish species and susceptibility. Mortality levels may reach 30 to 50% of the population during late summer epizootics, especially in fish-holding facilities with high loading of organic material, acidic pH and a water temperature over 25°C.[22] An estimated loss of 20 to 50 tons of bleak fish occurred during a 1970 epizootic of branchyomycosis in one lake in northern Italy.[17]

The disease is considered to be a major problem in commercial fish production in Europe. Not enough experience has been gained on morbidity and mortality among fishes of the United States to know how native fishes will respond to the disease. Species of fishes native to the United States may be more or less susceptible to the fungus than European or Asian fishes. Generally, however, branchiomycosis usually kills about 30% of the fishes during an acute or subacute epizootic, the remaining fishes making a complete recovery.[3]

Practical Aspects:

Individuals who have been most closely associated with branchiomycosis feel the disease is more of an environmental problem than a contagious disease. Care in stocking fish-holding facilities and reduction of organic matter loading of water or pond bottom, as well as good sanitation, disinfection and pond management, are es-

sential for control of the disease. Branchiomycosis has been placed on quarantine and restricted movement lists by many states of the United States. Some fish health persons feel it should not receive this notoriety. However, if the pathogen can be limited to particular parts of a country, fish culturists, fish managers and fishery administrators will not need to contend with it.

Epizootics of the disease among wild-ranging fishes are associated with eutrophication of the habitat. There are large numbers of water bodies in the southern and central United States which are eutrophying at a rapid rate. Temperatures in these waters range between 20 and 30°C during the late summer or early autumn. All such bodies of water are potential locations for a branchiomycosis epizootic if the pathogen is present.

Fish health people of the United States should take heed of experience with branchiomycosis in Europe and other parts of the world. The one presently available practical control procedure for this disease is quarantine, restriction of movement and a hope for containment of the fungus within the geographical area to which it has been confined.

Those parts of the United States which had epizootics of branchiomycosis have both commercial and governmentally controlled fish culture facilities. The bait minnow industry, for example, is a large and growing industry. Relying on shipping the product into most of the United States, where the minnows are subsequently used by sport fishermen. A pathogen widely distributed in the bait minnow culture area of the United States is a potential source of the pathogen, with a built-in method of movement throughout the country. Minnows may escape the sport fisherman and pass the pathogen along to native fishes in the body of water into which they escape. Would it not be more scientifically sound to attempt to control movement of such a pathogen before it is spread to all parts of the country?

Experience with elimination of the fungi from ponds in which bass were being reared was apparently successful. The pond bottom was dried and tilled for three years before fish were returned to the pond. The disease did not recur when fish were again stocked into the pond.[5]

Warmwater fish culture facilities are notorious for algal blooms and increased loads of organic matter during the warm period of each year. Each pond is a potential problem for the owner if *Branchiomyces* species are allowed to be introduced. Possibly the disease need not be quarantined or its movement restricted by government agencies, if fish culturists use care in importing fish for stocking and attempt to eliminate the fungal pathogen if it does appear.

Selected References

1. Alexeieff, A. 1914. "Sur le cycle evolutif d'une haplosporidie (*Ichthyosporidium gasterophilum* Caullery et Mesnil)," *Arch. Zool. Gen. N. et R.*, 54:30-44.

1a. Alderman, D. J. and J. L. Polglase. 1984. "A comparative investigation of the effects of fungicides on *Saprolegnia parasitica* and *Aphanomyces astaci*." *Trans. Br. Mycol. Soc.*, 83:313-318.

2. Amlacher, E. 1970. *Textbook of fish diseases*. T.F.H. Publ., Neptune, NJ. p. 166.

3. Anonymous. 1978. "Branchiomyces rides again," *Fish. Health Sec./Am. Fish. Soc. Newsletter*, 6(4):10.

4. Apazidi, L. K. 1959. "Development of the fungus agent of branchiomycosis of fish," *Veterinariya*, 39:37-39 (in Russian). Trans. by Howland, R. M., Div. Fish. Res., Bureau Sport Fish & Wildl. U.S. Dept. Interior, Washington, D.C.

4a. Bailey, T. A. 1984. "Effects of twenty-five compounds on four species of aquatic fungi (Saprolegniales) pathogenic to fish." *Aquacult.*, 38:97-104.

5. Barthelmes, D., T. Mattheis and J. Meyer. 1968. "Kiemenfaule bei Regenbogenforellen," *Dt. Fischerei-Ztg.*, 15:296-300.

6. Bauer, O. N., V. A. Musselius and T. A. Strelkov. 1969. *Bolezni prudovyk ryb (Diseases of pondfish)*. Izdatel'stvo "Kolos," Moscow (English trans., U.S. Dep. Commerce, 1973, TT 72-50070). 220p.

7. Caullery, M. and F. Mesnil. 1905. "Sur des haplosporidies parasite de poissons marins," *Compt. Rend. Soc. Biol. Paris*, 56:640-643.

8. Cline, T. F. and G. Post. 1972. "Therapy for trout eggs infected with saprolegnia," *Prog. Fish-Cult.*, 34:148-151.

9. Daniel, G. 1933. "Studies on *Ichthyophonus hoferi*, a parasitic fungi of the herring (*Clupea harengus*). I. The parasite as it is found in the herring," *Am. J. Hyg.*, 17:267-276.

10. Danko, G. and J. Szabo. 1966. "On the branchia putrifaction of carp," *Magyar. Allatorvosok Lap.* (December, 1966).

11. Davis, H. S. and E. C. Lazar. 1940. "A new fungus disease of trout," *Trans. Am. Fish. Soc.*, 70:264-271.

12. Dorier, A. and C. Degrange. 1961. "L'evolution de l'*Ichthyosporidium* (*Ichthyophonus*) *hoferi* (Plehn et Muslow) chez les salmonides d'elevage (Truite arcenciel et saumon de fontaine)," *Trav. Lab. Hydrobiol. Piscicult., Univ. Grenoble.*, 52.

13. Egusa, S. 1965. "The existence of a primary infectious disease in the so-called "fungus disease" in pond-reared eels," *Bull. Jap. Soc. Sci. Fish.*, 31:517-526.

14. Erickson, J. D. 1965. "Report on the problem of *Ichthyosporidium* in the rainbow trout," *Prog. Fish-Cult.*, 27:179-184.

15. Fijan, N. 1969. "Systemic mycosis in channel catfish," *Bull. Wildl. Dis. Assoc.*, 5:109-110.

16. Fish, F. F. 1934. "A fungus disease of fishes of the Gulf of Maine," *Parasitol.*, 26:1-16.

17. Grimaldi, E. 1971. "Heavy mortalities inside the populations of bleak (*Alburnus alborella*) in the lakes of northern Italy caused by a gill infection due to fungi of the genus *Branchiomyces*," *Riv. Ital. di Piscic. Ittiopat.*, 6:11-14 (*Sport Fishery Abs.* 13947, 1971).

18. Grimaldi, E., R. Peduzzi, G. Cavicchioli, G. Giussani and E. Spreafico. 1973. "Diffusa infezione branchiale de funghi attributi al genere *Branchiomyces Plehn* (*Phycomycetes saprolegniales*) a carico dell' ittiofauna di laghi stuati a nord e a sud delle Alpi," *Mem. Inst. Ital. Idrobiol.* 30:61-96.

19. Hofer, B. 1893. "Eine Salmonidenerkrankung," *Allg. Fischereizeitung*, No. 11.

20. Hoshina, T. and M. Oakubo. 1956. "Studies on saprolegniasis of the eel," *J. Tokyo. Univ. Fish.*, 42:1-13.

21. Lucky, Z. 1970. "The occurrence of branchyomycosis in the *Siluris glanis*," *Acta. Veterinaria Brno*, 39: 187-192.

22. Meyer, F. P. and J. A. Robinson. 1973. "Branchyomycosis: a new fungal disease of North American fishes," *Prog. Fish-Cult.*, 33:74-77.

23. Moore-Landecker, E. 1972. *Fundamentals of the fungi*. Prentice-Hall, Inc. Englewood Cliffs, NJ. 482p.

24. Neish, G. A. and G. C. Hughes. 1980. *Diseases of fishes. Book 6. Fungal diseases of fishes.* Snieszko, S. F. and H. R. Axelrod, eds. T.F.H. Publ. Inc., Neptune City, NJ. 159p.

25. Nolard-Tintigner, N. 1974. "Contribution a l'etude de la Saprolegniuse des poissons en region tropicale," *Acad. r. Sci. outre-mer, Cl. Sci. nat. med. (N.S.),* 19:1-58.

26. Pauley, G. B. 1967. "Prespawning adult salmon mortality associated with a fungus of the genus *Dermocystidium*," *J. Fish. Res. Bd. Can.,* 24:843-848.

27. Petit, A. 1913. "Observations sur l'*Ichthyosporidium* et sur la maladie qu'il provoque chez la truite," *Ann. Inst. Pasteur., Paris,* 27:986-1008, Pls. XIII-XIV.

28. Petit, A. 1911. "A propos du microorganisme producteur de la Trammelkankheit: *Ichthyosporidium* ou *Ichthyophonus*," *Compt. Rend. Soc. Biol., Paris,* 70: 1045-1047.

29. Plehn, M. 1912. "Eine neue Karpfenkrankheit und ihr Erreger *Branchiomyces sanguinis*," *Zentroalbl. f. Bakt. I. Orig.,* 62:129-135.

30. Reichenbach-Klinke, H. 1973. *Fish pathology.* T.F.H. Publ., Neptune, NJ. p. 102-123.

31. Ross, A. J. and W. T. Yasutake. 1973. "*Scolecobasidium humicola*, a fungal pathogen of fish," *J. Fish.* Res. Bd. Can., 30:994-995.

32. Sindermann, C. and A. Rosenfield. 1954. *Diseases of fishes of the western North Atlantic. I. Diseases of the sea herring (Clupea harengus). Res. Bull. 18. Dept. of Sea and Shore Fish.* Vicky-Hill Building, Augusta, ME. 23p.

33. Sindermann, C. J. and L. W. Scattergood. 1954. *Diseases of fishes of the western North Atlantic. II. Ichthyosporidium disease of the sea herring (Clupea harengus). Res. Bull. 19. Dept. Sea and Shore Fish.* Biol. Lab., Brandeis Univ. 40p.

34. Sprague, V. 1965. "*Ichthyosporidium* Caullery and Mesnil, 1905, the name of a genus of fungi or a genus of sporozoans?," *Syste. Zool.,* 14:110-114.

35. Srivastava, G. C. and R. C. Srivastava. 1976. "A new host record for *Branchiomyces sanguinis* Plehn," Dept. of Bot., St. Andrews Coll. Gorakhpur 273 001, India, Reprinted: *Curr. Sci.,* Dec. 20, 1976. 45(24):874.

36. Sun, S. H. 1962. *Introductory mycology.* John Wiley & Sons, New York City & London. 613p.

37. van Duijn, C. 1973. *Diseases of fishes.* Charles C. Thomas, Publ., Springfield, IL. 372p.

38. Wundsch, H. H. 1929. "Untersuchungen uber die Kiemenfaule bei Fischen. II. Eine besondere Art der "Kiemenfaule" bie Hechten un Scheien," *Zeit. f. Fish. u.d. Hilfs.,* 27:287-293.

Chapter VI

VIRUS DISEASES OF FISHES

The word "virus" was first used to describe a poison, toxin or soluble noxious agent. The term "filterable virus" was used because the supernatant from bacterial filtration indicated that a "filterable" noxious agent had passed through the filter. The term "filterable virus" has been changed to "virus" by common usage. Eventually, viruses were found to be particulate and not a soluble toxin or poison.

Diseases caused by infections of viruses in fishes have received intensive study since about 1960. This date can be contrasted to the fact that viruses involved with diseases of plants and higher vertebrates have been studied since 1892. The fish disease virologist has taken advantage of successes and failures of earlier virologists. Thus, the progress toward understanding fish viral diseases seems to have been more rapid than the early studies on plant and homeothermic animal viral diseases.

Study of viruses must take a different approach than the study of bacteria or fungi. This is partly because of the nature of the virus and partly because of viral structure and physiology. The size of viruses reduces the ease at which they can be observed, although the electron microscope permits observation of the virus in infected tissue and places these observations within the realm of diagnostic use.

Viruses do not have nuclei or the array of organelles used in the study of bacteria, fungi or other microorganisms. The single viral particle (virion) has no metabolic apparatus for maintenance or reproduction. The virion depends on the synthesizing structures of the host cell for replication. Viruses, therefore, are obligate parasites in the truest sense.

All virions are composed of nucleic acid, ribonucleic acid (RNA) or deoxyribonucleic acid (DNA) enclosed in a protein coat called a capsid. Capsids are either repeating protein molecules (called structural units) surrounding the nucleic acid of the virion or aggregates of structural units ·called capsomeres. The nucleic acid surrounded by the capsid is called a nucleocapsid. Some virions have an envelope surrounding the nucleocapsid: others have no such structure and are called "naked" viruses. Viral envelopes are drived from the host cell and contain lipid. Envelope lipids are responsible for sensitivity of the virion to treatment with ether or other solvents (Fig. 4).

The system of viral nomenclature has taken many directions over the years. Shape of the virion has been utilized. Nearly all viruses infecting animals are either spherical or rod-shaped. All spherical viruses have nucleocapsids which are actually an icosahedral (20-sided) shape. Rod-shaped virions have a helical nucleic acid symmetry. The orderliness of viral shape is confused by those viruses which do not belong to the icosahedral or helical symmetry. These are called "complex" or "binal" viruses. The Poxviruses are an example of this type of virus. Many Poxviruses are brick-shaped with an outer multilayered membrane-like organelle surrounding a biconcave core.

Early nomenclature of viruses was derived from the geographical area where the disease was first described or the virus first isolated. An example is the Egtved virus, first noted among trout near Egtved, Jutland. Another is the classification of a group of viruses, the first member of which was isolated near Coxsackie, New York. This group has been called the Coxsackie viruses.[1]

No official system of classification has been adopted, but the most used classification is on the basis of type of nucleic acid in the virion—i.e., riboviruses or deoxyriboviruses. These two classifications are subdivided by symmetry of the nucleocapsid, naked or enveloped, number of nucleic acid strands, size and shape, and number of capsomeres of icosahedral virions or diameter of the helix of helical viruses.[48] The system is useful to the fish health diagnostician because most of the viruses associated with fish viral diseases have been placed in this classification.[62]

Methods of maintaining viruses outside the host were devised during the early part of this century. The procedures were developed for use with viruses of humans and other higher vertebrates. Cell culture techniques in which human and laboratory homeothermic animal cells were maintained in vitro (within glass), were developed by 1950. Cell lines from piscine sources were more or less a novelty to laboratory practices with fishes through the 1950's. There were no standard cell lines, and fish health diagnosticians attempted to grow cell sheets from specific organs of fish as needed. The techniques were laborious and somewhat uncertain. Usually the cells were grown on longitudinally cut cover glasses, precariously and laboriously laid within culture tubes and the

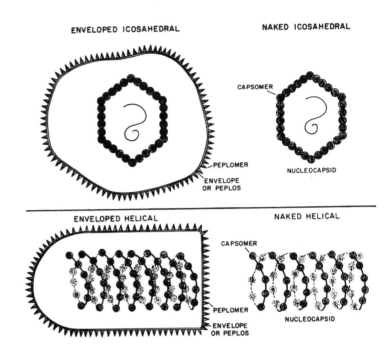

ENVELOPED ICOSAHEDRAL   NAKED ICOSAHEDRAL

CAPSOMER

PEPLOMER

ENVELOPE
OR PEPLOS

NUCLEOCAPSID

ENVELOPED HELICAL   NAKED HELICAL

CAPSOMER

PEPLOMER

ENVELOPE
OR PEPLOS

NUCLEOCAPSID

Fig. 4: Diagrammatic representation of typical viral particles.

tubes balanced on various kinds or racks. The development of a standard rainbow trout gonad cell line in about 1960 came at a time when research on fish viruses was expanding. The number of teleost cell lines available to the fish virologist increased to over 60 by 1980, and each year new cell lines continue to be initiated. Some of the cell lines have been through hundreds of passages and are available through the American Type Culture Collection in Bethesda, Maryland.[39a,91a]

Better glassware and plasticware have been devised for use in growing cell sheets and have been incorporated into the study of fish viruses.[97]

Methods of isolation and identification of fish viruses continue to be developed. Many of the methods utilize sheets of cells which are susceptible to cytopathologic effects from the virus. Viral dilution and inoculation into cell sheets, resulting in focal cell destruction (plaque formation),[104] have proved useful in estimating viral population and virulence. Antiserums have been prepared from some of the fish viruses and serum neutralization techniques found useful for identification of certain viruses. Fluorescent antibody techniques are being studied, but problems with purification of viral-induced antibody protein for fluorescent conjugation continue.[37]

The prevention and control of fish virus diseases are serious problems, especially among cultured fishes. There are no antibiotic or chemotherapeutic compounds which are effective virustats or virucides. Test and slaughter, quarantine and restriction of movement, and sanitation and disinfection procedures are the only practical control methods for fish virus diseases. One of the greatest problems in the control of fish virus diseases has been location of viral carriers in the tremendous populations of fishes found in many fish culture facilities.

Control of certain virus diseases of higher vertebrates has been possible by use of vaccines. This method continues to have limited use for control of fish viral diseases, even though much research has been performed on vaccine development.[12]

There is a growing list of virus diseases of fishes.[45,97] Some are economically or biologically important. Those diseases which have had the most thorough study or seem to be the most important among fishes will be discussed.

Infectious Pancreatic Necrosis

Infectious pancreatic necrosis, or IPN, is an acute to subacute highly contagious disease of young salmonid fishes. The disease was apparently known prior to 1940, but no publications were prepared until that year.[47] The disease was called acute catarrhal enteritis at that time because of the typical opalescent mucus plug characteristically found in the intestine of obvious cases of the disease. This name has a great deal of merit but was lost when tissue samples taken from fingerling brook trout in 1954 consistently demonstrated necrosis of pancreatic tissue.[110] The disease had occurred in several fish culture facilities in Connecticut, Pennsylvania and West Virginia, which suggested its infectious nature.

Early work on the disease led to the belief that IPN was not an infectious disease but was associated with rapid water temperature rise in the spring or with malnutrition of some sort.[20,47] Malnutrition was suspected because early workers saw no disease signs other than the activity of the fish prior to death and the complete stoppage of bile flow with a tremendous increase in mucus secretion in the intestine. The alimentary tract was always free of food or feces. Descriptions of these conditions were enough to demonstrate that all of the IPN epizootics of 1954 were the same as acute catarrhal enteritis, a disease considered as being noninfectious in the 1940's. Observations in 1954 strongly suggested that the disease was actually an infectious disease probably caused by a virus. Publications in 1957 and 1959 removed all doubt as to the viral nature of IPN and suggested that a virus of the Coxsackie group was the etiological agent.[75,76] The infectious pancreatic necrosis virus, or IPNV, was isolated *in vitro* in 1960, definitely establishing the disease as being caused by a virus.[101]

Etiological Agent:

The etiological agent of IPN is an unclassified virus.[62] The virus was initially placed into the Coxsackie group of piconraviruses, primarily because of its pancreatic tropicity. Subsequently this classification was refuted. Much evidence on the virus supports its classification as a Reovirus (respiratory-enteric-orphan virus) or a reovirus-like virus.[19,91a,106]

The IPNV is icosahedral 57 to 74 nm in diameter.[41,49,53a] It has a double stranded RNA genome.[106] Three serotypes of IPNV have been differentiated: VR299 (this major North American strain will cross react antigenically somewhat with two other North American strains; Buhl, Idaho and Powder Mill, N.H. strains) and two European strains designated Ab and Sp. Ab is also called the Denmark strain, and Sp the French strain. Sp is more closely related to North American virus and Ab more closely resembles the European eel virus (EEV).[51a] The three strains are important only from the standpoint of pathogenicity and species susceptibility.

The virus is resistant to heating at 60°C for 15 minutes and retains slight activity in physiological solutions held at 60°C for one hour.[95] The virus has been known to survive in air at laboratory temperature for 5 but not 6 weeks. It survives well in seawater, loss of one strain was only slight when held for 10 weeks at 4° or 10°C. One study demonstrated 99% of infectivity was lost in freshwater at 4°C over a 10 to 12 week period but residual infectivity was still present after 24 weeks.[21a] The virus is not effected by lipid solvents. It retains its viability in fish tissue frozen and stored at −20°C for five or more years and in 50% glycerin at 4°C for two and a half or more years. Replication of the virus is supported by trout gonad (RTG-2), fathead minnow (FTM), brown bullhead (BB or CCL) and many other cell lines. The virus replicates within the cytoplasm of cells and is neutralized by IPN antiserum.

Geographical Distribution:

Infectious pancreatic necrosis was first identified in the northeastern part of the United States. The disease has subsequently been diagnosed throughout the trout-rearing and some salmon-rearing areas of the United States and in Canada.[112] It was found in southern France in 1964[72] and has now been diagnosed in many parts of Europe, including the British Isles.[72] The disease is present in trout-rearing and some salmon-rearing facilities in Japan.[71]

Susceptible Species:

Infectious pancreatic necrosis is a disease of young trout and salmon. It was first identified in brook trout, the young of which are highly susceptible. The rainbow trout has approximately the same susceptibility as brook trout. Young cutthroat trout are the next most susceptible, with brown trout the least susceptible of the trout.[95] Young Atlantic salmon, coho salmon, masou salmon and other salmon species are also susceptible.[70,91] The most rapidly growing fry (alevins) of the species are more susceptible. Susceptibility among these fishes is greatest shortly after absorbing the yolk and initiation of active feeding (*i.e.*, swimup fry).

All trout and salmon species begin to lose susceptibility with age. Trout over six months of age, for example, are usually refractive to natural or laboratory infections of the virus. Some strains of rainbow trout lose susceptibility completely by the time they have reached six weeks of age. This is especially true if they are being reared in very hard water. These fishes do not demonstrate clinical signs of the disease but can become virus carriers.[79a]

The virus has been isolated from white suckers residing in the tailwaters of trout culture facilities in which the trout are IPN carriers. No clinical signs or mortality from IPN was noted in white suckers.[78] The virus has been associated with mortality in striped bass fry,[72a] southern flounder, Atlantic silverside, spot, Atlantic croaker, silver perch, hogchoker and striped mullet,[44a] all in estuarine waters. Evidence strongly suggested IPNV to be responsible for mortality in these fish, even though water salinity was greater 20⁰/₀₀ (parts per thousand). Epizootics with severe mortality in which IPNV was isolated have been reported in European and Japanese eel alevins in Japan.[53a] The IPN virus had been considered as a mortality factor in salmonids (trout, salmon and char) only. These epizootics indicate species of other fish families besides salmonids may be highly susceptible.

IPN virus has been isolated from carp, perch, roach, bream, pike, discus fish, zebra danio and goldfish.[1a,1b,2a,31a,53a] Fish from which the virus was isolated appeared to be healthy and asymtomatic.

Epizootiology:

The most important sources of IPNV are ovarian fluid of infected (carrier) female fishes and feces or intestinal discharge from clinical cases of the disease. Transmission is directly from gravid females to developing eggs. IPNV has been found in seminal fluid of the

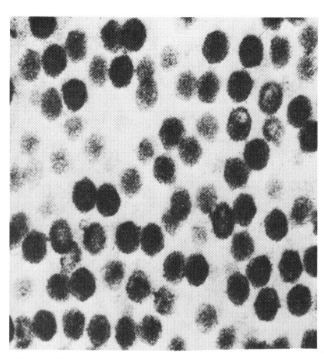

Fig. 5: Infectious pancreatic necrosis virus is icosahedral in shape, demonstrating six-sided structure in ultra-thin sections and viewed under the electron microscope. The virus is 55 to 57 nm in diameter. (282,000 X) Photo by Lightner.

male, so transmission is probably possible from infected males to eggs.[1a] Experiments demonstrated that much of the virus can be washed from the outside of the egg and that transmission must either be from viral particles which have penetrated the egg shell or from virus adhered to the outside of the egg so strongly that it cannot be washed away and remains to infect hatching fry.[95]

Clinical cases of IPN shed tremendous numbers of viral particles into the water. A million or more infectious doses have been demonstrated per milliliter of intestinal discharge from moribund fish. The virus is easily isolated from water discharged from fish culture facilities undergoing epizootics of the disease.

There is no evidence on the exact route IPNV is transmitted from infected host to noninfected host. Virus is probably passed by water from infected to noninfected fry. Nets, brushes or other hatchery utensils can carry the virus from infected fry or fingerlings to noninfected fishes even though no direct water exchange is made.

Water flowing from fish hatcheries in which epizootic IPN is occurring can carry the virus to noninfected fish. Fish surviving epizootics of IPN are usually IPNV carriers, or at least a high percentage of them will be carriers for their entire life and may serve as a source of virus. Thus, a trout or salmon culture facility contaminated with the virus can be a continuing source of the virus.

The incubation period for IPN is not known but depends on the virulence of the virus, water temperature, susceptibility of the host and other factors. Injection of tissue-cultured virus into fry at the life stage when alimentation begins will produce clinical IPN within five to seven days. Natural exposure to the virus or release of virus into water which subsequently flows to very young but feeding fry will cause the overt disease within one to two weeks. Peak mortality occurs after about four days to two weeks, depending on susceptibility and water temperature. The time at which infected fry begin to shed virus in feces is not known. Large quantities of virus continue to be shed for several weeks if the fish survives and will gradually subside to a continuous level, usually for the life of the fish.

IPN epizootics have ocurred at water temperatures as low as 4°C and as high as 18°C. The virus replicates slowly in RTG-2 cells held at 4°C. It replicates rapidly when incubated at 20 to 23°C, usually causing advanced cytopathic effects within 18 to 36 hours.[106] Extremely high mortality has been noted during epizootics of IPN among rainbow trout fry held at water temperatures between 10 and 15.5°C.

Transportation of IPNV-infected eggs or fishes from one geographical area to another has been, and will continue to be, a part of the epizootiology of the disease. There is much evidence to demonstrate that infected trout or salmon eggs have been responsible for transmitting the virus from IPNV-contaminated fishes within fish culture facilities to noninfected fishes within noninfected fish hatcheries.

Stocking of IPNV carrier fishes may be responsible for transmitting the disease to wild-ranging fish populations. The practice in many parts of the world of trapping upstream migrating spawning fishes as a source of eggs for fish culture can bring the virus into previously noninfected facilities if the virus had previously been released into the wild-ranging fishes.

No information is available regarding the effect of IPNV among incubation eggs, sac fry, swimup fry or alevin offspring of IPNV-infected wild-ranging salmonids. High mortality among IPNV-infected young may seriously reduce a year class among wild fishes.

The IPN virus may be transported mechanically by mammals and birds associated with water occupied by infected fish. IPN virus administered orally to mink, chickens and great horned owls was later isolated from feces of these animals.[77] IPN virus was isolated from feces of hatching gulls for up to seven days following oral administration of the virus.[53a] Thus fish-eating birds and mammals may be involved in transmission of the virus into previously noninfected geographical areas.

Disease Signs:

External signs of IPN among young salmonids include a reluctance to take food, gradual loss of equilibrium, swimming in spirals, sometimes violent flexing of the body as if in abdominal distress and lethargy. Fishes with advanced cases of the disease fall to the bottom or are swept downstream. Tapping on the trough or tank may cause the fry to attempt swimming, only to settle back to the bottom or be swept downstream. A trough containing infected fry will usually demonstrate all stages of the disease during an epizootic. Larger, faster growing young fishes are, as a rule, the first to die from IPN.

Young salmonids with acute or subacute IPN usually become dark in color, lose weight and develop anemia. The fishes may not demonstrate internal signs of the disease other than an alimentary tract filled with opalescent to clear mucus. The mucus may contain tremendous numbers of sloughed epithelial cells and other cellular debris from the intestinal walls. There is no bile staining of the mucus. Some reports state that a few of the victims have visceral hemorrhages, especially in the mesentery, visceral adipose tissue and pancreatic tissue.[106] There may be serous fluid in the abdominal cavity and behind the eyeballs, with exophthalmos and dropsy. The liver and spleen usually will be pale in color.

Diagnosis:

Diagnosis of IPN is dependent on history of the disease in the fish population, signs of disease, histopathology of various tissues, demonstration of the virus by electron microscopy and isolation and identification of the virus. The usual lethargic or spiral swimming activity of young salmonid fishes is suggestive of this disease. Necropsy of overt cases of IPN will usually demonstrate the opalescent to white color of the intestine, but quite often no other signs of the disease. The intestine will be filled with non-bile-stained mucus; the liver, spleen and gills will usually be pale in color. These signs are enough to make the diagnostician suspicious of IPN.

IPNV consistently causes necrosis of pancreatic tissue, some cases of the disease with only slight necrosis but others with marked or extreme histological change. Pancreatic tissue with advanced necrosis will have inclusions composed of either viral lattices or myelin figures (Pl. 15C). There may be necrosis in liver, kidney spleen or other organs, but the necrosis is not usually as extensive as that found in pancreatic tissue. Often the liver and kidney will be edematous (Pl. 15D).

Properly stained ultra-thin sections of pancreas and other tissues can be used under the electron microscope to demonstrate the virus. IPNV is an icosahedral-shaped virus appearing as a six-sided structure in ultra-thin sections and 55 to 74 nm in diameter (Fig. 5). The virus may be in lattices or single and diffuse throughout the cell, depending on the destruction which has occurred to the cellular elements (Fig. 6). Myelin inclusions may also be present in some pancreatic acinar cells (Fig. 7). These inclusions may or may not contain viral particles.

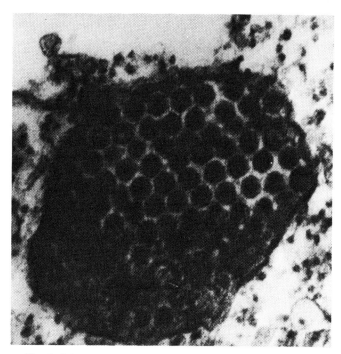

Fig. 6: Infectious pancreatic necrosis virus may appear within lattices in pancreatic acinar cells. (128,375 X) Photo by Lightner.

Fig. 7: Pancreatic acinar cells destroyed by infectious pancreatic necrosis virus may demonstrate inclusions (PL. 15C), which are composed of either lattices of viral particles or myelin figures (Fig. 6, above). (22,500 X) Photo by Lightner.

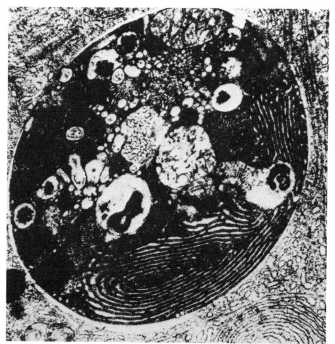

IPNV can be isolated into a number of teleost cell lines: RTG-2 (rainbow trout gonad), FHM (fathead minnow) BF-2 (bluegill fry), PG (northern pike gonad), WF-2 (walleye fry), GE-4 (guppy fry), SWT (swordtail embryo), GF-1 (bluestriped grunt fin), CHSE-114 (chinook salmon embryo), RBS (rainbow trout spleen), RTH-149 (rainbow trout hepatoma), STE-137 (steelhead trout embryo), ASH (Atlantic salmon heart), ASO (Atlantic salmon ovary), and possibly others.[91a] However, RTG-2 and FHM are usually the cell lines of choice. Incubation temperatures between 20 and 22°C is used for best replication. The usual procedure is to grind tissue suspected of containing the virus in a tissue grinder capable of rupturing cells and releasing viral particles. Sterile physiological saline or cell growth medium is used to assist in grinding the tissue. A bacteria-free filtrate or supernatant from centrifugation, with antibiotics and fungicides added to stop bacterial and fungal overgrowth, is inoculated into monolayer cell sheets in vitro. The virus will cause cytopathic effect (CPE) on susceptible cell sheets within 48 hours (Pl. 15E, 15F).

Presence and quantity of virus in a suspected tissue can also be detected by using a plaquing technique. Cell extract is serially diluted and an aliquot of each dilution inoculated into plaquing dishes prepared from susceptible cell sheets. The number of plaque-forming units (PFU) per unit volume of extract or unit weight of tissue can be determined. Presumptive identification is possible because of distinctive characteristics of plaques.[105]

Specific identification of IPNV is by serum neutralization test. IPNV antiserum is introduced to cell sheets with time allowance for absorbance of antibodies into the cells. A cell extract from fishes suspected of having IPN or material from cell sheets demonstrating CPE is inoculated into the antibody-absorbed cell sheets. IPNV antibodies will protect the cells in the cell sheet from CPE if the extract or inoculum has IPNV. Cells unprotected by the IPNV antibody will be destroyed.

Fluorescent antibody techniques for detection and identification of IPNV have been attempted, but no consistently useful procedure has been found. Purification of the IPNV antibody fraction from antisera prior to conjugation with fluorescent dye has been a problem not yet overcome. Indirect fluorescent antibody tests have been attempted for IPNV with limited success.[91]

A complement fixation test has been devised for IPN but has not received wide usage.[29] The procedure can be used to detect and identify the serological strains of IPNV after the virus has caused cytopathic effect in cell cultures. The test is completed within 24 hours, enhancing rapid diagnosis of the disease.

Therapy and Control:

There is no direct therapy for IPN. Reduction in water temperature may decrease rapidity of viral replica-tion and may be of some use in controlling part of the mortality.

The best control of IPN is prevention. Egg disinfection will not remove all virus from eggs. Therefore, eggs should be obtained from known IPNV-free brood fishes.

Test and slaughter and quarantine and movement restrictions will prevent the disease from being spread from one geographical area to another. Combination of test and slaughter with disinfection and sanitation has eliminated IPN disease from many fish culture facilities. Quite often epizootics of IPN disease cause high mortality among groups of susceptible fishes. The remaining fishes may be few in number. Slaughter and destruction of the fish carcasses is a minor task. This procedure, when combined with complete disinfection of the facility, will eliminate the virus, especially in hard-lined tanks, raceways or ponds (cement, fiberglass, butyl or other relatively impervious surface materials). Chlorine has been found useful. Chlorine used so that 10 mg of residual chlorine per liter remain after one hour of treatment in troughs, tanks, raceways and ponds filled completely with the chlorine solution is highly successful and relatively inexpensive. Tops of tanks and raceways should be kept wet with the chlorine solution for the entire hour-long treatment. All nets, brushes and other utensils should also be soaked in the chlorine solution for the hour treatment period. Incubators, trough stands and other equipment should be sprayed or dipped with a strong solution of chlorine. Water can be released from all fish-holding tanks after the chlorine has dissipated, usually within 24 hours.

Iodine compounds have been used to disinfect facilities and utensils. However, the cost of treating an entire fish culture facility with these compounds (polyvinylpyrrolidone-iodine) is quite high when compared to the use of chlorine for the same purpose.

An attempt was made to control IPN with virazole (1-D ribofluorosyl 1,2,4-triazole-3-carboxamide) using rainbow trout fry and known amounts of IPNV suspensions in flow through systems. Tanks receiving virazole dosages up to 0.4 mg per milliliter of water may have reduced mortality to some degree (45 to 55% mortality) as compared to 63% mortality in untreated control tanks.[71b]

Removal of fish from culture facilities and allowing the facility to remain dry for up to six months will usually eliminate the virus. This is especially useful in those facilities in which the water supply can be controlled and disinfected. Facilities receiving water from streams or from open springs may not be successfully disinfected.

Immunization for control of IPN has been considered possible, but no acceptable vaccine is available. Formal-in-killed and concentrated vaccines have been used experimentally with good success,[69a] but have not been successful under field conditions. Attempts are being made to prepare an anti-IPNV vaccine for brood-stock salmonids by cloning and expressing viral protein in *Escherichia coli* or yeast.[15a] Feeding of live but attenuated IPNV may also be possible for control of the disease. However, no consistently avirulent IPNV has been found.[91]

The use of resistant strains of fishes may be a possible way of controlling IPN. As an example, brook trout have been selectively bred for resistance to the IPNV at Pennsylvania State University since 1968. Fish exposed to the same strain of IPNV to which they were selected demonstrated 5% mortality when challenged with virulent IPNV; the most susceptible brook trout strains may suffer 95% mortality.[91]

Prognosis:

Morbidity levels among young susceptible salmonids usually reach 100% during epizootics. Mortality levels may reach 95 to 97% among the most susceptible fish species. Susceptibility is lost with age, and mortality of fishes three weeks to six months old may be minor. The fishes remaining alive following an epizootic, whether there has been high or low mortality, will be carriers of the virus for part or all of their life. As an example, an epizootic of IPN which occurred in Utah among rainbow trout caused 100% morbidity and 97% mortality. Those fish surviving the epizootic were moved to the laboratory and held for nearly three years. A sample of the surviving population was taken each three to six months following the epizootic and assayed for presence of the virus. No fish were found to be free of IPNV. Possibly higher carriers rates occur from survivors of epizootics in which high mortality levels are reached than among survivors of low mortality epizootics, since carrier rates of 35% or lower are noted among some surviving fish populations.

Practical Aspects:

IPN can usually be eliminated from fish culture facilities. This is desirable because elimination of the disease reduces mortality among fry and fingerlings susceptible to the disease and reduces the possibility of carrying the infection from an IPNV-contaminated facility to other facilities or to wild-ranging fishes. The expense of eliminating the disease may be much less over a long period of time than the sustained annual losses from the disease.

Practical IPN elimination from fish culture facilities may sometimes be almost a community effort, especially where salmonid-rearing facilities are relatively close together. Studies to determine if IPNV could survive passage through mammals and birds demonstrated that it will pass through mink, chickens, gulls and great horned owls.[29,77] There are probably many more mammals and birds which can spread the virus in this way. Therefore, if one fish culture facility scrupulously re-

moves the pathogen and a neighbor does not, the disease may be returned to the IPNV-free facility by birds or mammals.

The use of quarantine and restriction of movement of fishes has helped control the spread of IPNV and helped in its elimination within some geographical areas. Fish health personnel have successfully eliminated IPN from many parts of some states by disinfection, sanitation and quarantine and restriction of movement. State import stations along borders have been used to restrict salmonid shipments from entering without certification as being free of IPNV. Some states in the United States have also been successful in controlling IPN by stringent inspection, slaughter, disinfection and movement restriction within the state. Other states allow the disease to continue; the fish culturist sustains the losses in fishes but feels this is preferable to the time and expense of eliminating the disease.

Salmonid eggs infected with IPNV remain a major source of IPN movement within continents and throughout the world. Some state agencies have attempted to maintain a domestic source of all salmonid eggs. Thus no salmonid eggs need be brought into the state by government agencies. The practice has reduced the chances of bringing the virus to government-operated fish culture facilities. Stringent rules govern transportation of salmonid eggs from Europe and Asia into the North American continent, also reducing sources of IPNV. These practices do not reduce the possibility of commercial fish culturists bringing IPNV-infected salmonid eggs into a state.

IPN probably may never be completely controlled because of its wide distribution in the United States and Europe. Careful attention to sources of the virus can be used to hold the disease to the geographic area in which it presently occurs, without increasing the range any more than may naturally happen, until better methods of controlling the disease are devised.

Periodic inspections are necessary at trout and salmon hatcheries to determine the presence or absence of IPNV. These inspections should be conducted by a certified fish health inspector. A sample of each group (or lot) of fish is taken from the facility being inspected. A "lot" of fish is defined as fish of the same age, from the same egg source and sharing the same water. Samples of fish tissue or reproduction products (ovarian fluid or milt) is preferable to peritoneal washings or feces. A statistically valid number of fish from each lot should be taken, depending on the estimated IPNV carrier incidence. If IPN has been known to occur at a facility within the last year, the number of fish taken as a sample from the population is reduced, with a high percentage confidence limit still maintained (Table 12). The sample size must include a higher percentage of the population if IPN has never been known at a facility. Fish, fish tissue or fish reproductive product samples must be handled

TABLE 12

Estimated number of fish (sample size) which must be taken from a population with an assumed viral infection incidence to detect at least one IPN carrier at 95% confidence limits [a-9]

Population size[b]	Percent detectable disease carrier incidence[c]						
	0.5	1.0	2.0	3.0	4.0	5.0	10.0
50	46	46	46	37	37	29	20
100	93	93	76	61	50	43	23
250	192	156	110	75	62	49	25
500	314	223	127	88	67	54	26
1,000	448	236	136	92	69	55	27
2,500	512	279	142	95	71	56	27
5,000	562	288	145	96	71	57	27
10,000	579	292	146	96	72	57	27
100,000	594	296	147	97	72	57	27
100,000 or over	600	300	150	100	75	60	30

[a]From Amend, D. F. and G. Wedemeyer. 1970. *Approved procedure for determining absence of infectious pancreatic necrosis (IPN) virus in certain fish products.* FDL-31. U.S. Bur. Spt. Fish. Wildl., Div. Fish. Res. Washington, DC. 3p.

[b]Use sample size for the next larger population listed for intermediate population sizes

[c]Sample sizes can be rounded upward to an even five-fish interval to facilitate pooling

carefully and all tests performed according to prescribed procedures for best results.[9,23,30]

Infectious Hematopoietic Necrosis

The history of infectious hematopoietic necrosis (IHN) goes back to references of epizootics among cultured chinook and sockeye salmon during the 1940's and 1950's. Epizootics occurred among both salmon species at several fish culture facilities in the state of Washington. One facility was conducting nutritional studies in 1944, and experimental sockeye salmon were being fed adult salmon viscera. An unexplained mortality developed among these fish. The hemorrhagic signs of the disease were attributed to avitaminosis but could not be reproduced. The hemorrhagic disease recurred in 1948 and 1950 at several facilities. The disease was recognized as being caused by a distinct infectious entity in 1951, and its virus or virus-like nature was demonstrated in

1954.[67,86,98] The disease was called Sockeye Salmon Virus Disease (SSVD).

Meanwhile, epizootics of a recurring diseases were recorded as early as 1941 among chinook salmon at other salmon-rearing facilities.[66] Hemorrhagic areas developed in the fish and were quite similar to those noted in SSVD. A virus or virus-like filterable agent was demonstrated as the cause of the disease in 1959. The disease was subsequently called Oregon Salmon Disease (OSD).

Epizootics of a similar disease had been occurring at a salmon culture facility on the Sacramento River of California. Signs of the disease were similar to the others and a "filterable agent, highly resistant to antibiotics" demonstrated.[52] This disease was called Sacramento River Chinook Disease (SRCD).

A virus disease of sockeye salmon and rainbow trout, similar in pathology to SSVD, OSD, and SRCD, was recognized in 1968.[10] A better description of this disease was given in 1970, and the disease was named infectious hematopoietic necrosis (IHN) because of the primary pathological changes.[52] IHN is apparently common to all previous names given to the disease and has been accepted as the official nomenclature.[30]

IHN is an acute to subacute hemorrhagic disease of several salmonid species. The hematopoietic tissue of the spleen and anterior kidney is the primary tropic tissue, but other tissues of the body become target organs as the disease progresses.[7]

Etiological Agent:

Infectious hematopoietic necrosis virus (IHNV) is a Rhabdovirus which replicates in the cytoplasm of the infected cell. The size is given as 65 to 90 nm wide by 150 to 180 nm long, a size which accommodates SRCD virus (90 to 159 nm), OSD virus (91 X 181 nm) and the original measurement of IHNV (90 X 158 nm) (Fig. 8). The virus contains a single-stranded ribonucleic acid genome. IHNV (OSDV or SCRDV) is inactivated at 60°C for 15 minutes and by ether or chloroform. The virus is neutralized by IHN antiserum and to a very limited extent with viral hemorrhagic septicemia (VHS) antiserum. VHS virus is also a Rhabdovirus.[5]

IHNV does not survive at relatively high temperatures. It is inactivated when stored in 10% calf serum at 21°C within six weeks. It does survive storage in the same medium at 4°C for over 36 weeks.[5] Signs of the disease can be halted in fishes by raising the water temperature to above 15°C.[12] IHNV replicates in at least 15 cell lines,[91a] but CHSE-214 (chinook salmon embryo), RTG-2 (rainbow trout gonad) and FHM (fathead minnow caudal trunk) are the most often used cell lines. The optimum temperature for replication is between 13 and 18°C, with 20°C as maximum and 4°C as minimum temperatures.

Geographical Distribution:

IHN is enzootic along the west coast of the United States, from the Sacramento River to Kodiak Island, Alaska.[7] Epizootics of IHN have been reported in California, Oregon, Washington, Alaska, Idaho, Montana, Colorado, South Dakota, Minnesota, West Virginia and tentatively in Virginia.[107] The disease has been enzootic in salmon-rearing facilities along the Canadian Pacific coast. IHN is widely distributed in Japan, having been transported there first in shipments of sockeye salmon eggs from Alaska. A disease epizootic similar to IHN, and probably IHN, occurred in a fish culture facility in Australia after chinook salmon eggs were shipped from a salmon hatchery on the Sacramento River of California.

Susceptible Species:

Chinook salmon, sockeye salmon (also known as blueback or, the freshwater variety, kokanee salmon) and rainbow trout (including the anadromous steelhead rainbow trout) are primarily susceptible to the IHNV. The virus has been isolated from dog salmon in Japan during

Fig. 8: The virions of infectious hematopoietic necrosis are helical (a) or bullet-shaped (b) typical rhabdoviruses. Viral particle (c) demonstrates the apical pore. Photo by Amend and Chambers.

disease epizootics involving both rainbow trout and dog salmon fry. Experimentally inoculated cutthroat trout were susceptible to IHNV isolated from chinook salmon in one experiment, however no natural epizootics of IHN have been reported in this trout species.[53a]

The disease has not been reported in other salmon or trout species, even though other species have been present in fish culture facilities and in some cases shared the same water with IPNV-infected fish.[65,107]

IHN epizootics are usually found in fry or early juvenile salmonids. Fish over one year of age are nonsusceptible but can carry the virus without signs of the disease.

Epizootiology:

The major routes of natural transmission of IHN among susceptible fishes have been demonstrated to be oral, by contact (direct or contact with flowing infected water) and from parent to offspring through eggs. Susceptible fishes fed IHNV in the diet will readily develop the disease. Early experiments with sockeye salmon disease described feeding mixtures of infected fish ground with noninfected fish tissues to sockeye salmon. Up to 70% mortality occurred in a month's time. Experiments to determine if the disease could be transmitted by contact demonstrated direct contact to be more efficient than contact with contaminated water. Mortality levels between 90 and 70% were reported in either case following 30 days of contact.[86]

IHNV has been demonstrated in both ovarian fluid and milt taken from carrier brood fishes. Eggs obtained from carrier brood fishes are infected with the virus. This route of transmission has been responsible for moving IHNV over long distances (*i.e.*, west coast of the United States to West Virginia, California to Australia or Alaska to Japan[107]). Nothing is known of where the virus resides within or on infected eggs. The use of external disinfectants has not always removed the virus, indicating that either the virus is imbedded deeply in the pores of the egg shell or is within the membranes of the embryo.

The incubation period for IHN is temperature-related. The most rapid incubation time appears to be about 10°C, at which temperature mortality will begin in four to six days after experimental exposure. Highest incidence of mortality will occur for eight to 14 days after exposure and continue for several weeks.[90] The incubation period is longer at temperatures below 10°C and shorter above this temperature. No natural epizootics of IHN have been known to occur above 15°C.

The course of disease in very young susceptible fishes at 10°C is acute. The disease is of a more subacute nature at lower temperatures or in advanced fry or small fingerlings. The age of greatest susceptibility appears to be between one week and 35 days from the time of hatching.[4,90]

Mortality may be extensive; 80 to 100% has been reported. Virus is shed in feces during the clinical stage of the disease and subsides if the fish survives. The virus can be found in various organs of the body immediately following the acute or subacute stage. It can no longer be found in most body tissue during the late stages of recovery or in adult fishes. It is present, however, in reproductive products. A high percentage of both sexes surviving the disease will be carriers of IHN for the remainder of their life. A higher percentage of female sockeye and chinook salmon become carriers than the males of these species. Approximately equal numbers of male and female rainbow trout become carriers.[4] The carrier rate is somewhat related to season of spawning. Fall-spawning rainbow trout have a higher percentage of carriers than winter- or spring-spawning fish, but this does not seem to have any practical significance. IHNV accompanies eggs which have been obtained from either IHNV carrier females or fertilized by IHNV carrier males.

There is no evidence to judge the effect of stocking IHNV-infected fishes into wild-ranging fish populations. Stocked fishes, as IHNV carriers which survive the rigors of the natural existence, may produce IHNV-infected offspring. Fry mortality in redds may possibly be as great as mortality among very young cultured fishes, resulting in reduced recruitment to wild-ranging populations from natural production.

Disease Signs:

Gross signs of IHN are similar in sockeye or chinook salmon and rainbow trout. Early signs of the disease appear shortly after fishes begin feeding. Infected fishes become lethargic, usually are dark in color and swim erratically. Many swim feebly or frenziedly, some rolling slowly in the water, others maintaining a vertical position. Some cases of the disease develop exophthalmos and a distended abdomen. Some have distinct hemorrhagic areas behind the head on the dorsal surface, in the operculum, gill isthmus and at the bases of fins. There may be white to gray fecal casts extending from the anus. Some cases of the disease have no external signs other than lethargy or a dark color.[10]

Internally there may be serous fluid in the abdomen. The liver may be pale. The intestine can be filled with bile-stained mucus and with little or no food or feces. There may be petechial hemorrhages in the peritoneal lining, muscles and in the mesenteries and adipose tissue. The general appearance of the fish may be anemic. The kidney may be swollen and edematous.

Diagnosis:

Diagnosis of IHN is made on the basis of past history of the disease at the fish culture facility and source of eggs for the facility, fish species represented, disease signs, histopathology, electron microscopy and isolation and identification of the virus. Disease signs may suggest IHN, especially if the disease is present in sockeye or chinook salmon or rainbow trout held in water temperatures below 15°C.

Histopathology of IHN is similar in many ways to that caused by other salmonid viruses. However, IHN distinctively causes destruction of the hematopoietic tissue of the kidney and, in many cases, the spleen (Pl. 16A). This indicates that the primary target of IPNV in susceptible fishes is the hematopoietic tissues. There may also be necrosis in the pancreatic tissue, liver and stomach wall. Liver necrosis is generally focal in nature (Pl. 16B). There are usually extracellular and intracytoplasmic inclusions in necrotic pancreatic acinar cells.[114] Congestion and petechial hemorrhages appear in the myomeres and heart muscle and in many other tissues. Mucosal sloughing is present along the intestine, possibly contributing to the fecal casts.[10] Electron microscopy of kidney hematopoietic tissue demonstrates spindle- to bullet-shaped viral particles 65 to 90 nm in diameter by 150 to 180 nm in length. These findings may assist in presumptive diagnosis (Fig. 8).

IHNV replicates in RTG-2, FHM, CHSE-214 and other cell lines. FHM cells are preferred by some diagnosticians because the cells are more sensitive to the IHNV.[23] Other diagnosticians prefer RTG-2 cells for plaquing.[105]

IHNV is present in many tissues during acute and subacute stages of the disease. Whole infected fry can be ground with physiological saline or cell growth medium and a bacteria-free filtrate or centrifuge supernatant prepared. Centrifuge supernatant is much preferred because of viral reduction usually caused by membrane filtration. Antibiotics and fungicides are added to the tissue extract. Monolayered tissue culture cells are inoculated with tissue extract and incubated at 10°C. Cell destruction is usually advanced within two days to one week if IHNV is present.

Definitive diagnosis of IHN is possible using serum neutralization tests. Monolayered cells can be protected by IHN antiserum in tubes or plaquing plates. Plaque assay of virus is advocated by many diagnosticians because it is rapid and accurate. Characteristic plaques are produced by IHNV in RTG-2 cells.[105]

Fluorescent antibody tests are ideal for definitive diagnosis of viral diseases. However, a satisfactory fluorescent antibody test is not available for IHN diagnosis. An indirect fluorescent antibody test has been devised but has received limited use.[45]

Diagnostic procedures are important in the location of IHNV carrier fishes. The viral population reduces in most tissues over time following infection, active disease and recovery. Kidney and spleen are the best sources of the virus in fingerling-sized fishes and ovarian fluid or milt from "ripening or ripe" adult fishes. These products are handled in the same way as tissues used for diagnosis of epizootics. Serum neutralization and plaquing tests are used for definitive identification of IHNV carriers. The number of fish taken as a sample from a population of fish will determine competence in location of IHNV carriers (Table 12).

Therapy and Control:

There is no therapy for fishes during epizootics of IHN. Prevention of the disease is the best method of control. Location and elimination of IHNV carrier brood fishes will limit sources of the virus. There is a good chance that eggs taken from IHNV-infected fishes will be infected with the virus. Eggs suspected of IHNV infection may not be disinfected with iodophor compounds (polyvinylpyrrolidone-iodine).[8] Unfortunately, some salmonid eggs treated with these compounds have given rise to epizootics of the disease when hatched and the fry begin feeding. These epizootics could be the result of careless disinfection procedures or the possibility that the virus occurs within some eggs.

Experiments demonstrated that raising the water temperature to above 15°C and holding that temperature for two weeks stops mortality from IHN during epizootics

and may even eliminate the virus.[6] However, as with egg disinfection using iodophors, the virus is not completely removed and may reappear in the same fishes as a recurring epizootic or as IHNV carriers.

IHNV has been eliminated from some fish culture facilities by removing all fishes and disinfecting the entire facility as well as utensils used around fishes. The only fishes or fish eggs allowed on the facility after disinfection were those known to be free of the virus.

Control of IHN by immunization has not been possible. The most probable approach to this method of control is through use of live attenuated virus. An Oregon IHNV isolate, for example, was passed through STE-137 (steelhead embryo) cells over 40 times at an incubation temperature of 18°C, which greatly reduced its virulence. Kokanee salmon fry failed to develop fatal IHN when the attenuated virus was added to their water supply. Sockeye salmon fry were placed in contact with the attenuated virus for about 48 hours. Twenty-five days later they were challenged with a wild IHNV strain. Up to 90% of the fish were protected against fatal IHN injected peritoneally. The vaccination was effective against several isolates of virulent IHNV.[30b] Possibly such a product and a procedure for vaccination among the large numbers of fishes at some fish culture facilities will become available.

Prognosis:

Morbidity levels among IHN-susceptible fishes probably reaches 100% during epizootics of the disease. Mortality is usually high among fishes with transovarian infections. Reports of 80 to 100% mortality are not uncommon among fry of sockeye or chinook salmon and rainbow trout at water temperatures between 8 and 12°C.[5,86] Other epizootics have caused much lower mortality (less than 35%).[67] Mortality is usually rapid after initiation of the epizootic, building up to 50% of the population during the first two weeks and higher accumulated mortality within 45 days.

The percentage of surviving fishes from epizootics which become carriers of IHN cannot be predicted. Studies at one trout-rearing facility demonstrated an average carrier incidence of about 26% among brood fishes from which IHN epizootics occurred among progency.[45]

Practical Aspects:

Egg transmission is most important in the movement of IHN about the world by modern transportation systems. There is evidence that most, or possibly all, IHNV transmitted from parent fishes to offspring among rainbow trout is outside the egg shell and susceptible to proper disinfectant. Egg disinfection at 1:10,000 (100 mg/L) of iodine from iodophor compounds for ten minutes at water pH 6.0 or higher is sometimes effective in removing the virus and should be practiced to reduce the possibility of transmitting the virus on eggs.

Transmission of IHNV from infected fishes to noninfected fishes through contact with water carrying the virus has been proved possible.[4,115] Therefore, water flowing from fishes known to be infected with IHNV should not be used for fishes known to be free of IHNV downstream from infected fishes.

Early reports of SRCD and other similar diseases now known to be IHN indicated that fry had been fed raw ground adult salmon viscera. The oral route for transmission of the disease was strongly suspected as a source of the infective agent.[86] Since then, experiments have demonstrated definite fish to fish transmission of IHNV by feeding infected fish tissue to susceptible fry.[115] The fish culturist using fishes or fish products, and especially products from salmonid fishes, should pasteurize the fish products prior to adding them to the diet. IHNV is sensitive to heat, and a pasteurization temperature of about 55°C for 30 minutes should destroy all IHNV in fish products.

Natural epizootics of IHN among wild-ranging salmonids has not been reported. Possibly this is because high percentages of fry are lost in redds or shortly after emergence. Cultured salmonids known to harbor IHNV should not be stocked into wild populations, especially into water systems at temperatures of 15°C or below.

Viral Hemorrhagic Septicemia

Viral hemorrhagic septicemia (VHS) is an acute to chronic viral disease of rainbow trout. The first report of a disease that was apparently VHS was in Germany in 1938.[63,96] The disease was named Infectiose Nierenschwellung und Leberdegeneration (INuL). English translation of this name literally means infectious kidney swelling and liver degeneration, the major disease signs and pathology caused by the virus. A better description of the disease was given in 1949-50 when a previously unknown disease was found among cultured rainbow trout in eastern Jutland (Denmark). Epizootics were located near the township of Egtved, and the name Egtved disease was given.[63] Later observations indicated that Egtved disease was the same as INuL. A similar disease occurred among rainbow trout in parts of France in 1955.[15] This disease was called by several names: pernicious anemia,[15] infectious anemia, enterohepato-renal syndrome, popeye sickness, abdominal dropsy of trout and kidney swelling.[96] Modern opinion is that the disease reported among rainbow trout throughout various parts of Europe is viral hemorrhagic septicemia (VHS). The latter name became the official name of the disease in 1962.[96] The other names are used locally in some parts of Europe.

The etiology of VHS had been suggested as deficiency of vitamin B_{12} (cyanocobalamine) because of the pernicious (macrocytic, hypochromic) nature of the anemia present in moribund fish. Deficiency of thiamin (vitamin B_1) was also suggested because most cultured rainbow trout affected by the disease were being fed fresh herring.[63] Most fish flesh has thiaminase activity which destroys thiamin after death of the fish. Ocean-caught herring stored in the hold of fishing vessels continue to destroy their thiamin prior to being brought to the cultured trout. The viral nature of the disease was suggested in 1954 but met with much resistance. Ultrafiltration experiments in 1958 proved the viral origin of the disease.[11,22]

Etiological Agent:

Isolation of the virus in rainbow trout gonad (RTG-2) cells in 1965 proved the virus nature of the disease. Electron microscopy demonstrated it to be a conical (helical) virus with a diameter of 60 to 70 nm (average 65 nm) and 180 nm long. It was said to resemble the Coxsackie viruses and was variously called an Arbovirus,[11] Myxovirus[96] and Rhabiesvirus.[116] It was named *Rhabdovirus salmonis* in 1965,[117] a name which has not been accepted. However, the virus was classified as a Rhabdovirus in 1977.[62]

The official name of the virus which causes viral hemorrhagic septicemia is the *Egtved virus*.[30] The name varies from the usual nomenclature of naming the virus from the official name of the disease.

The Egtved virus has an optimum replication temperature of 12 to 14°C, minimum 4°C. The virus is extremely heat sensitive (inactivated at 60°C in 15 minutes, and loses at least 50% infectivity in 15 minutes at 31°C). It is rapidly destroyed by ether and chloroform, 50% glycerin and pH 3.5. The virus loses infectivity in dead fish tissue within 24 hours at 0°C but can be stored at −20°C for relatively long periods of time.[63] The virus will replicate in RTG-2 cells at pH 7.6 to 7.8, but not at pH 7.2.[33,96] It produces characteristic plaques in fathead minnow (FHM) cell monolayers. It will replicate on many other standard cell lines. The virus has an RNA genome and is neutralized by VHSV antiserum.[36a,53a,96]

Geographical Distribution:

VHS has been reported in various countries of Europe. It has been a particularly difficult problem in rainbow trout culture facilities of Denmark, France, northern Italy, Poland, Germany and other central European countries.[15,31,33,96] The virus has been brought to the United States for experimental purposes only and has not been permitted to escape from laboratories. *

Susceptible Species:

VHS is primarily a disease of rainbow trout. Brook trout have been experimentally infected by contact with Egtved virus-infected rainbow trout. No natural cases or epizootics are known among other fish species.

The virus has been inoculated into brown trout, brook trout and coho salmon intraperitoneally or intramuscularly. The same course of the disease follows as in rainbow trout.[63]

Rainbow trout of all ages are susceptible. There is high mortality among rainbow trout up to six months of age (200 grams).[31] The disease develops in fish older

* As of 1989, VHS has been reported in U.S.

than six months, but mortality among the population is considerably lower.

Epizootiology:

VHS is somewhat seasonal among cultured rainbow trout supplied water from streams or lakes. The greatest number of epizootics and highest mortalities occur during the winter months, gradually subsiding in the spring and occurring only sporadically in the summer and early autumn. Cooler water temperatures in November and December bring increased epizootics. The disease in trout culture facilities using spring water is less seasonal, especially in colder (7 to 11°C) water supplies.[63]

The major source of the virus is from infected rainbow trout. Large numbers of viral particles are shed from infected fish in feces and urine. Chronic or latent cases of the disease are probably the primary reservoir of the virus. The virus is carried over warmwater periods as latent cases of the disease.

Transmission of Egtved virus is by contact with virus-contaminated water. Experimental infections have been successful by brushing Egtved virus infected tissue homogenates onto the gills of noninfected rainbow trout. There is no evidence to indicate the virus is transmitted orally. Transmission of the virus with eggs is suspected but not proved.[96]

The incubation period for VHS is variable, depending on water temperature, age of the fish and route of transmission. Mortality among young rainbow trout experimentally injected intraperitoneally with bacterial-free filtrates prepared from Egtved virus-infected rainbow trout liver caused mortality in 13 days at 13°C. Mortalities continued for approximately four weeks. Normal rainbow trout in another aquarium receiving water which flowed across the injected fish began dying 14 days following the first mortality in the injected fish.[63] These results indicate transmission of the virus and incubation are almost as rapid by contact as by direct injection.

The incubation period is ten to 15 days when water temperature is 15 to 16°C. Fish receiving gill contact with the virus from infected tissue homogenates will begin to die in seven to 12 days, which is nearly the same incubation period as occurs in natural infections.[96]

Cases of VHS may be acute, subacute, chronic or latent. All cases of the disease are carriers of the virus and shed the virus at varying rates. The greatest period of viral release is during the clinical period. Latent cases of the disease are carriers of Egtved virus but may or may not shed the virus. Demonstration of the virus in latent cases is especially difficult.[11] Fish with latent VHS will begin to shed large numbers of viral particles when the latent stage changes to acute as a result of environmental stress.[96]

Viral hemorrhagic septicemia among susceptible hosts develops rapidly at water temperatures of 13 to 15°C. The mortality rate increases dramatically and gradually subsides. The virus can be found in all tissues of the body during the period of viremia and early recovery. Gradually the virus is lost from most tissues until it is found primarily in the spleen and posterior kidney as the period of recovery continues.[23]

There is no evidence that eggs from VHS survivors are involved in the epizootiology of the disease. Transportation of frozen Egtved virus-infected rainbow trout could carry the virus over long distances.[63] Stocking of Egtved virus-infected fish during the period of clinical disease and recovery could transmit the virus into wild-ranging fish populations. Water from fish culture facilities undergoing epizootics of VHS could carry the virus to wild-ranging fish and is probably a part of the recurrence cycle among stream-fed fish culture facilities.

Location of carrier fish is difficult with VHS. Apparently rainbow trout recovering from VHS have no neutralizing antibodies which might be used to identify them as survivors. Survivors of the disease are always suspected carriers of the disease.

Disease Signs:

VHS is a variable disease and disease signs vary with acute, subacute, chronic and latent cases. There is an early loss of appetite and erratic swimming; some fish move away from the group and remain motionless at the sides of the pond or at the surface. The fish usually become dark in color with all types of the disease. There are exophthalmos and distended abdomens from edematous fluid in tissues behind the eyeballs and in the abdominal cavity. The gills are pale in color. There may be dermal inflammation and hemorrhage in acute or subacute cases (Pl. 13C).

Internal disease signs of acute or subacute VHS are multiple hemorrhages throughout the muscle tissue, liver, visceral fat, gonads and other organs. The liver is pale in color, sometimes yellowish (Pl. 16C). The kidneys and spleen are swollen and congested. The digestive tract is empty. The stomach may be at pH 6 or 7 instead of the normal pH 1 or 2. There is edematous fluid in the abdominal cavity. There may be hemorrhages in the mouth and along the esophagus.[63]

Chronic cases of VHS appear different from acute cases of the disease. The fish are usually darker in color with exophthalmos and ascites (abdominal dropsy). Internal disease signs include greatly swollen kidneys and spleen; the liver is pale in color, with depletion of visceral fat (Pl. 16D).[96]

Diagnosis:

VHS is diagnosed by history of the disease in the geographical area of occurrence, host species, disease signs, histopathology and isolation and identification of the virus. VHS resembles other hemorrhagic diseases from both viral and bacterial orgin. Therefore, disease signs may be of little or no value for presumptive diagnosis but may be useful in the definitive diagnosis.

Histopathology of VHS is somewhat distinctive in that petechial hemorrhages and edema are found throughout the muscle and kidneys of acute or subacute cases of the disease.[115] There is also much edema in the spleen and liver. There may be pyknosis or more advanced necrosis in kidney, liver and spleen and cytoplasmic or nuclear inclusions in some cells.[96] Erythrocyte counts may be of assistance in diagnosis, being as low as 300,000 erythrocytes per cubic millimeter of blood.[96] Electron microscopy may be useful in presumptive identification of the virus except for its resemblance to other fish Rhabdoviruses, specifically the infectious hematopoietic necrosis virus.

Egtved virus may be isolated from kidney or splenic tissue by grinding the tissue with physiological saline and centrifugation to remove cellular debris. The supernatant is inoculated into monolayers of RTG-2 or FHM cells. Some diagnosticians prefer FHM cells because they appear to be more sensitive to the virus.[23,104] Egtved virus replicates best at pH 7.4 to 7.8 and hardly at all at ph 7.2 in RTG-2 cells.[97] The virus is neutralized by VHS antiserum. A fluorescent antibody test may be made on thin slices or squash preparations of infected tissues.[23a,37] Plaques formed in FHM cell sheets by Egtved virus are of assistance in identification of the virus.[105] The virus is ether sensitive, heat sensitive and will not survive in 50% glycerin.

Therapy and Control:

There are no therapeutic procedures for VHS. Prevention of the disease is the best control. Quarantine and restriction of movement of any fish suspected of having been in contact with Egtved virus should be stringently enforced. This is especially true when fish are to be moved from Europe to other continents. There is no evidence to demonstrate the absolute source of Egtved virus. Possibly native European poikilothermic animals are asymptomatic carriers of the virus. Therefore, any movement of poikilothermic animals from Europe should be done under very strict quarantine and after thorough viral examination.

Careful attention to sanitation and disinfection of all equipment around fish culture facilities is important in enzootic VHS areas. Some fish culturists state that better nutrition of rainbow trout, especially in relation to the B vitamins, vitamin E and vitamin A, assists in reducing severity of epizootics when they do occur.[40]

Experimentally infected rainbow trout produce antibodies against the Egtved virus; however, antibody production is lost in some fish by the time the fish become mature. Thus, serological surveys of fish populations to locate carriers of the virus are impractical for control of the disease.[24]

Prognosis:

Morbidity levels among rainbow trout in which epizootics are occurring is probably nearly 95%. Mortality levels among infected rainbow trout fry are usually between 9 and 25%. Mortality as high as 78% has been reported in Germany.[11] The disease may affect all ages of rainbow trout with no indication of loss of susceptibility with fish up to one year old.

Practical Aspects:

The absolute source of Egtved virus has not been determined. There are arguments which support the theory that it was, or is, present among certain native European, North Atlantic or Baltic Sea fishes. The rainbow trout is a relatively new introduction to the European continent and may have no natural resistance to the virus, which may explain its susceptibility. A similar argument could be made against the theory by use of the brook trout as an example of a North American native fish which should likewise have no natural resistance to the virus. The brook trout is susceptible to the virus, but does not readily become infected. Infections of Egtved virus in brook trout take long periods of time for the disease to develop. One experiment in which brook trout were placed in contact with infected rainbow trout produced the first mortality in nine weeks. Mortality occurred over an additional seven weeks, but eventually all of the 24 experimental brook trout died.[63]

The course of VHS disease in rainbow trout has been stated as a rapid increase in viral population in fish tissues during the clinical period, with gradual reduction until most organs are free of the virus as recovery progresses. Subsidence of viral replication and loss of virus from various organs of the body may explain why the virus has not been demonstrated on or in eggs taken from brood fish survivors of VHS epizootics. If ovaries are free of the virus, there will be little or no chance of egg contamination. It may also explain why the virus was not transported to the United States, Canada, Japan and other rainbow trout-growing countries of the world. Tremendous numbers of rainbow trout eggs were shipped to these countries during the 1950's and 1960's. Denmark was the supplier of millions of rainbow trout eggs through these years, yet the Egtved virus was apparently not transported with the eggs.

Saltwater-reared rainbow trout may also be carriers of the virus. Epizootics of VHS have occurred among this species reared in full-strength seawater. Fish in one such epizootic had 85% mortality, indicating severity in saltwater environments is just as great as in freshwater.[18a]

VHS is a disease which could be of tremendous economic importance throughout the world where rainbow trout have become the major trout reared for human consumption. Fortunately the etiological agent of this disease has remained on one continent, as far as anyone has been able to determine. Special efforts should be made to be sure that the virus is not moved from where it is at present to other trout-growing areas. VHS is one of the highly contagious diseases which has not been brought to North America. Fish health agencies should be especially alert to all possible ways this virus could enter the continent and devise methods to block entry, such as the U.S. Fish and Wildlife Service Title 50 fish importation restriction.

Channel Catfish Virus Disease

Channel catfish virus disease (CCVD) is an acute to chronic disease of channel catfish. CCVD first came to the attention of catfish culturists and fish health diagnosticians in 1968.[26] Large numbers of fry and fingerling channel catfish were dying during the summer of that year at one commercial and two federal catfish hatcheries in Alabama, Arkansas and Kentucky. External protozoa, *Flexibacter columnaris* and *Aeromonas hydrophila* infections at the commercial hatchery were thought to be the cause of mortality. Therapy for each of these pathogens did not reduce mortality. Likewise, a bacterial infection with *A. hydrophila* at one of the federal hatcheries did not respond to oxytetracycline therapy. The mortality at the other federal hatchery was thought at first to be caused by oxygen depletion from a heavy algal bloom, but the mortality was not relieved when better water was pumped into ponds to disperse the phytoplankton. These findings led to field and laboratory experiments to determine whether the disease was contagious.[26]

Contact and inoculation experiments using both infected and normal channel catfish proved the disease to be infectious. These experiments were followed by inoculation of bacteria-free filtrates prepared from infected catfish into four cell lines. Cytopathic effect occurred in brown bullhead (BB) cells. The disease was found to be caused by a virus in 1970.[28]

Reported epizootics of CCVD among channel catfish have increased (four in 1970, seven in 1971, 23 in 1972) and epizootics continue to be reported over an increasing range.[57]

Etiological Agent:

The etiological agent of CCVD is the channel catfish virus (CCV). The virus is a Herpesvirus. It is enveloped and the entire particles is 175 to 200 nm in diameter. The envelope contains 162 capsomeres. The icosahedral nucleocapsid is 95 to 105 nm in diameter, the core 40 to 50 nm (Fig. 9). CCV is inactivated by ether at 4°C in 24 hours and by chloroform in five minutes at room temperature.[93,100] It is inactivated at 60°C in 15 minutes. Studies demonstrated that it will not survive for three days in channel catfish tissue at 22°C. A gradual loss of viral activity occurs when the virus is stored in channel catfish tissue frozen at −20°C, and −80°C. All activity is lost in 162 days at −20°C, and only a low level of virus remains active after 210 days at −80°C.[61] The virus replicates at 33°C and 10°C, very slowly at the latter temperature. CCV replicates in BB (brown bulhead), CCO (channel catfish ovary) GDII (walking catfish gonad), KIK (walking catfish kidney) and GIB (walking

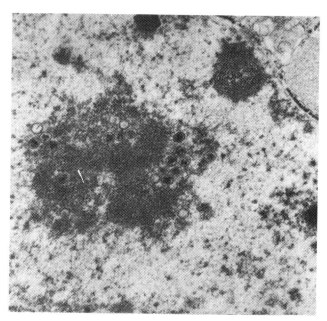

Fig. 9: The virion of the channel catfish virus is an enveloped herpesvirus, 175 to 200 nm in diameter with an icosahedral nucleocapsid. (20,000 X) Photo by Plumb.

catfish gill) cells but not in RTG-2 (rainbow trout gonad), FHM (fathead minnow) or BF (bluegill fry) cells. It is neutralized by channel catfish serum which contain CCV antibodies[30,54] and by CCV antiserum.

Geographical Distribution:

CCVD was first identified in Alabama, Kentucky and Arkansas. It has subsequently been found throughout the major channel catfish rearing areas of southern and southeastern United States. The disease has also been diagnosed in California and Honduras, Central America.[91]

Susceptible Species:

CCV is extremely host specific. The channel catfish is the primary susceptible species for CCVD. The blue catfish has been experimentally infected with the virus, and there have been instances of natural infections occurring in this species.[56] Attempts to infect the European catfish (which is not an ictalurid) met with failure.[53b] The virus is so host specific it will replicate in ictalurid cells only.

Epizootiology:

The source of CCV is not known. Older channel catfish which have survived CCVD are suspected. Certainly the host specificity of the virus suggests it can only be found in ictalurid fishes. Stocks of channel catfish with significant CCV neutralizing antibodies in the sera suggest these fish may have been previously in contact with the virus. It also suggests there may be latent viruses in certain tissues of the body.

Experiments have demonstrated that CCV is widely distributed in the tissues of the body during the acute stage of the disease. The virus is found in the kidney, skeletal muscle, liver, intestine and brain. The kidney seems to be the primary organ attacked, with other organs attacked as the disease progresses. Viral replication in the brain does not occur until late in the disease, probably accounting for erratic swimming in more advanced cases of CCVD.[59]

CCV can be isolated from infected fish only during epizootics and for a short time thereafter.[91] Methods of identifying suspected carriers of CCV continuously meet with failure. Those methods used to successfully identify carriers of infectious pancreatic necrosis virus (IPNV) and the viral hemorrhagic septicemia virus (Egtved virus) are of no value for detecting CCV among channel catfish. Experiments in which channel catfish were injected with CCV, and organ tissue samples, peritoneal washings and feces taken several weeks after injection, failed to yield the virus in any sample.[59]

The route of transmission of CCV among susceptible hosts is unknown. Transmission of the virus from parent to offspring through the egg is generally accepted as the route of transmission to very young fry. CCV-neutralizing antibodies have been found in channel catfish brood fish. The brood fish subsequently produced offspring with CCV.[58] The route of transmission of virus suggested for older channel catfish is contact with CCV-ladened water,[87] but whether entrance into the new host body is oral, absorbed through the gills or through other routes is speculative.

The incubation period for CCVD is dependent on temperature. The incubation period was found to be 48 to 72 hours at 30°C and ten days at 20°C among channel catfish experimentally injected with CCV. Fish developed the disease within 72 to 78 hours after contact with contaminated water at 22°C to 30°C.[87]

Mortality from CCVD among channel catfish is somewhat age-related. Fry and fingerlings are most susceptible. Susceptibility is almost entirely lost by one year of age and completely lost by two years of age. Size of fish does not appear to be as important as age, for example, fish 13 months of age but weighing only six grams were nonsusceptible. Subadult and adult channel catfish injected with viable CCV remain asymptomatic but develop CCV-neutralizing antibodies.[54] Survivors of CCVD epizootics undoubtedly are part of the epizootiology of the disease, but the exact way they are related is not known.

Disease Signs:

Channel catfish infected with CCV may swim erratically, sometimes rotating longitudinally as if attempting to maintain balance. They may remain motionless in the water with the body in a vertical position. There may be convulsions, followed by a quiet period during which they settle to the bottom of the container.

External signs of CCVD include petechial hemorrhages at the bases of fins and occasionally over much of the skin, more pronounced on the ventral surface.

Gills may be pale and hemorrhagic. The abdomen is distended and there is exophthalmos (Pl. 16E).[30,87]

The most striking internal sign os CCVD is the general hemorrhagic appearance of peritoneum, muscle, liver, kidneys, spleen and other visceral organs. The abdominal cavity is usually filled with yellowish edematous fluid. The alimentary tract is free of food. The intestinal tract is filled with yellowish bile-stained mucus. The stomach is distended with mucus secretions (Pl. 16F).[30,87]

Diagnosis:

Diagnosis of CCVD depends on history of the disease in the geographical area of occurrence, species of fish involved, disease signs, histopathology, plaque formation and serum neutralization. Epizootics of CCVD tend to follow in those catfish culture facilities with a previous history of the disease. Receipt of eggs from suspected brood fish may also be of use in the presumptive diagnosis. The fact that channel catfish are the only species involved in an epizootic among fishes in a facility with multiple species may assist in presumptive diagnosis.

Disease signs of CCVD may assist in diagnosis as evidence accumulates from other tests and observations. The diagnostician must keep in mind that the clinical signs of CCVD are not too different from those caused by certain bacteria (*Aeromonas* species and *Pseudomonas* species, for example).

The histopathology of CCVD is well documented.[44,54,60,103,113] The kidney, being a primary target for the virus, is damaged most rapidly following infection. There is necrosis in hematopoietic tissue and epithelium of proximal tubules. There is edema in glomeruli and other tubules. Necrosis is also present in pancreatic tissue. Massive hemorrhages are present in the spleen, submucosa of the gastro-intestinal tract and skeletal muscles. The liver is congested and with foci of necrosis. There may be intracytoplasmic inclusions in the liver cells affected by the virus. These histopathological findings are not too different from the histopathology noted in some of the salmonid virus diseases (IPN, VHS and IHN) but are quite distinctive for a virus disease in channel catfish.

Plaque formation in BB cells provides presumptive identification.[105] However, the only definitive identification of CCV is by the serum neutralization test.

Therapy and Control:

There is no therapy for CCVD. However, the virus is usually not a single entity in epizootics. Bacteria, fungi and animal parasites are usually opportunistic adjuncts to the epizootics. Therapy for removal of these pathogens may reduce mortality to some extent.

CCVD occurs during the warm part of the year when water temperatures are above 22°C. The suggestion has been made that cooler water might be added to facilities when possible to control or reduce mortality from

CCVD epizootics. Experiments using this method reduced mortality from 94% when fish were held at 28°C to 14% when fish were removed from 28°C water and placed in 19°C water 24 hours after being infected. Reduction of temperature as late as the time of first deaths from the disease reduced mortality to 78%.[55] These data indicate that early recognition of the disease is essential if temperature reduction is to be used for control of epizootics.

Another CCVD control procedure of great importance is the maintenance of channel catfish in specific pathogen-free water (uncontaminated well or spring water). Carefully decontaminated (ultraviolet or chemically treated) water may be helpful but has not been used in the control of this disease.

Careful selection of a channel catfish supplier to be relatively sure the brood fish are free of CCV is important in controlling epizootics of the disease in a fish culture facility and also in controlling geographical distribution of the disease. Eggs obtained from brood fish, a high percentage of which have significant virus-neutralizing capabilities, should be carefully disinfected. The iodophor compounds (polyvinylpyrrolidone-iodine) are recommended, even though nothing is known about the location of the virus in or on eggs. The fry hatched from a suspected brood fish source should be held so that if a CCVD epizootic develops the disease is limited to that group of fish.

The use of vaccines for control of CCVD has not been possible. Attenuated CCV has been prepared by serial passage of the virus in KIK (walking catfish kidney) cells.[50a] Possibly an attenuated live virus vaccine may be useful for mass vaccination but much more research is required.

Prognosis:

There is no evidence on morbidity levels of CCVD among young channel catfish, but it probably reaches nearly 100% during epizootics. Morbidity levels among subadult or older fish is entirely unknown because CCV infection among fish six months old or older remain asymptomatic even during the viremic stage. Mortality levels among channel catfish fry being held near 30°C can be as high as 90 to 94%.[55,58] Mortality levels are reduced with the age of the fish and lowered environmental temperatures.

Practical Aspects:

The common practice of rearing catfish in water which has been used for other purposes (returned irrigation water, runoff water from storms or similar sources) has probably been responsible for a number of CCVD epizootics. Catfish culturists have found that the channel catfish needs an uncontaminated water supply to remain healthy. Presence of adult catfish in water subsequently supplied to fry or fingerling channel catfish may cause CCVD epizootics among the small fish if the virus

has been known at that facility previously. Catfish culturists should use every precaution possible to lessen opportunities for CCVD epizootics until the exact nature of the carrier state of the virus is known.

Stocking or transporting channel catfish survivors of CCVD epizootics is not recommended, even though CCV has not been demonstrated in older fish. Egg transmission has been well documented. Transportation of channel catfish eggs from brood fish with high CCV neutralizing titers is also not recommended.

Lymphocystis Disease

Lymphocystic disease is a chronic, slowly developing viral disease of connective tissue cells. Only cells infected with the virus become hypertrophic, others near or attached to affected cells remaining unaffected. The tumorous growths are not malignant. The disease usually is not fatal to infected fishes.

The first report of lymphocystis disease was in England in 1874.[42] The disease was referred to as "multiple tumor" disease by a Scottish writer in 1884[43] and thought to have been caused by a "remarkable parasite" in an English scientific report in 1904.[111] An investigator declared the disease to be caused by a protozoan parasite in 1907.[13] The protozoan said to be involved was *Lymphocystis johnstonei*, the source of the modern accepted name of the disease even though the protozoan is not the etiological agent.

Confusion over the exact etiology of lymphocystis disease continued. A virus was suggested in a report in 1914. The report discussed the enlarged organelles of the hypertophic lymphocystis cells and suggested the "cytoplasmic network" (probably the inclusions) were the reaction products of a virus.[89] A positive Feulgen reaction for the cytoplasmic network within these cells was first reported in 1932, eliminating some of the doubt that the disease could be caused by a virus.[34] Lymphocystis disease in walleye (pike-perch) from Lake Erie was discussed by a comparative virologist in 1937. Strong arguments were given for viral etiology of the disease.[32] The contagious nature of the disease was demonstrated and the viral etiology theory further strengthened in 1939 by feeding lymphocystis-affected tissue to healthy fishes.[88] A publication in 1940 on the description of viruses known at that time listed lymphocystis disease among the known viral diseases of plants and animals.[74] The viral etiology concept continued. There was no doubt of etiology by the early 1950's.

Etiological Agent:

The etiological agent of lymphocystis disease belongs to the Iridovirus family.[35,62] It had formerly been placed in the Poxvirus group.[11] The lymphocystis disease virus (LDV) is a large, complex, naked virus with a deoxyribonucleic acid genome.[1,62,82,117] The nucleocapsid is icosahedral-shaped with several light and dark staining shells. The viral diameter averages 250 nm, with a range

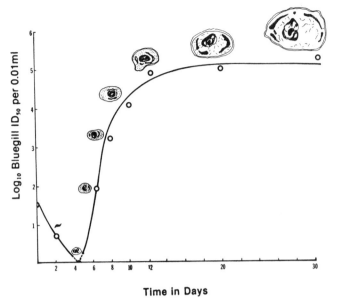

Y-axis label: Log$_{10}$ Bluegill ID$_{50}$ per 0.01ml

X-axis label: Time in Days

Fig. 10: The lymphocystis cell may grow to several hundred times the volume of normal cells. (From Wolf, Gravell and Malsberger)

of 200 to 300 nm.[82,117] Two strains of the virus have been identified from North Sea fish as distinguished by DNA cleavage patterns. Strain 1 was said to occur in flounder and plaice and Strain 2 in dabs.[30a]

LDV is located in the cytoplasm of infected cells, where it stimulates formation of bars of inclusion substance. Virions can be found in large numbers in contact with the inclusion substance.[85] This may account for the large amount of Feulgen staining material in most lymphocystic cells.

The virus replicates in bluegill (BF) and largemouth bass fry (LBF-2), silver perch swimbladder (SP-1), silver perch spleen (SP-2), sand seatrout fin (STF), spotted sea trout muscle (CYM) and Atlantic croaker fin (CrF) cells,[91a] and closely parallels development of lymphocystis disease in susceptible fishes. The virus replicates well at 23°C to 25°C, with demonstrated cell hypertrophy in about six days and the cellular capsule in about ten days.[102] Lymphocystis cells are mature in three to four weeks at this temperature (Pl. 17A, Fig. 10).

Geographical Distribution:

Lymphocystis disease has been reported in the central part of the United States, especially in and around the Great Lakes region. The disease is known over much of south-central and southeastern Canada, parts of South America, much of Europe and in North Sea, Baltic Sea, Barents Sea, North Atlantic and North Pacific.[94] The disease has been reported in fishes from the Gulf of California and Panama Bay.[46] This broad freshwater and marine distribution suggests the virus may be present throughout temperate and tempero-tropic parts of the world.

Susceptible Species:

Spontaneous lymphocystis disease has been reported in at least 81 species of fishes from 33 taxonomic families and seven taxonomic orders.[10a,38] The most susceptible species is the walleye (or pike-perch). Other members of the same family (Percidae), including the freshwater perches, sauger and darters are also highly susceptible. Probably all freshwater members of the sunfish family (Centrarchidae), including the sunfishes, basses, bluegill and crappie, are highly susceptible. Many of the shallow-water and bottom-feeding deep-sea fishes appear to be susceptible. Probably most of the bony (class Osteichthyes) aquarium fishes are susceptible. The disease has not been reported in the salmonid family (trout, salmon, char, whitefish and grayling).[94]

Epizootiology:

No studies have been made on the transmission of lymphocystis disease under natural conditions. Probably its transmission is similar among wild-ranging fishes as happens during experimental transmission in aquaria. The source of virus is shed or ruptured epithelial cells from infected fishes. The virus escapes from disintegrating infected cells. Minor injuries to skin and fins of susceptible new hosts are probably the portal of entry of the virus. The infection route is from contaminated water and bottom detritus into epithelial connective tissue cells. The virus begins replication within the newly infected cells causing a hypertrophic warty growth. These warts are usually on the parts of the skin and fins most vulnerable to abrasion and injuries, adding credence to the route of entry suggested above.

The oral route of transmission of lymphocystis disease may also occur. Lymphocystis cells have been reported along the gut and in the heart and other internal organs. These cells may be the result of the host feeding on LDV-infected fish tissue. Lymphocystis disease cases in which the hypertrophic cells are present internally are exceptions, and the cells are few rather than gathered into warts.[83]

The incubation period for spontaneous lymphocystis disease is usually several weeks. Incubation during experimental transmission of LDV depends on the viral population of the infecting material, the route of transmission and water temperature. The minimum incubation time for subdermal injection of LDV material in European perch was nine days and two weeks for walleye, both held at 25°C. Bluegills injected subdermally with LDV developed observable lesions in 12 to 15 days at 25°C and 37 days at 12.5°C.[94]

There are only a few cases of lymphocystis disease at any time among susceptible fish populations in which LDV is enzootic. Each diseased fish should be considered as a carrier. The nature of epithelial tissues is to maintain a continuous shedding of old cells to be replaced from lower levels of the tissue. Thus, lymphocystis cells are released into the water, maintaining a constant source of virus to the environment. The large, heavy lymphocystis cells fall to the bottom, where whole cells may be ingested by bottom-feeding fishes or spontaneously ruptured to release virus, which may infect abraded areas of the same host or new hosts. Those fishes which occupy the bottom of large bodies of water, such as open seas, the continental shelf areas of oceans or large freshwater lakes, are no doubt in greater contact with released LDV than fishes which occupy the surface areas.

Confinement of susceptible fishes to aquaria in which cases of lymphocystis disease are present increases the chance of infection of new hosts or reinfection of old hosts. Most aquarium fishes spend time on or near the bottom and become vulnerable in this way. Lymphocystis disease can become a continuous problem to the aquarist.

Lymphocystis disease is self-limiting. Any fish living with lymphocystis lesions for a few months to a few years without being destroyed by the disease will spontaneously slough the warty growth and remain free of the disease.

There is no indication that the virus is transmitted by fish eggs. Accepted egg disinfecting procedures should remove LDV which may accidentally accompany eggs from infected brood fishes. Transporting fishes with lymphocystis disease is a means of spreading the virus from one geographical area to another.

Disease Signs:

Lymphocystis disease is easily recognized because it occurs on the surface of the body. Lymphocystis lesions are rough, warty growths on skin and fins. The masses of lymphocystis cells may occupy large areas or may be few in number, creating small lesions which are usually white to gray-white or pinkish in color (Pl. 17B). Little or no magnification is needed to demonstrate the fine-grained texture of the lesions. Each of the grains is a tremendously enlarged lymphocystis cell. The lesion may develop its own blood supply, which accounts for the pinkish color of older, more developed lesions. Lymphocystis cells within the lesion may rupture and release virus particles into the water, or the entire lesion may rupture, releasing large numbers of lymphocystis cells. The skin at the site of the former lesion heals over, usually leaving a light-colored scar but with no other lasting effects.[83]

Diagnosis:

Diagnosis of lymphocystis disease is based on gross appearance of the lesions and histopathological evidence of epithelial connective tissue cell hypertophy. There is no need to isolate and identify the virus of lymphocystis disease, although isolation and identification will assist in diagnosis.

White to gray-white or pinkish warty lesions on the fins and skin of various parts of the body, and especially those parts most subject to minor injuries, are a pre-sumptive diagnosis for lymphocystis disease. Cut and stained sections of lymphocystis lesions which demonstrate the enormously enlarged (up to 500 times) connective tissue cells of the skin are a definitively positive diagnosis. All organelles are enlarged in the lymphocystis cell: nuclei, cytoplasm and cell wall (Pl. 17C). The cell wall usually is thickened to the point of being like a capsule. There are thread-like cytoplasmic inclusions.

Gross appearance of lymphocystis disease is similar to epithelial sarcomas of skin and fins. Sarcomas are neoplastic tumors. The diagnostician can easily differentiate between the gigantic hypertrophic cells of lymphocystis disease and the more normal-sized hyperplastic cells of sarcomas.

Additional diagnostic evidence can be obtained by viral isolation in BF cells and by electron microscopy of either the original host cells or tissue culture cells. LDV causes hypertrophy of BF cells, usually within two to three weeks at 25°C (Pl. 17A). Electron microscopy will demonstrate the virus to be an average 250 nm in diameter, naked and with an icosahedral nucleocapsid. There is no lymphocystis antiserum available for serum neutralization tests.

Plaque formation may be demonstrated using BF cells. LDV plaques are characteristic, demonstrating gross cellular hypertrophy.[105]

Therapy and Control:

There is no therapy for lymphocystis disease. Quarantine and restriction of movement, test and slaughter and disinfection and sanitation are the only methods for controlling lymphocystis disease. Fishes with lymphocystis disease should not be moved into lymphocystis-disease-free fish populations. Cases of lymphocystis disease among cultured bass, perch, sunfish or other highly susceptible fishes should be removed from ponds if possible and destroyed. Careful sanitation is essential in fish culture facilities with enzootic lymphocystis disease, especially if only one or a few of the fish-holding tanks are contaminated with LDV. Drying or complete disinfection with a strong disinfectant will remove the virus. A water supply known to be free of the virus will maintain fish free of lymphocystis disease following disinfection.

Control of lymphocystis disease among fishes in aquaria may be by removal of fishes with obvious signs of the disease. Expensive fishes may be held in quarantine until all signs of the disease disappear before returning them to the aquarium with other fishes. Several months may be necessary before all signs are eliminated.

Prognosis:

Morbidity levels of lymphocystis disease are quite low, even among the most susceptible fishes. The incidence of lymphocystis disease among wild-ranging walleye may be as low as less than 1% or as high as 30%. An increase in the number of LDV-infected walleye has been noted during spawning periods, possibly attributed to abrasions of skin and fins in shallow riffle areas of streams.[69] An incidence of lymphocystis disease as high as 10% has been reported among some of the Barents Sea bottom-feeding flatfishes.[83]

Mortality directly attributable to lymphocystis disease is negligible. Studies on tagged wild-ranging walleye with the disease indicated little or no effect on survival and probably no influence on the overall fish population.[69]

Practical Aspects:

The greatest practical problem from lymphocystis disease is esthetic. The appearance of lymphocystis lesions on fishes has caused removal and destruction of LDV infected fishes from the catch of commercial fishermen.[83] Modern processing of fishes into fish sticks or fish cubes can use LDV-infected fish because the virus is harmless to homeothermic animals, including humans.

Sportsmen catching LDV-infected fishes usually view the condition as a curiosity. Some LDV-infected fishes caught by sportsmen are destroyed if disfigurement of the fish is extreme.[83]

Lymphocystis disease becomes a problem to the aquarist because of the unsightly appearance of fishes with the disease. Transmission of the virus among fishes in close confinement of aquaria and among heavily populated tanks is more amenable than among wild-ranging fishes in large volumes of water. Introduction of a single LDV-infected fish into an aquarium containing other fishes may result in all fishes being infected with the virus. The chronic nature of lymphocystis disease and the relatively slow development of disease signs may culminate in infection of all fishes before the aquarist is aware of the disease.

Miscellaneous and Little-Known Virus Diseases of Fishes

Commercial availability of standardized fish cell lines in most technologically advanced countries of the world has resulted in viral isolation capabilities in many fish disease diagnostic and research laboratories. Routine inoculation of cultured fish cells with prepared tissue extracts taken from moribund or dead fishes during disease epizootics has become a common practice. Thus, many viral agents have been isolated which were never suspected previously. Many of the isolates are single isolates from one or a few fish. Others have been found to be distributed over a broad geographical area and isolated by numerous fish health diagnosticians or research people.

The five major virus diseases given previously in this chapter have been assigned an economic and biological importance, are widely distributed geographically and most susceptible hosts are known. Many other virus diseases have been studied. The viral etiology of some have been isolated, others have been observed by electron microscopy only. Those given in Table 13 are examples of miscellaneous and little-known virus diseases.[62,91a] They are listed here to give the reader an indication of the importance of viruses as pathogens of fish. The list is by no means complete since new viruses and viral diseases are being recognized continuously. Four of these diseases appear to be important to one or more species of fishes or have received more research than the others. These four diseases, viral erythrocytic necrosis disease, spring viremia of carp, pike fry Rhabdovirus disease and a disease caused by *Herpesvirus salmonis*, will be discussed.

Viral Erythrocytic Necrosis

Examination of the red blood cells of several species of marine fishes has demonstrated cytoplasmic inclusions. Electron microscopy of the erythrocytes of a gecko and a blenny revealed the inclusions contained icosahedral virions 200 to 250 nm in diameter.[79] A report in 1969 described inclusions in erythrocytes accompanied by massive erythrocytic destruction of Atlantic cod. The condition was termed piscine erythrocytic necrosis, or PEN, and the suggestion made that the condition was caused by a virus.[39] Two years later (1971) a report confirmed an icosahedral DNA-containing virus in electron micrographs of Atlantic cod erythrocytes.[81] The virions were found to be 300 nm in diameter. Erythrocytic degeneration of Atlantic herring was described in 1973.[73] The icosahedral shaped virus of herring measured 146 nm in diameter, considerably smaller than those reported from other species.[53] These data suggest the disease may be caused by a number of different/related viruses.

A similar hematological finding was reported in chum and pink salmon from Pacific coastal waters of North America in 1978. A study of virions was made and found to be icosahedral in shape with an average diameter of 190 nm (range 179-199 nm). The name viral erythrocytic necrosis, or VEN, was proposed because the name was more discriptive of the condition than piscine erythrocytic necrosis (PEN).[25a] The former name (VEN) has been more widely accepted.

Etiological Agent:

The etiological agent of both Atlantic cod and herring VEN has received considerable study. Virions from the two fish species are similar in structure but differ in size. The cod VEN virion is 310 to 350, average 330, nm in diameter. Herring VEN virions average 146 nm in diameter. Virions from Pacific salmon average 190 nm in diameter. All three are icosahedral and enveloped (Fig. 11).[25a,53,84] All three have been classified as Iridoviruses.[91a] All three are located in the cytoplasm of erythrocytes associated with inclusions. The inclusions can be observed in Giemsa-stained blood smears using light microscopy (Pl. 17D).[53]

PLATE 1

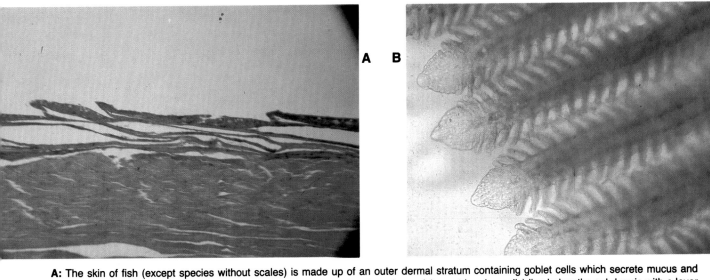

A: The skin of fish (except species without scales) is made up of an outer dermal stratum containing goblet cells which secrete mucus and surround the scales, and an inner subdural stratum. A stratum of melanophores (pigment-bearing cells) lies below the subdermis with a layer of facia (connective tissue) between the melanophores and the myomeres (body striated muscle).

B: Gill tissue of fish is a system of capillaries carrying blood from the afferent blood vessel on one side of the gill arch to the efferent blood vessel on the other side of the arch. The filaments have many lamellae, each separated so water can flow between them.

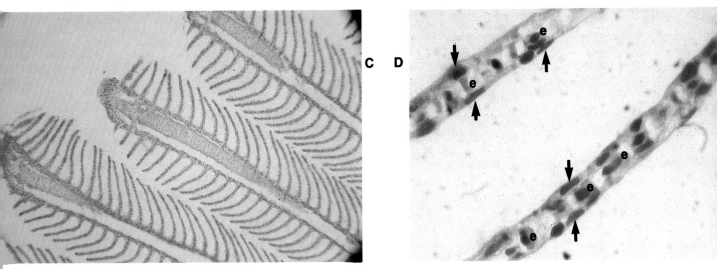

C: Note that the three gill filaments are supported by a cartilage; each gill filament supports several gill lamellae, which are the major respiratory structure of gills.

D: A lamellae is an individual capillary with one layer of squamous epithelial cells (arrows) separating erythrocytes (e) from water surrounding the lamellae.

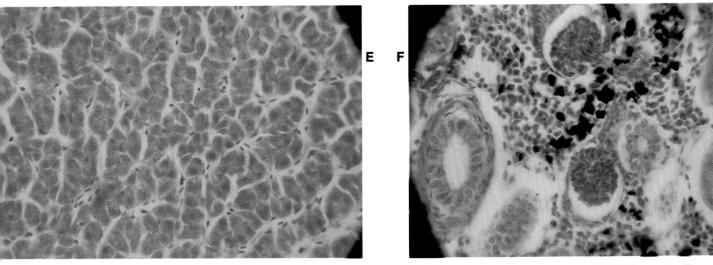

E: The liver of fish consists of hepatic cords, primarily hepatocytes, a network of blood vessels and hepatic ducts within the liver cords. The liver of fish is quite diffuse when compared to the liver tissue of higher animals. **F:** The mesonepheros kidney of most fish is made up of many renal corpuscles (glomeruli, Bowman's capsule, the proximal convoluted tubule, the distal convoluted tubule and collecting duct). The head kidney of fish also contains most of the hematopoietic tissue of the body. Melanin particles are usually found in kidney tissue.

PLATE 2

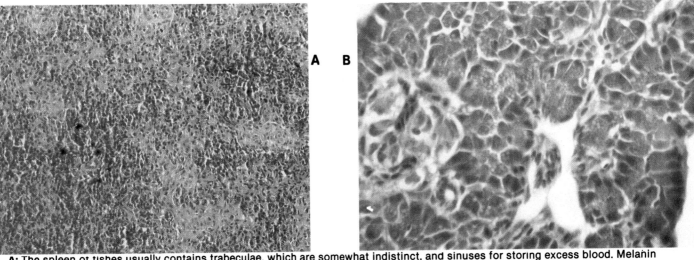

A: The spleen of fishes usually contains trabeculae, which are somewhat indistinct, and sinuses for storing excess blood. Melanin particles are normally found in the spleen of most fishes. **B:** Pancreatic cells of most fishes are cuboidal in shape and contain granules. The pancreas of fishes usually contains adipose tissue or may be surrounded by liver tissue.

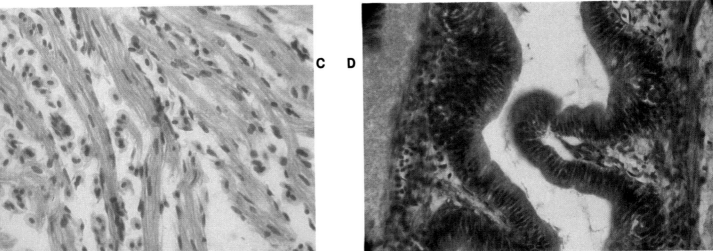

C: The atrium of fishes is quite diffuse when compared to cardiac tissue of higher animals. Muscle bundles are not closely packed together but lie apart, usually with many red blood cells between muscle bundles. **D:** The intestine of fishes contains a single muscle layer (tunica muscularis) with villi extending from the lamina epithelialis. Villar epithelium is formed and sloughed continuously.

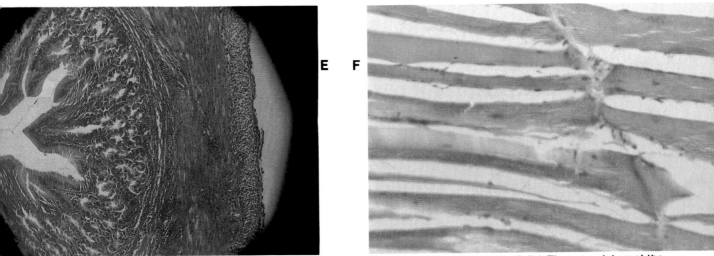

E: The inner lining of the stomach of most fishes contains an extensive stratum of villi (lamina epithelialis). The musculature of the stomach is made of two muscle layers. The outer surface of the stomach contains a single layer of connective tissue. **F:** The body muscles (myomeres) of fishes are made up of short muscle bundles attached at each end to other myomeres, but with a paucity of connective tissue. The myomeres act primarily by pulling the body in two directions.

PLATE 3

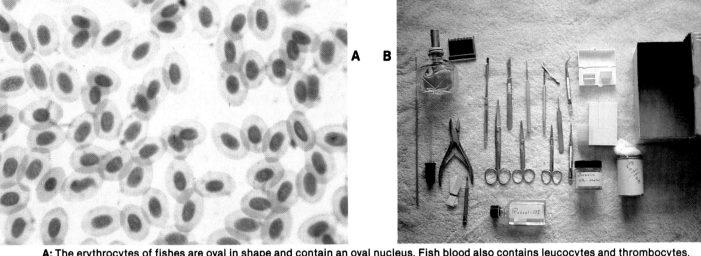

A: The erythrocytes of fishes are oval in shape and contain an oval nucleus. Fish blood also contains leucocytes and thrombocytes.
B: A necropsy kit containing all essential instruments is essential for fish necropsy.

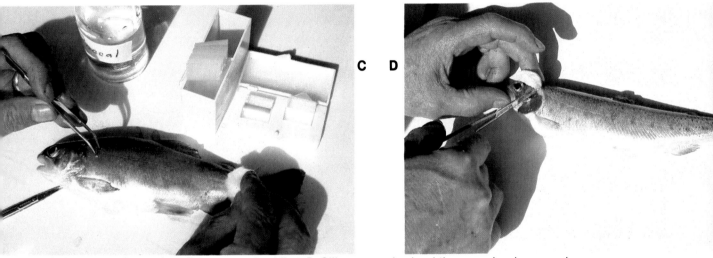

C: External surfaces of the fish are examined first. **D:** Gills are examined and the operculum is removed.

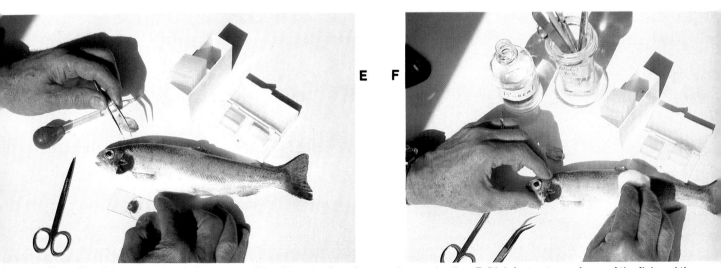

E: A gill arch is removed and placed on a slide with water for microscopic examination. **F:** Disinfect outer surfaces of the fish and the instruments if bacterial or fungal cultures are to be taken.

PLATE 4

 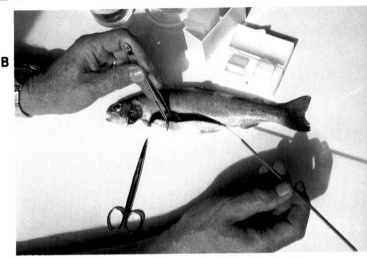

A B

A: The fish is opened along the swim-bladder. Cut about ¼ the distance between the lateral line and the most ventral abdominal surface. **B:** Remove tissue for bacterial examination first if cultures are to be made.

 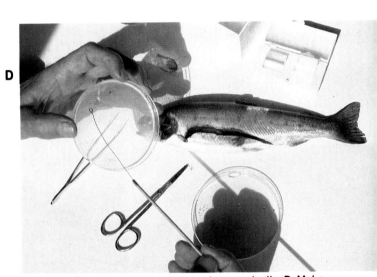

C D

C: Make squash smears of suspect tissue by pressing between two microscope slides, stain and examine microscopically. **D:** Make cultures of proven positive bacterial infected tissue.

E F

E: Examine other visceral organs. Take pieces of organs for histological examination as necessary. **F:** Remove a section of the body including the kidney.

PLATE 5

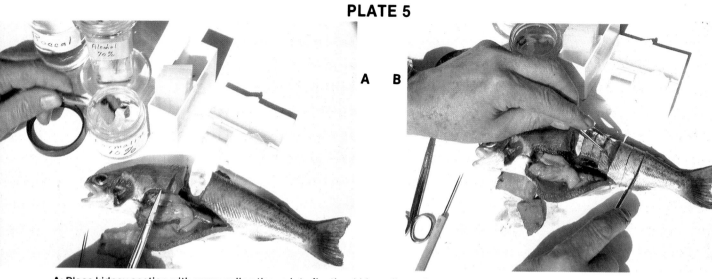

A: Place kidney section with surrounding tissue into fixative; kidney dissection can be completed after fixation. **B:** Slice through skin and muscle at intervals for observation of abscesses or other abnormalities.

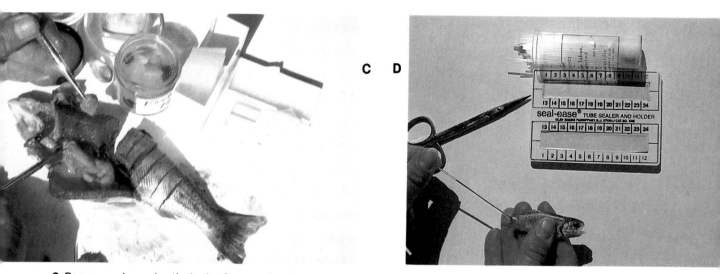

C: Remove and examine the brain after opening the skull. **D:** Collect blood from small fish by severing the caudal peduncle and filling hematocrit tubes or micropipettes as needed.

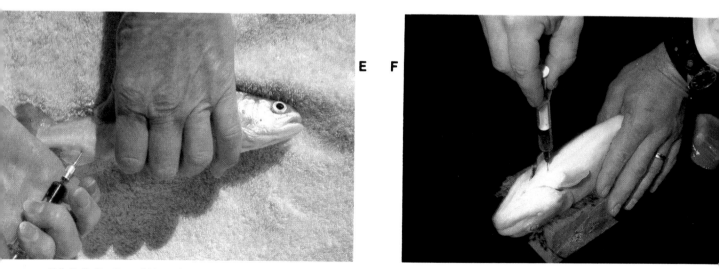

E & F: Collection of blood from relatively large fish can be accomplished by using a syringe and needle and entering the caudal vein (E) or the atrium (F). The fish should be anesthetized or held firmly. The needle may rupture the caudal vein or the heart, causing a damaging or fatal hematoma if the fish should move during the blood collecting procedure. Photo (F) by Dr. D.P. Anderson

PLATE 6

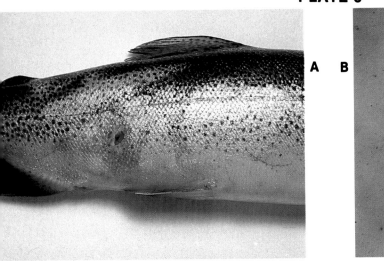 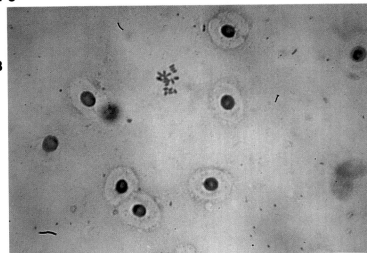

A: Signs of furunculosis range from minor to much more evident, depending on the nature of the case. Acute furunculosis may develop with few outward indications. Subacute or chronic cases usually demonstrate signs often associated with the disease: i.e., furuncles, much erythema at the base of the fins, in the mouth, and around the anus. **B:** *Aeromonas salmonicida* is a short oval to rod-shaped bacterium which usually appears as small masses of cells in kidney squash preparations. (Gram stain)

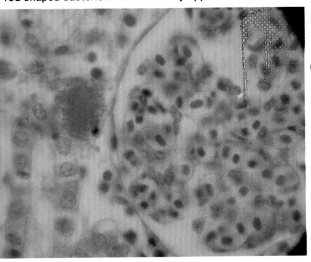 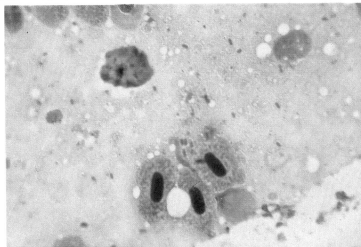

C: Histopathological lesions of furunculosis include masses of bacteria without leucocytic infiltration. The above illustration demonstrates a mass of *A. salmonicida* cells in kidney tissue. (H and E stain) **D:** Most aeromonads have cells 2.0 to 4.5 times longer than wide, occur singly or in pairs and can be observed in kidney squash preparations for septicemic cases of motile aeromonad disease. (Gram stain)

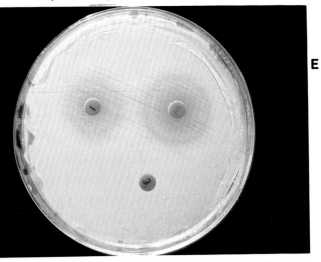 

E: Plate inhibition tests may serve as a guide to possible therapeutic drugs which can be used to control *Aeromonas* sp. infections in fish. The drug yielding the greatest zone of growth inhibition is usually the drug of choice for therapy. **F:** *Vibrio anguillarum* produces boil-like lesions in the muscles of susceptible fishes which break and leave large open sores.

118

PLATE 7

A: External disease signs of motile aeromonad disease are general erythema at the base of fins, in the mouth, within opercula and around the anus.

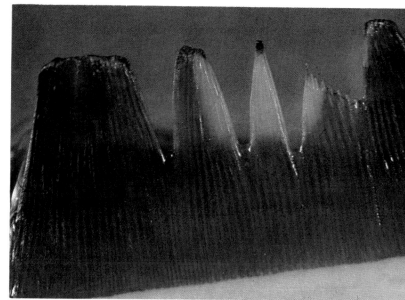

B: *Flexibacter columnaris* may invade gill tissue, causing necrosis of gill filaments.

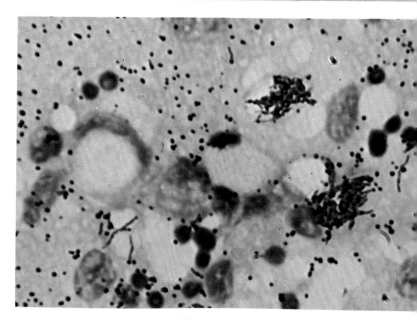

C: Long, acid-fast rod-shaped bacteria are present in kidney lesions of fish infected with *Mycobacterium marinum* or *Mycobacterium fortuitum*. Photo courtesy of Piscisan, Ltd.

PLATE 8

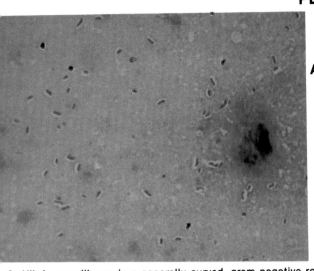 

A: *Vibrio anguillarum* is a generally curved, gram negative rod-shaped bacterium which can be seen microscopically in stained squash preparations taken from infected liver. **B:** Signs of enteric redmouth disease include darkening of the skin, unilateral or bilateral exophthalmos, erythema in fins or at the base of fins, general internal erythema, moderate amounts of serous fluid in the body cavity and swollen kidneys and spleen. Chronic cases usually demonstrate little or no visceral fat.

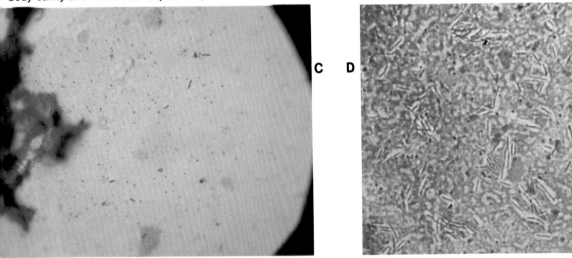 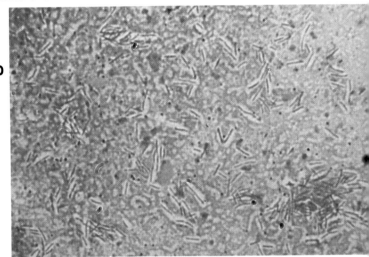

C: *Yersinia ruckeri* appears as a gram-negative, straight rod-shaped bacterium, occurring single or in pairs, in kidney squash preparations from infected fish. **D:** Gram-stained material scraped from the skin of fish infected with *Flexibacter columnaris* demonstrates long, slender, curved rod-shaped bacteria.

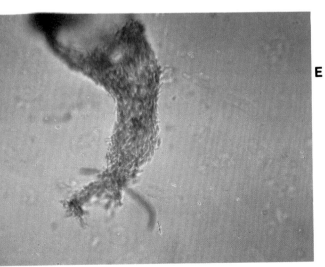 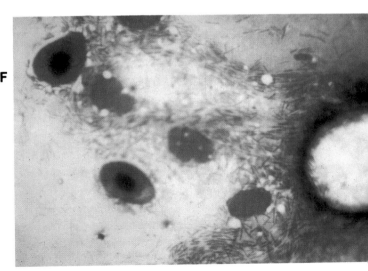

E: Examination of gill arches from fish infected with *Flexibacter columnaris* may reveal piles of bacteria protruding from the gill tissue. **F:** The flexibacteria from necrotic tissue of some cases of fin rot or peduncle disease are prolific. The bacteria are long slender, sometimes curved, gram-negative and nonsporeforming rod-shaped organisms.

PLATE 9

A: Fin rot may progress to peduncle disease by destroying the caudal fin and parts of the caudal peduncle. Those fish with caudal vertebrae exposed cannot survive. **B:** Warmwater strains of flexibacteria may involve aquarium fishes in the disease known as fin rot. The disease is usually secondary to malnutrition or other physiological imbalance.

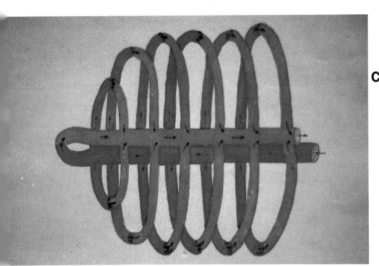
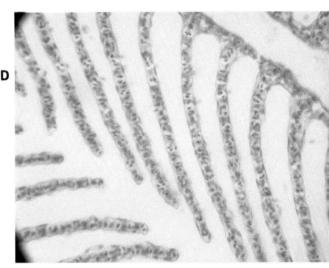

C: A gill filament of a fish is an intricate structure made up of capillaries and connective tissue. Blood returning from the body flows in the afferent side of the lamellae, those capillary loops extending into the water, and leaves as oxygenated blood from the efferent side. **D:** Gill lamellae are small, cylindrical capillaries with a lumen size not much larger than the red blood cells. The lamellar wall is one to two cells thick. Blood cells coursing through the capillaries (lamellae) are very close to the water for most efficient oxygenation.

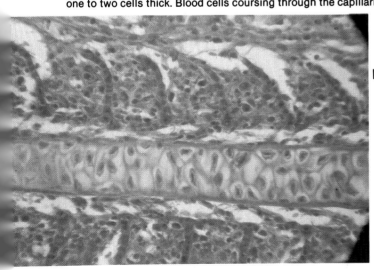

E: Gill hyperplasia occurs when irritants in the water cause the lamellar epithelium to proliferate. Hyperplastic cells fill the spaces between the lamellae and block or reduce flow of water between the lamellae. Blood oxygenation is obstructed. **F:** Gill hyperplasia resulting from excessive gill irritants in the water may be followed by bacterial invasion on the damaged gill. Masses of bacteria are found on gill filaments during an epizootic of bacterial gill disease.

PLATE 10

 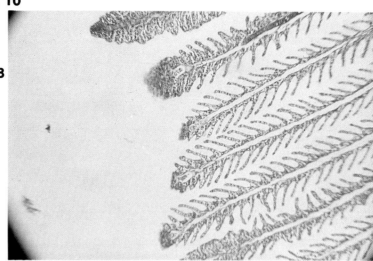

A: A section of gill arch mounted in water on a microscope slide and examined microscopically demonstrates the severity of gill hyperplasia. Individual lamellae should be distinct and separate (Note Pl. IC). **B:** Grade II gill hyperplasia is characterized by fusing of some lamellae, primarily at the distal ends of the filaments. Most of the lamellae are swollen. Prognosis of Grade II gill hyperplasia is that no mortality will occur if treated properly.

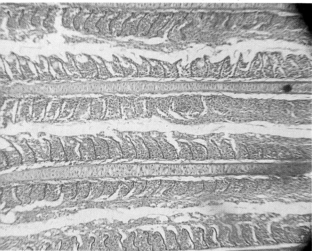 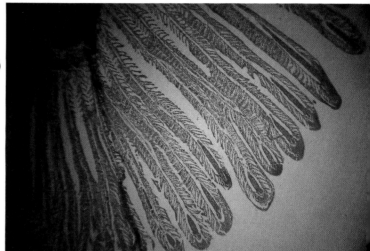

C: Grade III gill hyperplasia is quite severe. Most of the lamellae are fused but no filaments are fused. Prognosis of Grade III gill hyperplasia is that mortality can be controlled by use of external disinfectants and proper water management. **D:** Grade IV gill hyperplasia is characterized by fusion of most lamellae and some filaments. External disinfection is definitely recommended along with proper water management to reduce gill irritants. Biomass reduction should be delayed until fish can be moved safely.

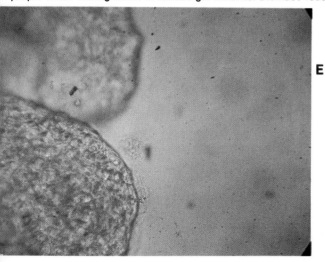 

E: Bacterial growth on gills infected with pseudomonad or aeromonad bacteria is white to gray-white, and tough and leathery. **F:** A few fish with bacterial kidney disease in a population may demonstrate abscesses opened to the exterior of the body.

PLATE 11

 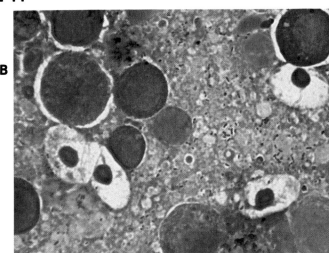

A: Internal lesions of bacterial kidney disease may appear in any visceral organ or tissue as white to gray-white purulent abscesses.
B: Gram-positive bacteria, many in the diplobacilli form, in squash preparations taken from suspected bacterial kidney disease lesions is a positive presumptive test for the disease.

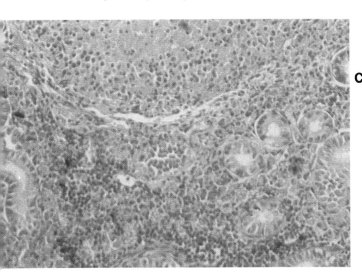 

C: A typical bacterial kidney disease lesion demonstrates classic necrosis. Cloudy swelling and pyknosis appear in the outer portions, cells in various stages of karyorrhexis or karyolysis inside of the outer areas and liquefaction or coagulation necrosis at the center of the lesion. **D:** These neon tetras have mycobacteriosis. The primary external disease signs are fin necrosis and loss of pigmentation.

E: Infections of *Mycobacterium marinum* may occur in and around the spinal column, causing spinal curvature. **F:** The lesion of ulcer disease (caused by *Haemophilus piscium*) is surrounded by a white to gray-white rim of necrotized skin and a dark to almost black center made up of tissue debris and blood cells. Photo courtesy of the Eastern Fish Disease Laboratory, Kerneysville, West Virginia.

PLATE 12

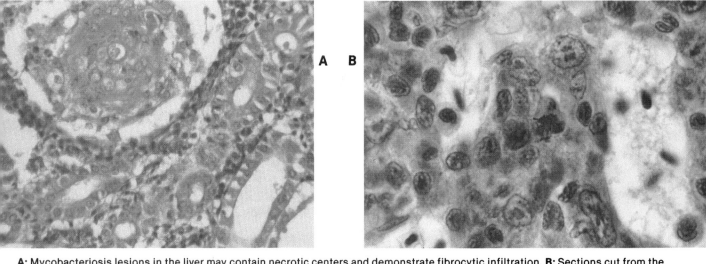

A: Mycobacteriosis lesions in the liver may contain necrotic centers and demonstrate fibrocytic infiltration. **B:** Sections cut from the kidney of fish suspected of mycobacteriosis and stained by the acid-fast technique may reveal discrete masses of acid-fast *Mycobacterium marinum*.

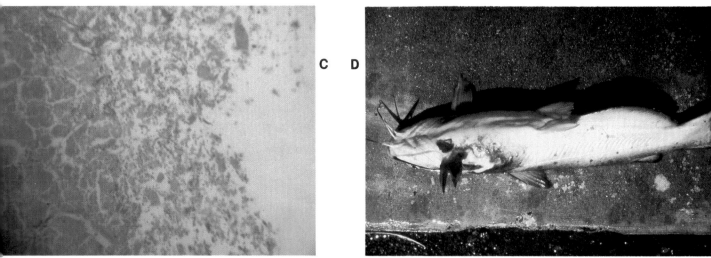

C: Histopathology of a lesion of ulcer disease (caused by *Haemophilus piscium*) includes degenerating myomeres, cellular debris and a tremendous increase in lymphocytes and polymorphonuclear leucocytes. **D:** Signs of edwardsiella septicemia in channel catfish are continually expanding lesions under the skin and into the underlying muscle. Cutaneous hemorrhage and erythema are present at the outer limits of the lesion. Photo by Dr. F.P. Meyer.

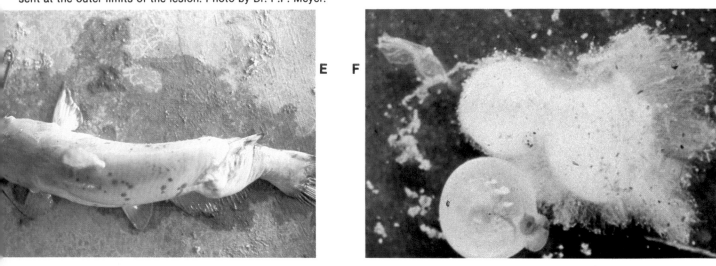

E: Enlarged lesions filled with gas and tissue debris are apparent in channel catfish with edwardsiella septicemia. Photo by Dr. T. Wellborn. **F:** Dead fish eggs are susceptible to saprolegnia invasion. Fungal mycelia may overgrow living fish eggs, suffocate them and then invade the dead eggs. Photo courtesy of Zool.-Par. Inst., Munich.

PLATE 13

A: Saprolegnia may occur where scales have been removed or where injuries are present. The disease sign is a cotton-like growth extending from the infected skin into the water. Each filament is a fungal hypha. Photo by Frickhinger.

B: Saprolegnia may invade injuries, growing on damaged skin and extending into underlying muscle tissue. The caudal peduncle of this guppy was injured and inoculated with a *Saprolegnia* isolate. Photo by Noland-Tintigner, permission of Acta Zool. et Pathol. Antverp.

C: Rainbow trout with acute viral hemorrhagic septicemia may demonstrate dermal and subdermal hemorrhages throughout much of the body. Photo by Dr. P. Ghittino.

PLATE 14

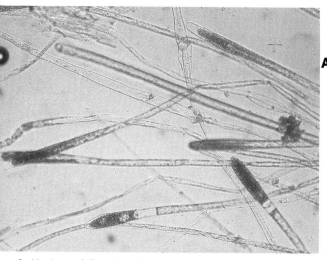 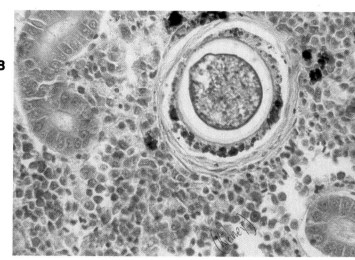

A: Hyphae of *Saprolegnia* sp. are nonseptate. Asexual reproduction is by far the most common means of reproduction among saprolegnia. Fertile hyphae have zoosporangia containing maturing zoospores. **B:** The quiescent stage cyst of *Ichthyophonus hoferi* in kidney tissue of a trout has a heavy cyst wall and a thick layer of host connective tissue.

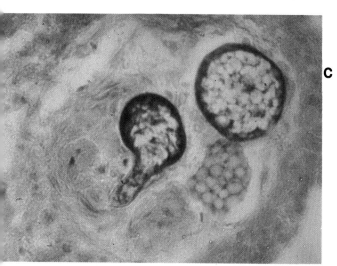 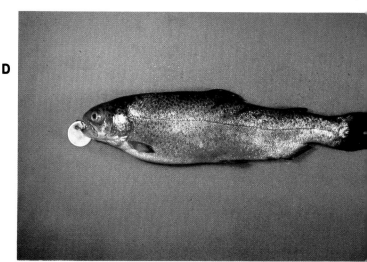

C: A germinating mother cyst of *Ichthyophonus hoferi* extends a plasmodium into surrounding liver tissue of a rainbow trout. Photo by Dr. H.H. Reichenbach-Klinke. **D:** Severe scoliosis and lordosis as well as rough, granulomatous appearance of the skin are external signs of ichthyophonus disease. Photograph by D. Erickson.

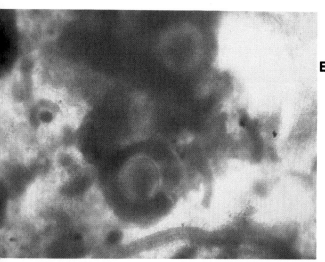 

E: Presumptive diagnosis of ichthyophonus disease is from disease signs and presence of spherical bodies with refractive double walls in squash preparations of infected tissue in water. **F:** The etiological agent of branchiomycosis destroys the blood supply to gills, producing necrosis. Necrotic areas in the gill appear white to brown or may appear denuded of soft tissues. Photograph by Dr. P. de Kinkelin.

PLATE 15

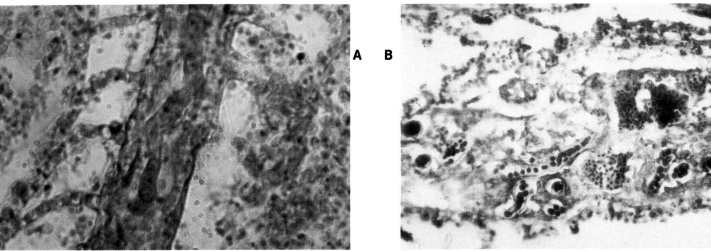

A & B: Demonstration of hyphae in gill capillaries (A) and measurement of fungal spores in cut and stained sections of gill (B) are used to identify *Branchiomyces*. Photos by Drs. Meyer and Robinson.

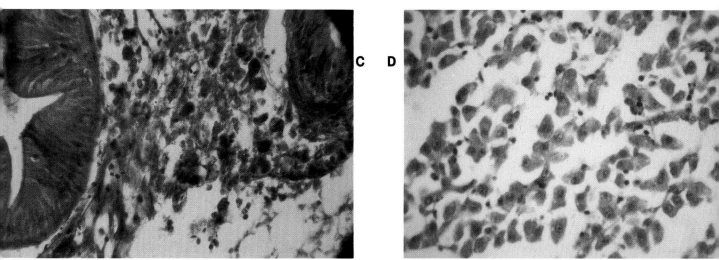

C: Infectious pancreatic necrosis virus may cause slight to extreme necrosis of pancreatic tissue. The extreme necrosis of pancreas caused by this virus will usually leave various sized, oval to round, dark staining inclusions. **D:** Liver edema is a consistent histopathological change in cases of infectious pancreatic necrosis of young salmonids.

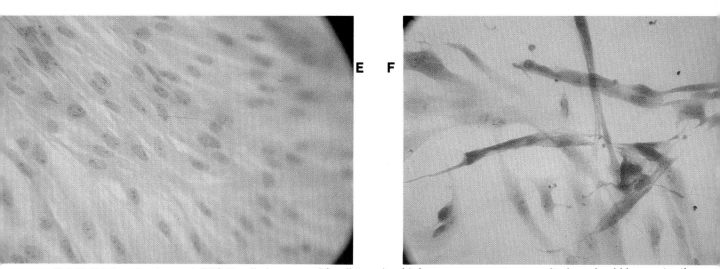

E & F: Rainbow trout gonad (RTG-2) cell sheets used for diagnosis of infectious pancreatic necrosis virus should be greater than 95% monolayered (E). Introduction of the virus will cause cytopathic effect to the cells (F).

PLATE 16

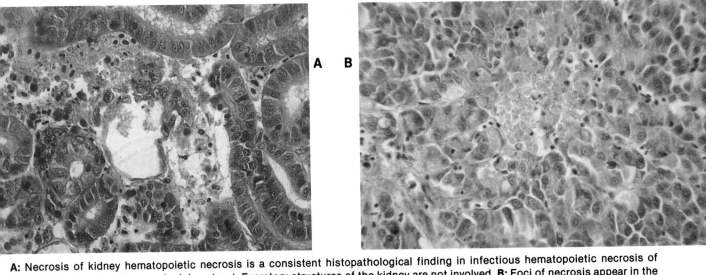

A: Necrosis of kidney hematopoietic necrosis is a consistent histopathological finding in infectious hematopoietic necrosis of sockeye or chinook salmon and rainbow trout. Excretory structures of the kidney are not involved. **B:** Foci of necrosis appear in the liver of sockeye or chinook salmon and rainbow trout with advanced infectious hematopoietic necrosis.

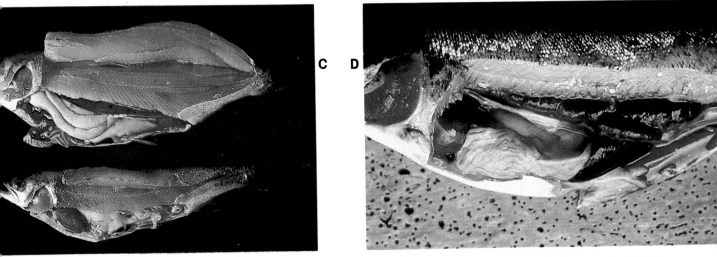

C: Internal signs of acute viral hemorrhagic septicemia include hemorrhages in most tissues. The liver and gills are pale in color. Photo by Dr. P. Ghittino. **D:** Chronic cases of viral hemorrhagic septicemia are sometimes referred to as the renal form of the disease because of the extensive swelling of the kidneys. The spleen is also swollen and the liver pale in color. Photo by Dr. P. de Kinkelin.

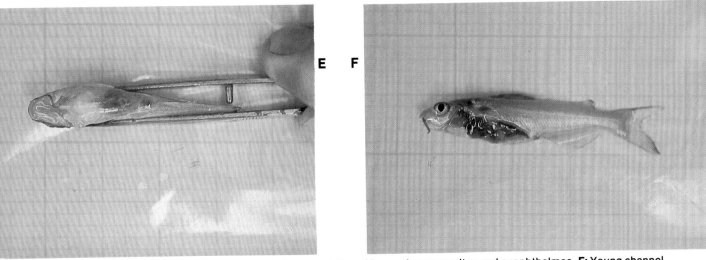

E: External signs of channel catfish viral disease include general dermal hemorrhages, ascites and exophthalmos. **F:** Young channel catfish infected with channel catfish virus develop a general hemorrhagic condition throughout the abdominal cavity. Photos by Plumb.

PLATE 17

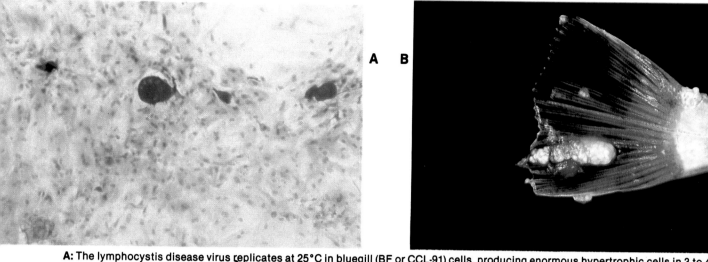

A: The lymphocystis disease virus replicates at 25°C in bluegill (BF or CCL-91) cells, producing enormous hypertrophic cells in 3 to 4 weeks. **B:** Lymphocystis disease appears as white to gray-white or pinkish warty lesions of fins and skin. The lesions are granular in appearance, each grain being a tremendously enlarged connective tissue cell. Photo by Dr. T. Hastein.

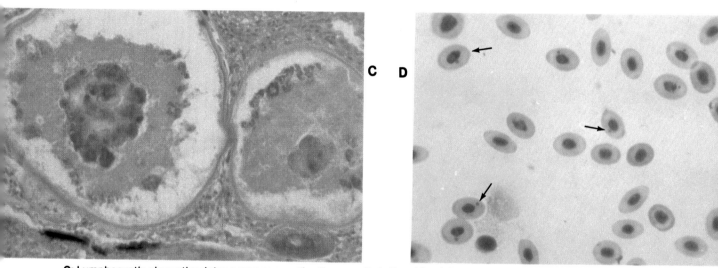

C: Lymphocystis virus stimulates some connective tissue cells in the skin of the host fish to enlarge. These enormous cells may be up to 500 times larger than normal. All elements of the cell are enlarged. Fine strands of inclusion material may appear in the cytoplasm of affected cells. **D:** Erythrocyte cytoplasmic inclusions in Giemsa-stained blood of Atlantic cod with piscine erythrocytic necrosis. Photo by Nicholson.

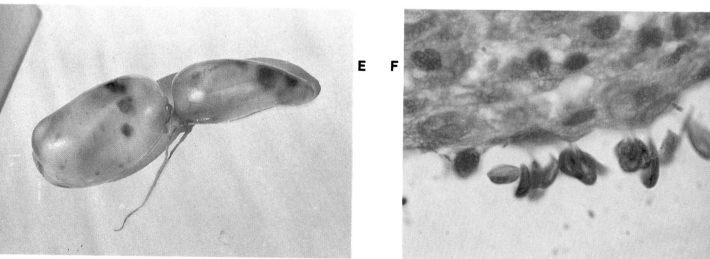

E: The swim-bladder of carp infected with *Rhabdovirus carpio* has hemorrhagic areas throughout the organ. The disease caused by *R. carpio* is called spring viremia of carp or swim-bladder inflammation disease. Photo courtesy of Zool.-Par. Inst. Munich. **F:** *Ichtyobodo necatrix* is a relatively small flagellated protozoan. The body is round or lentil-shaped with one pair of flagella. It may be found attached to the skin or gills of many freshwater fishes. Photo by Dr. T. Hastein.

PLATE 18

 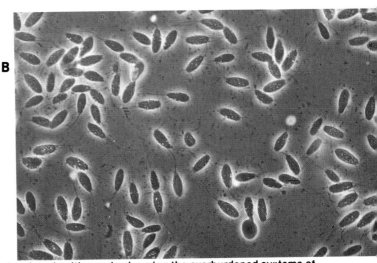

A **B**

A: *Hexamita salmonis* is an opportunist parasite, striking those fish already unhealthy and enhancing the overburdened systems of the fish. The result is increased emaciation and anemia. Fish in this condition may not take food. Photo by T. Hastein. **B:** *Hexamita intestinalis* in an intestinal smear using phase illumination. Photo by Frickhinger.

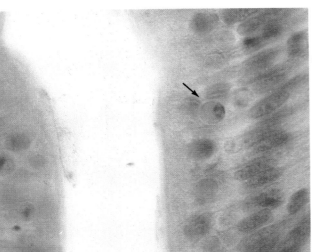 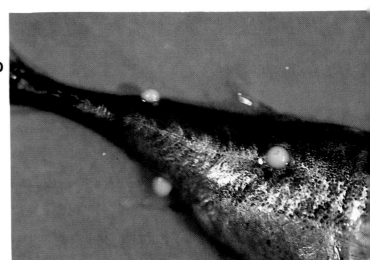

C **D**

C: *Hexamita salmonis* may reproduce by schizogony within the epithelial cells of the ceca. The organism may have a single large nucleus or the nucleus may have divided into several smaller chromatin particles. **D:** Cysts of *Glugea anomala*, a microsporan in the three-spined stickleback.

 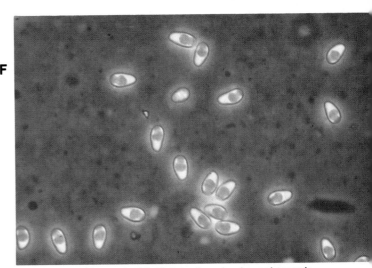

E **F**

E: Signs of microsporiasis may include alteration of body color as in this neon tetra infected with *Pleistophora hyphessobryconis*. Note the milky white area along the back indicating where underlying muscles are heavily infected with the protozoan. Photo by Ruda Zukal. **F:** Spores of *Pleistophora hyphessobryconis* taken from a cyst in neon tetra and observed unstained reveal a light-colored polar sac and darker polarplast at one end. Photo by Frickhinger.

PLATE 19

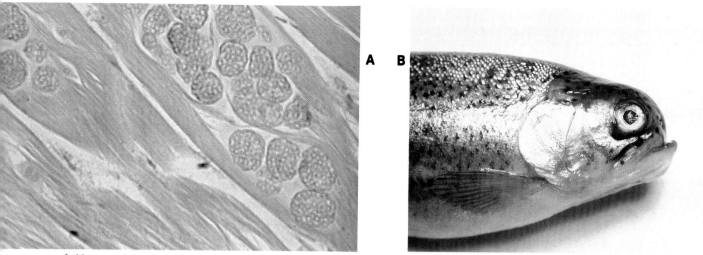

A: Masses of pansporoplasms of *Pleistophora hyphessobryconis* between muscle bundles of neon tetra. **B:** The skull of this rainbow trout has failed to grow to normal configuration from an infection of *Myxosoma cerebralis* during early life.

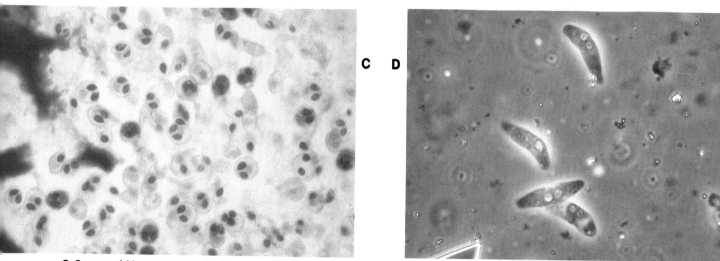

C: Spores of *Myxosoma cerebralis* are round to oval in shape with two well defined polar capsules and a lightly staining sporoplasm in cartilage or surrounded by bone. **D:** Trophozoites of *Ceratomyxa* sp. are widely arched with two distinct polar capsules. Photo by Frickhinger.

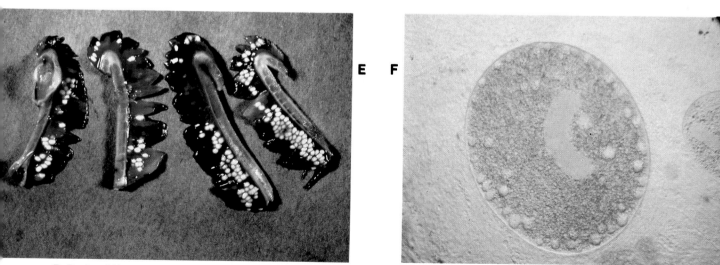

E: Cysts of *Henneguya psorospermica* in gill tissue may limit the respiratory capacity of the fish and cause debilitation or death. Photo by Dr. P. de Kinkelin. **F:** Mature *Ichthyophthirius multifiliis* with the typical crescent-shaped macronucleus.

PLATE 20

A: Young trout infected with *Myxosoma cerebralis* may develop darker pigmentation in the caudal area of the body because of damage to sympathetic nerves controlling pigmentation. Photo by Dr. S. F. Snieszko.

B: Radical skeletal deformation in rainbow trout infected with *Myxosoma cerebralis.* Note the deformed spinal column and the failure of the skull to grow to normal size. Photo by Dr. T. Hastein.

C: *Ceratomyxa shasta* may cause extremely large boil-like lesions in small coho salmon. Photo by J. Conrad.

PLATE 21

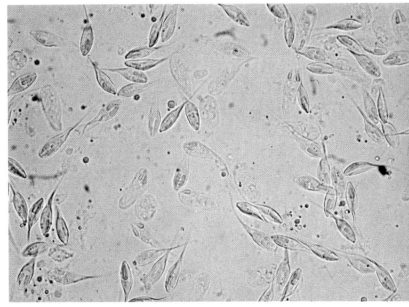

A: Spores of *Henneguya psorospermica* from the northern pike are fusiform in shape with an extremely long caudal process. Photo by Dr. T. Hastein.

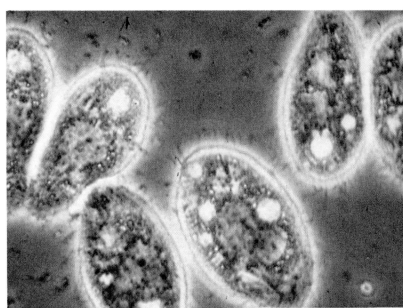

B: Ciliated tomites sometimes called swarmers or vagrant bodies are released from the mature cyst of *Ichthyophthirius multifiliis.*

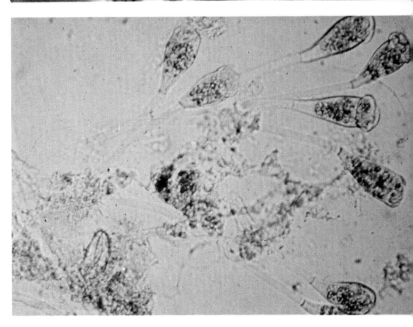

C: *Epistylis* sp. extends from attachment on the host surface into the surrounding water. The bell-shaped anterior end contains cilia used for gathering food. Photo by Dr. W. Rogers.

PLATE 22

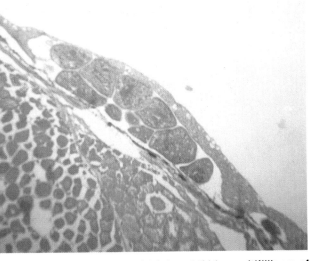

A: Multiple trophozoites of *Ichthyophthirius multifiliis* are often present in intradermal lesions of fishes. **B:** A fish with infections of *Ichthyophthirius multifiliis* has easily observable white spots in the skin containing one or more trophozoites. Photo by Frickhinger.

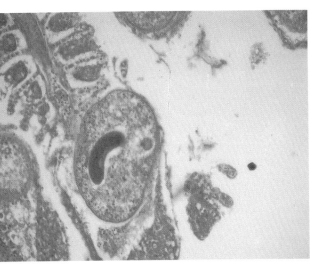
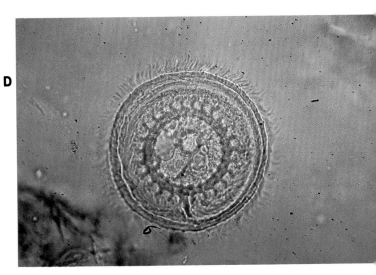

C: *Ichthyophthirius multifiliis* trophozoites may develop in gill tissue of the host. These organisms have a small micronucleus and a large crescent-shaped macronucleus. **D:** *Trichodina* spp. are among the most complex protozoa. The denticulate ring surrounded by a ring of cilia (ciliary girdle) gives this organism a distinctively symmetrical appearance.

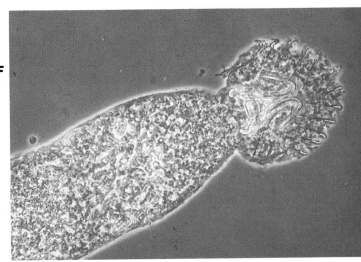

E: Fin necrosis and skin damage from gyrodactyliasis. Photo by Dr. T. Hastein. **F:** The opishaptor of *Gyrodactylus elegans* is armed with 16 marginal hooks and a pair of heavy median hooks. Photo by Frickhinger.

PLATE 23

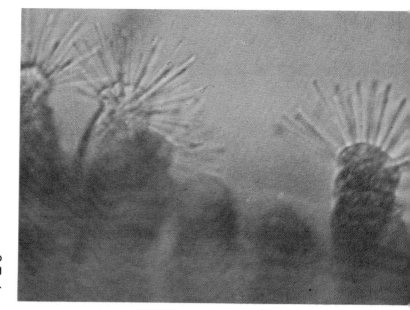

A: Young ciliated *Trichophrya* sp. attach to gill tissue of the host fish, lose the cilia and develop tentacles. Photo by R. Dexter.

B: *Epistylis* sp. colonies on the skin cause white to pinkish patches of slime. These organisms may open portals for opportunistic bacteria or fungi. Photo by Dr. W. Rogers.

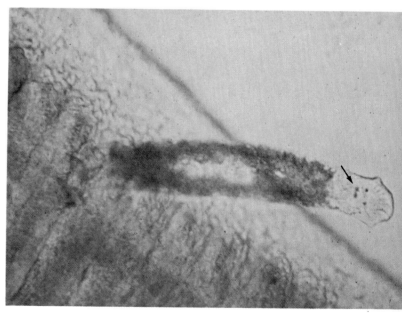

C: Pigment spots of *Cleidodiscus* sp., Monogenea on the gill of a channel catfish. Photo by Dr. F. P. Meyer.

PLATE 24

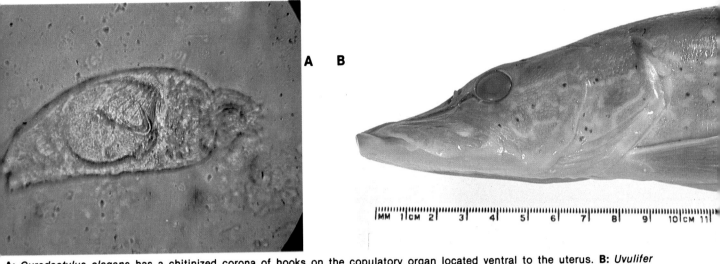

A: *Gyrodactylus elegans* has a chitinized corona of hooks on the copulatory organ located ventral to the uterus. **B:** *Uvulifer ambloplitis* metacercaria in the skin of fishes causes deposition of melanin around the trematode which results in appearance of black spots.

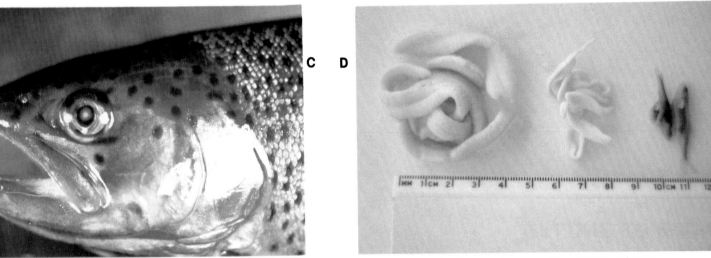

C: Metacercariae of the eye fluke, *Diplostomum spathaceum*, locate in the eye lens and retina causing parasitic cataract and may cause blindness. **D:** Size of *Ligula intestinalis* plerocercoids depends on size of the body cavity of the host fish. Note size variation from a large white sucker (left), from a 10 cm long yellow perch (middle) and fathead minnows (right).

E: *Piscicola* sp. can cause serious damage or death to young fish if the fish are attacked by large numbers of the leeches at any one time. Photo courtesy of Bayer. Biol. Versuchanstalt. **F:** Heavy infections of the large parasitic copepod *Lernaea elegans* may be extremely detrimental to small fishes.

PLATE 25

A: *Proteocephalus ambloplitis* in largemouth bass if present in the intestine in large numbers may cause emaciation, anemia, dark coloration, poor appearance and lost reproduction. Photo by Dr. C. Johnson.

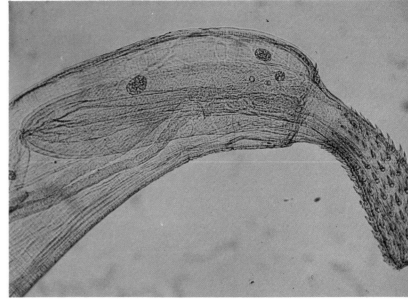

B: The proboscis and lemnisci behind the proboscis are distinctive characteristics of the Acanthocephala. Adult *Leptorhynchoides thecatus* (shown here) are found in the intestine of black bullhead. Photo by Dr. F. Meyer.

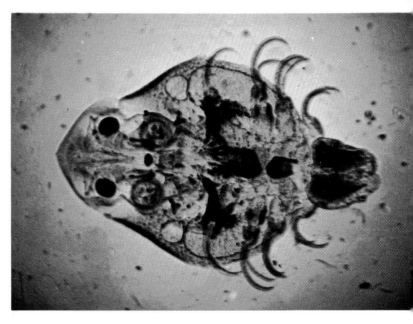

C: *Argulus* sp. (ventral view) has numerous hooks, barbs and spines, as well as suckers on the body and legs to assist in attachment to the host. Photo by Dr. E. Elkan.

PLATE 26

A: Adult female.

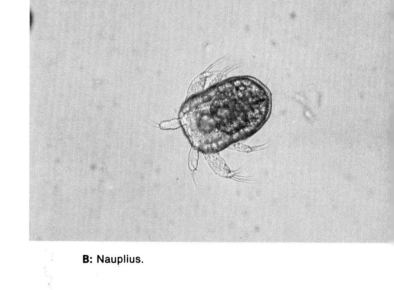

B: Nauplius.

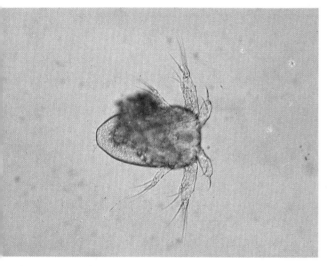

C: Metanauplius.

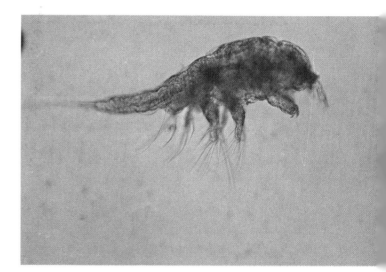

D: First copepodid.

E: Sixth copepodid female.

F: Sixth copepodid female with two sperma-tophores attached.

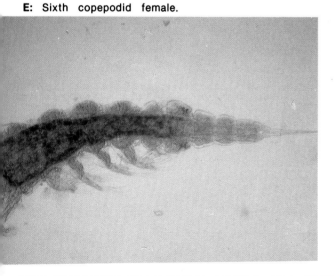

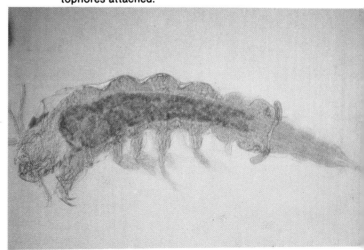

Life cycle of *Lernaea elegans*. Each copepodid stage is typified by addition of thoracic segments and appendages until the complete five segments and four pairs of swimming legs are present at the time of the third copepodid. The male sixth copepodid deposits a spermatophore on the genital segment of the sixth copepodid female and then dies. The female attaches to the host and begins producing eggs.

PLATE 27

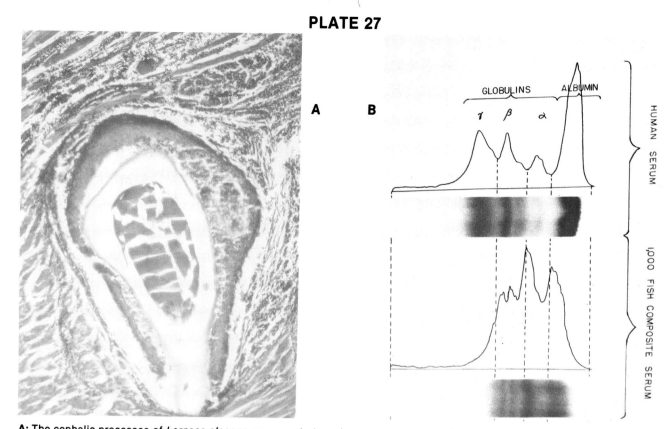

A: The cephalic processes of *Lernaea elegans* may penetrate various organs of the body, such as the muscle above, displacing vital tissue and creating tremendous inflammation and necrosis. **B:** Electrophoretic mobility of the serum proteins of rainbow trout compared to human serum proteins. Note the paucity or near lack of a fish globulin fraction with mobility equal to human gamma globulin.

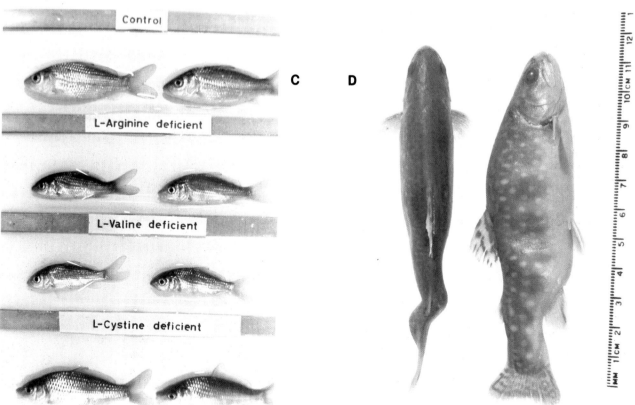

C: Reduction or removal of indispensable amino acids (arginine, valine) from carp's diet reduces growth. Growth continues at normal rate when required amino acids are present (control, top fishes) or when dispensable amino acids (cystine) are removed. **D:** Deficiency of dietary tryptophan causes transient lordosis and scoliosis. Normal body conformation returns on restoration of adequate tryptophan to the diet.

PLATE 28

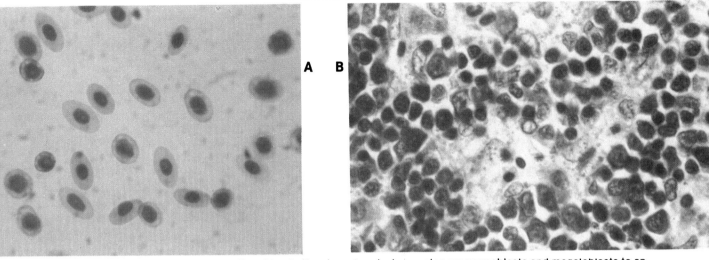

A: Presence of fat autoxidation products in the diet of trout alters hematopoiesis, causing pronormoblasts and megaloblasts to appear in circulating blood. **B & C:** Kidney damage from dietary fat autoxidation products includes focal necrosis of hematopoietic tissue (B) and nephrosis (C).

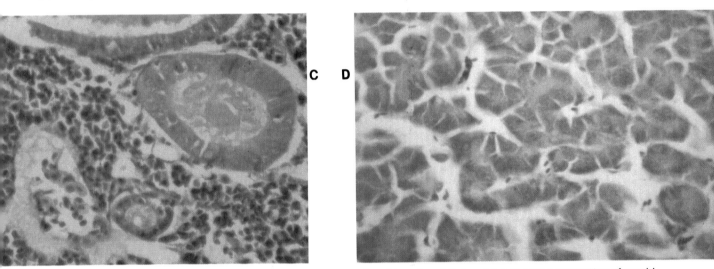

D: Autoxidation products at quantities greater than 10 mg of thiobarbituric acid per kg of dietary fat may cause deposition of ceroid in liver hepatocytes, which can be demonstrated histochemically by use of the acid-fast staining technique.

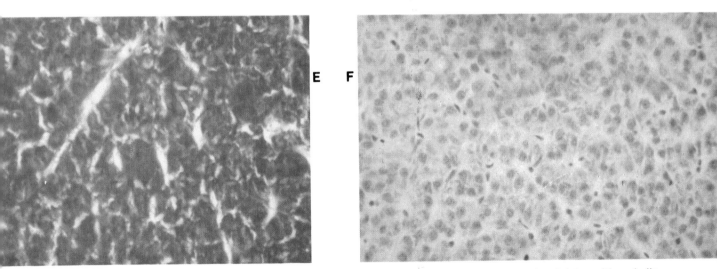

E & F: Liver glycogen storage can be estimated histochemically. Glycogen is demonstrated in liver tissue by staining with periodic acid-Schiff reagent without pretreatment with diastase (E), but fails to stain after diastase treatment (F).

PLATE 29

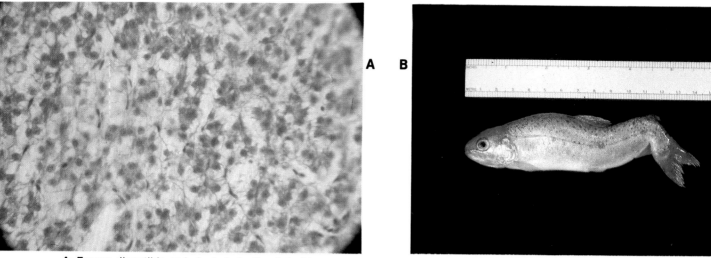

A: Excess digestible carbohydrate in the diet of trout causes liver hyperglycogenesis. Hepatocytes become filled with glycogen, possibly to the point where liver function is impaired. Liver glycogen in the above section of rainbow trout liver was 14% of the liver mass. **B:** Deficiency of ascorbic acid (vitamin C) causes scoliosis and lordosis in which vertebrae are permanently fused and misshapen.

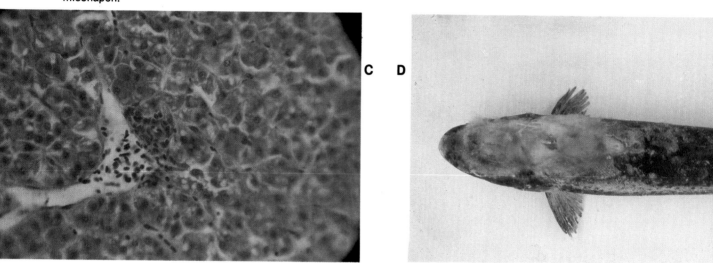

C: Deficiency of those vitamins responsible for normal blood formation (folic acid and vitamin B$_{12}$ for example) may cause extramedulary hematopoiesis in which primitive blood forming organs such as the liver (above) revert to hematopoietic function. **D:** Niacin deficiency in trout is typified by sloughing of epithelial cells, usually to a greater degree on the dorsal surface. The disease is known as back peel, back sore or sunburn disease, the latter name because sunshine enhances the pathology.

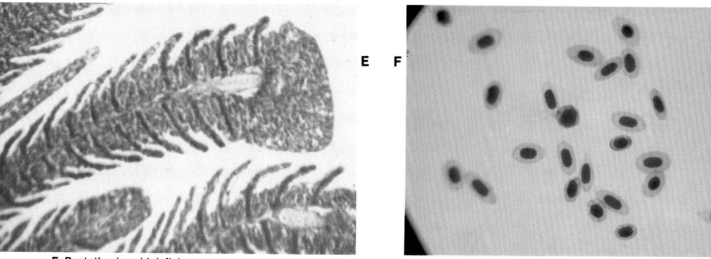

E: Pantothenic acid deficiency causes proximal lamellar hyperplasia. The condition can continue until gill filaments are extremely swollen and bulbous. **F:** Nutritional anemia, including iron deficient anemia, is hypochromic and microcytic in nature. A high percentage of juvenile and poorly formed erythrocytes in stained blood smears is also indicative of nutritional anemia.

PLATE 30

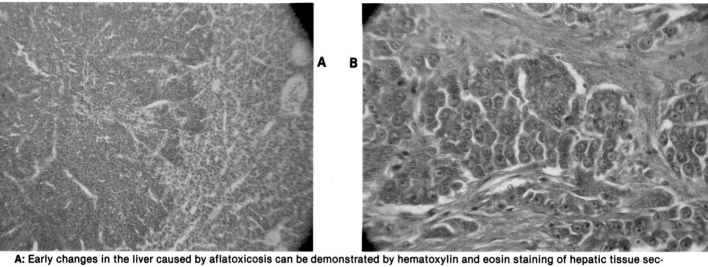

A: Early changes in the liver caused by aflatoxicosis can be demonstrated by hematoxylin and eosin staining of hepatic tissue sections. Large areas of basophilic-staining cells indicate initial change which will develop into hepatoma neoplasms. **B:** Nodular hepatoma formed in the liver of fish with aflatoxicosis may have little or no resemblance to the parent tissue. Anaplasia, increased mitosis and fibrous infiltration are a part of these hepatic cell carcinomas.

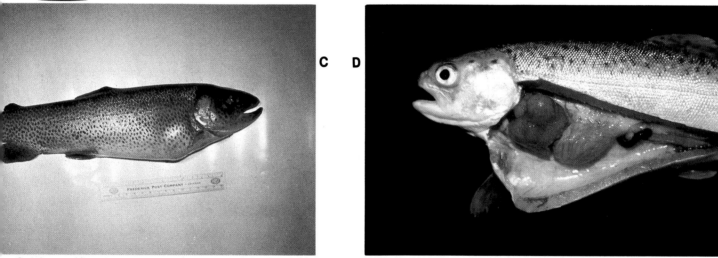

C: Advanced hepatoma causes enlargement of the liver, which may be visible through the body wall. The fish may become extremely emaciated. **D:** Hepatoma nodules may be present throughout the liver. Those near the surface are gray-white to yellowish color, and contrast with the normal deep reddish color of the liver.

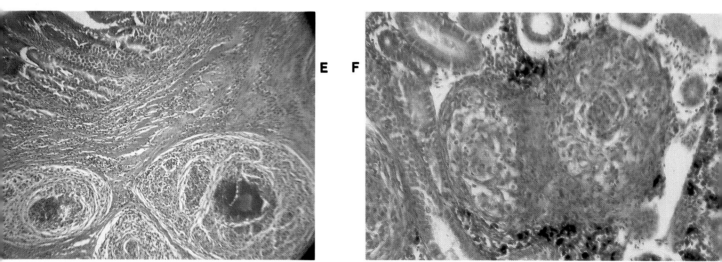

E & F: Benign fibromas, sometimes called visceral granulomas, are most often found in stomach musculature (E) and kidney (F) tissues. The cause of these tumors is not known.

PLATE 31

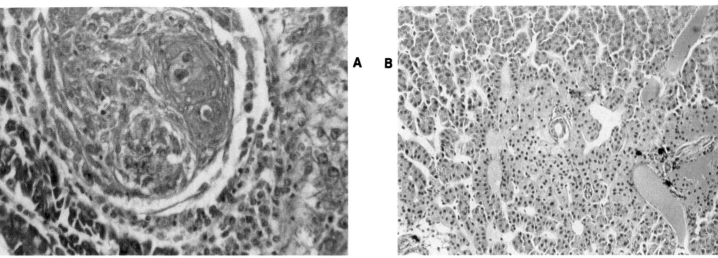

A: Benign tumors may be caused by oncogenic bacteria such as *Mycobacterium marinum* or *M. fortuitum*. **B:** Necrotic hepatic cells (necrotic foci above) surrounding blood vessels indicate the source of toxicant to be from blood.

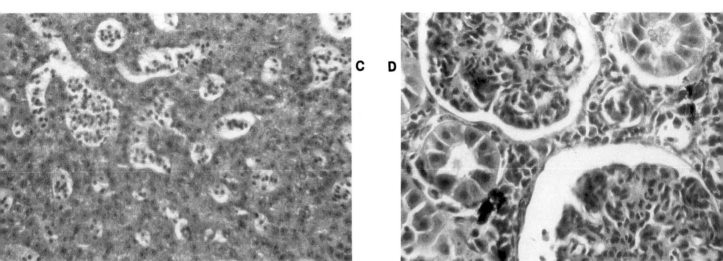

C & D: Accumulation of an irritant or toxic substance in an organ stimulates circulatory dilation and hyperemia. Liver (C) and glomerular (D) hyperemia indicate sublethal alteration of circulation caused by a toxic substance.

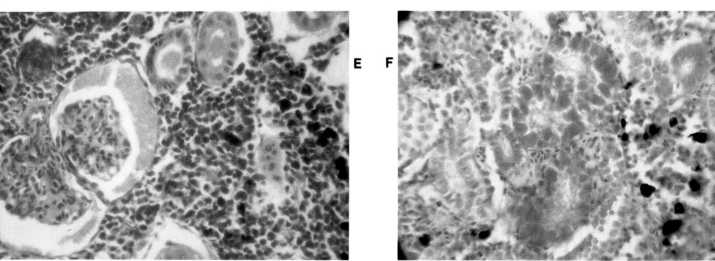

E: Nephrosis occurs when toxic substances alter glomerular permeability allowing blood plasma protein to seep into the excretory portion of the kidney. Protein casts in Bowman's capsule and excretory tubules are observed to indicate nephrosis. **F:** Hyaline degeneration in kidney excretory tubular epithelium may be caused by a high concentration of major ions dissolved in environmental water.

PLATE 32

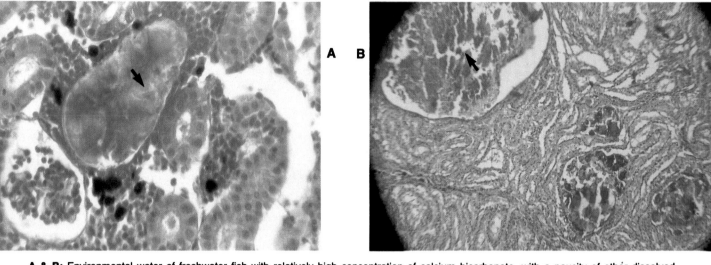

A & B: Environmental water of freshwater fish with relatively high concentration of calcium bicarbonate, with a paucity of other dissolved anions (chloride or sulfate) and near pH 7, may lead to urinary calculi (A) and/or pseudobranchial calcuil (B).

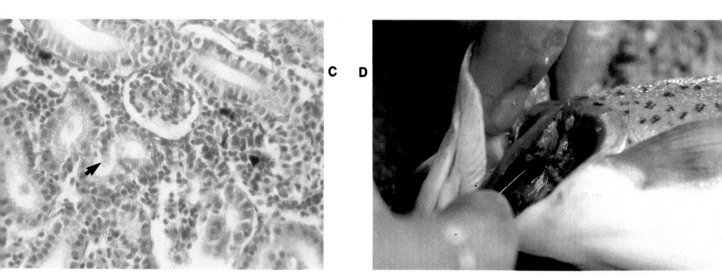

C: Sulfamerazine given at a relatively high dose level for a prolonged period of time causes severe kidney pathology including precipitation in excretory tubules, hyaline degeneration of tubular epithelium and nephrosis. **D:** Acute distress and death may result from placing fish into an intolerable pH. This fish was removed from water in a distribution tank at pH 7.4 and placed immediately into a spring-fed stream at pH 5.2. Note erythema and hemorrhages in the skin and fins and regurgitated food in the pharynx.

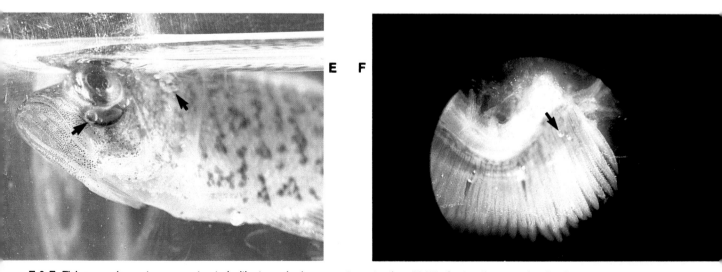

E & F: Fish occupying water supersaturated with atmospheric gases at greater than 104% of saturation may develop free gas bubbles around eyes, within tissues of the operculum, gill filaments, lips and other tissues. Gas pressure behind the eyeballs causes traumatic exophthalmos and hemorrhage. Photo "F" by U. S. F. & W. S. Leetown, W. Va.

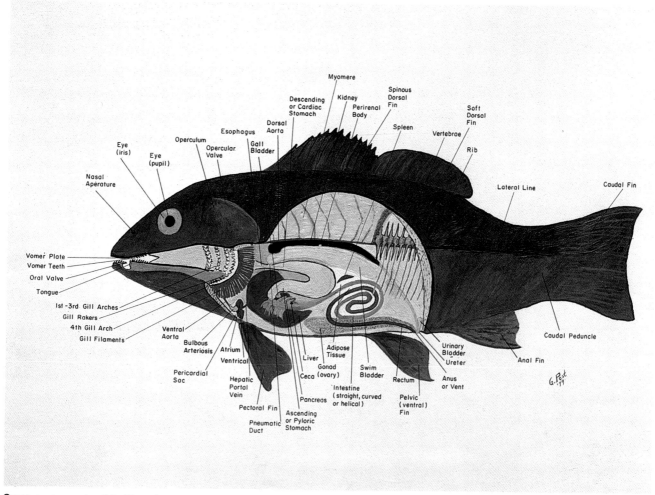

Gross anatomy of a fish. Note: Some anatomical structures may vary from this hypothetical diagram such as stomach shape, number of ceaca, presence of pancreatic tissue interspersed in liver tissue, fin variations and other differences depending on fish species.

TABLE 13

Examples of Miscellaneous viruses of fish[37a,62,64b,64c,71a,97]

Name of Virus	Abbreviation	Host(s)	Virus Characteristics
Herpesvirus Group:			
Herpesvirus salmonis	—	Adult rainbow trout; fry of land-locked sockeye salmon	175 nm diameter (may be indistinguishable from NeTVA)
Nerka virus	NeTVA	Fry of land-locked sockeye salmon	200 to 250 nm diameter (may be indistinguishable from *Herpesvirs salmonis*)
Herpesvirus cyprini	CHV	Carp pox in common carp	190-220 nm diameter
Herpesvirus vitreum	—	Walleye with hyperplastic dermal tissue	190 to 230 nm in diameter
Leukovirus Group:			
Esox lymphosarcoma-associated virus	—	Northern pike	Leukovirus Type-C particles
Orthomyxovirus Group:			
Eel virus—2	EV-2	European eel with stomatopapilloma	Orthomyxovirus-like, spheroid, pleomorphic, 80 to 140 nm diameter
Rhabdovirus Group:			
Eel Rhabdovirus—American	EVA	Young American eel at 20 to 27°C	Rhabdovirus; 143 nm length and 68 nm in diameter
Eel Rhabdovirus—European	EVEX	European eel	Rhabdovirus; 160 nm length and 73 nm in diameter
Grass carp Rhabdovirus	GCR	Young grass carp at 23°C	Rhabdovirus; 120 nm length and 70 nm in diameter
Rhabdovirus carpio	SVC	Spontaneous disease in carp; experimental infection in carp, guppy, pike fry and grass carp; mortality decreases below 17°C and above 20°C	Rhabdovirus; 189 nm length and 70 nm in diameter
Ribovirus			
Bluegill virus	BGV	Bluegill epitheliocystis	90 to 110 nm in diameter
Unclassified:			
Eel virus—European	EVE	European and Japanese eels at less than 20°C	Icosahedral, 68 to 77 nm in diameter
Eel virus—1	EV-1	European eel with stomatopapilloma	Icosahedral particles
European eel virus—stomatopapilloma	—	Blood of European eel with stomatopapilloma	Icosahedral; 55 nm in diameter

TABLE 13 (continued)

Name of Virus	Abbreviation	Host(s)	Virus Characteristics
Demonstrated by Electron Microscope Only:			
Epithelioma papillosum associated virus	—	Carp, with epithelioma papillosum; reported with other cyprinids	Herpes-like; enveloped particles 140 to 150 nm in diameter
Esox epidermal proliferation associated virus	—	Pike with epidermal lesions	Particles 120 nm in diameter, with 70 nm nucleoid
Viral erythrocytic necrosis virus	VENV	Erythrocytes of Atlantic cod, Atlantic herring and other marine species	Possible Iridovirus; icosahedral particles 310 to 360 nm in diameter
Walleye epidermal hyperplasia associated virus	—	Walleye epidermal tumor	Particles 80 nm in diameter; appear enveloped; budding particles observed
Walleye sarcoma associated virus	—	Walleye sarcoma	Particles 100 nm in diameter

Susceptible Species:

Twelve marine fish species from a geographical area ranging along the New England coast of the United States and the New Brunswick coast of Canada have been confirmed as susceptible to VEN. These species include alewife, herring, smelt, cod, spot, tautog, gunnel, sea raven, sculpin, seasnail and two species of flounder. Four other species have been suspected of being susceptible to VEN: one additional flounder species, windowpane, pout and two species of hake.[84]

VEN has been reported in chum and pink salmon taken along the Canadian Pacific coast.[25] Viral inclusions have been observed in blood from chum, coho and chinook salmon, and in steelhead rainbow trout in Oregon.[65a] Other fish species are no doubt susceptible to the disease, and additional hosts will continue to be reported.

Incidence and Importance:

Surveys to determine the incidence of VEN in susceptible fishes have demonstrated relatively high morbidity levels for wild-ranging fishes. Blood smears from cod taken along the central North Atlantic coast of the United States and Canada demonstrated erythrocytic cytoplasmic inclusions ranging from 11 to 16% (118 positive from 780 fish, or an average of 15% infected.)

Twenty-eight Atlantic herring taken near Boothbay, Maine demonstrated 11% incidence of severe erythrocytic degeneration. 57% of another 150 herring captured and held in the laboratory for six days had erythrocytic inclusions. 95% of 20 herring had erythrocytic inclusions 13 days after capture.[53] Examination of 1,412 anadromous smelt collected at 42 stream sites from Massachusetts through Nova Scotia and into New Brunswick Canada had 55.7% infection level.[72b]

A study was made to determine hematological variation in fish infected with VEN virus. Cod and herring with VEN inclusions in erythrocytes had lower erythrocyte counts, lower hematocrits and lower hemoglobin levels than noninfected fish.[64a] Pacific herring with heavily VEN virus-infected erythrocytes had skin hemorrhages but there was no mortality.[65a] Destruction of erythrocytes can be detrimental to survival or may be fatal. Wild-caught herring, as an example, had between 10 and 90% cytoplasmic inclusions in erythrocytes. One herring held in captivity for 16 days had 95% affected cells. There seemed to be some correlation between infection and presence of immature erythrocytes in the circulating blood. Herring normally have approximately 15% immature erythrocytes; VEN-infected fish had as high as 90% immature cells.[53] This indicates a tremendous loss of erythrocytes and stress on hematopoietic tissues to replace red cells for circulation. Additional research is needed on VEN before importance to fish populations can be judged.

Herpesvirus Salmonis Disease

A previously undescribed virus was isolated from ovarian fluid of apparently normal post-spawning rainbow trout in Washington State in 1974. The virus had general characteristics of the Herpesvirus group, the first Herpesvirus known in a coldwater fish species. The

PLATE 34

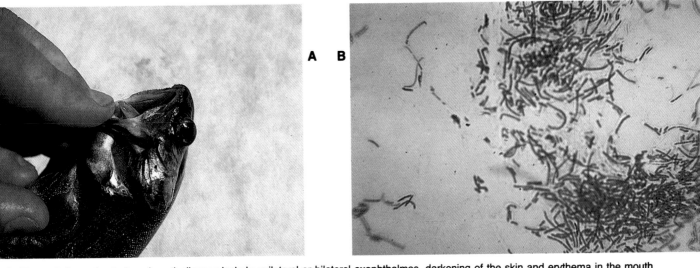

A: External signs of enteric redmouth disease include unilateral or bilateral exophthalmos, darkening of the skin and erythema in the mouth and base of fins. **B:** Pure cultures of *Flexibacter columnaris* clearly demonstrate long, slender, filamentous, curved, rod shaped, gram negative bacteria.

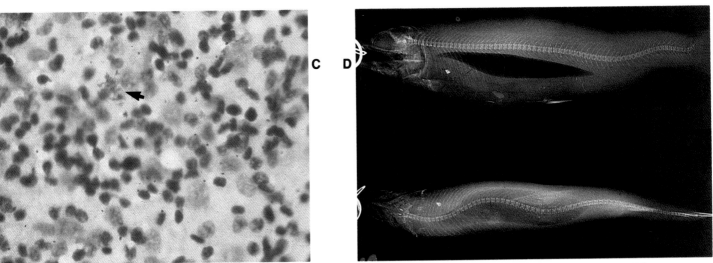

C: Sections cut from spleen of fish suspected of mycobacteriosis and stained by acid-fast technique reveals discrete masses of acid-fast *Mycobacterium marinum* (arrow). **D:** X-ray photographs of fish with ichthyophonus disease demonstrate vertebral column alteration both dorso-ventrally and laterally. Photograph by D. Erickson.

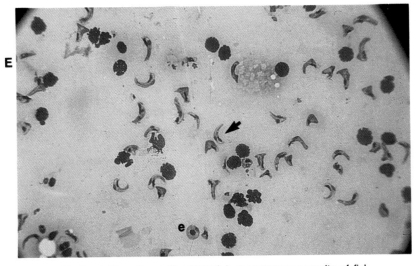

E: *Cryptobia salmonisitica* (arrow) is a protozoan parasite of fish blood (normal erythrocyte—e).

PLATE 35

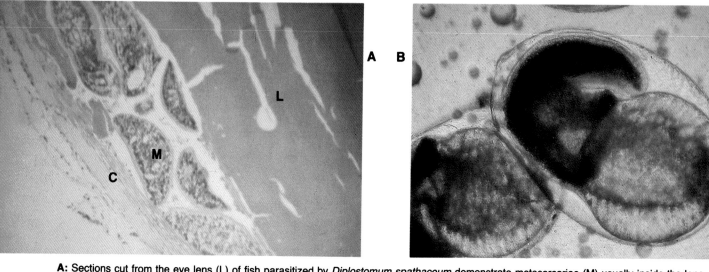

A: Sections cut from the eye lens (L) of fish parasitized by *Diplostomum spathaceum* demonstrate metacercariae (M) usually inside the lens capsule (C). **B:** Metacercariae of *Posthodiplostomum minimum* may appear as membrane enclosed organisms in wet mounts made from infected organs of fish.

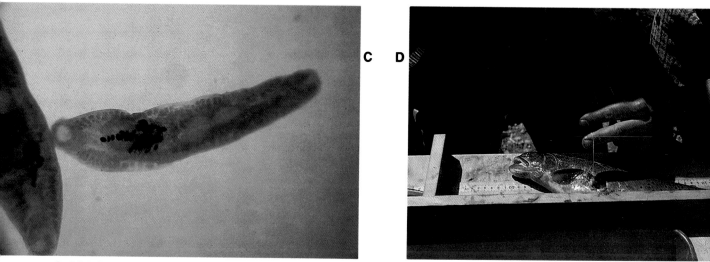

C: Adult *Crepidostomum farionis* are 2 to 6 mm in length and are found at various sites along the intestine of the host until reaching maturity (above) at which time they maintain themselves in the rectal area. Photograph by D. L. Mitchum. **D:** The plerocercoid stage of *Diphylobothrium cordiceps* is coiled in tissue of the alimentary tract or muscle and may be over 14 cm long.

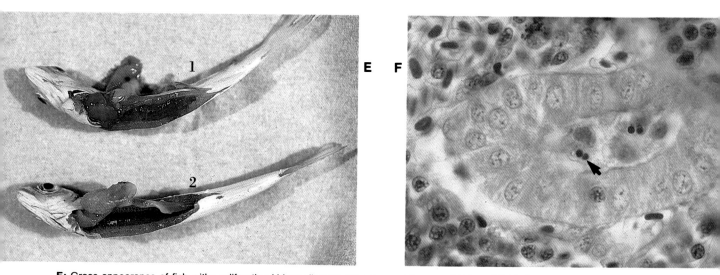

E: Gross appearance of fish with proliferative kidney disease (1) compared to normal kidney (2). **F:** PKX cells (arrow) appear in the lumen of uriniferous tubules of fish infected with proliferative kidney disease (Giemsa stain). Photographs E and F by Dr. R. P. Hedrick.

virus replicated in RTG-2 cells and was subsequently inoculated into very small rainbow trout fry.

Disease signs developed slowly in infected fry. The first death was 33 days post-inoculation. The disease proved to be 100% fatal to the inoculated fish. Infected fry became dark in color and some developed exophthalmos, a distended abdomen and extremely pale gills. There was edematous fluid in the abdomen of the fish. The liver, heart and spleen appeared edematous. The kidneys were light in color but were not swollen. All fish were extremely anemic.[109]

The primary target organs appeared to be liver and kidney. Histological preparations from the liver demonstrated edema, vacuolation, areas of necrosis and hyperemia. Skeletal and heart muscles were edematous, as was the kidney hemopoietic tissue. Kidney excretory tubules were filled with proteinaceous casts.[100a,109]

Etiological Agent:

The etiological agent has been named *Herpesvirus salmonis*. It is 175 nm in diameter, with an envelope and a 90 nm in diameter nucleocapsid. The virus is heat, chloroform and ether labile. Some infectivity persists on treatment at pH 10.0 but is lost at pH 3.0. Replication occurs between 5 and 10°C, inconsistently at 0 and 15°C and is lost completely at 20°C. The virus replicates in rainbow trout gonad (RTG-2), rainbow trout embryo (RTE-1), and chinook salmon (CHSE-214) cells. It replicates slowly in kokanee salmon (KF-1) cells and not at all in brown bullhead (BB), bluegill fry (BF-2) or fathead minnow (FHM) cells. It forms distinct plaques in RTG-2 cells, and intranuclear inclusions. The virus is not neutralized by infectious pancreatic necrosis, infectious hematopoietic necrosis or Egtved virus antisera.[99]

Susceptible Species:

The only fish species known to be susceptible to *H. salmonis* is rainbow trout.[108]

Incidence and Importance:

The incidence of infection of *H. salmonis* among susceptible fish is not known; neither is the importance of the virus among fish populations known. The virus is carried in ovarian fluid of apparently normal rainbow trout. This means that the organism could be transmitted to eggs and effect embryo development or newly hatched fry. Experiments demonstrated the susceptibility of rainbow trout fry to the virus following laboratory injection. Presence of this virus could explain some of the cases of significant mortality among rainbow trout fry held at cold water temperatures and in which no other etiological agent responsible for the mortality was found.

Pike Fry Rhabdovirus Disease

Northern pike culture has been practiced in North America, Europe and Asia. An ulcerative disease of the skin of adult pike is prevalent in European pike. The disease has been called by several names—red-disease,

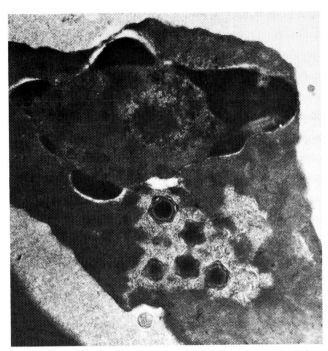

Fig. 11: Virions in erythrocytic cytoplasm of Atlantic cod piscine erythrocytic necrosis (PEN) disease. (20,000 X) Photo by Walker and Sherburne in J. Fish. Res. Bd. Can.

red-sore disease, pike pest and others. The etiology of the disease has variously been given as bacterial, protozoan, fungal and of other origins. A bullet-shaped virus was first reported from the kidneys of northern pike fry with red-disease in the Netherlands in 1973.[18,21] The viral isolate was sent to the Eastern Fish Disease Laboratory at Kearneysville, West Virginia for confirmation. Here the virus was found to replicate on rainbow trout gonad (RTG-2) cells. It grew well at 15°C and was classified as a Rhabdovirus.

Research between 1973 and 1975 demonstrated that a Rhabdovirus was truly a part of the etiology of the disease. The disease was named Pike Fry Rhabdovirus Disease (PFRD), a name used since that time.[17,21]

PFRD-affected pike fry demonstrate loss of equilibrium and erratic swimming. Hemorrhagic areas appear along the body, particularly above the pelvic fins. The fish develop exophthalmos and hydrocephalus.[16,92]

Histological preparations from affected fry demonstrate petechial hemorrhages in muscle, throughout the spinal cord, spleen, pancreas and hematopoietic tissue of the kidneys. The excretory portion of the kidneys has degenerative changes and necrosis. The excretory tubules may contain hyaline casts. The brain is edematous and the cerebro-spinal fluid contains erythrocytes.[92]

Etiological Agent:

The Rhabdovirus of PFRD is bullet-shaped, measuring 125 nm in length and 80 nm in diameter. It is chloroform and ether sensitive. Pike fry Rhabdovirus (PFR) replicates in RTG-2 and fathead minnow (FHM) cells between 14 and 24°C. Its entire range of replication temperatures is not known. Cytopathic effects of FHM cells appear within 24 to 40 hours at 20°C. The virus replicates well at pH 7.6, but the entire pH range of replication is not known. There is no PFRD antiserum available. The virus is not neutralized by *Rhabdovirus carpio* antiserum.[17,18,21,92]

Susceptible Species:

The northern pike is apparently the only species known to be susceptible to PFR. Adult pike are asymptomatic carriers of the virus and shed the virus into water. Young pike hatched from eggs previously in contact with PFR contaminated water suffered 100% mortality. Mortality began 14 days following hatching and continued for a week before all fry were lost. Incubation and fry holding temperature was 10.5°C.[17]

Incidence and Importance:

Epizootics of PFRD have occurred during the spring in many parts of the Netherlands. The incidence among northern pike is not known, even in those geographical areas in which it is enzootic. The virus can exist in water at 10°C for at least ten days.[17] The incubation period for northern pike eggs is about ten days at 10°C. Some viable particles of the virus would no doubt remain to infect fry on hatching, even if the virus cannot penetrate an incubating egg. Also, the disease can be transmitted from PFR-infected fry to normal pike fry. Movement of fish and fish eggs about Europe and the world has probably spread the virus, but the exact range is unknown.

The morbidity level among natural PFR-infected pike is unknown, nor is the incubation period known. Laboratory infection of pike fingerlings, in which PFR was inoculated intraperitoneally, yielded an incubation period of one to five days at 14°C and one to two days at 21 to 24°C.

The importance of PFRD is not known. Many of the epizootics of red-disease among hatchery-reared young northern pike in western Europe have been devastating to pike production for the year in which the epizootics occurred. There is no way of relating fry and fingerling mortalities for hatchery epizootics to wild populations of pike. The northern pike is not usually raised to maturity in culture facilities, as are certain other fish species. Hatching of northern pike eggs and rearing of pike fry are practiced primarily as adjuncts to natural reproduction. Fishery management biologists use hatchery-raised northern pike fry and fingerlings to initiate pike populations in natural waters where this species had not existed previously. The hatchery product has also been used to enhance natural reproduction of pike in those open waters which already have a pike population with limited spawning areas. Cultured pike in either case are used primarily as a sport fishery.

Most northern pike eggs are obtained from adult pike trapped from lakes, streams or partially confined water. PFR in hatchery-reared fry and fingerling pike could be transmitted to wild-ranging pike and from wild-ranging pike to eggs and fry. The disease could thus become important in the management of certain pike fisheries.

Spring Viremia of Carp

Spring viremia of carp (SVC) is an acute to chronic virus disease of several species of carp. The fact that most epizootics of the disease occur during the spring of the year, at a time when pond water begins to warm, adds credence to the name. Most epizootics of the disease occur during this period of the year, but the disease is also known to occur during cold water periods. Epizootics which develop during cold water periods are chronic in nature. Many warm water period epizootics are acute.[64]

SVC has been regarded as having a complex etiology. A disease known as infectious abdominal dropsy had been reported in carp culture over much of Europe. The disease was thought to be caused by bacteria. A virus etiology was postulated in the early 1950's. Experiments in the 1960's successfully transmitted the disease from infected to non-infected carp using bacterial-free filtrates prepared from kidney material of fish with infectious abdominal dropsy. Several workers at the time felt that a virus could explain infections of certain secondary bacteria usually associated with the disease.[51,64]

A virus was isolated from carp infected with infectious abdominal dropsy in 1971.[27] The virus was called *Rhabdovirus carpio* and has been subsequently accepted as the etiologic agent of SVC. Most workers feel there is a single etiology of infectious abdominal dropsy, or spring viremia of carp, and prefer to call the disease by its primary cause, spring viremia of carp virus (SVCV).

Another disease of cultured carp, known as swim-bladder inflammation, has also been prevalent among carp of Europe. A virus was isolated from fish with the disease in 1974. The virus has subsequently been found to be closely related to the SVCV.[14,80] Probably SVC is synonymous with both infectious abdominal dropsy and swim-bladder inflammation.

External signs of acute SVC include abdominal swelling and hemorrhages in the skin and around the anus. The gills are pale. Chronic cases may have hemorrhagic ulcers in the skin and more extensive edema.

Internal signs include profuse quantities of clear or blood-stained fluid in the abdomen. The liver is usually pale in color and may be hemorrhagic. The muscles are necrotic, and there are hemorrhages on the surface of the swim-bladder (Pl. 17E). The intestine is hemorrhagic and the kidney and spleen are swollen and hemorrhagic.[64]

Histopathology of carp tissue which results from experimental infection of SVCV is extensive. There are necrotic areas and extensive congestion in the liver and pancreas. Much desquammation is present in the intestinal epithelium. The spleen is congested. There is hyaline degeneration in kidney excretory tubules. The

PLATE 36

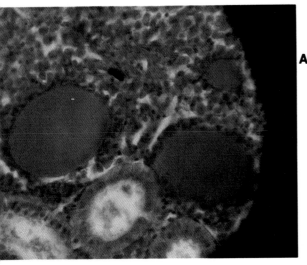
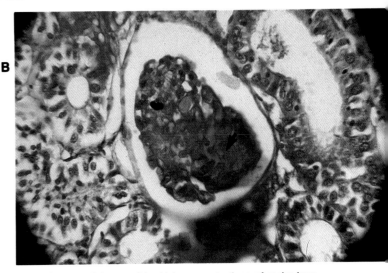

A: Some uriniferous tubules may be completely destroyed and replaced with hyaline material caused by high concentrations of major ions (especially sulfate ion) in environmental water. **B:** Environmental water of freshwater fish with relatively high concentrations of calcium bicarbonate and a paucity of other dissolved anions (chlorides and sulfates) may lead to urinary calculi in glomeruli and other parts of the kidney (arrows).

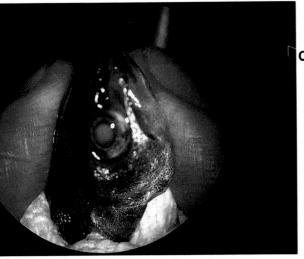

C: Nutritional cataract of the eye can be caused by deficiency of dietary zinc. Photo by Dr. H. G. Ketola. **D:** This rainbow trout was exposed while an embryo within its egg to 10 mg methylazomethanol acetate per liter of its environmental water. Liver and swimbladder neoplasms developed as illustrated by 9 months of age. Photo by Dr. J. D. Hendricks.

E: Piscidal compounds used to remove unwanted fish populations must be mixed evenly throughout the body of water being treated for best results. Photo by Dr. F. P. Meyer. **F:** Gravel or stones obtained from the pond or aquarium bottom during feeding may be too large to pass with the feces and cause obstructions along the intestinal tract or anus (above) leading to necrosis and death.

blood vessels of the swim bladder are extremely dilated (Pl. 17E). The pericardium demonstrates inflammatory response.[50]

Etiological Agent:

The etiological agent of SVC is a Rhabdovirus 189 nm in length by 70 nm in diameter. The virus replicates well in fathead minnow (FHM or CCL-42) and carp ovary cells at 20°C. It produces characteristic plaques in FHM cells.[104] SVCV is neutralized by *R. carpio* antiserum.[27] The virus will retain infectivity in carp ovary cells for more than a year at 4°C and in 50% glycerin for at least six months.[68]

The route of infection in susceptible fishes is apparently through the gills. Experiments in which common carp were submerged in 13°C water containing SVCV demonstrated viral particles in gill tissue two hours after submersion. The virus was found in the blood after six days and in various visceral organs (kidney, liver, spleen, heart and alimentary tract) in ten to 11 days. The virus began to shed in feces on 11 days post-infection, and the first deaths occurred at 20 days.

Susceptible Species:

Species of fishes susceptible to SVCV infection include the common carp, bighead carp, grass carp, pike fry, guppy and possibly tench.[3,48,64,68] Tench are thought by some investigators to be the source of the virus and to act as carriers. Other members of the family of fishes which include carp, Cyprinidae, may also be susceptible.

Incidence and Importance:

Probably the morbidity level among young carp is nearly 100% during epizootics in confined ponds. Mortality during epizootics may be 50 to 70% or higher.[11] Adult carp which have been in contact with the virus may develop viremia and display signs of the disease,

but there usually will be little or no mortality. Survivors of SVC have antibodies homologous to the virus. As an example, 25 to 30 gram carp were injected with SVCV and developed virus-neutralizing antibodies in about 30 days, and there was some mortality among these fish.[2]

SVC is enzootic over much of the carp-rearing areas of Europe. The disease is not known in the United States. The disease has a definite economic importance in those countries where the carp is an important fish. SVC has been said to be as important to the carp breeder of Europe as infectious pancreatic necrosis (IPN) is to the trout producer in the United States.[64]

Control procedures for SVC include quarantine, restriction of movement of infected fish, sanitation and disinfection. Careful disinfection of each pond after removal of all fishes has been recommended for reducing the incidence of the disease in enzootic areas.

SVCV is known to be transmitted from infected fishes to noninfected fishes through water. Certain external parasites (the fish louse *Argulus foliaceus*[1c] and the leech *Piscicola geometra* for example) are known to mechanitransmit the virus,[10] possibly other parasites may be involved in viral transmission as well.

Quarantine and movement restriction, especially from enzootic SVC geographical areas, should be practiced to prevent importation of the virus into other parts of the world. The carp is not a choice fish in the United States, but there are tremendous populations of this species throughout the country. The species may take on more importance for human food in the future, and for this reason the carp population in the United States should be protected from SVCV. Also, other members of the cyprinid family (daces, minnows, shiners and many others) native to the North American continent may be susceptible to *R. carpio*. Release of the virus into North American waters could cause catastrophic losses among these species.

Selected References

1. Acton, J. D., L. S. Kucera, Q. N. Myrvik and R. S. Weiser. 1974. *Fundamentals of Medical Virology*. Lea & Febiger, Philadelphia, PA. 350p.

1a. Ahne, W. 1983. "Presence of infectious pancreatic necrosis virus in the seminal fluid of rainbow trout, *Salmo gairdneri* Richardson." *J. Fish Dis.*, 6:377.

1b. Ahne, W. 1982. "Isolation of infectious pancreatic necrosis virus from zebra danio, *Brachydanio renio*." *Bull. Eur. Assoc. Fish Pathol.*, 2(1):8.

1c. Ahne, W. 1985. "*Argulus foliaceus* L. and *Piscicola geometra* L. as mechanical vectors of spring viremia of carp virus (SVCV)." *J. Fish Dis.*, 8:241-242.

2. Ahne, W. 1978. "Uptake and multiplication of spring viremia of carp virus in carp, *Cyrpinus carpio*," *J. Fish Dis.*, 1:265-268.

2a. Adair, B. M. and H. W. Ferguson. 1981. "Isolation of infectious pancreatic necrosis (IPN) virus from non-salmonid fish." *J. Fish Dis.*, 4:69-76.

3. Ahne, W. 1975. "A rhabdovirus isolated from grass carp (*Ctenopharyngodon idella* Val.)," *Arch. Virol.*, 48:181-185.

4. Amend, D. F. 1975. "Detection and transmission of infectious hematopoietic necrosis virus in rainbow trout," *J. Wildl. Dis.*, 11:471-478.

5. Amend, D. F. 1974. *Infectious hematopoietic necrosis (IHN) virus disease.* FDL-39, Div. Cult. Meth.

Res., U.S. Bur. Spt. Fish. Wildl., Washington, DC. 6p.

6. Amend, D. F. 1970. "Control of infectious hematopoietic necrosis virus disease by elevating water temperature," *J. Fish. Res. Bd. Can.*, 27:265-270.

7. Amend, D. F. and V. C. Chambers. 1970. "Morphology of certain viruses of salmonid fishes. II. *In vivo* studies of infectious hematopoietic necrosis virus," *J. Fish. Res. Bd. Can.*, 27:1385-1388.

8. Amend, D. F. and J. P. Pietsch. 1972. "Virucidal activity of two iodophors to salmonid viruses," *J. Fish. Res. Bd. Can.*, 29:61-65.

9. Amend, D. F. and G. Wedemeyer. 1970. *Approved procedure for determining absence of infectious pancreatic necrosis (IPN) virus in certain fish and fish products.* FDL-31, U.S. Bur. Spt. Fish. Wildl., Washington, DC. 4p.

10. Amend, D. F., W. T. Yasutake and R. W. Mead. 1969. "A hematopoietic virus of rainbow trout and sockeye salmon," *Trans. Am. Fish. Soc.*, 98:796-804.

10a. Amin, O. M. 1979. "Lymphocystis in Wisconsin fishes." *J. Fish Dis.*, 2:207-217.

11. Amlacher, E. 1970. *Textbook of fish diseases.* T.F.H. Publ., Neptune, NJ. 302p.

12. Anderson, D. P. 1974. *Diseases of fishes, Book 4: Fish Immunology.* S. F. Snieszko and H. R. Axelrod, *eds.* T.F.H. Publ., Neptune, NJ. 229p.

13. Awerinzew, S. 1907. "Zur Kenntnis von *Lymphocystis johnstonei* Woodcock," *Zool. Anz.*, 31:881-884.

14. Bachman, P. A. and W. Ahne. 1974. "Biological properties and identification of the agent causing swim bladder inflammation in carp," *Archiv. f. gesamte Virusforsch.*, 44:261-269. [In: Fish Health News (U.S. Fish. Wildl. Serv., Nat. Fish. Cent., Kearneysville, WV) 3(4):4-6.]

15. Besse, P. 1956. "L'anemie pernicieuse des truites," *Ann. Stat. Centr. Hydrobiol. Appl.*, 6:441-467.

15a. Bootland, L. M., R. M. W. Stevenson and P. Dobos. 1985. "Experimental induction of the carrier state in yearling brook trout: A model challenge protocol for IPNV immunization." *Proc. FHS-AFS, 1985 Ann. Meeting:* p. 8 (Abstract only).

16. Bootsma, R. 1971. "Hydrocephalus and red-disease in pike fry, (*Esox lucius* L.)," *J. Fish Biol.*, 3:417-419.

17. Bootsma, R., P. de Kinkelin and M. L. Berre. 1975. "Transmission experiments with pike fry (*Esox lucius* L.) rhabdovirus," *J. Fish. Biol.*, 7:269-276.

18. Bootsma, R. and C. J. A. H. V. Van Vorstenbosch. 1973. "Detection of a bullet-shaped virus in kidney sections of pike fry (*Esox lucius* L.) with red-disease," *Neth. J. Vet. Sci.*, 98:86-90.

18a. Castric, J. and P. deKinkelin. 1980. "Occurance of viral hemorrhagic septicemia in rainbow trout *Salmo gairdneri* Richardson reared in sea-water." *J. Fish Dis.*, 3:21-27.

19. Cohen, J. A., A. Poinsard and R. Scherrer. 1973. "Physico-chemical and morphological features of infectious pancreatic necrosis virus," *J. Gen. Virol.*, 21:485-498.

20. Davis, H. S. 1953. *Culture and diseases of game fishes.* Univ. Calif. Press, Berkeley and Los Angeles, CA. 332p.

21. de Kinkelin, P., R. Bootsma and B. Galimard. 1973. "Isolation and identification of the causative agent of red-disease of pike (*Esox lucius* L. 1766)," *Nature, Lond.*, 241:465-467.

21a. Desautels, D. and R. M. MacElvie. 1975. "Practical aspects of survival and distribution of infectious pancreatic necrosis virus." *J. Fish. Res. Bd. Can.*, 32:523.

22. Deufel, J. 1958. "Utersuchungen uber den Erreger der Infektiosen Nierenschwellung und Leberdegeneration der Forellen," *Arch. Fisch.*, 9:181-186.

23. Elliott, D. 1978. "Fish disease inspection and certification," *MFR Pap.*, 1302. [March. Fish. Rev. 40: 69-71.]

23a. Enzmann, P. J. 1981. "Rapid identification of VHS-virus from trout by immunofluorescence." *Int. Symp. Fish Biol.*, 49:57-62.

24. Eskildsen, U. K. and P. E. Vestergard Jorgensen. 1973. "On the possible transfer of trout pathogenic viruses by gulls," *Riv. It. Piscic. Ittiopat.*, 8: 104-105.

25. Evelyn, T. 1976. "Overview of viral diseases of salmonids," *In* Donson, M. and Kinkelin P. de. 1977. *Proc. Internat. Symp. Dis. Cult. Salm.*: 91-115. (Tavolek, Inc., Redmond, WA.).

25a. Evelyn, T. P. T. and G. S. Traxler. 1978. "Viral erythrocytic necrosis: Natural occurrence in Pacific salmon and experimental transmission." *J. Fish. Res. Bd. Can.*, 35:903-907.

26. Fijan, N. N. 1968. "Progress report on acute mortality of channel catfish fingerlings caused by a virus," *Bull. Off. Int. Epiz.*, 69:1167-1168.

27. Fijan, N. N., Z. Petrinec, D. Sulimanovic and L. O. Zwillenberg. 1971. "Isolation of the viral causative agent of the acute form of infectious dropsy of carp," *Vet. Arh. Zagreb.*, 41:125-138.

28. Fijan, N. N., T. L. Wellborn, Jr. and J. P. Naftel. 1970. *An acute viral disease of channel catfish. U.S. Bur. Spt. Fish. Wildl., Tech. Paper 43.* 11p.

29. Findlay, J. and B. J. Hill. 1975. "The use of the complement fixation test for rapid typing of infectious pancreatic necrosis virus," *Aquacult.*, 5:305-310.

30. Fish Health Section, McDaniel, D. (ed.). 1979. *Procedures for detection and identification of certain fish pathogens (Revised)*. Am. Fish. Soc., 5410 Grosvenor Lane, Bethesda, MD. 118p.

30a. Flugel, R. M. 1984. "Properties of fish lymphocystis disease virus." *Int. Sem. Fish Pathol.*, Tokyo, Jpn. p. 52 (Abstract only).

30b. Fryer, J. L., J. S. Rohovec, J. S. Tebbit, G. L. McMichael and K. S. Pilcher. 1976. "Vaccination for control of infectious diseases of Pacific salmon." *Fish Pathol.*, 10:155-164.

31. Ghittino, P. 1962. "L'ipertrofia renale e degenerazione epatica infettiva della trota iridea di allevamento," *Vet. Ital.*, 13:457-489.

31a. Hah, Y. C., S. W. Hong, M. H. Kim, J. L. Fryer and J. R. Winton. 1984. "Isolation of infectious pancreatic necrosis virus from goldfish (*Carassius auratus*) and chum salmon (*Oncorhynchus keta*) in Korea." *Korean J. Microbiol.*, 22:85-90.

32. Hyde, R. R. 1937. *Laboratory outline on filterable viruses*. Macmillan Co., New York City, NY. 85p.

33. Jensen, M. H. 1965. "Research on the virus of Egtved disease," *Ann. N.Y. Acad. Sci.*, 126:422-426.

34. Jirovec, O. 1932. "Engebnisse der Nuklealfarbung an den Sporen der Mikrosporidean nebst einigen Bemerkungen uber Lymphocystis," *Arch. f. Protist.*, 77:379-390.

35. Joklik, W. K. and H. T. Willett. 1976. *Zinsser microbiology, 16th ed*. Appleton-Century Press, New York City, NY. p.804-814.

36. Jorgensen, P.E.V. 1971. "Egtved virus: demonstration of neutralizing antibodies in serum from artificially infected rainbow trout (*Salmo gairdneri*)," *J. Fish. Res. Bd. Can.*, 28:875-877.

36a. Jorgensen, P. E. V. 1972. "Eptved virus: antigenic variation in 76 virus isolates examined by neutralization tests and by means of fluorescent antibody techniques." *Symp. Zool. Soc. London*, 30:330.

37. Jorgensen, P.E.V. 1974. "Indirect fluorescent antibody techniques for demonstration of trout viruses and corresponding antibody," *Acta. Vet. Scand.*, 15: 198-205.

37a. Kelly, R. K., O. Nielsen, S. C. Mitchell and T. Yammamoto. 1983. "Characterization of *Herpesvirus vitreum* isolated from hyperplastic dermal cells of walley, *Stizostedion vitreum* (Mitchell))." *J. Fish Dis.*, 6:249-260.

38. Lawler, A. R., J. T. Ogle and C. Donnes. 1977. "*Dascyllus* spp.: New hosts for lymphocystis, and a list of recent hosts," *J. Wildl. Dis.*, 13:307-312.

39. Laird, M. and W. L. Bullock. 1969. "Marine fish hematozoa from New Brunswick and New England," *J. Fish. Res. Bd. Can.*, 26:1075-1102.

39a. Lannan, C. N., J. R. Winton and J. L. Fryer. 1984. "Fish cell lines: Establishment and characterization of nine cell lines from salmonids." Ore. State Uni. Sea Grant Prog. Publ. No. *ORESU-R-84-018*. 6 p.

40. Liebmann, H. and H. Reichenbach-Klinke. 1964. "Untersuchungen zur Epidemiologie und Okologie der Forellenseuche," *Arch. Fischereiwiss.*, 15: 94-113.

41. Lightner, D. and G. Post. 1969. "Morphological characteristics of infectious pancreatic necrosis virus in trout pancreatic tissue," *J. Fish. Res. Bd. Can.*, 26:2247-2250.

42. Lowe, J. 1874. "Fauna and flora of Norfolk. Part IV," *Trans. Norfolk and Norwich Nat. Soc., Fish*: 21-56.

43. MacIntosh, W. C. 1884. "Diseases of fishes. I. Multiple tumours in plaice and common flounders," *Ann. Rep. Scot. Fish. Bd.*, p. 66.

44. Major, R. D., J. P. McCraren and C. E. Smith. 1975. "Histopathological changes in channel catfish (*Ictalurus punctatus*) experimentally and naturally infected with channel catfish virus disease," *J. Fish. Res. Bd. Can.*, 32:563-567.

44a. McAllister, P. E., M. W. Newman, J. H. Sauber and W. J. Owens. 1984. "Isolation of infectious pancreatic necrosis virus (serotype Ab) from diverse species of esturine fish." *Helgolander Meeresuntersuchungen* 37:317-328.

45. McAllister, P. E. 1979. "Fish viruses and viral infections," *In: H. Fraenkel-Conrat and R. R. Wagner, eds. Comprehensive virology*, 14:401.

46. McCosker, J. E. and R. F. Nigrelli. 1971. "New records of lymphocystis disease in four eastern Pacific fish species," *J. Fish. Res. Bd. Can.*, 28: 1809-1810.

47. McGonigle, R. H. 1940. "Acute catarrhal enteritis of salmonid fingerlings," *Trans. Am. Fish. Soc.*, 70: 297-303.

48. Melnick, J. L. 1973. "Classification and nomenclature of animal viruses," *Progr. Med. Virol.*, 15:380.

49. Moss, L. H. and M. Gravell. 1969. "Ultrastructural and sequential development of infectious pancreatic necrosis virus," *J. Virol.*, 3:52-58.

50. Negele, R. D. 1977. "Histopathological changes in some organs of experimentally infected carp fingerlings with *Rhabdovirus carpio*," *Bull. Off. Int. Epiz.*, 87:449-450.

50a. Noga, E. J., E. M. Walczak and J. X. Hartmann.

1978. "An attenuated virus vaccine for prevention of channel catfish virus disease." *9th Ann. FHS-AFS Workshop*:48.

51. Offhaus, K., G. Brunner and S. Redimuller. 1955. "Gedenken uber die Entstehung der Bauchwassersucht des Karpfens auf Grund bakteriologischer. Ergebnisse und elektrophoretischer Blutuntersuchungen," *Arch. Fischeriwiss.*, 5/6:316-327.

51a. Okamoto, N., T. Sano, R. P. Hedrick and J. L. Fryer. 1983. "Antigenic relationship of selected strains of infectious pancreatic necrosis virus and European eel virus." *J. Fish Dis.*, 6:19-25.

52. Parisot, T. J. and J. Pelnar. 1962. "An interim report on Sacramento River chinook disease: a virus-like disease of chinook salmon," *Prog. Fish-Cult.*, 24: 51-55.

53. Philippon, M., B. L. Nicholson and S. W. Sherburne. 1977. "Piscine erythrocytic necrosis (PEN) in Atlantic herring (*Clupea harengus harengus*): evidence of viral infection," *Fish Health News* (U.S. Fish Wildl. Serv., Nat. Fish. Res. Cent., Kearneysville, WV), 6:6-10.

53a. Pilcher, K. S., and J. L. Fryer. 1980. "The viral diseases of fish: A review through 1978." *CRC Crit. Rev. Microbiol.*, Part 1:287-363.

53b. Plumb, J. A. 1985. "Susceptibility of European catfish (*Siluris glanis*) to channel catfish virus." *FHS-AFS Newsletter* 13(2):7.

54. Plumb, J. A. 1973. "Neutralization of channel catfish virus by serum of channel catfish," *J. Wildl. Dis.*, 9:324-330.

55. Plumb, J. A. 1973. "Effects of temperature on mortality of fingerling channel catfish (*Ictalurus punctatus*) experimentally infected with channel catfish virus," *J. Fish. Res. Bd. Can.*, 30:568-570.

56. Plumb, J. A. 1971. "Channel catfish virus disease in southern United States," *Proc. 25th Ann. Conf. S. E. Game and Fish Comm.*, Oct. 1971. p. 489-493.

57. Plumb, J. A. 1971. "Southeastern cooperative fish disease project," Auburn University, Auburn, AL. *Newsletter 8.* p2.

58. Plumb, J. A. 1971. "Channel catfish virus research at Auburn University," *Prog. Rep. Series No. 95.* Agri. Exp. Sta., Auburn Univ., Auburn, AL. 3p.

59. Plumb, J. A. 1971. "Tissue distribution of channel catfish virus," *J. Wildl. Dis.*, 7:213-216.

60. Plumb, J. A., J. L. Gaines, E. C. Mora and G. G. Bradley. 1974. "Histopathology and electron microscopy of channel catfish virus infected channel catfish, *Ictalurus punctatus* (Rafinesque)," *J. Fish Biol.*, 6:661-664.

61. Plumb, J. A., L. D. Wright and V. L. Jones. 1973. "Survival of channel catfish virus in chilled, frozen and decomposing channel catfish," *Prog. Fish-Cult.*, 35:170-172.

62. Post, G. 1977. *Glossary of fish health terms.* Am. Fish. Soc., Bethesda, MD. 48p.

63. Rasmussen, C. J. 1965. "A biological study of Egtved disease (INuL)," *Ann. N.Y. Acad. Sci.*, 126:427-460.

64. Reichenbach-Klinke, H. H. 1973. *Fish pathology.* T.F.H. Publ., Neptune, NJ. 512p.

64a. Reno, P., D. Serreze, S. Hellyer and B. Nicholson. 1984. "Hematological and pysiological effects of viral erythrocytic necrosis (VEN) in Atlantic cod and herring." *Internat. Sem. Jpn. Soc. Fish Pathol.*, Tokyo, Jpn., p. 51 (Abstract only).

64b. Robin, J. and C. Dery. 1982. "The genome of bluegill virus." Can. J. *Microbiol.*, 28:58-64.

64c. Robin, J., and C. Lariviere-Durand. 1983. "Bluegill virs is a Ribovirus of positive-strand polarity." *Arch. Virol.*, 77:119-125.

65. Ross, A. J., J. Pelnar and R. R. Rucker. 1960. "A virus-like disease of chinook salmon," *Trans. Am. Fish. Soc.*, 89:160-165.

65a. Rohovec, J. S. and A. Amandi. 1981. "Incidence of viral erythrocytic necrosis among hatchery reared salmonids of Oregon." *Fish Pathol.*, 15:135-141.

66. Ross, A. J. and R. R. Rucker. 1960. *A "virus" disease of chinook salmon.* Fish. Leaf. 497. U.S. Fish Wildl. Serv., Washington, DC. 3p.

67. Rucker, R. R., W. J. Whipple, J. R. Parvin and C. A. Evans. 1953. *A contagious disease of salmon possibly of virus origin.* Fish. Bull. 76. U.S. Fish & Wildl. Serv., Washington, DC. 35p.

68. Rudikov, N. I., L. I. Grischenko and K. A. Lobuncov. 1975. "Vesennaja virus naja bolezj rhb," *Bjull. Ves. ord Lenina inst. erksp. vet.*, 20:16-19.

69. Ryder, R. A. 1961. "Lymphocystis as a mortality factor in a walleye population," *Prog. Fish-Cult.*, 23:183-186.

69a. Sano, T., K. Susuki and S. Fukuzaki. 1981. "Immune response in adult trout against formalin killed and concentrated IPNV." *Dev. Biol. Stand.-Fish Biologics*, 49:63-70.

70. Sano, T. 1973. "Studies on viral disease of Japanese fishes: IV. Infectious pancreatic necrosis of rainbow trout: susceptibility of freshwater salmons of genus *Onchorhynchus*," *Bull. Jap. Soc. Sci. Fish.*, 39: 117-120.

71. Sano, T. 1972. "Studies on viral disease of Japanese fishes. III. Infectious pancreatic necrosis of rainbow trout: geographical and seasonal distributions in Japan," *Bull. Jap. Soc. Sci. Fish.*, 38:313-316.

71a. Sano, T., H. Fukuda and M. Furukawa. 1985. "*Herpesvirus cyprini*: Biological and oncogenic properties." *Fish Pathol.*, 20:381-388.

71b. Savan, M. and P. Dobos. 1980. "Effect of virazole on rainbow trout *Salmo gairdneri* Richardson fry infected with infectious pancreatic necrosis virus." *J. Fish Dis.*, 3:437-440.

72. Scherrer, R. 1973. "Infectious pancreatic necrosis (IPN) of Salmonidae," *In* W. A. Dill (ed.). *Symposium on major communicable diseases in Europe and their control. FAO, Eur. Int. Fish Advis. Comm. Tech. Pap. 17, Suppl. 2:* 51-58.

72a. Schutz, M., E. B. May, J. N. Kraeuter and F. M. Hedrick. 1984. Isolation of infectious pancreatic necrosis virus from an epizootic occurring in cultured striped bass, *Morone saxatilis* (Walbaum)." *J. Fish Dis.*, 7:505-507.

72b. Sherburne, S. W. and L. L. Bean. 1979. "Incidence and distribution of piscine erythrocytic necrosis and the microsporidean, *Glugea osmerus* Mordox, from Massachusetts to the Canadian Maritimes." *Maine Dep. Mar. Res. Fish. Bull.*, 77(2):503-509.

73. Sherburne, S. W. 1973. "Erythrocyte degeneration in the Atlantic herring, *Clupea harengus harengus* L.," *U.S. Natl. Mar. Fish. Serv. Fish. Bull.*, 71:125-134.

74. Smith, K. 1940. *The virus.* Macmillan Co., New York City, NY. 176p.

75. Snieszko, S. F., K. Wolf, J. E. Camper and L. L. Pettijohn. 1959. "Infectious nature of pancreatic necrosis," *Trans. Am. Fish. Soc.*, 88:289-293.

76. Snieszko, S. F., E. M. Wood and W. T. Yasutake. 1957. "Infectious pancreatic necrosis in trout," *A.M.A. Arch. Pathol.*, 63:229-233.

77. Sonstegard, R. A. and L. A. McDermott. 1972. "Epidemiological model for passive transfer of IPNV by homeotherms," *Nature*, 237:104-105.

78. Sonstegard, R. A., L. A. McDermott and K. S. Sonstegard. 1972. "Isolation of infectious pancreatic necrosis virus from white suckers (*Catostomus commersoni*)," *Nature*, 236:174-175.

79. Stehbens, W. E. and M. R. L. Johnston. 1966. "The viral nature of *Pirhemocyton tarentolae*," *J. Ultrastr. Res.*, 15:543-554.

79a. Souter, B. W., A. G. Dwilow and K. Knight. 1984. "Infectious pancreatic necrosis virus: Isolation from asymtomatic wild arctic char (*Salvelinus alpinus* L.)." *J. Wildl. Dis.*, 20:338-339.

80. Tesarvik, J. F. 1977. "Studies in the relations between air bladder inflammation and infectious dropsy in carps," *Pr. VURH Vodnany*, 10:75-90. [*Fish Health News* (U.S. Fish Wildl. Serv., Nat. Fish Cent., Kearneysville, WV.), 7(4):182.]

81. Walker, R. 1971. "PEN, a viral lesion of fish erythrocytes," *Am. Zool.*, 11:707.

82. Walker, R. 1962. "Fine structure of lymphocystis virus of fish," *Virol.*, 18:503-505.

83. Walker, R. 1958. "Lymphocystis warts and skin tumors of walleye pike," *Rensslaer Rev. Grad. Stud.*, 14:1-5.

84. Walker, R. and S. W. Sherburne. 1977. "Piscine erythrocytic necrosis virus in Atlantic cod, *Gadus morhua*, and other fish: ultrastructure and distribution," *J. Fish. Res. Bd. Can.*, 34:1188-1195.

85. Walker, R. and R. Weissenberg. 1965. "Conformity of light and electron microscopic studies on virus particle distribution in lymphocystis tumor cells of fish," *Ann. N.Y. Acad. Sci.*, 126:375-385.

86. Watson, S. W., R. W. Guenther and R. R. Rucker. 1954. *A virus disease of sockeye salmon: Interim report. Sp. Sci. Rpt. Fish. No. 138.* U.S. Fish. Wildl. Serv., Washington, DC. 36p.

87. Wellborn, T. L., Jr., N. N. Fijan and J. P. Naftel. 1969. *Channel catfish virus disease.* FDL-18, Bur. Spt. Fish. Wildl. Div. Fish. Hatch., Washington, DC. 3p.

88. Weissenberg, R. 1939. "Studies on virus disease of fish. III. Morphological and experimental observations on the lymphocystis disease of pike perch, *Stizostedion vitreum*," *Zoologica, N.Y. Zool. Soc.*, 24:245-254.

89. Weissenberg, R. 1914. "Uber infectiose Zellhypertrophie bie Fischen (Lymphocysterkrankung)" *Sitz.-Ber. Klg. preuss. Akad. Wiss.*, 30:792-804.

90. Wingfield, W. H. and L. D. Chan. 1970. "Studies on Sacramento River chinook disease and its causative agent," *In* S. F. Snieszko, *ed. Symposium on diseases of fishes and shellfishes. Am. Fish. Soc. Spec. Publ., No. 5:* 307-326.

91. Wolf, K. 1976. "Fish viral diseases in North America, 1971-1975, and recent research of the Eastern Fish Disease Laboratory, U.S.A.," *Fish Pathol.*, 10: 135-154.

91a. Wolf, K. and J. A. Mann. 1980. "Poikilotherm vertebrate cell lines and viruses: A current listing for fishes." *In Vitro*, 16:168-179.

92. Wolf, K. 1974. *Rhabdovirus of northern pike fry. U.S. Fish Wildl. Serv., Fish Dis. Leafl. 37.* 4p.

93. Wolf, K. 1973. "Herpesviruses of lower vertebrates," *In* A. S. Kaplan, *ed. The herpesviruses.* Academic Press, New York City, NY. p. 495-520.

94. Wolf, K. 1968. *Lymphocystis disease of fish.* U.S. Bur. Spt. Fish. Wildl. FDL-13. 4p.

95. Wolf, K. 1966. *Infectious pancreatic necrosis (IPN) of salmonid fishes.* FDL-1, U.S. Bur. Spt. Fish. Wildl., Div. Fishery Res., Washington, DC. 4p.

96. Wolf, K. 1966. *Viral hemorrhagic septicemia of rainbow trout.* FDL-6, Bur. Spt. Fish. Wildl., Washington, DC. 4p.

97. Wolf, K. and J. A. Mann. 1980. "Poikilotherm vertebrate cell lines and viruses: a current listing for fishes," *In Vitro*, 16:168-179.

98. Wolf, K. 1958. *Virus disease of sockeye salmon. Fish. Leaf. 454.* Branch. Fish. Res., U.S. Bur. Spt. Fish. Wildl., Washington, DC. 3p.

99. Wolf, K., R. D. Darlington, W. G. Taylor, M. C. Quimby and T. Nagabayashi. 1978. "*Herpesvirus salmonis:* characterization of a new pathogen of rainbow trout," *J. Virol.*, 27:659-666.

100. Wolf, K. and R. W. Darlington. 1971. "Channel catfish virus: a new herpesvirus of ictalurid fish," *J. Virol.*, 8:525-533.

100a. Wolf, K. and C. E. Smith. 1981. "*Herpesvirus salmonis:* pathological changes in parenterally infected rainbow trout, *Salmo gairdneri* Richardson, fry." *J. Fish Dis.*, 4:445-447.

101. Wolf, K., C. E. Dunbar and S. F. Snieszko. 1960. "Infectious pancreatic necrosis of trout: I. A tissue culture study," *Prog. Fish-Cult.*, 22:64-68.

102. Wolf, K., M. Gravell and R. G. Malsberger. 1966. "Lymphocysts virus: isolation and propagation in centrarchid fish cell lines," *Science*, 151(3713: 1004-1005.

103. Wolf, K., R. L. Herman and C. P. Carlson. 1972. "Fish viruses: histopathologic changes associated with experimental channel catfish virus disease," *J. Fish. Res. Bd. Can.*, 29:149-150

104. Wolf, K. and M. C. Quimby. 1973. *Fish virology: Procedures and preparation of materials for plaquing fish viruses in normal atmospheres.* U.S Fish. Wildl. Serv. FDL-35, 13p.

105. Wolf, K. and M. C. Quimby. 1973. "Fish viruses: buffers and methods for plaquing eight agents under normal atmospheres," *Appl. Microbiol.*, 25:659-664

106. Wolf, K. and M. C. Quimby. 1967. "Infectious pancreatic necrosis, (IPN): its diagnosis, identification, detection and control," *Riv. It. Piscic. Ittiopat.*, 2:76-84.

107. Wolf, K., M. C. Quimby, L. L. Pettijohn and M. L. Landolt. 1973. "Fish Viruses: Isolation and identification of infectious hematopoietic necrosis in eastern North America," *J. Fish. Res. Bd. Can.*, 30:1625-1627.

108. Wolf, K., T. Sano and T. Kimura. 1975. *Herpesvirus disease of salmonids. U.S. Fish. Wildl. Serv., Fish. Dis. Leafl. 44.* 8p.

109. Wolf, K. and W. G. Taylor. 1975. "Salmonid viruses: a syncitium-forming agent from rainbow trout," *Fish Health News* (U.S. Fish. Wildl. Serv., Nat. Fish. Cent., Kearneysville, WV), 4(2):4; 4(3):8.

110. Wood, E. M., S. F. Snieszko and W. T. Yasutake. 1955. "Infectious pancreatic necrosis in brook trout," *A.M.A. Arch. Pathol.*, 60:26-28.

111. Woodcock, H. M. 1904. "Note on a remarkable parasite of plaice and flounders," *Rep. Lancashire Sea-fish Lab.* (1903).

112. Yamamoto, T. 1974. "Infectious pancreatic necrosis virus occurrence at a hatchery in Alberta," *J. Fish. Res. Bd. Can.*, 31:397-402.

113. Yasutake, W. T. 1975. "Fish viral diseases: chemical, histological and comparative aspects," *In* W. E. Ribelin and G. Migaki, eds. *The pathology of fishes.* Univ. Wis. Press., Madison. p.247-271.

114. Yasutake, W. T. and C. J. Rasmussen. 1968. "Histopathogenesis of experimentally induced viral hemorrhagic septicemia in fingerling rainbow trout (*Salmo gairdneri*)," *Bull. Off. Int. Epizoot.*, 69:977-984.

115. Yasutake, W. T. and D. F. Amend. 1972. "Some aspects of pathogenesis of infectious hematopoietic necrosis (IHN)," *J. Fish. Biol.*, 4:261-264.

116. Zwillenberg, L. O., M. H. Jensen and H. H. L. Zwillenberg. 1965. "Electron microscopy of the virus of viral hemorrhagic septicemia of rainbow trout (Egtved virus)," *Arch. ges. Virusforsch.*, 17: 1-19.

117. Zwillenberg, L. O. and K. Wolf. 1968. "Ultrustructure of lymphocystis virus," *J. Virol.*, 2:393-399.

Chapter VII
ANIMAL PARASITES
OF FISHES

Fishes evolved as the first vertebrate forms on earth. The relationship between fishes and invertebrates has thus existed longer than between invertebrates and any other vertebrate group of animals. The time, nearly half a billion years, has allowed not only the evolution of fishes but also the evolution of invertebrate animals which came into close association with fishes, some so closely associated that they actually inhabited external and internal structures of the fishes. The changes were gradual and usually took thousands and thousands of generations to arrive at the life stage present today. Many forms less adaptable or imperfect —as far as survivability and integration into the life of the host—become extinct. Consider the drastic alterations a free-living animal must undergo in order for its activity, anatomy and metabolism to integrate into the life cycle of its host.

The term *symbiosis* is used to describe the cohabitation between two dissimilar organisms. Some symbiotic relationships are so closely integrated that one animal is actually living in or on another animal. The term *mutualism* is used to describe those close associations in which both animals are benefited, *commensalism* for those in which one animal is benefited but the other is neither benefited nor harmed, and *parasitism* for those in which one animal lives at the expense of or harms the other.

Animals living in or on another animal (the host) today are the result of a tremendous biological history. They are the successful ones. The reason for success has been the subtle integration in which the host remained relatively unchanged and the other animal found a place to live, gain sustenance and reproduce. Those organisms which live at the expense of the host, but not at such great expense that all hosts are destroyed, are called parasites. The implication of the term parasite for some present day symbionts is that the host is harmed in some way, yet some are not usually detrimental to the animal in or on which they live. These organisms should be classified as mutuals or commensals and as parasites only when they do harm to, or at the expense of the host. Thus the broad term *parasite* can not always be accepted as destructive to the host. The student of parasitology must realize that not only is the relationship be-

tween many of these symbionts an association of long duration, but a marvel of adaptability between the two. Thinking of parasitism in this way explains why the most successful parasites have survived the milleniums, as have their hosts.[73]

Understanding the host-parasite relationship requires knowledge not only of the parasite but also of the host. The study of fish health places emphasis on the host side of the symbiotic relationship. Fishes have become, through evolution, hosts of myriads of symbionts. Some authors and parasitologists agree that fishes are the typical vertebrate host and can be used to demonstrate this relationship more advantageously than higher vertebrates.[73]

Hosts are classified by the purpose served to the parasite. Nomenclature of hosts is somewhat confusing. Parasitologists around the world have devised names to describe the way the parasite is served. The choice of host name is left to the individual parasitologist and has led to several names for each particular type of host. A *definitive* host, for example, is also known as the *primary* or *final* host. This is the host in or on which the parasite reaches adulthood. An *intermediate* host is also called an *alternate* or *secondary* host to describe a host in or on which the parasite passes a larval or nonsexual existence. There are variations among parasites which do not fit these terms directly and which further confuse nomenclature. As an example, a *transport* host is a type of intermediate host in or on which the parasite exists but no further development toward adulthood occurs.

Other hosts are described by the names *obligatory*, *mandatory* or *required*, being a host species which is absolutely essential for existence of a parasite. No other host species can serve either as the definitive or intermediate host. A *natural* host, as another example, has evolved with the parasite over so many generations that each has become accustomed to the other. Usually the natural host-parasite relationship has long ago become a mutualistic or commensalistic existence. The symbiont called the parasite may actually be of biological assistance to the host. Assistance may be subtle or straightforward. Some protozoans assist a fish host by utilizing host secretions or by devouring sloughed cells and keeping epithelial surfaces free of cellular debris. Others may stimulate host immune response to keep immunological competency at peak performance in case of attack by pathogens.

Another example of a host for animal parasites is the *temporary* host. A temporary host is a host in or on which the parasite lives briefly then leaves to become free-living. The temporary host is essential to development toward adulthood by the parasite. A *reservoir* host serves as a source of parasites for other hosts by harboring the parasite.

The parasite side of the host-parasite relationship must also be examined. Animal parasites of fishes appear in many forms, protozoan and metazoan, large and small, with simple or complex life cycles, all with tremendous reproductive potential and an adaptation to the host(s) in or on which they live. The parasite is classified by the way it integrates its life into the life of its host(s). The term *life cycle* is used to define the intricate association between the parasite and its host. The life cycle of a parasite is in actuality all stages of development in the life of the organism. The term life cycle is further segregated to simplify understanding of the symbiotic relationship between the two. A *continuous* life cycle, for example, is a life cycle in which the parasite remains in or on the host from generation to generation. There is no need for the parasite to leave the host. The parasite, in these cases, is designated a *continuous parasite*.

A second example of a parasite life cycle is *partial continuous*. The partial continuous parasite spends all its life on one host except for a brief time away from the host as an egg or cyst, only to recombine with the host after the egg hatches or the cyst returns to active life. Another important life cycle is the *intermediate* or *transport* life cycle. An intermediate parasite involve an intermediate host(s), and occasionally a transport host, in its life cycle. Each intermediate has an essential part to play in advancing the parasite toward attainment of adulthood and reproduction. The transport host in such a life cycle may not be essential but may serve as a place of survival with no advancement toward adulthood.

A parasite life cycle in which the host and parasite are in contact for a relatively limited part of the life span of the parasite is designated a *temporary* life cycle. The parasite develops to a stage of life during the encounter with the host which allows it to spend the remainder of its generation time away from the host. The temporary parasite may spend the greatest part of its generation time with the host, or the time may be brief. However, the period of time the symbionts are together is essential for existence of the parasite species. The parasite has become dependent on the temporary symbiotic phase of its life, and without the period of association with the host it cannot survive.

This brief introduction to the subject of parasitism may leave the reader with a different feeling for the parasite. Animals classified as parasites should be accepted for what they are today, remembering that each is a part of the ecosystem where it exists. Parasites have the capability for phenomenal reproduction given the opportunity. Their reproductive potential may result in epizootics of high intensity parasitism among fishes, sometimes spontaneously and sometimes from mismanagement on the part of fish culturists, aquarists, fishery managers and others involved with the fishery sciences. Those individuals concerned with fish health should be aware of the cause of parasitic epizootics among fish populations and of methods for controlling detrimental effects these organisms may cause to their hosts.

Parasitic Protozoa

Protozoa are animals comprised of a single cell capable of metabolism, reproduction and individual existence. The anatomy of protozoa is somewhat similar to the anatomy of any plant or animal cell having gross organelles such as nucleus, cytoplasm and cell wall. The protozoan cell has organelles or functions during some stage of development specifically adapted to movement. The protozoan thus becomes a different adaptation from cells which make up the body of higher plants and animals.

There are a tremendous number of porotozoan species, over 65,000 described and named. Protozoologists have classified them separately in the Animal Kingdom from other animals with bodies more complex than single celled bodies (Metazoa). Therefore, the Protozoa have been classified as a Subkingdom with the Metazoa into another Subkingdom (Table 14).[44]

Protozoa are the most primitive animals on earth and have adapted to every possible ecological existence. Some protozoa have adjusted to existence in or on other living organisms. Those symbiotic relationships involving protozoa and aquatic metazoa are more numerous than among the terrestrial metazoa. Part of the reason for success in aquatic relationships is because of the inability of most protozoa to resist drying. True, the protozoa which have adapted to terrestrial metazoan symbiosis developed the capability for withstanding periods of dryness, but adaptation to aquatic metazoan symbiosis did not require such extreme evolution. The bodies of aquatic organisms, in this way at least, proved to be more advantageous to protozoan symbionts, and fishes were no exception.

The first observation of protozoa was shortly after the invention of the microscope, approximately 1674 A.D.[50] The protozoa observed at the time were free-living but nonetheless brought about the study of these organisms. Parasitic protozoa of fishes were described as early as 1842.[16] Much of the study of protozoan parasites of fishes between that time and the present concerned identification, life cycle, host-parasite relationship and control procedures.

Protozoa living in or on fishes are a normal and natu-

TABLE 14

An abbreviated taxonomic scheme for the Subkingdom Protozoa with selected genera of interest to the fish health diagnostician.[27,44,53]

Phylum Class Order	Representative Genus or Genera	Characteristics

Sarcomastigophora
 Zoomastigophorea
  Kinetoplastida
 	
  Diplomonadida
 Sarcodina (Subphylum)
  Lobosea
   Amoebida
	Ichtyobodo
	Cryptobia
	Hexamita
	
	Acanthamoeba
	Entamoeba
	Vahlkampfia
	Schizamoeba
		Flagella; single nucleus; no spore formation; may form resistant cysts; asexual reproduction by binary fission, rarely sexual reproduction following conjugation
		
		Pseudopodia typically present; flagella when present restricted to developmental stages; body naked; asexual reproduction by fission, sexual reproduction by amoeboid gametes, may form cysts

Labyrinthomorpha Labyrinthulea Labyrinthulida	—	Spindle-shaped or spherical non-amoeboid cells; some genera have amoeboid cells which move by gliding; saprophitic or parasitic on algae, mostly in marine or esturine waters
Apicomplexa Sporozoea Eucoccidiida	*Eimeria* *Haplozoon*	Oocysts and schizonts formed; sexual and asexual reproduction common; merogeny inside the host, sporogeny outside the host; microgametes with two flagella
Microspora Microsporea Microsporida	*Pleistophora* *Thelophania* *Glugea* *Nosema*	Spores of unicellular origin, with or without polar filament; nucleus vesicular; single sporoplasm; spores with single valve

Acetospora
 Stellatosporea
  Occlusosporida
 	
  Balanosporida
	Marteilla
	
	Minchinia
	Urosporidium
		Spore with more than one sporoplasm; without polar capsule or polar filament; sporulation involves a series of endogenous budding producing sporoplasms within sporoplasms; spore wall entire
		
		Spore with one sporoplasm; spore wall interupted anteriorly by orifice; orifice covered by operculum or internally by diaphragm; sporoplasm without polar capsule or polar filament

TABLE 14 (*Continued*)

Phylum 　Class 　　Order	Representative Genus or Genera	Characteristics
Myxozoa 　Myxosporea 　　Bivalvulida	*Ceratomyxa* *Henneguya* *Myxidium* *Myxobolus* *Myxosoma*	Spores of multicellular origin with two to four polar capsules and sporoplasms; each polar capsule with coiled polar filament, polar filament function probably for anchoring to host
Ciliophora 　Kinetofragminophorea 　　Cyrtophorida	*Chilodonella*	Simple or compound cilia; body broad and dorsoventrally flattened; binary fission primary reproduction, sexual reproduction involves conjugation, autogamy and cytogamy
Suctorida	*Trichophrya*	Adult stage sessile; nutrition by suctoria tentacles; no stalk; reproduce by endogenous budding
Oligohymenophorea 　　Hymenostomatida	*Ichthyophthirius*	Body ciliation uniform and heavy at certain life stages; histophagous life stage; cysts common
Peritrichida	*Epistylis* *Schyphidia* *Trichodina*	Oral cilia field prominent; some species stalked and sedentary; some species with circlet of somatic locomotor cilia; primary reproduction by binary fission, sexual reproduction by complicated conjugation of micro- and macroconjugants

ral part of the world. Alteration of the environment of both host and parasite may be to the advantage of the parasite. Thus the extensive use of fish culture in the world today places many fish species under condition of high population density not present in nature. Protozoa usually present in low numbers on or in fishes residing in a natural environment may cause excessive parasitism if great care is not taken to provide suitable habitat and nutrition when the fishes are placed under culture. Appearance of excessive numbers of protozoan parasites among either cultured or aquarium fishes is an indication that acceptable habitat and/or acceptable nutrition for the fishes is not being provided.

There are epizootics of excessive parasitism from protozoa among wild-ranging fishes. Parasitic protozoa have probably been population-controlling entities among fishes down through the ages. Therefore, the fishery management biologist may wish to observe the epizootic as an indication that conditions are unsuitable to the fishes in some way but more suitable to the parasite.

The classification of protozoa for purposes of fish health investigation need not consider all the taxonomic breakdown necessary to the complete study of these organisms. The fish disease diagnostician needs a knowledge of the classification under the Subkingdom Protozoa: morphology used for identification, means of locomotion, life cycles, reproductive processes and possibly other factors. The tremendously large numbers of protozoan species identified have been placed into an orderly scheme of nomenclature to assist with each of these criteria.

The classification of protozoa, unlike classification of higher animals, is based almost entirely on present day organisms. There are few fossil remains of the protozoa to use for evolutionary relationships.

The subkingdom Protozoa is divided into seven phyla: Sarcomastigophora, Labyrinthomorpha, Apicomplexa, Microspora, Ascetospora, Myxozoa and Ciliophora. Each are further divided into the usual taxonomic classes, orders, families, genera and species. Characteristics of each phylum and classes under the phyla which are of interest to fish health are given in Table 14.

There are a large number of different species of protozoa parasitic to fishes. Some species have been known to cause unthriftiness, anemia, abnormal physiological changes, trauma, suffocation, other adverse conditions and death. Some may be responsible for secondary infections by bacteria, fungi or other animal parasites. Space is not available in this chapter to discuss each species of protozoan capable of causing dire effects on its host. Therefore, several specific protozoan-caused diseases will be discussed to demonstrate how these organisms have successfully become parasitic with fishes and those circumstances under which protozoa can become a problem to their host.

PATHOGENIC SARCOMASTIGOPHORA: ZOOMASTIGOPHOREA

Many species of flagellated protozoa occupy a habitat in or on the bodies of fishes. Relatively few of these protozoa are capable of becoming pathogens to their host.[4] The potential pathogens usually do not cause spontaneous diseases in wild-ranging fishes. Most instances when Zoomastigophorea become involved in pathogenesis among fishes are under confined situations. Fishes held in fish culture facilities and aquaria are especially susceptible to these organisms.

Certain species of the genera *Ichtyobodo (Costia), Hexamita, Oodinium, Amyloodinium, Trypanosoma, Trypanoplasma* and *Cryptobia* are potentially pathogenic.[4] All *Ichtyobodo, Oodinium, Amyloodinium* and some species of *Cryptobia* are ectoparasites occupying a place on skin, fins or gills. Ectoparasitic *Cryptobia* are found only on freshwater fishes. Other species of *Cryptobia* are found in the alimentary tracts of marine fishes. *Hexamita* sp. of fishes are all endoparasites usually found in the intestine, ceca or gall bladder of the host. Occasionally *Hexamita* sp. are found in the blood and body organs, especially in terminally ill fishes. This probably is because the extremely ill host can no longer maintain barriers against invasion from the alimentary tract to the bloodstream.[86]

Trypanosoma sp. and *Trypanoplasma* sp. of fishes are present in the blood. These organisms are found in freshwater and saltwater fishes throughout the world. They are two-host parasites, being transmitted by a leech vector. Trypanosomiasis has been diagnosed in many fishes, but usually with a low number of organisms in healthy fishes. Alteration of the host physiologically may result in increased numbers of the hemoflagellates and possible injury to the host.[4,50]

The two most widely known diseases of fishes caused by flagellated protozoa are costiasis (ichtyobodiasis) and hexamitiasis. These two diseases are discussed as examples of the relationship between flagellated protozoa and pathogenesis. Diseases caused by members of the other genera given above may be as important as ichtyobodiasis and hexamitiasis, but epizootics have been more limited. Certainly oodiniasis and crytobiasis should not be considered as having only minor potential pathogenesis (Pl. 34E). However, the reader is directed to more complete coverage of those diseases not given here.[4]

Ichtyobodiasis (Costiasis)

Ichtyobodiasis is a disease of fishes caused by excessive parasitism with one or more species of *Ichtyobodo*. The generic name *Costia* has been corrected to *Ichtyobodo*. Most literature pertaining to the disease, as well as the disease name costiasis, used the generic name *Costia*. However, the discussion here will use the more correct ichtyobodiasis. *Ichtyobodo* species are common inhabitants of the skin and gills of freshwater and marine fishes. These organisms are mutualistic parasites with their host when present in small numbers. Part of their sustenance is derived from sloughed epithelial cells and cellular debris from the host. However, adverse conditions within the host environment or poor health of the host may reduce the normal day-to-day mortality of *Ichtyobodo* and allow most to survive and to reproduce. The reproductive potential of *Ichtyobodo* is tremendous, and given the opportunity they can multiply at a phenomenal rate. They then cause adverse effects on the host by attacking living cells with detrimental or disastrous effects.

Etiological Agents:

There are two species of the genus *Ichtyobodo (Costia)* responsible for ichtyobodiasis, *Ichtyobodo necatrix* and *Ichtyobodo pyriformis*.[8] Both are relatively small for mastigophoran protozoa. *I. necatrix* is 10 to 20 micrometers long by 5 to 10 micrometers wide. *I. pyriformis* is slightly smaller, being 9 to 14 micrometers long by 5 to 8 micrometers wide. Both species have one pair of posteriorly directed axostyles and one pair of freely moving flagella. The axostyles are short and tightly attached to the body (Pl. 17F).[50] The free flagella are longer and are used for propelling the organism and attaching to the host.[73] The axostyles are used in feeding.[19] Both species have a small contractile vacuole and a rounded vesicular nucleus. The body of both *Ichtyobodo* species is lentile or pyriform shaped in profile. The body is concave on one side, thus forming a groove which leads anteriorly to a cytostome and attachment of the flagella.[50] Reproduction is primarily by longitudinal fission, though sexual reproduction following conjugation may occur. *Ichtyobodo* species form nonreproductive resistant cysts which are 7 to 10 micrometers in diameter.[107]

Geographical Distribution:

I. necatrix is by far the most common species and probably occurs worldwide on freshwater fishes. *I. pyri-*

formis has been reported in North America and parts of Europe.

Susceptible Species:

All species of freshwater fishes are susceptible to attack by *Ichtyobodo*. Fishes kept in aquaria or under crowded conditions of fish culture facilities and farm ponds are more susceptible to ichtyobodiasis than the same species of fishes residing under more favorable natural conditions. Epizootics of ichtyobodiasis are more common among coolwater and coldwater fishes. Tropical fishes held at water temperatures above 25°C do not have ichtyobodiasis. Young fishes of most species are more susceptible to ichtyobodiasis than older fishes.

Epizootiology:

Ichtyobodo species are obligate parasites. The trophozoite cannot survive long away from its host. *Ichtyobodo* are transmitted from fish to fish through water. Ordinarily the protozoan attaches to the skin or gills of its host by means of the flagella. Some individuals may be swept away to become attached to new hosts. Adverse conditions cause the trophozoites to encyst, sometimes on the fish and sometimes free in the water. Cysts revert to trophozoites when conditions become more favorable to the protozoa. Trophozoites derived from cysts must seek and find a host within a short time or they will die. Thus there are two sources of trophozoites for transmission to new hosts, those directly from host fishes and those derived from cysts. *Ichtyobodo* are spread from one geographical area to another by transporting infested fishes and water containing encysted *Ichtyobodo*.

Ichtyobodo live on the skin and gills of healthy fishes which are occupying a favorable non-polluted environment; there they occur in an apparently commensalistic state of symbiosis. The defenses of the host possibly keep the protozoan population reduced to an acceptable level. A change in the health of the host or a change in the environment to conditions usually associated with overcrowding in aquaria or fish culture (low dissolved oxygen, high ammonia content or other skin or gill irritant, low pH or other condition unsatisfactory to the host) allows survival of more of each generation of *Ichtyobodo*. The defenses of the host are overwhelmed and the protozoa revert to a parasitic existence in which the host is harmed.

Generation time of *Ichtyobodo* species is temperature dependent. Temperatures between 10 and 25°C favor rapid reproduction, and generations are produced in a matter of hours. Reduction of the temperature to below 8°C causes the organisms to encyst. The organisms apparently cannot survive above 30°C.[107]

Disease Signs:

Signs of ichtyobodiasis include a thickening of the mucus on those parts of the body most heavily infected with *Ichtyobodo*. The fish may refuse to eat because of irritated gills or skin. They may be lethargic and seek the sides of the tank or a corner with little or no interference from other fishes. Fish may roll in the water and rub against the bottom or the sides of the tank. Flashing is the term sometimes used for this activity because the sides of the body are turned toward the observer. Flashing and rubbing are apparently attempts to remove skin irritation caused by the parasite. Excessive parasitism with *Ichtyobodo* on the gills of fishes may cause excessive accumulation of mucus on the gills. Fishes in which gills but not the skin are attacked by the parasites may not demonstrate external signs other than alteration of the gills. The fish are listless, will not take food and do not flash or develop excess mucus on the skin.

Diagnosis:

Diagnosis of ichtyobodiasis is dependent on disease signs and observation of *Ichtyobodo* in slide preparations of gills or mucus from the skin. Skin scrapings from behind the pectoral or pelvic fins and along the dorsal side of the body behind the head and anterior to the doral fin are usually the most productive for observation of *Ichtyobodo*. Skin scrapings, gill arches or parts of gill arches are mounted on a microscope slide with one to three drops of water and a cover glass. The cover glass is pressed down gently to disperse the mucus or to spread gill lamellae. *Ichtyobodo* organisms are quite small and are best seen by the inexperienced observer using at least 450 magnification. The unattached organisms will be seen moving erratically among mucus and epithelial cells. They are transparent, and reducing the light by lowering the condenser of the microscope to spread the light may be necessary to make them more visible.

The diagnostician must judge the severity of each case of ichtyobodiasis. Preparation of materials taken from the fish and rapidity of observation of the material under the microscope are essential for correct diagnosis. *Ichtyobodo* species placed under the high intensity microscope light die rapidly. The organisms must usually be alive and moving in order for the diagnostician to observe them. Locating one to five *Ichtyobodo* organisms per low field (100 magnification) of the microscope, with many fields free of the organism, is considered by some individuals as being a normal and expected *Ichtyobodo* population on a healthy fish. Observation of over five organisms per low-power field is cause for concern. Well prepared material from heavily infested cases of ichtyobodiasis may demonstrate 50 or more organisms per low-power field. Thus the number of organisms observed in gill or skin preparations indicates severity of the disease.

Staining of *Ichtyobodo* species to make them more visible in skin and gill preparations is very difficult. These organisms are fragile and rupture when placed in various staining preparations. However, carefully prepared smears may be fixed in Shaudinn's fluid, transferred to ethyl alcohol and stained with several stains (iron hematoxylin, carmine and periodic acid-Schiff are examples).[4] Whole fish or the skin or gills of fish with ichtyobodiasis may be fixed in a good chemical fixative and later sections cut from the tissue and stained with suitable stains may demonstrate the organisms (Pl. 17F). However, skin or gill sections do not usually assist in assessing the severity of the disease.

Therapy and Control:

Therapeutic procedures for ichtyobodiasis are usually dependent on severity of the epizootic. Quite often an epizootic can be controlled by increasing water flow to cultured fishes, reducing biomass of fish to water volume, eliminating sources of skin or gill irritants or improving the health of the fish. Aquarists may control the disease by insuring efficiency of the filter and water conditioning system used in conjunction with the aquarium, altering pH to above neutral if it is acid, raising the temperature of the aquarium above 30°C or by insuring health of the fishes through proper nutrition.

Severe epizootics of ichtyobodiasis may be controlled by use of external protozoacides.[40] The wide geographical distribution of ichtyobodiasis has probably been responsible for development of a relatively large number of procedures which can be used for a variety of protozoacides to treat the disease (Tables 2 and 15). Each protozoacide given in Table 15 has been found to be effective when used with certain environmental conditions or water quality. The choice of protozoacide and method of external treatment are dictated by conditions under which fishes are to be treated. Small numbers of fishes may be dipped; large numbers are usually treated by a flush, bath or dynamic (flow-through) procedure.

Ichtyobodo species are normally found on the skin or gills of a wide variety of fishes. However, these organisms are considered by many fish culturists to be one of the most dangerous external protozoans. Epizootics of ichtyobodiasis on young channel catfish or salmonids may cause extremely high mortality within a few days if left untreated.[4,23,107] Mortality levels among young fishes may reach to greater than 90% if the fishes have been weakened by improper management or badly polluted water.[8]

Practical Aspects:

I. necatrix is widely distributed in the freshwaters of the world, and moving fishes known to harbor this protozoan is usually acceptable though such movement may serve to distribute strains of the organism more broadly. *I. pyriformis* apparently has a limited geographical distribution, and care should be taken to limit its movement through transporting fishes over long distances.

Many severe cases of ichtyobodiasis have resulted from the presence of adult fishes in the water supply of young fishes. This has occurred especially in trout and salmon culture. Therefore, young fishes being held in water supplies which also have older fishes should be managed to reduce overcrowding, malnutrition or other factors known to increase susceptibility to these protozoa.

Hexamitiasis

Hexamitiasis is a disease caused by excessive numbers of protozoa of the genus *Hexamita* in the alimentary tract of fishes. Many fishes of the world harbor alimentary *Hexamita*, but most have not been studied. *Hexamita* species are usually normal residents of the alimentary tract, primarily as commensalistic symbionts. Poor health of the host may lead to phenomenal reproduction of the protozoa.

Hexamitiasis is considered by many trout and salmon culturists as one of the most important diseases caused by flagellated protozoa. The disease has also been noted in other fish species, but most study has been given to the disease in salmonids. Therefore, the discussion which follows will concern those fishes in which the disease has been described but with emphasis on salmonid hexamitiasis, realizing that hexamitiasis may possibly occur in all species of freshwater or marine fishes.

Hexamitiasis has one synonymous name. The disease was known as octomitiasis until about 1960. The name was corrected to hexamitiasis after reviewing the nomenclature of the etiological agent.

Etiological Agent:

The etiological agent of hexamitiasis is any species of the genus *Hexamita*, formerly genus *Octomitus*. The reason for the change in generic name was a decision among taxonomists that somatic flagella should have no reference in nomenclature. Most *Hexamita* species have six anterior flagella and two posteriorly directed somatic flagella. Thus the name *Hexamita*, rather than the name *Octomitus* (from the total of eight flagella).[70]

Three species of the genus *Hexamita* have been described as pathogenic to fishes: *Hexamita salmonis*,[70] *Hexamita truttae*[107] and *Hexamita intestinalis*.[50] The first two, *H. salmonis* and *H. truttae*, are considered by some investigators as being the same.[107] An organism named *H. symphysodoni* was identified in the discus fish.[107] However, the name of this organism has never been accepted and is thought to be synonymous with *H. intestinalis*.[22] No doubt many members of the genus *Hexamita*, normal inhabitats of the alimentary tract of other fishes, can become pathogenic when conditions of the host favor the parasite.

Hexamita species are pyriform or oval in shape, tapering gradually toward the posterior end. Rounded individuals are quite common. The organisms are from 6 to 8 micrometers wide by 10 to 12 micrometers long. *Hexamita* species have three pairs of anterior flagella which vary in length but are about one and one-half times the length of the body. These flagella arise from the blepharoplast at the anterior end of the axostyles. A fourth

TABLE 15

Protozoacidal compounds and method(s) of use for control of ichtyobodiasis [40]

Compound	Dosage and Time	Method of Use	Remarks
★ Acetic acid	1:20 to 1:50 (2 to 5%) for 1 min or less	Dip	May be used daily as needed
★ Copper sulfate	1:250,000 to 1:1,000,000 (1 to 4 mg/L) for 1 hour	Bath or dynamic	Alkalinity of the water determines safe concentration of compound
	1:500 to 1:2,000 (500 to 2,000 mg/L) for 1 min	Dip	
★ Formalin	1:4,000 (250 mg/L) for 1 hour	Bath	Some fish species may be sensitive to formalin, so test a small number of normal fish before extensive use
	1:2,500 (400 mg/L) for 10 to 15 min	Dip	
Furacin	1:250,000 to 1:500,000 (2 to 4 mg/L) for 1 hour	Bath	May not be effective in cold (less than 12°C) water
Malachite green	1:15,000 (66.7 mg/L) for 10 to 30 seconds	Dip	May be used daily
	1:200,000 (5 mg/L) for 1 hour	Bath or dynamic	May be used daily
	1:10,000,000 (0.1 mg/L)	Continuous	In ponds
★ Potassium permanganate	Up to 1:250,000 (up to 4 mg/L) for 1 hour	Dip, bath or dynamic	Concentration depends on organic matter suspended in the water
Quinine hydrochloride	1:50,000 (20 mg/L) indefinitely	Bath	Place compound in water and allow to remain; detrimental to aquatic plants
★ Sodium chloride	1:30 to 1:50 (3 to 5%) for 1 to 2 min	Dip	Can be used daily
	1:100 (1%) for 20 to 30 min	Dip, bath or dynamic	Can be used daily
Temperature	—	—	Raise temperature above 30°C

*Approved for use with food-fish by the U.S. Food & Drug Administration (FDA).

pair of flagella arise from the axostyles at the extreme posterior end of the body. A pair of oval nuclei are present at the anterior end of the body. There is a delicate membrane surrounding the nucleus.

Hexamita species reproduce by longitudinal binary fission. The organism usually becomes round before dividing. *Hexamita* species may also reproduce by a type of schizogony within the epithelial cells of the ceca or intestine. The intracellular parasite begins division by developing a single large nucleus. It grows rapidly to many times the original size and eventually destroys the host cell. The single nucleus divides by splitting into five or six chromatin masses. Several divisions follow rapidly until there are numerous small merozoites making their way to uninfected cells, where the cycle is repeated. Occasionally the host cell disintegrates and the parasite passes into the lumen of the intestine. Schizogony furnishes a rapid means of multiplication since the entire process takes between 24 and 48 hours.[19]

Cysts of *Hexamita* species are occasionally formed in the intestine of the fish. The cysts are oval or spherical in shape, each containing a transparent membrane, paired nuclei, blepharoplasts and axostyles. Cysts of *H. salmonis* have also been observed in *in vitro* cultures of the organism, probably as a result of insufficient nutrients.[60] Cysts are quite resistant and can survive outside of the host for several weeks.[19]

Geographical Distribution:

H. salmonis occurs throughout the salmon and trout range of North America. *H. truttae* and *H. intestinalis* have been reported in various parts of Europe. Probably *Hexamita* species and the disease caused by these organisms can be found worldwide.

Susceptible Species:

There are a limited number of hosts from which hexamitiasis has been diagnosed. *H. salmonis* has been associated with pathological signs in most trout and salmon species. The organism may be found as a normal inhabitant of the lower alimentary tract of these fishes. *H. truttae* has been reported in several species of trout, angelfish, mosquitofish, discus fish, goldfish, golden rudd and black widow fish.[107] It has also been reported in burbot and the Siberian sterlet. *H. intestinalis* has been reported from brown trout and frogs.[50]

Epizootiology:

Transmission of *Hexamita* is probably by the oral route, although the anal route has been mentioned in the case of free-swimming flagellated forms of the organisms.[106] The latter route may sound somewhat improbable, but laboratory infection of normal rainbow trout with *H. salmonis* was possible using anal inoculation.[61] Oral transmission may involve the encysted stage taken accidentally with food.[19] The trophozoite stage, if taken orally, may possibly be destroyed by the ex-

tremely high acid of the stomach of most fishes (pH 1 to 2.5 in fishes with an acid stomach).

The flagellated stage of *Hexamita* makes its way to the lumen of the upper intestine or ceca. There it remains swimming freely in intestinal or cecal fluids. Reproduction goes on at the normal rate under most circumstances. A few of the organisms may enter epithelial tissue to follow schizogony in healthy fishes, but the number is not great. Most epizootics of hexamitiasis are initiated when fishes become unhealthy. Malnutrition, overcrowding with the usual conditions of anoxia and gill damage, or other reasons for poor health of the fishes may in some way initiate rapid reproduction of the flagellated forms as well as an increase in the number of organisms invading epithelial cells of intestine and ceca. Generation time for the flagellated form is thought to be approximately 24 hours.

Rapid reproduction of the parasite may enhance unthriftiness, anemia, anoxia and other physiological conditions within the fish. Eventually mortality above the normal expected mortality will begin. There is no indication that reinfection occurs from flagellated protozoa released in feces, partly because the fishes refuse to take food and partly because the entire intestinal tract is free of partially digested food or fecal material. Encysted *Hexamita* may be involved in reinfection or infection of members of the population not already infected but still taking food.

The water supply from fish populations suffering from an epizootic of hexamitiasis may carry large numbers of encysted and flagellated organisms to fishes downstream. However, hexamitiasis will not usually develop in the newly infected fishes if they are healthy.

H. salmonis seems to be present wherever trout or salmon are reared. There are times when a mystery surrounds the source of the organism. As an example, trout raised for the first time in a newly constructed fish culture facility with an enclosed well water source and cement-lined tanks and raceways habored *H. salmonis*. The source of the fish was eggs brought to the newly constructed hatchery building, disinfected on entrance, hatched and the fry reared in the usual manner. These cases strongly indicate that the protozoa, perhaps encysted, are passed in or on the egg.

Disease Signs:

Young fishes in a state of unthriftiness are the most susceptible to hexamitiasis. Signs of hexamitiasis also may be the signs of malnutrition, anemia, anoxia, gill hyperplasia or other physiological imbalance. Rapid reproduction of *Hexamita* in the intestine or ceca of the host is usually accompanied by dark coloration and listlessness. The fishes seek the sides or corners of the holding tank and refuse to take food. Hexamitiasis in trout or salmonrearing facilities is also indicated by inability of the fish to maintain a place in the flowing water, so they are swept downstream onto the lower dividing screen of the tank. Hundreds of such fish may be present around the lower screen area. Some are pressed against the screen and others are only barely able to hold a position away from the screen. Flashing of the fish is a common sign during epizootics of hexamitiasis. The fish appear as if excessive numbers of parasites in the gut are causing great pain. Many of these fish are emaciated, the body being extremely slender and the abdomen sunken, indications of nutritional deficiency. The gills are light in color. Internal examination reveals general anemia, a pale liver and reduction of hemoglobin pigment in the blood. The gut is usually free of food or feces but filled with mucus (Pl. 18A).

Diagnosis:

Disease signs, especially emaciation, anemia, dark coloration of the skin, lethargy and general unthriftiness of fishes, may assist in directing diagnostic investigation to a search for *Hexamita* species. Definitive diagnosis of hexamitiasis is by observation and identification of *Hexamita* organisms in the intestinal or cecal contents or from the gall bladder and occasionally the blood.

H. salmonis and *H. truttae* may be observed by removing the cecal area of the intestine of small fishes or ceca only from larger fishes and placing the tissue on a microscope slide with a few drops of water. The tissue is minced in the water with scissors or a sharp scalpel. A cover glass is placed on the minced tissue, pressed down lightly and observations made using low (100X) magnification of a compound microscope. *Hexamita* species are transparent, and either the light must be adjusted by lowering the condenser and scattering the light or phase contrast illumination used to make them visable. *Hexamita* species die rapidly under the intense illumination of the microscope and become almost impossible to locate if not moving. This is especially true when examining intestinal smears made from the gut of fishes in which food material is present. The organisms appear as small, rapidly moving lentile-shaped objects moving through the cecal, intestinal or tissue debris in the smear (Pl. 18B).

Histological preparations of ceca or intestinal tissue will demonstrate *Hexamita* organisms undergoing schizogony in cases of advanced hexamitiasis. The organisms are within epithelial cells of these organs. There may be but one large nucleus or the nucleus may have divided into several smaller chromatin particles (Pl. 18C).

A part of the diagnosis of hexamitiasis is a judgement of severity. The diagnostician must remember that low numbers of *Hexamita* are usually present in fishes. Therefore, treating fishes for a small number of these organisms may do more harm to the host than to allow the low-level parasitism to remain but concentrate on the other reason(s) for unthriftiness. A satisfactory system has been devised for estimating when a *Hexamita*

population within the fish is probably detrimental to the host and therapy indicated. A representative sample of fishes should be taken to estimate severity of the parasitism. Gut smears from each fish in the sample are examined for *Hexamita* in the prescribed manner as given above. Smears are observed under the low power (100X) of the microscope. Several low-power fields containing intestinal or cecal debris from each fish are examined and the number of *Hexamita* organisms estimated for each field. Severity is estimated on the basis of the average number of organisms per low-power field (Table 16).

There have been reports of finding *Hexamita* in the peritoneal cavity, heart, liver and blood of the discus fish; the description indicated the fish were near death.[1] Therefore, microscopic examination of organs other than the gall bladder, ceca and upper intestine may be useful for diagnosis of advanced cases of hexamitiasis.

Therapy and Control:

The wide geographical distribution of *Hexamita* species and the tremendous numbers of epizootics of hexamitiasis which have occurred in cultured fishes over the past half century have lead to numerous therapeutic procedures for the disease. Some of the therapeutic compounds used to reduce or eliminate *Hexamita* from the gut of trout and salmon are moderately toxic or create relatively high tissue levels of the drug. Therefore, the recommendation is made to treat those cases classified as marked or extreme in severity. Those epizootics in which fishes are generally classified as slight to moderate in severity should be controlled by management, nutrition or non-therapeutic procedures (Table 16).[19,40,60,61,84]

Therapy of marked or extremely severe cases and some epizootics judged moderate can be effected by adding the therapeutic drug to the diet. The diet-drug mixture is usually fed for three days; fishes are then fed a non-medicated diet for three days and a sample of fish examined. Three more days of drug-diet therapy are indicated if the infection has not been controlled. The reason for the three day drug-diet and three days normal diet followed by examination is to give the time necessary for all stages of the organism undergoing schizogony to be completed and flagellated stages released into the lumen of the intestine or ceca.

Two types of therapeutic compounds are used to control hexamitiasis, those which remove the flagellated and encysted parasites from the gut by mechanical means and those which kill the organisms *in situ*. Epsom salts (magnesium sulfate) is an example of a compound which causes peristalsis, flooding of the intestine with fluids derived from body fluids and mechanically removing the organisms through fecal discharge. There are several therapeutic compounds capable of killing flagellated forms of *Hexamita* species without excessive damage to the host (Table 17).

TABLE 16

Relationship between the average number of *Hexamita* organisms present in intestinal or cecal smears and the severity of infection

Number of Hexamita *sp. per Low-power Microscope Field*	*Severity of Infection*	*Remarks*
No organisms seen	Negative	None
Occasional field with 1 to 5 organisms	Slight	No treatment necessary
Average of 5 to 15 organisms	Moderate	No treatment unless primary cause for unthriftiness cannot be determined; keep close watch on further increase of parasites
Average of 15 to 30 organisms per field	Marked	Therapy necessary
Average of 30 to 100 organisms per field with some fields over 100	Extreme	Therapy essential

Prognosis:

Epizootics of hexamitiasis in salmonids are usually accompanied by 100% morbidity. Mortality among young, nutritionally deficient trout or salmon can reach nearly 100% of the population without therapy or alteration of the nutritional status of the fishes. High numbers of *H. salmonis* may be contributing to the mortality, but difficulty arises in demonstrating whether the parasite or the malnutrition is responsible. Reduction in *Hexamita* numbers followed by alteration of other possible causes for unhealthiness in the fishes can reduce mortality to less than 1% if diagnosis and therapy are accurate and rapid.

Practical Aspects:

Most trout and salmon culturists agree that adult fish should not be placed above young fish because this practice may result in excessive parasitism with *H. salmonis* among the younger fish. This may be true among other cultured fishes as well.

Some fish parasitologists feel that there are no true cases of hexamitiasis involving salmonids and *H. salmonis*, only cases where poor management or poor nutrition led to excessive parasitism.[106] However, experience indicates that mortality among young trout and salmon can usually be reduced by therapy for hexamitiasis.

One problem in the therapy of hexamitiasis is acceptance of the diet-drug mixture by the fish. During epizootics in which many of the fish are classified as ex-

tremely severe (30 to 100 *H. salmonis* per low-power microscope field, with some fields over 100), the fish may refuse to take food. These fish will probably be lost unless they can be stimulated to take the offering. However, there are usually some of the fish in the population which will take food. Reduction of *Hexamita* in these fish will be the first step back to health.

AMOEBIDA OF FISHES

Amoebas are relatively common symbionts of fishes. These organisms may be found on the skin or gills, occasionally in the intestinal tract and rarely in body tissues.[35,74,109] Those found on the skin or gills may or may not be normal inhabitants of the site on which they are found. Many are free-living forms displaced to the external surfaces of the fish; others are nonpathogenic inhabitants under all circumstances.

Spontaneous or secondary amebiasis has been reported occasionally in fishes. Species of the genera *Acanthamoeba*, *Entamoeba*, *Volkampfia* and *Schizamoeba* have been associated with fish losses, but usually as opportunists.[10,21,74,101]

APICOMPLEXA OF FISHES:

Coccidiosis

All members of the phylum Apicomplexa live in close relationship with a host. Those present in fishes belong to the order Eucoccidi and are usually referred to as coccidia—thus the name coccidiosis for infections of these

TABLE 17

Therapeutic compounds for therapy of hexamitiasis [19,40,61,84]

Therapeutic Compound	Dosage and Treatment Time	Remarks
Carbarsone	0.2% of the diet for three days	Carbarsone is an arsenical and should not be used for fishes which will subsequently be used for food
Calomel (mercurous chloride)	0.2% of the diet for three days	Mercury will accumulate to some degree in the tissues of the fish and be added to the environment on elimination from the fish
Cyzine (2-acetylamino-5-nitrothiazole)	1:50,000 (20 mg/kg) in the diet for three days	Product of American Cyanamid Company; relatively insoluble through gut wall into body tissues
Enheptin (2-amino-5-nitro-thiazole)	0.1 to 0.2% of the diet for three days	Product of American Cyanamid Company; relatively soluble through gut wall into body tissues
* Magnesium sulfate (Epsom salts)	0.2 to 0.3% of the diet for three days	Mechanically removes *Hexamita* organisms by purging the intestine

*Approved for use with food-fish by the U.S. Food & Drug Administration (FDA).

organisms when they become a pathological problem. Coccidiosis has not been throughly examined in the United States, but has received more attention in Europe. Piscine coccidiosis may become important as more is known about the disease and the host-parasite relationship.

Etiological Agent:

The etiological agent of coccidiosis of fishes is any species of two families, Eimeridae and Adeleidae.[10] One genus of Eimeridae, *Eimeria*, has a relatively large number of species reported from fishes of the world. Species of *Eimeria* are far more commonly found in fishes than species of the genus *Haplozoon*. All species of *Eimeria* and *Haplozoon* lead a partial-continuous life cycle. The only life stage outside of the host is the oocyst or sporocyst derived from the oocyst. Most other life stages of *Eimeria* species are in the intestinal or cecal epithelium of the host, though a few may be found in the liver, kidney, gonads or other organs. All *Haplozoon* sp. occupy blood cells of the host. Nothing is known of the host-parasite relationship of *Haplozoon* sp. in fishes except the location of reproductive stages (erythrocytes or leucocytes).

Over 40 species of *Eimeria* have been reported from fishes.[10,35] No attempt will be made to differentiate among the individual species.

Geographical Distribution:

Coccidiosis is probably worldwide in distribution.

Susceptible Species:

Eimeria species have been reported in the intestine, feces or from other organs of a wide variety of fishes (carp, goldfish, rudd, tench, herrings, trout, perch, cod, sculpin, Pacific mackerel, amurs, eels and many others). The organism has not been associated with disease except in a few instances. However, presence of these casual parasites suggests the possibility of coccidiosis in the fish host.

Epizootiology:

The infective entity of coccidiosis is the sporozoite in the oocyst. Coccidial oocysts of fishes usually sporulate (mature) inside the host fish (Fig. 12). Oocysts in fishes have a thin, cuticular oocyst wall, whereas those from terrestrial animals are thick and tough, probably to reduce drying. There is no need to reduce desiccation by aquatic oocysts.

The mature oocysts, usually with four sporocysts each with two sporozoites, are passed from the host. Some eimerian species release sporocysts from the oocyst, either inside the host or soon after excretion. The oocyst or sporocyst is ingested by a new host where sporozoites are released and enter cells of the suitable organ of the new host (Fig. 12). Each sporozoite transforms into a

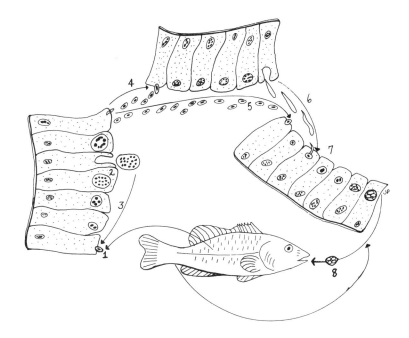

Fig. 12: Life cycle of a typical *Eimeria* sp.
1. Sporozoite passing into a host cell.
2. Schizogony producing a schizont with daughter merozoites.
3. Daughter merozoite to another host cell forming a new schizont.
4. Merozoite becomes a microgametocyte in a new host cell.
5. Merozoite becomes a macrogametocyte in a new host cell.
6. Flagellated microgametes make their way to a macrogamete.
7. Fertilization and a fertilized macrogamete, oocyst formed by sporogeny.
8. Oocyst excreted or ingested by a new host.

schizont in the host cell and begins to divide by multiple fission into a large number of daughter cells (schizogony). Merozoites are released from the cell to enter other cells, where they grow into new schizonts and duplicate the schizogony as before. Several asexual (schizogony) generations may occur before sexual processes begin. Some of the merozoites acquire sexual differentiation and transform to macrogametes. Other merozoites become microgametocysts and divide again to form a number of small flagellated microgametes. Flagellated microgametes released from a host cell actively move to find a macrogamete in another cell and a zygote is formed. The fertilized macrogamete (zygote) develops a cuticle and transforms into an oocyst. The nucleus of the oocyst divides into four daughter nuclei, which in turn develop into four sporocysts, each with a double membrane. An additional nuclear fission within the sporocyst produces two sporozoites. Thus there are four sporocysts, each with two sporozoites, within the oocyst. The oocysts are extremely capable of withstanding the rigors of external existence and remain viable for long periods of time, probably a year or more, or until swallowed by a new host (Fig. 12).[10]

The formation of merozoites, microgametes, macrogametes and oocysts is a continuous process within the host. Oocysts are released at a more or less constant rate. The coccidial reproductive success may be reduced or increased depending to some extent on the health of the host. Each fish infected with coccidia, therefore, becomes a carrier of the organism and a potential case of coccidiosis. There is no indication that infective units of

coccidiosis are carried with eggs. They can be transported over long distances in live fishes.

There is no information on temperature requirements of piscine coccidia. Each species of *Eimeria* has no doubt adapted to its natural host, and each coccidian species may be quite host specific.

Disease Signs:

Signs of coccidiosis include emaciation, lethargy and general poor health. Internal signs of coccidiosis include white blisters on the intestinal wall, the intestine swollen with fluid and the feces light in color and made up of many oocysts.[25,28]

Diagnosis:

Diagnosis of coccidiosis is dependent on disease signs, general histopathology of the organ in which the coccidia are in the reproductive state and identification of oocysts. Oocysts may be observed in intestinal scrapings or fecal smears viewed at magnifications of 200 to 400 X. They are usually round to oval in shape, have a thin double wall and are filled with spores and sporozoites. Identification to species is by size (length by width) and by internal structures. Descriptions of various species are then compared with the isolate.[10]

There may be tremendous numbers of oocysts in fecal casts or intestinal smears taken from cases of coccidiosis. Oocysts may be more difficult to locate from fishes without active coccidiosis. Oocysts can be concentrated in these cases by centrifugation and flotation. A small amount of feces taken from the suspected host is placed in water in a centrifuge tube. The feces is mixed thoroughly with the water and either allowed to settle for 24 hours or centrifuged at slow speed for three to five minutes. The supernatant is poured off, leaving the heavy materials at the bottom of the tube. The tube is filled completely with 60% sucrose (table sugar) solution, mixed thoroughly and a cover glass set on top of the tube touching the liquid in the completely filled tube. The cover glass should be left in this position for one to six hours, at which time it is removed and the wet side examined microscopically for presence of oocysts. The severity of coccidial infection can be judged by the number of oocysts found per unit weight of feces.

Therapy and Control:

There are no therapeutic procedures known for coccidiosis. Cases of active coccidiosis are rare and there has been little need to develop drug therapy for fishes. However, there are a number of coccidiostats used for higher vertebrates which may be acceptable for therapy of fish coccidiosis.

Prognosis:

Little information is known on morbidity or mortality predictions from epizootics involving coccidia. Two examples may serve to indicate morbidity levels. The first was an epizootic of disease in goldfish in Pennsylvania in which *E. aurati* was one of the parasites observed. The coccidian was demonstrated in seven of 29 fish.[28] *E. anguillae* was found during an epizootic of coccidiosis among eels in Auckland, New Zealand. Only emaciated individuals were examined. There was no mention of *E. anguillae* morbidity among the general eel population.[25]

Practical Aspects:

Coccidiosis has not been a problem among either confined or wild-ranging fishes of North America. However, fish disease diagnosticians need to be aware of this disease.

MICROSPORA OF FISHES:

Members of the phylum Microspora have been known in fishes since 1887, when *Glugea anomala* was described in sticklebacks.[12] Over 40 species are known in fishes today.[10] The microsporans are intracellular parasites with a tremendous reproductive capacity. The life cycle of all microsporans is monoxenous (requiring but one host). The only transmitting entity is spores composed of a valve and a polar filament. The polar filament is used to anchor spores to the host tissue until the sporoplasm is extruded through the everted filament.

Microsporiasis is characterized as a chronic condition in which masses of developing spores form within tissues of the host. The tumor-like masses appear as curiosities among stream, lake, estuarine or marine fishes or a definite morbid processes among certain cultured and ornamental fishes. The masses enclosing large numbers of spores may cause deformities of the integument or of the body, but with little effect on the host unless they occur in vital organs, interfere with movement or reduce ability to elude predation. Epizootics of microsporiasis caused by different microsporan species have been reported in fish populations as being of considerable economic importance because of food or angling value of the fishes.[12,89]

Etiological Agents:

The etiological agents of microsporiasis are species of at least two taxonomic families and a number of genera. Species of four genera are most often found infecting fishes: *Pleistophora*, *Nosema*, *Glugea* and *Thelohania*. The microsporans have such a wide distribution among fishes that space does not allow a discussion of each in this chapter. General characteristics of the microsporans and the host alteration caused by these organisms will be discussed.

All microsporans reproduce by binary fission and sporogony. Spores of microsporans are the smallest of protozoan spores. They are unique among the protozoa in being gram-positive with a small granule at the anterior end which is positive to the periodic acid-Schiff reaction (carbohydrate in nature). Each spore has a single polar filament coiled within the cytoplasm. Either one or two vesicular nuclei lie within the coils of the filament. Spores transmitted into new hosts increase in number by binary fission or schizogony at first. This is followed by sporogony in which sporonts are distinctively different from schizonts (Fig. 13). Enormous numbers of spores are produced, causing hypertrophy of the cells in which they occur, resulting in the formation of cysts. The cysts may be round, oval or elongate (Pl. 18D).

Geographical Distribution:

Species of the phylum Microspora are worldwide in distribution.

Susceptible Species:

Microsporans have been identified in a wide variety of host fishes. Some of the most commonly infected or economically important fishes include the neon tetra with *Pleistophora hyphessobryconis*, sticklebacks with *Glugea anomala*, steelhead (rainbow trout) with *Thelohania californica*, golden shiner with *P. ovariae*, whitefish and smelt with *Glugea hertwigi* and fathead minnow with *Nosema pimephales*.[12,87,89,99,100,107]

Quite often single cases of microsporiasis are reported to be found occasionally or widely distributed among a fish population, but usually they are of minor or no importance to maintenance of the population. Possibly all fishes are susceptible to infections of microsporans. Route of transmission and spore contamination on food may limit fish species susceptible to certain of the organisms. Carnivorous and scavenger fishes, as well as bottom-feeding fishes, are more susceptible to microsporan infections than those feeding on phytoplankton or other aquatic plants.

Epizootiology:

The transmitting unit of all microsporans is the spore.

Fig. 13: General life cycle of a microsporan
1. Spores taken into the new host orally or reinfection in the same host.
2. Sporoplasms enter the host cell and are called tropozoites at this stage.
3. The tropozoite reproduces by schizogony to an octonucleate schizont.
4. Nuclei divide again.
5. A sixteen-nucleate pansporoplasm forms. Each of the sixteen spores are released to complete the cycle.

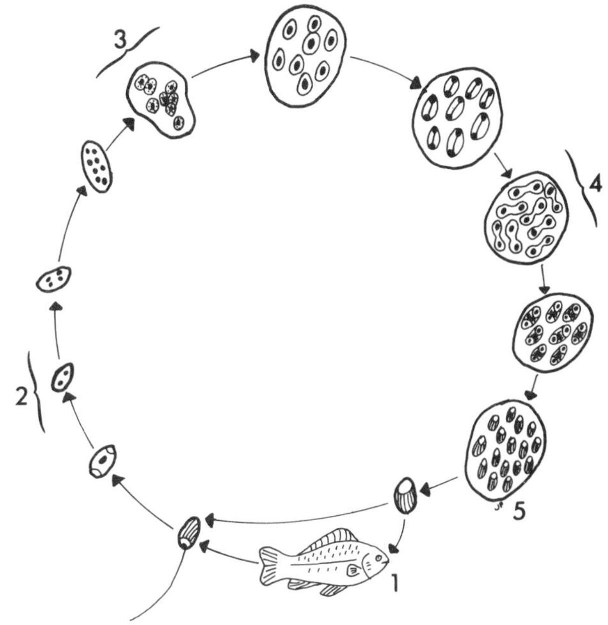

Spores are present in hypertrophic cells of the host fish until death of the fish. Disintegration of the tissue in which the spore is present releases spores. Ingestion of infected fishes by other fishes also releases spores from the infected host. Those released to the environment must be ingested by the new host, either directly or as contaminants on food. The spores are swallowed by the new host and the polar filament released by action of disgestive fluids. The sporoplasm is released either directly into the host cell or in close proximity to the host cell. It penetrates the intestinal epithelium by amoeboid movement and travels to the site of infection by means of the host's blood stream. The sporoplasm entering the host cell is called a trophozoite.

It begins division through multiple fission (schizogony) and produces a two, four, eight and sixteen nucleate schizont and pansporoplasms (Fig. 13). Multiple division and sexual fusion (sporogony) continue until tremendous numbers of spores are produced. The large numbers of spores enlarge the host cell until it may be large enough to see with the naked eye. Schizogony and sporogony continue for the life of the fish or until the cyst ruptures. There are indications that autoinfection occurs when cysts rupture internally.[12] Those cysts present in the skin and underlying fascia or muscle of the host may rupture to the outside and release spores into the water. At least one species of microsporan (*Thelohania ovicola*) is found in the eggs released from infected fish, another means of spore release not requiring death of the host fish.[89] The usual pattern, however, is death of the host fish before release of spores is possible.

Disease Signs:

The signs of microsporiasis depend on the part of the body infected by the pathogen. Those near the surface of the body, in skin, fascia or muscle directly underlying the skin, usually appear as white to gray-white tumorous masses called xenomas (Pl. 18E). The large multinucleate developmental stages and cysts made up of large number of pansporoplasms or spore stages are often visible with the naked eye. These masses may be present in any tissue of the body, usually depending to some extent on the species of microsporan involved. Each species has a usual site of infection.

Fishes with microsporiasis at an advanced stage of development may become lethargic, emaciated, may seek the surface if gills are involved, may become solitary or may have different body colors than are usual for that host species. Signs of *P. hyphessobryconis* in the neon tetra are accompanied by milky white areas in muscles underlying the skin, usually along the dorsal side of the body (Pl. 18E). The white areas are masses of developing *P. hyphessobryconis* observed through the skin.

Diagnosis:

Diagnosis of microsporiasis is by appearance of tumor-like cysts within cells of various parts of the body, observation of stained or unstained smears prepared from the cysts, histopathology of infected host tissue and identification of spores taken from the cysts. Host species and site of infection may also help in diagnosis.

Smears prepared from cysts will reveal oval to oblong spores (Pl. 18F). Spores of microsporans are quite small, ranging up to 7.5 micrometers long by 3.5 micrometers wide. Staining the spores with Giemsa or certain other stains may reveal inner structures of the spore useful for identification.

Sections cut and stained from tissue of fishes suspected of microsporiasis will reveal various stages of development of the microsporan and may be a definitive diagnosis for the disease. For example, tissue taken from a neon tetra infected with *P. hyphessobryconis* have large numbers of pansporoblasts and encysted spores within cells between muscle bundles (Pl. 19A). These findings are diagnostic for "neon tetra disease," a disease known to be specific for neon tetras and a few other fishes.

Therapy and Control:

There is usually no therapy for microsporiasis. Quarantine and restriction of movement will reduce the possibility of spreading the pathogen. Test and slaughter is also useful in aquaria in which only a few fishes have become infected with the particular species of microsporan. Removal of obviously infected fishes, disinfection of the aquarium and placing a fine mesh screen above the bottom may also be of assistance. The purpose of the screen is to keep fish from picking up food or other particles, including microsporan spores, from the bottom. The above-mentioned methods may also be practiced for controlling microsporiasis in fish culture facilities, especially those with cement or other hard-surface linings.

Prognosis:

Microsporiasis is usually an occasional finding among wild-ranging fishes. However, there have been reports of high levels of infection and mortality among some populations. Several epizootics of microsporiasis and mass mortality occurring among fishes in the upper reaches of the Amur and Volga Rivers have been reported from Russia.[10] Also, large numbers of gizzard shad were found dead along the shores of a lake in Ohio; 107 of 161 fish examined were infected with a microsporan.

The disease has also been responsible for high mortalities in cultured fishes. Almost a complete loss of 170,000 rainbow (steelhead) trout fingerlings occurred in California from *Thelohania californica.* A mortality of 75% was also reported in rainbow trout fingerlings in British Columbia from a similar organism. Spawning failures of golden shiners in Illinois were attributed to microsporan infection of the ovaries. The incidence of infection was 65% of the fish examined. No viable eggs were found in the infected females, suggesting that the fish had become sterile from the infection.[89]

Practical Aspects:

The most obvious problem from microsporiasis has been among ornamental fishes. Transportation of fishes from continent to continent or from country to country has served to move microsporans long distances. The aquarist should be alerted to the microsporans and the possibility of transmitting the organisms from host to host in the close confinement of aquaria. Fishes with obvious cysts should be removed as soon as they are noticed. Spores are not usually shed from intact fishes unless they are in the skin and the cyst ruptures. Aquaria which have fishes with microsporiasis, especially fishes with known ruptured cysts, should be thoroughly cleaned and disinfected prior to returning fishes to the tank.

Microsporans infecting ovaries or testes of host fishes may be responsible for reduced reproduction by not only reducing fecundity of the host but also contaminating the spawn with spores from degenerating eggs, producing an immediate source of infection to newly hatched alevins.

MYXOZOA OF FISHES:

All members of the phylum Myxozoa are parasitic to other animals. The myxozoans have been separated taxonomically from other cnidosporans or cnidocyst-producing protozoans. They are unique in that throughout much of their life cycle they demonstrate true multicellular existence. Many myxozoans are found in the urinary and gall bladders of the host (coelozoic). Many species are found in the parenchyma of soft tissues of the host (histozoic) but generally within the intercellular spaces. Occasionally intracellular (cytozoic) forms are found in muscle fibers.[67]

The Myxozoa are an extremely abundant and diverse group of organisms. Twenty-three genera are listed in Freshwater Fishes of North America.[35,118] Over 700 species have been identified in fishes. All species of the class Myxosporea occur in poikilothermic vertebrates, most of them in fishes. Most of the Myxozoa present in fishes have evolved into a successful commensalistic relationship. However, there are several significant parasitic pathogens to which the following discussion will be directed.

Species of five genera of the families Myxosomatidae and Myxobolidae have been responsible for significant losses in cultured fishes: *Myxosoma cerebralis, Ceratomyxa shasta, Henneguya* sp., *Myobolus argentens* and *Myotoulus notemigoni.* Species of at least ten other genera are commonly found in fishes: *Myxidium, Sphaeromyxa, Sphaerospora, Unicapsula, Auerbachia, Thelohanelus, Chloromyxum, Kudoa, Unicauda* and *Hexacapsula.* These protozoans are widely distributed, but usually with limited cases in fish populations at any one time period.

The genus *Henneguya* has at least 15 identified species widely distributed in the world.[10] Thus henneguyiasis is not a clearly defined disease. There are only a few species of *Ceratomyxa* recorded from fishes, but *C. shasta* has been responsible for epizootics in salmon culture facilities in the northwestern United States and Canada. The diseases caused by *Henneguya* sp. and *C. shasta* will receive limited discussion.

The disease caused by *Myxosoma cerebralis* has been and will continue to be a widely distributed disease in the world. The disease (whirling disease) has received much attention during the last two or three decades. This disease will be used as a major example of a myxozoan disease to demonstrate how these organisms affect the host, diagnosis of myxozoan diseases and how they may be controlled.

Whirling Disease

Whirling disease is a chronic debilitating, highly infectious disease of salmonids. The disease is apparently of central European origin and was not observed in the United States until 1956.[38] The disease was first reported in Germany in 1903. The name "whirling disease" was apparently given early in the century to describe the peculiar swimming activity of fishes with the disease. The causative organism has a tropicity for cartilaginous tissue of the host. Cartilage, and later ossified bone, in the skull and vertebral column becomes misshapen, which apparently alters inner ear control of balance or bends the body in such a way that the fish swims erratically in circles. The disease has also been called black tail disease when it occurs in young salmonids—lesions produced by the parasite alter innervation which controls pigmentation in the posterior third of the body.

Etiological Agent:

The etiological agent of whirling disease in *Myxosoma cerebralis*. Controversy remains as to whether the species actually belongs in the genus *Myxosoma* or *Myxobolus*. However, the two genera can be separated by presence or absence of an iodinophilus vacuole in spores; the iodinophilus vacuole is absent in *Myxosoma* and present in *Myxobolus*. Also, *Myxosoma cerebralis* is the only *Myxosoma* found in cartilage of salmonids.[26a,38] The parasite was first described in 1903 as *Myxobolus cerebralis*. The nomenclature changed to *Lentospora cerebralis* in 1905.[26,82] The latter name was used extensively until about 1952, when *Myxosoma cerebralis* came into common usage.

Spores of *M. cerebralis* are used primarily for identification and diagnosis. The spores are nearly circular in shape and 7 to 9 micrometers in length by about 5 micrometers thick. Each spore contains two prominent polar capsules, usually pyriform in shape and about 4 micrometers in length. A pronounced suture around the rim of the spore holds the two valves of the spore together. A single barely discernible polar filament is coiled inside each of the polar capsules. A single sporoplasm is present within the spore at the opposite end from the polar capsules.[54]

The spores are destroyed and probably killed by heating at 60 to 100°C for ten minutes, but not at 40°C. They are thought to be killed within 24 hours by 0.5 to 2.5% calcium oxide or 10 mg per liter of available chlorine. Irradiation with ultraviolet light at 35,000 micro-

watt seconds per square centimeter apparently destroys the spores in tanks containing water and live fishes.[33]

Geographical Distribution:

M. cerebralis was first identified in Germany.[26] Since then it has been reported throughout central and northern Europe, including Italy and all of the British Isles. It has been reported from Russia and Asia, South Africa, South America, New Zealand and North America.[105] Its first introduction into the United States was in central Pennsylvania. Frozen European trout with *M. cerebralis* was thought to have been brought to the United States and inadvertently fed to cultured trout at Brenner Springs, Pennsylvania, or whole fish or viscera discarded into the stream.

The first occurrence of whirling disease in the United States was in 1956. The pathogen has subsequently appeared in California, Connecticut, Massachusetts, Michigan, New Hampshire, New Jersey, New York, Ohio, Oregon, Virginia and West Virginia.[34,117,114B] Vigorous attempts have been made to eliminate the organism from most of the sites in the United States. Time alone will prove success of elimination procedures.

Susceptible Species:

Apparently all species of salmonids are susceptible to *M. cerebralis*. It has been diagnosed in rainbow trout, brown trout, brook trout, Atlantic salmon, chum salmon, pink salmon, seema salmon, malma salmon, chinook salmon, whitefish and grayling.[10,30,42] Young fishes may be more susceptible to the disease than older ones of the same species. Rainbow trout fry are susceptible to whirling disease infection three or more days after hatching. Egg stages are apparently not susceptible to infection.[88] Brown trout do not demonstrate signs of whirling disease unless they are infected at a young stage of their life. Lightly infected fish and fish a year old or older may not demonstrate signs of the disease but can become carriers.[30]

Epizootiology:

Whirling disease is transmitted by spores of *M. cerebralis*. Most spores within the cartilaginous tissues are trapped there until the fish dies. Spores which enter very young fishes and infect skeletal tissues prior to ossification of the bones are trapped within the bone as the fish ages.

The organism is not transmitted directly from fish to fish. There is little doubt the major route of transmission is orally. A transmission route through external body surfaces (gills or skin) is suspected since rainbow trout sac fry do not take food yet become infected if they are within an environment infected with *M. cerebralis*.[76] This strongly suggests transmission in which tubificid worms and free-swimming stages of the pathogen are involved (Fig. 14).

M. cerebralis spores harvested from recently dead fish, or whole ground fresh fish tissue containing *M. ce-*

175

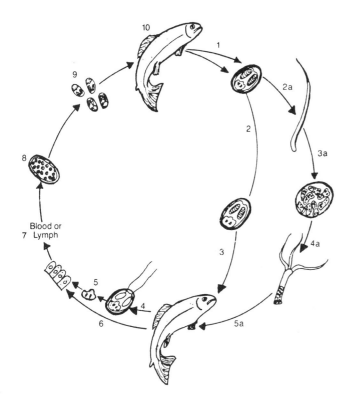

rebralis spores, have been pipetted directly into the stomach of susceptible fish which resulted in no transmission. Spores must be mature or "aged" (infective) prior to being pipetted into the stomach in order to reproduce the disease. Experimental attempts to transmit the organism met with failure until spores were "aged" by submerging them in pond bottom material for about six months. The bottom mud was autoclaved prior to addition of spores to eliminate any possibility of transmission from soil organisms.[102,105]

Other research has demonstrated transmission through an intermediate host tubificid (Annelida: Oligochaeta) worm.[56a] *M. cerebralis* spores enter gut epithelium of the worm, are transposed to an actinosporean sporocyst, and finally to a triactinomyxon with anterior epispore containing sporozoites (Fig. 14). Transmission is probably by ingestion of a tubificid worm in which the triactinomyxon stage is present in gut tissue. There is some evidence the free-swimming triactinomyxon may be taken in orally or possibly through gill or skin.[56b,114b,114c]

There is no direct experimental evidence on what happens to an infective spore or triactinomyxon once it is swallowed by the host. Mature spores treated with highly alkaline solutions (pH 10 to 12) will extrude the polar filaments.[65] This suggests that filament extrusion occurs in the alkaline conditions of the fish intestine.

There are some doubts about how the sporoplasm emerges from the spore and enters the hosts intestinal epithelium. The sporoplasm within intestinal epithelium is probably swept away by the blood stream, or possibly the lymphatic system, to organs in which further development can proceed.[91]

The sporoplasm probably enters cartilage at any place in the fish body, becomes a trophozoite and begins to reproduce by plasmotomy. A great number of spores are produced within the cartilage. Transmission to very young fishes, in which nearly all hard tissues are cartilage, is a fertile substrate for sporulation. Thus, young fishes are usually more affected by the spores and more apt to demonstrate deformed bodies.

The incubation period between exposure to infective spores and signs of whirling disease is 12 to 60 days, depending on water temperature and number of spores involved.[38,95] The sporoplasm, now called a trophozoite, has entered the cartilage, and lesions containing various stages of sporulation have developed (Fig. 14). Sporulation within the auditory capsule of the skull usually alters equilibrium. The fish attempts to move or tries to take food but can only move in a circular direction, becoming more frantic in these movements until exhausted.

Trophozoites entering cartilage in the vicinity of the 26th vertebra may alter caudal pigmentation through damage or pressure on sympathetic nerves controlling pigmentation.[38,95] These fishes develop the characteristic black tail if infected quite young in their lives (Pl. 20A).

Mortality may be quite high during the initial stages of the disease. Dead fish are a source of spores for transmission to other fish, after entering the intermediate tubificid host, or the period of aging to become infective. Fish surviving early stages of the disease continue to carry the spores for life. These fish are also a source of spores when they die. Spores of dead fish may be carried by water currents or remain on the pond bottom until infective or taken in by a tubificid.

Birds or aquatic mammals may be involved in the transmission cycle of whirling disease. Blue herons fed M. cerebralis-infected fishes passed the spores apparently unaltered. The spores were assumed to be viable because filament extrusion was possible by treating them with 2% potassium hydroxide.[39] Fingerling rainbow trout exposed to feces of mallard ducks and a black-crowned night heron which had been fed M. cerebralis-infected fish tissue developed whirling disease.[102]

There is no indication that M. cerebralis can be transmitted to eggs of infected fishes. Also, the protozoan is apparently not transmitted to eggs following spawning and during incubation, except as a contaminant.[41,88]

Disease Signs:

Signs of whirling disease depend on age of the fishes and severity of infection. A limited infection will usually cause no disease signs but the fishes will carry spores for life. These are the most dangerous fishes because detecting the infection is difficult. The most obvious signs in more heavily infected fishes is frantic swimming in a circle or appearance of darker pigmentation of the caudal peduncle and tail (Pl. 20A). Young fishes may become exhausted from the continuous circling and fall to the bottom. They will remain there until able to regain strength enough to continue swimming. Whirling signs tend to subside gradually for up to a year.[38] Fishes surviving the early stages of the disease develop misshapen bodies, particularly the head. Sunken areas are present above the eyes, and the mouth may be permanently bent or open. Those fishes with the black tail syndrome will usually have a radically deformed caudal area or curvature of the spine (Pl. 20B). The skull may fail to develop to normal size or conformation (Pl. 19B).

Diagnosis:

Diagnosis of whirling disease in fishes with obvious signs of the disease is not difficult. Definitive diagnosis is by signs of the disease and demonstration of spores in cartilage or bone of fishes known to be susceptible to the disease. Cut sections of the skull, gill arches and vertebrae stained with Giesma stain will reveal the spores located in cartilage or surrounded by bone (Pl. 19C). The polar capsules and lightly stained sporoplasm should be obvious in round to oval shaped spores. The spores of M. cerebralis are 7 to 9 micrometers in diameter and approximately 5 micrometers thick. Multinucleate trophozoites or developing spores may be seen in sections of cartilage from about one to four months after infection. Thereafter only spores or developing spores will be observable (Pl. 19C).

Demonstration of spores may also be possible by microscopic observation of gill arch tissue or the auditory capsule pressed between two microscope slides until the tissue is pressed out thinly. Unstained spores appear as refractile bodies 7 to 9 micrometers in diameter with two obvious polar capsules.[30] There are other species of myxozoans which resemble M. cerebralis, but M. cerebralis is the only one found in the skeletal tissue of salmonid fishes. M. squamalis occurs in the scales of salmonids in western United States. It is about the same size as M. cerebralis but has an obvious narrow ridge which parallels either side of the suture ridge. There are two species of Myxobolus with spores resembling M. cerebralis; each has an iodinophilous vacuole as do all Myxobolus sp. An iodinophilous vacuole is absent in M. cerebralis, as in all Myxosoma sp.

Location of M. cerebralis carriers is difficult, especially in lightly infected fishes. Several procedures have been developed to assist in diagnosis of the less obvious cases of whirling disease. One such procedure is by digesting skeletal tissue away from the spores by use of digestive enzymes. There are several modifications of the procedure, but the general sequence is to first remove as much of the soft tissues from skeletal tissue as possible, either with a scalpel or scissors or by heating at 45 to 50°C for five to ten minutes before removal. Gill tissue is usually used intact and placed with the cleaned skeletal tissue. The bony tissues and gills are minced or ground and treated with either pepsin—hydrochloric acid or trypsin—sodium hydroxide. The resultant digest is centrifuged, washed or treated with dextrose solution and the sediment examined microscopically for presence of spores.[51,58]

Another procedure for spore concentration is to first blend the head and gills of fishes suspected of being infected with M. cerebralis in a laboratory blender. The suspension is filtered to remove most tissue debris and the supernatant poured through a plankton continuous centrifuge. The spores and other small particles stick inside the centrifuge drum. Some of the collection is scraped off, placed under a microscope and examined for presence of spores.[75]

An immunodiffusion procedure has been attempted for identification of whirling disease carriers. The fluorescent antibody techniques show promise as a diagnostic procedure for whirling disease. Several difficulties must be resolved before the test is reliable.[57,79] Care must be taken to be absolutely sure spores are present in fish demonstrating other signs of whirling disease such as the black tail syndrome.[114a]

Therapy and Control:

There is no therapy for control of whirling disease. The disease can be reduced or eliminated by quarantine and restriction of movement, test and slaughter, and sanitation and disinfection. Legislation enacted in 1968 (Title 50, Wildlife and Fisheries Part 13) involving importation of fishes or fish eggs was extended to include whirling disease. This reduced importation of trout into the United States from Europe and other parts of the world in which whirling disease occurs. Careful testing of fishes in the United States for presence of *M. cerebralis* has been a part of the control plan. Fish found harboring the myxozoans have been destroyed and carefully disinfected, usually by deep burial or incineration. Studies have indicated that spores are not passed within the egg of infected fishes. However, contamination of eggs with water or mud may be possible.[76]

Attempts to destroy spores of *M. cerebralis* in the bottom of earthen ponds has been only partially successful. The theory of disinfection is to create an alkaline condition which causes the spore to extend filaments. The partially activated spore may then die. Consequently, calcium oxide (hydrated lime) and calcium cyanamide have been used. The number of spores is reduced but not eliminated.[41,42]

Chlorine levels of 10 mg per liter or Roccal will kill the spores *in vitro* (in glass). The use of these two disinfectants under conditions found in fish culture facilities has been of limited success, possibly because of the large amounts of organic matter which reduce available chlorine rapidly or inability of Roccal penetration under field conditions.[39,42]

Proof that fish-eating birds can pass *M. cerebralis* spores in feces following feeding on infected fishes indicates that control procedures involving any of the other methods will not be successful if fish-eating birds are allowed to fly from infected areas to disinfected facilities. Likewise, fish-eating birds may be responsible for transportation of viable spores over long distances, thus causing difficulties in attempts to control the spread of whirling disease.

Water supplies for fish culture facilities contaminated with spores of *M. cerebralis* may be treated with ultraviolet light to remove the infectivity. The water must flow past the illumination in a thin sheet because of reduced penetration by ultraviolet wavelengths. Evidence indicates that 35,000 microwatt seconds per square centimeter are necessary. Irradiation must be constant if this method is to be used for controlling the disease.[33]

Prognosis:

Morbidity among young salmonids being held in *M. cerebralis*-contaminated facilities will usually reach 100%. Mortality among heavily infected young salmonids varies greatly and may reach 100%. Severity of infection and age of fish determine mortality. Fishes not dieing directly from the disease may succumb to other problems. They may not be capable of taking food, thus malnutrition develops, followed by infections of other opportunistic organisms and death from secondary causes.

Salmonids infected at over one year of age will probably show no signs of infection nor will there be mortality, even if morbidity levels reach 100%. This is especially true with brown trout, possibly the natural host of *M. cerebralis*.

Practical Aspects:

Presence of whirling disease in the United States is a serious problem. Spreading this disease among all trout and salmon rearing facilities would be an extremely serious economic matter. Therefore, every effort should be made on the part of fish health personnel, fish culturists, fishery managers and fishery administrators to not only hold this disease to its present distribution in the United States, but to reduce its geographical distribution and possibly eradicate it.

The incidence of whirling disease in Michigan in 1968 can serve as an example of how the disease can be eliminated from a place where it had previously occurred. The disease was diagnosed in one commercial trout culture facility in central Michigan. Discharge water from the facility was released into a small stream which flowed into Lake Huron. The stream was inhabited by brook, rainbow and brown trout, all susceptible to the disease. A survey of wild-ranging fishes in the stream in late 1968 revealed that some of the fishes indeed, carried the spores of *M. cerebralis*.[119] A plan was set up to not only eliminate the trout population from the fish culture facility and disinfect the premises, but to eliminate the fish population from the entire length of the stream and tributaries on which the fish culture facility was located. The streams were treated in 1970 and there is no indication of disease recurrence.

Controlled experiments have been performed to determine, not only if tubificids can be intermediate hosts of *M. cerebralis* but which tubificids may be involved. These experiments have demonstrated *Tubifex* sp. can support transmission, but species of other genera of the family Tubificidae may also be capable of supporting the intermediate stage of *M. cerebralis*.[56b] The intermediate stage is specifically called the triactinomyxon stage. Species of the genus *Triactinomyxon* have long been known as parasites of tubificid worms, where the three appendage organisms originated was not known, but now *M. cerebralis* has been found to be one source (Fig. 14).

Tubificid worm culture has become a secondary industry to fish culture in the United States. Tailwater spilling from fish culture facilities is rich in nutrients with a load of fish feces and excess fish ration. Tubificids are grown in this environment, separated from bottom sediment, washed, and sold as an aquarium fish diet supplement. Great care is needed to be assured the worms or the water in which they are shipped do not carry the triactinomyxon stage of *M. cerebralis*. Also, further research is needed to determine if not only the *M. cerebralis* triactinomyxon stage, but possibly this stage of other Myxozoa (*Ceratomyxa, Henneguya, Myxobolus* and others) can be transmitted through tubificids.

Ceratomyxiasis Shasta

Infections of salmonid fishes by *Ceratomyxa shasta* are widely distributed in the northwestern parts of the United States and in British Columbia. This organism occurs among salmonid fishes in many river drainages where anadromous salmonids return from the ocean to spawn. The organism has also been reported in cultured nonanadromous salmonids as well. The disease is usually of no consequence to older fishes but can be devastating to very young salmonids.[111] The etiological agent may be found in many different organs of the body. Slight to moderate infections have no adverse effect on young hosts, but marked to extreme infections may cause rapidly developing pathology and death.

Etiological Agent:

The etiological agent of ceratomyxiasis shasta is *Ceratomyxa shasta*. It was first described in 1948 from fingerling rainbow trout in Shasta County, California.[72] Tissues of the fish contained both trophozoites and spores.

C. shasta is an obligate parasite and requires but one host for complete development. The spores are widely arched or double-wing shaped with rounded ends (Pl. 19D). The spores are 6 to 14 micrometers in length, with two polar capsules.[72] Each trophozoite contains two sporoblasts averaging 13 to 19 micrometers in diameter, and each sporoblast usually contains two to four spores. Attempts made to transmit spores directly from fish to fish met with failure, indicating the spores must remain outside of the fish body for a period of time for aging. The reason for this is unknown.

Susceptible Species:

Rainbow trout, cutthroat trout, brook trout, Atlantic salmon, coho salmon, chinook salmon, chum salmon and sockeye salmon are susceptible to *C. shasta*. Exposing these fishes to the protozoan for 43 to 60 days at water temperatures of 12.5 to 21.5°C resulted in 4 to 100% infections. Brook trout, cutthroat trout, rainbow trout, chum salmon and fall chinook salmon are most susceptible. Death may not occur in Atlantic salmon, but up to 30% may become infected if placed in contact with spores.[120]

Disease Signs:

Fishes with marked to extreme ceratomyxiasis shasta become sluggish and separate from the group. They usually seek the sides or corners of ponds or raceways. The abdomen may be distended with ascitic fluid. The anus may be distended and ooze mucus.[120] Internally there are tumor-like masses in one or more of the visceral organs. The intestine is more often affected than

other organs. The stomach, esophagus, cortex of the spleen, subcutaneous connective tissue, liver, kidney, heart, gonads, gall bladder or gills may contain white to gray-white masses filled with trophozoites and spores (Pl. 20C).

Diagnosis:

Diagnosis of ceratomyxiasis shasta is by disease signs and identification of spores and trophozoites within the lesions. Wet mounts of infected tissues, usually intestine, will reveal the characteristic arch-shaped spores. Trophozoites may have from one to many nuclei, depending on age. Species of host and history of presence of the myxozoan may be of assistance in diagnosis.

Therapy and Control:

No chemotherapeutic agents have been found for control of ceratomyxiasis shasta once it has appeared in susceptible fishes. Attempts to control the disease in fish culture facilities have been unsuccessful when the water supply cannot be disinfected. Removal of contaminated water and disinfection of all fish-holding facilities will assist in controlling recurrence of the disease.[94]

Practical Aspects:

Surveys conducted to determine distribution of *C. shasta* indicate that many lakes and streams of the northwestern United States are contaminated with the organism. All streams and lakes near the fish culture facility where ceratomyxiasis was identified in 1948 (Crystal Lake Hatchery, Mount Shasta, California) harbored *C. shasta*. Cages containing trout placed in these bodies of water resulted in positive transmission of the organism.[94]

A survey of the Columbia-Willamette-Deschutes River system and the coastal streams of Oregon demonstrated wide distribution of *C. shasta*. Incidence of ceratomyxiasis in the Deschutes River Basin ranged between 50 and 100% infection among salmonids. Salmonids taken from other streams in the state demonstrated infection levels of 0 to 64%.[93] A study to test a *C. shasta* recovery technique from the intestinal tract of nonfeeding, adult Columbia River spring chinook salmon in Idaho found a 94% infection level. Summer chinook salmon returning to the same place in Idaho were found to have 95% infection level.[10a] Other data indicate *C. shasta* to be widely distributed in northern California as well. Fishes taken from streams and lakes known to harbor the organism should not be transported outside the general geographical area in which they reside.

Ceratomyxiasis shasta has been responsible for high mortalities in young cultured salmonids. Complete mortality resulted in *C. shasta*-infected rainbow trout at the Crystal Lake trout hatchery in northern California.[94] Mortalities as high as 58% occurred in coho salmon at the Bonneville Salmon Hatchery on the Columbia River.[15] These reports demonstrate that ceratomyxiasis shasta can be a serious disease. Great care should be taken to at least hold distribution of *C. shasta* to its present confines.

Henneguyan Diseases

Species of *Henneguya* are among the most cosmopolitan myxozoans of freshwater fishes of the world. Many cases of henneguyiasis go unnoticed among fishes.[66] Cases of henneguyiasis among cultured fishes have caused losses or debilitation of fishes which limited survival.[59]

Etiological Agents:

Seventeen species of *Henneguya* were described in freshwater fishes of North America.[35] At least 18 species have been described in European fishes.[10,20]

Henneguya spores are characteristically oval or fusiform in shape, but a few are round. They have two long, whip-like caudal processes giving them a spermatozoan-like appearance (Pl. 21A). Measurement of the spores usually does not include the caudal process. Measurements should be from the anterior pole to the end of the spore cavity.[67] Sizes of spores range from 8 to 24 micrometers in length. The caudal process may be from 20 to 45 micrometers in length.

Susceptible Species:

A wide variety of freshwater and marine fishes have been reported with infections of *Henneguya* species—carp, channel catfish, stickleback, coho salmon, sockeye salmon, cisco, whitefish, yellow perch, northern pike and bluefish are examples.[35,59,64,66,67,92] Some *Henneguya* species appear to be host-specific, but others may be found in many fish species.

Disease Signs:

Henneguyiasis is often typified by formation of gross or microscopic opaque masses in various tissues of the body. Certain *Henneguya* species have limited tropicity, but others infect many organs. External examination of henneguyan-infected fishes may reveal cysts in the skin and gills (Pl. 19E). Liver, intestine, heart, muscle, kidney, spleen or other tissue may have lesions. Some infections are not serious to the fish unless it is in a vital organ. However, *H. postexilis*, an interlamellar *Henneguya*, can kill channel catfish fingerlings.

Various species of *Henneguya* produce different lesions in the host: intralamellar in gills, cutaneous underlying the skin, mandibular teeth lesions and gall bladder lesions. One type of henneguyiasis may be prevalent at one catfish farm, a different type at another farm.

Diagnosis:

Diagnosis of henneguyiasis can be made from gross appearance of the lesions and observation of spores. Small bits of the lesion may be spread on a microscope slide with a few drops of water and examined. Large numbers of characteristic henneguyan spores are a definite diagnosis (Pl. 21A).

Therapy and Control:

There are no chemotherapeutic agents known for control of henneguyiasis. The disease has been quite widespread with but a few cases, and therapeutic procedures are not usually warranted. Henneguyiasis has become somewhat of a problem in channel catfish culture in the United States. Cases of the disease involving gill tissue may cause anoxia, but attempts to treat the disease when gills are involved have usually caused additional mortality (Pl. 19E).[59]

No control procedures have been developed, even when henneguyiasis has been found in cultured fishes. Spores released from dead fishes or in feces (if cysts are present in tissues or secretory organs along the alimentary tract) probably maintain spores in earthen ponds. Movement of catfishes about the southern and southwestern United States is thought to have spread various species of *Henneguya*.

SPORE PRODUCING PROTOZOA OF DOUBTFUL CLASSIFICATION

Proliferative Kidney Disease

The name proliferative kidney disease (PKD) was given in 1974 to a disease of certain salmonids. A similar disease was described as early as 1906 in Germany. A much better description was given in 1924 and given the name "Amöbeninfektion der Niere." The 1924 report accurately described PKD. PKD has also been called "l'anémie infecteuse", l'amebiasi della trotta iridea," l'anémie perniceuse des truites" and "hepathonephrétique." Part of the confusion in nomenclature is probably because PKD often accompanies other diseases: Nephrocalcinosis, furunculosis, infectious pancreatic necrosis or viral hemorrhagic septicemia, for example. The number of diagnosed cases of PKD has increased dramatically since 1980 and has been considered as a serious economical disease of salmonid aquaculture in parts of Europe.[13a]

PKD was reported in Idaho (United States) in 1981. An outbreak of PKD was reported in 1983 at a California state fish rearing facility. Subsequent examination of records and prepared slide material indicated the disease may have been at the California site as early as 1958.[24a,24b,96b]

Etiological Agent:

The exact etiology of PKD is somewhat in doubt. Several authors have described protozoa as the cause, others suggest nutritional imbalance. A discription of the "parasitic" cells led three authors to designate them as "PKX," a term which is widely used to refer to these structures.[93a] The PKX structure is found in the lumen of kidney tubules of infected hosts, and in circulating blood and splenic tissue. It has been variously described as an amoeba, a myxozoan and an ascetosporozoan (Pl. 35F).

The earliest references to the disease (1924 and earlier) suggested an amoeba was the causative agent of a condition now described as PKD. Observers in 1977 described the presence of pseudopodia in the PKX structure.[23b]

The organism has been suggested as belonging to the phylum Myxozoa, because of presence of a polar capsule in intraluminal spores.[46a,46b] Discription of the PKX structure from electron microscopy include reference to electron dense bodies similar to haplosporosomes of *Marteilia refringens* (phylum Ascetospora, order Occlusosporida).[93a] Others suggest the haplosporosomes are similar to those found in the genus *Minchinia* or *Urosporidium* (phylum Ascetospora).

Present knowledge indicates the etiology of the disease is not nutritional imbalance, even though severe anemia accompanies the disease. Research since 1980 indicates the causative agent is probably a myxozoan because of presence of a polar capsule,[24b,46b] but exact classification remains to be settled.

Susceptible Species:

Rainbow trout (including the anadromous strain of steelhead trout) are the most susceptible hosts of PKD. The disease has also been found in brown and brook trout; coho, chinook and Atlantic salmon; grayling and pike.[22a,24c]

Disease Signs:

Fish with advanced PKD may become dark in color and swim erratically, often gasping at the water surface as if oxygen starved. They may have unilateral or bilateral exophthalmos and abdominal dropsy. Abdominal fluid may be pink or blood stained. Fish with advanced PKD are anemic and gills are light in color.

Internal gross pathology includes enlarged, light colored kidneys, sometimes along their entire length, but always with greatest change in the posterior kidneys (Pl. 35E). The spleen may be enlarged and light in color. The liver may be light in color and mottled. White nodules up to 10 mm in diameter are usually present in kidney; sometimes in liver spleen, muscle, peritoneum or other organs.[13a]

Diagnosis:

Diagnosis of PKD is by gross pathology, histopathology and hematology. Squash preparations of effected kidney tissue will have developing spores with polar capsules and refractile granules.[24a] Cut and stained sections of kidney tissue will have hypertrophic hemapoietic tissue. Secondary and tertiary daughter cells of the parasite may be present in tubule tissue. Spores may be present in the lumen of excretory tubules.[46b]

Anemia may be severe, with hematocrits as low as 11.0 and erythrocyte counts as low as 380,000 per cubic mm of blood. Blood smears will reveal a great increase in immature erythrocytes. Leucocyte counts may be 2 to 2½ times normal values.[13a]

Therapy and Control:

There are no therapeutic agents which can be used to control PKD. Prevention through quarantine and movement restriction is necessary. Fish culture facilities in which PKD is enzootic can reduce mortality by proper planning. Heavily infected fish are subject to being easily overstressed and handling, moving or other stressful procedures should be held to a minimum.[13a] No information is available on destroying affected fish populations in fish culture facilities and disinfecting facilities for control of the disease.

Practical Aspects:

PKD is a serious parasitic disease and every effort possible should be made to maintain it in its present geographical distribution. Fish with known PKD should not be transported or stocked into waters free of the organism. A study in California indicated the parasite was present in at least three drainages, but no explanation of how it occurred in each drainage could be given.[24b]

There is some doubt of how the organism is transmitted. It has been transmitted experimentally to noninfected rainbow trout by placing them in the same water with infected rainbow trout, whether caged above or on the pond bottom. The disease was not transmitted by feeding infected kidney tissue to noninfected fish or by contact with feces from infected fish.[21a] The disease can be transmitted by injecting blood or splenic tissue from infected rainbow trout intraperitoneally to noninfected rainbow trout.[46a]

The disease is seasonal. Water temperature is involved, not only in severity of infection but morbidity of the disease in a fish population. Highest morbidity and mortality among young rainbow trout appears to be in late spring or early summer in England. Water temperature of 16°C appears to allow full development of the disease but temperatures of 5 to 7°C completely stops development of the disease.[23b]

PATHOGENIC CILIOPHORA

There are many species of symbiotic protozoa of the subphylum Ciliophora associated with fishes.[10,27] Almost all reside in or on the skin or gills of the host. Most are cosmopolitan among fishes of the world with little or no host specificity. Many of these organisms may live as commensals or mutuals, causing no harmful effects on the host unless present on the fish in relatively large numbers. There are a few which cause limited skin or gill damage, even when present in small numbers, by penetrating skin or gill epithelium. Detrimental effects may be limited to minute destruction of the integument or may be more serious by opening a portal of entry for more severe pathogens.

Ciliophorans have the most complex body organization of the protozoans. All possess cilia, cirri or tentacles for locomotion or for use in feeding. Reproduction of those associated with fishes is primarily by binary fis-

TABLE 18

Genera of class Kinetofragminophorea and class Oligohymenophorea with species parasitic to fish.[35,44,53,73]

Ambiphyra
Apiosoma
Brooklynella
Carchesium
Chilodonella
Cryptocaryon
Epistylis
Ichthyophthirius
Scyphidia
Tetrahymena
Trichodina
Trichodinella
Tripartiella
Trichophyra
Vauchomia
Zoothamnium

---

sion, rarely conjugation. Spontaneous multiple fission occurs in only a few of these organisms, and then away from the host during a free-living stage of the life cycle (*Ichthyophthirius*). Some may produce resting stage cysts.

The fish disease diagnostician must be alert to these organisms living in or on outer surfaces of the fish body. Each should be catagorized and identified as found, especially those thought to be harmful to the host. There are more than 13 genera representing two classes of protozoans with cilia or tentacles which may be parasites of fish. Those genera in which species are sometimes detrimental are listed in Table 18. Protozoa with cilia or tentacles are quite often found on intensively reared fishes, and rarely can skin scrapings or gill mounts be examined microscopically without finding one or more species. Thus, a discussion of ciliates and suctorians inhabiting the outer surfaces and integument of fishes must be limited to examples of the commonly found genera and species. An attempt will be made here to demonstrate the life and life cycle of a few of those organisms occupying the outer layers of the skin and gills and of one organism which occurs within the dermal layers at one stage of life.

Ichthyophthiriasis

Ichthyophthiriasis is one of the most prevalent diseases of fishes. The disease has also been known as white spot disease or ich, white spot because of the visible white cysts in the host skin and ich as an abbreviation of ichthyophthiriasis. It occurs among cultured fishes, aquarium fishes and wild-ranging fishes. The disease is more common among coolwater and warm-water fishes than among coldwater fishes. Its wide distribution, common occurrence and relative ease of diagnosis have led to a thorough study of all of its ramifications in a wide variety of fishes and fish habitats.

Etiological Agent:

The etiological agent of ichthyophthiriasis is *Ichthyophthirius multifiliis*.[27,53] *I. multifiliis* is the largest protozoan found on fishes. The trophozoite, sometimes called the trophont, is oval to round in shape and 0.5 to 1 mm at the longest axis. Trophozoites are uniformly ciliated around the body and contain a characteristic crescent-shaped macronucleus in older individuals (Pl. 19F). The trophozoite encysts between dermal layers of the host skin (Pl. 22A). The mature trophozoite leaves the fish substrate and reproduces by multiple fission to produce tremendous numbers of tomites (sometimes called theronts or vagrant bodies) which are 30 to 45 micrometers long and uniformly ciliated (Pl. 21B).[27] Its optimum temperature for reproduction is 24 to 26°C. Reproduction in the mature trophozoite (cyst) occurs in about seven to eight hours at this temperature. Tomites released from the mature cyst must find a host within about 48 hours, and an entire life cycle is completed in about four days at 24 to 26°C. Multiplication within the cyst takes about 77 hours at 7°C, and a complete life cycle 35 to 40 days.

Geographical Distribution:

Ichthyophthiriasis is worldwide in distribution among freshwater fishes.

Susceptible Species:

Apparently all freshwater fishes are susceptible to infections with *I. multifiliis*, but some are more susceptible than others. The disease is more common among cultured and aquarium fishes than among wild fishes, the reason being ease of transmission of the etiological agent.

A disease similar to ichthyophthiriasis has been diagnosed in many species of marine fish. However, the etiological agent of the marine fish disease is *Crptocaryon irritans*.[27]

Epizootiology:

Tomites are the infecting units of ichthyophthiriasis. A somewhat complicated life cycle begins by release of tomites from the trophont (mature trophozoite). The ciliated, free-swimming tomite actively seeks a host. Those not finding a host within about 48 hours at 24 to 26°C will die. The successful tomite penetrates the skin of the host and produces an observable white spot (Pl. 22B).

The tomite matures into a trophont stage and leaves the fish. The ciliated trophont moves about for a short time and finally attaches to vegetation or falls to the bottom. It secretes a gelatinous sheath or cyst and begins reproduction by fission. Multiple fission continues until the cyst may contain up to 1,000 tomites (Fig. 15). The

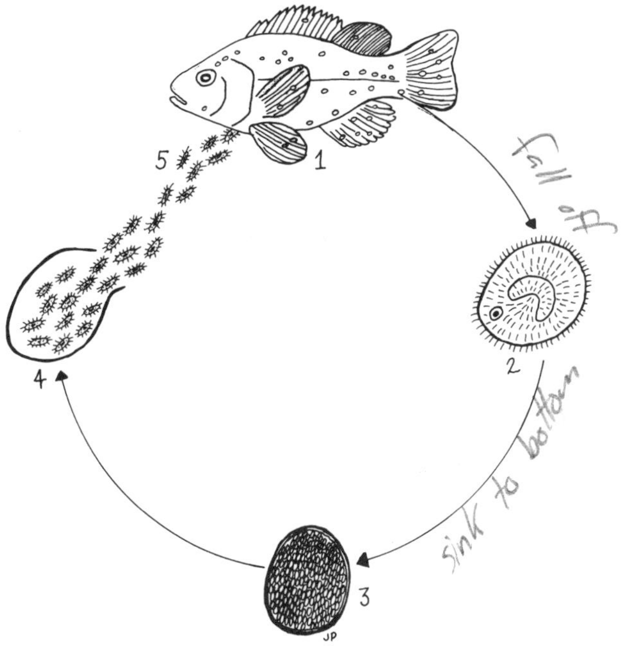

Fig. 15: Life cycle of *Ichthyophthirius multifiliis*
1. Trophozoites mature within the host skin.
2. Trophont (mature trophozoite) leaves the host and secretes a thick gelatinous coating.
3. Mature trophont produces 250 to 1,000 infecting units.
4. Tomites (swarmers or vagrant bodies) are released from the ripe trophont.
5. Tomites penetrate the host skin, develop into tomonts and into trophozoites.

cyst wall ruptures after complete development and releases the free-swimming, ciliated tomites to complete the life cycle and seek a new host (Pl. 21B).

Disease Signs:

Signs of *I. multifiliis* infection are small white spots in the skin and gills. Slight to moderate infections will not cause behavioral changes in the host. Marked or extreme infections may be accompanied by lethargy, listlessness, rubbing on the sides or bottom of the pond, raceway or aquarium and difficulty in obtaining oxygen if the gills are badly damaged.

Diagnosis:

Diagnosis of ichthyophthiriasis is by disease signs and identification of the protozoan. Presence of white spots is only presumptive since there are several other organisms or conditions to which the fishes may be subjected which cause similar signs. Proof of *I. multifiliis* can be made by removing one or more of the white spots from an infected fish, mounting on a microscope slide with a few drops of water and a cover glass, and observing under the microscope. *I. multifiliis* is quite large (0.5 to 1.0 mm) with a small micronucleus and prominent crescent-shaped macronucleus. Histological sections cut from ichthyophthiriasis-suspect gill tissue may assist in diagnosis. Observation of *I. multifiliis* trophozoites with the characteristic crescent-shaped macronucleus is definitive for this disease (Pl. 22C). Some of the more mature trophozoites can be placed in a watch glass with non-chlorinated water and incubated at 20 to 25°C for 24 to 72 hours. Large numbers of tomites can be observed following release from the trophont.

Therapy and Control:

The wide geographical distribution and large number of fish species susceptible to ichthyophthiriasis has led to a variety of therapeutic procedures in an attempt to control the disease.[18],[63] Usually the stages of *I. multifiliis* development within the fish dermal tissue cannot be removed by drug therapy. Those stages of the life cycle outside of the host are vulnerable to a number of chemotherapeutic agents (Table 19).

Ichthyophthiriasis is easily introduced to aquarium fishes and pond fishes by adding new fishes or aquatic plants. Tomites which have recently penetrated the skin will not be visible. Therefore, new fishes should be placed in quarantine for at least three days with a temperature of 24 to 28°C. Trophozoite cysts will become visible in that time. Careful examination of the fishes will then reveal the presence or absence of *I. multifiliis*. Fishes not demonstrating cysts should be safe to place into the aquarium or pond with other fishes.

Intermediate external stages in the life cycle of *I. multifiliis* may be attached to aquatic plants. Therefore, all plants being brought to an aquarium or pond from an unknown source should also be placed in a separate water supply for three or more days at 24 to 28°C (longer in colder water). Tomites will emerge and, finding no host, will die within two to three days after emergence.

Ichthyophthiriasis has also been a problem in trout, catfish and other food-fish culture. Control of the disease in large fish culture facilities is difficult. The organisms can often be removed or reduced in trout culture facilities by increasing the water flow to carry emerging tomites away before they can locate a host. The more

TABLE 19

Therapeutic procedures for control of ichthyophthiriasis[18,40]

Compound	Dosage and Time	Method of Use	Remarks
Formalin	1:5,000 (200 mg/L)	1 hour bath	Destroys tomites; other life stages may be affected; intradermal stages not affected
	1:50,000 (20 mg/L)	Continuous for 5 days	Destroys tomites as they are released, but will not affect intradermal life stages
Malachite green	1:666,000 (1.5 mg/L)	6 to 24 hour bath	Destroys tomites and possibly other external life stages, but will not affect intradermal life stages
Malachite green plus formalin	1:5,000,000 MG + 1:40,000 formalin (0.2 MG + 25 form. mg/L)	3 to 5 hour bath on alternate days	Destroys tomites as they emerge; will not control other external or intradermal life stages
Methylene blue	1:1,000,000 (1 mg/L) to 1:333,000 (3 mg/L)	Constant bath for 3 days	Destroys tomites as they emerge; will not affect other external or intradermal life stages
*Potassium permanganate	1:250,000 (4 mg/L)	30 minutes to 1 hour bath	Destroys tomites; no effect on other external or intradermal life stages
Quinine hydrochloride	1:50,000 (20 mg/L)	Add to water and leave until decomposed	Destroys tomites as they emerge, but will not control other external or intradermal life stages; remove aquatic plants before initiating treatment
*Sodium chloride	3% (30,000 mg/L)	1 hour bath daily for 7 consecutive days	Destroys tomites as they emerge, will not control other external or intradermal life stages
Temperature	32°C	5 days in aquaria	Destroys tomites as they emerge; probably weakens or kills other external or intradermal life stages

*Accepted by the U.S. Food and Drug Administration (FDA) for use with food-fish.

sluggish flow used in the culture of catfish, bass, sunfish and other fishes does not usually allow flow increase as a means of control. Chemotherapy is usually used for fishes being cultured in large ponds with a minimum water flow.

Life stages of *I. multifiliis* within the dermal tissues of a host fish are almost impossible to remove chemically without injuring or killing the host fish. Attempts to eliminate the encysted stage within the fish skin have met with failure. Experiments with hyperosmotic infiltration of various chemotherapeutic agents were unsuccessful. The mucus layer at the outside of the ectodermis is extremely difficult to penetrate. Dyestuffs which usually penetrate tissues quite easily will not penetrate the mucus layer. Several fish species placed in methylene blue, crystal violet or malachite green under normal pressure, vacuum infiltration (reduce pressure to one-tenth atmospheric pressure with rapid return to atmospheric pressure) and hyperosmotic saline at 16 milliosmoles osmotic pressure did not absorb the dyes past the mucus. Treated fishes were frozen immediately after the treatment and frozen sections cut and observed microscopically. Some dye could be seen at the extreme exterior surfaces of the mucus layer but none penetrated ectodermal cells. These experiments indicate the futility of attempting to remove dermal stages of *I. multifiliis* with external chemotherapeutics. Therefore, control of the organism must be concentrated on the life stages outside of the dermal tissues of the host.

There are indications that limited immunity results from sublethal infections of *I. multifilliis*.[63] Mirror carp have been infected with small numbers of tomites and found to be parasite free 21 days following exposure. They remained free of the parasite for eight months, even though they were held in infected water.[25a] This evidence led to an attempt at controlling ichthyophthiriasis by immunization procedures. *I. multifiliis* cannot be grown and harvested except by infecting host fish. *Tetrahymena pyriformis* is a close relative of *I. multifiliis* and large numbers can be grown in laboratory culture. Cultured *T. pyriformis* can be stripped of cilia and an immunizing agent prepared from cilia as well as an antigen from the whole cell. Results of experiments in which both the ciliary and whole-cell antigens were given to channel catfish intraperitoneally indicated good protection was given by the ciliary preparation. Mortality of immunized fish was near 11%, but was 100% in nonimmunized control fish on challenge with *I. multifiliis*.[23c] These results indicate a possibility for control of ichthyophthiriasis by immunization but much more research and development is needed.

Experimental evidence indicates *I. multifiliis* to be quite sensitive to ultra violet (UV) light. The minimum lethal dose of UV to tomites is about 100,000 microwatts per second per square centimeter. Cross infection was completely controlled in a water recirculation system of 36 aqaria with a UV light source of this magnitude.[23e]

Systemic drugs have been successfully used for control of intermediate subdermal stages of partial continuous parasites of homeothermic domestic animals. This method has apparently not been investigated for control of intradermal stages of *I. multifiliis* in fishes.

Prognosis:

Morbidity levels of *I. multifiliis* infections in fish populations usually reach 100% in aquaria and ponds. Some fishes may have only a few dermal stage organisms and others may have many. Generally fishes with small scales are more susceptible to infection than those with large scales.[91] Infections of *I. multifiliis* are somewhat seasonal, and infection levels may increase during autumn and winter in aquaria and during spring and fall in ponds because of the times of optimum temperature.

Mortality from ichthyophthiriasis may be caused by the parasite when the gills are extensively damaged. Alteration of the protective barrier of the skin by *I. multifiliis* may allow opportunistic bacteria or fungi access to underlying tissues and fishes may die from secondary infections. Fishes with large numbers of encysted *I. multifiliis* usually do not take food well, resulting in malnutrition and reduced vitality.

Practical Aspects:

The best control of ichthyophthiriasis is prevention. Fishes, plants, snails or other materials taken from one fish-holding unit to another should be kept in quarantine for at least a week, and two to three weeks are preferable.[63] The encysted organism is quite visible on fishes, especially the darker skinned species. Careful examination of fishes purchased from aquarium suppliers will reduce the possibility of moving the organism to non-infected aquaria.

The organism apparently does not accompany eggs of cultured fishes. Therefore, the fish culturist is safer in bringing eggs into a facility free of *I. multifiliis* than to bring in live fishes.

Warmwater and coolwater cultured fishes are more apt to have infections of *I. multifiliis*. This is because water temperatures over 12 to 15°C are more suitable for growth and reproduction of *I. multifiliis*. The organism has caused disastrous losses in trout culture facilities where the water warms to near 20°C, but usually the disease is rarely found in well managed salmonid culture.

CILIOPHORA: SESSILE AND MOTILE

There are numerous sessile (attached) and motile ciliates on the skin, fins and gills of fishes. These organisms are usually commensals but may become too numerous and may be responsible for dermal and branchial pathology.

Several genera of sessile and motile ciliates have been involved in epizootics of disease among fishes. The discussion here is limited to four selected genera: *Chilodo-*

nella, Trichodina, Epistylis and *Trichophrya.* These genera were selected because each is a characteristic protozoan form and each has on occasion contributed to pathology, either actively or as a passive opportunist.

Each of the four genera has one to many species of interest to the fish disease diagnostician. Again, space does not allow a discussion of each species, therefore generic reference will usually be made and species reference only because of definitive interest in a species.

Etiological Agents:

The characteristics of each genus will be used to describe the etiological agents of disease associated with sessile and motile ciliates.

Chilodonella (Chilodon)

The genus *Chilodonella* contains many species, two of which are found on the skin and gills of North American fishes. *Chilodonella* species are motile ciliates. The best-known species is *C. cyprini.*[19] It is typically heart-shaped, with the posterior end broader and slightly notched. The ventral side is flat with parallel ciliary rows. The dorsal surface is slightly convex and lacks cilia except in the oral groove at the extreme anterior end (Fig. 16). The oral opening is on the ventral side near the anterior end and is surrounded by a number of horny rods which extend for some distance into the body and gradually disappear. There is a large oval macronucleus in the posterior third of the body. A small micronucleus is near or within the macronucleus. The body size is 30 to 70 micrometers in length by 21 to 40 micrometers in width. Reproduction is primarily by binary fission. Species of *Chilodonella* exist over a wide temperature range, but 5 to 10°C appears to be near optimum for *C. cyprini.*[27]

Trichodina

Trichodina species are considered to be among the most highly complex of the protozoa commonly found on the skin and gills of fishes. The body is saucer- or bell-shaped (Fig. 17). The convex side is referred to as anterior or adoral and the concave side as posterior or aboral. The adoral side forms a complicated attachment organ known as the adhesive or sucking disk. The adhesive disk is a complicated skeletal structure arranged in the form of three concentric rings. The inner ring is the denticulate ring or corona. It is composed of denticles or tooth-like structures. There is a great variation in the number, size and shape of the denticles. A circular ribbon-like structure known as the striated band overlaps the hooks of the denticulate ring. The band appears as a series of radiating lines extending from the denticulate ring to near the edge of the disk. The outer ring forms the border and is composed of a thin flexible membrane which joins the striated band by an articulation on which it moves (Pl. 22D).

Just above and anterior to the border membrane is a row of fine cilia which are united for the greater part of

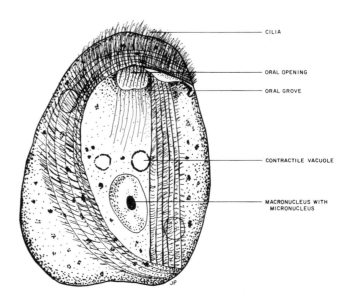

Fig. 16: Ventral view of *Chilodonella* sp.

their length to form a membranelle.[19,20] A marginal fold of granular cytoplasm, known as the velum, forms the outer edge of the body proper. Underneath the velum is a shallow groove to which is attached a band of long cilia. These cilia form the ciliary girdle. The organism moves about its host by means of the ciliary girdle, which also serves to propel it through the water (Pl. 22D).

The mouth is located at one side of the body and opens into the cytopharynx. The cytopharynx bears two parallel rows of long hair-like cilia which follow a spiral course to the mouth and into a groove around the adoral surface. A large horseshoe-shaped macronucleus is located in the endoplasm. The micronucleus is small and

Fig. 17: *Trichodina* sp. is saucer- or bell-shaped with an adhesive disk on the concave side for attaching to the surface of the host. Photo by Leteaux.

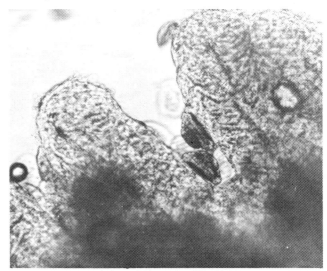

rounded or more commonly ovoid. It is located near the open end of the macronucleus.

Trichodina species reproduce by both binary fission and conjugation, binary fission being more common. Reproduction is not a simple procedure for these complex protozoa.[20]

Epistylis

There are many species of *Epistylis* on the skin, fins and gills of fishes, but North American species have not been studied. These organisms are sessile, being attached to the host by a transparent stalk. They characteristically appear on dichotomously branched stalks forming colonies (Pl. 21C).

Length of the stalk varies greatly among species. Fine surface striations occur on the posterior tip of the body and extend to the proximal tip of the stalk. The distal end of the stalk is the scapula. The gullet is short and narrow, with food particles usually visible in the gullet and cytoplasm. A macronucleus is usually visible as a broad concentric horseshoe-shaped organelle in the midportion of the body. The micronucleus is small and near the macronucleus. *Epistylis* species reproduce by longitudinal fission to produce a motile teletroch.[20]

Trichophrya

There are several species of *Trichophrya* which occur as commensals, usually on gill lamellae of fishes. The organisms are quite small and rounded, being 30 to 40 micrometers in length by 10 to 12 micrometers in diameter. These suctorians have developed tentacles rather than cilia in the mature forms, with 3 to 27 suctorial tentacles on the anterior end of the body.[27] Tentacles are used for gathering good, usually made up of plankton or host cells. The tentacles can be withdrawn into the body in times of stress but may be seen in gill mounts under the microscope (Pl. 23A).

The bodies of some *Trichophrya* species are orange to yellow-orange because of pigmented granules within the body. The body contains a large sausage-shaped macronucleus filled with a large number of spherules. There is a small, rounded micronucleus.

Trichophrya species reproduce by external and internal budding. A small individual is formed in a cavity or brood pouch. The fully developed bud is lenticular in shape and has a well-defined groove around the edge containing several rows of cilia. Each bud breaks free and becomes a free-swimming individual. Internal budding is accomplished by invagination from the body surface. The bud, containing the daughter nucleus, separates and eventually emerges. The newly formed and free-living bud either attaches to the host's gill immediately or swims about seeking a new host. The bud loses its cilia on attachment to the host and develops tentacles. Sexual reproduction by conjugation also occurs among *Trichophrya*.[19,27]

Geographical Distribution:

Species of *Chilodonella*, *Trichodina*, *Epistylis* and *Trichophrya* can be found worldwide among freshwater and marine fishes.

Susceptible Species:

The gills, skin and fins of fishes offer an ideal protected habitat for many species of ciliates. All freshwater fishes are particularly susceptible to habitation by *Chilodonella*, *Trichodina*, *Epistylis*, *Trichophrya* and species of other ciliate or suctorian genera (Table 18). The organisms are more commonly found on cultured and aquarium fishes, but examination of wild-ranging fishes may reveal various species from each of the four genera. Some species are widely distributed among a large number of fish species, while others are more host-specific, occurring on only one or a few host fishes within a limited geographical area. All species of these four genera and those ciliates of other genera (Table 18) are commensals, causing gill and dermal irritation or destruction when conditions allow increased numbers of the protozoans to exist.

Epizootiology:

Species of ciliates are usually present in small numbers on gill and dermal surfaces of healthy fishes. Overcrowding of fishes (in culture facilities, aquaria or in nature) and malnutrition may alter the host to the advantage of the ciliate. Water pollution and the accompanying body surface irritation may cause dermal or gill hyperplasia, with a tremendous increase in sloughed host epithelial cells. The normal food of most of the commensalistic or mutualistic ciliates is sloughed host epithelial cells or plankton. The increase in food supply is followed by an enormous ciliate population increase. Large numbers of *Epistylis* attached to the skin by a stalk or continuous movement of large numbers of *Chilodonella* or *Trichodina* may cause skin irritation. Large numbers of *Trichophrya* attached to gills may reduce oxygenation of the blood. The resulting pathology from poor water quality, malnutrition or other physical and biological reasons for abnormal dermal or gill epithelium is further affected by presence of an overpopulation of ciliates. The result may be excessive destruction of gill epithelium or dermal surfaces, which may lead directly to death or may be responsible for invasion of opportunistic bacteria, fungi or other animal parasites.

Disease Signs:

General signs of chilodoniasis, trichodiniasis, epistyliasis, trichophryiasis or excess numbers of other ciliates are a loss of appetite, listlessness or signs of anoxia if the gills are badly affected. The affected fish may become dark in color with slime patches at various locations on the surfaces of the body.

The sessile and motile ciliates cause dermal or gill irritation, epithelial hyperplasia and either excessive mucus secretion or regression of mucus release. The result may be the appearance of white to gray-white or pinkish slime patches on the dermal surface or gills (Pl. 23B). These slime patches may be somewhat localized or extensive over much of the body.

Diagnosis:

Diagnosis of excessive parasitism with sessile or motile ciliates is by observation of the organisms in wet mounts of material taken from the skin, fins or gills. These organisms are quite transparent and may be difficult to observe. Skin scrapings or gill arches from living but affected fishes should be quickly placed on a microscope slide with a few drops of water, a cover glass added and microscopic examination made prior to death of the organisms. Movement of the cilia assists in location. Exceptions are *Trichodina* species in that the more resistant and concentric denticulate ring may be as easily seen in dead or living organisms. Taxonomic classification may be made from observations, measurements and the use of published descriptions.[10,20,27,35] However, therapeutic procedures apparently do not vary from species to species or genus to genus.

Therapy and Control:

Prevention is the best control for excessive numbers of sessile or motile ciliates on fishes. Reduction of crowding and water pollution eliminates the possibility of skin or gill irritation which may lead to ciliate population increases. Proper nutrition of the fishes may also prevent excessive numbers of ciliates on skin and gills. Increasing water flow in fish culture facilities or more rapid filtration of water in aquaria may reduce ciliate populations.

Therapy with certain externally applied chemicals is usually effective against these organisms. Those chemotherapeutic compounds and treatment procedures used for other external protozoa are also effective against the ciliates (Table 15). Formalin, malachite green, sodium chloride, quinine hydrochloride and others used as dips or baths or dynamically will reduce the populations of sessile and motile ciliates on fish.

Prognosis:

Epizootics involving sessile or motile ciliates have been responsible for extreme mortality among cultured and aquarium fishes. High mortality epizootics have also been reported among wild-ranging fishes, especially during low water flow in streams with resultant concentration of fishes. Drawdown in reservoirs causes concentration of fishes, heavy use of remaining water, quite often heavy silt suspension from fish activity in shallow pools and increased ciliate populations on fishes.

Mortality levels up to 50% can be expected under severe conditions or of susceptible fishes. Therapy against developing ciliate populations, proper management of cultured and aquarium fishes or limiting the cause of increased reproduction of ciliates may reduce mortality levels in susceptible fishes to nearly zero.

Practical Aspects:

The fish disease diagnostician soon finds that sessile and motile ciliates are more common on fishes than had ever been suspected. Routine examination of ill fishes will usually reveal one or more species or genera of these organisms. Finding ciliates on the fins, skin or gills of fishes always involves making a decision on the exact nature of the infestation. Low numbers of a variety of ciliates will usually be considered as of no consequence, even when found during epizootics involving mortality. Other causes for the mortality should be sought. Epizootics of fish mortality in which large numbers of ciliates are found on the fishes should be controlled by reducing the ciliate population and at the same time attempting to reduce the primary cause for ciliate population increase. These organisms are not usually the primary cause of illness or mortality among fishes, only opportunists as are many other potential pathogens of fishes.

Epizootics of sessile or motile ciliates on fishes can occur at any time under improper management practices. The use of good water supplies for fish culture and aquaria is the first and foremost consideration in limiting epizootics from these protozoans. Static water-holding facilities such as aquaria and recirculating fish hatcheries are conducive to ciliate population increases. Proper installation and care of particulate filters will reduce numbers of ciliates on fishes in these facilities.

Ciliates and other protozoans have existed on the earth for a tremendously long time. They have been successful commensals or parasites on and in fishes, usually not damaging or destroying their hosts. The fish culturist, aquarist and fish manager should realize the tenacity and reproductive potential of these life forms and compensate by maintenance of healthy fishes in the most suitable water supply for the fish.

Platyhelminths of Fishes

The phylum Platyhelminthes is composed of three taxonomic classes: Turbellaria, Trematoda and Cestoda. The Turbellaria are almost all free-living and have no involvement in the diseases of fishes. All members of the other two classes live in a close relationship with host animals. The trematodes are known as *flukes*, the cestodes as *tapeworms*.

The trematodes and cestodes are widespread in nature. Every vertebrate either is or has been associated with one or more species of these flatworms. At times this relationship is detrimental to the host. Careful examination of the host-parasite relationship at other times may demonstrate the lack of visible detrimental effect the trematode or cestode has on its natural host. The relationship may be parasitic only on those occasions when unnatural hosts are involved or when excessive numbers of the parasite occupy a natural host body.[55] The fish disease diagnostician must assess each case with care.

Trematodes and cestodes are marvels of evolution. Consider the changes in body structure, reproduction and life cycle sequence necessary to transform from the free-living state to a state where existence is not possible without one or more animal hosts. The successful trematodes or cestodes are those able to fit existence into the habits and habitats of their hosts, the result of many thousands of generations together.

Trematodes and cestodes have the capability of producing disease in fishes, often from environmental alterations by human beings. Confinement alters the well-arranged natural plan for existence between the two, sometimes to the benefit of the trematode or cestode. The result is an active case of parasitism which requires examination, diagnosis and therapy. The translocation of fishes with their accompanying parasites intracontinentally or intercontinentally has been responsible for placing certain trematodes and cestodes in contact with unnatural hosts, sometimes with disastrous results on native fishes.[3] Thus, many of the commonly occurring disease problems involving trematodes or cestodes are associated with fish culture, holding of fishes in aquaria or placement of unnatural hosts in contact with potential parasites. Therapy or other control methods may be necessary at times when flukes or tapeworms are definitely responsible for adverse effects on fishes.

TREMATODA OF FISHES: MONOGENEA

Trematodes of the subclass Monogenea are usually found on the skin of lower aquatic vertebrates, especially fishes. Some inhabit the gill chambers, mouth cavity or other body cavities. Most are browsers, moving about on the body surfaces and feeding on dermal or gill debris. The Monogenea require but one host. All life stages are completed in a continuous life cycle. Translocation from one host to another may occur as an accident when a fluke inadvertently loses attachment to one host and is carried by water currents to another host, but those individuals not successful in locating another host will perish. Movement of eggs from one host to another may also serve in translocation.

Adult monogenean trematodes attach to the host by a specially adapted structure on the posterior end called a *haptor* (or *opishaptor*). This organ possesses sucking valves in some species, but hooks are always present. The opishaptor is used to attach and hold onto the hosts body surfaces. Hooks on the opishaptor are responsible for much of the damage to the host, penetrating into the surface layers of the skin or gills.[10,73] Large numbers of monogenean trematodes magnify skin or gill damage from the hooks, sometimes to the point of excessive trauma or opening portals of entry for opportunistic bacteria, fungi or protozoa which in turn may further damage the host (Fig. 18).

Most monogenean trematodes also have a means of attachment at the anterior end of their body called a *prohaptor*. The prohaptor is not armed with hooks but assists the opishaptor in holding onto the host by a sucking or adhesive function (Fig. 18).[10,73]

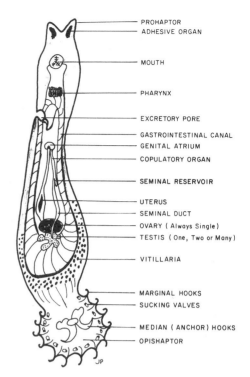

Fig. 18: Diagrammatic representation of a typical trematode of the subclass Monogenea.

Monogenean trematodes are hermaphroditic, having both male and female reproductive organs. Most are oviparous, producing eggs which are released, hatch and grow to adulthood in the water or on the same host as the parent. Other Monogenea are viviparous, larval flukes developing in the uterus until well along in development, at which time they are released to fend for themselves on the same host as the parent. Thus, generation to generation of either type may have a continuous relationship with a single host.

There are a tremendous number of monogenean trematode species on fishes of the world, in about 29 taxonomic families and six orders. Most are host-specific, although some species may be found on a relatively large number of host species. Many freshwater and marine forms exist.

Identification of Monogenea is by body size, anterior structures, opishaptor structure with accompanying armament, presence or absence of pigment spots, structures of the alimentary system, structures of the reproductive system, host species, location on the host and geographical location.[10,35]

Small numbers of monogenean trematodes cause little damage to their host, only an occasional scale pocket opened or epithelial cell altered. Large numbers cause trauma to skin and gills from incessant action of attaching hooks on the opishaptor, thus occurrence of large numbers of monogenean flukes on fishes comes to the attention of the fish disease diagnostician. The diagnostic problem usually is to determine why the large population of flukes has developed, usually finding the primary cause to be poor water quality, malnutrition or some other physiological alteration of the fish which gives the parasite an advantage in reproduction and survival. Most epizootics of excessive parasitism with these flukes are found on confined fishes, rarely on wild-ranging fishes. No attempt will be made to discuss each species or genus of Monogenea, but only to examine their host-parasite relationship collectively using a few specific examples to demonstrate host injury and capabilities of the flukes.

Etiological Agents:

Two commonly occurring Monogenea trematode families will be used to illustrate the effect of these organisms on a host if present in large numbers. Family Dactylogyridae and family Gyrodactylidae have characteristics which demonstrate the wide variability in the Monogenea and the tremendous number of species occurring on fishes.

Dactylogyridae

The family Dactylogyridae contains at least seven genera and over 150 recognized species on freshwater and marine fishes of the world. These organisms are never more than 2mm in length and most often between 0.2 and 0.5 mm. They all have seven pairs of marginal hooks and usually one pair of median hooks on the opishaptor; rarely species have two pairs. The dactylogyrids have two to four pigment (eye) spots located in the anterior fourth of the body. The ovary is round to oval in shape and the testes are unpaired. All dactylogyrids are oviparous with no uterus, only an ootype structure containing one egg at a time. The genus most commonly found on fishes is Dactylogyrus, its species sometimes known as gill flukes because most are located on the gills of their host. There are at least 100 identified species of Dactylogyrus. A widely distributed species is D. vastator.[10,35]

Gyrodactylidae

The family Gyrodactylidae is also a large group with three genera and over 100 recognized species. Gyrodactylids are found on many of the lower vertebrates (fishes, amphibians and reptiles) and also on invertebrates. At least 85 species have been identified on fishes. The gyrodactylids have eight pairs of marginal hooks on the opishaptor, with one or more pairs of median hooks and often two to six sucking valves. Those with sucking valves are oviparous, those without are viviparous. The gyrodactylids have a copulatory organ on the ventral midsection of the body which is a corona of chitinized hooks.[10] The most common genus on fishes is Gyrodactylus. Gyrodactylus species are small flukes rarely over 0.4 mm in length. All species of the genus are viviparous, with one to three daughter generations in the V-shaped uterus lying behind unpaired round testes. The

gastrointestinal canal has two intestinal trunks which terminate in blind sacs. Gyrodactylus species are usually on the skin or less commonly on gills of bony (teleost) fishes. The most widely distributed species is G. elegans.[10,35,73,91,107]

Geographical Distribution:

Species of Gyrodactylus and Dactylogyrus are worldwide in distribution.

Susceptible Species:

Probably all freshwater and many marine teleost fishes of the world act as host to at least one species of Dactylogyrus or Gyrodactylus. Quite often species of the two genera may be found at the same time on cultured fishes, especially if the fishes are overcrowded and unhealthy or in water of poor quality. Usually little or no harm is done to the host, but on occasion these flukes contribute to disease of the host if they become too numerous on a single host at any one time.[19,107]

Epizootiology:

Transmission of monogenetic trematodes from fish to fish is primarily by direct contact. The newly born young of Gyrodactylus leave the parent with a completely formed genital system, ready to occupy a place on the host of the parent or to be transmitted by contact to a new host.

Eggs of Dactylogyrus are not quite as apt to remain on the host of the parent. Some dactylogyrid eggs remain attached to gill epithelium, hatch and take up habitation on the parents host. Most are swept away by water flowing through the branchial chambers to become free-swimming larvae. The larvae are ciliated and actively swim or are carried by water currents in search for a new host. Some are successful, others die.

The reproductive abilities of the flukes and potential deleterious effect on hosts are enhanced by optimum water temperature. The generation time of D. vastator, for example, is only a few days at 22 to 24°C, during

Fig. 18a: Scanning electron micrograph demonstrating effects of *Gyrodactylus* sp. opishaptor hooks on the skin of a rainbow trout. Photo courtesy of Cone, D. K. and P. H. Odense, 1984.

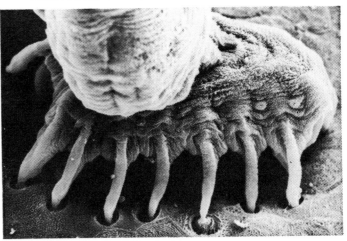

which eggs are produced, larvae hatched, a host located and adulthood attained. This time is extended to five or six months at temperatures of 1 to 2°C. The lifespan of the most vulnerable free-swimming stage is reduced at the higher temperature and prolonged at the lower temperature. Thus *D. vastator* may be a greater threat among cultured fishes at warmer water temperatures where reproduction is rapid. Success may be greater among wild-ranging fishes at lower temperatures because flukes have a longer time period to locate a host.

Sunlight has been found to reduce the lifespan of *D. vastator* free-swimming larvae. Nothing is known of the relationship of sunlight and survival of *G. elegans*. Environmental oxygen reduction has little or no effect on either *Gyrodactylus*, or *Dactylogyrus*. Depletion of dissolved oxygen low enough to affect or suffocate fishes apparently does not affect the flukes. They remain alive without altered behavior, and *D. vastator* even increases oviposition under reduced dissolved oxygen.

Disease Signs:

Signs of excessive parasitism with monogenean trematodes depend on the species of fluke involved, location on the host, environmental temperature and many other factors. Large numbers of *D. vastator* or other gill flukes cause loss of gill function and behavioral characteristics indicating partial suffocation. The fish become lethargic, swim near the surface, seek the sides of the pond and refuse food.

Large numbers of *G. elegans* or other skin-inhabiting flukes usually do not have the same effect as gill flukes. The fishes may rub against the bottom or sides of the holding facility. They may race through the water as if attempting to remove the irritant. Some may develop white to gray-white areas of thickening mucus on the skin, especially behind the fins or anterior to the dorsal fin. Some fishes may move to the sides of the pond or remain stationary. Closer examination may reveal damage to gills or skin. Gills may have areas of thickened mucus, hyperplasia, petechial hemorrhages and necrosis. Secondary infections of bacteria or fungi may also be present. The skin and fins may be somewhat altered with evidence of trauma and areas where scales and epithelium ooze pinkish serous fluid (Pl. 22E).[10,91,107]

Diagnosis:

Some monogenean trematodes are relatively large and can be seen without magnification, but others are microscopic. Skin scrapings or a piece of gill arch mounted with a few drops of water on a microscope slide can be used for location of the parasites. Identification is by use of various morphological characteristics and reference to taxonomic keys (Pl. 22F, 24A, 23C).[10,35]

Therapy and Control:

The best control procedures are careful management and balanced nutrition. Chemotherapy for these organisms is not usually satisfactory unless the primary cause of the increased fluke population is found and alleviated. A number of chemotherapeutic procedures have been found useful for therapy of *Gyrodactylus* or *Dactylogyrus* on fishes (Table 20). Elimination of the organisms is usually not possible, only reduction of the fluke population.

Prognosis:

Monogenean trematodes are often present on freshwater fishes, especially those in contact with open waters. The population of flukes is quite often much greater on confined fishes. Few, if any, culture facilities are free of these organisms because transportation of flukes into the facilities by birds, amphibians and reptiles is always possible. The major problem, then, becomes proper management of facilities in which fishes are held and maintenance of fish health.

High mortality levels may be associated with monogenean trematode ectoparasites. Proper care of confined fishes, with chemotherapy for those occasions when fishes in even the best-managed facility may become victims of high fluke populations, will hold mortality levels from this cause to less than 1% per year. Fishes which feed poorly or are unable to compete for a place in the pond where they can receive food are subject to excessive monogenean trematode parasitism. These fishes will usually demonstrate signs of several diseases besides monogenean fluke infestation.

Practical Aspects:

The fish disease diagnostician should attempt to identify the species of monogenean trematodes found on each fish species and in each geographical location. Diagnosticians in the United States have been especially lax in identification of ectoparasitic flukes on fishes. Species identification of the fluke has two purposes. Some fluke species are not susceptible to the usual therapeutic procedures, so attempts to treat them with a useless chemical may be time-consuming, expensive and of little help to the fishes. The other purpose is to obtain identification of the various genera and species of monogenetic trematodes on fishes at various locations in the United States. The usual diagnostic practice has been to note the presence of a monogenean fluke and prescribe a common treatment, sometimes with little or no reduction of the ectoparasite population. Also, identification and knowledge of the environment of each species (temperature, pH, salinity and other physical factors) may assist in knowledge of how to control these organisms when they become a disease problem.[68]

The detrimental effects of transporting monogenetic trematodes from one geographical area to another are as great as with most potential pathogens. Members of the Monogenea are easily moved from place to place with fishes, water and other vertebrates. Some notable examples are the movement of *Dactylogyrus extensus* from Europe to the United States with carp and *D. minutes* from

TABLE 20

Selected therapy for monogenean trematodes on fish

Compound	Dose Level	Time & Method	Results
*Acetic acid	5% (50,000 mg/L)	1 minute dip	Useful for aquarium fishes
*Ammonium hydroxide	1:2,000 (500 mg/L)	1 to 15 minute dip	Test fish species for safety before use on large numbers
*Formalin	1:4,000 (250 mg/L)	1 hour bath	No oftener than every third day
	1:6,000 (167 mg/L)	1 hour bath	Every other day for fishes sensitive to 1:4,000 formalin
#Malachite green	1:200,000 (5 mg/L)	1 hour bath	Each day for three days
	1:15,000 (67 mg/L)	Daily flush or 1 minute dip	Add to water inflow and allow to move through tank
#Malachite green + Formalin	1:400,000 (2.5 mg of malachite green/L) 1:6000 (0.167 mg of formaldehyde/L)	1 hour bath	Useful for cases in which formalin or malachite green alone do not control the organism
Mebendazole	1:100,000,000 (0.01 mg/L)	24 hour	Controlled *G. elegans* but not *D. vastator*[23d]
Mebendazole + Trichlorfon	1:2,500,000 (0.4 mg/L 1:556,000 1.8 mg/L) (0.4 mg/L 1.8 mg/L)	24 hour	Controlled both *G. elegans* and *D. vastator*[23d]
Methylene blue	1:350,000 (2.9 mg/L)	Indefinite	Add to water and allow to remain
Masoten	1:4,000,000 (0.25 mg/L)	Indefinite	Add to water and allow to remain
*Potassium permanganate	1:400,000 (2.5 mg/L)	Indefinite	Used as an alternate to formalin in ponds
*Sodium chloride	2.5% (25,000 mg/L)	1 hour bath	For fishes acceptable to high salinity
	0.7% (7,000 mg/L)	Indefinite	Kills free-swimming larval stages of many monogenean trematodes
Trichlorfon	1:625,000 to 1:2,500,000 (1.6 to 0.4 mg/L)	24 hour	Controlled *D. vastator* but not *G. elegans*[23d]

#May be lethal to certain fish species.
*Approved for use with food-fish by U.S. Food & Drug Administration (FDA).

Europe or Asia to the United States. Both have become established and are occasionally found with the host species on which they were brought to the United States. Europe has been the recipient of *Urocleidus dispar, U. similis* and *U. furcatus* from the United States with shipments of various fishes. An example of a deleterious transfer of a monogenean fluke occurred when sturgeon were moved from the Caspian Sea to the Aral Sea. Native sturgeon in the Aral Sea became heavily parasitized with a newly introduced parasite. Many died and the population remained depleted for more than 20 years.[3] Moving such organisms as the monogenean trematodes from one geographical area to another places them in contact with unnatural hosts, which may in turn have limited or disastrous results. There is never a way of predicting just what will happen.

DIGENEA

Digenean trematodes all have a complex life cycle with several successive larval generations, alternating sexual and asexual generations and changes of hosts to develop into the adult in its primary host. The life cycles of trematodes involving fishes may either use fishes as the primary hosts or as intermediate hosts. Adult trematodes may be found in the intestine, gall bladder, urinary bladder or more rarely in other organs. Nearly all digenean trematodes of fishes are hermaphroditic, having both male and female genital systems. Eggs produced in the primary host are released in feces, urine or by other routes. The eggs of *Salminicola* species, for example, are released into the blood of a fish to be passed along to the gills. The eggs hatch in the gills and the miracidia are released directly into the water (Fig. 19). Eggs passing out of the primary host either hatch into miracidia in the water or are eaten by the mollusk first intermediate hosts. Those hatching into miracidia in the water must actively seek a first intermediate host and penetrate its integument. Snails, clams or rarely annelid worms may act as first intermediate hosts; usually the intermediate host is limited to the species of trematode. The miracidium in the first intermediate host metamorphoses into a mother sporocyst or redia, which in turn may give rise asexually to one or more daughter sporocysts or daughter redia. Both mother and daughter sporocysts or redia produce a few to several hundred cercariae. The cercariae of most trematode species are shed from the first intermediate host into the water. The active, free-swimming cercariae seek the second intermediate host and penetrate its integument by actively boring through to underlying tissues. Cercariae of some trematode species enter the skin, others enter the cornea of the eyes and others enter the gill filaments or other structures. Some species of trematodes produce precocious cercariae in the mother or daughter sporocysts which can be released when fishes feed on the mollusk or annelid. A released cercaria survives the violent stomach environment to seek its tropic organ in its host.

The cercaria develops into a metacercaria in the second intermediate host and, when the second intermediate host is swallowed by a primary host, the life cycle is complete (Fig. 19).[10,35,36,43,68,73,78,98,107]

The digenean trematodes involving fishes are found primarily among wild-ranging fishes. Only occasionally are conditions acceptable to completion of the complicated life cycles of these organisms among confined fishes. These occasions usually involve rearing of pond fishes in which mollusks as well as aquatic birds have free access to fish-rearing facilities.

Fishes are involved in the life cycle of a tremendous number of trematode species. No attempt will be made to describe all of these, but three trematode species have been chosen to illustrate the host-parasite relationship between digenean trematodes and their host. Life cycles and host-parasite relationships of other trematode species, even though certain life stages differ from those illustrated, still have many points in common.

The fish disease diagnostician becomes involved with the Digenea when those species infect fishes and cause damage to the host. Most trematodes, however, have limited pathogenicity to the host, and the life stage of trematode development in the fish becomes a curiosity or interesting observation.

Etiological Agents (Selected):

Crepidostomum farionis

Crepidostomum farionis was chosen to illustrate a digenean trematode which is adult in the intestine of several fish species. *C. farionis* was first described in 1874 and has since been found in a wide variety of coolwater fishes of the northern hemisphere.

A *C. farionis* metacercaria initiates adulthood in the upper intestine, ceca, gall bladder or bile duct of its host. Its gradual metamorphosis makes it more capable of attachment to the active walls of the intestine as it gradually moves to the lower intestine and finally to the rectal area (Pl. 35C). Here it remains attached to the host by means of an anterior and a ventral suckers. The adult fluke is 2 to 6 mm in length with a maximum width of 2.5 mm.

Eggs appear in the uterus of adult flukes in 43 to 51 days in summer water temperatures and in 80 to 90 days when fishes become infected in early autumn. Eggs released in the feces hatch into ciliated miracidia. The first intermediate host can be several species of freshwater clams of the genera *Pisidium* and *Sphaerium*. A redia develops in the first intermediate host and in turn asexually divide into daughter redia. No sporocysts are produced. Ophthalmoxiphidiocercariae develop in the redia while remaining in the first intermediate host. The ophthalmoxiphidiocercariae are eventually released into the water and penetrate nymphal stage mayflies acceptable as second intermediate hosts. Several hundred arthropods, other than mayflies, in the same ecosystem with

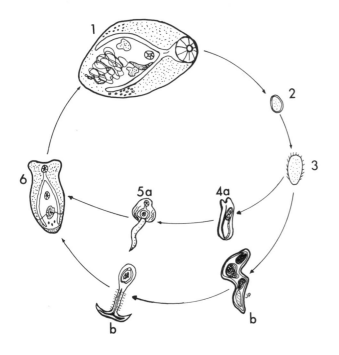

Fig. 19: Typical life cycle of Trematoda (Digenea).
1. Fully developed adult in the primary host.
2. Egg released in feces, urine or other routes from the primary host.
3. Free-swimming miracidium actively seeks a snail, clam, annelid or other invertebrate; egg is ingested by the invertebrate in some trematode species.
4. a. Miracidium metamorphoses to redia and to several daughter rediae in some trematode species.
   b. Miracidium transposed to mother sporocyst and asexually to daughter sprocysts, both mother and daughter asexually produce several hundred cercariae in some trematode species.
5. a. Ophthalmoxiphidiocercariae from redia actively seek a second intermediate host in some trematode species.
   b. Cercaria from sporocysts actively seeks a second intermediate host, or the second intermediate host ingests precocious cercaria within the first intermediate host in some trematode species.
6. Cercaria or ophthalmoxiphidiocercaria penetrates tissues of the second intermediate host and develop into a metacercaria. A primary host ingests the metacercaria along with the second intermediate host and the life cycle is complete.

C. farionis have been examined for *C. farionis* metacercariae, but no infection with this fluke has been found except in the mayflies.[9,49,104]

The life cycle of *C. farionis* is completed when fishes of the family Salmonidae ingest the mayfly nymph containing viable metacercariae. Experiments in which adult *C. farionis* in the intestinal tract of salmonid fishes were fed to other noninfected salmonids transferred the infection. Therefore, direct transmission is possible among these carnivorous fishes.[49]

The geographical distribution of *C. farionis* is North America, much of northern Europe and Asia. The fluke is especially prevalent in mountainous areas and in cold freshwater.

Fishes susceptible to *C. farionis* include all of the Salmonidae: trouts, salmons, chars, graylings and whitefishes. Many of these fishes have been found with natural infections and others have been experimentally infected.

Diplostomum spathaceum

Diplostomum spathaceum utilizes many species of fishes as a second intermediate host, the metacercariae localizing in eye tissue. Several fish-eating aquatic bird species, especially gulls, are the primary hosts of this fluke.

D. spathaceum was first described in 1819 in Europe. The worm was also described in the United States in 1928 but given the name *Diplostomum flexicaudum*, a name now considered synonymous with *D. spathaceum*.[78,108] The older name prevails, but much of the literature of the world used *D. flexicaudum* for the nomenclature of this organism.

The life cycle of *D. spathaceum* begins as an adult trematode in the intestine of gulls or other piscivorous birds. The body is 0.3 to 0.5 cm in length and distinctly divided into a flattened anterior forebody and a more cylindrical and narrower hindbody.[36,108] Eggs are shed and passed in feces to the water. They hatch in about 21 days at summer water temperatures into free-swimming ciliated miracidia (Fig. 19).

Miracidia seek aquatic snails for a first intermediate host; only lymnaeid snails are acceptable. The miracidia penetrate the hepatopancreas of the snail and metamorphose to a mother sporocyst, then to one or more daughter sporocysts. Each produces many cercariae which are released into the water. The free-swimming cercariae seek second intermediate hosts.

The usual route of transmission from the snail to the second intermediate host is through water and active penetration of the cercariae. However, much evidence points to the fact that transmission is possible by fishes feeding on snails containing precocious cercariae.[6,78] The cercariae penetrate the fins, skin, gills or cornea of the eyes. Some cercariae which enter skin, fins and gills enter the blood stream and are carried to the eyes within about 30 minutes from time of penetration. The cercariae become infective-stage metacercariae in 45 to 120 days, depending on water temperature.

Infected fishes are ingested by gulls or other piscivorous birds. Adult trematodes develop in the birds' intestine in three to five days. Eggs are produced within a short time after adulthood is reached (Fig. 19).[78,108]

The geographical distribution of *D. spathaceum* includes much of the temperate areas of North America, Europe, Asia and Africa. There have been serious infections of this trematode among wild-ranging fishes of the western United States and Europe.[77] It is most often found in coolwater and coldwater environments and is an occasional problem in warmwater pond culture.

Susceptible second intermediate host species of *D. spathaceum* include a wide variety of freshwater fishes, probably over 125 species. A survey in Utah Lake, Utah demonstrated the fluke in the eyes of ten species of fishes including four trout species, three species of suckers, one bass species, one chub species and one shiner species.[10,108]

Posthodiplostomum minimum

Posthodiplostomum minimum was chosen for discussion as another example of the host-parasite relationship between fishes and the metacercarial stage of trematodes because of its wide geographical distribution among a large variety of fishes in the United States. *P. minimum* was first described in 1921, and its life cycle has been carefully researched since that time.[7,35,55,98] The trematode has been known by several synonymous names: *Neodiplostomum minimum, Neodiplostomum orchilongum* and *Posthodiplostomum orchilongum.*

The life cycle of *P. minimum* begins as an adult in the intestines of several species of herons, loons and probably other piscivorous birds. It has been transmitted experimentally to domestic chickens.[36] The body of adult *P. minimum* is 0.3 to 0.5 cm in length and divided into two distinct segments, a more flattened forebody and a shorter, rounded hindbody. Subadult *P. minimum* are known to become sexually mature and produce fertilized eggs within 32 to 40 hours after being fed to experimental hosts. However, the time required from ingestion of infective-stage metacercariae to egg production is not known with certainty.[98]

Eggs are shed in the feces of the primary host. They hatch into ciliated miracidia in about three weeks. Miracidia probably do not exist more than one day if they do not find a suitable first intermediate host (several species of aquatic snails, usually of the genus *Physa*). The miracidia penetrate the integument of the host snail and develop into a mother sporocyst (Fig. 19). The mother sporocyst asexually produces several daughter sporocysts and each sporocyst can produce several hundred cercariae. About 28 to 34 days are required from penetration of the miracidium to development of a cercaria at summer temperatures of 21 to 29°C. As many as 840 to 8,940 cercariae may be released from a single infected snail in a 24-hour period.[7,37]

Infectivity of cercariae to fishes lasts no more than 24 hours after release from the snail. Cercariae apparently are not active enough at 15°C to infect fishes but can do so at 18°C or above.[37] Each cercaria actively raises a scale and enters under the scale pocket, causing some irritation to the fish. Blood, congestion and hemorrhage oc-

cur at the bases of fins or other places of cercarial penetration. The trematodes migrate from the point of entry to visceral organs of the fishes, usually within one to three hours after penetration. Metacercariae are located in any organ of the fishes' body, but are generally more numerous in the liver, kidney, heart, spleen and other organs of the abdominal viscera (Pl. 35B). Infective metacercariae develop in 18 to 30 days after cercarial penetration, depending on water temperature. All development is arrested at 16°C or less. The life cycle is then completed when the infective metacercariae are taken orally by certain herons, loons or other piscivorous birds.

P. minimum is found over much of the United States, especially in the warmer climates. It is not found in the alpine regions. It has been reported in over 100 species of North American fishes.[37,98]

Epizootiology:

The life cycle of each trematode species has evolved for successful transmission over thousands of generations. Piscivorous birds or carnivorous fishes are common links in the transmission cycle. Water quality, water temperature and presence of aquatic snails or other invertebrates are all essential to the life cycle of trematodes which parasitize fishes. Trematode species are found in freshwater and saltwater fishes. Some trematodes have adapted to cold water temperatures (i.e., *C. farionis* and similar organisms), while others are inhabitants of warm water (i.e., *P. minimum* and similar flukes). The tremendous diversity of trematodes is probably more prominent in fishes than among other animals of the world. Trematodes in which piscivorous birds are involved have an assured transmission cycle—not only are all links in the life cycle present at one time or another in and around aquatic environments, but mobility of birds can keep a ready supply of fertilized eggs in those bodies of water with the required snails and fishes necessary for continuation of trematode existence.

Disease Signs:

Signs of infection in fishes with trematodes are extremely varied. Quite often infections of the host fishes with either the metacercarial or adult stage of the trematode elicits no indications of disease. The relationship between presence of trematodes in fishes and overt disease is entirely related to the number of trematodes in any one fish host at any one time.

Signs of presence of trematodes in fishes may be evident to the observer. The appearance in the skin of black spots caused by melanin deposits around developing metacercariae may suggest the term "black spot disease." Black spot indications of trematode presence are noted with *Uvulifer* sp., *Neascus* sp. and many others (Pl. 24B). Visible white to yellow spots in the visceral organs, usually no larger than 1 mm in diameter, are often referred to as "white grubs" or "yellow grubs" and could be caused by several trematode species such as *P.*

minimum, Clinostomum marginatum, Nanophyetus salmonicola or others. Presence of several *D. spathaceum* metacercariae in the eye lens of susceptible fishes may cause obvious opacity of the lens, better known as parasitic cataract (Pl. 24C & Pl. 35A).

Diagnosis:

Diagnosis of digenetic trematode infections in fishes is by removal of the developmental stage, examination for morphology and the use of taxonomic keys for identification. Metacercariae are sometimes large enough to be seen with the naked eye or with no more magnification than a hand lens. Cysts containing the metacercariae are dissected and the metacercariae released (Fig. 20). Identification of the metacercariae to species is usually quite difficult, and transmission experiments may be necessary to obtain adults of the trematode species. The adult stage of those trematode species which use fishes as primary hosts are separated from the host and identified. Taxonomic keys usually give morphology and size of metacercariae as well as characteristics of the adult flukes.[10,35,36]

Most fish disease diagnosticians agree that natural hosts of digenetic trematode parasites are often not adversely affected by a small number of the stage of development characteristic to the host species. Diagnosis of overt disease thus becomes a decision of actual parasitic damage to the host.[110]

Therapy and Control:

There is no chemotherapy known for control of the metacercarial stage of trematodes in fishes. Reduction or elimination of a link in the transmission cycle may be effective in reducing numbers of flukes or in their complete elimination from a fish population. This may be possible in fish culture facilities but is usually impossible in large bodies of water. Attempts to eliminate snails have been made using copper compounds and certain phenolic compounds. Unfortunately, concentrations of these compounds necessary to destroy the snails are also often toxic to fishes.

Immunization of susceptible fish against digenean trematode cercariae may be possible, although impractical without much more information and research. One study demonstrated the potential for this method of control by harvesting metacercariae from *D. spathaceum* infected trout. They were washed, frozen, thawed, ground, sonicated and added to Freund's complete adjuvant. Experimental rainbow trout were injected with an equivalent volume equal to metacercarial protein in 10, 50, and 100 metacercariae. Fish receiving the equivalent of 10 metacercariae lived approximately 3½ months longer than nonimmunized control fish on challenge with viable *D. spathaceum* cercariae. Fish receiving 50 metacercariae equivalent survived almost eight months longer than control fish, and fish with 100 metacercariae equivalent had no mortality in 12 months following challenge. No information on metacercarial enumeration was given for any of the groups.[98a]

Fig. 20: The metacercaria of *Diplostomum spathaceum* can be separated from eye tissue by dissection. Taxonomic keys assist in identification of this trematode.

Adult trematodes in fishes may be removed by adding chemotherapeutic drugs to the diet. *C. farionis* was successfully removed from golden trout by feeding di-N-butyl tin oxide in food. A total dosage of 250 mg of the drug per kilogram of fish body weight given over a three-day period is recommended.[69]

Prognosis:

Many studies have been made in an attempt to estimate the effect of certain digenetic trematodes on their host. Quite often no correlation can be made between number of metacercariae per fish and fish growth or other physiological parameters. Mortalities among fishes caused by high incidence of metacercariae in the liver, kidney or other organ have been reported. However, other references suggest that more evidence is needed in these cases to substantiate mortality as being caused by the trematode. Infections of *P. minimum* up to 991 or 2,041 metacercariae per bluegill have been reported.[11,98] There are recorded cases in which as many as 2,000 metacercariae were present in a single six centemeter long fathead minnow. Slight mortality was occurring in this minnow population as a result of the excessive infection.[65a]

A study involving bluegill sunfish and infection of *Uvulifer ambloplitis* metacercariae in both a pond environment and in laboratory aquaria indicated fish with a heavy infection of metacercariae had significantly reduced body condition and reduced total body lipid. Heavily infected fish had increased oxygen consumption which gradually returned to normal in about 60 days from date of infection. Survival of fish with greater than 50 cysts per fish was reduced as water temperature reduced in autumn, probably associated with reduced feeding activity and entering the winter period with reduced body fat.[52a]

Certainly a few *D. spathaceum* per eye in susceptible fishes may be responsible for reduction of visual acuity. As many as 500 metacercariae of this trematode have been reported in one eye of a host fish. The fish was blind or nearly blind but still living.[10] Loss of vision caused by these trematodes may result in starvation or inability to elude predators (Pl. 35A).

Host alteration from adult trematodes in the intestines of fishes has not received as much study as effects of metacercaria. Adult flukes in the intestine may reach high numbers without causing obvious pathogenic effects. Infections of as high as 446 *C. farionis* in a fish caused inflammation of the intestinal wall.[110] Smaller numbers are thought to have no effect because they feed primarily on intestinal mucus. A study in which various physiological and blood chemistry parameters were used to test the effect of infections of 10 to 48 *C. farionis* per rainbow trout concluded that the non-infected control fish were in slightly better physiological condition than the infected fish. The flukes were said to have caused no serious conditions in the infected fish.[49]

Practical Aspects:

Trematodes in fishes probably occur in most wild-ranging fish populations. These organisms usually cause minimal over-all effects on reproduction, growth and survival. Excessively infected fishes taken by either commercial or sport fishermen may be discarded. However, proper management of exploited fish populations can usually be regulated to maintain a balance between flukes and fish hosts. An example of such a management practice occurred in Colorado. A heavily exploited sport fishing lake was continuously stocked with cultured rainbow trout to maintain a sufficient trout population. Many of the trout became infected with *D. spathaceum*. A study of the problem indicated that brown trout were more resistant to the fluke. Subsequently the stocking of rainbow trout in the lake was stopped and the trout population converted to brown trout. Metacercariae of *D. spathaceum* can be found in the eyes of brown trout but with less overt blindness.

CESTOIDEA OF FISHES:

Cestodes are a taxonomic class of organisms in which the adult stage usually lives in the intestinal tract of vertebrates. Intermediate stages live in a wide variety of body locations in both vertebrate and invertebrate hosts. The bodies of most cestodes are ribbon-shaped and divided into short segments called proglottids, thus the common name tapeworms. A holdfast organ at the anterior end is called the scolex; it is followed by a segment called the neck, and the remainder of the body is the strobila. The shape of the scolex and its organs of attachment is useful for identification. Each proglottid

is a complete reproductive unit, having both a male and a female genital system. The structures of the proglottids are also used for identification.

New proglottids are added to the strobila at the neck. Older proglottids become more mature toward the posterior end until those at the extreme posterior are nothing more than egg-production systems or sacs of eggs called gravid proglottids. Some cestode species release eggs continuously from gravid proglottids which remain attached to the stobila. The eggs pass out of the host with feces. Gravid proglottids of other species are released from the strobila to pass out with feces. Eggs are released when the proglottid decomposes or is torn apart by scavengers.

Nearly every vertebrate in the world has one or more cestode species with which they have evolved, and fishes are no exception. The natural host fishes live together with their cestodes, usually with little or no effect on the host. The cestode draws sustenance, a place of shelter and a place to reproduce from the host.

Many of the cestodes involving fishes have become host-specific, that is, specifically suited to only one host species. Host specificity may occur when the life history and feeding habits of the host are closely integrated with the life cycle of the cestode to the point that this is the only possible host for the cestode. Other cestodes are far less host-specific and are capable of completing their life cycles in a wide variety of fishes.

The life cycle of cestodes is extremely varied. Fishes may take the part of a primary host, an intermediate host or a transport host. Fishes in which the cestode is adult normally carry the worm in the intestinal tract. Those cestodes in which fishes are intermediate hosts live outside the alimentary tract, often in any or all organs and systems of the host (Pl. 35D). Intermediate host fishes may be damaged by only a few intermediate stage cestodes present in a vital organ such as the brain, eye or heart. However, intermediate-stage cestodes which remain in the body cavity, muscle tissue or other non-vital areas may have little or no effect even if present in large numbers.

The enormous numbers of cestode species which have evolved with fishes of the world cannot all be discussed here. Therefore, two selected species will be examined to illustrate two combinations of host-parasite relationships. One species, *Proteocephalus ambloplitis*, also called by the common name bass tapeworm, will be used as an example of a cestode in which fishes are the primary and intermediate hosts. *Ligula intestinalis* will be used as an example in which fishes play the part of intermediate host.

Etiological Agents (Selected):

Proteocephalus ambloplitis belongs to the family Proteocephalidae, a large family of cestodes with ten recognized subfamilies. The subfamily Proteocephalinae

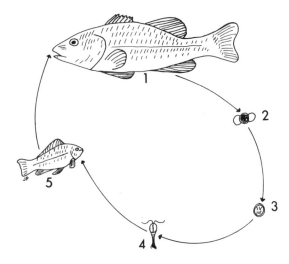

Fig. 21: Life cycle of *Proteocephalus ambloplitis*
1. Primary host, largemouth or smallmouth bass.
2. Egg passed in feces.
3. Develops to hexacanth embryo.
4. Hexacanth embryo ingested by copepod, develops to procercoid.
5. Copepod ingested by a variety of forage fish species, becomes a plerocercoid.
6. Forage fish with plerocercoid ingested by a bass, adult cestode develops in the intestine.

includes the genus *Proteocephalus* and nine other genera, each genus with several species, thus illustrating the reason why a representative of the family must be used in this limited chapter.[112,116]

Proteocephalid cestodes were first described in 1802 under the old composite genus *Taenia*. Not until 1891 did workers realize that some of the taenias were distinctly different. These were removed from *Taenia* and placed into a genus *Ichthyotaenia* in 1899.[2] Taxonomic clarification was finally made in 1914, when all species of the genus *Proteocephalus* were placed in the family Proteocephalidae, a classification which has been accepted by most parasitologists.[35,52]

P. ambloplitis has a complicated life cycle involving a piscine second intermediate host and a piscivorous primary host fish (Fig. 21). *P. ambloplitis* adults are found in the intestines of largemouth bass and smallmouth bass. The cestodes range in length up to about 150 mm and 1.5 mm in width. The strobila may contain up to 250 proglottids. The scolex has four functional cup-shaped suckers. A nonfunctional vestigial fifth sucker is also present at the extreme anterior of the scolex. The genital pores alternate irregularly on the proglottids and open laterally. Identification is made by morphological characteristics within the proglottids.[112,116]

Eggs are expelled from gravid proglottids and pass from the host in feces. The eggs mature in water to a hexacanth embryo, a small individual inside the egg having six hooks. Eggs with embryos are ingested by several species of copepods as the first intermediate host. The embryo becomes free of the outer egg membranes and, within a short time after ingestion, penetrates the intestinal wall of the host and begins development in the host hemocoel. The hooks are gradually lost and the procercoid forms. The metamorphosis takes between 24 and 80 days, depending on water temperature.

The life cycle of *P. ambloplitis* continues when the copepod is ingested by a fish. The most successful transmission occurs in a fish which serves as a forage-fish for the bass, but a variety of fishes such as sunfishes, shiners, minnows and even salmonids can serve the purpose of the cestode. The procercoid penetrates the intestinal wall of the second intermediate fish host. Some encyst in the wall of the intestine, others penetrate organs in the visceral cavity and some may eventually reach muscle tissue. Here they develop into plerocercoids, the next successive step in the life cycle. The life cycle is complete when the second intermediate host containing the infective plerocercoid is ingested by the primary host (Fig. 21).

P. ambloplitis has a geographical distribution over much of the United States, from Maine to Washington State and into the southern parts of the country. It is not usually found in alpine regions, but mainly in warmwater and coolwater environments. The cestode is found more often in lake and reservoir environments and has been associated with pond culture of bass throughout the midwestern and southern United States.

Ligula intestinalis belongs to the family Ligulidae, small family with two subfamilies and three genera. The Ligulidae are distinctive among cestodes for three reasons. They are not highly host-specific but can develop in a wide variety of second intermediate host fishes, primary host birds and mammals, and have even attained full adulthood in experimental artificial environments at temperature ranges between 36 and 42°C. The plerocercoid stage develops sexually in the second intermediate host, almost to a stage of egg production. These cestodes are very broad in shape and are often referred to as beltworms.[10]

L. intestinalis was first described in 1758 and has continued to generate interest among parasitologists. Adult *L. intestinalis* reside in the intestines of many species of aquatic piscivorous birds including gulls, terns, herons, grebes, loons and mergansers. Adult worms are 10 to 100 cm in length and 0.6 to 1.2 cm in width. They are

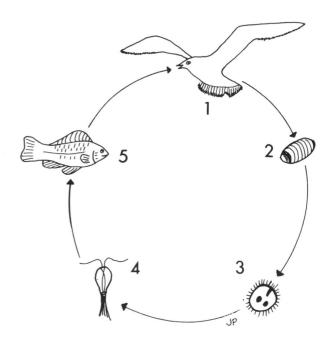

Fig. 22: Life cycle of *Ligula intestinalis*
1. Adult development completed 1 to 2 days following ingestion.
2. Operculated eggs passed in feces for 2 to 4 days, adult then dies.
3. Free-swimming coracidium released from egg in 5 to 8 days.
4. Coracidium ingested by a first intermediate host planktonic copepod, procercoid development complete in 10 to 15 days.
5. Copepod with procercoid ingested by second intermediate host fish, plerocercoid develops. Life cycle is completed when fish with plerocercoid is ingested by any of several species of aquatic piscivorous birds.

belt-like in shape without true segmentation of the strobila, thus pseudoproglottids are said to be present. The strobila has a distinct longitudinal groove along the middle of the ventral surface. Genital pores appear in or near the ventral groove from each of the 24 to 40 pseudoproglottids.

Completion of sexual development requires as little as 35 to 40 hours. Eggs are produced for two to four days, after which the worm dies. Eggs are passed out of the primary host in feces, and each hatches to a free-swimming coracidium. The coracidia are ingested by a wide variety of carnivorous first intermediate host planktonic copepods and migrate through the intestinal wall and into the body cavity. Here they develop into procercoids (Fig. 22). Second intermediate host fishes ingest the infected copepods, and the procercoid is released. The procercoid penetrates the intestinal wall and enters the body cavity, where development continues to the plerocercoid. A wide variety of fish species can serve as second intermediate host. *L. intestinalis* plerocercoids have been reported in many species of sunfishes, suckers, basses, minnows, shiners, chubs, dace, bream and many others, mostly in freshwater fishes but also in some brackish water and saltwater fishes.

Size development of the plerocercoid is limited by the size of the fish host. The plerocercoid(s) usually fill the space in the body cavity whatever the size of fish, being small in small fishes and large in larger fishes, almost to the point of appearing like different worm species (Pl. 24D). The plerocercoid is maintained in the body cavity of the fish probably for the life of the fish. Additional procercoids may be taken in and added to those already in the abdominal cavity; thus, plerocercoids of various sizes may be found in the same fish.

Plerocercoids continue to develop genital organs while in the second intermediate host until sexual development is almost complete. The life cycle of the cestode is completed when the fish containing the infective stage plerocercoid is ingested by a bird. Plerocercoids have been experimentally transmitted to a number of avian and mammalian species; however, most natural infections of *L. intestinalis* appear to be in aquatic birds.[1,10,35]

L. intestinalis is geographically ubiquitous, having been reported from all continents. The cestode is found primarily in wild-ranging fish populations, although it has been reported from cultured pond fishes in Europe, Asia and the United States.

Epizootiology:

Cestode transmission involving fishes depends on the species of hosts and worms involved. Transmission cycles always involve the food chain. Each stage of cestode development is associated with the food of the hosts. Development times for each cestode species differ, but those for life stages in poikilothermic vertebrates and invertebrates are temperature-dependent. Cestode populations in primary hosts involving aquatic invertebrates and fishes are usually quite seasonal. *L. intestinalis*, for example, is not found in primary host birds during winter months when lakes, ponds and reservoirs are frozen and plerocercoid-infected fishes are not available.

Infection levels of a fish with cestodes are somewhat related to age of the host fish. The plerocercoid stages of cestode development generally have a longevity of up to a few years. Thus, plerocercoid infection levels may continue to increase during the life of the fish as more procercoids are added to the plerocercoids already present in the fish. This is true of *L. intestinalis*. One study demonstrated that one-year-old yellow perch had 1.4%

infection incidence, two-year-old fish had 7.0%, three-year-old fish 18.5%, four-year-old fish 24.5% and five-year-old fish 24.0%.[81] The study did not indicate the severity of plerocercoid involvement, only age and infection incidence.

Longevity of adult cestodes is usually shorter than longevity of the plerocercoid. Most adults may live for less than a year in the primary host fish, as indicated by the annual egg production cycle over much of the temperate zones. Studies on five species of *Proteocephalus*, for example, indicated that eggs were shed primarily during three or more months between spring and autumn. This was thought to be because older worms were lost during late autumn and winter, to be replaced by younger worms in the spring and summer.[14,45]

Intensity of infection is important in the relationship between cestodes and fish health. The epizootiology of infection incidence is primarily dependent on numbers of each host species per unit of geographical area, water quality, water temperature and other general physical factors of the habitat. Overpopulation of fishes and/or invertebrate hosts tends to increase chances for successful transmission of a higher percentage of the cestodes. Cestode metamorphosis outside of homeothermic hosts is controlled by environmental temperature. Some stages of cestode development are enhanced by relatively warm water, but others are inhibited. Cold or cool water may be essential for metamorphosis of some cestode species but completely inhibitory for others. Turbidity, pH, alkalinity, hardness, pollution or other factors in the water may be responsible for more or less success in cestode transmission.

Disease Signs:

Excessive numbers of either adult or plerocercoid stages cestodes in fishes may cause reduced growth, emaciation, anemia, dark coloration, erratic swimming ability and susceptibility to secondary infections (Pl. 25A). Location of plerocercoids in vital organs of fish may be significant to survival. Only a few in the brain, heart, spleen, kidney, gonad or other organ may have a tremendous effect. Gonads, for example, may become atrophied and nonproductive from only a few plerocercoids.

Diagnosis:

The fish disease diagnostician must make an assumption of the effect of adult or plerocercoid stage cestodes on fishes. Other factors such as poor nutrition, overpopulation of fishes or presence of other disease entities in the fishes must also be considered. Presence of adult or plerocercoid cestodes may appear to be excessive but in actuality may not be. For example, as many as 68 plerocercoids of *Diphyllobothrium cordiceps* have been found in cutthroat trout in Yellowstone Lake, Wyoming. The number appeared to be excessive, yet no indication of deleterious effects could be found.[83] Compare this to re-

sults of a study in which a 55% reduction in growth of yellow perch was noted from infections with *L. intestinalis* plerocercoids.[81]

Therapy and Control:

The best control procedure for cestodes in cultured fishes is pond management. Draining and allowing ponds to dry completely will remove infected intermediate hosts and cestode eggs. Ponds that cannot be completely drained may be treated with chlorine or lime to destroy intermediate copepod hosts and cestode eggs.

Chemotherapy is effective when cultured fishes are being fed a mixed ration. Kamala, an ancient anthelminthic, fed at 0.1% of the diet for three days if dry rations are being fed, or up to seven days if wet rations are fed, will remove adult cestodes from fishes. Kamala is quite difficult to obtain in the United States.

Di-N-butyl tin oxide and di-N-butyl tin dilaurate are both effective in removal of adult cestodes from fish. Both are used at 0.5 to 0.6% of the diet. The ration is fed for three days so that a total dose of 250 mg of the drug is given per kg of fish. Yomesan, or phenasal, can also be used for removal of adult cestodes from fish by adding it to the diet and feeding at the rate of 50 mg per kilogram of fish for three days. Phenothiazine can also be used in the diet and fed at the rate of one gram per kilogram of fish body weight three times at two day intervals.[65b]

Mebendazole has been used experimentally to remove larval *P. ambloplitis* from the intestine and other organs of largemouth bass. An oral dose of 100 mg per kilogram of fish per day given for 14 consecutive days reduced tapeworm numbers by 90% compared to non-medicated control fish. One dose capsule implantation of 200 mg of mebendazole per kilogram of fish, or intraperitoneal injection of the same drug dose, both reduced tapeworm numbers by 95%.[8a]

There is no therapy for removal of plerocercoid stage cestodes from fishes. Pond management is the only alternative.

Cestode control in wild-ranging fishes has not been too successful. Attempts have been made to eliminate or reduce a link in the transmission cycle but have been of limited success even in small bodies of water. Increasing water flow, if possible, may be useful in removing both free-swimming stages of some cestodes and planktonic copepods which may be intermediate hosts.

Prognosis:

Direct mortality from cestode infections in fishes is usually quite rare. However, secondary effects such as unthriftiness, susceptibility to other diseases, evidence of malnutrition and other indications of poor health may be apparent in fishes with heavy burdens of cestodes. Wild fish population decline has been attributed to heavy infections of some cestodes, especially those which involve gonads and cause what has been called parasitic castration.[5,71,80]

Practical Aspects:

Cestodes are organisms which must be contended with among fishes. Presence of cestodes in natural host fishes is not usually destructive unless there is an upset in balance between the fish population and cestode survival. Cestodes have a tremendous reproductive potential, and an alteration in ecosystem balance which yields increases in cestode population by a fraction of a percent may be responsible for gross changes in the infection level of a fish population. Fishery biologists, managers and administrators should be aware of the potentiality of these organisms. Often heavily overfishing a fish population will reduce incidence of these worms among the remaining fishes. Cestodes among many wild fishes can be managed as the fish population is managed.

A practical aspect in relation to cestodes and the fishes they infect comes from the tendency to move fishes about the world without parasitological examination to be sure the fishes are uninfected. Cestodes may thus be inadvertently moved into fish populations in a new geographical area, only to discover the fish are sensitive to them. One of the best examples of what can happen if precautions are not taken came about when grass carp were moved from Asia to Europe and North America. A cestode, *Bothriocephalus acheilognathi* (*B. gowkongensis*), was moved with the fish. Those taken to Europe succeeded in being transported about until the cestode was present in many fish farms, causing heavy losses in cultured carp.[3] Those brought to the United States have been reported in golden shiners and fathead minnows, two of the most economically important bait minnow species in the United States. No assessment of damage to the bait minnow industry has been made, but the cestode may spread its range and become a management and economic problem. Careful parasitological examination of the grass carp prior to movement may have assured that the cestode was not transported. There is evidence of transferral of this cestode even though parasitological inspection was made, because the very youngest stage in the fish intestine is difficult to observe.[31]

Acanthocephala of Fishes

The phylum Acanthocephala is comprised of worms with an anterior proboscis covered with many hooks. These worms are often referred to as thorny-headed worms. Acanthocephalans are widely distributed. All are endoparasites in the digestive tract of vertebrates, the larval stages being found in invertebrate intermediate hosts.

The body of acanthocephalans is made up of the presoma (proboscis and associated structures) and the trunk. The trunk is more or less cylindrical in shape. There is no digestive tract or circulatory system, but a nerve ganglion and nerve fibers are present. The sexes are separate. The male usually has copulatory organs and a cement gland. The latter is used to seal the genital pore of the female immediately after fertilization. The female genital tract terminates in a vagina opening externally at the posterior end of the body.

The proboscis is used to a great extent for taxonomic classification. This organ is one of the most outstanding features of the worm, especially on first observation of the organism (Pl. 25B). Differentiation of shape of the proboscis is important, *i.e.*, round, oval or cylindrical. The number, shape, location and conformation of hooks on the proboscis are used to place various worms into taxonomic classes and orders. Classification depends on whether the hooks lie in rows, spirals or are randomly placed. Length and width of the hooks and their curvature are also used.[10,73,90]

Identification to genus and species depends on characteristics other than those of the proboscis. The worms have two fluid-filled sacs, called lemnisci, behind the proboscis (Pl. 25B). They are associated with extension and invagination of the proboscis and are also thought to have relationship to lipid metabolism. The shape, size and location of these organs, as well as total body conformation and other internal structures, assist in identification.

The alimentary epithelium of the primary host may sustain histopathological changes from attachment of the worms' thorn-covered proboscis. Serious infections in fishes with these worms can result in intestinal ulceration, areas of intestinal necrosis and possibly peritonitis. Acanthocephalans, as is true with other parasitic organisms, are not usually detrimental to the natural host unless they are present in large numbers. Those associated with fishes tend to be more a curiosity than a disease problem. This is not to say they cannot be responsible for fish losses, only that losses in fishes from acanthocephalans are quite rare.[1,10,35,73]

The life cycle of acanthocephalans involves crustaceans or occasionally mollusks and insects as the intermediate host, each acanthocephalan being somewhat host-specific in relation to their intermediate host. Eggs released from the female are swallowed by the intermediate host and fully formed larva or acanthor released. The acanthor uses its hooks to bore through the intestinal wall and into the hemocoel. It develops into an acanthella and becomes surrounded by a connective tissue capsule formed by the host. The acanthella then becomes a young thorny-headed worm or cystacanth inside its capsule. Sexual maturity of the worm is reached when the cystacanth is ingested by the primary host.[10,73]

Fishes can serve as primary hosts for those acanthocephalans which become sexually mature in the fishes. Fishes can also serve as reservoir hosts for acanthocephalans which are adult in marine mammals. Much more research is needed to determine the role of these worms in fish health, whether fishes are the primary or reservoir host.

Nematoda of Fishes

Parasitic nematodes (roundworms) are widely distributed among the plants and animals of the earth. Fishes are notorious for the variety of nematodes they carry. The phylum Nematoda has two taxonomic classes, Secernentea, formerly called Phasmidia, the Adenophorea, formerly called Aphasmidia. Class Secernentea has five taxonomic orders with ten suborders and 27 superfamilies. Class Adenophorea is much smaller, with two orders, two suborders and three superfamilies among the parasitic nematodes.[13,90] This may illustrate the tremendous number of genera and species of parasitic forms of nematodes which have evolved.

Nematodiasis, or disease related to nematodes, is surprisingly rare among fishes. A fish may be found with hundreds of nematodes of one or more species in various organs and tissues of the body yet living a relatively normal life. Nematodes of fishes have received only limited attention, and then not usually from the standpoint of disease. Zoologists and parasitologists have used nematodes of fishes for study and taxonomic classification since early times. Most nematodes are large enough to be seen without magnification, consequently they have been obvious to anyone doing necropsies on fishes for disease or parasitological surveys, or eviscerating and skinning them for human food. Many observations of nematodes in fishes are on the order of a curiosity or an inquiry into transmission to humans or domestic animals. Listing nematode findings of fishes from various geographical areas has also been popular.

Etiological Agents:

The etiological agents of nematodiasis are any nematode species present in vital organs of the fish host or in numbers detrimental to health. Nematodes are usually round in cross section, occasionally oval. The body is nonsegmented and cylindrical, fusiform or filliform in shape. The body has a well developed cuticle, muscular system and digestive system. Nematodes have a nerve ring, usually in the anterior one-fourth of the body, and nerve trunks leading from the nerve ring. They have an excretory system. The sexes are separate. Most male nematodes have a pair of chitinized spicules used for copulation. The shape, size and internal structures of the spicules and bursa assist in identification of nematodes (Fig. 23).

Geographical Distribution:

Nematodes may be found in fishes in fresh water and salt water in every climatic zone from Arctic to Antarctic and tropical areas of the world. Each nematode species has a definite geographical range.

Susceptible Species:

Nematodes are usually somewhat host-specific. Some nematode species may be found in one fish species, all fishes of a genus or in many different fishes over a relatively limited geographical area.

Epizootiology:

Life cycles of nematodes are extremely varied because each worm has evolved to fit into the life history of the host(s). The life cycles of most nematodes found in fishes have received little or no investigation. However, some general facts can be stated. The adult female nematodes living in the alimentary tract of fishes release eggs which pass from the host body in feces. Some female nematodes are anchored in the lower intestine of the host and extend themselves from the anus of the fish during the darkness to release eggs directly into the water. Other nematode species live in muscle or fascia directly under the skin, and eggs are released through a small hole in the skin into the water.

Some nematode species release eggs which are completely embryonated (containing a fully formed larval nematode). Others release eggs which must be embryonated outside of the host.

The life cycle of some nematodes is direct: eggs are released, embryonated outside the first host, ingested by a new host, the egg membranes digested away, releasing the larva which develops through several stages to an adult. Other nematode species have a more complicated life cycle, the egg requiring a period of time away from the host for embryonation before entering an intermediate host. The larva in the intermediate host must undergo several larval transformations before being infective to a new primary host.

Larval growth is by two to five molts, depending on nematode species. The larva sheds the cuticle at the time of each molt to be replaced by a new and larger cuticle. Nematodes which become adult in fishes usually spend the larval life in crustaceans during the period of molting. Certain nematode species may require a second intermediate host, usually a non-predatory fish, in which to attain the infective larval stage.

Certain fishes also serve in the role of second intermediate host for nematodes which later become adult in aquatic birds, mammals and even humans. The entire epizootiological scheme has been well advanced by each nematode species. The worm has been successful or it would not be present in its fish host today. The fish disease diagnostician usually must determine the life cycle of the nematode species found in uncommon fish hosts. Life cycles of more commonly found nematodes of fishes may or may not have been elucidated.

Disease Signs:

Signs of nematodiasis include anemia, emaciation, unthriftiness and reduced vitality when nematodes are too numerous in the alimentary tract. Raised areas under the skin or connective tissue-covered cysts in various organs may be visible when larvae are present in muscle or coiled within the cysts. Some larval forms of nema-

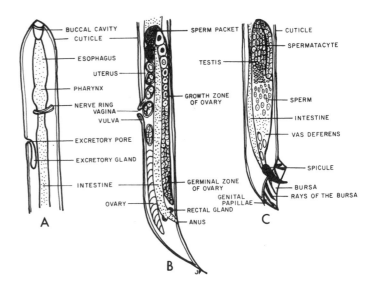

Fig. 23: Anatomy of a typical nematode
  A. Anterior body, both sexes
  B. Posterior body, female
  C. Posterior body, male

todes tend to wander, especially in an unnatural host, and may damage various body organs or systems in these wanderings. Partial paralysis, instability in water or other effects may be noted in these cases.

Diagnosis:

Diagnosis of nematodiasis is by examination and enumeration of the worms. The fish disease diagnostician must make assumptions on whether the nematode is actually causing the disease problem or whether other diseases are primary and the nematodes are innocent or extenuating. Diagnosis of cases involving actual nematodiasis is usually accompanied by identification of the worms.[13]

Therapy and Control:

Therapy of nematodiasis is sometimes possible in aquarium and cultured fishes. Phenothiazine used at 0.1% of the diet for three days may effectively remove the worms from the alimentary tract. Phenothiazine is a strong anti-niacin compound and should not be fed for more than three days. Tramisol used at 0.025 to 0.1% of the diet for seven days has also been found effective in removing alimentary nematodes. Nematodes encysted in various body organs or tissues cannot be removed by drug therapy.

Control methods useful for wild-ranging and confined fishes may be reduction or elimination of a link in the transmission cycle. Removal of fishes from ponds and either drying or disinfecting will eliminate the intermediate hosts, especially crustaceans. Eggs of most nematodes are resistant to drying and to some disinfectants. Usually eggs cannot survive for over six months to a year, and leaving a pond free of fishes for such a period of time will eliminate some nematode species.

Prognosis:

Observation of a few nematodes per fish in earthen ponds is quite common. Fishes with large numbers of

adult alimentary nematodes or large numbers of encysted or wandering larvae can cause mortality or contribute to mortality. Fishes with damaging nematode parasites may be a target for opportunistic bacteria, fungi or protozoans. Increased mortality may be from secondary infections, but is primarily the responsibility of nematodes.

Practical Aspects:

Transportation of fishes intercontinentally and intracontinentally has served to move nematodes from geographical areas of natural hosts to geographical areas with unnatural hosts. Undesirable movement can be controlled by careful parasitological examination prior to movement.

The question often arises in regard to food fishes with enzootic nematodes and the possibility of transmission of those nematodes to humans. Larval stage nematodes in marine fishes, for example, are usually intermediate for marine mammals and birds. A few cases of transmission of these nematodes to humans have been reported.[56] Humans are unnatural hosts of these worms, and the adult stage nematode may wander outside of the usual alimentary tract area, causing moderate to extreme damage to the human host. These cases are rare indeed but demonstrate the need for cooking, salting or pickling fish flesh which may have larval nematodes and is designated for human consumption.

Hirudinea of Fishes

Leeches of the taxonomic class Hirudinea (phylum Annelida) live in fresh waters of all continents except Antarctica and in all oceans of the world. Most leeches feed on worms, insect larvae, snails and other invertebrates. Others feed on blood of invertebrates and vertebrates. The latter are usually called predaceous parasites. Saltwater and freshwater fishes are the usual hosts of the latter, but they may also attack amphibians, aquatic reptiles, mammals and birds.[10,73] Those attacking fishes may cause considerable damage to the host, especially if the host is young or already has reduced vitality. Leeches can become a problem among fishes already disabled from other disease conditions. Although a completely healthy fish can elude these predatory organisms, sick fishes cannot.

Leeches take blood from their host, which can further reduce host vitality. The host may thus become more susceptible to other opportunistic pathogens. Leeches damage skin and scale pockets, opening portals of entry to secondary pathogens. Some of the hemoprotozoans may be transmitted directly by leeches.[1,73]

Leeches have long, slender, flexible bodies and actively swim for an attack on their prey. Skin and underlying tissue are traumatized to allow blood to flow into the leech's digestive system. The leech releases its hold on its prey when its digestive system is filled with blood. The wound gradually heals, but opportunistic pathogens can enter the wound at any time during the healing process.

Leeches are bisexual. The female leech is fertilized by the male through placement of packets of sperm in spermatophores into the atrium of the female. Sperm enters ovarian sacs, and the eggs are fertilized long after the male has left the female. Fertilized eggs are deposited in cocoons attached to aquatic plants, shells of mollusks, stones or other objects. Young individuals emerge and attack various aquatic organisms for sustenance.

Leeches attacking fishes are not host-specific. Usually any fish present in their environment is fair game. Some leeches prefer skin areas, others gill areas. Damage to skin and gills of the host depends on the number of leeches present at any time and the time between attacks necessary for healing of wounds caused by the leeches. Small fishes in earthen ponds are usually more vulnerable and susceptible to leech attack, probably because of the inability of small fishes to elude the attacker. Small fishes can be seriously damaged or killed by excessive numbers of leeches on their bodies or gills at any one time (Pl. 24E).

Leeches are not a usual problem, but occasionally the fish disease diagnostician is confronted with excessive numbers of these organisms on fishes. Rarely are wild-ranging fishes heavily attacked by these organisms. Large numbers of fishes confined to small ponds which also harbor leeches are more susceptible to attack. Leeches can be controlled in fish ponds by use of Masoten at 1:500,000 to 1:1,000,000 (0.5 to 1.0 mg/L) placed in the pond with the fish and allowed to dissipate. Sodium chloride used at 3.5% for one hour has also been found to be effective in removing freshwater leeches from fishes. Ponds with a high leech population may be drained and treated with chlorinated lime to destroy both living leeches and cocoons containing eggs. Allowing the pond to dry for a few weeks following lime treat-ment may also assist in eliminating various life stages of the worms.[1,40,90]

Crustacean Parasites

A tremendous number of crustaceans have evolved to become dependent on certain animals for existence. Those closely associated with fishes can cause disease problems. The phylum Arthropoda is an extremely large and diverse group. The class Crustacea includes numerous orders, many of which have species directly associated with fishes. One reference states that more than 1,000 species of copepods, branchiurans, isopods, amphipods and barnacles occur in or on fishes.[46] Many of them are lethal under certain circumstances, others debilitating and others of major importance to fish culture and the fishing industry.

Crustaceans possess an exoskeleton with jointed appendages and a segmented body. The digestive tract is complete, and the circulatory system consists mainly of a hemocoel. The brain is dorsal, paired nerve cords are ventral and each body segment has paired nerve ganglia. Malpighian tubules serve as excretory organs in most species. Respiration is by tracheae, gills or through body surfaces. The sexes are separate, all are oviparous.[73]

Many of the crustaceans which have become fish parasites no longer resemble free-living crustaceans. Bodies have been modified tremendously through evolution to bizarre shapes and with bizarre appendages, each modification serving a vital purpose for completion of the life cycle and survival of the crustacean. The modifications have been so extensive in many of the species that taxonomic classification is confusing.

The study of parasitic crustaceans of fishes is an enormous subject beyond the scope of this chapter. Therefore, much of the discussion which follows will relate to two selected organisms (*Lernaea elegans* and *Argulus* sp.) for a demonstration of the host-parasite relationship between certain crustaceans and their fish hosts and the complicated life cycle some must go through to exist.

Etiological Agents:

Copepoda

Members of the subclass Copepoda are the most numerous of the parasitic crustaceans. There are nine families of copepods which contain parasites of fishes (Table 21). Each family includes one or more genera. The family Lernaeidae has but one genus, *Lernaea*, with many species among the fishes of the world. *L. cyprinacea* has continued to be studied since its description in 1758, over 220 years ago.[10,35,73] There is much confusion over the name, *L. cyprinacea*. Usually the oldest nomenclature is considered to be the acceptable name. A discussion of the genus *Lernaea* in 1950 suggested that an organism found on goldfish in Ohio in 1931 and named *Lernaea carassii* was synonymous with *L. cyprinacea*, as was another organism called *Lernaea elegans* described in 1925. The belief was expressed that the species had

TABLE 21

Abbreviated taxonomic classification of major groups of parasitic crustaceans [10,35,46,73]

Group	Family	Representative Genus
Subclass Copepoda	Ergasilidae	*Ergasilus*
	Bomolochidae	*Bomolochus*
	Caligidae	*Caligus*
	Dichelesthioidae	*Eudactylina*
	Chondracanthidae	*Acanthochondria*
	Lernaeoceridae	*Lernaeocera*
	Lernaeidae	*Lernaea*
	Lernaeopodidae	*Salminicola*
	Sphyriidae	*Sphyrion*
	Philichthyidae	*Philichthys*
Subclass Branchiura	Argulidae	*Argulus*
Subclass Cirripedia	Rhizocephalidae	*Anelasoma*
Order Isopoda	Cymothoidae	*Cymothoa*

originated in Europe (where it was first described) and spread to Asia (where it was described as *L. elegans*) and then to North America (where it was described as *L. carassii*).[24,103] A further examination of all circumstances surrounding nomenclature of this organism indicates the true name to be *L. elegans*.[32] However, the name *Lernaea cyprinacea* is more widely used in North America and other parts of the world and this name will be used for discussion here.

The female *L. cyprinacea* becomes adult on a fish host following fertilization by the male. Female metamorphosis is complete when the body form of a typical copepod changes to a bizarre creature no longer resembling a copepod (Pl. 26A). The head region is thrust through the skin or gill epithelium of the host, often through the body wall or skull and into various organs. Metamorphosis of the head continues to form a structure known as the cephalic process. The cephalic process develops anchors which assist in holding the organism in place during the remainder of life (Pl. 26A).

The fertilized, attached female develops paired egg sacs near the posterior end of the body. Eggs are produced and added to egg sacs. Eggs in the sacs are arranged loosely enough to give space for developing embryos. The egg sacs are shed as the eggs mature. The eggs hatch and nauplii break out of the egg sacs (Pl. 26B).

The newly hatched nauplii are elliptical in shape,

about 140 micrometers long and 80 micrometers wide. The nauplii molt within 50 hours, depending to some extent on water temperature, to become metanauplii (Pl. 26C). Metanauplii are slightly larger, about 180 micrometers long by 85 micrometers wide, and spines appear at the base of each mandible. The first indication of body segmentation appears in the metanauplii. Twenty to 40 hours after metanauplii form, the exoskelton is shed again to form the first copepodid with a body about 230 micrometers long by 110 micrometers wide (Pl. 26D). The first copepodid has two pairs of swimming legs, and the antennulae become more segmented. The first copepodid must find a host within three days or it will perish.[47,113]

The first copepodid on a host's skin or gills continues to metamorphose. The second, third, fourth and fifth copepodid are formed, each with more body segmentation and with swimming legs. An additional abdominal segment is added at the fifth copepodid stage, the genital segment. The male, about 780 micrometers in length and 170 micrometers in width at this time, has developed a pair of testes in the thorax with sperm ducts leading to the genital segment. The female, about 1,040 micrometers in length and 200 micrometers in width, develops a long and heavy genital segment (Pl. 26E). Copulation occurs at the sixth copepodid stage of development. The male places two sac-shaped spermatophores on the genital segment of the female, leaves the female and dies (Pl. 26F). The fertilized female continues to metamorphose, increases rapidly in length and burrows into the integument or gills of the host. Anchor processes develop on the head, and the ovaries begin to move posteriorly from the anterior thorax to a point near the juncture of the thorax with the abdomen. The body continues to elongate, and cephalic horns branch from the head. The female is now in position to produce eggs (Pl. 26A).

Branchiura

Systematic classification of parasitic crustaceans is in a continual state of change. The branchiurans were classified as copepods originally, some taxonomists still feel they should be an order under the copepods, others feel they deserve the same rank as the copepods. The latter assumption will be used here, that subclass Branchiura is a valid taxonomic group. The subclass consists of about 130 species, about 100 of them belonging to the genus *Argulus*.[46]

Argulus sp. are the so-called fish lice. The body is flattened, with adaptations for attachment to the host and for feeding (Pl. 25C). The hooks and barbs on the body, cup-like suckers and stylet feeding apparatus may damage the host, especially when large numbers of these organisms appear on the same host.

The shape of the body of both male and female *Argulus* sp. is broad, flat and oval; sexes are about the same size. The head and thorax are closely attached to form a cephalothorax. Two complex faceted eyes are present in the head. The two maxillae are modified into sucker-like organs of attachment. The mandibles lie in a cavity on the ventral surface. Other modified mouthparts form the stylet, which is surrounded by a sheath and can be thrust out at will to pierce host tissue. The stylet lies between and slightly anterior to the eyes, between the modified mandibles.

The carapace of the cephalothorax is convex dorsally. There are four pairs of swimming legs which allow these organisms to maneuver in water and on the body of the host. The abdomen, sometimes called the caudal fin, is short, forming two rounded lobes closely attached to the thorax. Egg sacs are absent on the female (Pl. 25C).

Argulus lives on the skin, fins and gills of the host until full adulthood is reached. The fertilized female falls from the host and swims to aquatic plants and other submerged objects, to which eggs are attached by a sticky mucus material. The nauplius, metanauplius and first copepodid stages of most *Argulus* species develop in the egg. Other metamorphic stages include the second through the seventh copepodid, subadult and adult. The second copepodid has paired swimming legs on all four thoracic segments three to four days after hatching and actively seeks a host. The second copepodid is approximately 1 mm in length, with a body shape similar to the adult. Fourteen or more days are required for the argulid to reach the seventh copepodid stage, depending

on species and water temperature. The subadult molts several times before becoming adult, taking 14 to 16 days to complete metamorphosis. Mating then occurs, and the female again leaves the host to deposit eggs on submerged objects. The entire life cycle takes 40 to 100 days, depending on species and water temperature.[10,29,35,62,115]

Geographical Distribution:

L. cyprinacea is widely distributed in North America, Asia and Europe. It is found more often in cool and warmwater environments but has been reported on coldwater fishes. It is strictly a freshwater parasite. However, there are numerous other species of copepods parasitic on fishes in saltwater, brackish water and freshwater environments of the world.[32,47]

Argulids are found worldwide, in freshwater and saltwater environments. Fourteen species of *Argulus* have been reported on freshwater fishes of North America, and three species are reported from Europe.[10,29,35]

Susceptible Species:

L. cyprinacea has been reported on a variety of freshwater fishes, including carp, basses, sunfishes, freshwater salmonids, pikes, perches, shiners, catfishes, minnows and many others. *L. cyprinacea* is not at all host-specific, nor is it selective in the site of penetration of the host body. The female *L. cyprinacea* may embed the cephalic anchors in eyes, gills, opercula, fins, skin, lips or other body surfaces.

Argulids are parasitic primarily on teleost (bony) fishes in both salt water and fresh water. Some are also capable of living on amphibians.[46]

Epizootiology:

Transmission of both lernaeids and argulids can be through the water supply or by introduction of infected fishes. Amphibians moving from place to place may also be involved with transmission.

The free-swimming metanauplii of lernaeids or copepodids of argulids move about to some extent. Some may become attached to the plumage of birds and be moved short distances.

Copepodid stages of both lernaeids and argulids may be found on the same host. The copepodids are capable of swimming freely and may do so on occasion, thus changing hosts. The adult female of *L. cyprinacea* becomes completely immobile after attachment to the host. Female argulids have retained the capability of free locomotion away from the host, leaving the host to release eggs and then often returning to a different host.

Water temperature is important to the life cycle of all crustacean parasites of fishes. *L. cyprinacea* cannot complete the life cycle at 15°C or lower. *Lernaea* overwinter as larvae or adult females imbedded in host tissue, or possibly as eggs. Metamorphosis will not progress at any stage if the water temperature is 8°C or lower.[32]

Argulus sp. require a water temperature about 12°C.

Egg production ceases at 16°C or lower. These organisms hibernate on the body of the host below 8°C.[29]

Both lernaeids and argulids are sensitive to drying; 24 hours kills eggs, intermediate stages and adults. *Lernaea* sp. are sensitive to salinity, a salinity greater than 1.8% killing adult *Lernaea*, and even less salt kills other life stages. Argulids are not sensitive to salinity. Adults can withstand 3.5% salinity (seawater strength) but earlier life stages may be killed by less than 2%.

Almost all copepod parasites of fishes are sensitive to low pH. There are no records of these organisms occurring below pH 7.[32]

Disease Signs:

Copepods and branchiurans infesting the bodies of fishes are true parasites. Even small numbers of these organisms will cause behavioral and clinical changes in the host. Host damage is especially bad when small fishes are parasitized. For example, a single *L. cyprinacea* placed in the head region so the cephalic processes of the parasite penetrates the brain will be lethal.

Slight to moderate infestations of these organisms will cause fishes to rub against the sides and bottom of the pond or aquarium in an attempt to dislodge the irritating copepodid or adult parasites. Heavy infestations may cause fishes to become lethargic, seek the sides of the pond or aquarium and have difficulty in maintaining equilibrium. Some fishes may dart about as if attempting to dislodge the parasite, leaving them completely exhausted and swimming upside down (Pl. 24F).

Skin, fins and gills secrete excess mucus from irritation by copepodid stages crawling about and from movement of the spines, barbs and other organs. The place of attachment of *Argulus* adults may leave areas with the skin, fins and gill epithelium abraded from penetration of the stylet feeding organ. The surface is usually hemorrhagic and erythemic. Argulids apparently produce a hemorrhagic factor which they excrete from mouth parts. Extracts made from mouth parts of *Argulus coregoni* injected into the fins of fish caused marked hemorrhage. There was no erythrocyte lysis or cytotoxic effect of the extract.[96a] Sites of female *Lernaea* attachment may be inflamed around the parasite body or may cause tumor-like masses to build up around the parasite. The wounds remaining after female *Lernaea* have fallen away, heal slowly, demonstrating hemorrhagic and erythemic foci.

Diagnosis:

Adult copepod and branchiuran parasites of fishes are large and can be easily seen without magnification. Identification of the parasite is important not only for purposes of species range and host susceptibility, but also for purposes of treatment.

Identification of these organisms is based on morphology of the adult female. The male may be used for identification of *Argulus* species, but not for lernaeids since development does not go beyond the sixth copepodid stage. Morphological characteristics are used with published keys for family, genus and species identification.[10,17,35,62,114,115]

Nauplii, metanauplii and copepodid stages of these organisms are much more difficult to use for identification. They may be observed either in skin scrapings or gill mounts during routine necropsy and diagnostic procedures. There are no morphological keys for identification of the early stages of these organisms; however, descriptions of life cycles may be of some assistance, especially when accompanied by photographs.[47,96]

Lesions on skin, fins and gills associated with contact by these organisms may be of assistance in diagnosis. Histological sections of fish tissue invaded by penetrating copepod parasites may assist in determination of severity of parasite attack on the host. The cephalic horns of *Lernaea* may be embedded in vital organs such as the liver, spleen, heart, organs of the alimentary tract, eyes, skull, brain or others (Pl. 27A). The kidney is rarely involved because the vertebrae and ribs tend to protect it from penetration.[48,85,97]

Therapy and Control:

Prevention is the best control for crustacean fish parasites. Crustacean parasites present in the water system are difficult to remove. This is especially true in fish culture facilities. Adult stages of these organisms are generally no more affected by chemical treatment than the host. Attempts to eliminate the parasites may also damage the host fish. However, earlier life stages are usually more susceptible to chemical therapy.

Certain management practices may be of assistance in reducing, and in some cases eliminating, these organisms. Increased water flow through ponds may wash early life stages away before they can find a host. Removing places for female argulids to deposit eggs in ponds may also be of use in control. Draining and drying ponds will destroy all stages of these parasitic crustaceans.

The wide distribution of crustacean parasites in the world has led to numerous chemical control procedures. Some procedures are effective, but others are of little value. Those found most useful have been selected and are given in Table 22.[26b]

Prognosis:

All fishes in static ponds which harbor crustacean parasites will usually be infected if water temperature and water quality are acceptable to the crustacean parasite. Infection levels may range from one or a few crustacean parasites per fish to several hundred. However, one *Argulus* or one *L. cyprinacea* or similar crustacean parasite may kill a fish of two or three grams body weight.[10]

High mortalities have occurred among cultured catfish, goldfish, bait minnows, carp, trout and other fishes. Epizootics of crustacean parasites among wild-

TABLE 22

Selected procedures used for control of crustacean parasites on fishes

Compound	Dose Level	Time & Method	Remarks
Ammonium chloride	1:1,000 (1,000 mg/L)	4-hour bath	Useful for adults and early life stages; will not affect eggs.
*Benzene hexachloride (lindane)	1:8,000,000 (0.12 mg/L)	Indefinite	Add to the water and allow to dissipate; use one treatment only; removes all life stages.
**Masoten (neguvon)	1:4,000,000 (0.25 mg/L)	Indefinite	Add to water and allow to dissipate; use two applications at weekly intervals; removes all life stages.
Sodium chloride	3 to 5%	30-second to one-minute dip	Removes all life stages of *Lernaea*; some fish sensitive to strong salt solutions.
	0.8 to 1.1%	3 days	Removes all life stages of *Lernaea*; for use with fish sensitive to high salt solutions.
*Diflubenzuron	1:100,000,000 (0.01 mg/L)	Indefinite	Destroys naupli stages of *Lernaea cyprinacea*.

*Has not received clearance for use with any fish species.
**Has been cleared for use with bait minnows and aquarium fishes; not for food fishes.

ranging fishes have also occurred. Large numbers of fishes have been killed in streams, lakes, ponds and reservoirs. Mortality or contribution to mortality has also occurred among marine fishes from crustacean parasites.

These parasites also open portals of entry for a variety of opportunistic pathogens. Certain crustacean parasites have been involved as vectors of fish pathogens such as hemaprotozoans, bacteria and the virus of spring viremia of carp. The fishes may be lost because of secondary infection directly related to the crustacean parasites.

Fishes recovering from infestations of crustacean parasites which embed into body tissues are thought to be somewhat immune to a second attack by the same parasite species. However, this immune response has not been verified experimentally.[32]

Practical Aspects:

Transportation of fishes from geographical areas with enzootic crustacean parasites to non-infected areas has been responsible for widening the distribution of these organisms. Quite often inspection of fishes for interstate transportation does not include a conscientious effort to locate fish lice, anchor parasites or other crustaceans. The adult stages of these organisms may be obvious on fishes being inspected, but intermediate stages may be passed over. Observation of adult crustaceans by the fish health inspector are quite often ignored because these organisms are considered to be ubiquitous and therefore there is supposedly no reason to worry about moving them into a geographical area not already infected. This assumption has caused extreme problems when the fishes being inspected were later transported to a non-infected fish culture facility, lake, pond or reservoir. An example is brought to mind in which a load of trout was transported from Idaho to Colorado. The fish were certified as being free of certain diseases on a restricted list. The list did not include *Lernaea* species. The fish arrived at the delivery site, and the water temperature was properly adjusted before releasing them into the new holding facility. The fish culturist later recalled seeing these· long, slender objects with paired "appendages" (egg sacs) on some of the fish prior to their being released into the pond facility. The organisms had never been observed by the fish culturist, who also had no idea of the future consequences of a *Lernaea* infection at the facility. The delivery was made several years ago. Mortality directly related to *Lernaea* sp. has occurred, and some fish have been unsalable. Attempts to eliminate the parasite have failed; some parasites resist all such efforts. Much economic loss has resulted from the single unfortunate importation of fish.

Overcrowding fishes in fish culture facilities which also harbor crustacean parasites can be disastrous during warm-water periods of the year. Some fishes may die as a direct result of the crustacean infection, and others may be badly injured, which results in reduced growth, unthriftiness and loss of vitality. Those fishes which do survive to marketable size may be scarred and demonstrate ulcerated areas or lost scales. They may be unsalable as ornamental fishes, bait minnows or processed food fish.

Overcrowding of fishes, with subsequent increased crustacean parasite infestation, may also happen among wild-ranging fishes. Periods of low water flow in streams or excessive evaporation in ponds or lakes may concentrate fishes. These conditions quite often are present during late summer periods when water is warm, especially in arid parts of the world. Irrigation and flood control reservoirs are usually drained down during late summer, with crustacean parasites and fishes concentrated into the minimum pool. These situations are ideal for the parasite, and heavy fish losses may result. Reservoir engineers and fishery managers can plan reservoir construction so that the minimum pool is not an invitation to fish and parasite concentration.

Selected References

1. Amlacher, E. 1970. *Textbook of fish diseases*. T.F.H. Publ., Neptune, NJ. 302p.

2. Ariola, V. 1899. "Il gen *Scyphocephalus* Rigg. e proposta di une nuova classificazione dei cestodi," *Att. Soc. Ligust. Sci. Nat. Geogr. Genova.*, 10: 160-167.

3. Bauer, O. N. and G. L. Hoffman. 1976. "Helminth range extension by translocation of fish," *In* L. A. Page, ed. *Wildlife diseases*. Plenum Publ. Corp., New York City, NY. p. 163-172.

4. Becker, C. D. 1977. "Flagellate parasites of fishes," *In* J. P. Krier, ed. *Parasitic protozoa*, 1:357-416. Academic Press, New York City, NY.

5. Becker, C. D. 1968. "The bass tapeworm: a problem in northwest trout management," *Prog. Fish-Cult.*, 30:76-83.

6. Becker, C. D. and W. D. Brunson. 1966. "Transmission of *Diplostomum flexicaudum* to trout by ingestion of precocious metacercariae in molluscs," *J. Parasitol.*, 52:829-830.

7. Bedinger, C. A., Jr. and T. G. Meade. 1967. "Biology of a new cercaria for *Posthodiplostomum minimum* (Trematoda:Diplostomidae)," *J. Parasitol.*, 53: 985-988.

8. Benish, J. 1937. "Untersuchungen uber *Costia necatrix* Leclerc," *Zeit. f. Fisherei*, 34:755-770.

8a. Boonyaratpalin, S. and W. A. Rogers. 1984. "Control of the bass tapeworm, *Proteocephalus ambloplitis* (Leidy), with mebendazole." *J. Fish Dis.* 7:449-456.

9. Brown, F. J. 1927. "On *Crepidostomum farionis* O.F. Muller (*Stephanophiala laureata* Zeder), a distome parasite of the trout and grayling," *Parasitol.*, 19: 86-99.

10. Bykhovskaya-Pavlovskaya, E. I., et al. 1964. *Key to the parasites of freshwater fish of the U.S.S.R.* Trans. Israel Program for Sci. Trans., Nat. Sci. Found., Washington, DC. 919p.

10a. Coley, T. C., A. J. Chacko and G. W. Klontz. 1983. "Development of a lavage technique for sampling *Ceratomyxa shasta* in adult salmonids." *J. Fish Dis.*, 6:317-319.

11. Colley, F. C. and A. C. Olson. 1963. "*Posthodiplostomum minimum* (Trematoda: Displostomidae) in fishes of lower Otay Reservoir, San Diego County, California," *J. Parasitol.*, 49:148.

12. Canning, E. U. 1977. "Microsporidia," *In* J. P. Kreier, ed. *Parasitic protozoa: Babesia, Theileria, Myxosporida, Microsporida, Bartonellaceae, Anaplasmataceae, Ehrlichia, and Pneumocystis,* 4:155-196. Academic Press, New York City, NY.

13. Chitwood, M. B. 1969. "The systematics and biology of some parasite nematodes," *In* M. Florkin and B. T. Scheer, eds. *Chemical zoology,* 3:223-244. Academic Press, New York City, NY.

13a. Clifton-Hadley, R. S., D. Bucke and R. H. Richards. 1984. "Proliferative kidney disease of salmonid fish: A review." *J. Fish Dis.*, 7:363-377.

14. Connor, R. S. 1953. "A study of the seasonal cycle of proteocephalan cestode, *Proteocephalus stizostethi* Hunter and Bangham, found in the yellow pike-perch, *Stizostediom vitreum vitreum* (Mitchell)," *J. Parasitol.*, 39:621-624.

15. Conrad, J. F. and M. Decew. 1966. "First report of *Ceratomyxa* in juvenile salmonids in Oregon," *Prog. Fish-Cult.*, 28:238.

16. Creplin, F. C. H. 1842. "Psorosperms of *Acerina vulgaris* Wiegm.," *Arch. f. Naturge.*, 1:61-63.

17. Cressey, R. F. 1972. *The genus Argulus (Crustacea: Branchiura) of the United States. Biota of freshwater ecosystems. Identification Manual,* No. 2. U.S. Govt. Print. Off., Washington, DC. 14p.

18. Cross, D. G. 1972. "A review of methods to control ichthyopthiriasis," *Prog. Fish-Cult.*, 34: 165-170.

19. Davis, H. S. 1953. *Culture and diseases of game fishes.* Univ. of Calif. Press, Berkeley and Los Angeles, CA. 332p.

20. Davis, H. S. 1947. *Studies of the protozoan parasites of fresh-water fishes.* U.S. Fish Wildl. Serv. Fish Bull., 41. 29p and 224 fig.

21. Davis, H. S. 1926. "*Schizamoeba salmonis*, a new amoeba parasitic in salmonid fishes," *Bull. U.S. Bur. Fish.*, 42 (Doc. 988, 1925):1-8.

21a. D'Silva, J., M. F. Mulcahy and P. de Kinkelin. 1984. "Experimental transmission of proliferative kidney disease in rainbow trout, *Salmo gairdneri* Richardson." *J. Fish Dis.*, 7:235-239.

22. Elkan, E. and H. Reichenbach-Klinke. 1974. *Color atlas of the diseases of fishes, amphibians and rep-tiles.* T.F.H. Publ., Neptune, NJ. 256p.

22a. Ellis, A. E., A. H. McVicar and A. L. S. Munro. 1985. "Proliferative kidney disease in brown trout, *Salmo trutta* L. and Atlantic salmon, *Salmo salar* L. parr: histopathology and epidemiological observations." *J. Fish Dis.*, 8:197-208.

23. Fish, F. F. 1940. "Formalin for external protozoan parasites," *Prog. Fish-Cult.*, 38:1-10.

23a. Ferguson, H. W. 1981. "The effect of water temperature on the development of proliferative kidney disease in rainbow trout, *Salmo gairdneri* Richardson." *J. Fish Dis.*, 4:175-177.

23b. Ghittino, P., S. Andruetto and E. Vigliani. 1977. "L'amebiasi della trotta iridea d'Allevamento." *Riv. Ital. di Piscicult. Ittiopat.*, 12:74-89.

23c. Goven, B. A., D. L. Dawe and J. B. Gratzek. 1980. "Protection of channel catfish, *Ictalurus punctatus* Rafinesque, against *Ichthyophthirius multifiliis* Fouquet by immunization." *J. Fish Biol.*, 17:311-316.

23d. Goven, B. A. and D. A. Amend. 1983. "Mebendazole/trichlorfon combination: a new antihelmintic for removing monogenetic trematodes from fish." *J. Fish Biol.*, 20:373-378.

23e. Gratzek, J. B., J. P. Gilbert, A. L. Lohr, E. B. Shotts and J. Brown. 1983. "Ultraviolet light control of *Ichthyophthirius multifiliis* Fouquet in a closed system fish culture recirculation system." *J. Fish Dis.*, 6:145-153.

24. Harding, J. P. 1950. "On some species of *Lernaea* (Crustacea, copepods: parasites on freshwater fish)," *Brit. Mus. (Nat. Hist.) Bull. Zool.*, 1:1-27.

24a. Hedrick, R. P., M. L. Kent, J. S. Foott, R. Rosemark and D. Manzer. 1985. "Proliferative kidney disease in California: a second look." *FHS-AFS Newsletter*, 13(2):4-5.

24b. Hedrick, R. P., M. L. Kent, J. S. Foott, R. Rosemark and D. Manzer. 1985. "Proliferative kidney disease (PKD) among salmonid fish in California, U.S.A.: A second look." *Bull. Eur. Asso. Fish Pathol.*, 5:36-38.

24c. Hedrick, R. P., M. L. Kent, R. Rosemark and D. Manzer. 1984. "Proliferative kidney disease (PKD) in Pacific salmon and steelhead trout." *J. World Maricult. Soc.* 15:318-325.

25. Hine, P. M. 1975. "*Eimeria anguillae* Leger and Hollande, 1922, parasitic in New Zealand eels," *N.Z. J. Mar. Freshwater Res.*, 9:239-243.

25a. Hines, R. S. and D. T. Spira. 1974. "Ichthyophthiriasis in the mirror carp *Cyprinus carpio* (L.) V. Acquired immunity." *J. Fish Biol.*, 373-378.

26. Hofer, B. 1903. "Uber die Drehkrankheit der Regenbogenforelle," *Allgem. Fisch. Zeit.*, 28:7-8.

26a. Hoffman, G. L. 1985. "Addendum to fish disease leaflet 47." *FHS-AFS Newsletter*, 13(1):1.

26b. Hoffman, G. L. 1985. "Anchor parasite (*Lernaea cyprinacea*) control." *FHS-AFS Newsletter*, 13(4):4.

27. Hoffman, G. L. 1978. "Ciliates of freshwater fishes," *In* J. P. Kreier, ed. *Parasitic protozoa: Intestinal flagellates, histomonads, trichomonads, amoeba, opalinids and ciliates*, 2:583-632. Academic Press, New York City, NY.

28. Hoffman, G. L. 1965. "*Eimeria aurati* n. sp. (Protozoa: Eimeriidae) from goldfish (*Carassius auratus*) in North America," *J. Protozool.*, 12:273-275.

29. Hoffman, G. L. 1977. *Argulus, a branchiuran parasite of freshwater fishes. Fish Dis. Leafl.*, 49. U.S. Fish Wildl. Serv., Div. Fish Cult. Meth. Res., Washington, DC. 9p.

30. Hoffman, G. L. 1976. *Whirling disease of trout. U.S. Fish Wildl. Serv. Fish Disease Leaflet*, No. 47. 10p.

31. Hoffman, G. L. 1976. "The Asian tapeworm, *Bothriocephalus gowkongenesis*, in the United States, and research needs in fish parasitology," *Proc. 1976 Fish Farming Conf. and Catfish Farmers of Texas*. Texas A and M Univ., College Station, TX. p. 84-90.

32. Hoffman, G. L. 1976. *"Parasites of freshwater fishes. IV. Miscellaneous. The Anchor Parasite (Lernaea elegans) and related species." Fish Dis. Leafl.*, 46. U.S. Fish Wildl. Serv., Div. Cult. Method Res., Washington, DC. 8p.

33. Hoffman, G. L. 1975. "Whirling disease (*Myxosoma cerebralis*): control with ultraviolet irradiation and effect on fish," *J. Wildl. Dis.*, 11:505-507.

34. Hoffman, G. L. 1970. "Whirling disease of trout and salmon caused by *Myxosoma cerebralis* in the United States of America," *Riv. It. Piscic. Ittiopat.*, 2: 29-33.

35. Hoffman, G. L. 1967. *Parasites of North America freshwater fishes*. Univ. Calif. Press, Berkeley, CA. 486p.

36. Hoffman, G. L. 1960. *Synopsis of Strigeoidae (Trematoda) of fishes and their life cycles. Fish. Bull.*, 175, Vol. 60. U.S. Fish Wildl. Serv., Washington, DC. p. 439-469.

37. Hoffman, G. L. 1958. "Experimental studies on the cercaria and metacercaria of a strigeid trematode, *Posthodiplostomum minimum*," *Exp. Parasitol.*, 7: 23-50.

38. Hoffman, G. L., C. E. Dunbar and A. Bradford. 1962. *Whirling Disease of trouts caused by Myxosoma cerebralis in the United States. Spec. Sci. Rept. Fish*, No. 427. U.S. Fish Wildl. Serv., Washington, DC. 15p.

39. Hoffman, G. L., Sr. and G. L. Hoffman, Jr. 1972. "Studies on the control of whirling disease, *Myxosoma cerebralis*. 1. The effects of chemicals on spores *in vitro*, and of calcium oxide as a disinfectant in simulated ponds," *J. Wildl. Dis.*, 8:49-53.

40. Hoffman, G. L. and F. P. Meyer. 1974. *Parasites of freshwater fishes, a review of their control and treatment.* T.F.H. Publ., Neptune, NJ. 224p.

41. Hoffman, G. L. and J. J. O'Grodnick. 1977. "Control of whirling disease (*Myxosoma cerebralis*): effects of drying and disinfection with hydrated lime or chlorine," *J. Fish. Biol.*, 10:175-179.

42. Hoffman, G. L. and R. E. Putz. 1969. "Host susceptibility and the effect of aging, freezing, heat and chemicals on spores of *Myxosoma cerebralis*," *Prog. Fish-Cult.*, 31:35-37.

43. Hoffman, G. L. and R. E. Putz. 1965. "The blackspot (*Uvulifer ambloplitis*: Trematoda: Strigeoidea) of centrarchid fishes," *Trans. Am. Fish. Soc.*, 94: 143-151.

44. Levine, N. D., J. O. Corliss, F. E. G. Cox, G. Deroux, J. Grain, B. M. Honigberg, G. F. Leedale, A. R. Loeblich, III, J. Lom, D. Lynn, E. G. Merinfeld, F. C. Page, G. Poljansky, V. Sprague, J. Vavra and F. G. Wallace. 1980. "A newly revised classification of the Protozoa." *J. Protozool.*, 27:36-58.

45. Hopkins, C. A. 1959. "Seasonal variations in the incidence and development of the cestode *Proteocephalus filicollis* (Rud. 1810) in *Gasterosteus aculeatus* (L. 1766)," *Parasitol.*, 49:529-542.

46. Kabata, Z. 1970. *Diseases of fishes. Book 1: Crustacea as enemies of fishes.* T.F.H. Publ., Neptune, NJ. 171p.

46a. Kent, M. L. and R. P. Hedrick. 1985. "Transmission of the causative agent of proliferative kidney disease (PKD) with the blood and spleen of infected fish: Further evidence that the PKX parasite belongs to the phylum Myxozoa." *Bull. Eur. Asso. Fish Pathol.* 5:39-42.

46b. Kent, M. L. and R. P. Hedrick. 1985. "PKX, the causative agent of proliferative kidney disease (PKD) in Pacific salmonid fishes and its affinities with Myxozoa." *J. Protozool.*, 32:254-260.

47. Khalifa, K. A. 1973. *Tissue damage caused by Lernaea cyprinacea (a copepod parasite) and its developmental stages.* Unpubl. M.S. Thesis, Colo. State Univ., Fort Collins, CO. 91p.

48. Khalifa, K. A. and G. Post. 1976. "Histological effect of *Lernaea cyprinacea* (a copepod parasite) on fish," *Prog. Fish-Cult.*, 38:110-113.

49. Klein, W. D., O. W. Olsen and D. C. Bowden. 1969. "Effects of intestinal flukes, *Crepidostomum farionis*, on rainbow trout, *Salmo gairdnerii*," *Trans. Am. Fish Soc.*, 98:1-6.

50. Kudo, R. R. 1966. *Protozoology.* Charles C.

Thomas Publ., Springfield, IL. 1,174p.

51. Landolt, M. L. 1973. "*Myxosoma cerebralis:* Isolation and concentration from fish skeletal elements—trypsin digestion method," *J. Fish. Res. Bd. Can.*, 30:1713-1716.

52. LaRue, G. 1914. "A revision of the cestode family Proteocephalidae," *Ill. Biol. Monogr.*, 1:1-350.

52a. Lemly, A. D. and G. W. Esch. 1984. "Effects of the trematode *Uvulifer ambloplitis* on juvenile bluegill sunfish, *Lepomis macrochurus:* Ecological implications." *J. Parasitol.*, 70:475-492.

53. Levine, N. D. 1973. *Protozoan parasites of domestic animals and man.* Burgess Publ. Co., Minneapolis, MN 406p.

54. Lom, J. and G. L. Hoffman. 1971. "Morphology of the spores of *Myxoxoma cerebralis* (Hofer, 1903) and *M. cartilaginis* (Hoffman, Putz and Dunbar, 1965)," *J. Parasitol.*, 57:1302-1308.

55. MacCallum, G. A. 1921. "Studies in helminthology," *Zoopath., N.Y. Zool. Soc.*, 1:135-204.

56. Margolis, L. 1977. "Public health aspects of 'codworm' infection. A review," *J. Fish. Res. Bd. Can.*, 34:887-898.

56a. Markiw, M. E. 1986. "Salmonid whirling disease: Dynamics of experimental production of the infective stage—the triactinomyxon spore." *Can. J. Fish. & Aquat. Sci.*, 43:521-526.

56b. Markiw, M. E. and K. Wolf. 1983. "*Myxosoma cerebralis* (Myxozoa: Myxosporea) etiologic agent of salmonid whirling disease requires tubificid worm (Annelida: Oligochaeta) in its life cycle." *J. Protozool.*, 30:561-564.

57. Markiw, M. E. and K. Wolf. 1978. "*Myxosoma cerebralis:* Fluorescent antibody techniques for antigen recognition," *J. Fish. Res. Bd. Can.*, 35:828-832.

58. Markiw, M. E. and K. Wolf. 1974. "*Myxosoma cerebralis:* Isolation and concentration from fish skeletal elements—sequential enzyme digestion and purification by differential centrifugation," *J. Fish. Res. Bd. Can.*, 31:15-20.

59. McCraren, J. P., M. L. Landolt, G. L. Hoffman and F. P. Meyer. 1975. "Variation in response of channel catfish to *Henneguya* sp. infections (Protozoa: Myxosporidea)," *J. Wildl. Dis.*, 11:2-7.

60. McElwain, I. B. 1966. *Cyzine efficacy for trout hexamitiasis.* Unpubl. M.S. Thesis. Colo. St. Univ., Ft. Collins, CO. 35p.

61. McElwain, I. B. and G. Post. 1968. "Efficacy of cyzine for trout hexamitiasis," *Prog. Fish-cult.*, 30: 84-91.

62. Meehan, O. L. 1940. "A review of the parasitic crustacea of the genus *Argulus* in the collection of the U.S. National Museum," *Proc. U.S. Natl. Mus.*, 88(3087):459-522.

63. Meyer, F. P. 1966. *Ichthyopthirius multifiliis.* U.S. Fish Wildl. Serv., FDL-2. 4p.

64. Meyers, T. R., T. K. Sawyer and S. A. MacLean. 1977. "*Henneguya* sp. (Cnidospora:Myxosporida) parasitic in the heart of the bluefish, *Pomatomus saltatrix*," *J. Parasitol.*, 65:890-896.

65. Meyers, T. U., J. Scala and E. Simmons. 1970. "Modes of transmission of whirling disease of trout," *Nature*, 227:622-623.

65a. Mitchell, A. J., C. E. Smith and G. L. Hoffman. 1982. "Pathogenicity and histopathology of an unusually intense infection of white grub (*Postodiplostomum minimum*) in the fathead minnow (*Pimephales promelas*)." *J. Wildl. Dis.*, 18:51-57.

65b. Mitchell, A. J. and G. L. Hoffman. 1980. "Important tapeworms of North American freshwater fishes." *U.S. Dep. Int., Fish & Wildl. Serv. Fish Dis. Leafl.*, 59, 18 p.

66. Mitchell, L. G. 1978. "Myxosporidan infections in some fishes of Iowa," *J. Protozool.*, 25:100-105.

67. Mitchell, L. G. 1977. "Myxosporida," *In* J. P. Kreier, ed. *Parasitic protozoa: Babesia, Theileria, Myxosporida, Microsporida, Bartonellaceae, Anaplasmataceae, Ehrlichia and Pneumocystis*, 4:115-154. Academic Press, New York City, NY.

68. Mitchell, A. J. and G. L. Hoffman. 1978. "Species identification of fish parasites in diagnosis," *Proc. 3rd Biann. Fish Health Sec., Am. Fish. Soc.* p. 53.

69. Mitchum, D. L. and T. D. Moore. 1966. "Efficacy of Di-N-Butyl tin oxide on an intestinal fluke, *Crepidostomum farionis*, in golden trout," *Prog. Fish-Cult.*, 31:143-148.

70. Moore, E. 1922. "*Octomitus salmonis*, a new species of intestinal parasite in trout," *Trans. Am. Fish. Soc.*, 52:74-97.

71. Morrison, R. G. 1957. *The incidence and distribution of the bass tapeworm (Proteocephalus ambloplitis) in southern New Hampshire.* N.H. Game Fish Dept. Tech. Circ., No. 13. 33p.

72. Noble, E. R. 1950. "On a myxosporidian (protozoan) parasite of California trout," *J. Parasitol.*, 36: 457-460.

73. Noble, E. R. and Noble, G. A. 1971. *Parasitology: The biology of animal parasites.* Lea and Febiger, Philadelphia, PA. 617p.

74. Noble, E. R. and G. A. Noble. 1966. "Amebic parasites of fishes," *J. Protozool.*, 13:478-480.

75. O'Grodnick, J. J. 1975. "Whirling disease, *Myxosoma cerebralis*, spore concentration using the continuous plankton centrifuge," *J. Wildl. Dis.*, 11:54-57.

76. O'Grodnick, J. 1975. "Egg transmissions of whirling disease," *Prog. Fish-Cult.*, 37:153-154.

77. Palmer, E. 1939. "Diplostomiasis, a hatchery dis-

ease of freshwater fishes new to North America," *Prog. Fish-Cult.*, 4:41-47.

78. Palmieri, J. R. 1976. "Life cycle and incidence of *Diplostomum spathaceum* Rudolphi (1819) (Trematoda: Diplostomatidae) in Utah," *Great Basin Nat.*, 36:86-96.

79. Pauley, B. G. 1974. "Fish sporozoa: Extraction of antigens from *Myxosoma cerebralis* spores which mimic tissue antigens of rainbow trout (*Salmo gairdneri*)," *J. Fish. Res. Bd. Can.*, 31:1481-1484.

80. Pierce, U. D. Jr. 1972. "The bass tapeworm," *Maine Fish & Game Mag.*, Summer, 1972:B-311.

81. Pitt, C. E. and A. W. Grundmann. 1957. "A study into the effects of parasitism on the growth of the yellow perch produced by the larvae of *Ligula intestinalis* (Linnaeus 1758) Gmelin 1970," *Proc. Helminth. Soc., Wash.*, 24:73-90.

82. Plehn, M. 1904. "Uber die Drehrankheit der Salmoniden (*Lentospora cerebralis* Hofer, Plehn)," *Arch. Protistenkunde Bd..*, 5:145-166.

83. Post, G. 1971. *The Diphyllobothrium cestode in Yellowstone Lake, Wyoming. Res. J.*, 41. Univ. Wyo. Agri. Exp. Sta., Laramie, WY. 24p.

84. Post, G. and M. M. Beck. 1966. "Toxicity, tissue residue and efficacy of enheptin given orally to rainbow trout for hexamitiasis," *Prog. Fish-Cult.*, 28: 83-88.

85. Preece, A. 1972. *A manual for histological technicians. Third Ed.* Little, Brown and Co., Boston, MA. 428p.

86. Putz, R. E. 1972. *Biological studies on the hemoflagellates Cryptobia cataractae and Cryptobia salmositica.* U.S. Fish Wildl. Serv. Tech. Paper, No. 63. 25p.

87. Putz, R. E. 1969. *Microsporida of fishes.* U.S. Fish Wildl. Serv., Div. Fish. Res., FDL-20. 4p.

88. Putz, R. E. and G. L. Hoffman. 1966. "Earliest susceptibility age of rainbow trout to whirling disease," *Prog. Fish-Cult.*, 28:82.

89. Putz, R. E., G. L. Hoffman and C. E. Dunbar. 1965. "Two new species of *Plistophora* (Microsporidea) from North American fish with a synopsis of Microsporidea of freshwater and euryhaline fishes," *J. Protozool.*, 12:228-236.

90. Reichenbach-Klinke, H. 1973. *Fish Pathology.* T.F.H. Publ., Neptune, NJ. 512p.

91. Reichenbach-Klinke, H. and E. Elkan. 1965. *The principal diseases of lower vertebrates.* Academic Press, London and New York City. 600p.

92. Rogers, W. A. and J. L. Gaines, Jr. 1975. "Lesions of protozoan diseases of fish," *In* W. E. Ribelin and G. Migaki, eds. *The pathology of fishes.* Univ. Wis. Press, Madison, WI. p. 117-141.

93. Sanders, J. E., J. L. Fryer and R. W. Gould. 1970.

"Occurrence of the myxosporidian parasite, *Ceratomyxa shasta,* in salmonid fish from the Columbia River basin and Oregon coastal streams," *In* S. F. Snieszko, ed. *A symposium on diseases of fishes and shellfishes. Am. Fish. Soc., Spec. Publ.,* No. 5: 133-141.

93a. Seagrave, C. P., D. Bucke and D. J. Alderman. 1980. "Ultrastructure of a haplosporean-like organism: the possible causative agent of proliferative kidney disease in rainbow trout." *J. Fish Bio.*, 16:453-459.

94. Schafer, W. E. 1968. "Studies on the epizootiology of the myxosporidan *Ceratomyxa shasta* Noble," *Calif. Fish & Game*, 54:90-99.

95. Schaperclaus, W. 1954. *Fischkrankheiten.* AkademieVerlag. Berlin, Germany, 708p.

96. Scott, A. 1901. "On the fish parasites, *Lepeophtheirus* and *Lernaea*," *Proc. Trans. Liverp. Biol. Soc.*, 15: 188-241.

96a. Shimura, S. and K. Inoue. 1984. "Toxic effects of extract from mouth parts of *Argulus coregoni* Thorell (Crustacea: Branchiura)." *Bull. Jpn. Soc. Sci. Fish.*, 50:729.

96b. Smith, C. E., J. K. Morrison, H. W. Ramsey and H. W. Ferguson. 1984. "Proliferative kidney disease: first reported outbreak in North America." *J. Fish Dis.*, 7:207-216.

97. Smith, F. G. 1975. "Crustacean parasites of marine fishes," *In* W. E. Ribelin and G. Migaki, eds. *The pathology of fishes.* Univ. Wis. Press, Madison, WI. p. 189-203.

98. Spall, R. D. and R. C. Summerfelt. 1970. "Life cycle of the white grub, *Posthodiplostomum minimum* (MacCallum, 1921: Trematoda, Diplostomatidae), and observations on host-parasite relationships of the metacercaria in fish," *In* S. F. Snieszko, ed. *A symposium on diseases of fishes and shellfishes. Am. Fish. Soc., Spec. Publ.,* No. 5:218-230.

98a. Speed, P .and B. Pauley. 1985. "Feasibility of protecting rainbow trout, *Salmo gairdneri* Richardson, by immunizing against the eye fluke *Diplostomum spathaeceum*." *J. Fish Biol.*, 26:475-492.

99. Summerfelt, R. C. 1964. "A new microsporidian parasite from the golden shiner, *Notemigonus crysoleucas*," *Trans. Am. Fish. Soc.*, 93:6-10.

100. Summerfelt, R. C. and M. C. Warner, 1970. "Incidence and intensity of infection of *Plistophora ovariae*, a microsporidian parasite of the golden shiner, *Notemigonus crysoleucas*," *In* S. F. Snieszko, ed. *A symposium on diseases of fishes and shellfishes. Am. Fish. Soc., Spec. Publ.,* No. 5:142-160.

101. Taylor, P. W. 1977. "Isolation and experimental infection of free-living amebae in freshwater

fishes," *J. Parasitol.*, 63:232-237.

102. Taylor, R. L. and M. Lott. 1978. "Transmission of salmonid whirling disease by birds fed trout infected with *Myxosoma cerebralis*," *J. Protozool.*, 25:105-106.

103. Tidd, W. M. 1934. "Recent infestation of goldfish and carp with the 'anchor parasite,' *L. carassii*," *Trans. Am. Fish. Soc.*, 64:176-180.

104. Thomas, J. D. 1958. Studies on *Crepidostomum metoecus* (Braun) and *C. farionis* (Muller) parasitic in *Salmo trutta* L. and *S. salar* L. in Britain," *Parasitol.*, 48:336-352.

105. Uspenskaya, A. V. 1963. "Whirling disease of trout and salmon caused by *Myxosoma cerebralis* in the United States," *Riv. It. Piscic, Ittiopat.*, 2:29-31. (See G. L. Hoffman, 1970.)

106. Uzmann, J. R., G. J. Paulik and S. H. Hayduk. 1965. "Experimental hexamitiasis in juvenile coho salmon (*Oncorhynchus kisutch*) and steelhead trout (*Salmo gairdneri*)," *Trans. Am. Fish. Soc.*, 94:53-61.

107. van Duijn, C., Jr. 1973. *Diseases of fishes*. Charles C. Thomas Publ., Springfield, IL. 372p.

108. van Haitsma, J. P. 1930. "Studies on the trematode family Strigeidae (Holostomidae) XXIII: *Diplostomum flexicaudum* (Cort and Brooks) and stages in its life history," *Pap. Mich. Acad. Sci. Arts Lett.*, 13:483-516.

109. Voelker, F. A., M. R. Anver, A. E. McKee, H. W. Casey and G. R. Brenniman. 1977. "Amebiasis in goldfish," *Vet. Pathol.*, 14:247-255.

110. Wales, J. H. 1958. "Intestinal flukes as a possible cause of mortality in wild trout," *Calif. Fish & Game*, 44:350-352.

111. Wales, J. H. and H. Wolf. 1955. "Three protozoan diseases of trout in California," *Calif. Fish & Game*, 41:183-187.

112. Wardle, R. A. and J. A. McLeod. 1952. *The zoology of tapeworms*. Univ. Minn. Press, Minneapolis, MN. 780p.

113. Wilson, C. B. 1918. "The economic relations, anatomy and life history of the genus *Lernaea*," *U.S. Bur. Fish. Bull.*, 35:165-198.

114. Wilson, C. B. 1917. "North American parasitic copepods belonging to the Lernaeidae with revision of the entire family," *Proc. U.S. Natl. Mus.*, 53: 1-150.

114a. Wolf, K., M. E. Markiw, J. Machado, M. H. Galhano, J. Eiras and R. L. Herman. 1981. "Nonmyxosporidan blacktail in salmonids." *J. Fish Dis.*, 4:355:357.

114b. Wolf, K. 1986. "Salmonid whirling disease: Status in the United States, 1985." *J. Wildl. Dis.*, 22:295-299.

114c. Wolf, K. and M. E. Markiw. 1984. "Biology contravenes taxonomy in the Myxozoa: New discoveries show alternation of invertebrate and vertebrate hosts." *Science*, 225:1449-1452.

115. Yamaguti, S. 1963. *Parasitic Copepoda and Branchiura of fishes*. Intersci. Publ., New York City, NY. 1,104p.

116. Yamaguti, S. 1959. *Systema helminthum. II. The cestodes of vertebrates*. Intersci. Pub., New York City, NY. 860p.

117. Yasutake, W. T. and H. Wolf. 1970. "Occurrence of whirling disease in western United States," *J. Fish. Res. Bd. Can.*, 27:955-957.

118. Yasutake, W. T. and E. M. Wood. 1957. "Some myxosporidia found in Pacific northwest salmonids," *J. Parasitol.*, 43:633-642.

119. Yoder, W. G. 1972. "The spread of *Myxosoma cerebralis* into native trout populations of Michigan," *Prog. Fish-Cult.*, 34:103-106.

120. Zinn, J. L., K. A. Johnson, J. E. Sanders and J. L. Fryer. 1977. "Susceptibility of salmonid species and hatchery strains of chinook salmon (*Oncorhynchus tshawytscha*) to infections of *Ceratomyxa shasta*," *J. Fish. Res. Bd. Can.*, 34:933-936.

Chapter VIII

IMMUNE RESPONSE
IN FISHES

The immune response has been used to control infectious diseases since 1796, when a vaccine was used for smallpox in humans. The work of Koch and Pasteur during the middle and latter years of the 1800's demonstrated the usefulness of immunizing agents to reduce or eliminate certain diseases in animals, including humans.

The study of immune responses in fishes was apparently not attempted prior to 1903, when agglutinating antibodies against a bacterium were demonstrated in the blood of carp. Very few articles on immunity in fishes had been published by 1960.[11,17,38,46,48,49] The 1960 decade saw an increased interest in immunological studies of fishes, partly by comparative immunologists with a prime interest in evolutionary processes and partly by a few people with an interest in finding ways of controlling troublesome diseases among cultured fishes.

Evolution has been responsible for various basic biological responses in animals. The immune response no doubt came about as a protective mechanism. Animals evolving a usable immune capability necessary for survival in the accustomed environment have remained, while those without this capability perished. Fishes are the most primitive vertebrates, but they, too, had to develop an immune system proficient enough to react and protect them from attack by various microorganisms and animal parasites. Fishes living in various environments and under heterogeneous sociological structures developed acceptable immune response mechanisms for each condition. The solitary fish species living in a coldwater environment where pathogen generation time is extended does not need an effective immune response. These fish can allow ordinarily pathogenic bacteria to circulate in their bloodstream, generation time of the bacteria being so slow that there is no danger of it overwhelming its host. Fishes living in schools (where pathogens are easily passed from fish to fish) and at an environmental temperature conducive to rapid generation of microorganisms, need a more highly capable immune response system. Thus, the fishes of the world have developed a tremendous variation in immune substances, cells and organs.[15,18,27,31]

The host-pathogen relationship between infectious organisms and the host animal usually elicits a response in the host which serves to protect against ravages of the pathogen. All potential pathogens of fishes contain antigens: viral particles, bacteria or bacterial toxins, fungi or fungal toxins, and animal parasites. Antigens are complex substances, usually protein or protein-like polysaccharide, which stimulate immunological response in the animal. Antigens cannot stimulate this response unless they are within the tissues or body of the host.

Two types of immune response are elicited by most animals, probably including most fishes: a humoral response and a cellular response. The humoral response is described as a stimulation of serum protein molecular synthesis homologous or specific to the antigen causing the synthesis. These serum protein molecules (immunoglobulins) are called antibodies and circulate throughout the body, thus the name humoral. Cellular response to antigen stimulation is a sensitization of cellular elements of the reticuloendothelial system and phagocytic cells to the specific antigen. Both humoral antibodies and cellular immune responses are used by the animal to protect itself from infective agents of disease.[10,12]

Immunity of an animal to pathogens is a relative term. Some animals are completely *non-susceptible* to certain pathogens. Fishes, for example, are non-susceptible to the bacterium which causes bubonic plague of humans. Likewise, humans are non-susceptible to the infectious pancreatic necrosis virus of salmonid fishes. There is a fine line of distinction between the terms relative immunity, non-susceptibility and resistance.

Resistance of an animal to infection or disease-causing agents usually means there is a barrier within the host which allows the host to resist the pathogen. Resistance is used to describe those cases in which a host would be susceptible to the pathogen if the pathogen could pass the host's barriers. Resistance is usually associated with chemical or physical barriers. The mucus layer on the skin of fishes is both a physical and a chemical barrier to potential pathogens. It offers resistance to penetration of many microorganisms and contains a bactericidal substance useful in reducing bacterial flora on the skin. Entrance of certain pathogens through the alimentary tract of fishes may be blocked by the highly acid stomach or by intestinal epithelial barriers.

Natural immunity is attributed to inherited ability to produce antibodies against certain pathogens without actual stimulation by homologous antigens from the pathogens. Natural antibodies are the result of many generations of the host species living with the pathogen, to the point where a natural immunity has developed between the natural host and the potential pathogen.

Acquired immunity comes about when a host is stimulated by contact with antigens. Each generation of the host must be subjected to antigens of the pathogen before humoral or cellular immunity develops. Acquired immunity derived by the host in this way is called *active immunity*. Active acquired immunity can result from natural infections of pathogens or internal contact with antigens of the pathogen. Thus, the use of living avirulent strains of the pathogen, killed pathogens or antigens derived from killed pathogens can be used to establish relative immunity in the host against the pathogen without subjecting the host to the disease caused by the pathogen. Active acquired immunity is used when prepared antigens (bacterins, vaccines or other immunizing substances) are injected or caused to be absorbed into an animal. The animal becomes immune or partially immune without having to go through various stages of the disease.

One other type of relative immunity in animals is *passive immunity*. Passive immunity is described as immunity acquired from the use of antibodies produced by another animal. An animal subjected to antigens of a potential pathogen produces antibody proteins which circulate in the blood. The antibody proteins can be separated from the blood of the immunized animal, called the donor, and injected into a non-immunized animal, called the recipient. The recipient thus obtains a passive immunity from the donor. Passive immunity is usually a short-lived immunity but has found practical application in disease control among certain domestic animals and humans. Passive immunity has been used experimentally with fishes.[10]

The Immune System

There are several substances, cells and organs necessary for an animal to be immunologically competent. All of these elements are collectively called the immune system. A capable immune system in any animal must include organs of the reticuloendothelial system, with lymphocytes, plasmocytes and certain serum protein fractions. The reticuloendothelial system of fishes is composed of the anterior or head kidney, thymus, spleen and to some extent the liver.[28] The exact immunological activity of each organ is not entirely known in fishes. The function of similar organs in higher animals gives a clue to how they function in fishes. Therefore, some explanations given here are facts, others are conjectures.

The stem cells which become involved in the immune response are differentiated into two kinds of lymphocytes, B-lymphocytes and T-lymphocytes. B-lymphocytes, or B-cells, sometimes called bursa oriented cells, were given this name because they were first described in the bursa of Fabricius of the chicken. Lymphoid tissue in the Peyer's glands (patches) of the intestinal tract are thought to perform the same activity in mammals as

avian bursa of Fabricius tissue. There may be lymphoid-like tissue in the intestines of fishes capable of performing this activity, because orally administered bacterial antigens will stimulate production of homologous circulating antibody protein (Fig. 24).[10,12,15,17,18,40]

T-lymphocytes, or T-cells, also called thymus dependent cells, are found in the circulating blood of higher animals. T-cells of fishes have received only cursory study, and their exact activity is not well known in these animals.[9,10] T-cells are primarily responsible for the cellular immunity, usually referred to as cell mediated immunity.[3a,43a]

B-cells become involved in immune globulin (antibody protein) production through stimulation of splenic red-pulp and possibly liver of fishes. The liver of embryonic mammals contains stem cells, the activity of which is shifted to bone marrow at birth. The liver of fishes, either embryonic or throughout life, may also be an influential organ in immune response (Fig. 24).

The exact route for stimulation of antibody formation in fishes is not known, though all basic elements necessary for synthesis of these special proteins are present. Fishes have lymphocytes, macrophages, plasma cells and phagocytes, all essential to antibody formation. However, fishes do not have lymph nodes. A careful histological search failed to locate lymphoid tissue in various organs of rainbow trout outside of the thymus and hematopoietic tissue of kidneys and spleen.[28]

Fish may have a different system of cells useful for immune protection than higher animals. Lymphocyte-like cells present in the epidermal mucus and skin may be capable of cellular immune response, and a reason why contact between the outer surfaces of the fish body and immunizing substances elicits protection to the fish. These lymphocyte-like cells have been observed in several fish species, and may be present in all fish.[37a] Also, fish gills are known to have macrophages on or near the surface. These cells are no doubt important in eliciting and immune response with external contact immunogens.[3a,13]

The usual sequence of antibody formation begins by exposure of the animal to an antigen. The antigens of a bacterium will be used for purposes of explanation. A bacterium entering the body of a fish is either taken in by a phagocyte and transported to the splenic red-pulp or possibly to the anterior kidney, where antigens are released. Non-phagocytized bacteria may enter the spleen without assistance from the phagocytic cells. The antigens are released from phagocytes or from non-phagocytized organisms taken up by macrophages. The macrophages process the bacterium into all antigens, releasing them to B-cells and plasma cells. The plasma cells and B-cells are programmed to produce antibodies homologous to the antigens (Fig. 24).[10,12]

The serum proteins of fishes are varied among taxonomic groups. However, one common finding among

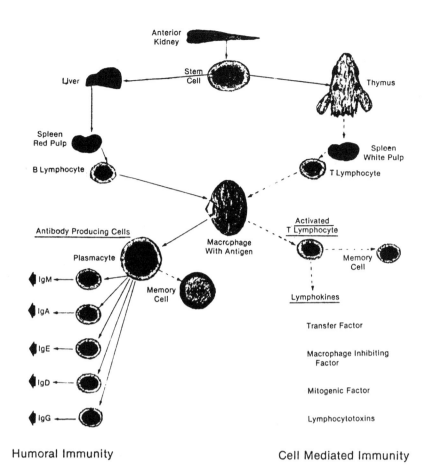

Fig. 24: The immune response in fishes. Routes with solid lines are known, routes with broken lines are speculative.

Humoral Immunity   Cell Mediated Immunity

fishes is the lack or near lack of certain globulins, especially those found as very important immune globulins of higher animals. Serum fractions of higher vertebrates include albumins and four globulins (alpha$_1$, alpha$_2$ beta and gamma). Most immune globulins of higher animals are present in the gamma and beta globulins. The near lack of gamma globulin in fish serum may illustrate why fishes are not as immunologically competent as higher vertebrates (Pl. 27B).[40,41]

An examination of the immunoglobulins and their usefulness in the immune response of higher vertebrates may assist in understanding the somewhat reduced relative immune response in fishes.[14] Research has indicated that the immunoglobulins of fishes are all macroglobulins, and that is about as far as direct correlation can be made. Fishes have little or no immunoglobulin fraction similar to IgG of higher animals. IgG is the most important component of antiviral, antibacterial and antitoxin bodies of higher animals and makes up about 80% of all immunoglobulins. The major immunoglobulin class of fishes with bacterial and viral antibody function is similar to IgM of higher animals.[45] Thus fishes will react differently to bacterial and viral antigens by forming an

IgM equivalent, with no IgG counterpart. Nothing is known for certain of immunoglobulins of fishes comparable to other immunoglobulin classes of higher animals: i.e., IgA, IgE and IgD. Table 23 lists the classes of immunoglobulins of higher animals (humans) and the known primary function of each class.[34] Some of these immunoglobulin functions are known in fishes, but immunoglobulin distribution and characterization are not known.[26,33,34,35,36,50]

Other substances involved in immune response or natural resistance have been identified in fish. Transferrin, lysozyme, interferon, complement and natural agglutinins and lysins display antimicrobial activity and have been identified in a wide range of fish species.[27a,45a]

Temperature and the Immune Response in Fishes

The body temperature of resting fishes is near the environmental temperature. Pathogen generation time is also temperature-related. Thus, fishes living in cold temperatures, less than 7°C, have little need for an immune response because pathogen reproduction, in most instances, is too slow to be detrimental to the host. Even toxin production by pathogens is slowed to the point it no longer is a threat. Therefore, the logical evolution of

TABLE 23

Immunoglobulin classes of higher animals (humans) and their function[10,12]

Class	Molecular Weight (dalton)	Percent of Antibody Protein	Function
IgG	148,000	80	Bacterial, viral and toxin type antibodies formed following initial IgM synthesis.
IgA	170,000 to 400,000	10 to 15	Antimicrobial activity in secretions of the various tracts, the main immunoglobulin in saliva and gastrointestinal secretions.
IgM[a]	870,000 to 970,000	7	IgM is the first antibody protein in circulation following stimulation by antigens from bacteria, virus or toxins, later to be reduced as IgG appears; IgM can bind complement.
IgD	200,000	less than 1%	Activity not known or characterized, but possesses antibody activity; does not bind complement.
IgE	200,000	less than 1%	Antibody of anaphylaxis and atopic allergies.

[a]The molecular weight of most bacterial and viral antibodies of bony fishes is greater than 800,000 daltons[13,14,26,33,44,50]

immune response has taken place with these fishes, because those residing in cold water (less than 7°C) do not produce immunoglobulins. Research with eels, for example, demonstrated that agglutinating antibodies were produced at 16 to 19°C but not at 7 to 11°C.[30] Agglutinating antibodies against sea urchin sperm in carp were demonstrated four days sooner at 28°C than at 15°C.[16]

Immune response time for antibody production is related to environmental temperature. Much of the research on immune responses in fishes has been done on coldwater fishes. Immune response is relatively slow in these animals. Rainbow trout at 15.5°C, for example, produced slight agglutination titers (1:2 or less) 28 days following injection of adjuvant suspended *Aeromonas hydrophila* antigens.[40] The immune response time seems to be more rapid in warmwater fishes being held in the higher ranges of temperature acceptability for these fishes. Humoral antibodies are demonstrable in as short a time as one week following injection of bacterial antigens.[21,26,45] The rapidity of the immune response is reduced, or ceases completely, in warmwater fishes at temperatures below 13 to 15°C.

Thus, the use of immunizing substances to develop active acquired immunity in fishes for control of disease must take into account the environmental temperature in which the fishes are living.[7,8] The species of fish and its optimum environmental temperature affect the magnitude and rapidity of immunizing response.

Age and Immune Competency

Immune competency develops slowly in mammals. Very young mammals obtain antibodies through the mother's milk for the first few weeks to six months of life, before immunological imprinting is possible and specific antibody synthesized. This is not the case in those fishes examined for age of immune competency. Rainbow trout and coho salmon are both known to be immune competent at an early age. Rainbow trout, for example, weighing 0.3 grams and 23 days after initiating feeding, developed A. (*liquifaciens*) *hydrophila* antibody when injected intraperitoneally with a bacterin suspended in saline or Freund's complete adjuvant 21 days following injection.[29] Juvenile coho salmon weighing 1.3 grams had demonstrable antibody against A. *salmonicida* four weeks after intraperitoneal inoculation of the antigen.[37] These data indicate that immunization of very young fishes is practical.

Bacterins and Vaccines for Fishes

Most of the immunizing substances developed for fish immunization have been bacterins. The most common bacterial pathogens have been used. Killed whole-cell suspensions and sonicated bacteria or antigens prepared from concentrated sonicated bacteria have found acceptance as immunizing substances for fishes.

Several methods of killing bacteria for bacterins have been put to practical use. The bacteria may be heat-killed, usually at 60°C for 60 minutes, killed with formalin at 0.45% formalin concentration, killed by overlaying the bacterial suspension with chloroform or killed with phenol, merthiolate or other chemicals.[1,23,32,40,43,44]

Suspensions of bacterial antigens for use as fish pathogen bacterins are prepared in saline or adjuvants. Freund's complete and incomplete adjuvants are most often used, but alum-precipitated bacteria added to lanolin or other types of adjuvants have also been used.

Monovalent bacterins are most often used. However, bivalent bacterins have been used experimentally.[19]

Practical viral vaccines for fish disease control have not been developed, even though much research has been done. The practical approach to viral immunization in fishes may be through the use of avirulent or attenuated viruses.[1,19,22,23] The virulence of a strain of infectious hematopoietic necrosis virus (IHNV) to sockeye salmon was reduced 100 fold after 41 passages in steelhead trout embryo cells and incubated at 18°C. Virulence was further reduced by 100,000 fold as compared to a wild strain of IHNV after 100 passages. Immunization of salmon using the further attenuated virus gave complete protection when challenged 30 and 60 days after vaccination. However, virulence was not reduced for rainbow trout possibly because rainbow (steelhead) trout cells were used to culture the virus.[34b] This phenomenon limits the potential use of attenuated viruses. One other problem is the potential for reversal of virulence of an attenuated virus.

The use of attenuated viruses may be more satisfactory when only one species of fish is susceptible to a virus. Channel catfish, for example, is the only species susceptible to the channel catfish virus (CCV). The use of a strain of CCV attenuated by growth on walking catfish kidney cells as a vaccine, protected channel catfish fingerlings against a virulent wild strain of CCV.[38a]

Killed virus vaccines have been used experimentally but with limited success. Viral hemorrhagic septicemia virus killed with B propiolactone and formalin was effective by intraperitoneal injection of one gram and 200 gram fish reared in seawater.[16b] Formalin killed infectious pancreatic necrosis virus (IPNV) injected into adult trout produced measureable humoral antibodies.[43b] Fish are known to maintain virus neutralizing capabilities and live virus inoculated into them usually cannot be reisolated.[16e] These findings indicate a possible method for controlling IPNV in brood trout and subsequent elimination of transmission to eggs produced by vaccinated fish.[16d] Immunization of fish against animal parasites may

also be possible. An immunizing substance prepared from ground trophozoites of *Ichthyophthirius multifiliis* and injected into channel catfish gave 100% protection on challenge with viable *I. multifiliis*.[24a] Further work demonstrated a suitable immunogen can be prepared from cilia of *Tetrahymena pyriformis*, a ciliate taxonomically similar to *I. multifiliis* and with heterologous antigens. Also, *T. pyriformis* is easily cultured and large numbers can be grown in the laboratory. Cilia can be harvested from trophozoites by cold osmotic shock, followed by mechanical removal by forcing them through a small aperture and floating the cilia away from the cells by centrifugation.[24b] The antigen injected into or given by bath treatment gave protection to fish after three to 10 weeks post injection or treatment.[16c,51]

Procedures for Active Immunization of Fishes

Practical immunization for control of diseases of fishes has been the hope of fish husbandrymen, aquarists and others who hold fishes in confinement. However, experimental and practical approaches to the use of immunizing substances with fishes have been examined only since about 1942.[3,40] Practical and laboratory experimentation usually determined that humoral antibodies were produced, but challenge to estimate protection to fishes against the pathogen was not done. Research reported in 1962 demonstrated humoral antibody titers could be produced by injecting or feeding bacterins prepared from *Aeromonas hydrophila* to rainbow trout and were protective against an LD_{90} of the viable and virulent homologous pathogen.[40,41] Reports of other research the following year (1963) demonstrated humoral antibody, homologous to *Aeromonas salmonicida*, protected brook trout against the pathogen.[32] There have been numerous reports since that time demonstrating fish immunoglobulins to be protective against homologous pathogens and practical immunization for control of diseases in fishes is possible.[5,19,22,25,29,47]

There are at least six ways immunizing substances can be given to fishes and produce protective immune responses. These are: parenteral injection, orally with food, hyperosmotic infiltration, iso-osmotic immersion, spray infusion and vacuum infiltration. Each method has advantages and disadvantages.

Parenteral Injection: Antigens are inoculated into fishes parenterally (intraperitoneally, intramuscularly, intravenously, subcutaneously or into other parts of the body) for purposes of developing humoral antibody. Parenteral injection usually produces a more rapid, and possibly a more protective, response to the pathogen than do other methods of antigen delivery. However, the disadvantage of parenteral injection is that it is usable only when small numbers of fishes are to be inoculated. Parenteral injection is usually impractical in large fish culture facilities because of the large numbers of fishes to be immunized. Mass injection is often used for immunization of brood fishes or other relatively large fishes. Manually operated automatic syringes attached to a reservoir of the antigen increase the number of fishes injected per hour or per day, but manual injection still has somewhat limited use. The impracticality of parenteral injection of large numbers of fishes has led to the development of other immunizing procedures.

Oral Immunization: The most practical immunizing procedure for immunizing large numbers of fishes is by feeding the antigen. Fishes absorb relatively large particles from their intestine. Leucocytic phagocytosis of digested or partially digested nutrients (especially neutral fats and polypeptides) from the gut for release into the blood stream or lymphatic system is known to occur in fishes. This important part of nutrient absorption lends itself well to the absorption of other particles. Bacterial cells, or bacterins prepared from bacterial cells, are probably also phagocytized and carried by the blood stream or lymphatic ducts to macrophages in antibody-producing organs (hemopoietic tissue of kidneys, spleen or thymus—Fig. 24) where homologous antibodies are produced. Phagocytosis explains why fishes can develop circulating antibodies homologous to orally administered bacterins.[47]

Oral immunization of trout was first demonstrated in 1942.[17] Trout were fed a bacterin prepared from *Aeromonas (Bacterium) salmonicida* and apparently developed moderate protection from furunculosis. Other research has demonstrated humoral antibody from bacterial antigens fed for long periods of time (70 to 272 days). Reduction, but not elimination, of mortality was possible when orally immunized fishes were challenged with viable homologous bacteria.[4,31,40,42,43] Research to determine the site of *Vibrio anguillarum* immunogen uptake by rainbow trout indicated the lamina epithelialis of lower intestine microfolds to be the only site. Immunogen feeding continued for 14 days and no bacterin was found in any other organ.[34a] Other experiments have demonstrated the lower intestine to be the site of oral bacterin uptake in other fish species as well.[16a,16c] These data indicate oral immunization for control of bacterial diseases of fishes is possible, but much more research is needed. Possibly oral immunization, combined with other methods of bacterin or vaccine delivery, may enhance or extend protection in fishes receiving the antigens.

Hyperosmotic and Direct Infiltration: An innovative mass immunizing procedure for fishes was reported in 1976. Rainbow trout were first placed into either urea or sodium chloride hyperosmotic solution (1,650 milliosmoles) for two minutes, then in hypo-osmotic bovine serum albumin (2% aqueous solution) for three minutes. Bovine serum albumin was detected in the blood of experimental fish at levels up to 0.2 mg per ml of blood. Bovine serum albumin was also taken into the blood of experimental trout when the two solutions (urea or sodium chloride at 1,650 milliosmoles and 2% bovine se-

rum albumin) were combined. The two-step procedure yielded higher levels of bovine serum than the one-step procedure.[2,20]

The procedure in which fishes are first subjected to a hyperosmotic solution then a hypo-osmotic suspension of antigen is usually referred to as "hyperosmotic infiltration." The procedure in which the immunizing agent is suspended in an iso-osmotic solution is called "direct infiltration." The uptake of bovine serum albumin by hyperosmosis has been extended to the use of bacterial antigens in place of bovine serum albumin. Both procedures have been used for mass immunization of trout against enteric redmouth disease (caused by the bacterium *Yersinia ruckeri*) and several fish species against vibriosis (caused by *Vibrio anguillarum*). Commercially prepared bacterins for these two diseases are licensed and available in the United States. The usual procedure for their use is to immerse small fish (100 to 1,000 fish per kg) in bacterin diluted according to the manufacturers directions. Groups of up to 100,000 fish can be handled quite easily through the immersion procedure. Bacterins are prepared to treat a given weight of fish per liter of bacterin. A primary immunization followed by an anamnestic booster immunization two to three weeks after primary treatment is recommended for best protection of fish.

Additional research has demonstrated these bacterins can be delivered to fish being immunized by spraying bacterin against outer surfaces of the fish body. Fish are placed in the upper end of a chamber which has a sloping floor. Bacterin is sprayed over them as they flip and flop along the inclined floor and drop out at the lower end. Larger fish can be treated by the spray process more economically and with less trauma using the spray process than by immersion. Manufacturers recommendations for diluting bacterins and time fish should remain in the spray should be followed for best results.

Immersion and spray procedures in which the prepared immunizing substance contacts outer body surfaces of the fish are known to produce protection for treated fish. Little or no humoral response is elicited following these immunizing procedures.[43a] Possibly leucocyte-like cells in skin and mucus are involved in a cellular response.[37a] Another theory for effectiveness of external contact immunization of fish is that gill macrophages may be involved in uptake of antigen followed by cellular immune response (Fig. 24).[3a]

There have been several controlled studies to determine protection given fish by outer body surface immunization. Sockeye salmon immunized against vibriosis by hyperosmotic immersion and direct immersion were challenged against a viable and virulent strain of *Vibrio anguillarum* 40 days after treatment. There was no mortality in fish treated by either method when the bacterin was undiluted. Nonimmunized control fish had 75 to 100% mortality. Fish treated by hyperosmotic immersion with bacterin diluted 1:1,000 (10^{-3}) had 0 to 5% mortality on challenge, mortality was 22% when bacterin was diluted one to one million (10^{-6}). Fish treated by direct immersion with the 1:1,000 (10^{-3}) dilution had 10 to 15% mortality and 95% mortality when the bacterin was diluted one to one million (10^{-6}).[6a] These results demonstrate the need for acceptable bacterial concentration in bacterins used for body surface immunization, as well as effectiveness of the two immunizing procedures.

Trout, salmon and possibly other fish species can withstand the tremendous change in osmotic pressure for the short hyperosmotic treatment period necessary for immunization. Experiments have demonstrated that many freshwater fish species cannot be placed in solutions of 1,650 milliosmoles osmotic pressure, even for a few seconds, without killing the fish. Thus, hyperosmosis used for fish immunization must be confined to those fishes capable of withstanding relatively high osmotic pressure.

Hyperosmotic infiltration, direct immersion and spray procedures for immunizing large numbers of fish are acceptable to use in fish culture. Research will continue on preparation of satisfactory immunogens against furunculosis, bacterial kidney disease, viral hemorrhagic septicemia, infectious hematopoietic necrosis, ichthyophthiriasis and many other infectious diseases. However, only *Y. ruckeri* and *Vibrio anguillarum* bacterins have been used successfully, possibly because of the limited number of serotypes of these organisms as compared to the abundance of serotypes of other bacterial pathogens.[6,22] The phenomenon in which an immune response can be brought out by body surface contact in fish will continue to be examined.

Vacuum Infiltration: A method of mass bacterin and vaccine delivery for immunization of fishes was reported in 1976.[1,5] The procedure was termed "vacuum infiltration" because fish were suspended in a saline suspension of bacterial or viral antigen(s) in a vacuum chamber. The fish and antigen suspension were subjected to three rapid reductions of atmospheric pressure with rapid return to ambient atmospheric pressure. The entire process takes approximately two to three minutes. Antigens are thought to be infused into fish tissue by the rapid changes in atmospheric pressure.

The vacuum infiltration method has been used to experimentally immunize coho salmon against infectious hematopoietic necrosis (IHN), enteric redmouth disease, vibriosis and furunculosis. Fish subjected to IHN antigens were said to have protection from viable IHN virus equal to that obtained from injection of antigen. Coho salmon immunized against vibriosis demonstrated a 4.3— fold reduction in mortality when subjected to viable *Vibrio anguillarum*, compared to non-immunized control salmon. Fishes immunized with *A. salmonicida* antigens by vacuum infiltration did not produce measur-

able homologous humoral antibodies and were not challenged, leaving doubt as to the effectiveness of the immunizing procedure for control of furunculosis.[1]

Vacuum infiltration has one major disadvantage: the procedure requires expensive equipment for performance. Mass immunization of fishes in a large fish culture facility would require a large vacuum chamber and high-capacity vacuum pump to perform the technique properly.

Amazingly, most fishes can withstand the tremendous alterations of pressure, i.e., ambient atmospheric pressure to pressures as low as 10 to 15 mm of mercury given three times over a period of two to three minutes. However, antigens suspended in saline may be fatal to many saline-sensitive fish species, even without added stress of pressure alteration. Experiments with saline-sensitive fishes (fathead minnow, carp, guppy and swordtail) indicate that fishes can withstand vacuum treatment. Possibly rapid alteration of atmospheric pressure alone may be useful for infusing bacterins and vaccines into saline-sensitive fishes.

Spray Infusion: The search for methods suitable for mass immunization of fishes led to development of a "spray infusion" procedure. Fishes are removed from the water and sprayed with bacterin under high pressure (100 pounds per square inch) using a sand blasting gun. A spray infusion using formalin-killed *V. anguillarum* antigens adsorbed on bentonite particles and blasted against coho salmon gave protection against vibriosis for up to 125 days. The spray infusion technique was more effective in controlling vibriosis in coho salmon than was oral immunization. A quadravalent immunizing agent containing two *Vibrio* organisms, *A. salmonicida* and *Renibacterium salmoninarum*, was infused into coho salmon and elicited agglutinin titers for all four. Furthermore, polyvalent immunizing agents exerted an adjuvant effect, each enhancing fish immune response to the other.[23,24] Spray infusion certainly is a promising mass immunization technique for fishes.

Duration of Active Acquired Immunity in Fishes
A major biological fact must be considered when using immunizing agents for control of infectious diseases of fishes—the elicited immune response appears to be of relatively short duration. Injection or infusion of an immunizing substance usually results in a measurable primary response if a suitable environmental temperature prevails. The primary response is usually of short duration, as demonstrated by reduction in antibody titer within a few weeks. Channel catfish held at 27 to 28°C, for example, elicited a primary response against injected *Flexibacter columnaris* antigens which slowly diminished after peak titers were reached in about three weeks. Secondary injections of antigen nine weeks after primary injection elicited an anamnestic response which far exceeded antibody titers developed from the primary injection. The experiment was terminated at 15 weeks, be-

fore duration of the secondary response was determined.[26] The experiment did prove that secondary injection or infusion of antigen is essential for maintenance of protective antibody titers in fishes, as in higher animals.

Fishes are capable of anamnestic response if the immunizing agent is given prior to loss of primary antibody titer. One or more booster injections or infusions are necessary to maintain protection. Rainbow trout held at 15.5°C, for example, required multiple (three to seven) injections of *A. hydrophila* bacterin to develop and maintain a protective antibody titer. Bacterin suspended in Freund's complete adjuvant and injected intramuscularly at 0, 10 and 17 weeks produced peak antibody titers by the 25th week. Antibody titers continued to reduce for the next 35 weeks, at which time only 20% of the fish were protected from challenge with an LD_{90} of viable *A. hydrophila*.[39,40]

Duration of protection from injected or infused immunizing substances has not as yet been properly addressed in fishes. Most experiments in which protective immunity is developed are terminated before protection durability is established. The experiments almost leave the impression that protective immunity has been demonstrated and the job is finished. However, reducing mortality from infectious disease in young fishes through immunization practices is of little value to the fish culturist if the same fish lose protection and die part-way through the rearing process. Also, fishes released from fish culture facilities during the terminal part of protection from certain infectious diseases may die from the disease before serving the purpose for which they were intended.

Immunization has become a more useful part in controlling mortality among confined fishes, very much as it has among other domesticated animals. More information is needed on the most useful organism species or serotypes, immunizing agent preparation and delivery to fishes, immunizing effect on fishes, and durability of protection derived from the immunization.

Selected References

1. Amend, D. F. 1976. "Prevention and control of viral diseases of salmonids," *J. Fish. Res. Bd. Can.*, 33: 1059-1066.

2. Amend, D. F. and D. C. Fender. 1976. "Uptake of bovine serum albumin by rainbow trout from hyperosmotic solutions: a model for vaccinating fish," *Science*, 192:793-794.

3. Anderson, D. P. 1974. *Fish immunology*. T.F.H. Publ., Neptune, NJ. 239p.

3a. Anderson, D. P., W. B. Van Muiswinkel and B. S. Roberson. 1984. "Effects of chemically induced immune modulation on infectious diseases of fish." *Chemical Regulation of Immunity in Veterinary Medicine*, Alan R. Liss, Inc. New York City, NY. p. 187-211.

4. Anderson, D. P. and J. R. Nelson. 1974. "Comparison of protection in rainbow trout (*Salmo gairdneri*) inoculated with and fed Hagerman redmouth bacterins," *J. Fish. Res. Bd. Can.*, 31:214-216.

5. Antipa, R. 1976. "Field testing of injected *Vibrio anguillarum* bacterins in pen-reared Pacific salmon," *J. Fish. Res. Bd. Can.*, 33:1291-1296.

6. Antipa, R. and D. F. Amend. 1977. "Immunization of Pacific salmon: comparison of intraperitoneal injection and hyperosmotic infiltration of *Vibrio anguillarum* and *Aeromonas salmonicida* bacterins," *J. Fish. Res. Bd. Can.*, 34:203-208.

6a. Antipa, R., R. Gould and D. F. Amend. 1980. "*Vibrio anguillarum* vaccination of sockeye salmon *Oncorhynchus nerka* (Walbaum) by direct and hyperosmotic immersion." *J. Fish Dis.*, 3:161-165.

7. Avtalion, R. R. 1969. "Temperature effect on antibody production and immunological memory in carp (*Cyprinus carpio*) immunized against bovine serum albumin (BSA)," *Immunol.*, 17:927-931.

8. Avtalion, R. R., Z. Malik, E. Lefler and E. Katz. 1970. "Temperature effect on immune resistance of fish to pathogens," *Bamidgeh*, 22:33-38.

9. Avtalion, R. R., E. Weiss, T. Moalem and L. Milgram. 1975. "Evidence of cooperation of T and B cells of fish," *Isr. J. Med. Sci.*, 11:1385. (Abst. *Fish Health News*, 6(3):152;1977).

10. Barrett, J. T. 1974. *Textbook of immunology. Second Ed.* C. V. Mosby Co., St. Louis, MO. 417p.

11. Bergman, A. 1911. "En Smittesam ogons jukdom keretomalaci, hos torsk vid sviriges sydkast," *Skand. Vet-Tijdscher.* (Cited in Pliszka, 1938.)

12. Boyd, R. F. and B. G. Hoerl. 1977. *Basic medical microbiology*. Little, Brown Co., Boston, MA. p. 191-208.

13. Cisar, J. O. and J. L. Fryer. 1974. "Characterization of anti-*Aeromonas salmonicida* antibodies from coho salmon," *Inf. Immun.*, 9:236-243.

14. Clem, L. W. 1971. "Phylogeny of immunoglobulin structure and function: IV. Immunoglobulins of the giant grouper, *Epinephelus itaira*," *J. Biol. Chem.*, 246:9-15.

15. Corbel, M. J. 1975. "The immune response in fish: a review," *J. Fish. Biol.*, 7:539-560.

16. Cushing, J. E. 1942. "An effect of temperature upon antibody-production in fish," *J. Immunol.*, 45: 123-126.

16a. Davina, J. H. M., H. K. Parmentier and L. P. Timmermans. 1982. "Effect of oral administration of *Vibrio* bacterin on the intestine of cyprinid fish." *Develop. Comp. Immunol. Suppl.*, 2:157-166.

16b. deKinkelin, P. 1982. "Viral hemorrhagic septicaemia." In: Anderson, D. P., M. Dorson and P. Dubourget, Eds. Antigens of Fish Pathogens., Assoc. Corp. *Etud. Med. Lyon.*, Lyons, France. p. 33-50.

16c. Dickerson, H. W., J. Brown, D. L. Dawe and J. B. Gratzek. 1984. "*Tetrahymena pyriformis* as a protective antigen against *Ichthyophthirius multifiliis* infection: Comparison between isolates and ciliary preparations." *J. Fish Biol.*, 24:523-528.

16d. Dixon, P. F. and B. J. Hill. 1983. "Inactivation of infectious pancreatic necrosis virus for vaccine use." *J. Fish Dis.*, 6:399-409.

16e. Dorson, M. 1982. "Infectious pancreatic necrosis of salmonids." In: Anderson, D. P., M. Dorson and P. Dubourget, Eds. "Antigens of Fish Pathogens.," *Assoc. Corp. Etud. Med.* Lyon., Lyon, France. p. 7-32.

17. Duff, D. C. B. 1942. "The oral immunization of trout against *Bacterium salmonicida*," *J. Immunol.*, 44: 87-94.

18. Ellis, A. E. 1977. "The leucocytes of fish. A review," *J. Fish. Biol.*, 11:453-491.

19. Evelyn, T. P. T. 1977. "Immunization of salmonids," *Proc. Inter. Symp. Dis. Cult. Salmonids.* Sponsored by Tavolek Inc., Redmond, WA. 21p.

20. Fender, D. C. and D. F. Amend. 1978. "Hyperosmotic infiltration: Factors influencing uptake of bovine serum albumin by rainbow trout (*Salmo gairdneri*)," *J. Fish. Res. Bd. Can.*, 35:871-874.

21. Frenzel, E. M. and H. Ambrosius. 1971. "Antihaptan antibodies in lower vertebrates," *Acta Biol. Med. Ger.*, 26:165-171.

22. Fryer, J. L., D. F. Amend, L. W. Harrell, A. J. Novotny, J. A. Plumb, J. S. Rohovec and G. L. Tebbit. 1977. *Development of bacterins and vaccines for control of infectious diseases in fish. Ore. State Univ. Sea Grant Coll. Prog. Publ.*, No. ORESU-T- 77-012, 10.

23. Fryer, J. L., J. S. Rohovec, G. L. Tebbit, J. S. McMichael and K. S. Pilcher. 1976. "Vaccination for control of infectious diseases in Pacific salmon," *Fish. Pathol.*, 10:155-164.

24. Gould, R. W. 1977. *Development of a new vaccine delivery system for immunizing fish and investigation of the protective antigens in Vibrio anguillarum.* Unpubl. Ph.D. Diss. Ore. State Univ., Corvallis, OR. 145p.

24a. Goven, B. A., D. L. Dawe and J. B. Gratzek. 1981. "*In vitro* demonstration of serological cross-reactivity between *Ichthyophthirius multifiliis* Fouquet and *Tetrahymena pyriformis* Lwoff." *Develop. Comp. Immunol.*, 5:238-289.

24b. Goven, B. A., D. L. Dawe and J. B. Gratzek. 1980. "Protection of channel catfish, *Ictalurus punctatus* Rafinesque, against *Ichthyophthirius multifiliis* Fouquet by immunization." *J. Fish Biol.*, 17:311-316.

25. Hara, T., K. Inoue, S. Morikawa and F. Tashiro. 1976. "Vaccination trials for control of furunculosis of salmonids in Japan," *Fish. Pathol.*, 10:227-235.

26. Heartwell, C. M., III. 1975. *Immune response and antibody characterization of the channel catfish (Ictalurus punctatus) to a naturally pathogenic bacterium and virus. U.S. Fish Wildl. Serv. Tech. Paper*, No. 85. 34p.

27. Heuzroth, H., E. Resch, R. Richter and H. Ambrosius. 1973. "Studies on antigenic similarity of immuno globulins," *Acta Biol. Med. Ger.*, 30:719 and 735.

27a. Ingram, G. A. 1980. "Substances involved in the natural resistance of fish to infection—A review. *J. Fish Biol.*, 16:23-60.

28. Khalifa, K. A. 1976. *Intracellular antibody formation and role of thymus in two teleosts.* Unpubl. Ph.D. Diss. Colo. State Univ., Fort Collins, CO. 92p.

29. Khalifa, K. A. and G. Post. 1976. "Immune response of advanced rainbow trout fry to *Aeromonas liquifaciens*," *Prog. Fish-Cult.*, 38:66-68.

30. Kiyokuni, M. and S. Egusa. 1969. "Immune response in Japanese eel to *Vibrio anguillarum*—1. Effects of termperature on agglutinating antibody production in starved eels," *Bull. Jap. Soc. Sci. Fish.*, 35: 868-874.

31. Klontz, G. W. and D. P. Anderson. 1970. "Oral immunization of salmonids: a review," *In* S. F. Snieszko, ed. *Symposium on diseases of fishes and shellfishes. Am. Fish. Soc., Spec. Publ.*, No. 5:16-20.

32. Krantz, G. E., J. M. Reddecliff and G. Heist. 1964. "Immune response of trout to *Aeromonas salmonicida*. Part 1. Development of agglutinating antibodies and protective immunity," *Prog. Fish-Cult.*, 26:3-10.

33. Marchalonis, J. J. 1971. "Isolation and partial characterization of immunoglobulins of goldfish (*Carassius auratus*) and carp (*Cyprinus carpio*)," *Immunol.*, 20:161-173.

34. Natvig, J. B. and H. G. Kunkel. 1973. "Human immunoglobulins: classes, subclasses, genetic variants and idiotypes," *Adv. Immunol.*, 16:1-59.

34a. Nelson, J. S., J. S. Rohovec and J. L. Fryer. 1985. "Tissue location of vibrio bacterin delivered by intraperitoneal injection, immersion and oral routes to *Salmo gairdneri*." *Fish Pathol.*, 19:263-269.

34b. Nicholson, B. L. 1982. "Infectious hematopoietic necrosis (I.H.N.)." In: Anderson, D. P., M. Dorson and P. Dubourget, Eds. Antigens of Fish Pathogens., Assoc. Corp. *Etud. Med. Lyon.*, Lyon, France. p. 63-79.

35. Nybelin, O. 1935. "Uber agglutininbildung bei Fischen," *Z. Immunit. Forsch.*, 84:74.

36. Ortiz-Muniz, G. and M. M. Sigel. 1968. "*In vitro* synthesis of anti-BSA antibodies by fish lymphoid organs," *Bact. Proc.*, M8, p. 66.

37. Paterson, W. D. and J. L. Fryer. 1974. "Immune response of juvenile coho salmon (*Oncorhynchus kisutch*) to *Aeromonas salmonicida* cells administered intraperitoneally in Freund's complete adjuvant," *J. Fish. Res. Bd. Can.*, 31:1751-1755.

37a. Peleteiro, M. C. and R. H. Ricards. 1985. "Identification of lymphocytes in the epidermis of the rainbow trout, *Salmo gairdneri* Richardson." *J. Fish Dis.*, 8:161-172.

38. Pliszka, F. 1938. "Untersuchungen uber die Agglutinine bei Karpfen. Zentr. Bakteriol. I," *Abt. Orig.*, 143:262-264.

38a. Plumb, J. A. and D. A. Jezek. 1982. "Channel catfish virus disease." In: Anderson, D. P., M. Dorson and P. Dubourget, Eds. Antigens of Fish Pathogens., Assoc. Corp. *Etud. Med.* Lyon., Lyon, France. p. 33-50.

39. Post, G. 1966. "Serum proteins and antibody production in rainbow trout (*Salmo gairdneri*)," *J. Fish. Res. Bd. Can.*, 23:1957-1963.

40. Post, G. 1963. *The immune response of rainbow trout (Salmo gairdneri) to Aeromonas hydrophila*. Publ. 63-7. Utah Div. Wildl., Salt Lake City, UT. 82p.

41. Post, G. 1962. "Immunization—a method of disease control in fish," *U.S. Trout News*, Sept.-Oct.:14-17.

42. Rohovec, J. S., R. L. Garrison and J. L. Fryer. 1975. "Immunization of fish for control of vibriosis," *Proc. 3rd U.S.-Jap. Aquacult. Spec. Publ. Reg. Jap. Fish. Res. Lab., Niigato, Japan.* p. 105-112.

43. Ross, A. J. and G. W. Klontz. 1965. "Oral immunization of rainbow trout (*Salmo gairdneri*) against the etiological agent of 'Redmouth Disease'," *J. Fish. Res. Bd. Can.*, 22:713-719.

43a. Sakai, M., T. Aoki, T. Kitao, J. S. Rohovec and J. L. Fryer. 1984. "Comparison of cellular immune responses of fish vaccinated by immersion and injection of *Vibrio anguillarum*." Bull. *Jpn. Soc. Sci. Fish.*, 50:1187-1192.

43b. Sano, T., K. Tanaka and Fukuzaki. 1981. "Immune response in adult trout against formalin killed concentrated IPNV." *Internat. Symp Fish Biologics: Dev. Biol.* Stds., 49:63-70.

44. Schachte, J. H., Jr. 1976. *Studies on the immunization of the channel catfish against two bacterial pathogens*. Ph.D. Diss., Auburn Univ., Auburn, AL. 84p.

45. Shelton, E. and M. Smith. 1970. "The ultrasturcture of carp (*Cyprinus carpio*) immunoglobulin: a tetrameric macroglobulin," *J. Mol. Biol.*, 54: 615-617.

45a. Smith, P. D. and R. Broun-Nesje. 1982. "Cell mediated immunity in the salmon: lymphocyte and macrophage stimulation, lymphocyte/macrophage interactions and the production of lymphokine-like factors in stimulated lymphocytes." *Develop. Comp. Immunol. Supp.* 2:233.

46. Smith, W. W. 1940. "Production of anti-bacterial agglutinins by carp and trout at 10°C," *Proc. Soc. Expt. Biol. Med.*, 45:726-729.

47. Snieszko, S. F. 1970. "Immunization of fishes: a review," *J. Wildl. Dis.*, 6:24-30.

48. Snieszko, S. and S. B. Friddle. 1949. "Prophylaxis of furunculosis in brook trout (*Salvelinus fontinalis*) by oral immunization and sulfamerazine," *Prog. Fish-Cult.*, 11:161-168.

49. Snieszko, S., W. Piotrowska, B. Kocylowski and K. Marek. 1938. "Badania bakteriologiczne i serologiczne nad bakteriami posocznicy karpi," *Rozpr. Biol.*, 16:15p.

50. Trump, G. N. 1970. "Goldfish immunoglobulins and antibodies to bovine serum albumin," *J. Immunol.*, 104:1267-1275.

51. Wolf, K. and M. E. Markiw. 1982. "Ichthyophthiriasis: Immersion immunization of rainbow trout (*Salmo gairdneri*) using *Tetrahymena thermophila* as a protective immunogen." *Can. J. Fish. Aquat.*, Sci. 39:1722-1725.

Chapter IX

NUTRITION AND NUTRITIONAL DISEASES OF FISHES

Proper nutrition is essential to the health of all animals, and proper nutrition of fishes is no exception. There are many diseases among fishes directly related to nutritional deficiencies and excesses. Also, malnutrition is implicated in many diseases involving pathogenic organisms. The fish disease diagnostician must be aware of the nutritional status of fishes in order to account for diseases basically nutritional in origin and complications caused by pathogens which are consequences of malnutrition. Estimating the role of malnutrition in disease epizootics involving opportunistic pathogens is essential to proper disease diagnosis.[43,44,45]

Wild-ranging fishes have a choice of a wide variety of foods and usually select a diet balanced to their nutritional requirements. These fish populations usually expand to balance the ratio of food supply to fish biomass, with little or no nutritional deficiency signs in the fishes except during times when the food supply is altered by climatic conditions, water quality, water quantity or other factors. A properly balanced food chain of plants to invertebrate animals to vertebrate animals to the top carnivorous animal runs its course among wild-ranging fishes, supplying all essential nutrients to each trophic level.[33] Thus, malnutrition is not as often a disease diagnostic problem among wild-ranging fishes as among confined fishes.

Confined fishes usually can be classified into three categories: those confined to ponds or other impoundments, those confined to a balanced ecosystem in aquariums and those held in intensive fish culture. Fishes confined to ponds and some aquariums may obtain part of their nutritional needs from the environment in the form of algae, other plants, invertebrate animals and occasionally vertebrate animals. The remainder of the nutrients must be supplied by the husbandryman. Fishes confined under intensive fish culture conditions or nonproductive aquariums must be supplied a ration containing all required nutrients each day, with no nutrients expected from the environment.

Two classes of diets have been used successfully to rear fishes in confinement with little or no signs of malnutrition. Diets designed to add nutrients to those obtained from the pond or aquarium environment are called *supplemental rations*. Rations for intensively reared fishes in which no nutrients are supplied from the environment are called *complete rations*. Formulation of acceptable supplemental rations is not difficult, because minor nutritional deficiencies in the ration are compensated by sources of those nutrients in the pond or aquarium. Complete rations must be formulated to meet all the nutritional requirements of the fish being fed and are more difficult to prepare. Formulations of complete rations are based on the quantitative expression of nutrient requirements of fishes and availability of the necessary components, as well as the digestibility of all feedstuffs and ingredients being used to prepare such diets. Mathematical formulation of a complete ration must be followed by ration preparation, analysis and actual feeding of the fish to be assured all nutrients are available.[19,26,51]

Physical preparation of the ration must also be considered to allow for presentation of the nutritionally balanced diet to the fishes in such a way that it can be ingested and digested.[44,45] Taste or palatability of the ration for each fish species must be considered. Fishes have a highly sensitive sense of taste, so the ration must pass the palatability test when presented to the fishes in order for it to be completely and continuously ingested.

The ration must be fed to the fish at prescribed time intervals because of a more or less limited stomach capacity. Stomachless fishes should receive the ration in small amounts but often; those with stomachs may sometimes be fed at extended intervals.

The amount of ration fed to confined fishes daily to maintain nutritional health depends on fish species, fish size, ration quality, water temperature and type of ration.[28,51] Feeding confined fishes an established feeding level each day is important. There are several ways feeding levels can be established. One method is based on a feeding chart in which fish size and water temperature are used to support the metabolic rate of the fish with all nutrient requirements for that metabolic rate. The feeding chart has many advantages, the major advantage being ration formulas can be prepared to match a minimum daily feeding level for the fish being fed, to each nutrient requirement for that fish species. A feeding chart has been used for most species of trout, but can be adapted to other fish species (Table 24).[11,51]

Other methods of estimating ration quantities to be fed each day include feeding to satiation, feeding for maximum conversion of food to fish tissue, feeding for best protein conversion and feeding for biological maintenance and appearance.[7] However, most fish nutritionists agree that the quantities of a nutritionally balanced diet fed to the fish daily should yield healthy fish with a ration conversion of 2.0 or less.[45]

Three types of prepared rations are used to feed confined fishes: moist, semimoist and dry. The type of in-

TABLE 24

Recommended amount of dry food to feed trout per day in percent of body weight[11,51]

	Number of Fish per kilogram										
Water Temp.	5,600 or less	5,600 – 670	670-190	190-83	83-43	43-26	26-16	16-11	11-8	8-6	6 or less
°C	Approx. Size, cm < 2.5	2.5-5.0	5.0-7.5	7.5-10	10-13	13-15	15-18	18-20	20-23	23-25	25
5.5	3.5	2.8	2.4	1.8	1.4	1.2	0.9	0.8	0.7	0.6	0.5
6.0	3.6	3.0	2.5	1.9	1.4	1.2	1.0	0.9	0.8	0.7	0.6
6.5	3.8	3.1	2.6	2.0	1.5	1.3	1.0	0.9	0.8	0.8	0.6
7.0	4.0	3.3	2.7	2.1	1.6	1.3	1.1	1.0	0.9	0.8	0.7
7.5	4.1	3.4	2.8	2.2	1.7	1.4	1.2	1.0	0.9	0.8	0.7
8.0	4.3	3.6	3.0	2.3	1.7	1.4	1.2	1.0	0.9	0.8	0.7
9.0	4.5	3.8	3.1	2.4	1.8	1.5	1.3	1.1	1.0	0.9	0.8
9.5	4.7	3.9	3.2	2.5	1.9	1.6	1.3	1.1	1.0	0.9	0.8
10.0	5.2	4.3	3.4	2.7	2.0	1.7	1.4	1.2	1.1	1.0	0.9
10.5	5.4	4.4	3.5	2.8	2.1	1.7	1.5	1.3	1.1	1.0	0.9
11.0	5.4	4.5	3.6	2.8	2.1	1.7	1.5	1.3	1.2	1.0	0.9
11.5	5.6	4.7	3.8	2.9	2.2	1.8	1.5	1.3	1.2	1.1	1.0
12.0	5.8	4.9	3.9	3.0	2.3	1.9	1.6	1.4	1.3	1.1	1.0
13.0	6.1	5.1	4.2	3.2	2.4	2.0	1.6	1.4	1.3	1.1	1.0
13.5	6.3	5.3	4.3	3.3	2.5	2.0	1.7	1.5	1.3	1.2	1.0
14.0	6.7	5.5	4.5	3.5	2.6	2.1	1.8	1.5	1.4	1.2	1.1
14.5	7.0	5.8	4.8	3.6	2.7	2.2	1.9	1.6	1.4	1.3	1.2
15.0	7.3	6.0	5.0	3.7	2.8	2.3	1.9	1.7	1.5	1.3	1.2
15.5	7.5	6.3	5.1	3.9	3.0	2.4	2.0	1.7	1.5	1.4	1.3
16.0	7.8	6.5	5.3	4.1	3.1	2.5	2.0	1.8	1.6	1.4	1.3
16.5	8.1	6.7	5.5	4.3	3.2	2.6	2.1	1.8	1.6	1.5	1.4
17.0	8.4	7.0	5.7	4.5	3.4	2.7	2.1	1.9	1.7	1.5	1.4
17.5	8.7	7.2	5.9	4.7	3.5	2.8	2.2	1.9	1.7	1.6	1.5
18.0	9.0	7.5	6.1	4.9	3.6	2.9	2.2	2.0	1.8	1.6	1.5
19.0	9.1	7.6	6.2	5.0	3.7	2.9	2.2	2.0	1.8	1.6	1.6
20.0	9.3	7.8	6.3	5.1	3.8	3.0	2.3	2.0	1.9	1.7	1.6

gredient used to prepare fish diets determines the type of diet. Moist rations are prepared from ingredients with a high moisture content (raw fish, meat products, wet vegetable products and similar ingredients). The moisture content of most moist rations is about 70%. Semimoist rations are prepared from dry products (dried fish products, cereal grains and other dry animal and vegetable products) added to ingredients with a high moisture content. The final moisture content of semimoist diets is approximately 35%. Dry rations are prepared from dry animal and vegetable products. The final moisture content is about 10%. The relationship between ration moisture and dry weight of the finished ration is important for purposes of establishing the amount of ration to feed daily in order to prevent malnutrition among the fish.

The most satisfactory rations prepared for fishes from natural or processed ingredients include supplements (crystalline vitamins, minerals, amino acids or other purified products). Supplements are added to balance deficits between nutrients in the combination of ingredients and the nutrient requirements of the fish species being fed. The fish disease diagnostician should be aware of types of diets fed to fishes, diet formulations, supplementation of diets, nutrient requirements of fishes and feeding practices.

The fish disease diagnostician should also be aware of the anatomy and physiology of the digestive tract of fishes because of the tremendous differences in alimentary structures and enzyme systems among fish species. Some pond-reared or intensively reared fishes are carnivorous, others herbivorous. Some have the usual complement of alimentary structures including stomach, ceca, intestine and rectum. These fishes conform to the usual physiology found among other animals with acid stomach secretions, bile alkalinization in the area directly below the stomach and the usual complement of digestive enzymes found among higher vertebrate animals. Other fishes have no organ which could be classified as a storage-bin type stomach, only a slight to moderate enlargement between the esophagus and intestine. There is no acid or acid-activated enzyme released in "stomachless" fishes. A stomachless fish maintains an alkaline reaction for the full length of the alimentary tract. Other fishes have a greater enlargement in the region of the stomach which could be classified as a definite stomach, but it remains alkaline at all times.[43,44]

The digestion of food by fishes is about the same as in other vertebrate animals, except in the stomachless fishes. Protein digestion begins in the stomach and continues in the ceca and intestine. Proteolytic enzymes similar to those in higher animals are found in fishes, except the stomachless fishes have no acid or acid-activated pepsinogen. Fishes have a complement of lipases and carbohydrases for digestion of fats and carbohydrates. Digested food is absorbed by simple diffusion, active transport and/or particulate phagocytosis.[44]

The biological rate at which food energy is utilized by an animal is called the metabolic rate. The metabolic rate of fishes is influenced by environmental temperature, body size or age, activity and other factors. Alterations of metabolic rate influenced by water temperature and body size or age are usually taken into account in the feeding of confined fishes. Increases or decreases in water temperature surrounding a fish will cause corresponding increases or decreases of the fish's body temperature and metabolic rate. The metabolic rate of fishes held at a constant temperature will decrease with age. The metabolic rate of fishes and subsequent dietary energy requirements should be considered whenever malnutrition-associated disease diagnoses are being made.[43,44,45,63]

Dietary Requirements

Information on the nutrient requirements of many of the confined and wild-ranging fishes is limited. The nutrient requirements for rainbow trout, chinook salmon and channel catfish are well known, and these data are used to estimate the requirements of other closely related fishes. Research continues on the nutrient requirements of eels, carps, several bass species and many other fishes. Examination of the diet being fed to confined fishes and comparison with nutrient requirements of the fish can assist in diagnosis of malnutrition-related diseases.[43,44,45]

Proteins and Amino Acids

Natural diets of most fishes are rich in protein. Thus, prepared rations fed to confined fishes must also have higher protein content than diets fed to most of the higher animals. The minimum protein requirement in a prepared fish ration is dependent upon the availability of amino acids from each protein source, often referred to as protein quality.[43,44,45] The gross protein requirement for those fishes in which requirements have been established range between a minimum of 25% for large (adult) channel catfish to 56% for small (young) chinook salmon. The recommended dietary protein level for seven fish species is given in Table 25.[9,14,41] However, the protein quality, protein digestibility and amino acid availability must be considered to insure that the protein content of a prepared ration is sufficient to meet the needs of the fish being fed.[44]

Amino acid requirements have been established for several fish species (Table 26).[4,9,13,14,47,56] An amino acid test diet in which amounts of all indispensable amino acids and several dispensable amino acids are added in crystalline form has been used to establish these levels. The test diet is balanced to support health and growth of the fishes being tested by adding essential fatty acids as well as other fats for energy, carbohydrates, required quantities of essential vitamins and minerals. The diet is fed to experimental fishes after leaving out one amino acid or adding that amino acid in serial quantities in order to demonstrate if the amino acid is indispensable or to determine the quantity necessary to support health and growth of the fishes.[21] Results of research indicate that ten amino acids are indispensable for those species of fish tested.[23] Two dispensable amino acids can reduce quantities of two indispensable amino acids necessary for health and growth of fishes: cystine will spare part of the methionine requirement, and tyrosine will spare part of the phenylalanine requirement (Table 26).[43,44,45,51]

Fats and Lipids

Dietary fats supply a major part of the energy of those fishes studied.[43] Phospholipids and steroid components of body organs also rely on dietary lipids for synthesis of supply.[44] Certain of the fatty acids are essential for health, growth and normal appearance of fishes.[8,45]

Hard (saturated) fats are not utilized well by fishes in cold water. Soft or liquid fats appear to be more satisfactory in the diet of coldwater fishes. Beef tallow has been found to be equal to highly unsaturated menhaden oil as an energy source when fed to warmwater fishes over 20°C. Triglycerides appear to be used more efficiently by catfishes and possibly other fishes than free fatty acids derived from triglycerides.[29,44,59]

Optimum levels of dietary fats for fishes have not been established. However, practical diets for catfish contain up to 12% fat, commercial carp diets contain 10 to 15% and prepared trout rations contain 3 to 15%.[44,45,53]

There is but one essential fatty acid in trout nutrition, and the same may be true for salmon, catfishes, carp and other fishes. It belongs to the linolenic acid family

TABLE 25

Recommended protein levels in percent of prepared diets (as-fed basis)[1a,44]

Species	Young[a] Fish	Subadult[a] Fish	Adult[a] Fish
Channel catfish	35-40	25-36	25-32
Rainbow trout	38-40	36-38	34-36
Chinook salmon	47-56	43-47	40-42
Carp	43-47	37-42	28-32
Eel	50-56	45-50	—
Ayu fish	44-51	45-48	—
Red sea bream	45-54	43-48	—
Smallmouth bass	45		
Largemouth bass	40-41		

[a]Protein fraction must have the necessary amino acid profile and amino acid availability to the fish receiving the ration. Reduced protein quality must be compensated by additional protein or supplemented with the necessary amino acid(s).

and has an 18:3w3 configuration, meaning it is an 18 carbon molecule with three double bonds, the first double bond being on the third carbon from the hydrocarbon end of the molecule. Rainbow trout require no less than 1.0% of the diet as this w3 fatty acid.[35] The linoleic fatty acid, 18:3w6, can reduce the w3 requirement by up to 10% (0.1% of the ration). Experiments with catfishes indicate the requirement for both the w3 and the w6 fatty acids may be much lower than for trout. Carp have a need for both linolenic and linoleic fatty acids. Best weight gain and food conversion have been obtained using 1% linolenic (18:3w3) and 1% linoleic (18:3w6) fatty acids in the diet. The 22:6w3 linolenic fatty acid may also be used as part of the essential fatty acid requirement of carp.[60] Additional research is needed on the essential fatty acid requirements of other fishes.[20,44] The best sources of essential fatty acids for fish diets are fish oils. Vegetable oils are low in the w3 acid but generally high in w6 acid (Table 27).

Carbohydrates

Fish species in which carbohydrate digestion and utilization have been studied indicate that fishes digest and metabolize carbohydrates at a lower rate than higher animals. Poor carbohydrate utilization by fishes probably has come about through evolution. Natural diets of carnivorous fishes are generally low in carbohydrate. These fishes no doubt have evolved to use proteins and fats more efficiently than carbohydrates. Herbivorous fishes may digest and metabolize carbohydrates better than carnivorous fishes, but only cursory research has been done on these fishes.

Carbohydrate molecular structure influences digestibility in carnivorous fishes. High molecular weight carbohydrate, such as starch, sucrose, lactose and others, are poorly digested by those fish species studied.[20,50] Excess digestible carbohydrate in the diet of most fishes increases blood sugar, liver glycogen storage and liver mass, sometimes to pathological levels. Maximum digestible carbohydrate for trout has been given as less than 20% of the diet because of reduced utilization of carbohydrates after absorption.[51] Other fish species may also require limiting digestible carbohydrate in the diet by using the approximate digestibility of the carbohydrate in each dietary ingredient (Table 28). Digestible carbohydrate can not be equated to the total nitrogen-free extract of a diet. Disease diagnosis, in which excess digestible carbohydrate is involved, thus requires a thorough knowledge of the ration formula.[43,51]

Dietary Energy

Energy utilization of fishes serves for body maintenance, growth and reproduction. Little or no energy is used by most fishes to maintain body temperature or position in the water, since the body temperature of most fishes is about the same as the environmental temperature and the bodies of most fishes have zero buoyancy with water. Energy for body maintenance is the first order of energy use in fishes. Energy for body maintenance must be satisfied before energy is available for growth.[45] Thus, energy values of the diet received by confined fishes become an important part in diagnosis of those diseases in which general malnutrition is apparent.

Caloric requirements for fishes have received only cursory attention. However, information available for

TABLE 26

**Amino acid requirements expressed as percent of the as-fed diet
for six species of fishes**[4,9,13,29a,43,44,45,51,53a,56,60a]

Amino Acid	Rainbow Trout	Chinook Salmon	Eel (young)	Carp (fry)	Coho Salmon	Channel Catfish
Arginine	2.5	2.4	1.7	1.7	2.4	2.6
Histidine	0.7	0.7	0.8	1.3	0.7	1.4
Isoleucine	0.9	0.9	1.5	1.0	—	2.4
Leucine	1.6	1.6	1.7	1.5	—	3.2
Lysine	2.0	2.0	2.0	3.5	1.5	1.2
Methionine	1.5[a]	1.5[a]	2.1[a]	1.2[c]	1.5[a]	2.1a
Phenylalanine	2.1[b]	2.1[b]	2.0[b]	4.0[b]	—	4.6
Threonine	0.9	0.9	1.5	2.4	—	1.8
Tryptophan	0.2	0.2	0.4	1.0	0.2	0.5
Valine	1.3	1.3	1.5	2.3	—	3.3

[a]Up to two-thirds of methionine may be supplied by cystine
[b]Up to one-fifth of phenylalanine may be supplied by tyrosine
[c]Methionine plus cystine

trout indicates that between 3,000 and 3,500 kilocalories of metabolizable energy are necessary per kg of diet, with about 100 mg of well balanced protein per kilocalorie of metabolizable energy. The ratio of dietary digestible energy to protein (DE in kcal:protein in percent of the diet) may be near 100 for the most economical trout diet.[53] Caloric requirements of other fishes may be similar to trout.

There is limited information on metabolizable energy of various feedstuffs for fishes. Physiological fuel values can be used to calculate approximate metabolizable energy of any feedstuff or finished ration if quantitative crude protein, crude fat and nitrogen-free extract are known. Physiological fuel values of average protein for fishes are about 5.0 kilocalories per gram, average fat about 8.0 kilocalories per gram and average carbohydrate about 3.8 kilocalories per gram.[45,58]

Vitamins

Vitamins essential to the survival of fishes must be supplied in sufficient quantities to confined fishes at intervals acceptable to needs of the fish. Much of the research on quantitative daily vitamin requirements of fishes has been done on trout, salmon, channel catfish, carp and eel.[2,12,19] These data were derived from the use of vitamin test diets nutritionally balanced to the fish being tested and by feeding of serial quantities of the vitamin being tested.[5,22] Information on quantitative vitamin requirements of those fishes studied is used to ex-

trapolate dietary vitamin quantities for other fishes having similar physiology.

Diets formulated for confined fishes must contain at least the minimum quantity of each essential vitamin, either present in ingredients used to prepare the ration or supplied as a supplement. The ration must then be fed in sufficient quantity and at regular intervals in order to maintain adequate biological storage of each vitamin to meet all the metabolic needs for the vitamins. Diet preparations in which one or more vitamins are deficient will sooner or later create deficiency signs of those vitamins in the fish. Vitamin deficiencies may result in well defined disease syndromes and death. Even partial deficiencies may result in increased susceptibility to infectious diseases.

Practical fish culturists express vitamin requirements of fishes by two methods: based on mg of each vitamin per kg of body weight per day and based on mg of each vitamin per kg of ration. The former method assumes a constant requirement for each vitamin regardless of size (or age) of the fish, which may possibly supply unnecessary quantities of vitamins as a fish's metabolism decreases with age. The latter method assumes that diet quantity will be reduced as the fish becomes larger (or older) and the requirement for each vitamin will be reduced proportionally, which may not always be true. Both methods have been found to be acceptable, and the method used is usually left to the individual preparing the ration formula.[51] However, the fish disease diag-

TABLE 27

Sources and percent of essential fatty acids for the diet of fishes [45]

| | Percent Essential Fatty Acids | | | |
| | Average | | Range | |
Source	18:3w3	18:3w6	18:3w3	18:3w6
Herring oil	21.6	1.4	18.7-26.9	0.9- 1.6
Menhaden oil	29.3	3.0	22.0-34.8	2.9- 4.4
Cod liver oil	25.9	2.3	24.3-27.4	2.0- 2.7
Salmon oil	27.1	2.6	18.9-31.4	1.6- 3.6
Soybean oil	7.1	50.3	4.9-10.1	39.5-55.6
Corn oil	1.1	55.8	0.1- 1.5	50.0-56.9
Linseed oil	45.6	17.7	42.0-50.0	8.0-21.0
Lard	0.8	9.9	0.2- 1.4	6.7-13.0
Beef tallow	0.4	2.5	0.2- 0.5	0.7- 3.8

nostician must be aware of the method used whenever diseases associated with vitamin deficiencies are suspected.

Data obtained from various studies on vitamin requirements of fishes have been combined (Table 29). These data have been found to be generally acceptable for maintenance of the vitamin requirements for most fishes. The ration formula usually has additional quantities of each vitamin, especially those fragile vitamins such as thiamin, pyridoxine, ascorbic acid and others, to allow for losses incurred during milling operations and storage of the ration.

Minerals

Fishes require the same mineral elements as higher animals, and each mineral has a similar function in metabolism.[48] However, there is a great difference in dietary requirements of certain minerals between fishes and higher animals, because fishes are capable of supplying part or all of these minerals from the water. Certain mineral ions readily diffuse from the water through gill tissue or skin, reducing the quantities of the elements which must be present in the diet. Diffusible ions include chloride, carbonate, sulfate, sodium, calcium, phosphorus, potassium, iodine and others. Copper, magnesium, iron, zinc, aluminum and similar less diffusible ions should be supplied by the diet.[45] Iodine is gill-diffusible but may be lacking in some natural waters, thus iodine is usually added to prepared diets. Phosphorus and calcium are often added to prepared fish diets, especially in those geographical areas in which natural waters are low in either of these elements.[38]

Only a few quantitative mineral requirements have been published for fishes. The iodine requirement for

trout is 0.6 to 1.1 mg per kg of ration.[45,65] Available phosphorus in the diet of eels should be 0.3%, of channel catfish, between 0.45 and 0.8% and of carp, between 0.6 and 0.75%.[1] The recommended requirements for channel catfish are: 150 mg zinc per kg of diet, 2.4 mg manganese per kg of diet, and 0.04% magnesium in the diet.[17a,17b,17c] Zinc requirements for rainbow trout are given as 15 to 30 mg per kg of diet, but levels as high as 170 mg zinc per kg of diet gave no measurable toxic effects.[47a,62a] Traces of selenium are required by fish. Levels of 0.15 to 0.38 mg of selenium per kg of diet yielded maximum levels of the selenium bearing enzyme glutathione peroxidase in blood of rainbow trout. No pathological effects were noted in rainbow trout given diets as high as 13 mg selenium per kg of diet.[27a] The

TABLE 28

Digestibility of certain carbohydrates by trout [43,51]

Carbohydrate	Percent Digestibility
Glucose	99
Glycogen	99
Maltose	92
Dextrin	80
Sucrose	73
Lactose	60
Starch (cooked)	57
Starch (raw)	38
Cellulose	10

TABLE 29

Vitamin requirements for fishes[19,20,43,44,45]

Vitamin	Requirements in mg/kg of Fish Body Weight Per Day[a]	mg/kg of Ration
Water Soluble		
Ascorbic Acid	3 to 5	100
B$_{12}$	0.0005 to 0.0007	0.02
Biotin	0.03 to 0.07	1
Choline	50 to 60	3,000
Folic Acid	0.15 to 0.20	5
Inositol	18 to 20	400
Niacin	3 to 7	150
Pantothenic Acid	1.0 to 1.5	40
Pyridoxine	0.2 to 0.4	10
Riboflavin	0.5 to 1.0	20
Thiamin	0.15 to 0.20	10
Fat Soluble		
A	75 iu	2,50 iu
E	1.0 iu	30 iu
K	0.1 iu	10 iu
D	72 iu	2,400 iu

[a]Based on the requirements of young fishes

TABLE 30

Mineral composition of a vitamin test diet[22]

Mineral Element	mg per kg of diet[a]
Aluminum	2
Calcium	3,800
Chloride	1,060
Cobalt	16
Copper	12.5
Iodine	5
Iron	220
Magnesium	1,095
Manganese	15
Phosphorus	5,170
Potassium	5,300
Sodium	1,380
Sulfur	1,500
Zinc	14

[a]Present in the diet but availability to the fish is unknown

assumption can usually be made that natural water and natural ingredient diets will supply all other minerals. Purified and test diets fed to fishes under experimental conditions contain a full complement of minerals to be assured that no mineral deficiencies will develop (Table 30). The diagnostician may estimate quantities of each mineral element in practical diets by consulting feedstuffs tables for each ingredient in the ration. Mineral salts may be added to make up deficiencies between the estimated quantities and those known to be acceptable in test diets.[3,5,22]

Bulk (Fiber)

A requirement for fiber in the diet of fishes has not been investigated extensively. Fiber has been demonstrated to be nonessential in the diet of channel catfish and trout.[34,43] Dietary fiber levels as high as 21% are known to reduce nutrient intake and impair digestibility of practical rations fed to channel catfish. Dietary fiber levels as high as 20% of rainbow trout diets increased food consumption, increased stomach evacuation time and increased stomach volume. Results of these experiments suggested dietary fiber levels for rainbow trout should be less than 10%.[27b] Other data indicate it should not exceed 4% for salmonids.[43]

Nutritional Diseases

Most nutritional diseases are chronic in nature, usu-

TABLE 31

Some diet-related biological and clinical findings considered by the author to be acceptable and normal for fishes receiving balanced nutrition

Biological or Clinical Response	Range of Normal or Acceptable Values
Conversion	≤ 2.0 kg ration per kg gain
Grams protein per kg gain	475 to 650
Kilocalories (kcal) per kg gain	3,600 to 5,530
Percent gain	5 to 300% per month (depending on age)
Percent mortality	< 0.1% per month
Blood hematocrit	≥ 42
Blood hemoglobin	≥ 10 g per dl
Erythrocyte count	≥ 1 million per cubic mm of blood
Blood glucose	70 to 120 mg per dl
Serum total protein	≥ 3.5 g per dl of serum

ally developing slowly over an extended period of time. Early disease signs may be subtle and difficult to interpret. This is especially true when moderate nutrient deficiencies or excesses are involved or when signs of the nutritional disease are masked by secondarily invading infectious organisms.

Diagnosis of many of the nutritional diseases requires observation of external and internal disease signs, quantitative clinical chemistry on blood or other body fluids or tissues from the affected fish, histopathological examination and histochemical procedures (Table 31). Analysis of the diet being fed to the fish for various nutrient components, vitamins and minerals, and comparison with the nutrient requirements of the species of fish may also be of assistance in diagnosis of the disease. Observation of the ration for particle size versus fish size receiving the ration may also offer clues to the deficiency.[43] Feeding practices may also be of value: number of times the ration is being offered to the fish each day, whether all fish in the pond, raceway, tank or trough able to obtain their fair share of the ration, and other indications of mismanagement. The statement is often made that the most satisfactorily balanced ration for a particular fish species will produce nutritional problems if proper feeding practices are not followed.

Pathological Syndrome Associated with Protein and Amino Acid Deficiency

Reduced protein, or the amino acids therein, in the diet of fishes affects biosynthesis of many essential nitrogenous compounds, including all enzymes, hormones such as thyroxin or adrenalin, melanin pigments, histamine, creatine and other cofactors, and many other vital substances. Certain amino acids derived from dietary protein are essential for oxidation and utilization of fats and carbohydrates and are sources of methyl groups essential in the formation of acetylcholine, nicotinamide, purines, pyrimidines and other substances.

Diagnosis of malnutrition involving protein or amino acid deficiencies is extremely difficult because of general alterations within the body. Many indications of protein and amino acid deficiency are nonspecific. Conversion of food to fish tissue may be greater than two (2.0), the percent gain in weight compared to time may be much reduced and mortality may increase to greater than expected (Table 31).

Clinical findings may demonstrate anemia (less than 750,000 erythrocytes per cubic mm of blood, less than 7.5 grams of hemoglobin per deciliter of blood, hematocrit less than 37 and abnormal erythrocyte appearance on stained blood smears) and total serum protein less than 3.5 grams per deciliter of serum (Table 31). Examination of the ration formula may assist in diagnosis, i.e., major protein sources, quantity of each indispensable amino acid and availability of each amino acid. Methods of processing major protein source ingredients in the ration may suggest amino acid availability. Many of these ingredients (fish meal, dried milk products, feather meal, meat and bone meal, cottonseed meal, soybean meal and others) are processed with heat, solvents, sprayed or by other procedures. Heat, for example, coagulates protein and may reduce digestibility for fish. Storage time of ingredients and the finished ration may indicate possible reduction in amino acid availability.

Many of the same diagnostic findings noted in protein

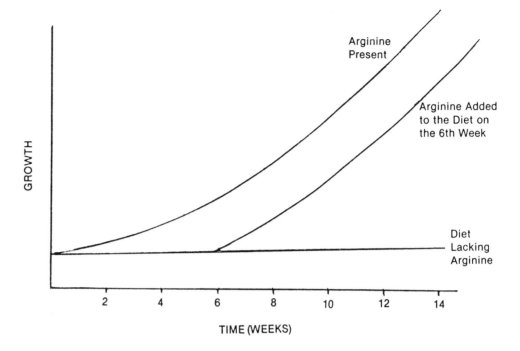

Fig. 25: Elimination of an indispenable amino acid (arginine in this case) from the diet will result in cessation of growth. Growth will be restored when the amino acid is added to the diet at an acceptable level.

and amino acid deficiency are similar to physical and functional alterations found in the diagnosis of diseases caused by other etiological agents. Probably the most common sign of protein and/or amino acid deficiency in fishes is reduction or cessation of growth. Limiting even one indispensable amino acid will affect growth. Feeding a diet in which an indispensable amino acid has been removed will cause growth to cease until the amino acid is restored to the diet (Fig. 25). Continued elimination of the indispensable amino acid will eventually cause mortality. Reducing or eliminating a dispensable amino acid from the ration will have no effect on growth (Pl. 27C).[10,23,43,56]

A specific pathological syndrome is associated with deficiency of the indispensable amino acid tryptophan. Deficiency of this amino acid will cause transient scoliosis and lordosis. Diets completely lacking in tryptophan will cause the condition in trout after about one month; possibly a similar effect will be noted in other fishes.

Studies to determine the cause of the extreme bending of the body indicate that collagen formation or connective tissue integrity is affected, allowing the notochord to bulge into intervertebral spaces. The body of a tryptophan-deficient fish may be extremely bent at certain times of the day and straight at other times. The extreme scoliosis and lordosis suffered by some fish (Pl. 27D) can be completely eliminated by restoring required quantities of tryptophan to the diet for one to two weeks.[31,32] Other signs of tryptophan deficiency include opacity of the lenticular part of the eye lens. This condition may also occur from deficiency of methionine, cystine or other sulfur bearing amino acid.[28a]

Excesses of leucine or isoleucine increases valine requirements, reduced growth and reduced food utilization. Five percent dietary leucine to lake trout caused significant reduction of liver fat content but could be returned to normal by feeding additional valine.[28b] No other undesirable effects of excesses of other amino acids have been noted in fish.

Pathological Syndromes Associated with Dietary Fats and Lipids

Pathological conditions occur in fishes from excess dietary fats, deficiency of essential fatty acid(s) and the toxic effect of rancidification (peroxidation) of unsaturated dietary fats. Feeding of highfat diets may cause fatty infiltration of the liver and excessive obesity.[49] The livers of fishes with fatty infiltration of the liver are yellowish to ochre in color, swollen and sometimes greasy in appearance. Touching the cut surface of the liver to water usually forms an oil film. The liver may be cut frozen and stained with a fat stain to demonstrate intracellular fat droplets for definitive diagnosis of this condition.[52] No microscopically observable fat droplets are present in normal fish liver. Liver malfunction may alter kidney function, leading to retention of body water. Edema of various organs, including the liver, often accompanies fatty infiltration of the liver.

Treatment of fatty infiltration is by reduction of dietary fats if it exceeds 18 to 20% of the diet or if much of the fat is saturated fat and the diet is being fed at cold water temperatures (10°C or less). Increasing choline in the diet may assist the fishes in metabolizing intracellular fat as dietary fat is being reduced.

Small trout have difficulty digesting and absorbing hard (saturated) fats if the fishes are in cold water. Fats obstruct the intestine and prevent elimination. Mortality may result. A similar condition may occur in other coldwater and coolwater fishes.[49]

Deficiency of linolenic family 18:3w3 fatty acid causes reduced growth, skin depigmentation, fin erosion and fainting in rainbow trout.[8,46] Similar signs of deficiency may occur in other fishes. The caudal fin appears to be more affected than the other fins. Secondarily invading bacteria or fungi may enhance the problem. The fainting or shock syndrome associated with deficiency of essential fatty acid is noted by rapid swimming induced by a stimulus (a sharp blow to the side of the tank or handling with a net). Rapid swimming is followed by immobility and loss of consciousness. The fish may float or sink to the bottom, remain motionless for a few minutes and then either recover or die. Fishes in this state of deficiency cannot survive handling or transportation.[8,57,60,61,62]

Reduced growth and increased levels of 5,8,10-eicosatrienoic acid, 20:3w9, occur as essential fatty acid syndromes in catfishes, eels and carp.[27] The requirement for essential fatty acids in catfishes must be quite low, because excellent growth rates have been obtained in long-term feeding studies in which beef tallow was the sole source of fat. The fishes did demonstrate high levels of 20:3w9 fatty acid in the tissue.[44,59]

Essential fatty acid deficiency syndrome can be eliminated by feeding at least 1% 18:3w3 linolenic acid to trout and salmon, but these quantities may not be so high with other fishes. The recommendation has been made that at least 5% fish oil, rich in linolenic 18:3w3 acid (Table 27), be added to salmonid rations to eliminate signs of essential fatty acid deficiency.[45]

The nature of prepared fish rations is that they usually contain high levels of polyunsaturated fats and oils. Unsaturated fats are subject to autoxidation (rancidification or peroxidation) in which peroxides and other toxic compounds are formed. Certain ration ingredients (dried blood meal, dried liver meal, dried meat scrap meal or other products high in hemoglobin content) catalyze autoxidation. The effects of the toxic compounds on trout have been known or suspected for a long time.[45,49] Autoxidation products produce a syndrome much like muscular dystrophy, a disease usually associated with deficiency of a-tocopherol. This is not surprising, since a-tocopherol acts as an antioxidant to retard autoxidation of unsaturated fats. The high levels of unsaturated fats in fish diets quickly utilize the a-tocopherol, so when the ration is fed, a-tocopherol deficiency is a part of the syndrome.[35,42,60]

Incomplete metabolism of fats by the fish's liver results in the formation of ceroid, an insoluble pigment. Ceroid is deposited in hepatic cord cells, which impairs liver function. Autoxidation products cause necrosis of kidney hematopoietic tissue, reducing or stopping hematopoiesis. Erythrocytes are released into the bloodstream (first as juvenile cells, then as pronormoblasts and even as young as the megaloblast stage) as the toxic effects of peroxidation products continue. Hematocrits as low as 7 and erythrocyte counts as low as 0.15 million per cubic mm of blood are not uncommon in advanced cases (Table 31). Liver malfunction causes kidney excretory malfunction, leading to nephrosis, fluid retention and edema.[35,64]

Diagnosis of rancid fat toxicity in fishes includes hematology, histopathology, histochemistry and analysis of the ration for autoxidation products. Affected fishes will usually have a reduced hematocrit and erythrocyte count. Examination of stained blood smears will reveal a paucity of older erythrocytes, with younger cells being more prevalent (Pl. 28A). Necrotic foci may be found in the kidney hematopoietic tissue, with edema and nephrosis (Pl. 28B, 28C). Ceroid may be demonstrated in liver hepatocytes (Pl. 28D). Analysis of the ration for autoxidation products, and especially thiobarbituric acids (TBA), indicates that values greater than 10 mg of TBA per kg of fat in the ration should be considered unacceptable for feeding those fishes known to be susceptible to these toxic products.

There is no specific treatment for fishes already affected by fat peroxidation products. Changing to a ration with less than one mg of TBA per kg of dietary fat may assist in bringing affected fishes back to health. However, experience has indicated that groups of fish in which a high percentage have hematopoietic necrosis, megaloblastemia and liver ceroid deposits may never return to normal.[15]

Prevention of the toxic condition caused by dietary autoxidation products is possible. All fats and oils to be used in fish diets and ration ingredients which contain unsaturated fats should be stabilized at the time of manufacture. Antioxidants such as butylated hydroxytoluene, ethoxyquin or santoquin can be used to prevent autoxidation. Unsaturated fats in rations prepared with catalytic ingredients (those containing hemoglobin or other catalytic products) may be protected by adding one of the above-mentioned antioxidants or up to five times more than the normally required quantity of a-tocopherol.[64] Quantities of butylated hydroxtoluene, ethoxyquin, santoquin or other similar antioxidants should not be greater than 0.02% of the finished ration, including the antioxidant present in ration ingredients and added directly to the ration. Stored rations prepared with unstabilized products and without added autoxidants will continue to produce peroxidation products with or without cold storage.[15,42]

Pathological Syndrome Associated with Dietary Carbohydrate

Excess digestible carbohydrates in the diet of trout and salmon causes hyperglycemia, liver hyperglycogenesis and increased liver mass. The degree of these conditions is important in determining if health of the fish is being impaired. Normal blood glucose in trout and salmon ranges between 70 and 120 mg per dl. Feeding of excess digestible carbohydrates may cause increases to greater than 300 mg of glucose per dl. The exact significance of hyperglycemia in fishes is not known, but hyperglycemic trout and salmon may be lethargic, seek the sides of the holding facility, swim near the surface of the water, become dark in color and/or refuse to take food.[45] Other fishes may react similarly, but no information on hyperglycemia on them is known.

Liver glycogen storage in normal trout and salmon ranges between 0.5 and 3.0% of the liver mass. Excess digestible carbohydrates in the diet may increase this level to greater than 17%. The exact effect of hyperglycogenesis on these fishes is not known, but it does contribute to the same syndrome associated with hyperglycemia. Groups of trout in which individuals have greater than 15% liver glycogen demonstrate increased mortality and increased susceptibility to diseases caused by bacteria, fungi and animal parasites. Liver glycogen of 17% may cause direct mortality.[43]

Increased liver mass accompanies hyperglycogenesis. Normal rainbow trout, for example, have a liver mass to body weight ratio of between 0.8 and 1.5%.[43] Trout with liver hyperglycogenesis may have livers which are greater than 3% of the body weight. A similar effect has been noted in red sea bream, plaice and yellow-tail.[45] Other fishes receiving a diet high in carbohydrate may react similarly.

Excessive glycogen in the liver of fishes, depending on severity, tends to cause liver malfunction and may contribute to kidney malfunction. Both liver and kidney malfunction may contribute to impairment of health.

Diagnosis of dietary carbohydrate-related pathology can be made by blood glucose and liver glycogen analyses. Estimation of liver mass to body weight ratio may also be of assistance in diagnosis. Histopathological examination of stained liver sections can be useful in the diagnosis of liver hyperglycogenesis. Liver hepatocyte vacuolation is dependent on glycogen content. Normal hepatocytes have no observable glycogen vacuoles (Pl. 1E), but the higher the glycogen content the greater the hepatocyte vacuolation (Pl. 29A). Proof that the hepatocyte vacuoles are filled with glycogen can be made histochemically. One slide of the suspected liver tissue is treated with diastase, which will remove glycogen if liver vacuoles are glycogen. The diastase-treated slide and an untreated liver tissue slide are stained with periodic acid-Shiff reagent. Glycogen remaining in the untreated liver sections will stain red to magenta with the periodic acid-Schiff reagent (Pl. 28E); the diastase-treated liver tissue has no glycogen and is stained by the counterstain only (Pl. 28F). The pathologist can usually make a judgment as to the relationships between liver glycogen, hepatocyte alteration and liver malfunction.

Pathological Syndromes Associated with Vitamin Deficiency

Formulation, preparation and storage of rations for confined fishes should take into account the requirements of each vitamin for the species of fish being fed. There should be a quantitative daily dietary intake of each of these essential nutrients necessary for maintenance of acceptable storage in tissues of the body. Depletion of the body storage of any single vitamin can be responsible for specific or general disease signs. Diagnosis of vitamin deficiencies is difficult, relying on all types of diagnostic techniques depending to some degree on the specific vitamin or vitamins suspected of being deficient. Gross signs, blood chemistry, hematology, tissue vitamin assay, gross pathology, histopathology and ration vitamin assay may be necessary for making a diagnosis.

Disease signs and gross pathology usually suggest which vitamin(s) may be deficient, and other diagnostic procedures are then used to complete the diagnosis.[6a] Results of research in which specific vitamins have been reduced or eliminated from the diets of fishes have demonstrated the usual signs, gross pathology and histopathology to be expected from specific avitaminoses (Table 32).[16,20,24,25,43,44,45]

Illustrative examples of selected vitamin deficiencies are given in Pl. 29B through 29E.

Assay for specific vitamins in the ration is important in diagnosis of vitamin deficiencies. Standardized methods for vitamin assay have been established by the Association of Vitamin Chemists.[17] Those vitamins which fluoresce at a particular wavelength of light can be determined fluorometrically; others are determined spectrophotometrically and others microbiologically. The quantity of a specific vitamin found by assay per unit weight of ration can be used to determine if the required amount of vitamin is being supplied to the fishes eating the ration (Table 29).

The relationship between folic acid assay quantity in a prepared trout ration and the folic acid requirement for trout is used below as an example to demonstrate the use of assay results for assistance in diagnosis of folic acid deficiency. Assay results of other vitamins can be used in the same way if the daily requirement is known for the vitamin in the fish species being fed.

Example: *Use of vitamin assay results in a prepared ration to assist in vitamin deficiency diagnosis.*

Rainbow trout in a raceway have developed macrocytic anemia, fragile caudal fins, are dark in color, demonstrate much reduced growth and are generally lethargic. Folic acid deficiency is suspected.

There are 1,000 kg of fish in the raceway. The aver-

TABLE 32

Signs of vitamin deficiency in fishes[43,45,66]

Vitamin	Signs
Water-soluble	
Ascorbic acid	Scoliosis; lordosis; impaired collagen formation; altered cartilage; capillary fragility; hemorrhagic exophthalmos; intramuscular hemorrhage; edema; anemia and loss of appetite;[a]
B_{12}	Hematologic disorders; fragile erythrocytes; poor growth; anemia;[b]
Biotin	Skin lesions (blue slime); muscle atrophy; spastic convulsions; erythrocyte fragility; poor growth
Choline	Poor growth; poor food conversion; hemorrhagic kidney and intestines; accumulation of neutral fats in liver
Folic acid	Poor growth; lethargy; fragile caudal fin; dark coloration; macrocytic anemia
Inositol	Poor growth; distended stomach; increased gastric emptying time;[c]
Niacin	Loss of appetite; lesions in rectum; muscle spasms while resting; hemorrhage in skin; skin lesions; anemia
Pantothenic acid	Clubbed gill filaments; proximal lamellar hyperplasia; loss of appetite; poor growth; exudate on gills
Pyridoxine	Nervous disorders (epileptiform convulsions); anemia; loss of appetite; edema in peritoneal cavity; blue-violet iridescent skin color; rapid rigor mortis; rapid and gasping breathing; flexing of opercles
Riboflavin	Corneal vascularization; cloudy lenses; reduced vision; abnormal pigmentation of iris; dark coloration; anemia; poor growth
Thiamin	Convulsions followed by body flexure and possible death; instability and loss of equilibrium; edema; poor growth
Fat-soluble	
A	Retinal alterations; exophthalmos; eye lens displacement; depigmentation; edema; poor growth
D	Tetany of white skeletal muscle; poor growth
E	Muscular dystrophy; ceroid in liver, kidney and spleen; edema; microcytic anemia; poor growth
K	Reduced blood clotting time

[a]Ascorbic acid may not be required by carp.[55a]

[b]B_{12} may not be essential in the diet of fish with cobalamine producing intestinal flora if dietary cobalt is sufficient.[35a]

[c]Inositol is not essential for channel catfish.[6b]

age size, as determined by weighing a representative sample of the fish and counting the number, is 540 fish per kg, and the water temperature is 16°C. The feeding level is 5.3% of the total fish weight in the raceway per day.

Folic acid assay in the ration indicates 2.2 mg of folic acid per kg of ration.

Determination of adequacy of the dietary folic acid as follows:

Minimum daily folic acid requirement—0.15 mg per kg of fish per day (Table 29).

Minimum folic acid for 1,000 kg fish—150 mg per day

Feeding level 5.3% fish body weight—53 kg ration per day

Ration folic acid assay results—2.2 mg per kg of ration

Therefore: 53 kg ration must contain 150 mg folic acid

But: 53 kg ration X 2.2 mg folic acid = 116.6 mg actual folic acid in 53 kg ration

Diagnosis: Folic acid is below the minimum daily requirement and could be responsible for the disease signs.

Pathological Syndromes Associated with Mineral Deficiencies

Mineral deficiency studies with fishes are difficult because all traces of each mineral to be studied must be removed from both food and water. Thus, only a limited number of mineral deficiencies are known or have been studied in fishes.[36]

Endemic goiter (thyroid hyperplasia) was first reported in brook trout in 1910. The condition was referred to at the time as thyroid carcinoma. Further studies on the condition linked thyroid hyperplasia to iodine deficiency.[18,39,40] The recommendation was made at the time that addition of iodized salt to the ration, usually at about 2% of the diet, would prevent goiter.

Quantitative studies in the middle 1960's indicated chinook salmon must be fed at least 0.6 micrograms of iodide per gram of dry ration to maintain maximum thyroid iodine storage and normal thyroid histology. Advanced parr required 1.1 micrograms of iodide per gram of ration during the smoltification period.[65] Possibly other anadromous fishes require similar quantities of iodine during transition from fresh water to salt water.

Definitive diagnosis of iodine deficiency is by histological examination of thyroid tissue and analysis for iodine storage in the thyroid area.[55] Moderate iodine deficiency can cause elongation of epithelial cells in the thyroidal tissue; a more advanced condition will be ac-

tual thyroid hyperplasia and enlargement. Observable swelling of tissue in the thyroid region (base of tongue to the last gill arch) may suggest iodine deficiency.[6,45,65]

Zinc deficiency has been implicated in the formation of cataracts in the eye lenses of rainbow trout. Trout fed a dry ration rich in a calcium-bearing feedstuff (a product prepared from the carcass of a fish following removal of two fillets and the liver) developed monolateral or bilateral cataracts within 18 weeks (Pl. 36C).[51a] Addition of zinc sulfate at 150 mg per kg of ration prevented cataract formation. Addition of calcium, phosphorus, sodium and potassium to the ration increased the severity of cataract formation if zinc was not supplemented. Removing supplemented manganese, copper and iron from the ration had no effect on cataract formation if zinc was present at an acceptable level.[30]

Feeding a ration with insufficient iron (1 mg iron per kg of ration) to carp for 15 weeks produced significantly reduced blood hemoglobin, hematocrit, mean corpuscular hemoglobin and mean corpuscular volume when compared to carp fed a ration with 199 mg iron per kg of diet. The percentage of immature erythrocytes was higher in fish fed the ration with insufficient iron. The results demonstrate carp fed rations with insufficient iron develop hypochromic microcytic anemia.[54] Other fishes probably respond similarly to dietary iron deficiency. Preparation, staining and microscopic examination of blood smears is an acceptable routine diagnostic procedure for estimating abnormalities of blood cells, including iron deficiency anemia (Pl. 29F). Other hematological procedures are also of diagnostic assistance.

Fishes require relatively large quantities of calcium and phosphorus, but both can be absorbed from food or water.[48] Quantities of soluble phosphorus in some natural waters are extremely low, so supplementation of phosphorus to the diet may be necessary. Deficiencies of phosphorus have been associated with lordosis and reduced skull growth in carp and with reduced growth, food conversion, bone ash and hematocrit in catfishes.[1,37,44] Diagnosis of phosphorus deficiency may be possible by observing skeletal deformities, hematology, blood phosphorus determination and analysis for phosphorus in both food and water.

Channel catfish fed a purified diet containing 0.004% magnesium developed magnesium deficiency signs including: loss of appetite, sluggish movements, muscle flaccidity and high mortality. Deficiency signs disappeared when the fish were given the purified diet containing 0.057% magnesium.[17c]

Deficiencies of other macromineral elements or ions (calcium, potassium, chloride, sulfate and sodium for example) and trace minerals (aluminum, copper, cobalt, manganese, molybdenum and others) have not been studied in fishes. Prepared rations offered to confined fishes should include sources of each, from food or water, to prevent deficiencies of these elements.

Selected References

1. Andrews J. W., T. Murai and C. Campbell. 1973. "Effects of dietary calcium and phosphorus on growth, food conversion, bone ash and hematocrit levels in catfish," *J. Nutr.*, 103:766-771.

1a. Anderson, R. J., E. W. Kienholtz and S. A. Flickinger. 1981. "Protein requirements of smallmouth bass and largemouth bass." *J. Nutr.*, 111:1085-1097.

2. Aoe, H., I. Masuda, I. Abe, T. Saito and Y. Tajima. 1971. "Water-soluble vitamin requirements of carp. VII. Some examinations on utility of the reported minimum requirements," *Bull. Jap. Soc. Sci. Fish.*, 37:124-129.

3. Arai, S., T. Nose and Y. Hashimoto. 1975. "Mineral requirements of eel," *Proc. Ann. Meet. Jap. Soc. Sci. Fish.* April 1-5, 1975. Tokoyo.

4. Arai, S., T. Nose and Y. Hashimoto. 1972. "Amino acids essential for the growth of eels, *Anguilla anguilla* and *Anguilla japonica*," *Bull. Jap. Soc. Sci. Fish.*, 38:753-759.

5. Arai, S., T. Nose and Y. Hashimoto. 1971. "A purified test diet for the eel, *Anguilla japonica*," *Bull. Freshwater Fish. Res. Lab., Tokyo*, 21:161-178.

6. Axelrad, A. A., C. P. Leblond and J. Isler. 1955. "Role of iodine deficiency in the production of goiter by the Remington diet," *Endocrinol.*, 56:387-403.

6a. Brunson, M. W. and H. R. Robinette. 1983. "Nutritional gill disease associated with starter feeds for channel catfish fry." *Prog. Fish-Cult.*, 42:119-120.

6b. Burtle, G. J. 1981. *Essentiality of dietary inositol for channel catfish*. Unpubl. Ph. D. Dissert., Auburn Univ. Auburn, AL. 42p.

7. Buterbaugh, G. L. and H. Willoughby. 1967. "A feeding guide for brook, brown and rainbow trout," *Prog. Fish-Cult.*, 29:210-215.

8. Castell, J. D., R. O. Sinnhuber, J. H. Wales and D. J. Lee. 1972. "Essential fatty acids in the diet of rainbow trout (*Salmo gairdneri*): growth, feed conversion and some gross deficiency symptoms," *J. Nutr.*, 102: 77-85.

9. Cowey, C. B. and J. R. Sargent. 1972. "Fish nutrition," *Adv. Mar. Biol.*, 10:383.

10. DeLong, D. C., J. E. Halver and E. T. Mertz. 1958. "Nutrition of salmonoid fishes. VI. Protein requirements of chinook salmon at two water temperatures," *J. Nutr.*, 65:589-599.

11. Deuel, C. R., D. C. Haskell, D. R. Brockway and O. R. Kingsbury. 1952. *The New York State Feeding Chart. N.Y. Cons. Comm. Fish. Res. Bull.*, No. 3. 61p.

12. Dupree, H. K. 1966. *Vitamins essential for growth of channel catfish. U.S. Bur. Spt. Fish. Wildl. Tech. Pap.*, No. 7. 12p.

13. Dupree, H. K. and J. E. Halver. 1970. "Amino acids essential for the growth of catfish," *Trans. Am. Fish. Soc.*, 99:90-93.

14. Dupree, H. K. and K. E. Sneed. 1966. *Response of channel catfish fingerlings to different levels of major nutrients in purified diets. Tech. Pap.*, No. 9, Bur. Spt. Fish Wildl., Washington, DC. 21p.

15. Fowler, R. E. 1978. *Uses of Cereco-II in rainbow trout rations.* M.S. Thesis, Colo. State Univ., Fort Collins, CO 60p.

16. Fowler, L. G. and J. L. Banks. 1970. *Tests of substitute ingredients and effects of storage on the Abernathy salmon diet, 1968. U.S. Bur. Spt. Fish Wildl. Tech. Pap.*, 47, Washington, D.C. 8p.

17. Freed, M. 1966. *Methods of vitamin assay. 3rd ed.* The Assoc. Vit. Chem. Inc. Interscience Publ., Div. John Wiley & Sons, New York City, NY. 424p.

17a. Gatlin, D. M. III, and R. P. Wilson. 1984. "Studies on manganese requirements of fingerling channel catfish." *Aquacult.*, 41:85-92.

17b. Gatlin, D. M. III, R. P. Wilson. 1984. "Zinc supplementation of practical channel catfish diets." *Aquacult.*, 41:31-36.

17c. Gatlin, D. M. III, E. H. Robinson, W. E. Poe and R. P. Wilson. 1982. "Magnesium requirement of fingerling channel catfish and signs of magnesium deficiency." *J. Nutr.*, 112:1182-1187.

18. Gaylord, H. R. and M. C. Marsh. 1912 "Carcinoma of the thyroid in salmonoid fishes," *Bull. Bur. Fish.*, 32: 364-524.

19. Halver, J. E. 1975. "Nutrient requirements of cold water fish." Proc. 9th Int. Congr. Nutr. *In: Food for the expanding world*, 3:142-157. S. Kargar AG, Basel, Switzerland.

20. Halver, J. E. (ed). 1972. *Fish nutrition.* Academic Press, New York City, NY. 713p.

21. Halver, J. E. 1957. "Nutrition of salmonoid fishes. IV. An amino acid test diet for chinook salmon," *J. Nutr.*, 62:245-254.

22. Halver, J. E. and J. A. Coates. 1957. "A vitamin test diet for long-term feeding studies," *Prog. Fish-Cult.*, 19:112-118.

23. Halver, J. E., D. C. DeLong and E. T. Mertz. 1957. "Nutrition of salmonoid fishes. V. Classification of essential amino acids for chinook salmon," *J. Nutr.*, 63:95-105.

24. Hashimoto, Y. 1975. "Nutritional requirements of warm water fish." Proc. 9th Int. Congr. Nutr. *In: Food for the expanding world*, 3:158-175. S. Kargar AG, Basel, Switzerland.

25. Hashimoto, Y. and T. Okaichi. 1969. *Vitamins as*

nutrients for fish. Transl. Publ. by J. Hoffman-La Roche and Co., Ltd., Basel, Switzerland. 40p.

26. Hastings, W. H. 1975. "Formula for extensive fish culture." Proc. 9th Int. Congr. Nutr. *In: Foods for the expanding world*, 3:208-214. S. Kargar AG, Basel, Switzerland.

27. Higashi, H., T. Kaneko, S. Ishii, M. Ushiyama and T. Sugihashi. 1966. "Effects of ethyl linoleate, ethyl linolenate and ethyl esters of highly unsaturated fatty acids on essential fatty acid deficiency in rainbow trout," *J. Vitaminol.*, 12:74-79.

27a. Hilton, J. W., P. V. Hodson and S. J. Slinger. 1980. "The requirement and toxicity of selenium in rainbow trout (*Salmo gairdneri*)." *J. Nutr.*, 110:2527-2535.

27b. Hilton, J. W., J. L. Atkinson and S. J. Slinger. 1983. "Effect of increased dietary fiber on the growth of rainbow trout (*Salmo gairdneri*)." *Can. J. Fish. Aquat. Sci.*, 40:81-85.

28. Huet, M. 1973. *Textbook of fish culture*. Fishing News (Books), Ltd. West Byfleet, Surrey, England. 43p.

28a. Hughes, S. G. 1985. "Nutritional eye diseases of salmonids: a review." *Prog. Fish-Cult.*, 47:81-85.

28b. Hughes, S. G., G. L. Rumsey and M. C. Nesheim. 1984. "Effects of dietary excesses of branched-chain amino acids on the metabolism and tissue composition of lake trout (*Salvelinus namaycush*)." *Comp. Biochem. Physiol.*, 78:413-418.

29. Kayama, M. 1966. "Fatty acid metabolism in fish," *Bull. Jap. Soc. Sci. Fish.*, 30:649-659. (Transl. Ser. Fish. Res. Bd. Can. No. 652, Queen's Printer, Ottawa, Can.)

29a. Ketola, H. G. 1982. "Amino acid nutrition of fishes: Requirements and supplementation of diets." *Comp. Biochem. Physiol.*, 73B:17-24.

30. Ketola, H. G. 1979. "Influence of dietary zinc on cataracts in rainbow trout (*Salmo gairdneri*)," *J. Nutr.*, 109:965-969.

31. Kloppel, T. M. 1974. *Tryptophan deficiency in rainbow trout*. M.S. Thesis, Colo. State Univ., Ft. Collins, CO. 43p.

32. Kloppel, T. M. and G. Post. 1975. "Histological alteration in tryptophan-deficient rainbow trout," *J. Nutr.*, 105:861-866.

33. Lagler, K. F. 1956. *Freshwater fishery biology*. Wm. C. Brown Co., Dubuque, IA. 421p.

34. Leary, D. F. 1972. *Fiber requirements of channel catfish*. Ph.D. Diss., Auburn Univ., Auburn, AL 89p.

35. Lee, D. L. and R. O. Sinnhuber. 1972. "Lipid requirements," *In* J. E. Halver (ed.). *Fish nutrition*, p. 145- 180. Academic Press, New York City, NY.

35a. Lovell, T. and T. Limsuwan. 1982. "Intestinal synthesis and dietary nonessentiality of vitamin B$_{12}$ for *Tilapia nilotica*." *Trans. Amer. Fish. Soc.* 111:485-490.

36. Lovell, R. T. 1975. "Nutritional deficiencies in intensively cultured catfish," *In* W. E. Ribelin and G. Migaki. *The pathology of fishes*, p. 721-731. Univ. Wis. Press, Madison, WI.

37. Lovell, R. T. 1974. *Phosphorus requirements of channel catfish fed all-plant diets in earthen ponds. Fish. Ann. Rep. Auburn Agri. Exp. Sta., Auburn, AL.*, 10:45p.

38. Lovell, R. T. 1971. *Calcium and phosphorus requirements of channel catfish. Vol. I. Fish. Ann. Rep. Auburn Agri. Exp. Sta., Auburn, AL.* 45p.

39. Marine, D. 1914. "Further observations and experiments on goitre in brook trout," *J. Exp. Med.*, 19:70.

40. Marine, D. and C. H. Lenhart. 1910. "Observations and experiments on the so called thyroid carcinoma of the brook trout (*Salvelinus fontinalis*) and its relation to ordinary goitre," *J. Exp. Med.*, 12:311.

41. Mertz, E. T. 1969 "Amino acid and protein requirements of fish," *In* O. W. Neuhaus and J. E. Halver, eds. *Fish in research*. p. 233-244. Academic Press, New York City, NY.

42. Murai, T. and J. W. Andrews. 1974. "Interactions of *a*-tocopherol oxidized menhaden oil and ethoxyquin on channel catfish (*Ictalurus punctatus*)," *J. Nutr.*, 104:1416-1431.

43. National Academy of Sciences. 1978. *Nutrient requirements of laboratory animals. Third revised edition*. Nat. Acad. Sci., Washington, DC. p. 84-96.

44. National Academy of Sciences. 1977. *Nutrient requirements of warmwater fishes*. Nat. Acad. Sci., Washington, DC. 78p.

45. National Academy of Sciences. 1973. *Nutrient requirements of cold water fishes*. Nat. Acad. Sci., Washington, DC. 63p.

46. Nicolaides, N. and A. N. Woodall. 1962. "Impaired pigmentation in chinook salmon fed diets deficient in essential fatty acids," *J. Nutr.*, 78:431-437.

47. Nose, T., S. Arai, D. L. Lee and Y. Hashimoto. 1974. "A note on amino acids essential for growth of young carp," *Bull. Jap. Soc. Sci. Fish.*, 40:903-908.

47a. Ogino, C. and G-Y. Yand. 1978. "Requirements of rainbow trout for dietary zinc." *Bull. Jpn. Soc. Sci. Fish.*, 44:1015-1018.

48. Phillips, A. M., Jr. 1959. "The known and possible role of minerals in trout nutrition and physiology," *Trans. Am. Fish. Soc.*, 88:133-135.

49. Phillips, A. M. and H. A. Podoliak. 1957. "The nutrition of trout. III. Fats and minerals," *Prog. Fish-Cult.*, 19:68-75.

50. Phillips, A. M., Jr., A. V. Tunison and D. R. Brockway. 1948. *Utilization of carbohydrates by trout. New York Cons. Dept. Fish. Res. Bull.*, No. 11. 44p.

51. Post, G. 1975. "Ration formulation for itensively reared fishes." Proc. 9th Int. Congr. Nutr. *In: Foods for the expanding world*, 3:199-207. S. Kargar AG, Basel, Switzerland.

51a. Poston, H. A., R. C. Riis, G. L. Rumsey and H. G. Ketola. 1978. "Nutritionally induced cataracts in salmonids fed purified and practical diets." *Mar. Fish.* Rev., 40(10):45-46.

52. Preece, A. 1972. *A manual for histological technicians. 3rd Ed.* Little, Brown and Co., Boston, MA. 428p.

53. Reinitz, G. L., L. E. Orme, C. A. Lemm and F. N. Hitzel. 1978. "Influence of varying lipid concentrations with two protein concentrations in diets for rainbow trout (*Salmo gairdneri*)," *Trans. Am. Fish. Soc.*, 107:751-754.

53a. Rumsey, G. L., J. W. Page and M. L. Scott. 1983. "Methionine and cystine requirements of rainbow trout." *Prog. Fish-Cult.*, 45:139-143.

54. Sakamoto, S. and Y. Yone. 1978. "Iron deficiency symptoms in carp," *Bull. Jap. Soc. Sci. Fish.*, 44: 1157-1160.

55. Sandell, E. B. and I. M. Koltoff. 1937. "Microdetermination of iodine by a catalylic method," *Mikrochim. Acta.*, 1:9-17.

55a. Sato, M., R. Yoshinaka and Y. Yamamoto. 1978. "Nonessentiality of ascorbic acid in the diet of carp." *Bull. Jpn. Soc. Sci. Fish.*, 44:1151-1156.

56. Shanks, W. E., G. D. Gahimer and J. E. Halver. 1962. "The indispensable amino acids for rainbow trout," *Prog. Fish-Cult.*, 24:68-73.

57. Sinnhuber, R. O. 1969. "The role of fats," *In* O. W. Neuhaus and J. E. Halver, eds. *Fish in research*. Academic Press, New York City, NY. p. 245-261.

58. Smith, R. R. 1976. "Metabolizable energy of feedstuffs for trout," *Feedstuffs*, 48(23):16-21.

59. Stickney, R. R. and J. W. Andrews. 1971. "Combined effects of dietary lipids and environmental temperature on growth, metabolism and body composition of channel catfish (*Ictalurus punctatus*)," *J. Nutr.*, 101: 1703-1710.

60. Takeuchi, T. and T. Watanabe. 1977. "Requirements of carp for essential fatty acids," *Bull. Jap. Soc. Sci. Fish.*, 43:541-551.

60a. Walton, M. J., C. B. Cowey and J. W. Adron. 1984. "The effect of dietary lysine on growth and metabolism of rainbow trout (*Salmo gairdneri*)." *Brit. J. Nutr.*, 52:115-122.

61. Watanabe, T., T. Takeuchi and C. Ogino. 1975. "Effects of dietary methyl linoleate and linolenate on growth of carp. II," *Bull. Jap. Soc. Sci. Fish.*, 41: 263-269.

62. Watanabe, T., O. Utsue, I. Kobayashi and C. Ogino. 1975. "Effect of dietary methyl linoleate and linolenate on growth of carp. I," *Bull. Jap. Soc. Sci. Fish.*, 41:257-262.

62a. Wekell, J. C., K. D. Shearer and C. R. Houle. 1983. "High zinc supplementation of rainbow trout." *Prog. Fish-Cult.* 45:144-147.

63. Winberg, G. G. 1956. *Rate of metabolism and food requirements of fishes. Fish. Res. Bd. Can., Trans.*, Series No. 194. Queen's Printer, Ottawa, Canada. 202p.

64. Woodall, A. N., L. M. Ashley, J. E. Halver, H. S. Olcott and J. Vander Veen. 1964. "Nutrition of salmonoid fishes. XIII. The a-tocopherol requirement of chinook salmon," *J. Nutr.*, 84:125-135.

65. Woodall, A. N. and G. LaRoche. 1964. "Nutrition of salmonoid fishes. XI. Iodine requirements for chinook salmon," *J. Nutr.*, 82:475-482.

66. Woodward, B. 1984. "Symptoms of severe riboflavin deficiency without ocular opacity in rainbow trout (*Salmo gairdneri*)." *Aquacult.* 37:275-281.

Chapter X

NEOPLASTIC DISEASES
OF FISHES

Each cell of an animal's body is characteristic for an organ or tissue of which it is a part. Each is capable of proliferation to allow for orderly growth, normal function and body maintenance. Cells lost to wear and tear, disease or injury are replaced at a controlled rate. Thus, structural stability and function are maintained in tissues, organs and the entire animal. Loss of the carefully regulated cellular proliferative growth in a tissue results in the appearance of tumor masses referred to as neoplasia (literally, new growth). The study of tumors is called oncology.[18]

The definition of a neoplasia as an abnormal growth of a cellular element of the body can easily be confused with the same definition for hyperplasia. The diagnostician must learn to differentiate between the two because neoplastic growth has far more serious disease implications than does hyperplastic growth. Hyperplasia is a controlled cellular proliferative process. The cellular population increases as does the size of the organ, but the normal structure of the organ is maintained. Neoplastic growth is not controlled and the organ differentiation is gradually lost (Table 33).

There are two broad types of tumors: benign and malignant. Benign tumors are considered to be less dangerous to the affected animal (or plant) than malignant tumors. The proliferative growth of a benign tumor is more subject to control than growth of a malignant tumor. Thus, a fish with a benign tumor may be only mildly affected, with complete recovery possible (Table 34).

Malignant tumors (cancers) are intracellular diseases in which altered cells are formed, transmitting altered cellular characteristics to succeeding generations of cells. Malignant cells proliferate rapidly, usually outgrowing normal cells of the same organ and overwhelming all structures and functions in the immediate vicinity of the tumor. Malignant tumor cells may break away from the parent tumor and move in the blood or lymph to other organs or tissues of the body, a phenomenon called metastasis. Malignant tumor (or cell) metastasis is a prime reason why this type of tumor is a dangerous disease. Metastasis is known to occur with malignant tumors of fishes but usually to a lesser degree than in homeothermic animals. There are other characteristics of malignant tumors which make them a serious problem to the effected animal (Table 34).[18]

Tumors are also classified by origin, using the prefix relating to or synonymous with the tissue of origin and a suffix, -oma. Benign tumors of epithelial tissue, for example, are called epitheliomas or papillomas if derived from single-layered cells as in the skin or adenomas if derived from glandular epithelial tissue. Malignant tumors of epithelial tissue origin are referred to by cell type, such as basal cell or squamous cell, and carcinoma. Benign tumors originating from connective tissue likewise are named for origin, such as fibromas if from fibrous tissue, lipomas if from adipose tissue, chondromas if from cartilage or osteomas if from bone. Malignant tumors derived from connective tissue are fibrosarcomas from fibrous tissue, liposarcomas from adipose tissue, chondrosarcomas from cartilage and osteosarcomas from bone. Benign tumors from nervous tissue cells, for example, are ganglioneuromas, and malignant tumors of the same cells may be neuroblastomas or sympathicoblastomas, depending on position of the cells in the body tissues. Complete listings and nomenclature of all tumors can be found in various pathological publications.[1,37]

Oncology of fish tumors is a relatively recent study, and the numbers of tumors expected to be found among fishes may be quite small, yet the fish disease diagnostician should be aware of neoplasias and the implications to the health of fishes. Literature dealing with fish neoplasias is widely spread but has been referenced into bibliographies which assist in locating this information.[4,20,21] Examination of these bibliographies demonstrates that neoplasms reported in fishes often appear as single occurrences. Also, a specific type of neoplasia may occur randomly in the world, usually affecting one or a few individuals over a wide geographic area. This makes a discussion of neoplasms among fishes much too complicated and lengthy to cover completely here. The reader is referred to other references if more information is needed about specific neoplasias or geographic areas in which they have occurred in various fish species.[4,20,21]

The formation of a Registry of Tumors in Lower Vertebrates as a part of the National Museum of Natural History in Washington, D.C., in 1965 has been of assistance in the understanding of fish neoplasias. The registry also offers an identification service where specimens can be sent for diagnosis and registry.[17]

TABLE 33

General characteristics of neoplasia and hyperplasia [18]

Hyperplasia	Neoplasia
Abnormal multiplication of normal cells in a normal arrangement	Abnormal multiplication of abnormal cells in an abnormal arrangement
Occurs in direct response to extracellular stimulus	No immediate exciting cause evident
Regresses when stimulus removed	Persists
Cells are typical for those of the organ or function	Cells are atypical, undifferentiated, anaplastic[a] and pleomorphic[b]
Cells are organized	Cells in varying degree of organization
Usually involves multiple tissue elements	Usually involves one tissue element
Tends to be diffuse	Tends to arise from a single focus

[a]Anaplastic: loss of normal differentiation organization and function
[b]Pleomorphic: occurring in various distinct forms

TABLE 34

General characteristics of benign and malignant neoplasms

Characteristics	Benign	Malignant
Cellular	Relatively normal	Abnormal in varying degrees of differentiation, anaplastic, pleomorphic
Histological	Relatively normal	Abnormal, with varying degrees of a tissue type
Mitosis	Slight increase in mitotic rate	Usually a great increase in mitotic rate
Growth rate	Relatively slow but increased over normal	Much more rapid than normal
Manner of growth	Expansive but restricted	Invasive growth, unrestricted and destructive
Limitations	Usually encapsulated or confined	Never encapsulated or confined
Metastasis	Never	Usual or common
Blood supply	Normal or reduced from normal	Moderate or marked increase from normal
Necrosis	Occasionally at center of the tumor	Usually present
Ulceration	Not usual	Frequent, with hemorrhage
Recurrence after removal	Not usual	Usual
Impairment of function	Not usual	Usual

Causes or Possible Causes of Neoplasia

The cause or causes of tumors in fishes, as in other living organisms, remain obscure. Usually no single etiology can be found. These cellular changes come about from multiple causes and effects spaced out over an extended period of time. Some of the interacting causes could include age, heredity, immunologic factors, presence of carcinogens or irritants, trauma, oncogenic viruses and others.

Most animals reaching old age become more susceptible to cellular metabolic and reproductive aberrations. The statement has often been made that any animal living long enough will probably develop some kind of a tumor. This may not be entirely true, particularly in fishes, because fishes age differently from homeothermic vertebrates in that they continue to grow throughout life— there is no regulatory mechanism which stops growth at a usual age. Yet certain types of tumors never appear prior to a certain age in fishes and could be considered to be age-related.[12,18]

Heredity or intrinsic causes of tumors have been demonstrated in fishes. The eastern brook trout, for example, was reported to be susceptible to thyroid "carcinoma."[13] Further study on epizootics of enlarged thyroids in these fish demonstrated that they were not neoplastic but were thyroid hyperplasia caused by iodine deficiency.[5,12,13,25] Other reports specifically state that the tumors were cancerous in nature.[20,21,22] Hereditary causes have been demonstrated as being a factor in melanotic cancer of platyfish-swordtail hybrids. Complex genes contributed by each parent are responsible for these melanomas.[5,15] A study of neurilemomas and neurofibromas in a population of goldfish at Case-Western Reserve University in Cleveland, Ohio indicated hereditary tumor susceptibility. No carcinogenic substance or oncogenic virus could be found. Bluegills and largemouth bass in the same pond remained free of the tumors during several years of study.[26] Another example of hereditary influence on oncogeny is the fact that rainbow trout are highly susceptible to aflatoxin contamination in the food. Certain strains of rainbow trout, the Mount Shasta strain for example, appear to be even more sensitive to these carcinogenic substances than other rainbow trout strains.[11] Channel catfish are resistant to carcinogenic effects of aflatoxins.

There are frequent references of tumors induced by viruses. Such tumors as lymphocystis and certain papillomas or proliferative benign neoplasms regress when fishes recover from the viral infection.[20] *Herpesvirus cyprini* produces papilloma tumors of the skin of carp, usually called carp pox. Incidence of this tumor may reach as high as 30% of carp populations.[25a,33a]

Presence of carcinogenic substances in the environment of fish is known to produce neoplasms in fish. Surveys of fish populations in or near sources of industrial pollutants reveal moderate to severe oncogenic effects to the fish. Brown bullheads from the Fox River in Illinois had 12.2% incidence of tumors. The Fox River is highly polluted with a variety of industrial pollutants.[6a] Atlantic tomcod were found to have an incidence of 25% hepatoma (liver cell carcinoma) in the highly polluted Hudson River Estruary near New York City. Analysis of water from the area revealed 11 to 100 mg of polychlorinated biphenyl compounds per liter, which were thought to cause or enhance tumor incidence.[28a] Studies of waters near highly industrialized areas of the Great Lake basin suggested increased incidence of several neoplasias: gonadal tumors, liver tumors, skin papillomas, and thyroid hyperplasias.[4a]

Carcinogen induced tumors may occur as a result of water management for fish culture. Chlorinated and dechlorinated water from a coolant tower of a paper mill, for example, caused low level neuroblastomas in coho salmon fingerlings reared in the water.[22a]

Fish age and susceptibility to tumor inducement has received only cursory examination. There were indications that liver cell carcinoma (hepatoma) could occur after aflatoxin contaminated diets were fed to young rainbow trout, especially those of the Shasta strain, and removal of the aflatoxin contamination after feeding a short time.[12] Further examination of this phenomenon indicated the carcinogenic effect of aflatoxins or similar compounds, can alter liver cellular metabolism in rainbow trout embryos if incubating eggs are subjected to contact for a few minutes to one hour. Fish hatched from these eggs and reared under conditions completely removed from any possibility of contact with these compounds have a high incidence of hepatoma.[17a,17b,17c] Thus, aquatic pollutants may induce changes in fish cells while the fish are embryos or very young, not only rainbow trout but possibly other fish species as well (Pl. 36D). Appearance of tumors may not occur until later life, long after the tumorogenic compound has been eliminated. The fact must be kept in mind that age, heredity, oncogenic viruses, presence of carcinogenic substances or other factors do not act alone to cause metabolic and reproductive changes among organ cells which create neoplasias.

The remainder of this chapter will be devoted to those neoplasms which are either common or which, on occasion, caused great losses among cultured fishes. Other publications should be referred to for descriptions of other tumors.[18,19,20]

Malignant Tumors of Fishes

Malignant neoplasms have involved nearly all organs and cell types among fishes. However, incidence of malignant tumors among fishes is usually quite low, with reports of specific neoplasms among widely divergent fish species and scattered geographic areas. Thus many of the reported malignancies of fishes are primarily of scientific or comparative interest with little or no actual effect on the entire fish population.[8] Research has continued on specific causes of malignant tumors among fish. Many mutagenic and tumorogenic compounds have been identified.[17a]

There have been instances when many individuals in a population suffered from a specific malignancy. This has been especially true when the cause was a carcinogen and susceptible individuals were present. Such was the case of epizootic hepatoma (malignant liver tumor) among cultured salmonids. The high incidence of hepatoma among cultured trout can serve as an example of an epizootic malignancy among fish.

Hepatoma (Liver Cell Carcinoma)

The first report of hepatoma in rainbow trout was as early as 1933.[16] Epizootics of hepatoma in California trout hatcheries between 1937 and 1942 were reported, but the significance was not understood.[31] Trout diets at the time were primarily made from meat and fresh meat products. Cottonseed meal began to be added to these moist diets as a protein supplement during the latter part of the 1930's. The diets produced an occasional tumor in the liver of rainbow trout receiving the mixtures. These occurrences were interesting at the time but became more important later.[30]

The advent of complete dry, pelletized rations for trout in the middle 1950's utilized various vegetable meals, cottonseed meal being one such ingredient. Another significant change which came about during this time was the wide-scale use of mechanical cotton pickers. Cotton was left in the field longer after the bolls had opened in order to make mechanical picking more efficient, as compared to hand-picking several times for each field during harvest. Moisture in the cotton seeds in the opened bolls and contamination with ubiquitous spores of *Aspergillus flavus* served to make the seed media for fungal growth and toxin production. Also, the rapid harvest of cotton and subsequent ginning left large quantities of cottonseed to be processed into oil and meal. The large volumes of cottonseed awaiting processing often were stored under tarpaulins or plastic sheets in the direct rays of the sun, creating ideal conditions of moisture and heat for *A. flavus* growth. Thus some of the cottonseed meal added to dry, pelletized trout rations was contaminated with the toxins produced by the fungus, known collectively as aflatoxins.

Several reports of epizootic hepatoma appeared in the United States and several European countries in 1960. The liver tumors appeared in rainbow trout seven months of age or older. Morbidity as high as 85% was reported at some fish culture facilities. The exact etiology was not known at the time, but conferences held between interested people were set up to define all possible causes. The hepatoma conferences were of definite significance because they brought together many scientists and other interested people to solve the problem. Probably there had been no such effort to solve a disease

problem in fishes since formation of the Furunculosis Committee in 1928.

Research was assigned to each interested group. Viral etiology, pesticides, nutritional imbalance, genetic differences, cultural methods and several environmental factors proved negative.[9] Direct toxicity or carcinogenesis was found to be the cause. The source of carcinogen was not known until about 1962, when hepatomas were induced in the livers of rainbow trout fed moldy cottonseed meal in a test diet. Aflatoxin-contaminated cottonseed meal experiments with ducks and rainbow trout later definitely proved the etiology.[28,34]

Etiological Agents:

The major etiological agents of epizootic hepatoma are aflatoxins, those toxins produced by *A. flavus*. However, fish species, heredity and age are important as well. There are four major biologically active aflatoxins produced by the fungi: B_1, B_2, G_1 and G_2. These compounds are chloroformsoluble; B_1 and B_2 fluoresce blue under long-wave ultraviolet light and G_1 and G_1 fluoresce yellow-green.[31] Five other *A. flavus* mycotoxins are known: M_1 and aflatoxicol (both are metabolites of B_1); B_{2a} (a metabolite of B_2), Q_1 and P_1. All are carcinogenic but only limited studies have been done on these toxins.[17a,26a,27,33]

Test diets incorporating single aflatoxin fractions (B_1, B_2, G_1, G_2 and M_1) and crude aflatoxin (the natural mixture of toxins produced by *A. flavus*) fed to rainbow trout has demonstrated the relative carcinogenicity of each (Table 35).

Geographical Distribution:

Aflatoxicosis and resultant epizootic hepatoma among trout have been reported in the United States, France and Italy.[14] However, cases of the disease may possibly be found in all areas of the world where *A. flavus* contaminated feedstuffs are incorporated into the diet of susceptible fishes.

Susceptible Species:

All strains of rainbow trout appear to be susceptible to aflatoxin-induced hepatoma. Some strains are more susceptible than others. The Mount Shasta strain of rainbow trout is the most susceptible in that dosages as low as 0.4 microgram of aflatoxin per kg of diet have induced 14% hepatoma in 15 months.[6] Certain strains of rainbow trout appear to be less susceptible to aflatoxin hepatocarcinogenesis. Cutthroat trout and eastern brook trout are less susceptible than the rainbow trout, but cases of hepatoma have been reported in these species. The brown trout is apparently the least susceptible of the trout.[30]

The five species of North American salmon appear to be relatively nonsusceptible to aflatoxin hepatocarcinogenesis. However, hepatoma has been reported in sockeye salmon fed a diet containing both aflatoxin and

TABLE 35

Dietary aflatoxin carcinogenic to rainbow trout

Aflatoxin Fraction	(ppb)[a] Dose	Percent of fish with hepatoma (at 12 months)	Incidence in percent (at 16 months)
B_1	4	25	35
B_1	8	70	80
B_1	20	78	—
B_2	20	5	0
G_1	20	5	0
G_2	20	0	0
M_1	16	70	95
Crude	20	38	57

[a]mcg aflatoxin per kg of diet

cycloprene triglyceride.[30] Other fish species have been reported to be resistant to this type of tumor. Channel catfish, for example, fed diets relatively high in aflatoxins failed to develop hepatoma.

Epizootology:

Aflatoxin contamination from mold growth on feedstuffs can occur prior to harvest, during processing or during storage. *A. flavus* growth on feedstuffs is enhanced by warm temperatures and moist conditions. Some strains of the fungus are more productive in the mycotoxins than others. Those producing the toxins may do so on or in a wide variety of feedstuffs. Peanut meal, wheat products and corn products have been implicated in epizootic hepatoma as well as cottonseed products. Many of these feedstuffs are processed into dry or moist rations to be used for the culture of fishes. *A. flavus* growth on prepared fish rations may also yield aflatoxins which may subsequently be fed to susceptible fishes.[7]

Aflatoxins absorbed from the diet in the alimentary tract are passed to the liver. The initial effect on the liver is a gradual change in normal architecture. Some hepatocytes enlarge slightly, stain poorly and die. They are replaced with smaller hyperplastic cells which stain more deeply with basic dyes (Pl. 30A). The hyperplastic cells multiply with indifference to normal liver structure. There is a loss of normal sinusoids and development of trabecular hepatoma. The non-capsulated tumor often invades, enlarges and destroys normal liver tissue until there is little or no resemblance to the parent tissue (Pl. 30B). Necrosis occurs within the nodular tumor followed by hemorrhage and fibrosis. Similar nodules may appear throughout the liver until much of the normal liver tissue is lost.[2,3]

Hepatoma metastasis is not common but does occur. Some of the nodular tumors invade surrounding organs (kidney, stomach, spleen, ceca and pancreas) by contact, primarily compressing the normal cells of the neighboring organ until that area of the organ is destroyed. The tumor then extends into the invaded organ. True metastasis, in which tumor cells break free and are carried by blood or lymph to other organs of the body, also occurs in affected fishes, but to a lesser degree than is usually expected of a malignancy.[4]

Fishes affected by hepatomatous neoplasia continue normal growth and activity until destruction of liver tissue alters metabolism beyond the capability of health maintenance by the individual. Also, nodular tumors may press against vital organs such as the esophagus, stomach or hematopoietic structures of kidneys, reducing their normal function and leading to death.

Disease Signs:

There are no outward indications of aflatoxicosis or hepatoma during early stages of tumor growth. Fish appear normal and healthy. Later, enlargement of the liver may be visible through the body wall and the fish may lose weight and become emaciated (Pl. 30C).

Early hepatomas may be visible on or in the liver as small gray-white or yellowish nodular areas. The nodules enlarge as the disease progresses. Some may occupy much of the liver mass, and some may have contacted surrounding organs with destruction of the area of contact (Pl. 30D). Only occasionally will hepatoma neoplasms be found in organs far removed from the liver.

TABLE 36

Incidence of hepatoma in rainbow trout fed rations with various levels of cottonseed meal for 25 months [9]

Dietary Cottonseed Meal Content (%)	Incidence of Hepatoma (%)
0.0[a]	0
7.8	10
12.5	14
21.0	35
30.5	72
31.0	55 and 70[b]

[a]There were no hepatoma cases reported at three fish culture facilities in which no cottonseed meal was present in the ration

[b]Results from two fish culture facilities

Diagnosis:

Diagnosis of hepatoma is by external and internal signs and histopathology. Presence of multiple gray-white to yellowish nodular lesions in the liver of susceptible fishes which have been fed diets prepared from moldy feedstuffs is presumptive for hepatoma. The neoplasms are recognized because their color contrasts with the deep reddish color of normal liver tissue.

Definitive diagnosis of hepatoma is by oncology of the tumors. Hepatoma is a liver cell carcinoma, and classic identification of a malignant tumor must be made (Table 34). Liver cells will be anaplastic, with an increase in mitotic figures (Pl. 30B). The hepatic cells of advanced nodular hepatoma are usually enlarged and growing randomly with complete loss of normal liver architecture. Areas of necrosis, fibrosis, hemorrhage and hemosiderosis are commonly found within the tumor (Pl. 30B).

Therapy and Control:

There is no therapy for hepatoma once established in fishes. Epizootic hepatoma can be controlled in succeeding generations of cultured fishes by eliminating aflatoxins from the ration. Feeding moldy feedstuffs or finished rations is not recommended. Much research has been done on methods of aflatoxin detection in suspect feedstuffs. Thus, feedstuffs free of aflatoxins can be specified in ration preparation to be used for the most aflatoxin-susceptible fishes.

The toxicity of aflatoxins can be deactivated by treating feedstuffs with ammonia under increased atmospheric pressure and in combination with heat and moisture. Ammonia treatment may be a practical means of controlling aflatoxicosis and subsequent hepatoma in fishes and other domestic animals.[6]

Prognosis:

Morbidity of epizootic hepatoma may reach to greater than 70% of rainbow trout at fish culture facilities where aflatoxin-contaminated rations have been fed.[9] Data obtained from the examination of rainbow trout which had received rations containing cottonseed meal for 25 months, during the hepatoma epizootic of the early 1960's in western United States, serve to demonstrate hepatoma incidence (Table 36). Morbidity of hepatoma was directly related to the quantity of apparently aflatoxin-contaminated cottonseed meal in the ration. Those fish receiving no cottonseed meal had no hepatoma. Rations with nearly 30% cottonseed meal produced the highest incidence of hepatoma, nearly 70% of the population.[9]

Mortality from hepatoma eventually is the same as the morbidity if the fish are allowed to live their life span.

Practical Aspects:

Epizootic hepatoma among rainbow trout in the United States during the latter 1950's and early 1960's served to alert trout culturists and commercial trout diet producers to the adverse effect of mold contaminants in food. More careful monitoring of ration ingredients for fishes and other animals has resulted.

Occasional cases of hepatoma had been reported in trout, ducks, turkeys, sheep and other animals prior to the late 1950's, but the cause was unknown. These trout hepatoma epizootics served two major purposes in the study of animal diseases: diagnosis of hepatoma in all animals including humans, and a demonstration of the usefulness of a united effort among fish health people in solving mutual problems.

Benign Tumors of Fishes

Benign tumors have been identified from many fish species throughout the world. Most cases are from individual fish, widely distributed and with but little or no effect on a fish population. Benign tumors caused by oncogenic viruses or bacteria may be more numerous than those of other etiology. Lymphocystis, for example, may occur at a relatively low morbidity rate among certain fishes, but usually does not exceed 30% even among the most susceptible fishes.[32] Infections of *Mycobacterium fortuitum* or *M. marinum* stimulate production of tumor-like masses in kidney, liver, spleen or other tissues (Pl. 31A). However, the incidence of mycobacteriosis in a wild-ranging fish population is usually quite low, with but a few fish affected at any time.[23]

Certain copepod parasites embedded in the skin of host fishes may stimulate fibromas to form around the place of attachment. Environmental conditions in which fishes are crowded and water temperature is suitable to the parasite may be conducive to a high incidence of this type of benign epithelial tumor. Papillomas are wart-like tumors found on the skin, lips, opercula, fins or other external parts of the body. Papillomas may be numerous among certain bottom-feeding fishes. The etiology of most papillomas of fishes is not known.[4a,20,21]

Visceral granuloma is the chronic development of benign fibromas within the body cavity of affected fishes. These tumors have been reported from many fish species.[17,20,21] However, the highest incidence has been found in cultured Eastern brook trout populations.[19,24,29,35,36] The etiological agent of visceral granuloma is not known, but granulomas in general are usually caused by certain infectious organisms (viruses, bacteria, fungi, animal parasites) and foreign bodies entering tissues. Viral and mycotic etiology have been suggested, but transmission experiments have proved unsuccessful. The increased use of natural ingredient feedstuffs in the preparation of rations for cultured fishes has also been suggested as a possible cause for these tumors. Initial appearance of most tumors in affected fishes is in stomach and/or cecal tissue, and particles from the diet could enter these tissues and cause formation of foreign body-induced tumors. Certain of the particles could also enter other nearby tissues as well, the kidney being the organ most often affected outside of the stomach and ceca. Granulomatous lesions in the visceral organs of wild-ranging fishes may also have been induced by food particle penetration.[10]

Visceral granulomas appear as many small, discrete, white to gray lesions usually in stomach, pyloric ceca and/or kidney, but may also be located in liver, spleen, heart and body muscles. Lesions have also been reported in gill tissue, eyes and tongue.[35] The microscopic appearance of each nodule is a proliferative mass of fibrous tissue, sometimes surrounded by a fibrous capsule and often with a necrotic center. Giant cells may also be found within the tumors (Pl. 30E, 30F).

Compendium:

Routine examination of fishes may reveal other types of tumors than those briefly mentioned above. Each should be identified and registered. The fish disease diagnostician may wish to employ the services of a pathologist knowledgeable in tumor identification (oncologist) to assure correct nomenclature of those tumors found.[16] Specific information on fish species, genetic factors, environmental factors and geographical location as well as type of tissue involved, should accompany information on the tumor(s).[17] Thus, the study of neoplasia in fishes may eventually reach a stage of understanding which may assist in understanding neoplasias in all animals, including humans.

Selected References

1. Ackerman, L. V. and J. A. del Regato. 1970. *Cancer: Diagnosis, treatment and prognosis. Fourth ed.* Mosby Press, St. Louis, MO. 1,049p.

2. Ashley, L. M. 1970. "Pathology of fish fed aflatoxins and other antimetabolites," *In* S. F. Snieszko, ed. *A symposium on diseases of fishes and shellfishes.* p. 366-379. *Spec. Publ.,* No. 5. Amer. Fish. Soc., Bethesda, MD.

3. Ashley, L. M. 1967. "Histopathology of rainbow trout aflatoxacosis," *In* J. E. Halver and I. A. Mitchell, eds. *Trout hepatoma research conference papers.* p. 103-120. U.S. Dept. of Health, Ed., Welf. and U.S. Fish Wildl. Serv. Res. Rep. 70, Washington, DC.

4. Ashley, L. M. and J. E. Halver. 1963. "Multiple metastasis of rainbow trout hepatoma," *Trans. Am. Fish. Soc.,* 92:365-371.

4a. Baumann, P. C. 1984. "Cancer in wild freshwater fish populations with emphasis on the Great Lakes." *J. Great Lakes Res.* 10:251-253.

5. Becker, F. F (ed.). 1975. *Cancer. I. A comprehensive treatise.* Plenum Press, New York City, NY. 524p.

6. Brekke, O. L., R. O. Sinnhuber, A. J. Peplinski, J. H. Wales, G. B. Putnam, D. J. Lee and A. Ciegler. 1977. "Aflatoxins in corn: Ammonia inactivation and bioassay with rainbow trout," *App. Environ. Micro- biol.,* 34:34-37.

6a. Brown, E. R., J. J. Hazdra, L. Keith, I. Greenspan, J. B. G. Kwapinski and P. Beamer. 1973. "Frequency of fish tumors found in a polluted watershed as compared to nonpolluted Canadian waters." *Can. Res.,* 33:189-198.

7. Ciegler, A., S. Kadis and S. J. Ajl., eds. 1971. *Microbial toxins.* Vol. 6. Academic Press, Inc., New York City, NY.

8. Dawe, C. J. and J. C. Harshbarger. 1975. "Neoplasms in feral fishes: their significance to cancer research," *In* W. E. Ribelin and G. Migaki, eds. *The pathology of fishes.* p. 871-894. The University of Wisconsin Press, Madison, WI.

9. Dollar, A. M., E. A. Smuckler and R. C. Simon. 1967. "Etiology and epidemiology of trout hepatoma," *In* J. E. Halver and I. A. Mitchell. *Trout hepatoma research conference papers.* p. 1-17. Res. Rep. 70. U. S. Fish Wildl. Serv., Washington, DC.

10. Dunbar, C. E. and R. L. Herman. 1971. "Visceral granuloma in brook trout (*Salvelinus fontinalis*)," *J. Nutr.,* 101:1445-1451.

11. Halver, J. E. 1969. "Aflatoxicosis and trout hepatoma," *In* L. A. Goldblatt, ed. *Aflatoxin-scientific back- ground, control, and implications.* p. 265-306. Academic Press, New York City, NY.

12. Halver, J. E. and I. A. Mitchell, eds. 1967. *Trout hepatoma research conference papers.* U.S. Dep. Health, Ed., Welf. and U.S. Fish Wildl. Serv. Res. Rep. 70.199p

13. Gaylord, H. R. 1916. "Further observations on so-called carcinoma of the thyroid in fish," *J. Cancer Res.,* 1:197-204.

14. Ghittino, P. and F. Ceretto. 1962. "Studio sulla eziopatogenesi dell'epatoma della trota iridea de allevamento," *Tumori,* 48:393-409.

15. Gordon, M. 1950. "Heredity of pigmented tumours in fish," *Endeavour,* 9:26-34.

16. Haddow, A. and I. Blake. 1933. "Neoplasms in fish: a report of six cases with a summary of the literature," *J. Path. Bacteriol.,* 36:41-47.

17. Harshbarger, J. C. 1965-1978. *Activities report registry of tumors in lower animals.* Reg. Tumors. Lower. An., Nation. Mus. Nat. Hist., Smithsonian Inst., Wash-ington, DC.

17a. Hendricks, J. D. 1982. "Chemical carcinogenesis in fish." In: Webster, L. J., Ed. *Aquatic toxicology,* Raven Press, New York City, NY. p.149-211.

17b. Hendricks, J. D., J. H. Wales, R. O. Sinnhuber, J. E. Nixon, P. M. Loveland and R. A. Scanlan. 1980. "Rainbow trout (*Salmo gairdneri*) embryos: A sensitive animal model for experimental carcinogenesis." *Federation Proc.,* 39:3222-3229.

17c. Hendricks, J. D., R. A. Scanlan, J. L. Williams, R. O. Sinnhuber and M. P. Grieco. 1980. "Carcinogenecity of N-Methyl-N'-nitro-N-nitrosoguanidine to the livers and kidneys of rainbow trout (*Salmo gairdneri*) exposed as embryos." *J. Nat. Cancer Inst.,* 64:1511-1519.

18. Hopps, H. C. 1964. *Principles of pathology. Second ed.* Appleton-Century-Crofts, New York City, NY. 403p.

19. Herman, R. L. 1971. *Visceral granuloma.* FDL-32. U.S. Fish and Wildl. Serv. Washington, DC. 4p.

20. Mawdesley-Thomas, L. E. 1975. "Neoplasia in fish," *In* W. E. Ribelin and G. Migaki, eds. *The pathology of fishes.* p. 805-870. The University of Wisconsin Press, Madison, WI.

21. Mawdesley-Thomas, L. E. 1972. "Some tumours of fish," *In* L. E. Mawdesley-Thomas, ed. *Symposium of the zoological society of London.* Vol. 30, p. 191-284. Academic Press, New York City, NY.

22. Mawdesley-Thomas, L. E. 1969. "Neoplasia in fish-a bibliography," *J. Fish. Biol.,* 1:187-207.

22a. Meyer, T. R. and J. D. Hendricks. 1984. "A limited epizootic of neuroblastoma in coho salmon reared in chlorinated-dechlorinated water." *J. Nat. Cancer Inst.* 72:299-309.

23. Parisot, T. J. 1958. "Tuberculosis of fish," *Bact. Revs.,* 22:240-245.

24. Post, G. and W. G. Hepworth. 1960. *Diseases and parasites of fish*. Federal Aid to Fish Restoration. Proj. No. FW 3-R-7, Wyo. Game and Fish Comm. p. 10.

25. Radulescu, I., D. G. Vasiliu, E. Ilie and S. F. Snieszko. 1968. "Thyroid hyperplasia of the eastern brook trout, *Salvelinua fontinalis* in Romania," *Trans. Amer. Fish. Soc.*, 97:486-488.

25a. Sano, T., H. Fukuda and M. Furkawa. 1985 "*Herpesvirus cyprini*: Biological and oncogenic properties." *Fish Pathol.*, 20:381-388.

26. Schlumberger, H. G. 1952. "Nerve sheath tumors in an isolated goldfish population," *Cancer Res.*, 12: 890-899.

26a. Schoenhard, G. L., J. D. Hendricks, J. E. Nixon, D. J. Lee, J. H. Wales, R. O. Sinnhuber and N. E. Pawlowski. 1981. "Aflitoxicol-induced hepatocellular carcinoma in rainbow trout (*Salmo gairdneri*) and the synergistic effects of cyclopropenoid fatty acids." *Cancer Res.*, 41:1011-1014.

27. Sinnhuber, R. O., J. D. Hendricks, J. H. Wales and G. B. Putnam. 1977. "Neoplasms in rainbow trout, a sensitive animal model for environmental carcino- genesis," *Ann. N.Y. Acad. Sci.*, 298:389-408.

28. Sinnhuber, R. O., J. H. Wales, J. L. Ayres, R. H. Engebrecht and D. L. Amend. 1968. "Dietary factors and hepatoma in rainbow trout (*Salmo gairdneri*) I. Aflatoxins in vegetable protein feedstuffs," *J. Nat. Cancer. Inst.*, 41:711-718.

28a. Smith, C. E., T. H. Peck, R. J. Kauda and J. B. McLaren. 1979. "Hepatomas in Atlantic tomcod (*Microgradus tomcod* Walbaum) collected in the Hudson River estuary, New York." *J. Fish Dis.*, 2:313-319.

29. Snieszko, S. F. 1961. "Hepatoma and visceral granuloma in trouts," *N.Y. Fish and Game J.*, 8:145-149.

30. Wales, J. H. 1970. "Hepatoma in rainbow trout," *In* S. F. Snieszko, ed. *A symposium on diseases of fishes and shellfishes*. p. 351-365. Spec. Publ. No. 5, Amer. Fish. Soc., Bethesda, MD.

31. Wales, J. H. and R. O. Sinnhuber. 1966. "An early hepatoma epizootic in rainbow trout, *Salmo gairdneri*," *Calif. Fish & Game*, 52:85-91.

32. Walker, R. 1958. "Lymphocystis warts and skin tumors of walleyed pike," *Rennsselaer Rev. Grad. Stud.*, 14:1-5.

33. Wogan, G. N. 1967. "Isolation, identification and some biological effects of aflatoxins," *In* J. E. Halver and I. A. Mitchell, eds. *Trout hepatoma research conference papers*. p. 121-129. Res. Rep. 70. U.S. Fish Wildl. Serv., Washington, DC.

33a. Wolf, K. 1983. "Biology and properties of fish and reptilian herpesviruses." In: Roizman, B., Ed. *The Herpesviruses*. 2:319-366. Plenum Press, New York City, NY and London, Gr. Br.

34. Wolf, H. and E. W. Jackson. 1963. "Hepatomas in rainbow trout: descriptive and experimental epidemiology," *Science*, 142:676-678.

35. Wood, E. M. and W. T. Yasutake. 1956. "Histopathology of fish. IV. A granuloma of brook trout," *Prog. Fish-Cult.*, 18:108-112.

36. Wood, E. M., W. T. Yasutake and W. L. Lehman. 1956. "A mycosis-like granuloma of fish," *J. Infect. Dis.*, 97:262-267.

37. World Health Organization. 1976. *International classification of disease for oncology. First ed.* W.H.O. Geneva, Switzerland. 131p.

Chapter XI

DISEASES CAUSED BY TOXIC SUBSTANCES

The waters of the world have always been a place where suspended materials, dissolved compounds and ions, and products of biological degradation remained, some for relatively short periods of time, others for extended periods.[31,115] Water, the major solvent of nature, retains natural substances as well as those synthesized or partially synthesized by man.

Modern civilization is capable of bringing about the most complex kinds of environmental changes.[35] This is not to say that all environmental changes have been modern, but only to suggest that release of substances foreign to nature has accelerated greatly during the industrial age. Various substances released from modern complex human societies and entering waters may produce alterations in survivability of aquatic organisms residing within such a polluted environment, because many are highly toxic. Thus, fishes are in the unenviable position of being within a constantly changing ecosystem which may at some time either alter their physiology or biochemistry or induce changes in their bodies resulting in increased susceptibility to other disease agents.[15,16]

Both wild-ranging fishes and those held in confinement may accidentally or intentionally be exposed to a great many substances. Attempts have been made over the last several decades to classify toxic relationships between aquatic pollutants, or naturally occurring substances in water, and fishes. The results of these studies have been placed in a semblance of order by classifications used by toxicologists, as well as terms to demonstrate relative toxicity as it relates to the aquatic environment (Table 37). Not only have these toxicological classifications been of value to those concerned with toxicology, but they have also been useful as a method of estimating pathological diagnoses of sublethal or lethal effects on fishes.

The use of toxicological terms (Table 37) for describing the relative effect of a toxicant should be accompanied by information on as many interrelated factors affecting toxicity as possible.[9] Environmental temperature, pH, dissolved oxygen concentration and presence of substances which could either enhance toxicity (synergism) or reduce toxicity (antagonism) should be known. A substance, for example, may be lethal to a particular fish species at a given concentration in soft water (water low in calcium, magnesium and similar ions usually referred to as hardness) but have no measurable physiological effect during short-term exposure in the presence of relatively high calcium and magnesium content. Aquatic pH may shift the calcium-magnesium ratio to favor magnesium, which may also alter relative toxicity. Presence or absence of organic matter in water may cause tremendous alteration of toxicity of some potential toxicants. Many of the results reported on toxicity of various suspended materials and dissolved compounds, ions or elements in existing literature seem to be inconsistent, but in actuality they seem to conflict only because environmental parameters were different or not measured or reported.[26,27,28]

Many of the materials present in water and considered to be toxic to fishes in one way or another can be categorized into seven major groups (Table 38). These substances may cause pathological, physiological or adverse biological changes which affect survival of individuals or of the population. Much of the literature relating to the toxic effect(s) on fishes concerns lethality, that is, at which concentration or in what quantity is the substance lethal. These data are useful for the purpose intended. However, a toxicant which does not kill individual fishes at a specific concentration over a specified time may still have permanent adverse effects which interfere with health or the ability to survive and reproduce. Contact with substances which leave the affected fish relatively normal in appearance and activity but destroys reproductive capabilities may have far-reaching effects on an entire population by reducing or eliminating recruitment of new individuals to the population. Thus, the final result may be as damaging to the population as a concentration which kills many or all individuals quickly.[52]

Diagnosis of diseases in fishes caused by toxic substances usually includes observation of appearance and activity prior to death, gross signs of disease before and after death, histopathological observations and analysis of water, food and/or fish tissues for the suspected toxicant. The remainder of this chapter will discuss selected toxic or potentially toxic substances related to the major groups of substances given in Table 38 and methods which may be useful for diagnosis of their effect(s) on fishes.

Oxygen-Depleting Materials

Aquatic environments have an inherent capacity to

TABLE 37

Toxicological terms used to estimate relative toxicity of substances or ions to fishes or other organisms[92]

Term	Definition
TL_m	Median tolerance limit where 50% of the individuals survive in the presence of a specified concentration of a toxicant, usually for a specified time.
LD_{50}	That concentration of a toxicant in the water or given parenterally or orally which kills 50% of the individuals, usually within a specified time.
ED_{50}	That dose of a toxicant which brings about the toxic effect intended in 50% of the individuals, usually within a specified time.
MATC	Maximum acceptable toxicant concentration which will cause an adverse physiological effect.
AF	Application factor, or the relationship between the TL_m concentration and the MATC concentration. The AF of a toxicant is computed by dividing the MATC concentration for a given organism species by the TL_m for that same species.

dissolve gases from the atmosphere. Oxygen is the major aquatic life-sustaining gas involved in this exchange. However, the ability of a body of water to dissolve oxygen is directly related to atmospheric pressure and inversely related to aquatic temperature; i.e., a higher atmospheric pressure induces higher dissolved oxygen content in open water, but a higher aquatic temperature causes reduced solubility of gases.[18,93] These physical factors become a vital part of the capacity of any open water to accept oxygen-depleting materials, assimilate them and continue to maintain dissolved oxygen concentrations suitable for support of fishes.[31]

Minimum limiting dissolved oxygen concentrations for each species of fish depend on a wide variety of physical and chemical factors under which the fishes are capable of survival. Thus, the minimum limiting oxygen concentration is not an absolute value. It is dependent upon temperature and the related metabolic rate of the fish as well as the inherent metabolic rate associated with age; health of the fish, especially health of gill tissue through which oxygen must diffuse; activity of the fish and subsequent oxygen requirements to sustain that activity; and many other factors. There have been extensive studies on oxygen requirements of fishes. Space does not permit a more complete examination of the subject, and the reader is referred to other literature.[28,29,34,123] However, examples of recommended

threshold values of dissolved oxygen of a few selected fishes are given in Table 39.

Accidental or intentional addition of oxygen-depleting materials, as well as presence of degrading organic materials in water (decaying algae, other aquatic plants or animal tissue), may absorb and utilize dissolved oxygen at a more rapid rate than it can be restored from the atmosphere. Photosynthetic activity of aquatic plants under the dark part of the cycle may reduce dissolved oxygen in water. The result may be depletion of dissolved oxygen to concentrations below the minimum survival level and asphyxiation or suffocation of fishes.

Release of oxygen-depleting material is often responsible for extensive fish-kills. Data obtained from 7,492 fish-kill incidents in the United States between 1961 and 1975 indicated that 25% (1,894) of the incidents were caused by low dissolved oxygen concentrations. Release of sewage into water bodies harboring fishes led all sources in the number of oxygen depletion fish-kill incidents in which one million or more fishes were killed (133,000,000 in all), with 23 reported incidents.[30] Industrial release of food products was responsible for over 42 million fishes killed, paper products over 2.3 million and manure-silage drainage over 7.5 million killed. Ninety percent of the fishes killed were classified as nongame fishes, but nonetheless, the fishes were a part of the biological assets of the ecosystem in which they

TABLE 38

**Major groups of substances potentially toxic or damaging to fishes,
with a few examples to demonstrate each group**

Group	Examples
Oxygen-depleting materials	Domestic wastes, effluents containing slaughter house wastes, effluents from milk and milk product processing plants, runoff from animal feeding lots, paper mill effluents containing oxygen binding inorganic and organic substances, effluents from sugar refineries, effluents from breweries and distilleries, and others.
Toxic metals	Aluminum, arsenic, antimony, cadmium, chromium, copper, iron, manganese, mercury, lead, uranium, zinc and others.
Naturally occurring major ions usually present in water	Ions of calcium, magnesium, sodium, potassium, sulfate, carbonate (bicarbonate), chloride. These make up 95 to 99 + % of all dissolved ions in most natural waters. The combination usually found in natural waters is designated as "total residue" or "salinity," depending on whether the description is for fresh water or salt water.
Toxic gases	Ammonia, chlorine, bromine, hydrogen sulfide, carbon dioxide, ozone and others.
Toxic organic compounds	**Amines, amides, alcohols, aldehydes, cresols, cyanides, ketones, fats and fatty acids, phenols, petro-**chemicals, solvents, tars, organic acids or salts such as citrates, malates, tartrates, oxalates, salicylates and others.
Pesticides	Insecticides: Chlorinated hydrocarbons, organophosphates, carbamates, metallic elements, metallic compounds and natural organic compounds. Algicides Herbicides Piscicides
Therapeutic compounds	Terramycin, sulfamerazine, malachite green, masoten, formaldehyde, quaternary ammonium compounds and all other bactericides, fungicides, protozoacides and others are toxic to fishes to some extent even if used as directed. They may be extremely toxic if used incorrectly.

TABLE 39

Minimum threshold values of dissolved oxygen for some selected fish species [34] [77]

| Species | Dissolved oxygen concentration in mg/L for survival of all individuals | |
	Summer	Winter
Pike	6.0	3.1
Largemouth Bass	5.5	4.7
Black Crappie	5.5	1.5
Yellow Perch	4.2	1.4
Green Sunfish	3.3	3.5
Black Bullhead	3.3	1.1
Median concentration	4.2	3.1

lived. These results indicate the tremendous potential for destruction of aquatic animal life which can occur as a result of release of oxygen-depleting materials.[30]

Diagnostic Procedures:

Diagnosis of the cause for mortality among fish populations as a result of depleted oxygen is difficult. Signs of partial suffocation in fishes (surfacing and gulping air, crowding into areas where water spills over dams or riffles, moving to shallow water, reduction of activity and lethargy) may be the first indication that the dissolved oxygen concentration is below or near the minimum survival level for the fish species involved. Anoxia leaves no pathological changes in fish tissue which can be observed grossly or microscopically. Therefore, accurate dissolved oxygen analysis of representative samples of water from the area, and at the time in which fishes are affected, is essential to proper diagnosis. Collection of information on other factors which may influence the minimum dissolved oxygen concentration for survival (temperature, pH and other dissolved substances) is necessary for accurate diagnosis. Oxygen demand analyses on water or effluents containing oxygen-depleting materials can be of assistance in locating the cause of depleted dissolved oxygen and subsequent anoxia of fishes. Two such analyses are used: biochemical oxygen demand (BOD) and chemical oxygen demand (COD).[5]

The BOD analysis is a measurement of the biological decomposition accessibility of organic wastes, certain inorganic substances such as biological oxydizable nitrogen and some reducing ions which react with molecular oxygen. The BOD test is based on analysis for the initially saturated dissolved oxygen content in completely filled bottles of effluent or polluted water compared to the residual dissolved oxygen in similar bottles of the material after a recommended five-day incubation period of 20°C.

The BOD test is somewhat complicated by the fact that many effluents or pollutants have the capability of depleting all dissolved oxygen in the closed bottles prior to five days of incubation. These materials must be diluted using oxygen-saturated dilution water, usually referred to as seed water. Seed water may be prepared from distilled water, natural unpolluted water or prepared mineral water plus a seeding of organisms most commonly found associated with the type of effluent or pollutant being examined. Dilutions are made serially in an attempt to obtain that concentration of effluent or pollutant which will utilize between 40 and 60% of the dissolved oxygen during the incubation period. Results are used to calculate the oxygen-depleting capability of a known volume of the effluent or pollutant. These data are reported as mg of BOD per liter and can be used to estimate the capabilities of a receiving body of water to assimilate a quantity of the effluent or pollutant and either deplete the dissolved oxygen below minimal concentration for survival of aquatic organisms or leave sufficient dissolved oxygen for their survival.[5]

The COD analysis is a measurement of that portion of organic matter in an effluent or pollutant susceptible to oxidation by a strong chemical oxidant. COD analyses are especially useful for industrial wastes or effluents which are toxic and unsuitable for support of seed organisms used in the BOD test. Samples which have organic matter available to bacterial degradation and no toxic matter present may demonstrate similar results for both COD and BOD tests.

The usual procedure for COD analysis is to reflux a known quantity of effluent with standardized potassium dichromate and sulfuric acid. Certain substances or ions in the sample may interfere with oxidation of organic matter by chromic acid. Interferences may be overcome by addition of other substances to the refluxing mixture, silver or mercury sulfate, for example, to control interference of chloride ions in the sample.

The usual reflux time is two hours. Excess potassium dichromate in the mixture is determined by titration. The quantity of oxidizable organic matter in the sample is a measure of the oxygen equivalent of reduced potassium dichromate. Results are reported as mg COD per liter of sample and can be used in the same way as results of BOD tests to estimate the demand for molecular oxygen of a water body receiving the effluent or pollutant.[5]

Toxic Metals

Metallic elements occur throughout the earth's crust, and fishes have always been subjected to contact with them. Industrialization has accelerated release of metallic elements or ions into water bodies, often in extremely high concentrations. This has brought about a more thorough examination of the effects of various metallic elements on fishes as well as improvements in analytical methods for qualitative detection and quantitative estimation of these elements in water.

Contamination of soils and waters with metallic compounds or elements may lead to toxemias in fishes and result in direct mortality, biological accumulation, chronic toxicity and subtle changes in physiological functions leading to an inability to survive. Chronic toxicity of some metals may lead to loss of reproductive capabilities, body malformations, inability to prevent predation and susceptibility to infectious organisms.[7,9,23,57,67,89]

Much research has been done and reported in scientific literature on the toxic effects of metallic elements on fishes. These data are used by diagnosticians, fishery biologists, toxicologists and many others to estimate the effects of metallic substances on fish populations. Data given for metal toxicity from both laboratory and open waters are not absolute values but depend on conditions under which the data were obtained. Total water hardness, pH, temperature, presence of other dissolved substances and other factors alter toxicity of most metals to fishes. Conflicting results obtained by various researchers can usually be explained when these factors are taken into consideration. Space does not allow a complete listing of toxic data for metallic substances in this chapter, but a selected few are given as examples (Table 40).

Metals dissolved in water usually have several chemical species; some may be toxic and others may not. The pH of water is extremely important in governing chemical species and solubility. High pH may cause some metals to form hydroxides or carbonate species which may be relatively insoluble. These compounds tend to precipitate or remain as particulates suspended in water and may or may not be toxic.[57,78] Other metals may form species more soluble at high pH.[33] Thus, the conditions under which the tests were run to obtain toxicity data are extremely important, and the information given in Table 40 is suggestive to toxicity. More thorough exami-

nation of the metallic compounds and aquatic conditions involved must be made when diagnosis of fish-kills or sublethal effects of toxic metals on fishes is being investigated.

Sources of Toxic Metals

Sources of toxic metals are many and varied. Toxic metals may occur naturally in waters from springs, wells, flowing streams, lakes or estuaries. Water moving through aquifers or along stream beds may pass ore bodies and dissolve sufficient substances to cause toxic problems in fishes residing in the water downstream from the ore bodies. This process may have caused certain parts of streams, lakes or other bodies of water to be free of fish life.

Another similar source of metallic substances results from mining industries opening ore bodies and causing release of water. Some mine drainage water is high in toxic metals. Some of these waters have low (acid) pH, increasing solubility of metals. Coal mine drainage water quite often is highly acid and has dissolved metallic substances from coal beds.[86]

Spoils piles, slag and rubble removed from mines may be a source of toxic metals. These materials are usually accumulated at the portal of the mine or near processing structures. They may release toxic metals as natural precipitation percolates through the piles to be released at some point at a lower elevation from the pile. Some streams may be devoid of aquatic animal life for several kilometers below mine waste piles.

Release of metallic compounds by industries is a potential source of these toxic substances. Metal plating, photographic processing, metal fabrication, smelters, chemical industries, electric generating plants and many others have been involved in release of toxic metals. Some metals are released directly into water bodies and some into the air as particulate effluents to fall to the ground and be carried into water bodies with runoff water. Surveillance of all industries potentially capable of polluting the aquatic environment is necessary to prevent toxic metal hazards to fish life.[120,124]

Mining and metals were responsible for 485 reported fish-kills in the United States between 1961 and 1975. An estimated 12.5 million fishes were killed by these sources of water pollution.[30]

Diagnostic Procedures:

Toxic metals may cause death or sublethal effects to fishes in a variety of ways. Many metallic compounds or ions accumulate in body tissues, especially liver, kidney, gill, heart, spleen and bone. Pathological changes in these organs occur which can be observed microscopically. Also, quantitative analysis of these body tissues may indicate toxic accumulations of the metal(s) involved. Analysis of water, bottom sediment and food organisms from where the fishes came may also be useful in diagnosis.[5,111]

TABLE 40

Toxicity of several metals to fishes

Element	TL_m (mg/L)	Probable Safe Concentration (mg/L)	Extenuations
Aluminum[33,68,85a]	0.3 (24 hr)	≤ 0.1	Maximum solubility 0.05 mg/L: at pH 7, at least 5 mg/L at pH 9
Antimony[114]	12 to 20 (96 hr)	—	Antimony potassium tartrate toxicity to fathead minnow
Arsenic[70] as arsenite[54a]	1.1 to 2.2 (48 hr) 14.1 to 14.4 (29 da)	≤ 0.7 —	May be concentrated in aquatic food chain as an additional source under natural conditions
Cadmium[101]	0.01 to 10.0	≤ 0.001	Related to water hardness, environmental factors, fish species and others
Chromium[31,89]	5.0 to 118.0 (96 hr)	≤ 0.05	Related to water quality; depends on valence (hexavalent or trivalent chromium) and chemical species
Copper[69]	3.0 to 7.0 (48 hr)	≤ 0.015	Related to water hardness, synergisms and antagonisms of other substances in the water anf fish species
Iron[26]	0.1 to 10.0 (24 to 48 hr)	≤ 0.03	Solubility of iron is related to pH; iron hydroxides precipitate onto gills and suffocate fishes at pH 7 or higer; toxicity is related to hardness
Lead[31,89]	1.0 to 7.0 in soft water, 400+ in hard water (96 hr)	≤ 0.03	Solubility of lead related to pH; toxicity related to water hardness
Manganese[26]	2.2 to 4.1 (24 hr)	—	Permanganates are much more toxic than other manganese species; manganese compounds are unstable and precipitate as manganese oxides or hydroxides at pH above 7.5
Mercury[31]	1.0	average total mercury 0.0005	Biological accumulation 0.5 mcg Hg per g of wet weight aquatic organism
Nickel[31,80a,80b,89]	5 to 43 (96 hr)	≤ 0.03	Toxicity is related to water hardness
Silver[21,68,80a,103] as sulfide + thiosulfate complex[53a]	0.004 to 0.2 280 to 360 (96 hr)	0.0001 to 0.0005 16 to 35	Toxicity is related to organic loading of the water, silver, species and other factors
Uranium[68,113]	2.8 to 135.0 (96 hr)	—	Toxicity is related to water hardness
Zinc[21,31,89,124a]	0.87 to 33.0 (96 hr)	≤ 0.05	Toxicity is related to water hardness and to synergism or antagonism of other substances in the water

Sublethal effects of metal poisoning are much more difficult to diagnose. Accumulation of toxic metals in fish tissue may border on quantities thought to be toxic, yet only enough to arouse suspicion. Reproduction may be reduced but not completely eliminated. Fish body conformations may indicate malnutrition but not emaciation. Histopathological examination may demonstrate serious degenerative changes in vital organs, not unlike toxemias resulting from other causes (Pl. 31B, 31C, 31D, 31E). Hematological and blood chemistry values may be low but border on normal values for the fish species involved. Enzymatic analysis may indicate reduced activity of some enzymes but still within ranges of normal. Often analysis of the fishes' environmental water, bottom sediment or effluents coming into the water body may lead to positive diagnosis of the problem.[103,104a]

Water analysis for components which relate directly to quantitative toxicity of metals to fishes is important. The relationship between total hardness and pH to metal toxicity has been discussed. Other water quality factors, such as alkalinity (a measurement of carbonaceous and hydroxyl anions), total dissolved solids, settlable or suspended solids and substances thought to be antagonistic or synergistic to the toxicity of a suspected metal should be determined.

Toxicity of Naturally Occurring Ions Usually Present in Water

Most natural waters of the world contain three major dissolved anions (chloride, sulfate and carbonaceous ions). Four major cations (calcium, magnesium, sodium and potassium) are usually present as well. Various combinations of these anions and cations make up 95 to 99+% of the total dissolved substances in most natural waters. The remainder of the total dissolved substances include a large number of "trace" elements and ions (nitrate, phosphate, silicate) and trace minerals (metallic ions, selenate, iodide, fluoride and others). These ions serve vital purposes in the mineral metabolism of all animals and plants. Fishes require a complement of each for normal existence. However, presence of the major ions at relatively high concentrations or in combinations not usually encountered by fishes may cause direct toxemia or subtle changes resulting in reduction of fish populations. Many fishery biologists, for example, have often recognized the correlation between high salinity of natural waters and the standing crop of fish food organisms.[84] The discussion here will concern direct toxic effects of the major ions to fishes.

The primary major anion of ocean water is chloride, and the major cation is sodium. These two elements make up more than 98% of the dissolved elements in seawater. Marine fishes evolved with the capability of existence in a concentration of sodium chloride as high as 3.5%. Special physiological adaptations allow them to retain water and excrete salt, since seawater is hyper-

tonic to their blood and body fluids. Sharks and rays are exceptions; their blood and body fluid are isotonic to seawater. Marine fishes cannot survive in freshwater because salts are rapidly lost as there is little or no physiological mechanism for salt retention. Many freshwater fishes cannot survive in seawater for the opposite reason—they have adapted to retain salt and excrete water, even in seawater. Toxemia results in either case.[45]

Much of the research involving toxicity of major ions to fishes has been done on freshwater fishes and freshwater systems. Freshwaters of the world have a much different complement of major ions than seawater, depending on geological structures in or near the source of water. Rising continents and receding oceans left many land areas with beds of limestone, gypsum, Glauber's salt and other carbonate and sulfate compounds of calcium, magnesium and sodium. Sodium chloride was leached away to remain in seawater, except in some areas of the world. Upthrusts formed mountains, with much of the old sub-sea beds removed by erosion to leave bare granite and other silicate rocks open to rainfall. A different type of anionic system becomes possible in natural waters of the land as compared to ocean water.[45,68]

Toxicity of major ions dissolved in water is dependent upon total dissolved solids and the combination of ions which make up the total dissolved solids. Carbonate (or bicarbonate) salts of calcium, magnesium and sodium are more toxic to fishes if they occur singly than if the water also contains chloride or sulfate salts of these cations. Sulfate salts are less toxic to freshwater fishes than carbonate (or bicarbonate) salts, and chloride salts are the least toxic (Table 41). However, tolerance to higher concentrations of either sulfates or chlorides by freshwater fishes appears to be enhanced if there is a well balanced mixture of all major cations and anions (Table 41).[36,68]

About 5% of the fresh waters of the United States supporting mixed fish populations have total dissolved solids of less than 72 mg/L, 50% of less than 169 mg/L and 95% under 400 mg/L.[68] Total dissolved solids concentration between 5,000 and 10,000 mg/L may be limiting to freshwater fishes, depending on ionic complement in the water, fish species and previous acclimation of the fishes to higher concentrations.[60]

Diagnostic Procedures:

Diagnosis of major ion toxicity to fishes is difficult. Examination of the history of circumstances leading up to fish mortality may be useful, especially if the water body is in an arid geographical area. Concentration of salts in the water often occurs during periods of low rainfall. Toxic concentration of salts may then cause serious physiological changes or death to fishes.

There is little information available on how increased salinity affects fishes, except in relation to osmotic pressure and relative increases or decreases of body water

TABLE 41

LC$_{50}$ values and confidence limits for bicarbonate, chloride and sulfate
salts of calcium, magnesium and sodium and combinations of certain
salts to rainbow trout exposed for six weeks [44,74,113]

Salt(s)	LC$_{50}$ (mg/L)	Confidence Limits[56] (mg/L)	Remarks
CaCl$_2$	4,782	4,138- 5,526	———
MgCl$_2$	———	———	17.5% mortality in 6 weeks at 7,500 mg/L
NaCl	10,452	8,040-13,589	———
Ca(HCO$_3$)$_2$	121	105-140	———
Mg(HCO$_3$)$_2$	80	63-101	———
NaHCO$_3$	250	———	———
CaSO$_4$	———	———	20% mortality in 6 weeks at 2,100 mg/L
MgSO$_4$	8,857	8,029-9,769	———
Na$_2$SO$_4$	5,006	4,411-5,681	———
Ca(HCO$_3$)$_2$ - 1.0 part with CaSO$_4$ - 23.2 parts	———	———	30% mortality in 6 weeks at 2,000 mg/L
Ca(HCO$_3$)$_2$ - 1.0 part with MgSO$_4$ - 23.2 part	2,366	1,987-2,817	———
Na$_2$SO$_4$ - 39.0 parts NaCl - 7.2 parts MgSO$_4$ - 6.4 parts Ca(HCO$_3$)$_2$ - 5.0 parts CaSO$_4$ - 2.5 parts KCl - 1.0 part	5,499[a]	5,012-6,033	———

[a]thought to be an average combination of these compounds found in naturally
occurring water in which sulfate is the major anion

and salts.[45] However, toxicity of bicarbonate ions in environmental water, for example, may block excretion of bicarbonate ions through gills, resulting in alkalosis.

High concentrations of major ions in environmental water of fishes may alter kidney function, causing edema and hyaline degeneration of kidney tubule epithelium (Pl. 31F). Altered kidney function may lead to edema in other organs, which can be observed histologically.

Water in which the total dissolved solids are made up primarily of calcium bicarbonate, with a paucity of other major anions (chloride or sulfate), and a pH near neutral may be especially conducive to formation of calcareous deposits in kidney glomeruli and excretory tubules and in pseudobranchia. Histological examination of the kidney and pseudobranchia is used to demonstrate calcareous deposits (Pl. 32A, 32B).

Analysis of water for total dissolved solids and major ions which make up the total dissolved solids is necessary for diagnosis of problems related to major dissolved ion toxicity to fishes. Other factors in the water, especially pH, may also be useful for diagnosis.

Toxic Organic Compounds

There is a tremendous number of organic compounds released into the waters of the world as pollutants which may be toxic to fishes. Water analysis procedures usually separate them into a variety of fractions including oil and grease, organic carbon absorbable, phenolic compounds, pesticides (including metabolites of pesticides), polychlorinated biphenyls, phthalate esters, phosphate esters and others. Specific organic compounds are often of direct concern. The complexity of the problem of potentially toxic organic materials to fishes must be stressed, but a thorough discussion cannot be given here.[31,54,68]

Oil and Grease

Oil and grease may be present in water as an emulsion or as minute particles suspended in water. The materials are derived from industrial wastes, lubricating oils, petroleum products, decomposition of algae or other aquatic plants and many other sources. Normally insoluble oils and greases may be emulsified or saponified by detergents, alkalies or other chemicals in the water. Heavy fractions of petroleum oils may remain insoluble but still exert an effect on fish life.

Oil and grease act as toxicants to fishes in a variety of ways. They may act directly on external surfaces of the fish; gills may be coated and cause asphyxia; sense organs (cornea of eyes, olfactory papillae or delicate structures in lateral line cells) may be damaged or destroyed.[31,68] Oil and grease or emulsified materials may be absorbed or ingested by fishes and cause either death or sublethal effects which decrease their survival.[112] These materials may coat plankton or the pond bottom and destroy fish food organisms.[54] They may deoxygenate water and cause fishes to be killed by asphyxiation.[31,68]

The toxicity of crude oils (petroleum) is difficult to interpret because they contain such a variety of compounds, both organic and inorganic.[22] Composition varies with geological structures from which they are derived. However, the aromatic group of compounds appears to be the major group of acutely toxic compounds in most crude petroleum (Table 42).[13,75,104]

Fish held in sublethal concentrations of the water soluble fractions of crude oil may develop pathological conditions in various organs: increased numbers of epithelial goblet cells, corneal lesions, gill lamellar hyperplasia and filament fusion, liver hyperemia, increased numbers of kidney and splenic macrophages, and delayed spermatogenisis.[112] Increased concentrations of tissue hydrocarbons have also been found. Fish exposed to sublethal levels of crude oil for extended periods of time usually grow more slowly and probably cannot survive the rigers of a natural environment as well as unexposed fish.[50a,124b]

Organic Carbon Absorbable

Organic carbon absorbable represents a large list of organic compounds absorbable on activated carbon. These compounds normally are lost during analytical procedures for oil and grease. Thus, they represent the

TABLE 42

Acute toxicity of selected organic compounds or substances to certain fishes [13,31,61,65,75,104,109]

Source of Compound	LC_{50} Concentration (mg/L)
Oil and grease:	
Gasoline	91 (24 hr); 40 (96 hr)
Diesel fuel	167 (96 hr)
Bunker oil	1,700 (168 hr)
Cutting oil	14,500 (96 hr)
Organic carbon absorbable:	
Benzene	23 to 32 (6 hr)
Kerosene	2,990 (24 hr)
Naphthylene	165 (48 hr)
Acrylophenone	10 ($<8\frac{1}{2}$ hr)
Heptane	4,924 (48 hr)
Cyclohexane	31 (96 hr)
Isoprene	75 to 118 (96 hr)
Phenolic compounds:	
Phenol	7.5 to 56 (24 to 48 hr)
o-Cresol	2.3 to 29.5 (24 hr)
m-Cresol	6.4 to 24.5 (24 hr)
p-Cresol	4.0 to 21.2 (24 hr)
Resorcinol	14 (24 hr)
o-Xylenol	13 to 30 (24 hr)
Hydroquinone	0.3 (48 hr)
Polychlorinated biphenyls:	
Aroclor® 1242	5,430 (96 hr)
Aroclor® 1248	5,750 (96 hr)
Aroclor® 1254	42,500 (96 hr)
Examples of other organic compounds and mixtures:	
Detergent:	
Alkalate sulfonate	3.3 to 6.4 (96 hr)
Phthalate esters:	
di-n-Butyl phthalate	731 to 1,300 (96 hr)
Phosphate esters:[a]	
Pydraul 115E	45 to >100 (96 hr)
Pydraul 50E	0.72 to 3.0 (96 hr)
Houghtosafe 1120	1.7 to 43 (96 hr)

[a]From hydraulic fluid

more volatile aliphatic and aromatic hydrocarbons as well as a number of ill-defined potentially toxic organic substances in water.

Organic carbon absorbable is further subdivided into those compounds which can be redissolved from activated carbon by chloroform (carbon-chloroform extract or CCE) or ethyl alcohol (carbon-alcohol extract or CAE).[5,14,31] Examples of substances included in the CCE and CAE are substituted benzene compounds, kerosene, polycyclic hydrocarbons, acrylonitrile, hydrazines, benzopyrenes, and others (Table 42).[42a,42b,75,124b]

The effect(s) of mixtures in CCE and CAE fractions on fishes cannot be stated specifically. Extractions from each source of polluted water will have an entirely different composition from those found in polluted water from other geographical areas. However, recommendations have been made to limit the CCE to no more than 0.3 mg/L and CAE to no more than 1.5 mg/L in public water supplies.[5,31] These recommendations may be acceptable levels for minimum effective concentrations to fishes when compared to the selected compounds given in Table 42.

Phenolic Compounds

Phenolic compounds are defined as hydroxy derivatives of benzene and its condensed nuclei.[5] These compounds are derived from processing coal, petroleum, wood distillation, many chemical industries and from domestic and animal wastes. Many phenolic compounds are more toxic than pure phenol, but the toxicity of pure phenol is often used as a guide to toxicity of other phenolics to fishes when no other data are available. The toxicity of pure phenol varies widely between fish species and under varying environmental conditions (Table 42).[87a]

Phenolic compounds may cause direct mortality or sublethal effects which may lead to serious alteration of fish populations. Pure phenol, for example, was found to cause extensive damage to the reproductive system of rainbow trout in seven days at a concentration of 6.5 mg/L.[76] Examples of other phenolic compounds which may have adverse or lethal effects on fish include cresols, xylenols, resorcinol and hydroquinone (Table 42).

Phenolic compounds in relatively high concentrations cause immediate damage to gill epithelium. Absorption by fishes leads to liver and kidney focal necrosis (Pl. 31B), edema, anemia and death. Diagnostic procedures for phenol or phenolic compound toxicity include histopathology and analysis of water or effluents which may have led to toxic effects on the fish.[5,76]

The U.S. Environmental Protection Agency recommends a maximum permissible concentration of phenolic compounds in water for fishes and wildlife to be no greater than 0.1 mg/L. Thus, concentrations in water or effluents suspected of having caused mortality among fishes which are greater than this quantity should be considered as suspected cause for mortality or adverse effects among fishes residing there.[31]

Polychlorinated Biphenyls

Polychlorinated biphenyls (PCB) are a group of stable compounds used in lubricants, heat exchangers, waterproofings, hydraulic fluids, plasticizers and for many other purposes. They may have one to ten attached chlorine atoms, making possible over 200 compounds. However, primarily eight biphenyls have been manufactured in the United States, all under the trade name Aroclor®, and each designated with a four-digit number (1221, 1232, 1242, 1248, 1254, 1260, 1262 and 1268). The last two digits of each formulation designate the percent chlorine.[37] There are at least two triphenyls, designated by the numbers 5442 and 5460, and another Arochlor®, 4465, which is a mixture of biphenyls and triphenyls.[31] Experiments have indicated that the higher the percent chlorine in the formulation, the lower the toxicity to fishes (Table 42).[31] These compounds are extremely stable and therefore persist in an ecosystem or in tissue of animals for a long time.

PCB's have been found in body tissues of fishes throughout the world.[87] The greatest problem in fishes does not appear to be the acute toxicity, which seldom occurs in the natural environment, but the chronic accumulation and subtle physiological damage caused by these compounds. Accumulations of PCB's from the environment may represent a greater hazard than if taken in with food. Experiments indicate that residues of PCB in fish body tissue can be as great as 100,000 times the concentration of the compounds in water surrounding them.[65,81]

Probably the greatest hazard to fish life is effects on reproduction. PCB residues in eggs have been related to egg mortality. Residues in salmon eggs, for example, in which 0.4 to 1.9 mcg of PCB's were present per gram of egg weight, caused 16 to 100% mortality respectively.[49] Reproduction did not occur in fathead minnows exposed to 8.3 mcg/L of either Aroclor® 1242 or Arochlor® 1254. Reproduction was possible at 5.4 mcg/L or less of Arochlor® 1242 and 1.8 mcg/L or less of Arochlor® 1254.[81]

PCB compounds may inhibit or enhance carcinogenicity of certain known carcinogenic compounds. Arochlor® 1242 or 1254 were added to diets which also contained diethylnitrosamine (DEN) and fed to rainbow trout for one year. Approximately 40% of the trout receiving Arochlor® 1242 developed hepatic (liver) cell carcinoma, compared to 10% of the fish receiving DEN alone. Arochlor® 1254 increased hepatocellular carcinoma to 20%, twice the incidence of DEN alone.[103a] Carcinogenesis of aflatoxin B_1 was inhibited by addition of Arochlor® 1254 to the diet.[103b]

Research has suggested that accumulations of PCB's in fish tissue should not exceed 0.5 mcg per gram of tissue because of the relationship between residue effect on reproduction and other possible physiological damage. Also, recommendations have been made that maximum concentrations of PCB's in water should not exceed 0.002 mcg/L.[31]

Examples of Other Organic Substances Possibly Toxic to Fishes:

Detergents are common pollutants in sewage and industrial wastes. These compounds are used primarily as cleaning agents. Detergent compounds prior to 1965 were tetrapropylene derivatives of alkylbenzene sulfonates (ABS). These compounds tended to accumulate because of nondegradability. However, a shift was made after 1965 to use of detergent formulations containing the more biodegradable linear alkalate sulfonates (LAS). LAS compounds are generally more toxic than ABS compounds but have the major advantages of nonaccumulation in ecosystems, including the tissues of fishes (Table 42).[88] Recommendations have been made that for safety of aquatic life in open water, LAS detergent concentrations should be no greater than 0.2 mg/L at any time or place.[31]

Phthalate esters are a group of compounds used widely as plasticizers, especially in polyvinyl chloride (PVC) plastics. These compounds accumulate in water, bottom sediment and aquatic organisms near industrial and heavily populated areas. Toxicity is relatively low (Table 42). However, recommendations have been made, in order to protect fishes and their food supply in open waters, that concentrations of these compounds should not exceed 0.3 mcg/L.

Phosphate esters are a group of compounds which are candidates for replacement of PCB's. These compounds are used as lubricants, oil additives, plasticizers and in hydraulic fluids and may become more commonly used in the future. They are mixtures of aryl and alkyl phosphates. All are extremely resistant to thermal degradation and oxidation, which makes them desirable for industrial use but undesirable from the standpoint of potential ecosystem accumulation. Phosphate esters depress cholinesterase activity in body tissues and in this respect act as organophosphate insecticides. The 96-hour LC_{50} of three phosphate esters found in hydraulic fluid ranged between 0.7 and 45 mg/L to four fish species (Table 42). Channel catfish were more tolerant than bluegill, fathead minnows or rainbow trout.[83] The possible wide usage of these compounds should be watched closely by fish health personnel, fishery biologists and fishery administrators.

Toxic Gases

Gases which may be toxic to fishes are derived from many sources, such as pollutants from industries, domestic wastes, animal feedlots, water treatment plants and other human activities. Others may be derived from natural sources such as from bacterial degradation of or-

ganic matter in water, normal excretions from aquatic organisms, photosynthesis or from springs or volcanic activity. The most common gases dissolved in water which cause toxic effects to fishes include ammonia, chlorine, hydrogen sulfide, carbon dioxide and ozone. Each acts as a toxicant in different ways, and diagnosis of the toxic effect of each becomes necessary on occasions.

Ammonia

Ammonia is released as a pollutant from a variety of industrial and cleaning processes. It may also be released from bacterial degradation of organic matter. Ammonia gas is soluble in water in the form of ammonium hydroxide to the extent of about 100,000 mg/L at 20°C. It dissociates into ammonium and hydroxyl ions and into un-ionized ammonia. The un-ionized component of ammonia solutions is the primary toxicant to fish (Table 43). Un-ionized ammonia concentration increases with pH (Fig. 2). The toxicity of ammonia to fish was discussed in Chapter III under "Bacterial (Environmental) Gill Disease."

Kidney pathology has also been observed in fish held in low concentrations of unionized ammonia for long periods of time. Ceroid deposits in the excretory portion of the kidneys have been reported. Hyaline droplets (Pl. 31F) in proximal excretory tubules appears to be quite common in fish held for up to 90 days in 0.2 to 0.4 mg of unionized ammonia per liter or concentrations as low as 0.01 to 0.07 mg/L for 7 to 11 months.[23a,112a]

Nitrification products of ammonia, especially nitrites, and their toxicity to fish have been studied. The major problem associated with nitrite toxicity is related to formation of methemoglobin in blood and subsequent reduction of oxygen carrying capacity. Young channel catfish, for example, were exposed to 1,2,3,4, and 5 mg of nitrite (in sodium nitrite) for 24 hours. The mean methemoglobin concentrations (percent of the total hemoglobin) was 35,79,79,85 and 90 percent, respectively.[47a] The 96 hour LC_{50} of nitrite (as nitrite ion) to rainbow trout was found to be 0.2 mg/L at pH 6.4 and 1.7 mg/L at pH 9.0.[100a] The toxicity of nitrite to fish is reduced by disolved chloride in environmental water. Addition of salt (sodium chloride) to the water at nitrite: chloride molar ratios of 0.06 to 0.25 can reduce percent methemoglobin in the fish to levels considered safe.[110a]

Chlorine

Chlorine and chloramines are released into open water from sewage treatment plants, power plants, paper mills and many other industries. Water treatment plants add chlorine to water to increase potability for human consumption. The use of water from potable sources (tap water) for aquariums, fish culture or ornamental ponds without allowing time for chlorine dissipation or adding substances such as thiosulfates to quickly bind chlorine will often result in death to fishes. The toxicity depends primarily on the quantity of residual chlorine.

Toxicity of chlorine to fishes depends to some extent on fish species and presence of organic matter or other material which may combine with chlorine. Threshold concentrations of residual chlorine in water receiving sewage effluents appear to be about 0.04 to 0.05 mg/L. However, fecundity may be effected after long-term exposure to the lower concentration (0.04 mg/L). The highest concentration demonstrating no measurable effect is about 0.016 mg/L.[126]

Recommendations have been made that natural waters in which fishes exist should not exceed 0.003 mg of residual chlorine per liter (Table 43). Short term contact of fishes should be at a residual chlorine level of no greater than 0.05 mg/L for up to 30 minutes in any 24-hour period.[31]

Fishes affected by excess residual chlorine demonstrate distress, attempt to avoid the area of chlorine contamination and often lose equilibrium after extreme exertion, followed by death. Concentrations of as little as 0.001 mg of residual chlorine per liter will usually cause avoidance behavior in most freshwater fishes.

Diagnosis of residual chlorine toxicity is made by observation of signs of distress in the fishes and by water analysis. Several rapid and accurate analytical procedures for residual chlorine are useful for diagnosis. The ortho-tolidine procedure is acceptable for detection of residual chlorine concentrations which cause acute toxicity, but it may not be sensitive enough to measure concentrations causing chronic toxicity.[5]

Hydrogen Sulfide

Sulfides are present in effluents from sewage treatment plants, paper mills, meat packing plants, chemical plants and other industries. Sulfides also occur as the result of bacterial action on bottom sediments and organic matter in ponds, lakes or other bodies of water. Springs, seeps and deep wells coming from geological structures high in sulfides may also contain toxic levels of hydrogen sulfide.

Hydrogen sulfide is soluble in water to about 4,000 mg/L at 20°C. It dissociates in relation to pH, as $H_2S \rightleftharpoons HS^- + H^+$. About 99% will be H_2S at pH 5, about equally divided at pH 7 and about 99% HS^- at pH 9. The toxicity of hydrogen sulfide to fishes is greater at lower pH levels.

Hydrogen sulfide formed in bottom sediments of water bodies used by fishes for spawning may have transient concentrations of this toxicant which reduce or destroy hatchability of fish eggs or kill young and juvenile fishes. Hydrogen sulfide analysis of water samples taken near the bottom of lakes with heavy accumulations of sludge or organic matter may demonstrate the reason for poor fish production.

The LC_{50} of hydrogen sulfide for the young of several

TABLE 43

Accepted maximum concentrations of toxic gases in water which support fish life[31,118]

Gas	Maximum Concentration for continuous exposure (mg/L)
Un-ionized ammonia	0.01
Chlorine (total residual)	0.003
Hydrogen sulfide	0.002
Ozone	0.002
"Free" carbon dioxide	< 60.0

freshwater fish species ranges between 0.0018 to 0.032 mg/L (Table 43).[46] The LC_{50} for developing eggs of the same species ranges between 0.037 and 0.071 mg/L.[108]

Diagnosis of hydrogen sulfide toxicity in fishes is primarily by the relationship between fish mortality and the results of hydrogen sulfide analysis on the water. Water samples taken for sulfide analysis should be taken with minimum aeration and agitation because oxygen taken into the sample from the atmosphere will rapidly reduce sulfide by chemical action. Samples should either be analyzed immediately on collection or preserved by the addition of zinc acetate solution to bind all sulfides into inert zinc sulfide.[94] A subsample used for analysis of total sulfide must contain a representative quantity of suspended solids, including the zinc sulfide.

Ozone

Ozone is being used as a replacement for chlorine to disinfect water for potability, sewage effluent treatment, power plant coolant water, disinfection of water for fish culture and a variety of other applications where its high oxidative capacity is of value.[12,40,82] However, studies have indicated that this gas may have serious adverse effects on fishes. Experiments made as early as 1930 indicated concentrations of ozone as low as 0.03 mg/L were lethal to minnows.[47] The cause for mortality was not determined until later, when studies demonstrated severe hydromineral imbalance and massive gill lamellar destruction in rainbow trout subjected to ozone concentrations as low as 0.007 mg/L for 96 hours. The 96-hour treatment with 0.007 mg of ozone per liter reduced plasma sodium to 80% of pre-treatment levels and increased hemoglobin to approximately 140%, hematocrit to about 154% and plasma glucose to over 1,200% of pre-treatment levels. Chronic exposure to 0.005 mg of ozone per liter for three months caused mild polycythemia and hyperglycemia, with significant lymphocytopenia and gill hypertrophy.[40]

These data indicate that increased use of ozone and subsequent release into open water should be monitored

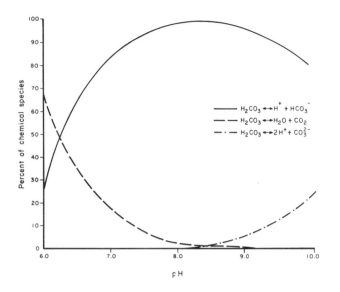

Fig. 26: Relationship between carbonaceous species and pH.

for toxic effects on fishes. An accepted maximum concentration of ozone in water supporting fishes should not exceed 0.002 mg/L (Table 43).[40]

"Free" Carbon Dioxide

Limnological measurement of so-called "free" carbon dioxide is a measurement of titratable ionized and unionized carbonaceous substances in water. The procedure measures the sum of carbon dioxide existing as carbonic acid, bicarbonate and carbonate. Carbonic acid exists at a relatively low pH and dissociates into carbonate at a relatively high pH (Fig. 26).

The actual toxicity of "free" carbon dioxide is caused by the inability of fishes to eliminate bicarbonate ion through gills, with a consequent reduction in dissolved oxygen uptake.[45,91] Some fishes, for example, are unable to remove dissolved oxygen at 50% saturation if "free" carbon dioxide is between 90 and 175 mg/L. Most fishes can extract dissolved oxygen if "free" carbon dioxide is below 60 mg/L (Table 43).[41]

"Free" carbon dioxide content of most surface waters seldom exceeds 10 mg/L, but some ground waters may contain far above this level. Fishes subjected to intolerable levels of "free" carbon dioxide lose equilibrium, develop anoxia and die with little or no activity. However, fishes are capable of detecting slight changes in "free" carbon dioxide gradients and will avoid levels as low as 1.0 to 6.0 mg/L, if possible.[46]

There are several analytical methods for estimating "free" carbon dioxide in water. The titrimetric and nomographic methods are most often used.[5]

Pesticide Toxicity to Fishes

Pesticides are synthetic and natural compounds used to control animal and plant life considered adverse to human society. Only natural pesticide compounds, such as rotenone, pyrethrum, lead arsenate and arsenic tri-

chloride, were used prior to 1900. Several synthetic pesticides had been incorporated into thousands of different formulations for control of "pests" by 1971.[31]

Pesticides have assisted human survival in many ways: increased crop yields; reduced losses of crops in storage or transit; improved quality of food and fiber; reduced human death rates in many parts of the world; protected clothing, carpeting, wood and other products from termites and other destructive organisms; controlled bad odor and tastes in municipal water. The examples are endless. The honest and intelligent use of pesticides has made tremendous contributions to human welfare. These compounds have, on occasion, been responsible for adverse effects on both plants and animals, including fishes.

The major source of pesticides in water is from runoff from treated land, industrial discharges and domestic wastes. Other sources include fallout from atmospheric drift and precipitation, and application of pesticides to water surfaces either intentionally or accidentally. Many of the pesticides have relatively low solubility in water and tend to absorb onto suspended or sedimentary materials or organisms in water bodies. Many have an affinity for, and accumulate in, animal and plant lipids. Some are extremely stable and remain in ecosystems for exceptionally long times. Fishes may accumulate these compounds either by direct absorption or through the food chain. The transfer of pesticide residues from prey to predator in the food chain can result in residues in higher trophic levels many times greater than residues in water or sediments.[39]

The majority of pesticides are insecticides or herbicides.[31] Probably insecticides have had more inadvertent adverse effects on fishes than any other pesticides. Therefore, the discussion which follows is a brief examination of a few insecticidal and herbicial compounds to demonstrate toxic effects on fishes.

Insecticides can be categorized into four major groups, each group having distinct characteristics and toxicological effects: chlorinated hydrocarbons, organophosphates, carbamates and natural compounds. The relationship between fishes and toxicity, tropicity and persistency of members of each category will be discussed.

Chlorinated Hydrocarbon Insecticides

Chlorinated hydrocarbon insecticides are a class of synthetic organic compounds relatively insoluble in water and highly soluble in organic solvents. All are resistant to oxidation or other molecular alteration. Their characteristic solubility in biological lipids makes them a special toxicological problem among animals.

Chlorinated hydrocarbon insecticides were among the first synthetic compounds to be used for this purpose, and 2,2'-bis (p-chlorophenyl) 1,1',1''-trichlorethane, better known as DDT, was one of the earlist. DDT has subsequently been used for a variety of pest control functions, some of which allow it or its metabolites to enter aquatic systems and fishes.[71]

Other chlorinated hydrocarbons found useful as insecticides during the 1940's, 1950's and 1960's include such compounds as chlordane, dieldrin, endrin, heptachlor, lindane, methoxychlor and toxaphene. Each has become a specific toxicological problem in fishes when used for pest control. This class of compounds is no longer used as insecticides by governmental agencies of the United States, except in special instances where other insecticides are unusable.[31]

The toxicity of chlorinated hydrocarbon insecticides is partly because of their fat solubility and accumulation in tissues high in lipids. Fishes may accumulate relatively large quantities of these compounds over a summer season with little or no toxic effect, because the compounds accumulate in adipose tissue. Body fats mobilized from adipose cells during periods of reduced availability of food release stored chlorinated hydrocarbon insecticides or their metabolites.[71] They may then be absorbed by tissue with the next higher lipid content, often nervous tissue. The result may be destruction of nerve cells, causing partial or complete paralysis. Some may be absorbed into other vital tissues (liver, kidney, or spleen) and cause foci of necrosis or general toxemia within the organ. Death may result, or anatomical or physiological changes which may lead to death.

Diagnosis of acute or chronic chlorinated hydrocarbon insecticide toxicity in fishes may be by history of toxicant release(s), paralytic signs in the fish, histopathological changes and analysis of tissues, especially adipose tissue or brain, for the suspected compound. Chronic effects of chlorinated hydrocarbon insecticides on fishes vary with the compound. Toxaphene, for example, reduces growth and survivability. Toxaphene reduces collagen formation, the major component of organic matrix in connective tissue, and results in lordosis and scoliosis. These effects have been noted at extremely low doses (0.6 mcg/g of fish body weight).[72,110] Studies on the chronic effects of DDT indicated a marked increase in mortality and reduced number and volume of eggs, with smaller and less vigorous fry of cutthroat trout.[2]

Toxicity of chlorinated hydrocarbon insecticides varies greatly with fish species and strains within species. Live golden shiners resistant to endrin, for example, accumulated 64 times more endrin in the blood than endrin-killed susceptible shiners.[59] This can be demonstrated by performing toxicity tests side by side using exactly the same materials (toxicant, dilution water and randomly selected fishes) in the same test vessels and at the same time (Table 44).[99]

Physiological condition of the fish, source or quantity of food available to the fish, aquatic temperature and other aquatic parameters are somewhat responsible for relative toxicity of these compounds. Examples of the

TABLE 44

Relative 96-hour TL$_m$ of DDT and endrin to four salmonid species[99]

Fish Species	DDT (mcg/L)	Endrin (mcg/L)
Rainbow trout	1.72	0.40
Cutthroat trout	1.37	0.19
Brook trout	11.90	0.59
Coho salmon	18.65	0.77

toxicity of eight selected chlorinated hydrocarbon insecticides to rainbow trout and fathead minnow are given in Table 45.[31] Toxicity of other insecticides can be found in selected references.[31,50,68,117,124a]

Organophosphate Insecticides

Organophosphate compounds used as insecticides are oily, relatively volatile, relatively insoluble in water and soluble in organic solvents. Most are absorbed through unbroken skin, respiratory tissue and from the digestive tract of animals. Many of those used as insecticides are non-persistent, losing toxicity within a short time after application, especially in warm, moist conditions.

The primary toxicological effect of organophosphate insecticides to fishes is binding of cholinesterases, most important being acetylcholinesterase (AChE). AChE is essential for destruction of excess acetylcholine (ACh) at muscle-nerve synapses following muscle contraction. Nerve impulses entering endplates opposite muscle fibers cannot continue on to the muscle until ACh is se-

TABLE 45

Relative toxicity of selected chlorinated hydrocarbon insecticides to rainbow trout and fathead minnow [31]

	Acute LC$_{50}$ in mcg/L	
Insecticide	Rainbow Trout	Fathead Minnow
Chlordane	44	56
DDT	7	19
Dieldrin	10	16
Endrin	0.6	1.0
Heptachlor	19	56
Lindane[a]	27	67
Methoxychlor	62.6	7.5
Toxaphene[b]	11	14

[a]Lindane has been prescribed for removal of copepod parasites from fishes

[b]Toxaphene has been used as a piscicide

TABLE 46

**Percent residual brain AChE activity versus activity index and time
for recovery of normal AChE activity in three salmonid species
following contact with sublethal amounts of malathion[98]**

Malathion Concentration (mcg/L)	Residual Brain AChE (%)[a]	Activity Index (Time)	Activity Index (%)[a]	Time for Complete AChE Recovery (days)[a]
Brook trout:				
0	100.0[c]	29:18[b]	100.0	
40	68.4	24:31	83.7	
90	51.4	16:15	55:5	
120	24.3	8:35	29.3	25
Rainbow trout:				
0	100.0[d]	35:20	100.0	
55	81.5	34:12	97.7	
112	50.6	23:15	66.3	
175	28.1	13:26	29.0	35
Coho salmon:				
0	100.0[e]	43:06	100.0	
100	71.9	41:07	95.4	
200	52.0	33:03	76.7	
300	29.0	20:58	48.7	42

[a]Compared to nontreated fish of the same species
[b]Minutes:Seconds
[c]Percent residual AChE obtained in 7 days exposure
[d]Percent residual AChE obtained in 10 days exposure
[e]Percent residual AChE obtained in 9 days exposure

creted into the synapse. ACh secretion allows nerve impulses to continue, resulting in muscle contraction. Normally, muscle bundles remain in a state of contraction because of continued nerve impulse transmission until voluntarily stopped by the central nervous system and hydrolysis of remaining ACh within the synapse by AChE. Organophosphate insecticides firmly attach to AChE, eliminating the effectiveness of this enzyme for hydrolysis of remaining ACh. The muscle bundles remain in a continuous state of contraction until completely exhausted.[51,80]

The organophosphate-AChE bond is firm. Normal AChE activity can only be restored by synthesis of unaffected AChE. Synthesis of AChE continues at a regular pace in the body at all times; therefore, restoration of normal quantities of AChE takes time. Not only are the amounts of organophosphate insecticides present in the animal body as acute doses important for toxicological reasons, but also the frequency of exposure to subacute quantities is important as well.[98] Agricultural use of these insecticides may require several applications to crops during a growing season because of the rapid loss of toxicity to the target organism. Each application may produce a residual effect among animals inhabiting the ecosystem, with incomplete recovery between organophosphate insecticide applications. The animal may die or be killed as an indirect result of sublethal insecticidal toxicity.[98]

There are two related sublethal effects of organophosphate compounds to fishes: 1) loss of physical strength and stamina; and 2) incipient scoliosis and lordosis, probably resulting from altered muscular control.[119] Loss of physical strength and anatomical deformities may have a direct relationship to the ability of wild-ranging fishes to elude predators and seek food, both extremely important factors in survival.

TABLE 47

Acute toxicity of selected organophosphate insecticides to some fish species [3,31]

Compound Name	Fish Species	96-hr LC$_{50}$ (mg/L)
Diazinon	Fathead minnow	7.8
	Brook trout	0.77
	Bluegill	0.46
Dursban®	Rainbow trout	0.011
Fenthion® (Baytex)	Fathead minnow	2.4
	Largemouth bass	1.54
	Rainbow trout	0.93
Guthion®	Fathead minnow	0.093
	Largemouth bass	0.005
	Rainbow trout	0.014
Methylparathion	Fathead minnow	8.9
	Largemouth bass	5.22
	Rainbow trout	2.75
Malathion	Fathead minnow	9.0
	Largemouth bass	0.285
	Rainbow trout	0.17
Parathion	Fathead minnow	1.6
	Largemouth bass	0.19

The severity of stamina loss caused by organophosphate insecticide treatment, and subsequent time required to regain normal stamina, was tested by exposing three salmonid species to sublethal concentrations of malathion in water. The treatment period was long enough to reduce brain AChE in selected groups to approximately 75, 45 and 25% of normal. Groups of 20 fishes from each of the three treatments were then placed in water flowing at a constant 26.67 cm per second (0.875 ft/sec) until 75% of the fishes could no longer maintain the swimming position and were swept downstream. The time required for loss of swimming ability was recorded and used to calculate an activity index. There was a nearly proportional relationship between loss of AChE activity and loss of physical stamina (Table 46). The time required for recovery to normal AChE activity and physical stamina was also established, and ranged between 25 and 42 days, depending on spe-

cies. These findings demonstrate the need for careful planning of organophosphate insecticide release where it may enter water containing fishes so complete or nearly complete recovery of tissue AChE activity is restored before subsequent insecticide applications are made.[98]

Organophosphate insecticides vary greatly in toxicity to different fish species. The compound diazinon, for example, is 17 times more toxic to the bluegill than to the fathead minnow (95-hr LC$_{50}$ bluegill 0.46 mg/L; fathead minnow 7.8 mg/L). Malathion is 45 times more toxic to brown trout (96-hr LC$_{50}$ 0.2 mg/L) than to the fathead minnow (96-hr LC$_{50}$ 9.0 mg/L). Examination of other organophosphate compounds and toxicity to fishes will demonstrate a similar relationship (Table 47).[3,31]

There is also a great variation in toxicity between compounds to the same fish species. Parathion, for example, is about 5.5 times more toxic to fathead minnows than malathion (96-hr LC$_{50}$ for parathion 1.6 mg/L; malathion 9.0 mg/L). Examples of the relationship between the acute toxicity of other selected organophosphorous compounds are given in Table 47.[3,31]

Diagnosis of organophosphate insecticide poisoning in fishes is primarily by tissue AChE activity compared to normal AChE for the type of body tissue and fish species being analyzed and for the residual organophosphate compound or its metabolites.[71] Brain tissue from fishes suspected of having been in contact with organophosphate compounds has been found to be more satisfactory for AChE assay than other tissues or body fluids. Fishes selected for AchE assay must be living or just dying at the time of collection. Body tissue to be used for AChE assay should be removed quickly and either analyzed immediately or frozen; it should remain frozen until analysis.

Analysis of body tissues or whole fish bodies for organophosphate compounds or metabolites should be used for diagnosis if the fishes have been dead for more than a few minutes at environmental temperatures above 10°C. An involved sample cleanup and standardization of chromatography equipment are necessary if an organophosphate compound or its metabolites are used for diagnosis.

Histopathology has been suggested as being of assistance in diagnosis of organophosphate poisoning in fishes. This method can only be used as an adjunct to other methods of diagnosis.[6]

Carbamate Insecticides

Carbamate insecticides are highly toxic to a wide variety of insects and crustaceans but have a relatively low toxicity to most vertebrates. These compounds have intermediate persistence when compared to persistent chlorinated hydrocarbon and nonpersistent organophosphate insecticides.[64] Applications of carbaryl (Sevin®), for example, maintain insecticidal activity up to three weeks. Furthermore, its toxicity to fishes is up to 250

TABLE 48

96-hour LC$_{50}$ concentrations of carbaryl and zectran to fishes [31,99]

Fish Species	Carbaryl [a] (mg/L)	Zectran (mg/L)
Rainbow trout	1.47 to 4.34[b]	10.20
Brook trout	1.07 to 1.45	—
Cutthroat trout	1.50 to 2.17	—
Coho salmon	0.76 to 1.50	—
Largemouth bass	6.40	14.70
Channel catfish	15.80	11.45
Black bullhead	20.00	16.70
Bluegill	6.70 to 11.00	11.4 to 16.7
Yellow perch	0.75	2.48

[a]Registered trade name Sevin
[b]Ranges are results from two authors

times less than DDT. The carbamate compounds should prove to be safer insecticides for use in aquatic environments supporting fishes than many now in use.

Carbamate insecticides are cholinesterase inhibitors. Acetylcholinesterase (AChE) is the most important enzyme inhibited by carbamates because of its function in voluntary muscle contraction (an explanation of this function was given under organophosphate insecticides).[85]

Carbamates react somewhat differently from the organophosphates in that a relatively weak bond is formed between the carbamate and AChE, and the affected fishes may not need to synthesize a full complement of AChE because some is released from carbamate bonding to continue normal AChE activity. Fishes affected by carbamate intoxication recover normal body functions more rapidly than those affected by organophosphates. Chronic toxicity to fishes from carbamate insecticides is not as great a problem because of the constant AChE release.[94] Acute toxicity of two carbamate compounds to several species of fishes is given in Table 48.

Diagnostic procedures for carbamate insecticide intoxication in fishes is by assay for AChE activity in selected body tissue taken from affected fishes. Interpretation of results is difficult because of the weak bonding between the carbamate compound and AChE. Tissue AChE must be done immediately after sample collection for most accurate results. However, release of AChE from carbamate bonding can be slowed by storing tissue samples on dry ice, but the time between sample collection, freezing and analysis should not exceed 24 hours.

Even then, some bonding release may have occurred, and results should be interpreted accordingly.

Other methods for diagnosis of carbamate intoxication in fishes have not been possible. No histopathological changes could be observed in the spot fish, even after five months of exposure to 0.1 mg of carbaryl per liter. Growth rate of the insecticide-exposed fish was comparable to that of non-exposed fish.[58]

Herbicides

There are a large number of terrestrial herbicidal compounds in use, each a possible pollutant to aquatic ecosystems. Several aquatic herbicides are used to remove unwanted aquatic plants from waterways (streams, ponds, lakes and other bodies of water). The toxicity to fishes of each compound registered for use in the United States is relatively low compared to insecticidal compounds (Table 49).

Many of the aquatic herbicides are relatively persistent. Diquat and paraquat, for example, may be found in bottom sediment or bottom soil for up to six months after application.[32] Some aquatic herbicides are applied to water bodies in granular form, the formulations being designed for slow and continuous release of the herbicide to the water. The solubility of most herbicides is quite low, but granular formulations tend to maintain maximum concentration of the herbicide for longer periods of time than those formulations applied to the water surface. Bottom-feeding fishes may be subjected to contact with herbicidal compounds continuously for several weeks or months.[31,32,48]

The herbicide 2,4-dichlorophenoxyacetic acid (2,4D) absorbed by fish is eliminated rapidly. The half-life (time for half the compound to be excreted) in rainbow trout was found to be 2.4 hours. Injected doses of 2,4-D were excreted rapidly in urine. Approximately 80% of the compound appeared in urine within 24 hours. The herbicide was present in bile for up to 96 hours.[18a]

Diagnosis of herbicide intoxication to fishes is difficult. Residue analysis for the suspected herbicide or its metabolites is recommended.[71]

Natural Organic Pesticides

There are several naturally occurring organic compounds used as pesticides which are also toxic to fishes. The toxicity of two such compounds, rotenone and pyrethrum, will be discussed as examples.

Rotenone has been known for its insecticidal effects since antiquity. This compound is a complex organic molecule found in the root tissue of several plant species. Most rotenone used commercially as an insecticide comes from cube and derris roots. Often commercially available rotenone insecticide is called cube root or derris root.

Rotenone is almost insoluble in water but can be emulsified or suspended in water. Powdered derris or cube root can also be suspended in water for use as a

TABLE 49

Acute toxicity of some herbicidal compounds to fishes[17,31,48,79]

Herbicide	Fish Species	Acute Toxicity (mg/L)	LC_{50} Time (hr)
Aqualin	Bluegill	0.08	24
	Brown trout	0.024	24
Dacthal	Bluegill	700.0	48
Dalapon (sodium)	Bluegill & fathead minnow	290.0	96
Dicamba	Bluegill	20.0	48
Dichlobenil	Bluegill	20.0	48
Diquat	Bluegill	350	96
	Largemouth bass	7.8	96
	Rainbow trout	11.2	96
2,4 D	Fathead minnow	5.6	96
Endothal (sodium)	Bluegill	120	96
	Fathead minnow	110	96
	Largemouth bass	120	96
Hydrothal Plus	Bluegill	3.5	48
Silvex	Bluegill	1.1	48

spray in insect control or in vats for dipping domestic animals. Rotenone is extracted from the plant roots with organic solvents and the concentrated solution formulated into water-emulsifiable suspensions. Most commercially available rotenone preparations have been adjusted to a 5% rotenone concentration.

The lethal concentration of rotenone to fish is 0.02 mg/L. This concentration will usually kill most fish within 24 to 48 hours.

Diagnosis of rotenone introxication in fish is by analysis of water for rotenone.[24a,95] Usually there is no pathological findings which indicate rotenone poisoning. However, fish effected by rotenone demonstrate signs of anoxia. Gills are bright red in color, not dark red as is often observed in cases of anoxia.

Pyrethrum is a combination of pyrethrins, allethrins and cinerins present in dried flowers of *Chrysanthemum cinerariaefolium*. The pyrethrum used in some parts of the world is nothing more than dried and ground flowers, which contain between 0.3 to 5.0% of the active chemicals. The active compounds are soluble in organic solvents and are extracted and mixed with synergists and activators to enhance insecticidal activity.

The toxicity of pyrethrum or its active compounds to fishes has received only cursory research. Two mg of pyrethrins per liter will cause noticeable effects in carp, and 5 to 10 mg/L will cause paralysis and death. One mg of pyrethrins per liter killed guppies in five hours.

The lethal threshold for pyrethrins to juvenile Atlantic salmon appeared to be about 9 mcg/L.[1,31,127] Nothing is known of diagnostic procedures to be used for determination of pyrethrum toxicity to fishes.

Piscicides

There are several compounds used for elimination of unwanted fish populations. These compounds are referred to as piscicides. Piscicidal compounds must be somewhat selective in toxicity (i.e. much more toxic to fish than other organisms), be acceptable for use at low concentrations and have a relatively short half-live (be eliminated from ecosystems rapidly leaving no undesirable intermediate compounds). They must be relatively inexpensive.

Compounds used as piscidies include two compounds registered for fishery use in the United States (rotenone and antimycin), and several others. There are selective toxicants such as lampricides, effective against larval lamprey in tributary streams leading into the Great Lakes, and Squoxin, selective against squawfish of the upper Columbia River tributaries. Other compounds which have been used include salicylanalide, 2-digerany-lamino-ethanol (GD-174) and toxaphene.[62b]

Complete removal of undesirable fish populations is often difficult to attain. The pH, temperature and chemistry of water being treated may effect toxicity of certain piscicides. Method(s) of application of the compounds to water bodies may also effect success. Great care must be taken in applying the toxicant to all parts of the water body, and it must be mixed thoroughly with the water (Pl. 36E).

Characteristics of rotenone and antimycin will be given here, as well as a note on the use of toxaphene and its undesirable characteristics.

Rotenone is highly toxic to a wide variety of arthropods and gill-breathing vertebrates. Its toxicity to homeothermic, air-breathing animals is relatively low. These characteristics make rotenone a desirable insecticide. Its high toxicity to fishes also makes it a useful fish control chemical.

The 96-hour LC_{50} of rotenone to fathead minnows is approximately 0.006 mg/L and to channel catfish about 0.47 mg/L.[19,20] Most piscicidal applications use rotenone at approximately 0.05 mg/L (1.0 mg/L of a 5% rotenone emulsion or plant root).

Research on the toxicity of rotenone to fishes in the 1940's suggested the compound caused lamellar constriction and subsequent blockage of blood circulation.[38] Later research indicated this was not true. The most probable toxicological effect is that rotenone blocks electron transport in gill tissue by oxidation of the major cytochrome systems (A, A_3, B and C).[55] Fish affected by rotenone exhibit signs of anoxia by surfacing, gulping of air and loss of equilibrium.

Rotenone use for removal of undesirable fish populations is worldwide. Fishery biologists apply the piscicide, wait for the fish to die and rotenone toxicity to dissipate, and restock with a more desirable species. Rotenone toxicity dissipates at a relatively constant rate in water and appears to be regulated primarily by water temperature. Rotenone residues can be detected quantitatively by a chemical method, although the method does not appear to be entirely satisfactory in all waters.[24a,95] Use of a time-temperature-rotenone concentration curve may be of assistance in judging when rotenone toxicity dissipation is complete (Fig. 27).[96] Baskets of a few fishes of the same species to be restocked should be suspended near the bottom of the water body for a few days to prove rotenone dissipation prior to subjecting large numbers of fishes to possible toxic residues of rotenone in the water.

Desirable fish populations may be destroyed by accidental release of rotenone in water. An incident comes to mind in which fishes in a small stream were killed for approximately 14 kilometers downstream when cattle were released from a dipping vat and immediately crossed the stream. Inadvertent spraying of rotenone for control of insects has also caused accidental fish-kills.

Antimycin is an antibiotic compound toxic to a wide variety of organisms including yeasts, fungi and fish. It is absorbed on gills of fish and subsequently taken by the blood to other organs of the body. It blocks electron transport in mitochondria of cells. Fish affected by anti-

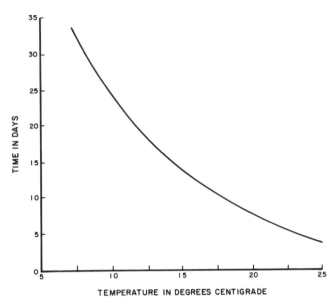

Fig. 27: Time in days for a rotenone concentration of 0.05 mg/L to become nonlethal to most fishes at various water temperatures.[96]

mycin become disoriented, surface and become unable to respond to stimuli. The 96 hour LC_{50} ranges between 0.05 mcg/L for rainbow trout to 20.4 mcg/L for channel catfish at pH 7.5.

The recommended concentration used to remove unwanted fish is 5 to 50 mcg/L. Toxic effect is pH and temperature related, being less toxic at higher pH (8.5 to 9.5) and low temperature (10 to 12°C).[36a]

The half-life of antimycin is primarily pH dependent ranging between 310 hours at pH 6 to 6.5 and 10 hours at pH 9. The half-life is somewhat influenced by water temperature but to a much lesser degree.[62a]

Estimation of residual antimycin in water is difficult. Yeast assay or gas chromatography is used to determine if antimycin has dissipated to safe levels so desirable fish can be restocked.[1a] Baskets of a few live fish of the same species to be restocked should be suspended at various places in the water body to prove safety of restocking.

Toxaphene (chlorinated camphene) was widely used for insect control during the early 1950's. Its toxicity to fishes was recognized, and the product was used for destruction of unwanted fish populations. Toxaphene's characteristic persistence in aquatic environments assured a more prolonged piscicidal action than the more often used rotenone.[43] Also, both toxaphene and rotenone were used at about the same toxicant level (0.02 to 0.05 mg/L), but toxaphene was much less expensive. The main disadvantage of toxaphene for this purpose was that some water bodies treated with the prescribed quantity of toxaphene were not safe to restock with desirable fishes for one or more years. Gradually information regarding biological accumulation of toxaphene and other chlorinated hydrocarbon insecticides in aquatic systems became known, especially accumulations in higher trophic levels. None is used as a piscicide in the United States today.

Toxicity of Therapeutic Compounds

Chemical compounds (drugs) used for controlling the growth or for killing infectious organisms which cause pathological effects on or in fishes also exert antibiological effects on the fishes being treated. The reason why these drugs are useful therapeutics is because they produce antibacterial, antifungal or antiparasitic effects at concentrations which do not cause permanent toxicological effects to the host. Therapeutic concentrations and time of use for each drug have been found by experimentation.

The recommended dose levels and treatment times for some therapeutic compounds are near the lethal level for certain fishes. Each drug exerts a sublethal effect on the host but does allow the host to survive. So, the use of drugs for control of diseases among cultured, ornamental and other confined fishes becomes the choice between possible mortality from the pathogen and the sublethal effect of the drug being used.

The most useful drugs are those which produce transient toxicity in the host when used at the prescribed dose level for the prescribed time. Pathology and toxemias produced by the drug should be reparable and completely reversible, and drug residues in body tissues should be completely eliminated within a reasonable time after withdrawal of the drug. The discussion which follows describes potential toxic effects of several chemical compounds used for disease therapy in fishes.

Antibiotic Compounds

Antibiotics such as choramphenicol, oxytetracycline (Terramycin®) and erythromycin, administered orally at the prescribed dosage for ten or more days, repress the number of erythroblasts in hematopietic tissue.[53] The effect may be mild or severe, depending on fish species. These antibiotics clear body tissue rapidly after the drugs are withdrawn. Erythropoiesis is restored when the drugs are eliminated from the hematopoietic tissue. Prolonged treatment or the usual ten-day treatment series offered to fishes at intervals more often than a two-week nonmedicated period may cause moderate to severe anemia.[100]

Fry hatched from eggs which had previously been exposed to chlortetracycline demonstrate abnormalities in growth and development.[102] This compound is known to concentrate in bone, which may account for skeletal defects.

Some fish species are more sensitive to adverse effects from chloramphenicol than others. Atlantic salmon, for example, developed reddish hive-like sores in the skin following an injected dose of 18.7 mg/kg of body weight. This same dose did not produce adverse effects in rainbow trout or brown trout.[8]

Kanamycin is an antibiotic compound used to control certain bacterial infections in fishes. The recommended oral dose is 20 mg of kanamycin per kg of fish per day for 21 days. However, a study in which 20 mg of kanamycin sulfate per kg of body weight was administered intraperitoneally to steelhead (rainbow) trout once each week, one group for three weeks and another group for five weeks, produced acute toxic effects in both groups. Other groups of steelhead administered half the dose (10 mg/kg) in the same way also became acutely ill, and many died. Necropsy of the fish demonstrated yellowish, blood-streaked fluid in the abdominal cavity and small hemorrhages in the liver. Microscopically, the livers of most fish had focal hemorrhages and hepatic cells pyknosis. Kidney tubular epithelial degeneration was common.[66] These findings indicate the need for establishing safe dose levels of drugs to be administered to fishes. Kanamycin is not widely used, but its toxic effect to steelhead (rainbow) trout demonstrates that it can be highly toxic to some fish species.

Erythromycin has been used for control of bacterial kidney disease in salmonids. The recommended dose is 100 mg/kg of fish body weight per day for 21 days. Toxic effects have been observed in rainbow trout given this dose in food after feeding 14 to 21 days. Pathological changes have been demonstrated in epithelial linings of the proximal excretory tubules of kidneys. However, cell injury is reversible.[44a]

Sulfonamide Compounds

Several of the sulfonamide compounds have been used as chemotherapeutic drugs for control of certain bacterial diseases of fishes. Improper or prolonged use of these drugs can cause serious renal pathology usually related to crystallization of the compounds into the excretory portion of the kidney (Pl. 32C).

The most often used sulfonamide drug is sulfamerazine. The oral dosage of sulfamerazine is usually recommended at 220 mg/kg (10 g/100 lb) of fish per day for 14 days. This dosage and prolonged treatment time may be responsible for renal damage in some fishes. Cutthroat trout broodfish, for example, developed edema and hemorrhages in renal tubules after receiving this dose level for the prescribed 14 days. Males seemed to be more severely affected, which was attributed to the combined stresses of bacterial infection, drug treatment and reproductive activities.[107] Some fish pathologists will not use the sulfonamide drugs because of potential pathological effects.[100] However, use of the modified dose rate for sulfamerazine (0.264 g SM/kg of body weight for three days, followed by 0.154 g of SM/kg of body weight for 11 days) reduces the possibility of pathological effects.

Nitrofuran Compounds

Two examples of nitrofuran compounds used for disease control in fishes are furazolidone and furanace. No direct pathology was found after feeding four salmonid species 35 mg of furazolidone per kg of body weight for 21 days. Tissue levels up to 7.0 mg of the drug were found per kg of body tissues and cleared rapidly when the drug was withdrawn.[42]

Furanace is used primarily as an externally administered chemotherapeutic. Most fish species appear to accept the recommended dose level for the prescribed time (2 mg furanace/L). However, channel catfish may be exceptionally sensitive to furanace, because skin lesions appeared after three or four days of treatment with 0.5 mg of furanace per liter. The lesions began as dull areas on the skin and increased until the skin and underlying muscle were eroded, some exposing the vertebrae.[73] Another experiment demonstrated mortality and increased rate of skeletal and body anomalies in mummichogs subjected to a concentration of 2.0 or more mg of furanace per liter. The reason for the adverse effect was not determined.[122]

Alimentary Parasiticide Compounds

Enheptin has been used for control of intestinal flagellated protozoa in fishes. This compound is usually administered at 0.1% of the diet for three days. The LD_{50} of enheptin administered in this way was found to be 200 mg/kg of body weight when given for ten days. Lethal doses caused liver hemorrhages, hepatic cell necrosis and hyaline degeneration in kidney tubular cells. However, doses of 125 or less mg/kg of body weight for six days produced no observable pathology. Enheptin tissue residues of up to 143 mg/kg of kidney tissue were found after feeding the drug for six days at the 125 mg/kg per day dosage and did not completely clear from the tissues for over 140 days.[97]

Thiabendazole has been administered in the diet for control of nematodes in fishes. This compound, although relatively insoluble in water, can be absorbed through alimentary epithelium in quantities high enough to cause liver and kidney degeneration.[100]

External Disinfectant Compounds

Quaternary ammonium compounds have been used for many years to control external bacterial infections on fishes. However, these compounds can be extremely toxic if used incorrectly. The bactericidal ingredient in roccal, for example, has a 48-hour LC_{50} concentration ranging from 1.12 mg/L for channel catfish to 3.40 mg/L for brook trout. Toxicity to bluegill, lake trout, brown trout and rainbow trout ranges between these two concentrations. The recommended dose level for roccal is 4.0 mg/L (1:250,000 of the 50% formulation) for one hour, a therapeutic level relatively close to an acute toxic level for this drug.

Formalin appears to be quite toxic to some fish species, especially to rainbow trout. A survey conducted among 73 trout culture facilities in the United States indicated that 23 facilities had toxicity problems with formalin, including immediate and delayed mortality. Twenty-two of the 23 facilities reporting formalin toxicity involved toxicity to rainbow trout.[90]

The 96-hour LC_{50} concentration for formalin is approximately 72 microliters of formaldehyde solution per liter for rainbow trout. Channel catfish are reportedly even more sensitive to formalin (96-hour LC_{50} about 64 microliters of formaldehyde solution per L). Green sunfish appear to be the most tolerant to formalin treatment (96-hour LC_{50} about 173 microliters of formaldehyde solution per L).[11]

Solutions of malachite green can be toxic to fishes. The acute 96-hour LC_{50} concentration of malachite green to bluegills (the most sensitive fish tested) is 0.035 mg/L. Coho salmon may be the least sensitive to malachite green, with an acute 96-hour LC_{50} concentration of 0.382 mg/L.[10] Malachite green has been found to be extremely toxic to eggs and fry of largemouth bass, and the recommendation is made that malachite green not be used with this species.[125]

Malachite green has been found to produce inflammation of alimentary epithelium, gills and skin. This compound is known to block digestive enzymes in the intestine, which may account for reduced consumption of food in many fish species following therapy with malachite green.[100] Malachite green is also known to increase blood plasma magnesium, but the significance of this action is unknown.[125]

Copper sulfate is used to control algae in fish ponds and as a bactericide and parasiticide. Copper sulfate can be extremely toxic to fishes. Lethal concentrations of copper sulfate depend on alkalinity of the water. The acute 48-hour LC_{50} concentration of copper sulfate to bluegills was found to range between 3.1 mg/L in low-carbonate water to 44 mg/L in high-carbonate water.[68] The compound is known to produce kidney necrosis, destruction of hematopoietic tissue, increased liver fat and inhibition of certain digestive enzymes.[100]

Cutrine is an algicide prepared from chelated copper. Chelation is presumed to reduce copper toxicity to fishes; however, this is doubtful when copper concentrations are compared. The 96-hour LC_{50} for cutrine to largemouth bass, for example, has been found to be between 6.4 mg of copper/L (70 microliters of cutrine per L) and 0.198 mg of copper per liter (2.2 microliters of cutrine per L).[105]

External Parasiticide Compounds

Masoten (Neguvon) is used in water to control monogenean flukes and external copepod and branchiuran parasites. Masoten is an organophosphate compound and as such produces the same antiacetylcholinesterase effect as organophosphate insecticides. The acute 96-hour LC_{50} concentration of masoten to fathead minnows is about 50 mg/L.[68] The recommended dose level is 0.25 mg per liter for one hour, used up to four times per week, a dosage far below the 96-hour LC_{50}. However, using the recommended dose level too often may deplete body acetylcholinesterase and produce general loss of physical abilities in the fish.

Anesthetic Compounds

Several anesthetic compounds have been found useful for many fishery-related activities. These compounds are used whenever reduction of fish movements is desired. However, some may have adverse effects if used improperly. The acute 96-hour LC_{50} concentration of quinaldine sulfate, for example, ranges between 6.8 mg/L for largemouth bass to 72.5 mg/L for carp. Other fish species tested range between these concentrations.[25,63]

The acute 24-hour LC_{50} concentration of tricaine-methane sulfonate (MS-222) also varies with fish species. The lake trout 24-hour LC_{50} has been found to be 33.8 mg/L, and the more tolerant largemouth bass is 63.0 mg/L.[62] MS-222 was found to produce slight hypoglycemia and a slight increase in hematocrit, blood potassium and blood magnesium. All hematology and blood chemistry levels were restored to normal in four to 24 hours after termination of anesthesia.[106]

Mixtures of quinaldine sulfate and MS-222 have been found to be more satisfactory anesthetics than either compound used alone. However, the toxicity of both compounds seems to be increased by mixing. Mixtures containing a quinaldine sulfate to MS-222 ratio of 1:4 had a 96-hour LC_{50} concentration ranging between 8.6 to 34.5 mg/L for carp and 4.2 to 16.9 mg/L for lake trout. The 96-hour concentration for nine other fish species ranged between these values.[24]

Clearance time for MS-222 from fish body tissue has been investigated to demonstrate residual effects. Muscle tissue in four deeply anesthetized salmonid species ranged between 6 and 72 mg of MS-222 per kg of tissue immediately after removal from the anesthetic. Residues of 0.8 to 32 mg of MS-222 per kg still remained 24 hours post-anesthesia.[116]

Carbonic acid, sometimes referred to as "free" carbon dioxide, is used as an anesthetic. Ionized carbonic acid suppresses bicarbonate excretion from the gills, resulting in mild anoxia. Most fish species can tolerate up to 600 mg of carbonic acid per liter for up to 15 minutes. Fishes removed from carbonic acid solutions quickly return to normal. There is no undesirable tissue residue with this anesthetic (Fig. 26).[91]

Egg Disinfectant Compounds

Chemical compounds used for disinfection of eggs to prevent transmission of egg-borne diseases may cause increased egg and fry mortality. Studies using Wescodyne® and Betadine® indicated that adding these compounds to water containing eggs during the water hardening process produces significant mortality and crippling of fry at hatch. No mortality or crippling of fry occurred when 25 to 100 mg of iodine (from these compounds) per liter were used for disinfection of eggs after the water hardening process and in water between pH 6.0 and 8.0. The recommended treatment for egg disinfection is 100 mg of iodine per liter for 15 minutes in water with the above-mentioned pH range.[4] However, experience has indicated that these compounds should not be used within three days of hatching for salmonid eggs. The compounds may cause early egg pip and fry unable to emerge completely from the shell.

Merthiolate (thimerosal) is also used for disinfection of fish eggs. This compound has 49.6% mercury in its molecule and has the potential for mercury accumulation in the embryo. The toxicity of mercury to embryonic fish cells is not known. Many experiments have been conducted on toxicity of various organo-mercury compounds to older fishes and the relative mercury accumulation associated with that toxicity determined. These data have been used to establish a maximum acceptable mercury accumulation in aquatic organisms as 0.5 mg of mercury per gram of wet weight tissue.[31] Nothing is known of the mercury absorbance into fish embryos when merthiolate is used for egg disinfection at the prescribed dose for the recommended time.

Acriflavin has been used as a fish egg disinfectant since the 1930's. It has been generally replaced for this purpose by the iodophors and merthiolate. Acriflavin is an intense yellow-orange dye which produces a prolonged stain in the eggshell when used to disinfect eggs at the prescribed dosage for the recommended time. Nothing is known of absorption by the embryo or of any toxic effects if it is absorbed.[121]

Selected References

1. Adlung, K. G. 1957. "The toxicity of acaricidal agents to fish," *Naturwissenschaften*, 44:471.

1a. Abidi, S. L. 1982. "High-performance liquid chromatographic resolution and quantification of a dilactone antibiotic mixture (antimycin A)." *J. Chromatog.*, 234:187-200.

2. Allison, D. T., B. J. Kallman, O. B. Cope and C. VanValen. 1964. *Some chronic effects of DDT on cutthroat trout.* Res. Rep. 64. U.S. Fish Wildl. Serv., Washington, DC. 30p.

3. Allison, D. T. and R. O. Hermanutz. 1977. *Toxicity of diazinon to brook trout and fathead minnows.* Environ. Protect. Agency Rept. No. EPA-600/3-77- 060. 69p.

4. Amend, D. F. 1974. "Comparative toxicity of two iodophors to rainbow trout eggs," *Trans. Am. Fish. Soc.*, 103:73-78.

5. American Public Health Association, American Water Works Association, and Water Pollution Control Federation. 1980. *Standard methods for examination of water and waste water.* 15th ed. Amer. Publ. Health Assoc., Washington, DC. 1,134p.

6. Anees, M. A. 1978. "Hepatic pathology in a freshwater teleost (*Channa punctatus* (Bloch)) exposed to sub-lethal and chronic levels of three organophosphorus insecticides," *Bull. Environ. Contam. Toxicol.*, 19:524-527.

7. Bengt-Erik, B. 1975. "Vertebral damage in fish induced by pollutants," *In* J. H. Koeman and J. J. T. W. A. Strik. *Sublethal effects of toxic chemicals on aquatic animals.* p. 23-30. Elsevier Sci. Publ. Co., New York City, NY.

8. Bennett, V. E. 1975. "A possible reaction of Atlantic salmon (*Salmo salar*) to injected chloramphenicol," *Prog. Fish-Cult.*, 37:114.

9. Benoit, D. A. 1975. "Chronic effects of copper on survival, growth, and reproduction of the bluegill (*Lepomis macrochirus*)," *Trans. Am. Fish. Soc.*, 104: 353-358.

10. Bills, T. D., L. L. Marking and J. H. Chandler, Jr. 1977. *Malachite green: its toxicity to aquatic organisms, persistence and removal with activated carbon.* U.S. Fish Wildl. Serv. Invest. Fish Control No. 75. 6p.

11. Bills, T. D., L. L. Marking, and J. H. Chandler, Jr. 1977. *Formalin: its toxicity to nontarget aquatic organisms, persistence and counteraction.* U.S. Fish Wildl. Serv. Invest. Fish Control No. 73. 7p.

12. Blogoslawski, W. J. and M. E. Stewart. 1977. "Marine applications of Ozone water treatment," *In* E. G. Fochtman, R. G. Rice and M. E. Browning, eds. *Forum on ozone disinfection.* p. 266-276. Intnat. Ozone Inst., Syracuse, NY.

13. Blumer, M. 1971. "Oil contamination and the living resources of the sea, Number R-1," *In: FAO Fish. Rept.*, 99:101. Food & Agri. Org. U.N., Rome, Italy.

14. Booth, R. L., J. N. English and G. N. McDermott. 1965. "Evaluation of sampling conditions in the carbon absorption method (CAM)," *J. Am. Water Works. Assoc.*, 57:215-220.

15. Brungs, W. A., R. W. Carlson, W. B. Horning II, J. H. McCormick, R. L. Speaker and J. D. Yount. 1978. "Effects of pollution on freshwater fish," *J. Water Pollut. Con. Fed.*, 50:1582-1637.

16. Brungs, W. A., J. H. McCormick, T. W. Neiheisel, R. L. Spehar, C. E. Stephan and G. N. Stokes. 1977. "Effects of pollution on freshwater fish," *J. Water Pollut. Con. Fed.*, 49:1425-1493.

17. Burdick, G. E., H. J. Dean and E. J. Harris. 1964. "Toxicity of aqualin to fingerling brown trout and bluegills," *N.Y. Fish Game J.*, 11:106-114.

18. Cairns, J., Jr., A. L. Buikema, Jr., A. G. Heath and B. C. Parker. 1978. *Effects of temperature on aquatic organism sensitivity to selected chemicals.* Va. Water. Res. Research Cent., Va. Polytech. Inst., Blacksburg, VA. OWRT Proj. B-084-VA, VPI-VWRRC- Bull. 106. 88p.

18a. Carpenter, L. A. and D. L. Eaton. 1983. "The disposition of 2,4-dichlorophenoxyacetic acid in rainbow trout." *Arch. Environ. Contam. Toxicol.*, 12:169-173.

19. Clemens, H. P. and K. E. Sneed. 1959. *Lethal doses of several commercial chemicals to fingerling channel catfish. Spec. Sci. Rept. Fish.*, No. 316. U.S. Fish Wildl. Serv., Washington, DC. 10p.

20. Cohen, J. M., L. J. Kamphake, A. E. Lemke, C. Henderson and R. L. Woodward. 1960. "Effects of fish poisons on water supplies. Part 1. Removal of toxic materials," *J. Am. Water Works. Assoc.*, 52: 1551-1566.

21. Cope, O. B., ed. 1978. *Colorado fisheries research review.* Colo. State Publ. Code DOW-R-R-F76-77. 64p.

22. Copeland, B. J. and T. C. Dorris. 1964. "Community metabolism in ecosystems receiving oil refinery effluents," *Limn. Oceanog.*, 9:431-445.

23. Crandall, C. A. and C. J. Goodnight. 1962. "Effects of sublethal concentrations of several toxicants on the common guppy, *Lebistes reticulatus*," *Trans. Am. Microsc. Soc.*, 82:59-73.

23a. Daoust, P. Y. and H. W. Ferguson. 1984. "The pathology of chronic ammonia toxicity in rainbow trout, *Salmo gairdneri* Richardson." *J. Fish Dis.*, 7:199-205.

24. Dawson, V. K. and L. L. Marking. 1973. *Toxicity of mixtures of quinaldine sulfate and MS-222 to fish.* Invest. Fish Control No. 53, p. 1-11. U.S.

Bur. Sport Fish. Wildl., Washington, DC.

24a. Dawson, V. K., P. D. Harmon, D. P. Shultz and J. L. Allen. 1983. "Rapid method for measuring rotenone in water at piscicidal concentrations." *Trans. Amer. Fish. Soc.*, 112:725-727.

25. Dixon, R. N. and P. Milton. 1978. "The effects of the anesthetic quinaldine on oxygen consumption in an intertidal teleost (*Blennius pholis* L.)," *J. Fish. Biol.*, 12:359-369.

26. Doudoroff, P. and M. Katz. 1953. "Critical review of literature on the toxicity of industrial wastes and their components to fish. II. The metals, as salts," *Sew. Ind. Wastes*, 25:802-839.

27. Doudoroff, P. and M. Katz. 1950. "Critical review of the literature on the toxicity of industrial wastes and their components to fish. I. Alkalies, acids and inorganic gases," *Sew. Ind. Wastes*, 22:1432-1458.

28. Doudoroff, P. and D. L. Shumway. 1970. *Dissolved oxygen requirements of freshwater fishes.* Food Agri. Org. of United Nations. Fish. Tech. Pap. 86. 291p.

29. Doudoroff, P. and C. E. Warren. 1965. "Dissolved oxygen requirements of fishes," *In* C. M. Tarzwell, ed. *Biological problems in water pollution—third seminar, 1962.* p. 145-155. U.S. Public Health Service, Div. Wat. Sup. Pollut. Cont., Cincinnati, OH. PHS Pub. 999, WP-25.

30. Environmental Protection Agency. 1978. *Fish kills caused by pollution—fifteen year summary, 1961-1975.* EPA-440/4-78-011. 78p.

31. Environmental Protection Agency. 1973. *Water quality criteria 1972.* Series EPA-PB-236 199. 594p.

32. Frank, P. A., and R. D. Comes. 1967. "Herbicidal residues in pond water and hydrosoil," *Weeds*, 15: 210-213.

33. Freeman, R. A. and W. H. Everhart. 1971. "Toxicity of aluminum hydroxide complexes in neutral and basic media to rainbow trout," *Trans. Am. Fish. Soc.*, 100:644-658.

34. Fry, F. E. J. 1960. "The oxygen requirements of fish," *In* C. M. Tarzwell, ed. *Biological problems in water pollution.* U.S. Dept. Health, Ed., Welf., Taft. Sanit. Eng. Cent., Cincinnatti, OH. p. 106-109.

35. Gardner, G. R. 1975. "Chemically induced lesions in estuarine or marine teleosts," *In* Rebelin, W. E. and G. Migaki. *The pathology of fishes.* p. 657-693. The Univ. Wis. Press, Madison, WI.

36. Garrey, W. C. 1916. "The resistance of fresh-water fish to changes of osmotic and chemical conditions," *Am. J. Physiol.*, 39:313-329.

36a. Gilderhus, P. A. 1972. "Exposure times necessary for antimycin and rotenone to eliminate certain freshwater fish." *J. Fish. Res. Bd. Can.* 29:199-202.

37. Gustafson, C. G. 1970. "PCB's prevalent and persistent," *Environ. Sci. Technol.*, 4:814-819.

38. Hamilton, H. L. 1941. "The biological action of rotenone on freshwater animals," *Iowa Acad. Sci.*, 48:467-479.

39. Hannon, M. R., Y. A. Greichus, R. L. Applegate and A. C. Fox. 1970. "Ecological distribution of pesticides in Lake Poinsett., South Dakota," *Trans. Am. Fish. Soc.*, 99:496-500.

40. Harris, W. C. 1972. "Ozone disinfection," *J. Am. Water Works Assoc.*, 64:182-183.

41. Hart, J. S. 1944. "The circulation and respiratory tolerance of some Florida freshwater fishes," *Proc. FL. Acad. Sci.*, 7:221-246.

42. Heaton, L. H. and G. Post. 1968. "Tissue residue and oral safety of furazolidone in four species of trout," *Prog. Fish-Cult.*, 30:208-215.

42a. Henderson, V., J. W. Fisher and R. A'llessandris. 1981. "Toxic and teratogenic effects of hydrazine on fathead minnow (*Pimephales promelas*) embryos." *Bull Environ. Contam. Toxicol.*, 26:807-812.

42b. Hendricks, J. D., T. R. Meyers, D. W. Shelton, J. L. Casteel and G. S. Bailey. 1985. "Hepatocarcinogenicity of benzo(a)phrene to rainbow trout by dietary exposure and intraperitoneal injection." *J. Nat. Cancer Inst.*, 74:839-851.

43. Henegar, D. L. 1966. *Minimum lethal levels of toxaphene as a piscicide in North Dakota lakes.* Invest. Fish Control No. 3:3-16. U.S. Fish Wildl. Serv., Washington, DC.

44. Hepworth, W. G. 1965. *Effects of the salinity of natural waters on various species of trout.* Fed. Aid. Wyo. Proj. FW-3-R-12, WP Job No. 1F. Wyoming Game Fish Comm., Cheyenne, WY. p. 34-36.

44a. Hicks, B. D. and J. R. Geraci. 1984. "An histological assessment of damage to rainbow trout, *Salmo gairdneri* Richardson, fed rations containing erythromycin." *J. Fish Dis.*, 7:457-465.

45. Hoar, W. S. and D. J. Randall. 1969. *Fish physiology. Vol. 1:Excretion, ionic regulation and metabolism.* Academic Press, New York City, NY. 465p.

46. Hoglund, L. B. 1961. *The relations of fish in concentration gradients.* Inst. Freshwater Res., Drottningholm, Sweden. Rep. No. 43. 147p.

47. Hubbs, C. L. 1930. "The high toxicity of nascent oxygen," *Physiol. Zool.*, 3:441-460.

47a. Huey, D. W., B. A. Simco and D. W. Criswell. 1980. "Nitrite-induced methemoglobin formation in channel catfish." *Trans. Amer. Fish. Soc.* 109:558-562.

48. Hughes, J. S. and J. T. Davis. 1962. "Comparative

273

toxicity to bluegill sunfish of granular and liquid herbicides," *Proc. 16th Ann. Conf. S. E. Game Fish Comm.*, p. 319-323.

49. Jensen, S., N. Johansson and Olsson. 1970. "PCB-indications of effects on salmon," *PCB Conference, Stockholm, Sweden, Sept. 1970*. Swedish Salmon Res. Inst. Rep. No. LFI MEDD 7, 1970.

50. Kenaga, E. E. 1979. "Acute and chronic toxicity of 75 pesticides to various animal species," *Down to Earth*, 35(2):25-31. Dow Chemical Co., Midland, MI.

50a. Khan, R. A. and J. Kiceniuk. 1984. "Histopathological effects of crude oil on Atlantic cod following chronic exposure." *Can. J. Zool.* 62:2038-2043.

51. Koelle, G. B. and G. Gilman. 1949. "Anticholinesterase drugs," *Pharmacol. Rev.*, 1:166-216.

52. Koeman, J. H. and J. J. T. W. A. Strik. 1975. *Sublethal effects of toxic chemicals on aquatic animals.* Elsevier Scientific Publ. Co., New York City, NY. 234p.

53. Kreutzmann, H. L. 1977. "The effects of chloramphenicol and oxytetracycline on hematopoiesis in the European eel (*Anguilla anguilla*)," *Aquacult.*, 10:323-334.

53a. LeBlanc, G. A., J. D. Mastone, A. P. Paradice and B. F. Wilson. 1984. "The influence of speciation on the toxicity of silver to fathead minnow (*Pimephales promelas*)." *Environ Toxicol. Chem.* 3:37-46.

54. Leeuwangh, P., H. Bult and L. Schneiders. 1975. "Toxicity of hexachlorobutadiene in aquatic organisms," *In* J. H. Koeman and J. J. T. W. A. Strik. *Sublethal effects of toxic chemicals on aquatic animals.* p. 167-176. Elsevier Sci. Publ. Co., New York City, NY.

54a. Lima, A. R., C. Curtis, D. E. Hammermeister, T. P. Markee, C. E. Northcott and L. T. Brooke. 1984. "Acute and chronic toxicity of arsenic (III) to fathead minnows, flagfish, daphnids and amphipod." *Arch. Environ. Contam. Toxicol.* 13:595-601.

55. Lindahl, P. E. and K. E. Oberg. 1961. "The effect of rotenone on respiration and its points of attack," *Exp. Cell. Res.*, 23:228-237.

56. Litchfield, J. T., Jr. and F. Wilcoxon. 1949. "A simplified method of evaluating dose-effect experiments," *J. Pharmacol. Exper. Thera.*, 96:99-113.

57. Lloyd, R. 1960. "The toxicity of $ZnSO_4$ to rainbow trout," *Ann. Appl. Biol.*, 48:84-94.

58. Lowe, J. I. 1967. "Effects of prolonged exposure to Sevin® on an estuarine fish, *Leiostomus xanthurus* Lacepede," *Bull. Environ. Contam. Toxicol.*, 2: 147-155.

59. Ludke, J. L., D. E. Ferguson and W. D. Burke. 1968. "Some endrin relationships in resistant and susceptible populations of golden shiners, *Notemigonus crysoleucas*," *Trans. Am. Fish. Soc.*, 97:260-263.

60. Mace, H. H. 1953. "Disposal of wastes from water treatment plants," *Publ. Works.*, 84:73, 88-100.

61. MacPhee, C. and R. Ruelle. 1969. *Lethal effects of 1,888 chemicals upon four species of fish in Western North America. Univ. of Idaho, For. Wildl. Range Expt. Sta., Bull.*, No. 3, 112p.

62. Marking, L. L. 1967. *Toxicity of MS-222 to selected fishes. Invest. Fish Control*, No. 12. 11p. U.S. Bur. Sport Fish. Wildl., Washington, DC.

62a. Marking, L. L. and V. K. Dawson, 1972. "The half-life of biological activity of antimycin determined by fish bioassay." *Trans. Amer. Fish. Soc.* 101:100-105.

62b. Marking, L. L. and T. D. Bills. 1981. "Sensitivity of four species of carp to selected fish toxicants." *Amer. J. Fish. Manag.* 1:51-54.

63. Marking, L. L. and V. K. Dawson. 1973. *Toxicity of quinaldine sulfate to fish. Invest. Fish Control*, No. 48. 7p. U.S. Bur. Sport Fish. Wildl., Washington, DC.

64. Mauck, W. L., L. E. Olson and J. W. Hogan. 1977. "Effects of water quality on deactivation of mexacarbate (Zectran®) to fish," *Arch. Environ. Contam. Toxicol.*, 6:385-393.

65. Mayer, F. L., Jr. 1972. "Special report on PCB's," *In:Progress in sport fishery research 1970.* p. 33-36. U.S. Fish Wild. Serv. Washington, DC.

66. McBride, J., G. Strasdine and U. H. M. Fagerlund. 1975. "Acute toxicity of kanamycin to steelhead trout (*Salmo gairdneri*)," *J. Fish. Res. Bd. Can.*, 32:554-558.

67. McFarlane, G. A. and W. G. Franzin. 1978. "Evaluated heavy metals: a stress on a population of white suckers (*Catostomus commersoni*), in Hamell Lake, Saskatchewan," *J. Fish. Res. Bd. Can.*, 35: 963-970.

68. McKee, J. E. and H. W. Wolf. 1963. *Water quality criteria.* Resource Agency Calif., State Water Qual. Con. Bd., Publ. No. 3-A, 548p.

69. McKim, J. M. and D. A. Benoit. 1971. "Effects of long-term exposures to copper on survival, growth and reproduction of brook trout (*Salvelinus fontinalis*)," *J. Fish. Res. Bd. Can.*, 28:655-662.

70. Meinick, F., H. Stoof, and H. Kohlschutter. 1956. *Industrie-Abwasser. 2nd Ed.* Gustav Fischer Verlag. Stuttgart, Germany. 527p.

71. Menzie, C. M. 1978. *Metabolism of pesticides, update II. Spec. Sci. Rep.-Wildl.*, No. 212. U.S. Fish & Wildl. Serv., Washington, DC. 381p.

72. Mehrle, P. M. and F. L. Mayer. 1977. "Bone development and growth of fish as affected by toxaphene," *In* I. H. Suffet, ed. *Fate of pollutants in air and water environments.* p. 301-314. Wiley Interscience Publ., New York City, NY.

73. Mitchell, A. J., J. M. Grizzle and J. A. Plumb. 1978. "Nifurpirinol (Furanace: P-7138) related lesions on channel catfish *Ictalurus punctatus* (Rafinesque)," *J. Fish. Dis.*, 1:115-221.

74. Mitchum, D. L. 1960. *An experimental study of the toxicity of calcium carbonate, calcium sulfate, magnesium carbonate and magnesium sulfate to rainbow trout.* Unpubl. M.S. thesis, Uni. of Wyo., Laramie, WY.

75. Middleton, F. M. and A. A. Rosen. 1956. "Organic contaminants affecting the quality of water," *Publ. Health Rep.*, 71:1125-1133.

76. Mitrovec, U. U., V. M. Brown, D. G. Shurben and M. H. Berryman. 1968. "Some pathological effects of sub-acute and acute poisoning of rainbow trout by phenol in hard water," *Water Res.*, 2:249-254.

77. Moore, W. G. 1942. "Field studies on the oxygen requirements of certain fresh-water fishes," *Ecol.*, 23:319-329.

78. Mount, D. I. 1966. "The effect of total hardness and pH on acute toxicity of zinc to fish," *Air Water Pollut.*, 10:49-56.

79. Mount, D. I. and C. E. Stephen. 1967. "A method of establishing acceptable toxicant limits for fish—malathion and the butoxyethanol ester of 2,4-D," *Trans. Am. Fish. Soc.*, 96:185-193.

80. Nachmansohn, D. and M. A. Rothenberg. 1945. "Studies on cholinesterase. I. On the specificity of the enzyme in nerve tissue," *J. Biol. Chem.*, 158: 653-666.

80a. Nebeker, A. V., C. K. McAuliffe, R. Mshar and D. G. Stevens. 1983. "Toxicity of silver to steelhead and rainbow trout, fathead minnows and *Daphnia magna.*" *Environ. Toxicol. Chem.*, 2:95-104.

8ob. Nebeker, A. V., C. Savonen and D. G. Stevens. 1985. "Sensitivity of rainbow trout early life stages to nickel chloride." *Environ. Toxicol. Chem.* 4:233-239.

81. Nebeker, A. V., F. A. Publis and D. L. Defoe. 1971. *Toxicity of polychlorinated biphenyls (PCB) to fish and other aquatic life.* Environ. Protec. Agency, Nat. Water Qual. Lab., Duluth, MI.

82. Nebel, C., R. D. Gottschling, R. L. Hutchinson, T. J. McBride, D. M. Taylor, J. L. Pavoni, M. E. Tittlebaum, H. E. Spencer and M. Fleishman. 1973. "Ozone disinfection of industrial-municipal secondary effluents," *J. Water Pollut. Con. Fed.*, 45: 2493-2507.

83. Nevins, M. J. and W. W. Johnson. 1978. "Acute toxicity of phosphate ester mixtures to invertebrates and fish," *Bull. Environ. Contam. Toxicol.*, 19: 250-256.

83a. Nimi, A. J. 1983. "Biological and toxicological effects of environmental contaminants to fish and their eggs." *Can. J. Aquat. Sci.* 40:306-312.

84. Northcote, T. G. and P. A. Larkin. 1956 "Indices of productivity in British Columbia lakes," *J. Fish. Res. Bd. Can.*, 13:515-540.

85. O'Brien, R. D. 1963. "Organophosphates and carbamates," *In* R. M. Hochster and J. H. Quastel, eds. *Metabolic inhibitions*, 2:205-241. Academic Press, New York City, NY.

85a. Ogilvie, D. M. and D. M. Stechey. 1983. "Effects of aluminum on respiratory response and spontaneous activity of rainbow trout, *Salmo gairdneri.*" *Environ. Toxicol. Chem.* 2:43-48.

86. Parsons, J. D. 1977. "Effects of acid mine wastes on aquatic ecosystems," *Water Air Soil Pollut.*, 7:333- 354.

87. Peakall, D. B. and J. L. Lincer. 1970. "Polychlorinated biphenyls—another long-life widespread chemical in the environment," *Biosci.*, 20:958-964.

87a. Phipps, G. L., G. W. Holcombe and J. T. Fiandt. 1981. "Acute toxicity of phenol and substituted phenols to the fathead minnow." *Bull. Environ. Contam. Toxicol.*, 26:585-593.

88. Pickering, Q. H. 1966. Acute toxicity of alkyl benzene sulfonate and linear alkylate sulfonate to eggs of the fathead minnow *Pimephales promelus*," *Air Water Pollut.*, 10:385-391.

89. Pickering, Q. H. and C. Henderson. 1966. "The acute toxicity of some heavy metals to different species of warmwater fishes," *Infl. J. Air Water Pollut.*, 10: 453-463.

90. Piper, R. G. and C. E. Smith. 1973. "Factors influencing formalin toxicity in trout," *Prog. Fish-Cult.*, 35:78-81.

91. Post, G. 1979. "Carbonic acid anesthesia in aquatic organisms," *Prog. Fish-Cult.*, 41:142-144.

92. Post, G. 1977. *Glossary of fish health terms.* Am. Fish Soc. Bethesda, Md. 48p.

93. Post, G. 1970. "Determination of inert gases in water," *Prog. Fish-Cult.*, 32:170-173.

94. Post, G. 1967. *Methods of sampling and preserving field specimens for laboratory examination or analysis.* Pruett Press Inc., Boulder, CO. 73p.

95. Post, G. 1955. "A simple color test for rotenone in water," *Prog. Fish-Cult.*, 17:190-191.

96. Post, G. Unpubl. *Time versus temperature in rotenone dissipation.* Dept. Fish. Wild. Biol., Colo. State Univ. Ft. Collins, CO. 12p.

97. Post, G. and M. M. Beck. 1966. "Toxicity, tissue residue, and efficacy of enheptin given orally to rainbow trout for hexamitiasis," *Prog. Fish-Cult.*, 28:83-88.

98. Post, G. and R. A. Leasure. 1974. "Sublethal effect of malathion to three salmonid species," *Bull. Environ. Contam. Toxicol.*, 12:312-319.

99. Post, G. and T. R. Schroeder. 1971. "The toxicity of four insecticides to four salmonid species," *Bull. Environ. Contam. Toxicol.*, 6:144-155.

100. Reichenbach-Klinke, H. H. 1975. "Lesions due to drugs," *In* W. E. Ribelin and G. Migaki, eds. *The pathology of fishes.* p. 647-656. Univ. of Wisconsin Press, Madison, WI.

100a. Russo, R. C., R. V. Thurston and K. Emmerson. 1981. "Acute toxicity of nitrite to rainbow trout (*Salmo gairdneri*): Effects of pH, nitrite species and anion species." *Can. J. Fish. Aquat. Sci.* 38:387-393.

101. Schweiger, G. 1957. "The toxic actions of heavy metal salts on fish and organisms on which fish feed," *Arch. Fisch. Wiss.*, 8:54; *Water Pollut. Abs.*, 34:9, 1744 (1961).

102. Seaman, E. A., V. J. Norton and T. E. DeVaney. 1959. *Registration and clearance of chemicals for fish culture and fishery management. Trans. 99th Annual Meeting of Am. Fish. Soc.* 73p.

103. Shaw, W. H. R. and B. R. Lowrance. 1956. "Bioassay for the estimation of metal ions," *Anal. Chem.*, 28: 1164-1166.

103a. Shelton, D. W., J. D. Hendricks and G. S. Bailey. 1984. "The hepatocarcinogenicity of diethylnitrosamine to rainbow trout and its enhancement by Aroclors 1242 and 1254." *Toxicol Letters*, 22:27-31.

103b. Shelton, D. W., J. D. Hendricks and R. A. Coulombe. 1984. "Effect of dose on the inhibition of carcinogenesis by Arochlor 1254 in rainbow trout fed aflatoxin B." *J. Toxicol. Environ. Health*, 13:649-657.

104. Shelton, R. G. J. 1971. "Effects of oil and dispersants on the marine environment," *Proc. Roy. Soc. London., Biol. Sci.*, 177:411-422.

104a. Sippel, A. J. A., J. R. Geraci and P. V. Hodson. 1983. "Histopathological and physiological responses of rainbow trout (*Salmo gairdneri*) to sublethal levels of lead." *Water Res.*, 17:1115-1118.

105. Skea, J. C. and H. A. Simonin. 1979. "Evaluation of cutrine for fish culture," *Prog. Fish-Cult.*, 41:171- 174.

106. Soivio, A., K. Nyholm and M. Huhti. 1977. "Effects of anesthesia with MS-222, neutralized MS-222 and benzocaine on the blood constituents of rainbow trout (*Salmo gairdneri*)," *J. Fish. Biol.*, 10:91-101.

107. Smith, C. E., J. E. Holway and G. L. Hammer. 1973. "Sulfamerazine toxicity in cut-throat trout broodfish *Salmo clarki* (Richardson)," *J. Fish. Biol.*, 5:97-101.

108. Smith, L. L. and D. Oseid. 1971. *Toxic effects of hydrogen sulfide to juvenile fish and fish eggs. Proc. 25th Purdue Univ. Ind. Waste Conf.*

109. Stalling, D. L. 1972. "Analysis of organochlorine residues in fish: current research at the Fish-Pesticide Laboratory," *In* A. S. Tahori, ed. *Pesticide Chem., Meth. Residue Anal.*, 4:413-438. Gordon and Breach Sci. Pub., New York City, NY.

110. Stickel, L. F. and J. J. Hickey. 1977. "Toxicological aspects of toxaphene in fish: a summary," *Trans. 42nd. N. Am. Wildl. Nat. Res. Conf., Wildl. Manage. Inst., Washington, DC.* p. 365-373.

110a. Schwedler, T. E. and C. S. Tucker. 1983. "Empirical relationship between percent methemoglobin in channel catfish and dissolved nitrite and chloride in ponds." *Trans. Amer. Fish. Soc.*, 112:117-119.

111. Tafanelli, R. and R. C. Summerfelt. 1975. "Cadmium-induced histopathological changes in goldfish," *In* W. E. Ribelin and G. Migaki, ed. *The pathology of fishes* p. 613-645. Univ. of Wis. Press, Madison, WI.

112. Tagatz, M. E. 1961. "Reduced oxygen tolerance and toxicity of petroleum products to juvenile American shad," *Chesapeake Sci.*, 2:65-71.

112a. Thurston, R. V., RC. C. Russo, R. J. Leudtke, C. E. Smith, E. L. Meyn, C. Chakoumakos, K. C. Wang and C. D. Brown. 1984. "Chronic toxicity of ammonia to rainbow trout." *Trans. Amer. Fish Soc.* 113:56-73.

113. Tiernan, M. W. 1962. *A study of the toxicity of various salts to rainbow trout.* Unpubl. M.S. thesis, Univ. of Wyo., Laramie, WY.

114. Tarzwell, C. M. and C. Henderson. 1960. "Toxicity of less common metals to fishes," *Ind. Wastes*, 5:12.

115. van Duijn, C. 1973. *Diseases of fishes 3rd edition.* Charles C. Thomas, Publ., Springfield, IL. p. 293-307.

116. Walker, C. R. and R. A. Schoettger. 1967. *Residues of MS-222 in four salmonids following anesthesia. Invest. Fish Control*, No. 15. 11p. U.S. Bur. Sport Fish. Wildl., Washington, DC.

117. Webb, W. E. 1961. *Toxicity of certain pesticides to fish.* Fed. Aid. Proj. FW-34-R-2, ID Fish Game Dept., Boise, ID. 12p.

118. Wedemeyer, G. A., N. C. Nelson and W. T. Yasutake. 1979. "Physiological and biochemical aspects of ozone toxicity to rainbow trout (*Salmo gairdneri*)," *J. Fish Res. Bd. Can.*, 36:605-614.

119. Weiss, C. M. 1959. "Response of fish to sub-lethal exposures to organic phosphorus insecticides," *Sew. Ind. Wastes*, 31:580-593.

120. Wiener, J. G. 1978. "Aerial inputs of cadmium, copper, lead and manganese into a freshwater pond: relations to a nearby coalfired power plant," *Bull. Ecol. Soc. Am.*, 59:65.

121. Willford, W. A. 1967. *Toxicity of 22 therapeutic compounds to six fishes. Invest. Fish Control*, No. 18. 10p. U.S. Bur. Sport Fish. Wildl., Washington, DC.

122. Williams, G. Jr., R. C. Simmonds and J. F. Boyd. 1975. "Effects of the antimicrobial furanace on *Fundulus heteroclitus* embryos," *J. Fish. Res. Bd. Can.*, 32:69-71.

123. Winberg, G. G. 1960. "Rate of metabolism and food requirements of fishes," *Fish. Res. Bd. Can. Trans. Ser.*, 194:1-202.

124. Wisseman, R. W. and S. F. Cook, Jr. 1977. "Heavy metal accumulation in sediments of a Washington lake," *Bull. Environ. Contam. Toxicol.*, 18:77-82.

124a. Woltering, D. M. 1984. "The growth response in fish chronic and early life stage toxicity tests: A critical review." *Aquat. Toxicol.*, 5:1-21.

124b. Woodward, D. F., P. M. Mehrle, Jr. and W. L. Mauck. 1981. "Accumulation and sublethal effects of a Wyoming crude oil on cutthroat trout." *Trans. Amer. Fish. Soc.*, 110:437-445.

125. Wright, L. D. 1976. "Effect of malachite green and formalin on the survival of largemouth bass eggs and fry," *Prog. Fish-Cult.*, 38:155-157.

126. Zillich, J. A. 1972. "Toxicity of combined chlorine residuals to fresh water fish," *J. Water Pollut. Con. Fed.*, 44:212-220.

127. Zitko, V., W. G. Carson and C. D. Metcalfe. 1977. "Toxicity of pyrethroids to juvenile Atlantic salmon," *Bull. Environ. Contam. Toxicol.*, 18:35-41.

Chapter XII
DISEASES OF
MISCELLANEOUS ORIGIN

Diseases Caused by Physical Factors

Development and existence of life on this earth was, and still is, an indication that organisms are compatible with their surroundings under most circumstances. The existence of various species of plants and animals is possible within narrow environmental limits. Life is usually adversely affected or even destroyed whenever environmental conditions exceed those limits. Generally, fishes fill a particular niche within environmental limits, and excessive alteration in these limits leads to physiological and biochemical changes within the fish beyond their ability to survive. The fish are either killed as a direct result of the physical alteration or their systems damaged to the point where they are vulnerable to other diseases. Diagnosis of diseases associated with physical factors is sometimes necessary and helpful in understanding what measures are needed to improve environmental conditions for the fishes.

The most common diseases of fishes related to physical factors are associated with osmotic pressure, environmental temperature, hydrogen ion concentration (pH), dissolved air and mechanical trauma. These factors are often disregarded as causes of diseases in fishes, but alterations of any beyond the limits of fish health can be as devastating to a fish population as infections of other non-infectious diseases.

Osmotic Pressure

The osmotic pressure of pure water exerts a force on living cells equal to one atmosphere. Living cells are made up of a variety of chemical compounds either bound into organelles or suspended and dissolved in cellular fluids. The net effect, when a living cell is placed into pure water, is a higher osmotic pressure inside the cell than outside. The semipermeable cell wall may allow some substances within the cell to diffuse out, but the greatest effect is in diffusion of water into the cell to equalize osmotic pressures. The result is a flooding of the cell, often until it bursts.

Consider a number of cells of various types bound together into a living organism, a fish. Subjecting the fish to external osmotic pressures below the osmotic pressure of the entire organism tends to do the same thing as happens to a single cell. The fish must either develop capabilities for excreting excess water and retaining all diffusable cellular components, or its cells will become flooded and will no longer function properly. The opposite occurs when a fish is placed into water of high osmotic pressure, seawater for example, with an osmotic pressure of about 6.5 atmospheres. Marine fishes must eliminate diffusable substances, salts, and retain cellular water, otherwise their cells will collapse from loss of water and retention of salt. Fishes have developed mechanisms to help them control their internal osmotic pressure against the outside water or salt gradient. The skin, mucus and gill membranes have adapted to meet these requirements.[11,14,15,21,24]

Fishes of the world have each evolved to withstand a relatively narrow range of osmotic pressure and can satisfactorily occupy that range. Many freshwater fishes are killed by immersion in sea water, because salts are taken into cells accustomed to retaining salts, and water is lost from cells accustomed to losing water. Marine fishes placed into fresh water are also killed because of the rapid alteration of cellular salts and water.[18]

Fishes are often subjected to change in osmotic pressure or water salinity concentrations and may succumb because of physiological changes in their body and cells. The brackish water (or estuarine) fishes and fishes living in freshwater relatively high in dissolved salts are usually capable of existence in a broader range of osmotic pressures than those which evolved in very high or very low osmotic pressures. Catadromous or anadromous fishes are capable of acclimating to the opposite ends of the osmotic pressure (water salinity) conditions, especially so at particular times of their lives.[8,19,24,27,33]

Another important factor relating to osmotic pressure and fish survival involves ova. Eggs released by female freshwater fishes are flaccid and must absorb water. This process is called water-hardening. Eggs of freshwater fishes subjected to water with a relatively high salinity cannot absorb water against the relatively high osmotic pressure within the egg and die from the effect.[32]

Diagnosis of adverse effects of osmotic pressure on fishes is difficult. Freshwater fishes subjected to high salinity concentrations become lethargic, seek the shoal areas of the pond or lake or may even attempt to leave the water by beaching themselves. There usually is no external or internal gross pathology. Microscopic histopathology may indicate saline toxicity (Pl. 31F, 32A, 32B) but no observable effects directly related to osmotic changes.

There has been much research on determination of osmotic and ionic concentrations of fish body fluids or certain gill enzymes (Na^+, K^+, ATPase, for example) and relating the results to normal for the fish species involved.[33] Using these data for assistance in diagnosis of unacceptable osmotic pressure in fishes has not been possible.

Analysis of water for total dissolved solids, total salinity or specific conductance as it relates to dissolved salts may indicate ranges tolerated by the fish species involved. These water analyses are important in seawater aquariums for maintenance of health among saltwater fishes.

Temperature

Each fish species has an inherent temperature range within which it can survive, grow and reproduce.[12] Coldwater (psychrophilic) fishes cannot survive temperatures above 25°C, and existence of many is limited by a temperature of 20°C. Coldwater fishes continue a normal and active life at temperatures where water is most dense, 4°C. These fishes live at temperatures as low as 0°C, but their metabolism, growth and reproduction are slowed or stopped at these low temperatures. Their eggs and offspring may not develop or survive well at these colder temperatures.[12]

Warmwater (thermophilic) fishes can live continuously at temperatures as high as 33 to 35°C, but their metabolism is much reduced at 20°C, and some are incapable of living at temperatures of 5 to 10°C because of complete cessation of metabolism. Most warmwater fishes do not reproduce below 15°C but can do so above 22°C. There is a large group of fishes, usually referred to as coolwater (mesophilic) fishes, capable of living at a broad range of temperatures. These fishes survive and grow between 0° and 30°C, and many complete reproduction between 10° and 30°C. [2,3,4,9,12,16]

Natural waters of the world which support fish life must range between temperature requirements for the fish species living there. Temperature requirements must also be maintained in fish culture facilities, aquaria and ornamental ponds for support of the fish species to be held there. Changes in environmental temperatures which occur too rapidly or are beyond the normal survival range of fishes may cause thermal trauma. Disorders in fishes arising from thermal trauma include effects on the cardiovascular system, the nervous system, changes in the colloidal state of proteins and reduction or cessation of enzymatic activities. Thermal trauma may result in permanent impairment of body functions or death.[7]

Fishes are often subjected to thermal trauma from natural causes. Fishes residing in polar oceans, for example, do so at temperatures near, or even a few tenths of a degree below, the freezing point of water, because salt water has a lower freezing point. Blood in these fishes continues to flow because of the salts and colloidal proteins present in their body fluids. They may on occasion be subjected to ice thrombi in blood vessels, ruptured cells caused by freezing and thawing and other disorders associated with thermal trauma. Some fishes may be subjected to the other extreme, excessively high temperatures resulting from a high air temperature in contact with water surfaces and direct absorption of the sun's heat. Thermal trauma can cause disorders and death to these fishes as well.[5]

Many modern technological operations produce excess heat which is released into natural waters. Fish species living within aquatic environments where excess heat is released may die because of thermal trauma and be replaced by more heat-tolerant species.[9,17]

Thermal adaptation of fishes, sometimes called tempering, is necessary when changing from ambient temperature to a new temperature several degrees above or below their present temperature. Thermal adaptation should be done slowly, usually no more rapidly than 1°C per two minutes. Slow adaptation will allow physiological functions to alter slowly, with a minimum of thermal stress. Also, fishes taken from one water temperature and placed into a higher or lower temperature usually should not be subjected to immediate changes of more than 2 to 3°C to reduce thermal stress.[16]

Fish eggs also should not be subjected to rapid changes in temperature. They must be adapted slowly, and the same rule applies as for fish—1°C per two minutes—or excessive or total mortality may result.[12]

Diagnosis of thermal trauma in fishes and fish eggs is difficult. Diagnosis must be made primarily on records of water temperature to which the eggs or fishes have been subjected. There are no consistent external or internal signs or pathological findings.

Hydrogen Ion Concentration (pH)

Natural waters have a variety of dissolved substances, each acts as a buffer to some degree. The buffering effect of the array of dissolved substances determines its hydrogen ion concentration or pH. Fishes existing in aquatic environments have adapted to a range of pH within which they are capable of survival. The acceptable limits of pH for most fishes to live continuously is about 6.2 to 9.2. However, some fish species may be subjected to transient pH levels of 5.4 to 10.2 without causing death. More tolerant fish species are capable of existence outside these ranges. Carp, for example, may live continuously between pH 4.0 and 9.5, with transient pH ranging between 3.3 and 11.0.[5,6,22]

Excessively high or low pH may be directly responsible for death or for stresses which may result in death from secondary causes. Many toxic substances become more toxic to fishes at high or low pH levels.[5,6,22]

Pathological problems arising from excessively high or low pH may involve: maintenance of normal pH of body fluids and alteration of the acid-base balance; inability to excrete bicarbonate ion or absorb oxygen; and trauma to skin, gills and other external body surfaces.[5] Fishes subjected to excessively high or low pH may become frantic, seek the shoal areas and even become beached in an attempt to remove themselves from irritating effects on skin and gills. Skin and fins may become erythemic and develop ruptured surface capillaries (Pl. 32D). They

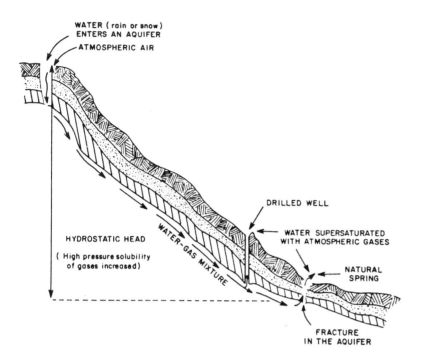

WATER (rain or snow)
ENTERS AN AQUIFER
ATMOSPHERIC AIR

HYDROSTATIC HEAD
(High pressure solubility
of gases increased)

WATER-GAS MIXTURE

DRILLED WELL

WATER SUPERSATURATED
WITH ATMOSPHERIC GASES

NATURAL
SPRING

FRACTURE
IN THE AQUIFER

Fig. 28: Water and atmospheric air enter aquifers and move to a lower elevation. Atmospheric air becomes more soluble as pressure increases. Water released from springs or wells may be super-saturated with these gases, causing gas bubble disease or gas embolism in fishes living in the water.

may cough or attempt to clear their gills; some may regurgitate food by this action.

Diagnosis of the effects of high or low pH on fishes is primarily by signs of distress in the fish, possibly hemorrhages in external body surfaces and by analysis of environmental water for pH. Water bodies with a large volume of aquatic plants may become extremely alkaline after exposure to long periods of sunlight. Water analysis for pH in these cases should be done in late afternoon to find the most alkaline pH to which fishes are subjected. Some spring waters may be highly acid or alkaline and may be involved in fish losses.

Fishes stocked from fish culture facilities directly into natural waters may be subjected to immediate pH change which can cause extreme pH trauma.[23a] One such instance involved release of fishes from a distribution tank with water at pH 6.9 into a lake with an afternoon transient pH 10.2. The fishes exhibited all signs usually noted in pH trauma, and many died. Another instance involved stocking of fishes from water of pH 7.4 into a spring-fed stream at pH 5.2. All fishes in the group exhibited pH trauma and were dead within a short time (Pl. 32D). Fish to be placed in aquaria are often subjected to rapid pH change and may either die soon after release into the tank or receive such severe trauma they may suffer delayed mortality. Mortality may be eliminated or reduced by gradually acclimitizing fish to extreme pH change.[23a] Fisherybiologists, ornamental fish fanciers and fish disease diagnosticians should be aware of the disease and injury caused by excessive changes in environmental pH.

Sublethal effects resulting from low environmental pH have been examined in relation to atmospheric acid pollution brought down by precipitation. Some studies have demonstrated increase numbers of fish with deformaties (fin aberrations, bone abnormalities and others) among fish populations residing in softwater lakes with reduced pH. The suggestion has been made that reduced pH in softwater may result in altered calcium metabolism producing major bone deformities in some fish.[1a,15a,16a,34a]

Supersaturation of Atmospheric Gases in Water

The effects of supersaturation of water with atmospheric gases had been a problem, primarily in fish culture facilities, until construction of high dams and other operations where atmospheric air was mixed with water under relatively high pressure.[12,13,36] Fish culturists were aware of this problem, especially in fish-holding facilities supplied with water from springs or wells.[31]

Mixing of atmospheric air and water under pressure increases solubility of all gases. Sudden release of pressure on the water-gas mixture allows the gases to gradually escape back to the atmosphere until the pressure and gas solubility are equalized. Fishes living in water during the period of pressure-dissolved gas equalization may develop a disease known as gas bubble disease or gas embolism. These diseases are characterized by formation of bubbles of gases trapped between or within tissues or in the circulatory system.[23,28]

There are several ways atmospheric air can enter water and later create gas bubble disease or embolism in fishes. Natural precipitation on the land and subsequent seepage into rock strata or aquifers may carry atmospheric air with it. Aquifers are solid layers of rock lying at an incline which allows water to move downward, under or within the layers until reaching a fracture. There

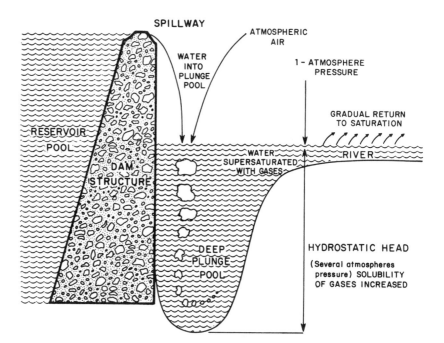

Fig. 29: Water falling over the spillway of a high dam carries atmospheric air into the plunge pool. Increase of pressure toward the bottom of the plunge pool increases solubility of gases. Pressure release as the water moves into the downstream area allows a gradual release of gases back to the atmosphere, but fishes residing in the area of gas supersaturation are subject to gas bubble disease or gas embolism.

the water returns to the land surface as a spring. Springs are always at a lesser elevation than the water source, which allows for a certain amount of hydrostatic pressure between the intake and release point. Atmospheric air entrained in the water becomes more soluble as the hydrostatic pressure increases. Water escaping from the aquifer fracture is placed in a pressure-gas equalization situation, and fishes living in the water are subjected to development of gas bubble disease or embolism (Fig. 28). Wells drilled into aquifers may release water in the same way as if it were released from a fracture, with a similar result on fishes residing in the water.

Water spilling over a high dam and falling into deep plunge pools at the base of dams carries bubbles of atmospheric air with it. The water-air mixture is placed under relatively high hydrostatic pressure as it nears the bottom of the plunge pool. Gases become more soluble, and as the dissolved gas-water mixture surfaces to flow downstream, it is in a state of pressure-gas equalization. Fishes residing in this water are subjected to development of gas bubble disease or embolism. Great fish losses are attributed to gas bubble disease under these conditions (Fig. 29).[13,36]

All gases are more soluble in water at lower temperatures and lose solubility as the temperature rises. Rapidly increasing the temperature of water causes supersaturation of dissolved gases. Gas bubble disease may occur among fishes in water bodies receiving heated effluents or other conditions which produce relatively rapid heating of environmental water.[1,16]

The diagnostician can usually predict if water will cause gas bubble disease or embolism by analysis for total dissolved gases.[12,29,36] Generally, gas bubble disease is chronic when water contains air between 105 and 140% of saturation. Gas embolism is usually acute to subacute and causes rapid fish kills when atmospheric air is present in water of more than 140% of saturation.

Gas bubble disease is characterized by appearance of observable gas bubbles in body cavities, often behind the eyes (causing exophthalmos) or between layers of surface tissue (such as in the skin of the opercula or lips) (Pl. 32E). Analysis of gases collected from these bubbles indicates they are formed of all the gases found in the atmosphere and in about the same proportions. The intratissue gas bubbles are large enough to be seen without magnification. Gas embolisms are characterized by the presence of relatively small bubbles of gas within gill capillaries or in other parts of the circulatory system.[28,34,35]

Diagnosis of gas bubble disease or gas embolism in fishes can usually be done by gross and microscopic examination for bubbles of gas behind eyeballs, in tissues and in the circulatory system. Underwater eye removal from fishes with exophthalmos will release an observable bubble of gas for positive diagnosis of gas bubble disease. The severity of the problem can be determined by gross appearance of the fishes and by determination of the quantity of gases released from a known volume of water. These data can be used to determine the relationship between water temperature and atmospheric pressure compared to expected solubility of atmospheric air and the quantity of dissolved gases obtained from the water sample, usually expressed as percent of saturation.[29,31,36]

Analysis of the gas may also be of assistance; i.e. relationship between inert gases (nitrogen, argon, xenon and others) and gases which are absorbed or excreted by fish (oxygen and carbon dioxide for example).[29]

A more modern method for determination of these quantities is by a total gas meter which display water temperature, barometric pressure and percent gas saturation. Calculations can also be made for quantitative dissolved inert gases and oxygen in the water.

Sunlight and Sunburn Disease

Dorsal skin pathology (sunburn) has been reported in fish exposed to intense sunlight. Placing sunshades over ponds, or reducing intensity of sunlight in other ways, eliminates the problem. Spectral wavelengths most often involved with skin lesions of fish are in the ultraviolet (UV) range of 280 to 320 nanometers.[5a] UV light sources used for control of pathogenic organisms in water supplies for fish culture facilities is another source of damaging light rays for fish. Fish should be held well away from such UV light sources.

Anomalies, Genetic Diseases and Teratology

Anomalies and genetic aberrations are most noticeable among cultured fishes. Adverse genetic changes also occur among wild-ranging fishes, but individuals capable of survival may be lost to predation or from inability to sustain themselves and thus fail to reproduce the anomalies.[10] Selective breeding of cultured fishes is a relatively new art, except among ornamental fishes. Selective breeding among intensely reared food fishes (rainbow trout, channel catfish, carp and others) has been practiced scientifically, with careful selection of broodfishes and records kept of desirable hereditary characteristics, since the 1960's. Commercial broodfish operators select primarily for desired body conformation, balanced features, ability to accept prepared diets and rapid growth.

Heritable anomalies can affect a relatively large part of a fish population in the more sheltered conditions found among cultured fishes. The anomalies may or may not be limiting. Those with little or no effect are allowed to continue in the population. Some strains of salmonids, for example, have a high percentage of individuals in the population with the liver on the left side of the abdominal cavity, the normal position being on the right side. There is no apparent adversity from the organ being on the left side, and the fish survive, grow and reproduce as well as those with the more normal conformation. Occasionally desirable abnormalities appear, such as finlessness or extremely large and flowing fins among ornamental fishes.[25,26]

Genetic anomalies which do affect health, growth and survival of individuals in a population should be removed if possible. Determining heritability of the anomaly may be quite difficult. Production of fish eggs to supply the many commercial and governmental fish hatcheries of the world is a large operation in many countries. These eggs are taken from selected brood-

fishes and are usually incubated for a few days before being transported to various other geographical areas. They may be subjected to a variety of adverse environmental conditions during spawning, early incubation, transportation and final incubation. Contact with toxic substances (certain pesticides, heavy metals or therapeutic compounds), low dissolved oxygen, excessively high or low temperatures, pH or other conditions which could adversely affect development of the embryo may cause deformations easily mistaken for genetic anomalies. Some deformations of body or body structures are not observable until the fishes are partially grown. These older fishes could have been in contact with physical or chemical factors responsible for the deformation. Thus, the diagnostician must make a careful analysis of the deformity to determine absolute dependence on heredity before any attempt to eliminate the condition can be made.[10,15a,34a]

Mechanical Trauma

Injuries from mechanical trauma can lead to death or subsequent infections. Netting cultured or aquarium fishes may be responsible for breaking the dermal and mucus barriers of the skin, allowing entrance of pathogens. The use of mechanical devices to grade fishes into various sizes, lift them from holding containers into distribution tanks and many other handling operations may also cause trauma. Holding and sorting broodfishes prior to spawning, as well as the actual process of stripping eggs and milt, often injure skin and fins, which subsequently leads to invasion of pathogens. Constant fighting among male broodfishes during the spawning season tends to result in many cases of injury.

Eggs of many species of fish are subject to mechanical injury and death during certain periods of incubation. The blastoderm of an early embryo advances a germ ring to surround the yolk during development. Embryos are especially subject to damage from physical shock prior to complete closure of the germ ring.[20,30]

Cultured or aquarium fishes being fed sinking, pelleted rations are often forced to obtain food from the pond bottom. Gravel or small stones from the pond bottom may be swallowed along with the hard, pelleted food during frenzied feeding. Stones too large to be passed with feces may lodge in the anus and cause necrosis in that region of the body, leading to infections and death (PL.36F). This problem may become of major importance unless care is taken by the fish culturists or aquarist in selecting the correct size of gravel for the pond or tank bottom.

Close confinement of cultured fishes lures scavenger or piscivorous birds or mammals to prey upon them. Often, relatively large numbers of fish are injured when these animals attempt to feed and deliver only glancing blows to the fishes.

Overcrowding of fishes in cultural facilities or aquaria

leads to many traumatic problems. There are usually dominant fish in any group which fight with others challenging dominance. Injuries from bites are common under these conditions. Fins and skin injured in this way may be subject to entrance of pathogens. Cannibalism is also common in overcrowded conditions in which fishes of widely varying sizes are present.

There are a variety of other ways fishes can become injured. Each case of injury becomes a potential infection or mortality problem. The fish culturist or aquarist should guard against mechanical injury to fishes, but if injuries do occur, therapy should be given commensurate with the most likely invading bacteria, fungi or other pathogenic organisms until the injury has healed.

Selected References

1. Adair, W. D. and J. J. Hains. 1974. "Saturation values of dissolved gases associated with occurrence of gas-bubble disease in fish in a heated effluent," *In* Gibbons, J. W. and R. R. Sharitz, eds. *Thermal ecology.* p. 59-78. U.S. Atomic Energy Comm. Nat. Tech. Inf. Serv. No. CONF-730505.

1a. Beamish, R. J., W. L. Lockhart, J. C. Van Loon and H. H. Harvey. 1975. "Long term acidification of a lake and resulting effects on fishes." *Ambio.*, 4:98-102.

2. Black, E. C. 1953. "Upper lethal temperatures of some British Columbia freshwater fishes," *J. Fish. Res. Bd. Can.*, 10:196-210.

3. Brett, J. R. 1941. "Tempering versus acclimation in the planting of speckled trout," *Trans. Am. Fish. Soc.*, 70:397-403.

4. Brett, J. R. 1956. "Some principles in the thermal requirements of fishes," *Quart. Rev. Biol.*, 31:75-87.

5. Brown, M. E. 1957. *The physiology of fishes. Vol. 1: Metabolism.* Academic Press, New York City, NY. 447p.

5a. Bullock, A. M. and R. J. Roberts. 1981. "Sunburn lesions in salmonid fry: A clinical and histological report." *J. Fish Dis.*, 4:271-275.

6. Burrows, R. E. 1964. *Effects of accumulated excretory products on hatchery reared salmonids. Fish. Res. Rep.*, 66. Bur. Sport Fish. Wildl., Washington, DC. 12p.

7. Cech, J. J. Jr., D. W. Bridges, D. M. Rowell and P. J. Balzer. 1976. "Cardiovascular responses of winter flounder (*Pseudopleuronectes americanus* (Walbaum) to acute temperature increase," *Can. J. Zool.*, 54: 1383-1388.

8. Clarke, W. C. and J. Blackburn. 1977. *A seawater challenge test to measure smolting of juvenile salmon. Environ. Can. Fish. Mar. Serv. Tech. Rep.*, No. 705. 11p.

9. Coutant, C. C. 1971. "Thermal pollutions—biological effects," *J. Water Pollut. Con. Fed.*, 43:1292-1334.

10. Dawson, C. E. 1964. "A bibliography of anomalies in fishes," *Gulf Res. Rep.*, 1:308-399; Supplement 1,1966, 2:169-176; Supplement 2,1971, 3:215-239.

11. Evans, D. H. 1975. "Ionic exchange mechanism in fish gills," *Comp. Biochem. Physiol., A: Comp. Physiol.*, 51:491-495.

12. Environmental Protection Agency. 1973. *Water quality criteria 1972.* Series EPA-PB-236 199. p. 163-164 and p. 135-139.

13. Ebel, W. J. 1969. "Supersaturation of nitrogen in the Columbia River and its effects on salmon and steelhead trout," *U.S. Bur. Comm. Fish., Fish. Bull.*, 68(1):1-11.

14. Fletcher, C. R. 1978. "Osmotic and ionic regulation in the cod (*Gadus callarias* L.) II. Salt balance," *J. Comp. Physiol., B: Biochem. Syst. Environ. Physiol.*, 124:157-168.

15. Fletcher, C. R. 1978. "Osmotic and ionic regulations in the cod (*Gadus callarias* L.) I. Water balance," *J. Comp. Physiol., B: Biochem. Syst. Environ. Physiol.*, 124:149-155.

15a. Fromm, P. O. 1980. "A review of some physiological and toxicological responses of freshwater fish to acid stress." *Environ. Biol. Fishes*, 5:79-93.

16. Fry, F. E. J. 1967. "Responses of vertebrate poikilotherms to temperature (review)," *In* Rose, A. H. ed. *Thermobiology.* p. 375-409. Academic Press, New York City, NY.

16a. Jagoe, C. H. and T. A. Haines. 1985. "Fluctuating asymmetry in fishes inhabiting acidified and nonacidified lakes." *Can. J. Zool.*, 3:130-138.

17. Krenkel, P. A. and F. L. Parker, eds. 1969. *Biological aspects of thermal pollution.* Vanderbilt Univ. Press, Nashville, TN. 407p.

18. Leggett, W. C. and R. N. O'Boyle. 1976. "Osmotic stress and mortality in adult American shad during transfer from saltwater to freshwater," *J. Fish. Biol.*, 8:459-469.

19. Lasserre, P., G. Boeuf and Y. Harache. 1979. "Osmotic adaptation of *Oncorhynchus kisutch* Walbaum. I. Seasonal variations of gill Na and K

ATPase activity in coho salmon, O-age and yearling, reared in fresh water," *Aquacult.*, 14:365-382.

20. Leitritz, E. 1963. *Trout and salmon culture. Fish. Bull.*, No. 107. Calif. Dept. Fish Game, Sacramento, CA. 169p.

21. Marshall, W. S. 1978. "On the involvement of mucous secretion in teleost osmoregulation," *Can. J. Zool.*, 56:1088-1091.

22. McKee, J. E. and H. W. Wolf. 1963 *Water quality criteria. Second ed.* Resour. Bd. Calif., Water Qual. Con. Bd. Publ. No. 3-A. p.234-237.

23. Miller, R. W. 1974. "Incidence and cause of gas-bubble disease in a heated effluent," *In*: J. W. Gibbons and R. R. Sharitz, eds. *Thermal ecology.* p. 79-93. U.S. Atomic Energy Comm. Nat. Tech. Inf. Serv. No. CONF-730505.

23a. Murray, C. A. and C. D. Ziebell. 1984. "Acclimation of rainbow trout to high pH to prevent stocking mortality in summer." *Prog. Fish-Cult.* 46:176-179.

24. Naiman, R. J., S. D. Gerking and R. E. Stuart. 1976. "Osmoregulation in the Death Valley pupfish *Cyprinodon milleri* (Pisces: Cyprinodontidae)," *Copeia*, 1976:807-810.

25. Nelson, J. S. 1971. "Absence of the pelvic complex in ninespine sticklebacks, *Pungitius pungitus*, collected in Ireland and Wood Buffalo National Park Region, Canada, with notes on meristic variation," *Copeia*, 1971:707-717.

26. Nelson, J. S. and F. M. Atton. 1971. "Geographic and morphological variation in the presence and absence of the pelvic skeleton in the brook stickleback, *Culaea inconstans* (Kirtland), in Alberta and Saskatchewan," *Can. J. Zool.*, 49:343-352.

27. Oguri, M. and Y. Oashima. 1977. "Early changes in the plasma osmolality and ionic concentrations of rainbow trout and goldfish following direct transfer from fresh-water to sea water," *Bull. Jpn. Soc. Sci. Fish.*, 43:1252-1257.

28. Pauley, G. B. and R. F. Nakatani. 1967. "Histopathology of "gas bubble" disease in salmon fingerlings," *J. Fish. Res. Bd. Can.*, 24:867-871.

29. Post, G. 1970. "Determination of inert gases in water," *Prog. Fish-Cult.*, 32:170-173.

30. Post, G., D. V. Power and T. M. Kloppel. 1974. "Survival of rainbow trout eggs after receiving physical shocks of known magnitude," *Trans. Am. Fish. Soc.*, 103:711-716.

31. Rucker, R. R. 1972. *Gas-bubble disease of salmonids: A critical review. Tech. Pap.*, No. 58. U.S. Fish. Wildl. Serv., Washington, DC. 11p.

32. Shen, A. C. Y. and J. F. Leatherland. 1978. "Effect of ambient salinity on ionic and osmotic regulation of eggs, larvae, and alevins of rainbow trout (*Salmo gairdneri*)," *Can. J. Zool.*, 56:571-577.

33. Spaargaren, D. H. 1976. "A comparative study on the regulation of osmotic, ionic and organic-solute concentrations in the blood of aquatic organisms," *Comp. Biochem. Physiol.*, A: Comp. Physiol., 53:31-40.

34. Shirahata, S. 1966. "Experiments on nitrogen gas disease with rainbow trout fry," *Bull. Freshwater Fish. Res. Lab. (Tokyo)*, 15:197-211.

34a. Spry, D. J., C. M. Wood, and P. V. Hodson. 1981. "The effects of environmental acid on freshwater fish with particular reference to the softwater lakes in Ontario and the modifying effects of heavy metals. A literature review." *Can. Tech. Rep. Fish. Aquat. Sci.*, No. 199.

35. Westgard, R. L. 1964. "Physical and biological aspects of gas bubble disease in impounded adult chinook salmon at McNary spawning channel," *Trans. Am. Fish. Soc.*, 93:306-309.

36. Weitkamp, D. E. and M. Katz. 1977. *Dissolved atmospheric gas supersaturation of water and the gas bubble disease of fish.* Envir. Infor. Serv. Inc., Mercer Island, WA. 107p.

APPENDIX

Conversion of Weights and Measures:

Unit	Gallon	Quart	Pint	Pound	Ounce	Fluid Ounce	Cubic Inch	Cubic Foot	Milli-liter	Liter	Gram	Kilo-gram
1 gal	1.0	4.0	8.0	8.337	133.52	128.6	231.0	0.1337	3,785.4	3.785	3,785.4	3.785
1 qt	0.25	1.0	2.0	2.086	33.38	32.0	57.749	0.0334	946.36	0.95	946.35	0.946
1 pt	0.125	0.5	1.0	1.043	16.69	16.0	28.875	0.0167	473.18	0.47	473.18	0.473
1 lb	0.12	0.48	0.96	1.0	16.0	15.35	27.67	0.016	453.59	0.454	453.59	0.454
1 oz	0.0075	0.03	0.06	0.0625	1.0	0.96	1.73	0.001	28.3	0.03	28.35	0.028
1 fl oz	0.0078	0.031	0.062	0.062	1.04	1.0	1.8	———	29.57	0.03	29.41	0.029
1 cu in	0.0043	0.017	0.035	0.036	0.573	0.554	1.0	———	16.39	0.016	16.3	0.016
1 cu ft	7.481	29.922	59.848	62.428	998.848	957.48	1,728.0	1.0	28,316.0	28.316	28,316.58	28.316
1 ml (cc)	0.0003	0.001	0.002	0.002	0.035	0.034	0.061	———	1.0	0.001	1.0	0.001
1 liter	0.264	1.057	2.1134	2.205	35.28	33.815	61.025	0.0353	1,000.0	1.0	1,000.0	1.0
1 gram	———	———	0.002	0.0022	0.0353	0.034	———	———	1.0	0.001	1.0	0.001
1 kilogram	0.2642	0.0661	0.033	2.205	35.27	34.902	———	———	1,000.0	1.0	1,000.0	1.0

Relationships between proportion, parts per million, and percent

Proportion	Parts per Million	Percent (%)	Proportion	Parts per Million	Percent (%)
1:100	10,000	1.0	1:50,000	20	0.002
1:500	2,000	0.2	1:100,000	10	0.001
1:1,000	1,000	0.1	1:250,000	4	0.0004
1:4,000	250	0.025	1:500,000	2	0.0002
1:5,000	200	0.02	1:1,000,000	1	0.0001
1:10,000	100	0.01	1:4,000,000	0.25	0.000025
1:25,000	40	0.004	1:10,000,000	0.1	0.00001

Miscellaneous Conversion Factors

1 meter = 100 centimeter = 3.281 feet = 39.37 inches
1 centimeter = 10 millimeter = 0.394 inches
1 inch = 2.54 centimeters = 25.4 millimeters
1 cubic foot per second = 448.8 gallons per minute = 1,698.7 liters per minute
1 cubic foot per minute = 7.4805 gallons per minute = 28.314 liters per minute

1 part per million = 1 milligram per liter = 1 microgram per milliliter
1 part per billion = 1 microgram per liter
Degrees Centigrade = $0.556x$ (°F −32)
Degrees Fahrenheit = (°C x 1.8) + 32

INDEX

Page numbers printed in italic refer to illustrations.

Pathogenic vibrio, 41-47
Pathological syndromes of dietary deficiency, 232-237
PCB (polychlorinated biphenyls), 259
Peduncle disease, 13, 54-56, *121*
PEN (piscine erythrocytic necrosis), 112, 147, *150*
Pesticide toxicity, 266-269
Pestis rubra anguillarum, 7
Pestis salmonum, 7
PFR (pike fry rhabdovirus), 150-151
PFRD (pike fry rhabdovirus disease), 150-151
pH (Hydrogen ion concentration), *144*, 279-280
Phenolic compounds, 259
Phosphorus deficiency, 237
Piconraviruses, 95
Pike fry rhabdovirus (PFR), 150-151
Pike fry rhabdovirus disease (PFRD), 150-151
Piscicides, 267-268
Piscicola sp., *136*
Piscine erythrocytic necrosis (PEN), 112
PKD, (Proliferated kidney disease), 180-181
"PKX," *149, 180,* 181
Platyhelminthes, 188-201
Pleistophora, 172
    hyphessobryconis, *130, 131,* 172-173
    ovariae, 172
Plerocercoid, *136,* 199
Polychlorinated biphenyls (PCB), 259-260
Polyvinyl chloride (PVC), 259, 260
Posthodiplostomum minimum, *149, 175,* 195-197
Posthodiplostomum orchilongum, 195
Poxvirus, 93
Preservation methods, 11-12
Primary host, 159
Proboscis, *137,* 201
Procercoid, 198
Proglottid, 197
Prohaptor, 189
Proliferative kidney disease, (PKD),180-181
Protein deficiency, 232
Proteins, 227
Proteocephalus, 197, *198,* 200
    ambloplitis, *137,* 197-198
Proteus, 70
Protozoa, 160, 180
Protozoan diseases, 160-188
    amebiasis, 169
    ceratomyxiasis, 179
    chilodiniasis, 186
    coccidiosis, 169
    epistyliasis, 187
    henneguyiasis, 180
    hexamitiasis, 165
    ichthyophthiriasis, 182
    ichtyobodiasis, 163
    microsporiasis, 172
    trichodiniasis, 186
    trichophryiasis, 187
Pseudomonad septicemia, 44-47
Pseudomonads, 44
Pseudomonas, 44
    fluorescens, 44-47
    species, 39, 98
PVC (polyvinyl chloride), 259, 260
Pyrethrum, 267

Q
Quarantine, 16-17
Quaternary ammonium compounds, 240
Quinaldine sulfate, 271

R
Rations, 225-227
Redia, 193
Reduction of transmission link, 18
Renibacterium, 60
    salmoninarum, 60-64, 69, 72, 221
Reovirus, 95
Required host, 160
Reservoir host, 160
Resistance, 215
Reticuloendothelial system, 216
Restriction of movement, 16-17
Rhabdovirus carpio, *129,* 151
    salmonis, 104
Round worms, 202
Rotenone, 266-68

S
Sacramento River chinook disease, (SRCD), 100
Sacramento River chinook disease virus (SRCDV), 101
Salminicola sp., 193
Salmonella, 70
Sanitation, 17-18
Saprolegnia, 81, *124, 125, 126*
    parasitica, 82
Saprolegniasis, 81-84, *124-5*
Sarcomastigophora, 163
Schizamoeba, 169
Scolex, 197
Scoliosis, *126, 129, 141*
Secernentea, 202
Sockeye salmon virus disease (SSVD), 100
Spermatophores, *138*
Sphaeromyxa, 174
Sphaerospora, 174
Spray infusion, 221
Spring viremia of carp (SVC), *129,* 151-153
Spring viremia of carp virus (SVCV), 151, 153
SRCD (Sacramento River chinook disease), 101
SRCDV (Sacramento River chinook disease virus), 101
SSVD (sockeye salmon virus disease), 100
Streptococcus, 72
    agalactiae, 72
    faecalis, 72
    species, 72
Streptococcus septicemia, 72-73
Streptothrix asteroides, 68
Sulfamerazine, 269
Sulfonamides, 269
Sunlight disease, 282
Supersaturation of atmospheric gases, 280-281
Supplemental ration, 225
Symbiosis, 159
Systemic treatment, 22-25

T
Taenia, 198
Temperature, 217, 279
Temporary host, 160
Teratology, 250
Terramycin®, 269
Tetrahymena pyriformis, 219
Test and slaughter, 16
Thelohanelus, 174
Thelohania, 172
    californica, 172, 174
    ovicola, 173
Therapeutic compounds toxicity, 269
Thermal adaptation, 279
Thermal trauma, 279
Thiabendazole, 270

Thiobarbituric acids (TBA), 234
Thorny-headed worms, 201
Tomites, *133*
Toxaphene, 268
Toxic gases, 260-262
Toxic metals, 254-256
Toxic organic compounds, 257-260
Toxicity (naturally-occurring ions), 256-257
Transmission link (destruction), 181
Transport host, 159
Trauma, 282-283
Trematoda, 189-197
Triactinomyxon, 178
Tricainemethane sulfonate (MS-222), 271
Trichodina, *134,* 186-187
Trichodiniasis, 186-187
Trichophrya, 186, 187
    species, *135*
Trichophryiasis, 187-188
Trypanoplasma, 163
Trypanosoma, 163
Tuberculosis, 7
Tubifex sp., 178
Tumors, 243-247
Turbellaria, 188

U
Ulcer disease, 69-70, *123*
Unicauda, 174
Unicapsula, 174
Urocleidus dispar, 193
Urocleidus turcatus, 193
Urocleidus similis, 193
Urosporidium, 181
Uvulifer ambloplitis, *136,* 196
Uvulifer sp., 195

V
Vaccines, 218-219
Vacuum infiltration, 18, 221
VHS (viral hemorrhagic septicemia), 104-107
Vibrio, 41, 70
    anguillarum, 41-47, *118,* 220, 221
    species, 39
Vibriosis, 7, 41-47
Virus diseases, 93-112, 146-147, 150-151, 153
    channel catfish virus, 107
    herpesvirus salmonis, 147, 150
    infectious hematopoietic necrosis, 100
    infectious pancreatic necrosis, 94
    lymphocystis, 109
    pike fry rhabdovirus, 150-151
    piscine erythrocytic necrosis, 112
    spring viremia of carp, 151, 153
    viral erythrocytic necrosis, 112, 147
    viral hemorrhagic septicemia, 104
Viral erythrocytic necrosis (VEN), 112, 147
Viral hemorrhagic septicemia (VHS), 101, 104-107, *125, 128*
Virus, 93, *94*
Vitamins, 229-230, 235
Volkampfia, 169

W
Wescodyne®, 21, 271
Whirling disease, 175-179
White spot disease, 182

Y
Yersinia, 47
    ruckeri, 47-54, *120.* 221
Yersiniosis, 47-54

Z
Zinc deficiency, *152,* 237
Zoomastigophorea, 112, 145